MUSKOX LAND

Ellesmere Island
in the Age of Contact

University of Calgary Press
Parks and Heritage Series
ISSN 1494-0426

MUSKOX LAND

Ellesmere Island
in the Age of Contact

Lyle Dick

UNIVERSITY OF
CALGARY
PRESS

University of Calgary Press
2500 University Drive N.W.
Calgary, Alberta
Canada T2N 1N4
www.uofcpress.com

National Library of Canada Cataloguing in Publication Data

Dick, Lyle
Muskox land

      (Parks and heritage series, ISSN 1494-0426 ; 5)
      Includes bibliographical references and index.
      ISBN 1-55238-050-5

   1. Ellesmere Island (Nunavut)—History. 2. Inuit—Nunavut—
Ellesmere Island—History. 3. Ellesmere Island (Nunavut)—Discovery
and exploration. 4. Acculturation—Nunavut—Ellesmere Island—History.
I. Title. II. Series.
FC4345.E55D52 2001   971.9'5   C2001-911198-3
F1144.E44D52 2001

 We acknowledge the financial support of the Government of Canada
through the Book Publishing Industry Development Program (BPDIP)
for our publishing activities

This book has been published with the help of a grant from the Humanities and Social Sciences
Federation of Canada, using funds provided by the Social Sciences and Humanities Research
Council of Canada.

 The Canada Council for the Arts
Le Conseil des Arts du Canada

Printed and bound in Canada by Friesens.
∞ This book is printed on acid-free paper.

Front cover: "Kood-look-to [Kridtluktoq] Coming from Fort Conger with Dog Team," 1909.
Colourized lantern slide image courtesy of the Peary-MacMillan Arctic Museum, Bowdoin
College, Donald B. MacMillan Collection No. 3000.32.12 ("North Pole 35")

Cover Design by Kristina Schuring
Page design and layout by Larie Stoley

This book is dedicated to my mother and father,
and to RTF.

CONTENTS

PART FOUR

Conclusion:

List of Figures

20. Inughuit men building an *iglooyah* at Eureka Sound, during Donald B. MacMillan's Crocker land Expedition, 1913-17. Credit: American Museum of Natural History, Donald B. MacMillan Collection, Crocker Land, 1913-17, Negative no. 233531.

21. Building a snow-block wind break on the trail. From Harry Whitney, *Hunting with the Eskimos* (1910), p. 288.

22. "Native skin tents at Bache Detachment, Ellesmere Island, NWT, ca 1926." National Archives of Canada, Photo no. PA-102670.

23. "Eskimos matching their dogs," Etah, ca 1920s. Credit: American Museum of Natural History, Donald B. MacMillan Collection, Crocker Land, 1913-17, Negative No. 232625.

24. Route of Qitdlarssuaq's Journey, ca 1850-60.

25. "Ka-ko-chee-ah with bow and arrow," Etah, northern Greenland, Credit: American Museum of Natural History (New York City), Donald B. MacMillan Collection, Crocker Land Expedition, 1913-17, Negative no. 230920.

26. The *Proteus* in the ice at the entrance to Discovery Harbour, August 1881. Credit: U.S. National Archives, RG 27, Lady Franklin Bay Expedition Records (Washington, DC), Box No. 17. Photographer: George W. Rice.

27. "The *Roosevelt* lies trapped among rough ice floes off the barren coast of Ellesmere Island. Members of the crew can be seen standing on the ice near the bow of the ship." Credit: National Geographic Society (Washington, DC), Robert E. Peary Collection, Project No. 02116, Consecutive No. 3159, Picture Id. No. 123658A, Picture Rec. Id. No. 132029.

28. One of the sledging parties of the HMS *Discovery*, prior to their departure to explore the coast of Lady Franklin Bay, 1876. The sledge weights were as much as 450 kg. National Archives of Canada, Photograph no. C-52571.

29. The *Discovery* anchored at Lady Franklin Bay, with the depot and observatories on shore, September 1875. National Archives of Canada, Photograph No. C-25921.

30. "Lat. 81° 44' N. The people who did not leave the ship in the early spring sledding season. A discarded face protector on snow bank, 1876." Photograph by Thomas Mitchell, National Archives of Canada, Photo No. C-4588.

31. The expedition house at Fort Conger under construction. Note the vertical board-and-batten siding, high ceiling and extensive attic space. Photograph by George Rice. Credit: U.S. National Archives (Washington, DC), RG 27, Lady Franklin Bay Expedition Records Box No. 17.

32. The completed house at Fort Conger, showing canvas additions. Note that the banking of sod has only been brought part way up the walls. Photograph by George Rice. Credit: U.S. National Archives (Washington, DC), RG 27, Lady Franklin Bay Expedition Records, Box No. 17.

33. "First Communication with the Natives of Prince Regents Bay as Drawn by John Sackheouse and Presented to Captain Ross, August 10, 1818." National Archives of Canada, Photograph no. C-119412. Handcoloured aquatint by John Sackeuse, 1818–19. Plate originally published in John Ross, *A Voyage of Discovery, Made under the Orders of the Admiralty, in His Majesty's Ships* Isabella *and* Alexander, *for the Purpose of Exploring Baffin's Bay and Inquiring into the Probability of a North-West Passage*, Vol. I (1819).

34. Map of the route of the expedition of Elisha Kent Kane, 1853-55.

35. View of Cape Louis Napoleon, U.S. National Archives (Washington, DC), RG 401, Series XPX-1898-8892-2.

36. Map of the route of the expedition of Isaac Israel Hayes, 1860-61.

37. Map of the route of the expedition of Charles Francis Hall, 1873.

38. The HMS *Discovery* in wintering quarters, Lady Franklin Bay, 1875-76. National Archives of Canada, Photograph no. C-52573.

60. "Padlunga, Klishook [Qisuk] and Inacosea [Inoqusiaq] — Arctic Highlanders who spent the winter 1923-1924 at Craig Harbour, Ellesmere Island, NWT." National Archives of Canada Photo no. PA-102279.

61. "New detachment at Bache Peninsula, Ellesmere Island, NWT," 1926. Photograph by L.D. Livingston. National Archives of Canada Photo no. PA-111799.

62. "Klishook [Qisuk] - Arctic Highlander at Craig Harbour, Ellesmere Island, NWT, ca 1924." National Archives of Canada Photo no. PA-102279. Photographer: T. Tash.

63. "Noo-ka-ping-wa [Nukappiannguaq] and dead square flipper seal, Off Cairn Point." Photo courtesy of the Peary-MacMillan Arctic Museum, Bowdoin College (Brunswick, Maine), Photograph no. 285.

64. "Eskimo man and woman at Bache Peninsula, Ellesmere Island, NWT," late 1920s. National Archives of Canada Photo no. PA-102650.

65. "Landing supplies at RCMP Detachment, Craig Harbour, Ellesmere Island, NWT, August 1925." National Archives of Canada Photo no. PA-102444.

66. Routes of RCMP Patrols on Ellesmere Island and adjacent islands, 1922-1940.

67. "View taken from a point about 81° W. between Bay Fiord and Flagler Fiord [Ellesmere Island] (taken towards south)." Photograph by Christian Vibe, Van Hauen Expedition, May 1940. National Archives of Canada Photo no. C-137056.

68. "Robert Edwin Peary, full-length portrait, standing on deck of ship or dock, facing left, distributing gifts to Eskimos, Greenland." Library of Congress (Washington, DC), Photo no. LC-USZC4-7505

69. "Eskimo with kometaho," Credit: American Museum of Natural History (New York City), Donald B. MacMillan Collection, Crocker Land, 1913-17, Negative no. 231657.

70. "Peary on the main deck of steamship *Roosevelt*." Library of Congress (Washington, DC), Photo No. LC-USZC4-7507.

71. "Matt Henson (of Peary's crew) in Arctic costume on deck of the *Roosevelt* on arrival at Sydney, Nova Scotia." Library of Congress (Washington, DC), Photo no. LC-USZC4-7506.

72. "Etah,1898." Photograph showing the interconnected complex of structures at Peary's wintering complex in 1898. U.S. National Archives, RG 401(1)(A), Papers Relating to Arctic Expeditions, 1886–1909, Greenland - Ellesmere Island, 1898–1902, Photograph No. 401-1/1898/ 8985, "Etah, 1898."

73. Aerial view of Fort Conger in 1979, showing the outlines of the surviving shelters of Peary's wintering complex of 1900. The outline of Peary's wintering tent and its passageway to Dr. Dedrick's shelter are visible on the left side of the complex, while on the other side of Dedrick's dwelling the remains of the former tunnel connection to the Inughuit shelter are visible. The depression in the right centre is the site of the former kitchen, which the outlines of Greely's big house of 1881 appear in the upper right corner of the photograph. Parks Canada, Western Canada Service Centre, Cultural Resource Services, Winnipeg.

74. Plan of Peary's wintering complex at Fort Conger, showing the spatial relationships of its constituent structures.

75. "Hans Hendrik, Esquimaux dog-driver, with his son and daughter, 1875." National Archives of Canada Photo no. C-52497.

76. Map showing the spatial distribution of "pibloktoq" episodes on Ellesmere Island and northern Greenland.

77. Matthew Henson and unidentified Inughuit woman on the deck of the SS *Roosevelt*, 1908–09. National Geographic Society (Washington, DC), Robert E. Peary Collection, Project No. 02116, Consecutive No. 2105, Picture Id. No. 122369A, Picture Record No. 130975.

Acknowledgements

This book's preparation was made possible by the contributions of many individuals and institutions. I wish to acknowledge the financial support of the Aid to Scholarly Publications Programme of the Social Sciences and Humanities Research Council of Canada. Parks Canada contributed resources for research and publication to enable the important human history themes of Quttinirpaaq National Park of Canada to be interpreted to park visitors and other Canadians. The support of the Arctic Institute of North America and its director, Karla Williamson, is appreciated. I would like to acknowledge the role of Susan Buggey, formerly Chief of Historical Services for the Prairie and Northern Region of Parks Canada, under whose direction the concept of the book was initially developed and who first proposed and supported the oral history of Grise Fiord. More recently, I was able to complete the text of the manuscript with the backing of Dr. Martin Magne, Manager, Cultural Resource Services, and Orysia Luchak, Director, Western Canada Service Centre of Parks Canada. The assistance of Elizabeth Seale, Nancy Anilniliak, John Webster, and Vicki Sahanatien, all with the Nunavut Field Unit of Parks Canada, was essential to the project's success and has been much appreciated. In addition to contributing resources to help underwrite the book's publication, the Field Unit also enabled me to visit Grise Fiord and Resolute Bay in May 2001 to report to these communities on the status of the book project. I would also like to thank Bill Thorpe and Renee Wissink, two former Chief Park Wardens for Ellesmere Island National Park Reserve, the forerunner of Quttinirpaaq, who assisted me in my field work in the park in 1989. As an enthusiast of High Arctic History, Renee often shared historical references with me and encouraged the completion of the book. Thanks are also due to Ellen Lee and Peter Priess, archaeologists and colleagues who collaborated in the inventory and assessment of the cultural resources within the park area at that time. Our field work received logistical support from the Polar Continental Shelf Project of Natural Resources Canada, which was essential to its success and is appreciated.

I benefited from early advice from Dr. Milton Freeman, Professor of Anthropology at the University of Alberta, Minnie Freeman, and Dr. Rick Riewe, Professor of Zoology at the University of Manitoba, all experts on the history of Grise Fiord. Ms. Freeman made the key recommendation to contact Martha Flaherty to assist in the oral history project. I would also like to thank Dr. Riewe for his kind permission to reproduce three maps of the major travelling and hunting routes of the Grise Fiord Inuit, previously prepared for the Inuit Land Use and Occupancy reports. Other specialists who kindly shared their knowledge were Dr. Peter Schledermann and Dr. Karen McCullough, who read several chapters and provided incisive comments. Their long-term archaeological studies on the east coast of Ellesmere Island have helped shape my understanding of the complex pre-contact period of Aboriginal occupation on Ellesmere Island. Recently, Larry Audlaluk of Grise Fiord read the chapters on Inuit occupation of Ellesmere Island since 1950 and shared his extensive knowledge of the community's history, which improved the balance and coverage of Inuit history in this section of the book. I would also like to acknowledge the critical commentary of three anonymous assessors for the University of Calgary and the Humanities and Social Sciences Federation of Canada.

At the University of Calgary Press, Walter Hildebrandt, Director, encouraged me to submit the manuscript and provided considerable assistance throughout the process of review and production. The assistance of John King, Production Editor, throughout the production process, is also sincerely appreciated. I wish to acknowledge the assistance of Larie Stoley, who produced the book's layout, and Kristina Schuring, who designed the cover. Thanks are also due to Dr. Renée Fossett, who designed the book's index.

Archival assistance and advice was provided by Marjorie Ciarlante of the U.S. National Archives, Bill Perry and Barbara Shaddock at the National Geographic Society, Doug Whyte at the National Archives of Canada, the staff at the Manuscript Division of the Library of Congress in Washington, and the staff of the Rare Book Room at the Bowdoin College Library in Brunswick, Maine. The late Dr. Irene Spry, Professor of Economics at the University of Ottawa, drew my attention to the papers of Sir George Nares, which she had played a role in securing for the National Archives of Canada.

I wish to acknowledge the encouragement of Dr. Susan Kaplan, Dean of Arts and Director of the Peary–MacMillan Arctic Museum and Arctic Studies Centre at Bowdoin College, in Brunswick, Maine, who invited me to present some of my research findings in the First Annual Peary Polar Exploration Lecture in 1994. Ms. Molly Laird, assistant curator at the Peary-MacMillan Arctic Museum at Bowdoin College, was very helpful in locating a series of colourized lantern slides from Donald B. MacMillan's collection, which are reproduced on the cover and as illustrations for this book. I am indebted to John Pawlyk, Exhibit Designer with the Service Centre, who designed and prepared most of the maps in this book, Kathy Lauseman, who drafted the chart on the seasonal cycle at Grise Fiord for this publication, David Elrick, who drafted several Figures for the book and Wayne Duford, who drafted the map showing the spatial distribution of "pibloktoq" episodes. As well, Alice Gavin kindly assisted in the reproduction of plates from Kane's *Arctic Explorations* and Greely's *Three Years in Arctic Service*, revised and re-drafted many maps and graphs, and shared her knowledge of RCMP history in the Arctic. I also wish to thank Rachel Running, who assisted with the orders of historical photographs from various repositories in Canada and the United States.

Throughout the process of researching and writing the manuscript, I have benefited greatly from the continued advice of Ron Frohwerk, whose support and encouragement was essential to its completion. He assisted in the research at Bowdoin College and was instrumental in helping me to forge a link with this institution. I would also like to acknowledge the influence of one of my early teachers, the late Professor W.N. Hargreaves-Mawdsley, former Head of the Department of History at Brandon University, who taught me that one can never do enough reading in history.

Some of the material in this book appeared in two previously published articles. I would like to acknowledge the permission of the *Society for the Study of Architecture in Canada Bulletin* to republish excerpts from "The Fort Conger Shelters and Vernacular Adaptation to the High Arctic," and the journal *Arctic Anthropology* and its publisher, the University of Wisconsin Press, which consented to the re-use of portions of "'Pibloktoq' (Arctic Hysteria): A Construction of European-Inuit Relations?", both cited in the Bibliography. I also wish to acknowledge the critical and editorial comments of the following individuals who read drafts of the article on "pibloktoq": Ron Frohwerk, Margaret Conrad, Susan Kaplan, Rolf Gilberg, Jennifer Brown, Elizabeth Legge, Sheila Butler, Gerald Friesen, Albert Haller, the late Richard Condon, and two anonymous reviewers for *Arctic Anthropology*. Both Susan Buggey and Ron Frohwerk provided critical feedback on the paper on the Fort Conger shelters. I would also like to thank Ruth Sandwell, who read a draft of the manuscript and offered insightful feedback regarding the presentation of thematic material.

The oral history with current and former residents of Grise Fiord was made possible through the approval of the Advisory Committee for Ellesmere Island National Park Reserve and the efforts of Larry Audlaluk, Liza Ningiuk, and Iga Kigugtak, who carried out the interviews at Grise Fiord. Larry served as local co-ordinator for the project and his advice and assistance has been very much appreciated. I am also indebted to Martha Flaherty, who carried out the interviews with former residents of Grise Fiord following their return to Inukjuak, Quebec. Ms. Flaherty also prepared the transcriptions and the translations of the interviews into English. I have also drawn on the Pond Inlet oral history project co-ordinated by Lynn Cousins, who made available transcripts and translations of interviews with former residents of Grise Fiord who had returned to Baffin Island. Particular thanks are due to Abraham Pijamini, a respected Elder at Grise Fiord, who as chair of the Park Reserve Advisory Committee gave his support to the project in 1989. At our meeting with the community in May 2001, Mr. Pijamini drew my attention to the particular importance of caching in enabling Inuit to survive in this challenging environment.

Finally, I would like to acknowledge the contribution of many people who shared their knowledge in the interviews cited in this book: Edith Patsauq Amaroalik, Anna Nungaq, Samwilly Elaijasialuk, the late Gamaliel Aqiarak, Martha Kigugtak, the late Tookilkee Kigugtak, Markusie Patsauq, Rynee Flaherty, Martha Flaherty, the late Annie Pijamini, Abraham Pijamini, Samuel Arnakallak, Ningiuk Killiktee, the late Simon Akpaliapik, the late Ross Gibson, Robert Pilot, Sharon Richardson, and the late Robert Christie. Their words remind us that history, the thing itself, is a not merely an abstraction but also the concrete, lived experience and memory of each individual.

Note on Orthography and Terminology

The names of Inughuit or Inuit individuals mentioned in this book were recorded by European observers as the nearest equivalent as it sounded to the writers' Western ears. Wide variations in spelling have generated considerable difficulty in linking different references to the same person. For the Inughuit names, I have followed the official Greenlandic orthography provided in the appendix to Kenn Harper's *Give Me My Father's Body* (pp. 236-40), supplemented by the genealogical table in Guy Mary-Rousselière's *Qitdlarssuaq: l'histoire d'une migration polaire* (inside back cover). For the spelling of the names of Inuit residents of Ellesmere Island, I have followed the spelling provided by the oral history interviewees at Grise Fiord and Inukjuak, supplemented by the advice of Larry Audlaluk of Grise Fiord.

In referring to Aboriginal peoples, this discussion uses the term Inughuit for the Indigenous people of the Thule District of northwestern Greenland (also known as Avanersuaq); Inuit for the Indigenous inhabitants of the Canadian territory of Nunavut; and West Greenlanders for the Aboriginal inhabitants of the west coast of Greenland, as far north as Melville Bay. Occasional references to the Aboriginal inhabitants of coastal arctic areas of Alaska, on the other hand, conform to the American usage of the term "Eskimo." Each of these terms is consistent with the definitions provided in the *Handbook of North American Indians*, Vol. 5, "Arctic, " referred to in the endnotes.

Introduction

This book is the result of the author's inquiries over several years into the history of Ellesmere Island and the High Arctic. It explores how two cultures came into contact in this region in the nineteenth and twentieth centuries, how they were changed, and why in other respects they emerged relatively unaltered by this experience. It began as a project to provide historical background to assist in the protection and presentation of cultural resources in Ellesmere Island National Park Reserve of Canada. The initial focus of study was the series of European expeditions to Ellesmere Island and the adjacent territories of the High Arctic in the era of North Polar exploration. A review of the literature suggested that previous writing had focussed rather narrowly on the exploits of the European or Euro-American explorers, with comparatively little reference to the role of their Inuit participants. The undertaking then expanded to encompass a study of the cultural background and interactions of both groups participating in this quest—Aboriginal and European. This shift in emphasis required further refinements when it became apparent that it involved the participation of members of diverse cultures, including the Inughuit of Northwest Greenland, West Greenlanders, Canadian Inuit, British nationals, Americans, Euro-Canadians, and others. It also soon became apparent that the history of the High Arctic could not be understood without a treatment of its physiography, climate, and ecosystems, each of which has played a pivotal role in its human history.

The undertaking was further complicated by the conflicting perspectives in the work of historians of the Arctic. A survey of the historiography of just one theme—the history of North Polar exploration—revealed distinctive traditions of writing on the expeditions in the literature of different countries. As well, a search of unpublished materials in various archives in Canada and the United States indicated a significant divergence between the official record of the explorers and their private journals and diaries. Over time, the focus extended beyond the specific subject matter to a more ambitious undertaking, a re-framing of many of the issues of contact. For example, in approaching the expeditions of Robert Peary, the question evolved from the standard issue of whether Peary actually reached the North Pole in 1909 to matters of perhaps greater consequence: How did Peary position himself in terms of knowledge and technique to be able to survive in the polar environment? What knowledge and expectations did the Europeans and Aboriginal peoples bring to these encounters? What did they take away from the exchange? How did Inuit respond to the contact experience, and what impact did Inuit have on the larger European societies that sent expeditions to the region? How, in turn, was the physical environment affected by contact, and what effects did it exert on the participating cultures? What lasting changes were brought about by the interchange of these cultures? For that matter, were these changes as enduring as might appear on the surface?

The research methodology was to assemble data from a wide range of unpublished archival documents and oral history sources before consulting secondary works late in the process. The objective was to assemble first-hand accounts as the building blocks of a new approach to historical writing, rather than integrate these stories into the pre-existing frameworks of arctic historiography. To redress the lack of Aboriginal perspectives in the primary textual and photographic sources, I worked with members of the community of Grise Fiord to plan an oral history so that Inuit voices would be represented in the story. These interviews, recorded between 1989 and 1991, underscore the fact that arctic history is not merely a set of stories set in the past, but an ongoing process that continues into the present day. For interpretive guidance, I also consulted the work of arctic social scientists, especially the learned writings of Dr. Milton Freeman, which have been particularly useful in reconstructing the patterns of human experience represented in the historical sources.

However, this book is a work of history, and so it needed a framework for approaching issues of change over time, within which the diversity of High Arctic history could be encapsulated. Generally, it has seemed to me that Fernand Braudel's structural, multi-dimensional approach to temporality offers the most compelling model for addressing the complexities of historical continuity and change. This is not to endorse all of Braudel's interpretations, which belong to a particular era, but rather to acknowledge the continuing relevance of his methodological innovations in the treatment of historical time, which have enduring importance for the study of history. In the familiar register of narrative history, time has often been distilled into a single path, a play-by-play recounting of lived experience as it might have appeared to an individual, whether the historical subject, the writer, or an assumed reader. Following Braudel, I approach the issue of time in a more complex way, not as a single temporal register but rather as in the times of history. This approach is based on the view that at any given moment in history, there is no single present. A historical event comprises the intersection of many presents, each of which bears on the unfolding of a particular occurrence and its interrelationships with other events. These issues surface on multiple levels, not only in discussions of individual agency in biographical and narrative history, but also on the level of social history, as it relates to the role of groups or cultures, and also on the macro-scale of environmental history.

The variety of factors influencing human history is mirrored in the multiplicity of voices and perspectives brought to bear on its interpretation. History, the thing itself, is never experienced from a single perspective; no two individuals view it in exactly the same way. In reconstructing the Europeans' experience of history, this book has relied on a wide range of textual and iconographical documents, including unpublished manuscripts, primary published accounts, government reports, books, articles, and historical photographs. The primary research has been particularly comprehensive for the study of expeditions that actually reached northern Ellesmere Island, the area of Quttinirpaaq National Park of Canada. An exception is the first part of the book on the physical environment of Ellesmere Island, where I have largely relied on the specialist knowledge of climatologists, geographers, archaeologists, and ecologists in sketching out the role of the natural environment, buttressed by relevant primary references relating to climatic history and ecology.

The reconstruction of Inuit perspectives was another matter. Clearly, the documentary record could not adequately represent the experience of Aboriginal peoples in the contact situation. They were often omitted from the discussion, and when they were referenced, the documentary sources presented Aboriginal people through the eyes of the Europeans or Euro-North Americans who generated these records and images. A rare exception is the memoirs of Hans Hendrik, the West Greenlander who served on three of the nineteenth century expeditions, and whose account of his own experiences was published in 1878. To access Inuit perspectives of history, however, it would be necessary to look beyond the printed page to the oral record. Only by incorporating the testimony of Inuit would it be possible to give due consideration to their role and contributions in history. Beyond an expansion of the base of information, this was an essential step if the study were to move beyond the treatment of Inuit participants as subjects of study—persons about whom others speak—to an acknowledgement of their status as speaking subjects, or persons who speak on their own behalf.

This study deals on a micro-scale with a global historical phenomenon, the contact between Western and Indigenous peoples. As in so many other areas of the world, Indigenous people in the Arctic confronted numerous pressures brought about by developments in transportation, communications, and the export of Western concepts and technologies. In documenting these assorted influences, I have sought to examine both the medium- and long-term benefits and disadvantages of cultural exchange.

The history of Ellesmere Island is a story of life on the margins of history. A place more remote from the networks of the world's economies and populations would be difficult to imagine. And yet, for a few decades in the late nineteenth century and early twentieth century, it was a focus of attention for innumerable armchair explorers fascinated by the race to reach the North Pole and the exotic arctic world evoked in publications by or about explorers. It is a story of the relationships between two cultures, one large, powerful and connected to international trade, diplomacy, and communications; the other local, largely self-contained, and characterized by pragmatic strategies organized around hunting and the seasons. To understand this relationship, this book attempts to place their interactions within the appropriate contexts of nature, culture, circumstance, and perspective.

Accordingly, the book is organized into four parts. Part I introduces two of the principal *dramatis personae*, that is, the natural environment, consisting of physical geography, climate, and ecology; and the cultures who came into contact in this environment, the Inuit and European peoples. I have used the term "Continuities" to characterize the role of these players, as environment and culture comprise two relatively stable, albeit variable factors, each of which has exerted a marked influence on the human history of the High Arctic. Part II comprises a narrative accounting of the events of polar exploration which brought these two cultures into contact. This section is entitled "Circumstance," a term that seems to capture the play of chance and personality associated with narrative history, as well as the often ephemeral nature of the short-term history of events. Part III is an investigation of the interplay of culture and the environment in the contact era, as well as an assessment of the historical impact of the interface of these forces. Among the issues examined are material and technological exchanges between Inuit and Europeans, intercultural relations, the demographic impact of contact, and the effects of contact on wildlife in the High Arctic. This section is entitled "Change," as it is at the level of culture or ecology that significant transformations in human history can be identified and traced over time. Specifically, adjustments in the material and technological repertoire or the population levels of a society may be considered reliable indices of enduring social or cultural change. The book concludes with Part IV, a series of chapters on the more recent history of Ellesmere Island, focussing on the history of the Inuit community of Grise Fiord since 1951. This section incorporates the three major historical registers introduced earlier in the text, including the factor of circumstance, which brought Inuit from Quebec and Baffin Island to a region they had never before experienced; change, as they were obliged to make a major adjustment to a new environment, and finally continuity, as the adaptation of Inuit to life on Ellesmere Island was enabled by the application of long-standing techniques and vernacular traditions of living in the arctic environment, as developed and refined over hundreds of years.

Partly to underscore the relationships between human history and arctic ecology, and partly to acknowledge that the island had been named and utilized by Aboriginal people before the arrival of Europeans, I have chosen the title "Muskox Land" for this book. This term is the English translation of *Umingmak Nuna*, the name given by Inuit and Inughuit to Ellesmere Island prior to contact with Western explorers in the nineteenth century. It was a term that still had currency with Inughuit in the 1930s. As this book focusses on the theme of contact, I have chosen not to treat other recent aspects of the human history of Ellesmere Island, including the establishment of the High Arctic Weather Stations at Alert and Eureka around 1950 and the military history at the Alert Base from the late 1950s. For the history of the impressive scientific research program conducted by the Defence Research Board in this region between 1951 and 1974, readers are encouraged to read Geoffrey Hattersley-Smith's *North of Latitude Eighty*[1] or my own research bulletin on the cultural resources of the Defence Research Board camps in northern Ellesmere Island.[2] Moreover, in the discussion of the earlier expeditions to the region, I have decided not to treat their role in arctic science, as a good overview of their contributions is already available in Trevor Levere's *Science and the Canadian Arctic: a Century of Exploration, 1818-1918*.[3]

I hope this book will help readers enhance their understanding of the human history of this remote yet fascinating region, the High Arctic. Readers may also be encouraged to reflect on larger issues beyond the study of a specific region, including the nature of historical time and the need for critical engagement with its many entanglements and ambiguities. At least, this history of Ellesmere Island may show that the past is never played out in a single progression but rather in a counterpoint of different rhythmic elements. If we can isolate these component rhythms and discern how they interacted with one another historically, it may be possible to reconstruct an image of the past that does justice to its rich diversity.

CONTINUITIES

The Natural Environment, Culture, and Human History

The first part of this book is concerned with the continuities of history, the major forces that, however imperceptible to observers in the short term, nevertheless exerted an enduring and continuing impact on human societies in the High Arctic. Historical continuities can include long-range economic patterns such as the establishment of material opportunities or relative depravation confronting a group in a particular era. Fernand Braudel's *The Mediterranean*[1] and David Hackett Fischer's *The Great Wave*[2] are examples of this kind of "long-wave" analysis of economic trends. For the purpose of this book, I have chosen to focus on two other structural factors evident throughout the roughly 200 years of the region's post-contact history: the natural environment and culture.

That the natural environment played a role in Ellesmere Island's human history seems self-evident, although its dimensions are not fully understood. A generation ago, environmental issues were not within the repertoire of North American historians. In 1949, the publication of Fernand Braudel's *The Mediterranean* brought the study of the natural environment to the fore of European historical scholarship. In the last two decades, North American and British historians, too, have begun to explore the ecological relationships bearing on the history of this continent. With the rise of environmental history, such issues as climatic change, the degradation of environments through human interventions and other topics have begun to be explored.[3] There is little consensus on the focus for methodology or topics in this field. Much remains to be studied, especially the forces exerted by climate or geography on human history and the complex interrelationships of nature and culture, including the impact of humans on ecosystems and the influence of ecology on human history.

For the purpose of this study, the natural environment is defined as a combination of physical geography, climate, and ecology. An operating hypothesis has been that these physical factors have exerted far-reaching effects on the history of human populations inhabiting the High Arctic. Far more than the backdrop to human history, the environment is conceived as a major agent of history that unavoidably influenced the decisions and actions of the people operating within it.

This is not to argue a kind of environmental determinism, as such factors as culture, individual personality and circumstance are also given due weight in the following discussion. Accepting that there is a plurality of influences bearing on historical events, the structures of the natural environment can and do impose limits on the range of choices available to an individual or group at a particular point in time.

This section has also been structured to address long-term continuities of culture in the High Arctic. It must be acknowledged that "culture" is a problematic term with a wide range of meanings.[4] The *Concise Oxford Dictionary* provides a deceptively simple definition: "the customs, civilization, and achievements of a particular time or people,"[5] but this definition does not capture the enduring qualities of culture. A culture might initially belong to a particular time, people, or place, but can continue to inhabit the consciousness of its members long after they have travelled to a new place. A culture might develop in response to economic, technological, environmental, and ideological factors, but could persist well after these factors have ceased to influence it. The intellectual historian Richard Slotkin has provided another working definition: "it will be useful to think of culture as denoting those works and practices that have to do with the assigning or attribution of meaning and significance to the things, persons, and happenings of the material world."[6] However, culture is not merely a process of assigning meanings, but it also encompasses the concrete material and technological approaches of a group toward their environment. Incorporating both material and intellectual/ideological components of culture, the anthropologist David Bidney has offered another definition: "culture may be described denotatively as comprising the historically acquired actual and ideal forms of behaviour, feeling, and thought of members of society, as well as the products of these processes ...."[7] For this book, the term "culture" is used to depict the manifold ways human societies both think about and function within their environment, including their approach to and relationships with other cultures and the ecosystem.

Generally, the contact era of the High Arctic brought together two groups of cultures, European or Euro-American peoples on the one hand and Aboriginal peoples on the other. The Aboriginal peoples included West Greenlanders, the Inughuit, formerly known as the "Polar Eskimos" of northwestern Greenland, and Inuit of Canada's Arctic Archipelago, now living within the Territory of Nunavut. While individual differences of experience between these two groupings should not be minimized, European and Aboriginal peoples brought markedly distinctive cultural assumptions and ways of knowing to the contact experience. The post-contact human history of this region cannot be understood without reference to the diverging practices, systems of belief and material culture contributed by the two participating cultures and the ways their respective traditions were integrated and yet retained many distinctive differences even in the context of contact.

It is acknowledged the concept of culture cannot fully explain human motivation and action. Human history is also the product of individual consciousness, personality, and behaviour. While culture sets general parameters for human activity, this concept alone cannot enable us to predict how a particular person will react in specific circumstances. For that reason the second part of this book, under the rubric "Circumstance," addresses the issues of personality and circumstance in the treatment of expeditions to Ellesmere Island in the nineteenth and twentieth centuries. Yet even the very notion of individualism, so central to the self-concept of the explorers, was itself part of the nineteenth century cultural inheritance of the expansionist British, Anglo-American, and later, Anglo-Canadian, cultures that sponsored these expeditions. As will perhaps become evident in this study, the power of culture to mould individuals to respond in particular ways to their environment should never be underestimated, even when they imagine themselves to be the agents of change.

1
Geography and Climatic History of Ellesmere Island

As in other arctic regions, the physical environment of Ellesmere Island defines much of the scope of possible human activity within its territories. We might begin by positioning this land mass geographically, at the summit of the High Arctic. Ellesmere Island is the most northerly island in the Canadian Arctic Archipelago and, apart from the tip of neighbouring Greenland, which extends a mere 50 kilometres beyond its arctic flank, it is also the most northerly land mass in the world. Ellesmere's northern extremity — Cape Columbia at approximately 83° North latitude — is less than 800 kilometres from the North Pole. While the island stretches more than 750 kilometres to the south, even its southern coasts are in the vicinity of 77° North latitude. This fact of Ellesmere's extreme northernness, coupled with its proximity to both Greenland and the other arctic islands, may be viewed as defining characteristics of its natural and human history in all periods, including the present (Figure 1).

Geography: Land, Seas, and Coasts

Beyond its polar positioning, the island's physical geography and relationships to particular waters can also be seen as defining characteristics. In broad outline, it is a mountainous mass of rocky terrain, surrounded by ocean waters, and incised by fiords and channels extending far into the heart of the island. To the east, a succession of narrow channels separate Ellesmere from Greenland. On the island's southern flank, the waters of Jones Sound divide it from Devon Island. Along its western coasts Eureka Sound carves a channel between Ellesmere and Axel Heiberg islands. To the north, Ellesmere's broad coastline is bounded by the Arctic Ocean, there being no land lying between it and the northern islands of Siberia some 2,100 km distant, on the far side of the pole.

Not only is it surrounded by salt water, the island has one of the most extensive coastlines for its size in the world. Much of the interior is deeply gouged by some of the world's longest fiords, products of ancient glacial spillways. Among the most spectacular examples are the channels of Greely Fiord and Nansen Sound. Together, they form a continuous waterway in a broad arc between the northern part of Ellesmere Island, sometimes known as Grant Land, the island's central section to the south, and Axel Heiberg Island to the west. These and other fiords and inlets function to allow maritime access deep into the heart of the island.

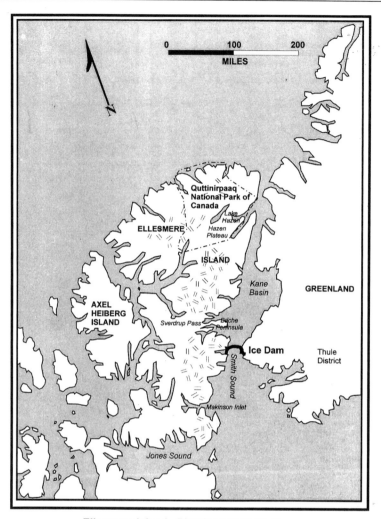

Ellesmere Island - Physiographic Features

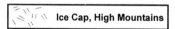 **Ice Cap, High Mountains**

Figure 1: Map of Ellesmere Island, showing the location of mountains and ice caps

Ellesmere is the most mountainous of the arctic islands as it possesses both the highest and the longest alpine ranges in eastern North America. Its surface area of 213,000 km^2 is only slightly smaller than the island of Great Britain.[1] This combination of factors — high mountains and a relatively large land mass — has enabled the development of quasi-continental climatic pockets contrasting with the overriding Arctic marine climate. The continental effect is particularly pronounced in Ellesmere's northern region, where a series of lofty cordilleran ranges coincides with the island's area of greatest breadth. These conditions help produce interior micro-climates of a markedly different character from those of the coasts facing the Arctic Ocean only 150 km to the north or the non-mountainous islands of the Queen Elizabeth group many hundreds of kilometres to the south.

Ellesmere Island is the site of the largest ice caps in Canada; combined its glaciers cover 83,000 km^2 or 40% of its surface area and comprise more than half the total ice cover of the Arctic Islands.[2] The largest of the Ellesmere ice caps, covering about 25,600 km^2, is in the most northerly part of the island. Sometimes referred to as the "Grant Land Ice Cap," this ice field extends from the heads of Otto and Hare fiords in the west to within 40 km of the Lincoln Sea to the northeast. To the north, the ice stretches to the coastal ranges, where its outlet glaciers push out into fiords opening to the Arctic Ocean. Among the island's other large ice caps is the Agassiz Mer de Glace, located between the Hazen Plateau and the Sverdrup Pass to the south. The pass also defines the northern margin of the third largest ice sheet on Ellesmere Island, which pushes out to the sea in three directions: to Buchanan Bay to the north, Smith Sound to the east, and along the northern coast of Makinson Inlet to the south.

The extent of glacial ice on Ellesmere Island is remarkable. Not only does it cover a broad surface area, the ice is often very thick, measuring well over 900 m deep over much of the Grant Land ice cap, and as deep as 1,300 m in some areas.[3] The tremendous weight of the ice has depressed the Earth's crust many dozens of metres. In areas of post-glacial emergence, isostatic rebound is pushing the land gradually upward toward pre-ice-age levels. Despite a warming trend in the twentieth century, glaciologists believe that Ellesmere's ice cover is nearly as extensive as it was during the last ice age, ca. 12000 to 10000 years BP (Before the Present).

Proximity to the other Queen Elizabeth Islands and to Greenland has given Ellesmere Island a pivotal role in the history of the High Arctic. Its southwestern tip is separated from North Kent Island by a narrow 4 to 8 km channel of turbulent water named Hell Gate by the

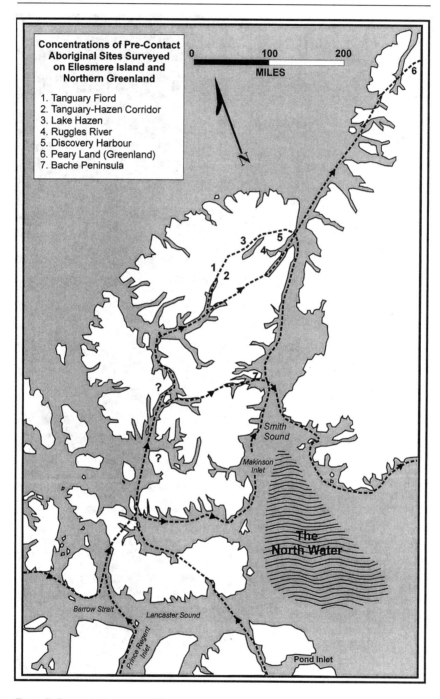

Figure 2: Pre-contact routes to Ellesmere Island and Greenland

Sverdrup expedition of 1898-1902. North Kent Island, in turn, is only 10 to 12 km across the Cardigan Strait from Devon Island's Grinnell Peninsula. Located athwart the eastern mouth of Jones Sound, Coburg Island similarly functions as a stepping stone between Ellesmere and Devon Islands. In this case, the southern tip of Coburg Island is about 20 km across Lady Ann Strait from Devon Island's northeastern coast, and only 11 km, across Glacier Strait, separates this island from a glacial foot off Ellesmere Island's southeastern shore.[4] On Ellesmere's western flank, Eureka Sound defines a narrow channel separating it from Axel Heiberg Island that closes to within 13 km along the Grinnell Land coast. On Ellesmere's east central coast, the waters of Smith Sound narrow at Cape Isabella to a 46-km-wide channel between the island and Greenland. Farther north, the two land masses are separated by the 19-km-wide Robeson Channel.

In pre-contact eras, these slender straits were the crossings by which various Native groups reached Ellesmere Island (Figure 2). They included the early "small-tool" cultures of 3000 to 4000 years BP and the Thule culture after 1000 BP. Each of these cultures migrated to Ellesmere Island from the south and west and proceeded along its coasts or overland en route to Greenland. There are a limited range of possibilities in access routes to Ellesmere Island, and similar routes must have been followed successively by all Aboriginal groups travelling to this land, from the Paleo-Eskimo cultures to the Thule people, the forerunner culture of today's Inuit. Most archaeologists and anthropologists have accepted the hypothesis that the majority of Greenland's current population is descended from Thule immigrants who passed through Ellesmere Island and spread along the Greenland coast. After a lapse of several centuries, Inuit from Baffin Island began again to cross these channels by the mid-nineteenth century and perhaps earlier. Around this time, Europeans also appeared in this region and began to utilize the narrow channels for marine navigation and, following the lead of the Inuit, for sledge travel.

The polar positioning of the Ellesmere Island contributed to these human migrations, as the freezing of the sea ice enhanced linkages between the islands of the Arctic Archipelago and Greenland. For up to nine months of the year, the sea ice freezes to form a variable surface over which travellers can travel between these land masses. Even so, sea-ice formation in the channels and straits between Ellesmere Island and other land masses is not always guaranteed, as ocean currents accelerate through the narrow passageways, opening leads and denying access to sledge travellers.

The physiography of Ellesmere Island is the product of complex geological processes operating over millions of years. As reconstructed by geologists, these processes have been varied, including folding, uplift, volcanic activity, and sedimentary deposits, resulting in a complex collection of landforms. As summarized by the geologist H.P. Trettin, the major geological regions of Ellesmere Island include the Franklinian Mobile Belt, a zone of Cretaceous volcanic and instrusive rock covering the northwestern area of Ellesmere; adjacent regions of sedimentary and volcanic rocks of deep water basins in the area of the Hazen Plateau; the syntectonic clastics of the Sverdrup Basin; the Franklinian Shelf stretching from southern Ellesmere Island, north to Greely Fiord, thence to the eastern coast of the island; and a smaller region of Canadian Shield comprising the landforms of southeastern Ellesmere Island.[5] Overall, the land masses of the Arctic Archipelago have been shaped by two periods of uplift, one before the Pleistocene era and characterized by faulting, during which the overall character of the islands was established. The other, later period of uplift probably related to isostatic rebound after the partial melting of the great ice caps following the last ice age.[6] Beyond the geological forces, climate has played a key role in the development of Ellesmere Island's landforms as cooling contributed to the great buildup of glacial ice, both depressing and scouring its rocky surfaces as the ice sheets spilled out into drainage basins, in the process carving the sides of mountains and valley floors. The erosional effects of glacial run-off in the warmer months further shaped this stark polar landscape over the millennia.

In the 1950s, geographer Andrew Taylor prepared a series of monographs on the physical geography of the Queen Elizabeth Islands. In broad outline, notwithstanding much improved recording of various features since that time, Taylor's division of northern Ellesmere into three major regions — the Grant Land Highlands, the Greely-Hazen Plateau, and the coastal sedimentary plateau — still seems an appropriate framework from which to approach its physiography.

Northern Ellesmere Island's physiography is dominated by a large belt of fold mountains across most of its northern flank. The spine of the Grant Land Mountains is the imposing United States Range and a series of smaller, connected ranges, including the Osborne Range, Garfield Range, British Empire Range, and Challenger Mountains.[7] Collectively, these ranges impart an extremely rugged character to much of the island's land mass. Rising to heights exceeding 2,600 m, the United States Mountains actually comprise two parallel ranges separated by a valley that follows the southwest to northwest strike of the ranges. The considerable height of these uplands and consequent low

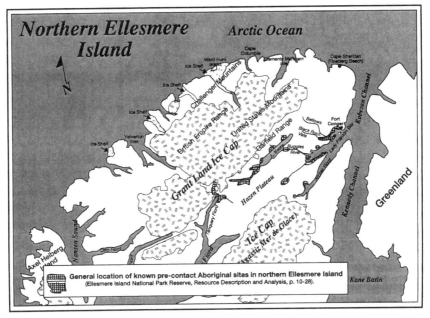

Figure 3: Map of Northern Ellesmere Island, showing the location of major features and the areas of pre-contact Aboriginal sites in this region

levels of solar radiation have enabled the build-up of the massive Grant Land Ice Cap. Engulfing many mountains, the ice cap has created a distinctive landscape of glaciers and nunataks or isolated mountain peaks surrounded by ice and snow. At its summit, the ice field rises above the mountains and presents a smooth, unbroken surface.[8] Two deep passes intersect the range and divide the ice cap into three segments. To the east, Piper Pass runs between Clements Markham Inlet and the Hazen Plateau, and, to the west, a pass connects the heads of Yelverton Inlet to the north and Tanquary Fiord to the south (Figure 3).

North of the United States ranges are the British Empire Mountains, a 48-km-wide cordilleran band that runs roughly from Yelverton Inlet to the northwest to within a few miles of Clements Markham Inlet on the northeastern coast. As Andrew Taylor has noted, this is not a true chain of mountains, but rather a mountainous area of disconnected peaks. Slightly lower than their United States Range counterparts, the British Empire Mountains vary between 1,300 and 2,300 m above sea level. These mountains are also largely surrounded by the ice cap and typified by nunataks projecting above the surface.[9]

The most northerly mountains on Ellesmere Island are the Challenger Mountains, a coastal range sandwiched between the British Empire Range and the Arctic Ocean. Here the Grant Land Ice Cap reaches its northern terminus. The range is lower in elevation than the interior ranges, and its peaks are generally between 1,000 and 1,500 m. As a result of increased solar radiation at lower altitudes, the Grant Land Ice Cap has largely retreated from the coastal areas, and glaciers persist only near the summits of the range.[10]

The Garfield Range of mountains that hugs the northern shore of Lake Hazen acts as a barrier between the lake and the Grant Land ice cap and nunataks of the United States Range to the north. To the east, the chain extends across the Hazen Plateau while, to the west, it runs virtually to the head of Tanquary Fiord. The mountains, which tower as much as 1,500 m above Lake Hazen, typically consist of steep snow-free slopes facing south, with north-facing slopes of shallow gradients covered in snow and ice. At intervals, the range is bisected by broad valleys 5 to 8 km in width that are occasionally filled by glacial tongues, such as the monumental Henrietta Nesmith Glacier that descends to within 4 km of Lake Hazen near its northwestern end.[11]

To the southwest, the Conger Mountains are a structural continuation of the Garfield Range. They were named by American Adolphus Greely, who sighted them during a sledging expedition to the interior of northern Ellesmere Island in 1882.[12] The mountains begin about 16 km west of Mount Osborne, which borders the Henrietta Nesmith Glacier and marks the terminus of the Garfield Range. Skirting the southern edge of the great Grant Land ice cap north of the head of Tanquary Fiord, the Conger Range continues into the highlands north of the head of Hare Fiord.[13] The over-all extent of the range is about 180 km. Nearly all its peaks are ice-covered, although most of the southern slopes are ice-free. Many of the valleys between the peaks are filled with glacial tongues spilling out to the south from the Grand Land Ice Cap. The glaciers that descend to the floors of the Lewis and Macdonald river valleys are met by tongues cascading from the smaller Viking Ice Cap west of the head of Tanquary Fiord. In some cases, they create a spectacular effect, such as the Scylla and Charybdis glaciers, which almost touch at the valley floor.

Beyond their effects on the interior climate of northern Ellesmere Island, these highlands have produced an additional natural effect. At higher elevations, snow has accumulated to produce the glacial ice caps which are the source of water for all the rivers and streams of the island, enabling the growth of vegetation and production of a food base for the terrestrial mammal populations. At the same time, the upland regions are a series of polar deserts, unproductive of plant or animal life, and little more than a backdrop to the human history events that unfolded beneath their forbidding peaks.

Below the Grant Land Highlands, a broad plateau of varying elevation and gradient stretches to the coast in virtually all directions. To the north, the coastal plateau is a succession of sedimentary peaks in an advanced stage of erosion. Along the northeastern coast, the plateau is a lower extension of the Hazen Plateau and, along the eastern coast, facing Robeson Channel, the plateau ends abruptly in steep cliffs up to 500 m high, with high scree embankments. To the southeast, the coastal terminus of the plateau varies from rounded peaks in the area of Discovery Harbour to precipitous cliffs and scree slopes along the coasts of the various tributary fiords of Lady Franklin Bay: Archer, Conybeare, and Chandler fiords. To the southwest, the deeply incised coastal walls of Greely Fiord and its major tributary channels, Borup, Otto and Hare Fiords, present similarly steep cliffs rising to heights of up to 1,000 m or more.[14] In the case of Tanquary Fiord, the channel cliffs rise as mountain peaks as high as 1,600 m above the head of the fiord. The Grant Land Mountains are also incised by several wide valley systems forming extensive coastal lowlands. At Tanquary Fiord, several river valleys converge to form a large 300 km^2 lowland. At the head of Clements Markham Inlet on the northeast coast, large outwash plains combine with raised deltas to form another major coastal lowland.[15]

The other major physiographic region of note in northern Ellesmere Island is the Hazen Plateau, a large tableland stretching from near the head of Greely Fiord in a northeasterly direction to the coastal plateaux between Lady Franklin and Black Cliffs bays. The Hazen Plateau separates the Grant Land Mountains and Ice Cap to the northwest from the Agassiz Ice Cap and Lady Franklin Bay to the southeast. Measuring approximately 400 km from southwest to northeast, and 100 km or more in width from Lady Franklin Bay to the highlands to the northwest, it comprises approximately 26,000 km^2.[16] The Hazen Plateau is one of the largest ice-free regions on Ellesmere Island. Its fortuitous positioning on the leeward side of the Grant Land Mountains has fostered unusually productive micro-climates, assuring it a strategic role in the human history of the High Arctic.

The outstanding physical feature of the Hazen Plateau is Lake Hazen, a huge freshwater lake located in a trough along the southeastern flank of the Garfield Mountains. Approximately 80 km in length and between 5 and 13 km in width, it is the largest lake in the world north of the Arctic Circle. The lake functions as the principal drainage basin for glacial runoff flowing to the south off the Grant Land Ice Cap. Lake Hazen is connected to the sea by the Ruggles River, its principal outlet, which flows in a southeasterly direction to the head of Chandler Fiord. Historically, this connection enabled arctic charr to reach and populate the lake, although these migrations have apparently now ceased. For more than 4,000 years, the Ruggles River has also offered a vital access route for humans travelling from the eastern coast to the Hazen region.

Major drainage channels on the plateau generally run in a northwest to southeast direction, perpendicular to the main strike of the plateau. They form steep-sided canyons, particularly on the south side of the lake, where the rivers cut through the raised southern rim of the plateau. A major exception is the Dodge River, flowing into Conybeare Fiord, which runs parallel to Archer Fiord, a tributary channel to Lady Franklin Bay.[17]

Given the rugged topography that characterizes much of Ellesmere Island's interior, its coasts have assumed a particular importance throughout its human history. They have served as the major approachways for newcomers in all historical eras up to the Second World War. As well, coastal fiords and inlets have provided access to connecting valleys leading to the interior and its comparatively rich game animal resources. The coasts have also been the sites of settlements for all groups occupying the island, particularly the cultures relying primarily on maritime resources, such as the Thule-Inuit and Inughuit. Even government installations of Euro-North Americans, initially dependent on supply by sea, have clung to the island's coasts.

The coastline of Nares Strait has been of particular importance to human movements and occupation. Really a series of channels separating Ellesmere Island's eastern coasts from northwest Greenland, the Nares Strait is the popular name for the waters between Baffin Bay to the south and the Arctic Ocean on the north. Most of the shoreline along this rugged stretch from Smith Sound to the island's northeastern tip at Cape Union is characterized by high cliffs alternating with steep slopes of eroded bedrock.[18] Ubiquitous erosion is reflected in high scree slopes along much of this coastline. But for the presence of sea ice that freezes fast to the shore in three of the four seasons, much of the coast would be impassable. Along numerous stretches between Smith Sound and the Arctic Ocean, Ellesmere Island's sheer embankments and boulder-strewn shores render coastal land travel virtually impossible between July and mid-September.

In comparison with the steep-walled character of the Robeson Channel coastline, Ellesmere Island's northeastern coasts are unusually low-lying and regular. This coast defines the northeastern boundary of the Hazen Plateau and is characterized by flat shores behind which undulating hills rise gradually to the plateau's height of 600 m or higher. Apart from Lincoln Bay to the south and Dumbell Bay and Hilgard Bay to the north, the coast runs in a generally smooth arc between these features.

Ellesmere Island's northern coast is characterized by a succession of craggy mountains intersected by numerous fiords. The fiords are the flooded extensions of deep straight-walled glacial valleys butting through the cordilleran wall of mountain ranges from the Grant Land Ice cap.[19] In several of the fiords, such as Disraeli Fiord and McClintock Inlet, the outlet glaciers push well beyond the heads of the fiords. Among the most remarkable features along this coast are several ice shelves or large floating rafts of ice frozen fast to the coast and extending out into the Arctic Ocean. In the northern hemisphere, ice shelves are found only along the northern coasts of Ellesmere Island and Greenland. The largest example on Ellesmere is the Ward Hunt Ice Shelf that presently extends about 35 km north off the mouth of Disraeli Fiord and 15 km beyond Ward Hunt Island. Lengthwise, it stretches approximately 80 km from west to east between McClintock Inlet and Markham Fiord. A fixture for the last 3,500 years, the Ward Hunt Ice Shelf is the source of various ice islands that calved from the shelf between the 1940s and the 1980s.

In the fall, rapidly dropping temperatures produce a remarkable and indispensable feature hugging the coasts of the High Arctic regions, the ice foot. The product of tidal action, this feature consists of a belt of ice formed between the high- and low-water marks of the tides. Supplemented by multi-year ice that forms in, or is carried to, the mouths of many fiords and inlets that cut into the coastline, the ice foot was historically the principal travelling surface along the length of the island. All pre-contact Aboriginal groups travelled along it and were emulated by European and North American explorers during the exploration era, ca. 1850 to 1940.

The term "ice foot" was coined by the party of the American Elisha Kent Kane, who learned of its importance from the Inughuit of northwest Greenland while in close contact with this group in the 1850s. According to Kane, the term was adapted from the Danish *eis-fod* to designate the land-fast shore ice of arctic regions. While this feature disappeared during the summer months in more southerly latitudes, he observed:

> in this our high northern winter harbor, it is a perennial growth, clinging to the bold faces of the cliffs, following the sweeps of the bays and the indentations of rivers. This broad platform, although changing with the seasons, never disappears. It served as our highway of travel, a secure and level sledge-road, perched high above the grinding ice of the sea, and adapting itself to the tortuosities of the land. As such I shall call it the "ice-belt."[20]

Taking the Inughuit practice as an example, Kane utilized the ice foot as a travelling surface in his own sledging excursions. He was followed in this practice by various explorers and their parties, especially by Robert E. Peary at the end of the century. Throughout the polar exploration era, the importance of the ice foot along Ellesmere

Figure 4: "Crossing the Ice Belt at Coffee Gorge." Illustration from Elisha Kent Kane, *Arctic Explorations*, Vol. I, Plate between pp. 92-93.

Island's east coast was evident in its designation as the "Highroad to the North Pole"[21] (Figures 4 and 5).

For much of the year, the surface of the Arctic Ocean and nearby waters of the Arctic Archipelago is covered with sea ice. Even in late summer, two thirds of the surface of the Arctic Ocean is covered with ice, and comparable levels of sea ice have been recorded in the channels surrounding Ellesmere Island. During the period between September and May, most of these waters appear entirely covered in ice, yet the ice of the Arctic Ocean, Nares Strait, and Jones Sound is constantly in motion, propelled by tides, currents, and winds. Periodically leads of open water open between floes, only to close again as the tides or winds shift.

The surface of the polar ice pack is highly irregular, consisting of a complex amalgam of new and old ice floes. Dramatic collisions occur when floes are driven together by currents, winds, and tides. As two floes smash together, rafting typically occurs as one slides over its counterpart, often for considerable distances, before its advance is halted. The collision of two floes typically produces a jagged surface of pressure ridges or hillocks of ice, presenting considerable obstacles to human attempts to traverse them. As well, wherever ice floes raft or are broken apart by a collision with another floe, a corresponding area of open water is generated to compensate, generating leads which also present obstacles to surface travellers. The pressure of moving floes is particularly great along the coast, where the ice is driven against the land. In these cases, "since the

Figure 5: "Ka-ko-chee-ah and Ah-now-kan on the ice foot, Port Foulke, northern Greenland." Credit: American Museum of Natural History (New York City), Donald B. MacMillan Collection, Crocker Land, 1913–17, Negative No. 231541.

land is immovable, the ice gets crushed and heaped into a jagged chaos that can hardly be conceived by those who have not seen it."[22]

Along the coast, a belt of fast ice develops beyond the ice foot in places where the configuration of the coast and its subsurface features are conducive to its formation. Fast ice is ice that freezes fast to the coast and is generally not dislodged by melting in the spring and summer. It forms in places where the coastline is irregular, the bottom is shallow, or the presence of small islands inhibits ice movement. Generally, the outer margin of fast ice corresponds to the edge of the continental shelf, where the ocean floor rapidly drops off from the shelf's shallower depths of 10 to 20 fathoms (20-35 m). Beyond the fast ice is found pack ice. This ice is much more variable in its surface character and movements, subject as it is to the action of tides, wind, and currents, particularly in the months between June and January. Generally, in most areas around Ellesmere Island, the pack ice stabilizes by February, but this is not always the case. For example, in early February 1927, members of the RCMP detachment at Bache Peninsula attempted to cross Smith Sound to Greenland but were forced back when they found the ice was in motion.[23] In places where the depth of the ocean is less than 20 m, hummocky ice may be stranded, forming high ridges adjacent to the fast ice. The most level areas of pack ice are found out in the ocean far from land. Here, protected from the effects of colliding ice floes, the ice is less likely to be pressed together. In places nearer the shore where the ice floes raft, the pressure can pile peaks up to 19 to 22 m above sea level.[24]

In polar regions, ocean waters freeze and thaw according to their own seasonal rhythms. Rapid warming of water during the 24-hour daylight of summer delays the seas' freezing until well after the change of seasons. Data from expeditions to Nares Strait since 1850 suggest that ice movements in the Ellesmere–Greenland channel generally cease during the first three weeks of January. Occasionally, as in 1970-71, the ice in Nares Strait does not freeze fast until February, with more or less continuous opening of leads, ridging of pressure ice, and refreezing up to that time.[25] Once frozen solid, the sea ice remains frozen until late spring, as thawing is delayed by extremely cold temperatures, deflection of solar radiation, and the long winter. Beginning with the ice foot's melting in May, pack ice recedes until channels become navigable by mid- to late July. At the same time, climatic variability produces a wide range of possible results, depending on the year. In a milder year, the ice can break up early; in a cold year, Nares Strait may not thaw sufficiently to enable vessels to penetrate the channel even in the summer.

A similar pattern has been observed for the Arctic Ocean, where pack ice freezes more or less into a congealed mass by February, to become increasingly unstable with the return of warmer weather after May. Even so, ocean currents and winds, sometimes in concert with the subsurface structure of the ocean floor, can cause leads or cracks in the ice pack to open in any season (Figure 93). In the age of North Polar exploration, this came into play during Robert Peary's last two polar expeditions. Striking out across the ice pack in late February and early March in 1906 and 1909, in both years Peary encountered a large stretch of open water, which he named the "Big Lead." A recurrent feature even in the coldest months, this lead characteristically formed in the ice pack where the continental shelf of the Arctic Ocean drops off to greater depths.[26]

For Aboriginal travellers, seasonal shifts in sea ice historically created opportunities and imposed constraints on surface travel in the region. Travel on the coastal ice foot needed to be planned on a seasonal basis to take advantage of the surface ice when adequately frozen in the colder months and to avoid becoming stranded when melting produced "rotten" ice in the summer and early autumn. In the age of exploration, the more sagacious European visitors who studied and emulated Inuit methods likewise adapted their travel patterns to the rhythms of sea-ice formation and ablation.

In the predominantly maritime environments of the Queen Elizabeth Islands, both natural and human history have been heavily influenced by the surrounding ocean waters. The sea is the home of much of the region's wildlife and food resources. Historically, it provided the surface for much of the human transport in the region, whether by boat in areas of open water or by sledge or foot over the sea ice that covers the saltwater channels in three of the four seasons. Ocean currents have also been responsible for bringing driftwood to the shores of Ellesmere and other islands. For the Independence cultures who first inhabited the island, driftwood was an essential material for use in making weapons, sledge frameworks, and shelter supports. In the last 1,000 years, the maritime culture of the Thule-Inuit relied on the currents to break up the ice pack in the colder months, enabling marine mammals to be hunted along the floe edge. Generally, oceans have played determining roles in the region's climate, although the effects have varied according to which of two great bodies of water has exerted the dominant influence on air masses in the region at a given point in time, the Arctic or the Atlantic oceans.

The saltwater channel between Ellesmere Island and Greenland has been one of the most important transportation waterways throughout High Arctic history. Running in a southwest to northeast direction, it afforded the only continuous route from Smith Sound to the north. In warmer months, apart from periods of sea-ice buildup, the waters of this channel can be navigated in good weather. In favourable conditions, at particular points such as Smith Sound, the narrowing channel can be crossed by boat, although prevailing north-south currents bearing ice floes and icebergs present considerable hazards and difficulties to craft of any size. In pockets along the eastern coasts of Ellesmere Island, these waters remain open during the winter, enabling various wildlife species to overwinter and, hence, fostering opportunities for occupation by Aboriginal populations depending on these animals for subsistence.

In the pre-contact era, far more viable than ocean navigation was travel over the ice surfaces that cover these channels during most of the year. During the region's brief summers, members of the Thule culture followed the ice foot along the coast and crossed the straits of Smith Sound and Robeson Channel by dog team. Alternately, in periods of open water, they travelled in skin boats, either kayaks or umiaks. In addition to transport, hunters used these boats to pursue such sea mammals as walruses and narwhals. After the Thule-Inuit of the High Arctic ceased making boats some time after 1600, these waters were not navigated again until large European vessels sailed to the Thule region after 1800.

While occasionally yielding access by ships to the Arctic Ocean, the Ellesmere–Greenland channel has proved a problematic, often treacherous route. Moving pack ice carried from the Arctic Ocean south through Nares Strait is prevalent throughout the brief navigation season between late July and September. Even during these few favourable months shore-fast ice typically extends far out into Kane Basin from the Greenland coast. Icebergs are numerous in the channel as they calve from the 100-km-wide Humboldt Glacier directly into Kane Basin. Further north the Petermann Glacier calves many other icebergs into Hall Basin, adding to the flotilla of hazards. The dangerous character of moving pack ice in the channel is compounded by weather conditions. Fog is a recurrent problem for shipping due to the combination of open water and pack ice that persists much of the year. The latter part of the navigation season also coincides with the period of greatest wind turbulence in the fall,[27] when opposing Atlantic and Arctic air masses collide to generate severe storms. Of Nares Strait, explorer Robert Peary wrote:

> There is probably no place where ice navigation is so hazardous as in the Smith Sound, or American route to the pole, where the heaviest of ice, swift currents, narrow channels, and iron shores make the pressures sudden, erratic, almost continuous, and of great intensity. The negotiation of the three hundred and fifty miles [560 km] of virtually solid ice of all conceivable shapes and sizes that lie between Etah and Cape Sheridan presents problems and difficulties, which will test the experience and nerve of the ablest navigator, and the powers of the strongest vessel that man can build.[28]

For many thousands of years, the dominant saltwater body influencing Ellesmere Island's environment has been the Arctic Ocean. This cold mediterranean sea is bordered by the circumpolar lands and islands of Greenland, North America, and the vast Eurasian continent.[29] While comprising only 2.8 percent of the Earth's saltwater surface, the ocean exerts a powerful influence, not only over the climate of arctic regions but over the northern hemisphere as a whole. Since the last ice age, the ocean's surface has been largely covered by the polar ice pack, an agglomeration of multi-year floes in more or less constant motion between January and June. Deflecting the oblique rays of solar radiation, the pack ice combines with the Earth's rotation to generate a cold high pressure cyclone which dominates the winter climate of the entire arctic region.

Ocean currents exert a major influence on the climate and weather of Ellesmere Island. The ocean's influence derives partly from its subsurface structure, in conjunction with prevailing wind patterns, which produces currents with far-reaching effects. Beyond the continental shelves of the circumpolar land masses, which spread far to the north of Eurasia, the greater part of the ocean floor is covered by the Abyssal Plain, a vast triangular trough 3,100 to 4,650 m in depth. It extends from north of Greenland in a southwesterly direction across the northwestern flank of Canada's arctic islands to the Beaufort Sea. Here, the edge of the trough pushes west toward Siberia's Taymyr Peninsula and back toward Greenland, to the north of Franz Josef Land and Spitsbergen. The Abyssal Plain is bisected by the Lomonosov Ridge, a long narrow plateau that thrusts as high as 3,000 m above its floor to within 1,000 to 2,000 m of the surface and stretches from the Siberian shelf across the pole to its terminus in the Lincoln Sea about 250 km north of Ellesmere Island.[30]

The waters of the Arctic Ocean circulate in a generally clockwise direction, driven by the high pressure vortex that forms to the northwest of the Canadian archipelago. Here the subsurface features come into play as the water moves from the Chukchi Sea to the vicinity of the ridge of the Eurasian continental shelf and along its axis to move out of the ocean in a cold current along the east coast of Greenland. The continental shelf north of Franz Josef Land and Spitsbergen plays a role in channelling the water toward its primary outlet in the north Atlantic, while the arctic cyclone also drives some of the water to the west of Greenland to produce a prevailing southerly current through Nares Strait between Greenland and Ellesmere Island (Figure 6).[31] The Lomonosov Ridge is also a factor in deflecting some of this water into the channel.

Remote as it is from temperate latitudes, Ellesmere Island's climate and animal populations, at least on its productive southeastern marine flank, are also heavily influenced by warm Atlantic water. Here the dominant influence is the West Greenland current, a combination of cold Arctic and warmer Atlantic waters, that flows north along Greenland's west coast. These waters initially combine southwest of Iceland, where the cold East Greenland current meets an offshoot of the warm Atlantic Gulf Stream. Together, these waters form the Irminger Current, which flows in a southerly direction, rounds the southern tip of Greenland and shifts northward as the West Greenland current. The waters are not really mixed but layered, with the cold Arctic water flowing on top of the warmer Atlantic undercurrent.[32]

The effects of the West Greenland current on animal life in the Davis Strait/Baffin Bay regions are important and varied. The warmer Atlantic waters are credited with carrying larger concentrations of phytoplankton and zooplankton to higher latitudes of the Baffin Bay region than would otherwise be expected. Both forms of plankton are the basis of arctic food chains on which sea mammals ultimately depend. Moreover, as archaeologist Moreau Maxwell has pointed out, contact between the cold and warmer waters and the two marine biomes overlapping, produces richer food resources than are generated by a single current.[33]

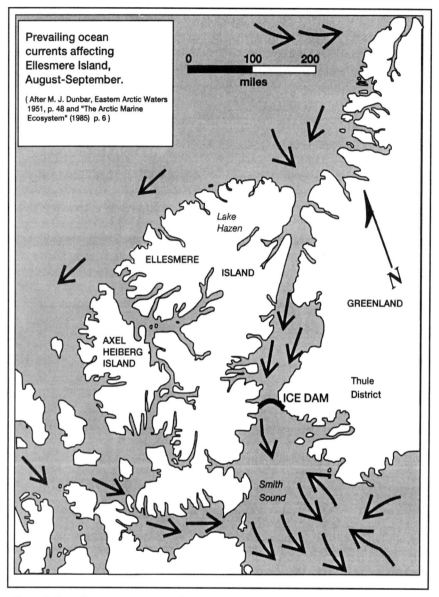

Prevailing ocean
currents affecting
Ellesmere Island,
August-September.

(After M. J. Dunbar, Eastern Arctic Waters
1951, p. 48 and "The Arctic Marine
Ecosystem" (1985) p. 6)

0   100   200
miles

Lake
Hazen

ELLESMERE
ISLAND

GREENLAND

AXEL
HEIBERG
ISLAND

Thule
District

ICE DAM

Smith
Sound

N

Figure 6: Prevailing ocean currents affecting Ellesmere Island, August – December

A further aspect to the physical environment is the factor of wind. In various seasons, the region periodically experiences high winds, which, combined with very low temperatures, can pose major hazards for its inhabiting populations. Ellesmere Island is dominated by two quasi-permanent air systems. One system is a low-pressure area varying between sites in the Labrador Sea and Baffin Bay and is at maximum depth in the winter. The other is a centre of high pressure positioned over the Arctic Ocean, also at maximum height in winter. The prevailing winds are easterlies, blowing most heavily in the winter.[34] At Fort Conger, during the U.S. Lady Franklin Bay expedition to northern Ellesmere Island, this party recorded wind speeds of 104 kmph on 16 January 1882, with gusts of 130-145 kmph. In 1958, a team of scientists based at Lake Hazen, in the interior, recorded a storm on 17-18 January with winds of 65-80 kmph.[35]

Some of the most turbulent weather has been reported in the autumn, when arctic and southern air masses collide to produce ferocious winds. Such is the importance of wind that the Inughuit, the inhabitants of northwestern Greenland, traditionally designated different groups and their homelands by the names of different kinds of wind. Writing about the era before the First World War, the Dane Knud Rasmussen described the effects of just one of the winds characterizing this area:

> I received so violent a blow in the back that I was unable to get up for a moment, but when at last I succeeded in rising to my knees, I saw that all the many sledges which a moment ago had driven in a long string one behind the other, were swept together into one huge pile.... As it was quite impossible to stand upright, not to mention driving, we let ourselves be blown up on land with sledges and dogs, until we found some little shelter in a clough [ravine] by a broad tongue of ice where the sledges could be anchored and the dogs tethered. Hardly was this done when the *Föhn*, with the roar of a hurricane, swept down upon us from the mountains and the inland-ice and made us suspect that the world itself was going under.[36]

Beyond the difficulties imposed on land travel by gale-force winds, the winds greatly increased the risks of travel on both sea ice and water. Rasmussen also observed that high winds produced "huge fissures in the ice, frothing white, and a few hours after the outbreak there was open sea where shortly before we had driven our sledges."[37] To Rasmussen, this incident well illustrated the importance of understanding the role of the wind, especially for the Inughuit, a hunting people dependent on the sea.

Climate and High Arctic History

Climate is another great environmental factor that, in concert with physical geography, broadly establishes the opportunities for, and limits to, viable human occupation.[38] In a harsh and marginal natural environment such as Ellesmere Island, we would expect climatic factors to assume a particular importance, especially for cultures dependent on the region's natural resources.

While most observers agree on the importance of climatic factors in human history, establishing the nature and chronology of climatic history is more problematic. The writings of a number of arctic climatologists suggest that, as in other regions, the High Arctic climate has undergone major oscillations of varying duration and intensity.[39] If these scientists are right, climatic change has occurred and recurred on a grand scale, manifested in long-term trends lasting centuries or millennia; in the medium term of 30 to 60 years;[40] and in the short term, through fluctuations lasting 5 to 10 years. Such variations are believed to have played an important role in establishing opportunities for and impediments to viable human occupation. Dramatic shifts have also been recorded from one year to the next, with either positive or negative consequences for the region's wildlife and dependent human populations. Seasonal patterns are highly variable, but nevertheless influenced by the larger climatic cycles, their complex rhythmic counterpoints of warming and cooling, moisture and dryness, ice formation and ablation.

On the broadest scale, the Arctic climate is the product of a complex of factors developing over millions of years, focussing on northward drift and consequent cooling of the land masses ringing the polar regions. Continental cooling caused increased mean surface winds to bring warm, moist Atlantic air over the circumpolar land surface. The Atlantic air, precipitating, produced large continental ice shelves, which, in turn, cooled arctic air masses to help produce surface pack ice over much of the Arctic Ocean. Both terrestrial and marine ice masses deflected solar radiation back to an almost cloudless atmosphere less capable of absorbing long-wave radiation. In this way, the build-up of ice over much of the circumpolar land and sea contributed to a self-sustaining polar climatic environment within which cooling continental and marine influences were mutually reinforcing.

Within this broad climatic structure, dramatic oscillations between climatic warming and cooling cycles have been recorded over the last 700,000 years.[41] One of the principal techniques by which climatic trends have been measured has been ice-core analysis. This method involves drilling into a glacier and extracting a cylindrical core for dating analysis of its layers by various methods. Christian Vibe's earlier attempts to identify patterns in the arctic climate were in part extrapolated from Lauge Koch's compilation of empirical reports of sea ice levels in the waters off eastern Greenland.

It is acknowledged that identifying regional climatic cycles based on the analysis of ice cores or sea ice conditions is a broad-brush undertaking that can overlook significant local differences. Beyond the variability of the physical environment, cultural groups historically differed in terms of the suitability of their material responses to High Arctic conditions. Geographer John D. Jacobs has proposed a useful concept, climatic stress, as an indicator of viable human activity in the Arctic. The degree of climatic stress on humans working outdoors in the winter is indicated by a combination of meteorological and other variables. These include: wind-chill, a combination of temperature and wind speed that approximates the loss of heat from the body, and the clothing unit (clo), a measure of the amount of insulation required to maintain body heat at a given metabolic rate.[42] It would seem self-evident that, in colder cycles, accumulated climatic stress exceeds the stress levels of warmer periods; theoretically there would be a threshold beyond which humans could not viably function for extended periods. However, the threshold itself is variable according to the insulating qualities of clothing and its capacity to limit the effects of wind-chill through the organization of activities according to the weather. This reminds us that the role of culture, as well as nature, must be factored into any assessments of the impact of the physical environment on human history; these issues are explored in the following four chapters.

For the human occupation of the Arctic Islands, the critical climatic shift apparently occurred about 11000 BP when a warming trend precipitated the retreat of the ice caps and the development of both terrestrial species clusters in non-glaciated areas and favourable marine habitats in adjacent waterways. Ice-core analysis by climatologists situates the post-glacial optimum in the High Arctic at 4000 to 5000 BP, followed by a general cooling trend.[43] These studies also reveal shorter warming intervals within the broader context of climatic deterioration during the last 4,000 to 4,500 years. For example, an ice core from Meighan Island to the west of Axel Heiberg Island indicates a protracted interval of negative mass balance (net ablation exceeding accumulation), indicating climatic improvement between ca. 660 and 2000-2500 BP. This sample corresponds to another ice core from an Ellesmere ice cap, which similarly shows a general warming interval between 700 and 2400 BP.[44]

Carbon dating of driftwood found at various locations in the High Arctic reveals the periodic breakup of the pack ice in the region's channels during the last 4,000 years. Driftwood was a vital source of fuel and materials for weapons and tent supports for the Independence cultures and their Thule-Inuit successors. For example, archaeologist Eigil Knuth has carbon-dated driftwood charcoal found at Independence Fiord off the north coast of Greenland to 3600 to 4700 BP, indicating its use by the Independence I culture between ca. 3600 and 4000 BP. Knuth has noted that occupation of this region at that time must have coincided with a warmer climatic interval, when reduced levels of pack ice in the Arctic Ocean enabled driftwood from Siberian rivers to reach the northern shores of Greenland.[45]

The presence of driftwood also confirms that, at various intervals since initial occupation, High Arctic waterways were sufficiently open to enable the exploitation of marine mammal resources. Biologists have established that ringed seals shift locations in response to ice conditions,[46] requiring Thule-Inuit populations dependent on seals to move accordingly. In northeast Ellesmere Island, driftwood samples dated to 3650 BP suggest relatively open waters during the summer months, as do samples from Disraeli Fiord dated to 3400 to 3000 BP. Marine mammals were also an ancillary food source of some importance to the earlier "small-tool" cultures.

Geographers Thomas Stewart and John England have used driftwood to identify more recent climatic warming trends at ca 1000 BP, coinciding with re-occupation of the High Arctic by the Thule culture.[47] One thousand years ago, the waters between Ellesmere Island and Greenland were sufficiently free of ice to permit extensive summer hunting of marine mammals, including whales from kayaks or umiaks. Moreau Maxwell has inferred that up to the late sixteenth century these channels were sufficiently open to permit summer hunting from boats as far north as 80° North latitude on the Ellesmere side and farther north on the Greenland side.[48] Hunting at these remote latitudes took place during summer excursions from base settlements in the Smith Sound regions of both Ellesmere and Greenland. The temporary character of the Thule excursions to the Lady Franklin Bay region is evidenced by the extant record of numerous tent rings, indicating temporary, mild-weather occupations. The presence of several Thule stone dwelling remains around Lady Franklin Bay and at Lake Hazen suggests that some of the migrating families wintered on occasion in the north and possibly remained for several years in succession.[49] However, even during the climatic optimum, long-term occupation of northern Ellesmere Island was problematic.

Between AD 1400 and 1600, climatic deterioration produced progressively colder summers as the Little Ice Age developed. Increased pack ice made hunting from boats difficult and eventually impossible in more northerly locations. Despite the worsening conditions, a few families continued to press into the far north beyond the limits of viable occupation and hunting. Eigil Knuth discovered an umiak frame, carbon dated to ca. AD 1490, on the north coast of Greenland, where it was apparently abandoned due to lack of open water.[50] On the Ellesmere side, archaeological sites at Lady Franklin Bay and Lake Hazen excavated by Moreau Maxwell document the poignancy of a few families' futile attempts to survive during this period of a descending climatic juggernaut.[51]

With the further advance of the Little Ice Age, serious consequences were in store generally for High Arctic populations. The progressively cooling climate forced most resident populations of the Thule culture to withdraw from the Arctic Archipelago,[52] and Greenland's populations fragmented into small isolated groups. Areas where coastal travel was difficult became uninhabited and communication between certain areas ceased altogether.[53] The most striking example was the complete loss of contact after AD 1600 between the Inughuit of northwestern Greenland and other populations south of Melville Bay.

Beyond longer climatic trends, some scholars have argued that medium-term episodes of 30 to 100 years have also had critical effects on High Arctic wildlife and, by extension, humans depending on them. Danish scientist Christian Vibe asserted that the climate of this region is in a cycle of three distinct phases, each lasting roughly 50 years, heavily influenced by sunspot activity.[54] The phases represent general trends of cooling, warming, or stagnation ("pulsation"), each with distinctive effects on animal populations.

Vibe's model may help explain some of the most important climatic trends affecting the faunal and human histories of northwestern Greenland and Ellesmere Island over the last 250 years. Between approximately AD 1740 and 1810, the regions bordering Baffin Bay were experiencing a succession of drift ice pulsation and melting episodes. Increased precipitation covered winter foraging grounds with an ice crust, causing the decimation of muskox and caribou populations in these areas. At the same time, these conditions were favourable for the hunting of marine mammals in more northerly regions, as leads and polynyas expanded and remained open during the crucial winter and spring months.[55]

Meanwhile, a great buildup of sea ice in northern Baffin Bay after AD 1600, compounded by drifting ice during the pulsation and melting episodes after 1740, caused congested ice conditions to persist south of the North Water for the balance of the eighteenth century. These conditions forced the Greenland whale (*Balaena mysticetus*) to the south, beyond the reach of the Inughuit, but easily accessible to European whalers. Heavier sea ice also prevented communication between Inughuit and West Greenlanders and delayed contact with Europeans who could not penetrate the ice barrier in Baffin Bay. Whaling began in Davis Strait in 1719 and continued for nearly 100 years. The whalers ventured as far north as Melville Bay but, due to the ice conditions, were unable to follow the whales to their summer habitats in northern Baffin Bay. In 1818, the ice jam broke, a delayed reaction to a warming cycle that ended in the early nineteenth century, enabling two British ships to cross Melville Bay to reach Cape York in Avanersuaq or the Thule District, the homeland of the Inughuit.[56]

Around 1810, a cold, dry, stable climatic episode began and persisted until roughly 1860. Colder temperatures caused drift ice to clog in the channels between Ellesmere Island and Greenland, leaving Baffin Bay navigable in the summer and enabling whalers to extend their whaling grounds to the north. In the channels of the Canadian Arctic Archipelago to the west, however, the ice conditions were heavily congested, explaining in part the stranding of the Franklin expedition and its disastrous conclusion. This drift ice stagnation cycle was favourable to muskox and caribou populations in northern coastal areas but forced the ringed seal, a mainstay of the Inughuit, to the south of the Baffin Bay pack ice in winter. As a result, polar bear populations also dropped in these areas.[57] When Europeans encountered the Inughuit in the early nineteenth century, they found them living in difficult circumstances, eking out a marginal existence based on an unreliable supply of seals, among other resources, and largely cut off from other Inuit groups.

Thus, the climate established the preconditions of the first meeting of Europeans and Inughuit since their Thule ancestors' possible contact with Norse sailors 600 years before. It was to be a fateful encounter for the human history of Ellesmere Island. Over the succeeding 200 years, European explorers, scientists, and adventurers, accompanied by Inughuit, Inuit, or West Greenland Aboriginal guides, hunters, and labourers, negotiated the island's rugged coasts and criss-crossed its interior. The eventual synthesis of Aboriginal environmental knowledge and European technology enabled effective exploration but placed heavy stress on the island's wildlife resources, particularly muskoxen. Throughout this period, the climate continued to exert an irresistible force. Accommodated but never overcome, it continued to play a major role in all acts of the unfolding drama.

2
High Arctic Ecosystems and Human History

The ecosystem is another powerful environmental factor influencing arctic history. A popular dictionary defines ecosystem as "a biological community of interacting organisms and their physical environment."[1] This definition omits the historical dimension. Ecosystems are not in a state of perpetual equilibrium, but instead comprise a dynamic set of changing relationships between organisms which, in theory, could be charted over time. Such interrelationships may for a period establish a degree of equilibrium among the species, but disturbances in any of the components can upset the balance, with consequences for all species in the system. Humans occupy an important and often pivotal role in the ecosystem. But while human history has often been influenced by the natural environment, it has also been driven by ideological factors that are not reducible to the natural ecosystem. Beyond natural forces, the human factor is captured in a current definition of cultural ecology: "a pattern of purposive behaviour involving a matching of resources with objectives, a transforming of natural phenomena in order to meet these objectives, and a capacity to think about this process objectively without actually going through the physical steps."[2]

Over the course of High Arctic history, the region's ecosystems have exerted profound impact on the lives of its inhabitants. These ecosystems have established limits on natural resource use, with far-reaching effects on population levels, social organization, and distribution of all peoples occupying the region. While a thorough examination of these ecosystems is beyond the scope of this study, a survey of some of their principal features can enhance our understanding of the human history of this region over many thousands of years.

The ecosystems of the High Arctic are of relatively recent origin, as they emerged in the brief time span since glacial retreat 8000-10,000 BP. Partly because of their recent development, and partly because of the harsh physical environment, High Arctic ecosystems have been characterized by a lack of species diversity,[3] i.e., there are comparatively few animal species and short food chains from the simplest forms of life to the predators at the summit of the system.

Some ecologists have explained the low diversity of Arctic ecosystems as a consequence of the relatively short period of time they have been in existence. According to this argument, arctic ecosystems, having started as recently as the Pleistocene era, are still in an undeveloped or immature state.[4] Whether the lack of diversity has contributed to an inherent instability in the arctic ecosystem continues to be debated.[5] What is not in dispute is that the populations of its major mammal species have fluctuated widely over time, often as a consequence of climatic change.

As an extreme polar environment, Ellesmere Island is on the margins of viable existence for most of the species that inhabit its lands, waters, and surrounding oceans. Not only does it possess a limited range of flora and fauna, the populations of the respective species are small in comparison with more southerly latitudes. High Arctic faunal populations tend to be widely dispersed, forced to roam over large expanses in search of the limited food resources on which they depend. Fluctuations in population are particularly evident among terrestrial species.[6] Food chains are short and major changes in the population of one species are likely to have dramatic effects on other populations. In these conditions, uncertainty of access to food resources has promoted greater randomness of animal movements, complicating the efforts of both predators and hunters to sustain their numbers.

If this brief characterization of the arctic ecosystem approximates the reality, it may help explain the recurrent disjunctions in the region's human history. Humans in every historical era have depended heavily on the region's mammal resources for subsistence. Any major disruption in the availability of game animals therefore could not fail to have major disruptive effects on the people inhabiting it.

A further refinement appears to be required. Specialists have characterized arctic ecosystems not so much as a single system, but as a congeries of ecosystems, each one interacting with the others, but also operating as distinctive entities. Anthropologist Milton Freeman has identified at least three sub-systems of arctic ecosystems: terrestrial, freshwater, and marine subsystems. For human history, two of these have particular relevance: the terrestrial and the marine.

The terrestrial sub-system comprises an interdependent set of mammals, birds, insects, and plant species, while the numbers and range of flora and fauna are limited by the extent of nutrients to sustain them.[7] In terms of terrestrial habitats, Ellesmere and neighbouring islands have been referred to as an "arctic desert"[8] or "polar desert."[9] Prevailing northwesterly winds and low atmospheric humidity resulting from the comparative lack of open water in the Arctic Ocean produce some of the most arid environments in Canada. Orographic precipitation is highest along the Ellesmere northern coast, which receives annual precipitation of 8 to 10 cm. On the leeward side of the Grant Land Mountains, only 2 cm of precipitation reaches the Lake Hazen area, an extraordinarily low rate.[10] The growing season is short in all regions of the island. The number of annual snow-free days varies from an average of only 45 days on the north coast to 77 days in the Eureka–Tanquary corridor. Even in July, cold air masses forming over the Arctic Ocean dominate the weather of the Queen Elizabeth Islands 90% of the time, and there is no month that is free of freezing temperatures.[11] These areas have been characterized as "the ultimate climate and substrate limit for plant development,"[12] an inhospitably barren zone in which vegetation is often either absent or not visible to the untrained eye. I remarked on the sparse distribution of flora and fauna over such huge tracts of land. Beyond the climatic constraints, plant growth is also inhibited by the prevalence of exposed bedrock, surficial debris, and thin marginal soils. Extensive upland and glaciated areas are particularly devoid of vegetation. Even in the more favourable growing conditions of the sheltered valley floors, the vegetation is never abundant in comparison with regions south of the tree line. Consequently, the numbers of mammalian herbivores depending on such vegetation for forage, and of carnivores feeding on the herbivores, are relatively few and far between. Owing to the comparative meagreness of the grazing grounds and their scattered distribution, the major ruminants such as muskox and Peary caribou range over wide areas, never foraging for long in a single location.[13]

Notwithstanding the polar desert conditions of Ellesmere Island, human occupation has been made possible by two remarkably productive, but atypical, ecological zones. Known as arctic oases and ocean "polynyas," these unusually rich biological areas have supported enough game mammals throughout the year to provide indispensable food resources to the human populations periodically inhabiting the region.

The largest arctic oasis in the High Arctic extends in a southwesterly to northeasterly arc from the Eureka lowlands to the Hazen Plateau, a distance of roughly 320 km. Here, the sheltered interior valleys of Ellesmere Island have fostered an unusual level of plant growth for this high latitude. For example, in the inner lake Hazen Basin, plants such as *Salix arctica*, *Dryas integrifolia*, *Saxifraga oppositifolia*, *Drab cinerea*, *Erysmum pallasii*, and *Oxyia dignya* grow in relative abundance. On the protected north side of the lake, favourable microclimates, fostered by warm temperatures during the brief summers, are enhanced by the moisture of many streams flowing off the Grant land Ice Cap and support a number of additional plant species.[14]

The comparatively rich plant growth in the interior regions is particularly associated with the muskox (*Ovibos moschatus*). The largest grazing mammal of the High Arctic, it was historically the most important land-based game animal on Ellesmere. These hairy ruminants are found exclusively in Canada's arctic regions and in Greenland. In the 1960s, there were an estimated 1,500 muskoxen on Canada's mainland and another 8,500 on the Arctic Islands, with perhaps 4,000, or nearly half of these living on Ellesmere Island.[15]

The extremely low winter precipitation received in interior regions of Ellesmere Island, such as the Eureka–Tanquary–Hazen corridor, is a boon to the resident muskox population. Sleet conditions can spell starvation for muskoxen in coastal areas of Ellesmere and Greenland, since the covering of plants by ice or an ice crust over a snow layer makes it difficult for the animals to uncover the vegetation with their hooves. Northern Ellesmere Island is sufficiently distant from Baffin Bay that it escapes most of the winter precipitation generated by the interface of Atlantic and Arctic water. In the summer, low precipitation is also not an impediment, as the plant communities on which the muskox feeds are watered primarily by glacial runoff that collects in the wet meadows of valleys or deltas.[16] In protected areas, these conditions foster a surprisingly lush growth of such plants as *Carex aquatilis* and *Eriophorum scheuchzeri*.[17] Particularly luxuriant growth of vascular plants has been recorded in such sheltered places as the valleys to the north of Lake Hazen on the southern flanks of the United States Mountains, which are prime muskox grazing areas.[18]

The muskox feeds by wrapping its tongue around plants such as sedges and ripping out the leaves or stems or by biting off the leaves and twigs of arctic willow that creeps along the ground in high latitudes. Feeding is concentrated in three topographical and vegetation communities, including wet sedge meadow, dry slope tundras, and willow thickets on the flat tundra. Muskoxen do not overgraze their summer foraging grounds but slowly make their way along the region's short river systems and lake shores and across the tundra. Zoologists have argued that a particular requirement for sustaining a muskox population in the High Arctic is the presence of lowland meadows with adequate sedges and grasses to support both summer and winter forage,[19] which are also of importance to grazing Peary caribou.[20]

Typically, muskox herds consist of a bull, several cows and calves, but solitary bulls are also common. In winter, the muskoxen are reportedly less mobile than in summer, as they stay in one place longer to more fully exploit less abundant grazing opportunities and to conserve energy.[21] The fact that they do not migrate in the winter and also remain within limited grazing areas was probably of crucial importance to the Independence cultures who largely relied on muskox meat for subsistence when they wintered in this region 3,000 and 4,000 years ago. Further, the tendency of muskoxen to retreat into a stationary defensive circle when confronted by attackers is a characteristic that has made them relatively easy prey for hunters in all historical periods.

Biological research suggests that populations of High Arctic ungulates have been significantly affected by changing weather patterns. For example, studies of caribou and muskoxen, respectively, carried out during the winters of 1970-71[22] and 1973-74[23] indicated a serious decline of their populations in areas of the Queen Elizabeth Islands. In 1973-74, record winter snowfall levels coincided with dramatic reductions in the numbers of surviving muskox calves. Harsh winters not only depleted the number of yearling calves but also inhibited the production of calves in the next breeding season and their chances of survival.[24] Other weather conditions, including late spring thaws, have also been cited as factors limiting muskox populations in the High Arctic.[25] For the early Paleo-Eskimo cultures, who relied on muskoxen, the consequences of such reductions of an already limited game resource must have been dramatic.

The Peary caribou (*Rangifer tarandus pearyi*) and other mammals including arctic fox and arctic hares, have also played a role in supporting human populations on Ellesmere Island. However, the small resident populations of caribou, and the small size of the other species, ensured that their contribution to human history was of secondary importance to the muskox.

While of lesser historical importance to the cultures occupying the region, freshwater ecosystems have played a role in the human history of the High Arctic. As with the terrestrial ecosystems of the region, High Arctic freshwater ecosystems are characterized by much lower productivity than their counterparts at more southerly latitudes, which is reflected in slow rates of zooplankton production.[26] For residing human populations, the principal species taken was the arctic charr (*Salvelinus alpinus*), the most northern of freshwater fishes. Arctic charr include the anadromous variety, which migrates to the ocean in the spring and returns to fresh water in the fall, and the resident variety, which passes its entire life span in fresh water. Anadromous charr take a long time to reach maturity, 10-13 years, and live as long as 30 years.[27] A study of landlocked and anadromous charr in Lake Hazen, undertaken in 1958, showed that the resident fish in this far northern location took an even longer time, 18 to 20 years, to reach their maximum size.[28] Due to the long developmental cycle, charr are particularly sensitive to stresses such as resource extraction, as populations need many years to regenerate. While it was long believed that the charr of Lake Hazen comprise both anadromous and resident populations, a recent study suggests that all the fish spend their entire cycle in the lake. This interpretation characterizes the lake as a "closed system," without inputs of energy from outside its boundaries. If accurate, this study indicates that the lake's ecosystem may be even more sensitive to disruption than was previously believed.[29]

In the High Arctic, anadromous charr begin their return migration in late July or early August, sometimes peaking as late as early September.[30] Historically, this was a prime period for fishing. When they inhabited the interior of northern Ellesmere Island, both the Independence and Thule peoples fished in Lake Hazen, other small lakes, and rivers to supplement their diet of mammal flesh. The presence of fish bones at the sites of former dwellings adjacent to the shores and banks of these interior water bodies indicates not only the need for fresh water but the fact that fish resources were utilized by all cultures historically occupying this region.[31] One example is the surviving ruins of a Thule stone dwelling at the source of the Ruggles River at the eastern end of Lake Hazen. Despite severely cold winter temperatures, the strong current resists icing over and historically afforded opportunities to fish in the dark period.[32] During the era of North Polar exploration, American Robert E. Peary engaged Inughuit to stage hunting excursions to the island's interior, where they secured a considerable number of charr with the traditional spearing technique of their ancestors.

Given the unpredictable and often low productivity of the land, marine ecosystems have assumed a particular importance for human subsistence in polar regions. Like its terrestrial counterpart, the marine ecology of the region has been characterized by relatively small populations of organisms, sparsely distributed. The limited productivity of the waters around Ellesmere Island is confirmed by a comparison of primary phytoplankton production estimates for sites on Ellesmere Island and at more southerly latitudes. Measuring the weight of carbon produced through photosynthesis per unit area of ocean surface, geographer Maxwell Dunbar recorded the following differences in biomass:[33]

Regional Production (grams of carbon per square metre per year)

Dumbell Bay (northern coast, Ellesmere Island)	9-12
Jones Sound (southern coast, Ellesmere Island)	20, 35
Frobisher Bay, Baffin Island	41, 70
Gaspe Current, Gulf of St. Lawrence	385

As phytoplankton and zooplankton are the base of the marine food chain, the low overall productivity of the seas around Ellesmere Island is apparent.

Despite the marginal productivity revealed in Dunbar's tabulation, some waters, especially in areas where polynyas occur, have been remarkably rich environments. In affording year-round access to food resources, High Arctic polynyas have played a role in human history comparable to terrestrial oases. A polynya is defined as an area of open ocean water and ice floes, surrounded by compacted multi-year sea ice, which typically remains open during the winter. Why these anomalies recur perennially is not fully understood although winds, upwelling of warmer subsurface water, and ocean currents have been cited as contributing factors.[34] Whatever their specific causes, the ice edges of these polynyas are particularly rich habitats for a variety of marine mammals and birds throughout the winter.

The largest and most famous polynya in the North American Arctic is the North Water of Smith Sound and northern Baffin Bay (Figure 7), also known to nineteenth century whalers as the "Cape York Water."[35] This large expanse of open water and circulating new ice is kept open in winter when pack ice carried south by the current between Ellesmere Island and Greenland becomes congested and forms an ice plug in Smith Sound. Aided by the prevailing northerly winds, the current nevertheless continues to carry away new ice as it forms to the south of the ice dam. Another contributing factor may be the upwelling of warmer Atlantic water from the West Greenland current as it comes into contact with the denser Arctic waters, but this hypothesis awaits verification.[36]

The boundaries and extent of the North Water vary from year to year although the northern limit is relatively fixed as it is determined by the ice plug that characteristically forms in Smith Sound or the southern part of Kane Basin. Commonly, the North Water appears in a roughly triangular formation as it fans out from Smith Sound to the south along the east coast of Ellesmere Island and to the southeast near the coast of the Hayes Peninsula, comprising the Thule region of Greenland. During some winters, the southern edge of the North Water is in the vicinity of the mouth of Jones Sound between Coburg Island and the northeastern end of Devon Island. In other years, it extends as far south as the mouth of Lancaster Sound and thence across Baffin Bay to northwest Greenland.

Other recurring polynyas around Ellesmere have included the Hell Gate–Cardigan Strait waters between southeastern Ellesmere and Devon Island's Grinnell Peninsula, and a series of polynyas along the island's east coast north of Smith Sound. Two of these, the straits between Pim

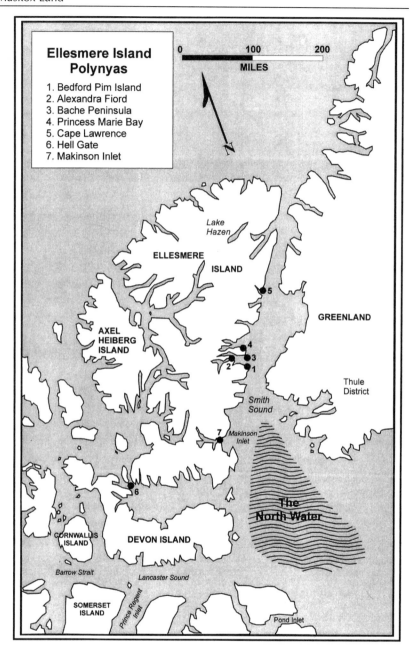

Figure 7: Location of polynyas around Ellesmere Island, August – December

Island and the Johan Peninsula and the mouth of Flagler Fiord, form at the narrows between two larger bodies of saltwater, where tidal pressure both breaks up the pack ice and inhibits the formation of new ice. Two additional shore-fast polynyas occur at the eastern end of Bache Peninsula and on the north shore of the peninsula at the mouth of Alexandra Fiord (Figure 7).[37] Another is located at Makinson Inlet on the southeastern coast of Ellesmere Island.[38] Apart from the polynyas that normally remain open throughout the year, other pockets of exposed water open at full and new moons in the late winter and spring. Danish scientist Christian Vibe attributed the presence of these polynyas to tidal action,[39] although the fact that the ocean current is strongest near the coast[40] presumably plays a role in their formation. Other factors include the constriction of flowing water between two land masses and the presence of comparatively shallow water.[41] These open areas of water offered vital hunting opportunities for the Inuit and earlier Aboriginal groups. At least three such lunar polynyas are typically found along the eastern coast of Ellesmere Island, north of Smith Sound. They include a tidal opening off the Darling Peninsula between Dobbin and Scoresby bays and another south of Fort Conger (Figure 7).

The polynyas have been winter refuges for mammals as diverse as polar bears, narwhals, and beluga whales, as well as a wide variety of birds. At different periods of the region's climatic history, Aboriginal peoples adjacent to the North Water shifted their hunting patterns according to the availability of major game mammals inhabiting these waters. For example, the bowhead or Greenland whale (*Balaena mysticitus*) was hunted by Thule culture between 1000 and 600 BP alongside the hunting of pinnipeds or fin-footed mammals. With climatic deterioration after AD 1400 and the build-up of drift ice in Baffin Bay, the whales moved south, a fact reflected in diminishing quantities of baleen in post-1400 archaeological sites. By AD 1600, Thule whaling had ceased in the High Arctic, and this people had become almost entirely dependent on seals and walrus. Around this time, their strategies shifted as they developed the technique of breathing-hole hunting, enabling them to establish wintering sites in the inner fiord areas far from the floe edge, in addition to the other settlements adjacent to the floe edge of the region's polynyas.[42]

In the last 500 years, pinnipeds became the most important game species for the Inuit inhabitants of Greenland and Ellesmere Island. Among the principal pinnipeds hunted by the Thule-Inughuit were ringed and bearded seals. Historically, this culture used bearded seal skins in making a variety of items including dog-team harness and traces, harpoon lines, and the soles of boots. Its skins were also used in building both kayaks and umiaks, which are larger boats.[43]

Historically, the ringed seal (*Phoca hispida*) or jar seal has been the most numerous and widely distributed marine mammal in the High Arctic.[44] The zoologist with Robert Peary's 1893-95 expedition to northern Greenland described the ringed seal as the "staple of the Arctic Highlanders."[45] On Ellesmere Island in the 1950s, RCMP personnel at the Alexandra Fiord detachment described this animal as the "most abundant" marine mammal in that area of the Smith Sound region.[46]

The ringed seal congregates in areas of suitable fast ice along the outer coast and in sounds, bays, and inlets in the High Arctic. These are places for breeding and raising their young, which the mothers place above the ice in lairs hollowed out in the snow near breathing holes. During the winter, adults and older infants continue to hunt under the ice in bays or fiords by keeping breathing holes open. In the spring, the seals come out onto the ice to bask in the sun and to moult their hair. While adults remain under the ice in the fiords and bays by maintaining a number of breathing holes, the younger seals stay at the floe edge. Characteristically, the seals rest in groups on the ice, near their breathing holes or adjacent to leads or cracks in the ice.[47]

The bearded seal or square flipper seal (*Erignathus barbatus*) is found largely in arctic regions where shallow banks are free of land-fast ice during the winter. The bearded seal congregates by several shore-fast polynyas and moves out onto moving ice to rest and to reproduce in the spring. Historically, its range has included the floe edge skirting the entire coastline of Greenland between Melville Bay and Cape Inglefield on Kane Basin and probably also the entire eastern coast of Ellesmere Island. Vibe noted that this seal could also be found in the fiords of the region, including Lady Franklin Bay adjacent to Fort Conger.[48] In the twentieth century, RCMP game reports indicated a particular concentration in the Smith Sound region, especially the areas to the north and south of Bache Peninsula,[49] while large numbers have also congregated in Jones Sound and near its mouth between Coburg and Ellesmere Islands.[50]

The walrus (*Odebenus rosmarus*) also frequents arctic areas of shallow banks free of winter land-fast ice. The Smith Sound region is one of two major summer feeding grounds for walrus along the entire axis of Davis Strait and Baffin Bay. According to Christian Vibe, female walrus also winter in that vicinity of the North Water. In the spring and summer, they follow a migration pattern first to the northwest along the Greenland coast of Kane Basin to Cape Kent, then to the northwest along the floe edge to the Bache Peninsula area of Ellesmere Island. Walrus feed on the rich resources of Buchanan Bay and the Ellesmere coast, before migrating further to the south in the autumn.

Distinctive for their tusks and whiskers, walruses are the largest of the pinnipeds. Males extend to more than three metres in length and average 910 kg, with a maximum weight of about 1,180 kg. Like bearded seals, they move out on to the pack ice to rest and breed. Characteristically, they huddle together on ice pans, an apparent adaptation to conserve heat. Based on his observations, American Elisha Kent Kane, who spent two winters in the Thule District in the 1850s, surmised that walruses stayed in the area of the North Water throughout the year. Isaac Israel Hayes, who spent the winter of 1860-61 in this area, remarked that in February: "The walrus had been very numerous in the open waters outside the harbour all through the winter, and their shrill cry could be heard at almost any time from the margin of the ice."[51] Walruses have also been known to overwinter in the Cardigan Straits polynyas at the western entrance to Jones Sound and in the Flagler Fiord polynyas of Kane Basin to the north,[52] described by a RCMP officer at Alexandra Fiord in 1961 as the favoured "summer feeding grounds" of this species.[53]

The polar bear (*Thalarctos maritimus* Phipps) has historically been the principal predator of the ringed seal and a number of other mammals of the High Arctic. Ubiquitous in arctic regions, polar bears generally are found in regions where their prey congregate. One of the principal breeding grounds of the species is the region of Kane Basin,[54] on both the central coast of Ellesmere Island and areas of Greenland on the other side of the channel. Historically of some importance to the Inughuit for meat, polar bears were primarily hunted for their thick fur, used in making pants for both men and children.

The narwhal (*Monodon monoceros*), a whale best-known for the long lance-like tooth which extends from the head of adults, has been common to the area of the North Water. Over the last hundred years, it has been reported to winter in Baffin Bay and Davis Strait, and to migrate gradually to the north with the ice break-up in the warmer months. In the Smith Sound region, large herds of narwhals have been sighted at various times and locations along the eastern coast of Ellesmere Island, especially within its bays and fiords.[55] George A. Clark, a zoologist with Robert E. Peary's 1893-95 expedition to northern Greenland, observed that in the spring the narwhals initially gravitated around the leads and the belt of shore water before the general break-up late in the season.[56] During Robert Peary's return from Cape Sheridan in 1909, his surgeon Dr. John Goodsell observed several narwhals near their ship while sailing in Robeson Channel adjacent to the northeastern coast of Ellesmere Island.[57]

In the 1940s Danish scientist Christian Vibe observed narwhals summering in Kane Basin, some apparently migrating along the ice edge as far north as the Lincoln Sea, on the threshold of the Arctic Ocean.[58] Of these northern migrants, one herd proceeded to the north coast of Greenland's Inglefield Land, while others summered in Lady Franklin Bay in the vicinity of Fort Conger. They returned south with the approach of autumn and freezing of the pack ice. Even after the formation of fast ice in the autumn, many of these animals have been observed to winter in such areas as Alexandra Fiord by breaking the ice to maintain breathing holes.[59] Others, trapped by the fast ice in northern Baffin Bay, were sighted off Cape Parry in the early 1890s.

The beluga or white whale (*Delphinapterus leucas*) also summers in the inlets and channels of the region, but inhabits a more restricted range than the narwhal and pursues a different seasonal migration path. In the autumn, belugas swim north from Lancaster Sound into Jones Sound and along the coast of Ellesmere Island before crossing the northern areas of Baffin Bay to Greenland.[60] From there, they move along the coast to the south and winter off the Greenland coast. In the spring, belugas reverse this route.[61] Belugas also have been observed overwintering in the North Water. In March 1978, two biologists identified 402 belugas inhabiting this area, mostly in narrow leads near the southeastern shores of Devon Island and along the floe edge of Jones Sound. Farther north, a RCMP officer spotted a herd of about 1,200 belugas near Pim Island in Smith Sound on 5 April 1978.[62]

In addition to mammals, the High Arctic polynyas have also been important habitats and refuges to migrating birds. Among other species, the nesting islands near Whale Sound were the home to thousands of dovekies (*Uria grylle*). Observed by Hayes wintering in the region in the 1850s,[63] dovekies and numerous other types of bird were hunted by Inughuit and probably also by their Thule ancestors.

The Seasons and Arctic Human History

An important factor bearing on arctic ecosystems is the seasonal cycle. High Arctic seasons are characterized by stark differences between summer and winter conditions, with dramatic oscillations in the availability of food for most organisms.[64] On Ellesmere Island, the seasonal cycle consists of very long, harsh winters and fleeting summers, separated by the brief intervals of spring and autumn. At the far northerly latitudes of the island, snowfall comes as early as late August and does not melt until the next June's thaw. Another distinctive feature is the dramatic seasonal shift in daylight levels occurring at such northerly latitudes.

Dramatic shifts from summer productivity to winter scarcity have demanded special adaptations, of which only a limited number of species have proved capable. Persisting organisms have confronted the stress of seasonal fluctuations in various ways. Some have developed the capacity to store enough energy during the productive season to last until the next, while surviving at low metabolic levels during the intervening period. Zooplankton, the foundation of the marine ecosystems, has adjusted by growing to a larger body size than in other regions, and by producing larger eggs in greater numbers. Other small organisms, such as plankton or insects, have breeding cycles regulated to occur only once a year, synchronized with the brief summers.[65]

This raises the issue of the effects of arctic seasons on human populations. Since the work of French sociologist and ethnologist Marcel Mauss 100 years ago, various writers have attempted to explain Inuit cultures and their adaptations in relation to climate and seasonal variations.[66] Using data on various peoples, including the Inughuit of northwestern Greenland, Mauss discerned two distinctive patterns of seasonal life, organized around summer and winter.[67] In the summer, greater mobility occasioned by perpetual daylight, milder temperatures, and open ocean waters fostered a general dispersion of Inuit across their territories, as families separated from their compatriots during the intensive food procurement activities of this season.[68] On the other hand, the harsh character, reduced mobility, and resource constraints of winter occasioned the development of a communal response to scarcity, as Inuit came together in this season to share food, fuel, even sexual partners. This pattern of alternating dispersion and nucleation was repeated endlessly, a perfect social adaptation to environmental necessity.

Mauss's work provides an insight into the character of life in this region and the adaptive strategies of the Aboriginal cultures that have inhabited it. Humans have always been obliged to accommodate to the region's distinctive seasonal cycles. Each season presents its own challenges and opportunities. In this most stringent of the Earth's climates, a keen knowledge of the seasons and how best to exploit them has often meant the difference between survival and extinction, with little margin for error.

For the region's human inhabitants, a particular requirement has been the need to develop strategies for coping with the harsh conditions of polar winters. Winters in the High Arctic are extremely cold, particularly in the interior areas where more continental conditions obtain. The readings of the only two parties to winter in the interior of northern Ellesmere Island in recent centuries are instructive. At Lake Hazen, a hunting party with Robert Peary's expedition recorded daytime temperatures of –64° in February 1900.[69] During the winter of

1957-58, a wintering party with the Defence Research Board recorded temperatures as low as –70° C in the same area. Coastal areas have also recorded very low winter temperatures; at Discovery Harbour on the northeast coast, members of the Greely expedition recorded a minimum of –62.1° F in February 1882.[70] Despite these severe temperatures, the presence of archaeological remains of winter habitations of both the Independence and Thule cultures in the interior of Ellesmere Island shows that the extreme conditions of these areas did not completely inhibit human occupation.

Perhaps the greater limiting factor was the lack of light during the High Arctic winters. Apart from moonlight, the winters here are periods of near-total darkness. In the northern sections of Ellesmere Island, the sun disappears over the horizon in mid-October, not to return again before the end of February, a sunless season lasting four and a half months. On the northern coast in 1875, Captain George Nares of the British Arctic Expedition remarked on the "unparalleled intensity and duration of darkness," persisting at that latitude for 142 days.[71] In 1930, at Bache Peninsula on the central coast of Ellesmere, an RCMP constable recorded a dark period of four months between 18 October and 23 February.[72] On the southern coasts of the island on Jones Sound, some 700-800 km away, the sunless period is shorter, lasting slightly more than three months. Since there is a gradual transition of twilight, providing a degree of illumination, the period of total darkness is of shorter duration, about two and a half months. During the winter, some light is afforded by the moon, enabling inhabitants to travel and even hunt to a limited degree.

Archaeologist Eigil Knuth speculated that, during the dark period, hunter families of the Independence cultures (ca. 3000 and 4000 BP) passed a sedentary existence within their skin shelters. They subsisted on accumulated stocks of the flesh of land mammals such as ermine, lemmings, and polar bears, which they had hunted in the period leading up to the disappearance of daylight in the autumn. In his analysis of artifacts from their settlement sites, Knuth observed a general absence of nearby meat caches. He inferred that the Independence peoples must have kept stores of dried meat or pemmican close at hand, probably within their dwellings.[73] Subsequent Aboriginal groups, the Inuit, Inughuit and their ancestors, the Thule people, were more active during the winter than their predecessors. With an economy centred on marine mammal resources, the Inughuit often located winter settlements near polynyas to afford access to seals and other species even during the dark period. The lack of daylight in this season presumably prevented them from venturing too far from their wintering settlements in this season, although in the Smith Sound region the Inughuit could utilize moonlight during two weeks of each winter month to travel and hunt.[74]

Spring arrives late in the High Arctic. The return of daylight in late February or March coincides with a continuation of very cold weather virtually until May. The persistence of colder weather ensures that the pack ice remains fast frozen, limiting opportunities for the hunting of marine mammals to the floe edge of the North Water or smaller polynyas where ocean currents typically open cracks or leads in the ice pack in this season.

At the same time, the combination of daylight and fast sea ice allowed increased mobility, as hunters moved beyond the immediate vicinity of wintering settlements. Persisting sea ice facilitated traversing fiords, bays, and channels, while the ice foot enabled spring forays along the coasts. Several Thule culture archaeological sites in the vicinity of Lady Franklin Bay in northern Ellesmere Island are apparently traces of temporary shelters erected during spring forays by Aboriginal hunters based in the Smith Sound region to the south. They apparently travelled to the north along Ellesmere Island's eastern coast, via the ice foot. Since the ice foot in this area largely melts by mid-June, these forays would probably have been staged during the months of April and May. If so, these parties might have resembled the more recent excursions undertaken by Inughuit hunters since the time of Peary.

With the appearance of ringed seals on the surface of the sea ice in April, Aboriginal hunters were afforded enhanced opportunities to hunt these animals. Whether early Aboriginal cultures hunted seals from the sea ice is not certain, although archaeological evidence of harpoons at various sites, including those of the Independence culture,[75] suggests that they had the capability to do so. What is clear is that at the time of contact in the nineteenth century, Inughuit groups had fully integrated sea-ice hunting of both seals and walruses in their hunting regimes.[76]

High Arctic summers are a period of heightened activity for most of the region's organisms, as they hurry to build up their reserves in preparation for the long winter. For a few fleeting weeks in July and August, the summers bring an efflorescence of life to the High Arctic. Average daytime highs above 0° C combine with 24-hour daylight to warm the ground and raise the surface temperature of the ice caps, the source of the region's rivers. When it finally arrives, summer appears suddenly "with an abrupt bursting forth of the ravines and a general rush of torrents to the sea."[77]

Melting glacial run-off gathers in the valley bottoms in lakes and pools fostering rapid plant growth, and, in turn, supporting muskox and caribou populations. Summer is also a period of intensified feeding for marine mammals. In June, numerous species, including walruses and several types of seals, harp, bearded, and ringed, move to the north as the frozen mass of sea ice begins to recede and leads open up near the coasts.[78] In the same month, numerous species of migrating birds, including snow geese, American brants, and eider ducks, begin to arrive from the south.[79]

For the Thule-Inughuit culture, the difficulties of hunting during the dark season required redoubled efforts during the short summers to stockpile meat and other food resources for the winter. In June, auks and eggs were collected on the island seabird rookeries in the Thule District.[80] By July, Inughuit families were moving to their summer camps in preparation for summer hunting activities. August was typically the month for hunting walruses, narwhals, and belugas from kayaks.[81] Analysis of faunal remains at sites of the Independence cultures excavated by Knuth and spear fishing tools excavated by Maxwell indicate that these peoples also hunted a range of marine mammals and fished for arctic charr in the summer or early autumn.[82] By late August, Inughuit turned their attention to hunting caribou, whose skins were then in optimal condition following moulting and renewal of their coats.[83] Late summer was another prime period for fishing charr in streams and spawning lakes.[84]

In the polar region, autumn comes early and strikes with particular force. During this season, colliding air masses produce unstable and very rough weather, with marked effects on coastal travel, hunting, and navigation. The stormy weather peaks in the month of October and generally persists until the freezing of the sea. American hunter Harry Whitney, who spent the winter of 1908-09 at Etah, on the Greenland coast of Smith Sound, wrote that "heavy winds and terrific snow storms swept over us with only brief intermissions."[85] More recently, polar explorer Wally Herbert described the polar autumn as "one of the worst periods of the year," consisting of "four or five weeks of intermittent high winds and tempestuous seas, when the salt-spray beats up from the rocks below each village and rains down on the Eskimos' houses and their huskies lying outside."[86]

Due to the increased risk of hunting disasters, the High Arctic autumn presented particular challenges to Aboriginal inhabitants. In such conditions, hunting from kayaks or umiaks was highly dangerous, while hunters at the floe edge confronted the risk of being stranded adrift when ice floes were dislodged by high winds or the driving ice pack.[87] Travel along the ice foot was imperilled by waves that could sweep a hunter and his dog team away in an instant. Nevertheless, the Inughuit continued hunting marine mammals on the ocean, as well as caribou and muskoxen on land, for as long as weather and travelling conditions permitted. This was also the period of "smooth-ice hunting," when seals were caught on the recently formed sea ice by resourceful hunters who approached them stealthily with soft bearskin undersoles on their boots.[88]

Adaptation and High Arctic History

A central notion in cultural ecology is the concept of adaptation, essentially the process by which organisms establish beneficial relationships with their environments.[89] Social scientists have identified at least three levels of human adaptation: behavioural/cultural, physiological, and genetic/demographic.[90] This post-contact human history of Ellesmere Island is primarily concerned with the first level of adaptation, i.e., behavioural adaptations of individuals and the cultural responses of groups. Cultural adaptations include such aspects as the adoption of technology, changes in social organization, and ideological changes, i.e., changes in the outlook or world view of a group. Human beings adapt to their environments by providing solutions to environmental problems, improving the effectiveness of solutions, developing adaptability, and increasing their awareness of environmental problems.[91]

In terms of behavioural change, archaeologist Karl Butzer has identified three types of adaptive systems. The first, adaptive adjustment, refers to the capacity of societies to respond to short-term economic or social crises, such as epidemics or famines. It involves relatively minor adaptations aimed at re-establishing a pre-existing state of equilibrium, such as the stability of a group's population and its health. The second type, adaptive modification, involves a significant change of strategies within an adaptive system. In this case, a group might adopt or abandon cultural practices according to either internal or external influences. Such adaptations will usually have a regional impact on subsistence practices, settlement patterns, and population levels. Adaptive modifications may also result in changes to cultural patterns, such as ethnic or linguistic identity. The third type, adaptive transformation, involves the development of dramatic new adaptive strategies, including changes in "social behaviour, technology, and resource utilization." According to Butzer, such changes have "continental or global repercussions for subsistence, settlement or demography."[92] All three types of adaptations are represented in the history of Ellesmere Island over the past 200 years.

An emerging consensus among students of human ecology is that diversity is the key to sustaining population levels.[93] One of the ways that animal species develop greater diversity is by increasing the range of their habitat. Human populations can be made more viable by extending their range of natural resource use, the number of organisms they utilize, or the efficiency and effectiveness of resource exploitation through improvements in technology or its application. At the same time, as anthropologist Robin Ridington has argued, it is important not to reduce technology to a set of artifacts and tools, but rather, to view it more broadly as a complex of adaptive strategies encompassing knowledge of the environment (including topography, mineral resources, and seasonal changes), world views, and belief systems.[94] While material items such as weapons, sledges, and boats are important artifacts of hunting cultures, an even more fundamental requirement is "the technique of being able to carry the world around in your head."[95]

A more complicated issue is whether adaptive strategies can sustain the larger ecosystem as well as individual species. In adapting to their environment, humans are the perhaps the only species with the potential to pose a systemic threat to the survival of other organisms. While the difficulty of reconstructing the ecological impact of earlier hunting cultures must be acknowledged, it is reasonable to suppose that the small numbers of occupants and the inherent limitations of their technological repertoire limited the numbers of game harvested to sustainable levels. Anthropologist Robert Paine has hypothesized that subsistence hunters exploit local animal populations until yields are reduced to a level of diminishing returns. They then move on to another locality to repeat this pattern. The low point in yields is not too low to inhibit the reproduction of the animals, and faunal populations rebound quickly. While this hypothesis has yet to be thoroughly tested in High Arctic contexts, it may explain in part how Aboriginal peoples have managed to live in this sparse ecosystem for extended periods without depleting the resources on which they depend for survival.[96]

The importance of adaptive strategies to successful occupation of the High Arctic is illustrated by the history of a series of Aboriginal peoples inhabiting this region over more than 4,000 years. The work of a series of archaeologists working in northern Ellesmere Island — Eigil Knuth[97] of Denmark, Moreau Maxwell[98] of the United States, and Patricia Sutherland[99] of Canada — has greatly expanded our knowledge of these cultures and changes in their way of life over time. The picture of early life on Ellesmere has also been significantly enhanced by the work of Peter Schledermann[100] and Karen McCullough[101] in their archaeological investigations on the central Ellesmere coast. In the late 1950s, Maxwell excavated a series of sites in the vicinity of Discovery Harbour and Lake Hazen, while Knuth conducted extensive fieldwork in both northern Greenland and Ellesmere Island in the 1950s and 1960s. In a series of studies on the "small-tool" cultures, which he labelled Independence I and II peoples, Knuth reconstructed a picture of the hunting economies of the region's earliest inhabitants. For the purpose of clarification, according to Sutherland, Knuth's Independence II culture corresponds to the Early Dorset phase of arctic occupation.[102] Knuth found evidence that, while they hunted various land and sea mammals, these peoples depended heavily on the muskox as a food source.[103] More recently, Sutherland, in excavating the Rivendell site at the western end of Lake Hazen, has discerned a combination of characteristics of both Independence I and Early Dorset cultures, suggesting both continuity of occupation and adaptation to changing cultural and ecological contexts.[104]

The small-tool cultures had very small populations. Organized into small hunting bands, they spread out along the great expanse of the Eureka Upland, from Axel Heiberg Island and west-central Ellesmere Island on the west, across the Hazen plateau of northern Ellesmere, to Peary Land, in the northern extremity of Greenland. Knuth and Sutherland argued that the Independence I culture inhabited the area about 4000 years BP, while its successor arrived about 1,000 years later, approximately 3000 BP. At the same time, other archaeologists have pointed out that the pre-contact history of the region was very complex, comprising a diversity of cultures and population movements. In his analysis of burin tools represented in the sites investigated in the Smith Sound region, Peter Schledermann identified six different cultures of the Arctic Small Tool Tradition: Independence I, Independence I/Saqqaq, Pre-Dorset, Saqqaq, Early Dorset, and late Dorset.[105]

Arriving long after the retreat of the last glacial advance, the Independence I culture found an island not significantly different in appearance from the one encountered by visitors today. Then, as now, Ellesmere was a polar desert with a regime of cold climate, low precipitation, and generally limited species diversity. Yet, what might represent a low level of biological productivity in one region constitutes relative abundance in another. While the High Arctic was already in the process of cooling from the post-glacial optimum, Ellesmere's climate was far more inviting at these intervals than it was subsequently to become.

Settlement patterns of "small-tool" cultures expressed their distinctive subsistence strategies to respond to the region's natural environment. As interpreted by Eigil Knuth, the small-tool cultures did not dwell for extended periods at any of their camps. The non-permanent character of their dwellings reflected their reliance on the muskox and the need to move on when food supplies were exhausted in the vicinity of their camps. Another essential precondition of survival during the long, dark and severe winters was an adequate supply of fuel. In coastal areas, such as the fiord settlements in northernmost Greenland, the Independence cultures relied on driftwood, but in interior regions, they needed to supplement this source with the roots and trunks of *salix arctica*. Fires were also maintained with the use of fatty bones and muskox droppings.[106]

Another factor determining the location of settlements was access to fresh water during the colder seasons. Wintering on the coast and in the interior of the Eureka Uplands region, the Aboriginal people established settlements along the shores of lakes and rivers, where they could chip ice fragments for drinking water. Figure 2 shows the general location of pre-contact archaeological sites in northern Ellesmere Island, invariably places with ready access to fresh water.

The wintering dwellings of the Independence cultures were skin tent shelters characteristically erected around mid-passage hearths. The lack of more substantial, insulated structures seems surprising in this harsh environment. It can be explained partly by the need of Aboriginal occupants to hunt game animals in all seasons, particularly muskoxen. Pursuing this peripatetic ruminant required a high degree of mobility. In search of game, the Independence peoples fanned out into the interior valleys and the Hazen plateau. The nature and size of their dwellings were determined by the maximum weight of skins and tent supports they could drag or carry with them. On locating one or more herds of muskoxen, they erected these temporary shelters for a time, to be collapsed and moved when the surviving animals moved on to other pastures. In surveying the distribution of Paleo-Eskimo settlements in northern Ellesmere Island, the archaeologist Patricia Sutherland found that more than three-quarters of their sites were located in the interior,[107] suggesting both mobility and utilization of the region's resources in all the seasons. In the winter, the Independence peoples inhabited skin tents in the interior areas where temperatures of –70° C have been recorded.

The adaptability of these cultures is indicated in Sutherland's work on the Rivendell site at Lake Hazen. Occupied in the period 3500 to 3000 BP. this site produced artifacts indicating contact and exchange with the Paleo-Eskimo cultures to the south. In assessing Sutherland's findings, Robert McGhee has noted the similarity of artifact forms between these cultures, including a soft stone lamp reminiscent of the lamps of the Saqqaq culture of southwestern Greenland and bone lance heads with incisions for fastening stone blades, analogous to the lance heads of the Dorset culture at sites to the south.[108]

With the migration of the Thule people to Ellesmere Island around AD 1100, an advanced hunting culture was positioned to make the most effective adaptation to this region up to that time. If the settlement patterns of the Independence I people were oriented to interior lakes and river valleys where they hunted land mammals, the Thule people and their successors, the Inuit and Inughuit, were drawn to the ocean polynyas, as their cultures stressed the procurement of marine mammal resources.

Between ca. 1000 and 1450 AD, the Thule people hunted baleen whales throughout the Arctic, although in recent years the belief that whaling was a mainstay has been superseded by the interpretation that it represented one among many procurement strategies.[109] Arctic specialists apparently agree that when whales were available, it was a major source of food, bones for dwelling roof supports and kayak frames, and ivory for weapons and tools. One of the most dramatic artifacts of the Thule whaling era was the largely intact wooden structure of an umiak, located by Danish Archaeologist Eigil Knuth in Independence Fiord in the far northern region of Greenland, which has been dated to the fifteenth century. The location of this artifact suggests that the channels between Ellesmere Island and Greenland were generally open at least up to ca. AD 1450.[110] However, ringed seals were a much more common and reliable source of subsistence. As climatic deterioration clogged the High Arctic sea channels with ice, the whales were forced farther south, obliging the Thule people of the region to adjust their hunting regimen. They replaced whale hunting with a more diversified exploitation of a variety of sea and land mammals, principally seals. This shift in itself was evidence of the adaptability of their culture.[111]

Thule material culture was characterized by the development of a wide range of a sophisticated tools from the very limited store of available materials to ensure an effective exploitation of both marine and terrestrial food sources. Their technology incorporated a number of advantages over their Paleo-Eskimo predecessors, including effective weapons for hunting sea mammals and the use of sled dogs for surface transport. The use of dogs greatly enhanced overall mobility to enable the exploitation of game sources inaccessible to the "small-tool" cultures. The Thule people also showed resourcefulness in acquiring new materials to facilitate their capacity to exploit the resources of this remote region. An example was their use of iron. In a series of archaeological investigations of Thule sites on Ellesmere Island's Bache Peninsula in the area of Smith Sound, Peter Schledermann found more than

50 Norse artifacts, including pieces of chain mail.[112] Acknowledging the possibility that these materials were traded through middlemen, Schledermann and Karen McCullough have presented a compelling case that the Thule residents of Ellesmere Island instead acquired them through direct trade with Norse Greenlanders who had sailed from the south.[113] In either case, the presence of the Norse artifacts demonstrated the pragmatic capacity of the Thule people to incorporate new materials into their material culture.

Iron was also obtained through an extensive pre-contact trade in meteorite iron, which originated in the Thule district and spread across the Arctic Archipelago to the Canadian mainland.[114] The Aboriginal inhabitants of the Smith Sound region used their ready access to iron to improve their tools and boats. In 1899, Robert E. Peary wrote of the remains of three kayaks found by his Inughuit employees on Ellesmere Island's eastern coast between Carl Ritter Bay and Cape Lawrence. The fittings of the boats were unlike any they had previously seen. The Inughuit reported to Peary that the makers of these kayaks had good knives and iron drills. Whether it was meteorite iron or iron from trade with Europeans is not known, but its presence provided further evidence of the adaptability of this culture.[115]

For both the Inughuit and their ancestors, winter shelter took the form of quasi-permanent stone and sod winter dwellings. Other pragmatic reasons might help explain the form of their wintering settlements, including the need to hunt co-operatively during the colder months of autumn, winter, and spring. Further, the periodic practice of grouping of more than one family in a single winter dwelling enabled greater warmth and conservation of scarce fuel. Conversely, the comparative abundance of summer both enabled and required a dispersion of individual family units. The families spread out across a wide range to enable optimal exploitation of game resources during the fleeting opportunities presented by the warmer months. Their mobility was perfectly expressed in their form of summer shelter—the skin tent.

Patterns of Aboriginal Occupation on Ellesmere Island

Historians and archaeologists are accustomed to look for patterns to impose meaning on the chaos of undigested data encountered in the course of research. Does the progression of human occupations of Ellesmere Island over 4,000 years yield to the impulse to generalize, to find common meanings in their different histories? This question has inspired hypotheses from a variety of archaeologists and ethnohistorians, who have looked for commonalities in the experience of the inhabiting cultures.

A feature common to all Aboriginal groups inhabiting the High Arctic in every era was their practice of nomadism. Nomadism is defined as a way of life involving moving the entire community and its belongings over extended distances. For arctic peoples, the sparse populations and perpetual movement of the region's animals demanded a high level of mobility by all inhabiting human populations. They needed to be constantly on the move, adjusting their areas of resource use according to the movements of the game species. Their nomadism entailed the transport of all materials necessary to sustain life—clothing, skins for tents and bedding, hunting, cutting, and scraping tools, and sufficient provisions to sustain the group in intervals between the successful procurement of game. It was the only viable response to an ecosystem in which game species were both broadly dispersed and inclined to roam over vast expanses of territory.

To effectively exploit the small number of animals available, Aboriginal inhabitants also needed to avoid too much specialization. While faunal remains at their former camps indicate that while the Independence peoples emphasized hunting muskoxen and the Thule-Inuit people relied heavily on marine mammals, all cultures of the High Arctic secured game from a range of both marine and terrestrial species. Such diversification required the development of a wide variety of hunting tools and a repertoire of techniques to ensure an adequate response to the region's sparse resource base.

As hunting peoples, all of Ellesmere Island's Aboriginal occupants needed to adapt to the region's natural ecology and to adjust to its frequent and unpredictable privations. Viable human occupation of this region required strategies of resource use closely attuned to the seasonal cycle, the feeding characteristics, and migration patterns of the major game animals. Other essential adaptations included the development of flexible forms of social organization oriented to hunting, high levels of mobility, and limiting groups to small bands capable of developing sustainable strategies of natural resource use. As well, the material culture of a succession of occupying cultures was largely derived from products of the animals they hunted: clothing and bedding from skins of muskox, fox, seals, and polar bear, and projectile points and sledge runners from walrus ivory (Figure 8).

At the same time, there were marked differences in the capacity of the respective hunting groups to utilize the available game sources. Of all pre-contact groups to occupy Ellesmere Island, the Thule-Inuit cultures appear to have made the most effective adaptation to the region and its ecology. The Independence and Dorset cultures, lacking the advantage of technologies of rapid pursuit, such as dog-drawn sledges

Figure 8: Thule culture sledge found by Lieutenant Adolphus Greely at Cape Baird in northern Ellesmere Island, 81°30' N. lat. US National Archives (Washington, DC), RG 27, Lady Franklin Bay Records, Box No. 17.

and kayaks, relied instead on stealth and their own legs to capture their game.

Even so, even the superior technology of the Thule culture was no match for the overriding impact of the climate, which forced the majority of the forerunners of the Inughuit in the region to abandon the High Arctic during the cooling era of the Little Ice Age after ca. AD 1450. Perhaps even this withdrawal exemplified this resourceful group's adaptation to the region's exacting climate. Archaeologist Patricia Sutherland has unearthed evidence of Thule stone dwellings in the Eureka Upland area up to ca. AD 1700, suggesting that at least a few Thule families continued to visit northern Ellesmere Island even well after the onset of climatic deterioration.[116] The great majority, however, apparently made only seasonal use of this most stringent of Ellesmere Island's regions, and eventually even this limited use ceased with the further advance of climate cooling. In interpreting the archaeological evidence, Peter Schledermann has concluded that Smith Sound was the major hearth region for Ellesmere's Thule populations until ca. AD 1700-1750.[117] Here, proximity to the North Water and other polynyas gave them continuing access to marine mammals despite increasing pack ice levels. With their traditional knowledge of Ellesmere Island and its resources, this group probably continued to make occasional excursions across Smith Sound in the warmer months, sometimes reaching northern Ellesmere in the course of these seasonal trips, with only very rare instances of wintering on Ellesmere Island.[118] Eventually, travel to Ellesmere Island ceased altogether at some point before contact, although the historical memory of the island persisted long after they had ceased to visit it. As discussed in Chapter 4, it was an environment that both Inuit from Baffin Island and Inughuit in northern Greenland continued to remember especially for its rich resources of muskoxen, although the resident Thule population retreated from occupation of Ellesmere Island after ca. AD 1700, perhaps becoming absorbed into the Inughuit in settlements on the northwestern Greenland coast. This was the environment in which they were living when Europeans arrived in the early nineteenth century.

The Continuing Role of the Polar Environment: Two Examples from the Contact Era

As has been noted, the polar region is characterized by a harsh physical environment, dominated by winters of severe cold and 24-hour darkness and an autumn period of intense storms and dwindling daylight. The examples of "pibloktoq" (arctic hysteria) and depression, two reported disorders of the contact era, both with a seasonal dimension, serve to illustrate the continuing impact of the High Arctic environment on human populations. These phenomena indicate some of the psychological aspects of life in the High Arctic environment, at least as experienced by Aboriginal and Western cultures in the contact era. It is acknowledged that social or cultural factors were probably also at play in reports of psychological distress. Still, these examples are suggestive of the potentially wide-ranging impacts of this extreme environment on people, demanding coping strategies to mitigate its effects.

Few Europeans who wintered in the High Arctic were immune to the physiological and psychological effects of the polar winter,[119] described by Donald MacMillan as "this so-called long dark, dreary arctic night, the night that drives men mad."[120] Various expedition accounts record the recurrent distress of Europeans and Americans during this season of perpetual darkness. Members of these parties particularly displayed evidence of depression at the onset of the long arctic night, as hunting activity lessened, and they were increasingly confined to the expedition quarters.

The polar winters apparently exerted psychological effects on all Europeans, whether endowed with hardy or brittle constitutions. In reviewing his journal for the months of January and February 1854, Elisha Kent Kane noted that it was "devoid of interest." He wrote: "In the darkness and consequent inaction, it was almost in vain that we sought to create topics of thought, and by a forced excitement to ward off the encroachments of disease. Our observatory and the dogs gave us our only regular occupations."[121] Kane added that "the influence of this long, intense darkness was most depressing."[122] Of the dark polar winter, Kane's compatriot William Godfrey wrote: "As might be expected, in view of their situation, our men were terribly affected with the blue devils."[123]

While commanding the Lady Franklin Bay Expedition of 1881–84, Lieutenant Greely reported that his American subordinates frequently experienced depression, malaise, and listlessness during this season. He attributed the malaise to the physiological effects of months of continuous, perpetual darkness. As days became darker in the autumn, several men, including officers, began to sleep in as late as the afternoon:

> That the long-continued darkness exercised a depressing influence on most of the party was evident to every observing person. Naturally, no one was inclined to admit that he was personally affected, but no one escaped this influence. The most marked signs among us were tendency to insomnia, indisposition to exertion, irritability of temper, and other similar symptoms abnormal to our usual characteristics both mental and physical."[124]

For his part, Greely had difficulty limiting his sleep to a set pattern and applying himself consistently to his "mental work." He acknowledged periodic "irritability of temper, which required a continued mental struggle to repress."[125] Frequently confined to their expedition quarters by the darkness or severe cold of this season, the men displayed the signs of "cabin fever." In January 1882, during the first winter at Fort Conger, Dr. Octave Pavy likened his daily routine to "a white bear in its cage." Elaborating, he spelled out the sources of his unhappiness: "our room, the society, the atmosphere, the gas, the warmth, the air, the unpleasantness of the commander come up within me."[126]

Even Robert E. Peary, a person of remarkable fortitude in innumerable situations, was affected by the long polar night. In early 1901, while wintering at Fort Conger in northern Ellesmere Island, he recalled the "uncontrollable nightmares of apprehension which used to come over me at the [Anniversary] Lodge in the winter of '94 and '95 [1894 and 1895]." Six years later, and confronting "the continuation of the darkness" and "mental tension" occasioned by the death of the one of the Inughuit women, and its anticipated effects on his other Aboriginal guides, Peary acknowledged a growing sense of foreboding.[127]

Regarding the mental state of Peary's men during the dark winter of 1900-01, Peary's expedition surgeon Dr. T.S. Dedrick observed that the lack of light had a depressing effect on all members of the party. He wrote: "It is a poor time for [Matthew] Henson to sit in the dark evenings. Very unadvisable in fact for him to feel on short allowance of light. In fact, the Esk[imo]s the same."[128] On March 10 Peary wrote of his surgeon in his diary at Fort Conger:

> Dr. looking & feeling badly (mentally) this morning said I would have to write down whatever I wanted him to do as he could remember nothing. Yesterday a similar remark, that if I would tell him what to do he could do it but he could do nothing himself. It cannot but be a bit depressing to have a physician who says he considers entire party in a bad way & is in a blue funk himself. He has the same drawn worried look that he had at Conger for 2 weeks or so after we arrived 2 years ago. He appears to intimate that on 10 days at Conger will break him up as he has no appetite. This is not a very favourable state of mind for him to be in.[129]

The extent to which these reported episodes of depression related to cultural patterns, physiological reactions, or variations in individual psychology is unclear. However, the prevalence of melancholia and lassitude in the winter suggests both psychological and physiological reactions to protracted winter darkness. To distinguish between environmental and other factors, we also need to study the particular ways in which European cultures responded to the polar environment. How they dealt with the many stresses posed by the physical environment holds the potential to illuminate both the outcomes of their exploration efforts and the suitability of their approaches to living in the Arctic.

A second phenomenon with an apparent seasonal relationship, reported in exploration literature, was recurrent hysteria among the Inughuit of Northwest Greenland. Various European visitors who wintered in northern Greenland commented on a general gloom and depression among Inughuit in the fall, peaking in the month of October. This period, which marks the last few weeks of dwindling sunlight before the undelivered darkness of polar winter, is characterized by extremely rough weather before the sea freezes. During this time, according to American big-game hunter Harry Whitney, "heavy winds and terrific snow storms swept over us with only brief intermissions."[130] At this time, Inughuit men and women reportedly displayed pronounced symptoms of melancholy and anxiety. However, there was one key difference between the genders. As soon as feasible, the men, whose primary responsibility was to secure game for the family and the community, left on hunting trips. The women, charged with domestic tasks, were confined to the settlements and their tiny dwellings. In Whitney's view, their anxiety was heightened by the considerable risk of hunting disasters in this season.[131]

It was in this context that Whitney reported witnessing several episodes of "pibloktoq," or arctic hysteria. He was in the *igloo* of Qulutana (Kulutinguah) in the presence of this man's spouse Torngi (Tongwe) and another woman. The two women cried for the return of their partners. They were very short of food, having been obliged to kill three of their dogs that day to eat, "an additional cause for worry." Later that night he was awakened by Torngi's screams. He wrote that she was "shouting at the top of her voice — shrill and startling, like one gone mad."[132]

In the same era as Whitney, explorer Dr. Frederick Cook made similar observations of prevalent depression and hysteria among the Inughuit in this season. After the "forced hilarity of their annual sporting event in the late autumn he observed a general onset of depression as the sun waned and disappeared. In Cook's view, with the freezing of the ocean and the out-migration of many sea mammals, "the Eskimos unconsciously feel the grim hand of want, of starvation, which means death, upon them."[133] He noted also the reappearance of shamanism at this time and related the sounds of sorrow that characterized this period. He wrote: "Out of the sombre, heavy air began to issue a sound of many women sobbing. From the indistinct distance came moaning, crooning voices. Sometimes hysterical wails of anguish rent the air and now and then frantic choruses shrieked some heartaching despair." A physician, Cook offered a generalized diagnosis: "The psychology of this period depression partly lies, undoubtedly, in this instinctive dread of death from lack of food and the natural depression of unrelieved gloom."[134]

A tabulation of the seasonal distribution of primary reports of "pibloktoq" compiled from a range of unpublished and published sources appears to bear out the inference that arctic hysteria was particularly concentrated in the summer and fall.[135] Of 39 episodes identified by month, more than two thirds occurred in a four-month period beginning in July. They peaked in October, when more than one fourth of the episodes were reported (Figure 9). While the sample remains small, this tabulation provides some quantitative support for the reports that hysteria was particularly concentrated in the period leading up to the disappearance of the sun.

Whatever the specific origins of the explorers' depression or Inughuit "pibloktoq," these phenomena suggest that the unusual and extreme conditions of the High Arctic environment could exert far-reaching effects, perhaps intensifying reactions of distress rooted in other causes. We must be careful not to leap to conclusions that smack of "environmental determinism." As various writers have pointed out, the entire issue of hysteria is loaded with the encrusted baggage of nineteenth century patriarchy[136] and the reports of hysteria cannot easily be separated out

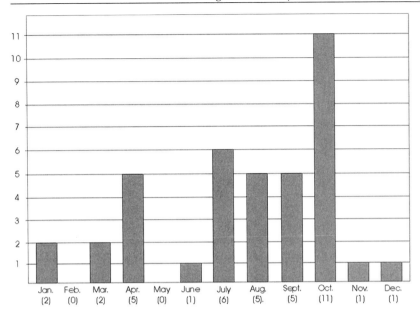

Figure 9: Distribution of reported "pibloktoq" episodes by month. This graph illustrates the seasonal distribution of "pibloktoq" episodes, as reported in the primary sources. It comprises 39 of the 40 reported cases; one episode could not be identified by month and was left out of the tabulation. There are no obvious sampling biases, as all episodes have been included for which there was eye-witness testimony, and which could be situated in time (year) and place. These episodes were reported by Euro-Americans or Europeans who were then spending at least one year in close contact with the Inughuit. Their extended contact would seem to rule out the possible skewing of results according to summer voyages to the Arctic and associated fieldwork, for example. Reproduced from Lyle Dick, "'Pibloktoq' (Arctic Hysteria): A Construction of European-Inuit Relations?" *Arctic Anthropology*, Vol. 32 No. 2 (1995), Appendix B, pp. 30-42.

from the mindset of the European observers who wrote about it. In seeking to solve the mystery of "pibloktoq," as well as other fascinating phenomena of the contact era, we also need to study the cultures that participated in the exchanges of contact, the subject of the next part of this book, as well as the dynamics of intercultural relations, treated in Part III. Provisionally, however, these examples point to the power of the High Arctic environment to influence human history in more ways than has been previously acknowledged. Its force was such that no arctic traveller could ignore it and, ultimately, only groups that studied its characteristics, opportunities, and constraints, developed the potential for long-term survival in this region of extremes.

3
Inughuit Culture in the High Arctic, 1800–1900

Inughuit Culture in the Nineteenth Century

From the contact era to the present, the people with the most enduring relationship to Ellesmere Island have been the Inughuit of northwest Greenland. They are the most northerly branch of the Inuit circumpolar culture of arctic North America and Greenland, hence, the most northerly people in the world. The Inughuit developed from their predecessors, the Thule culture, who spread across the Arctic from Alaska to Greenland around 900–1000 years BP. While differing in a number of respects from the way of life of their counterparts in other arctic regions, the Inughuit at the time of contact possessed a material and intellectual culture with affinities to all groups within the Inuit family of cultures. In terms of population, they were a very small branch of Inuit culture overall, as they reportedly numbered only about 140 individuals in the entire Thule region in the mid-nineteenth century.[1]

Who were these people, unknown to the outside world before 1818? Before the modern era, they were known by a wide variety of names. Captain John Ross referred to them as the "Arctic Highlanders,"[2] a term which continued to have currency throughout the nineteenth century. The German ethnographer Emil Bessels called them the "Itanese,"[3] after Etah, the name of the most northerly settlement of Inughuit. American anthropologist A.L. Kroeber called them "the Smith Sound tribe of Eskimo."[4] To Danes Knud Rasmussen and Peter Freuchen, they were the "Polar Eskimos,"[5] while American explorer Robert E. Peary, expressing his own proprietary notions, called them the "Peary Eskimos" and "my Eskimos."[6] The members of this people called themselves *Inughuit*, meaning "great and powerful human beings."[7]

When John Ross arrived at Cape York in 1818, the Inughuit asserted that they had never before encountered "white men." Was this in fact the first face-to-face meeting of the two cultures? Based on their discovery of a series of Norse artifacts at sites on the eastern and western coasts of Pim Island, archaeologists Peter Schledermann and Karen McCullough have inferred that members of the Thule culture in the Smith Sound region might have had direct contact with Norse visitors from southern Greenland. As well, Patricia Sutherland has interpreted the discovery of a bronze set of scales in western Ellesmere Island as indicating the presence of a Norse trader in the region. Whether Norse visitors encountered these High Arctic people directly or the artifacts made their way north through Aboriginal trade may be difficult to establish conclusively. No textual documentation of prior contacts between Europeans and Inughuit has apparently yet been unearthed.

At the point of contact the Inughuit were in difficult straits, lacking important materials for sledge and house construction, and had lost the knowledge of a number of skills vital to the survival of their culture. A comparison of pre-1800 Inughuit archaeological artifacts with their 1850s toolkit reveals a "dramatic decrease in technological complexity" in relation to the immediately preceding era.[8] Their diminished material capacity even included the loss of boat-building skills. When British mariner Peter Sutherland accompanied an expedition in search of Sir John Franklin to Cape York in 1850, he found some Inughuit resorting to inflating sealskin bladders to fashion a crude vessel on which one or two individuals could sit to paddle.[9] Sutherland observed that, to hunt caribou, Inughuit men were using a simple sling or were even obliged to throw rocks, which sometimes yielded results when an animal was injured and then taken by a group of hunters rushing in to finish it off.[10]

What can account for such a dramatic change in material capacity? Environmental factors appear to have been decisive. As noted in Chapter 1, a general climatic cooling ensued during the Little Ice Age after AD 1450, contributing to increased levels of pack ice in the waters of the High Arctic. As a result, driftwood, on which the Inughuit depended for the construction of *igloo* roof arches, kayak frames, and various tools, failed to reach the Thule region. These problems were worsened as congested sea ice also drove the Greenland whale farther south, beyond the reach of Inughuit hunters. This meant that they were also deprived of whale ribs, an alternative material used in the construction of kayaks, assorted weapons, and roof supports.

Beyond the long-term cooling cycle, climatic research suggests that this group's material difficulties were compounded by a cold climatic cycle of shorter duration during the first half of the nineteenth century. In this period, the ringed seal was probably forced to migrate to the south, drawing polar bears with it, thus reducing the game animals available to the Inughuit.[11] Ice congestion in the fiords made hunting narwhal by kayak difficult or impossible and may have contributed to the loss of boat-building skills. Concurrently, congested pack ice in Baffin Bay prevented the prevailing currents from delivering driftwood to northwest Greenland, cutting off an important supply of materials for both sled and boat construction.

Archaeologist Karl Butzer has theorized that when population pressures come face to face with technological constraints and limited resources, a curtailment of population results.[12] In the case of the Inughuit, the very small population of perhaps 150 reported around 1850, combined with the presence of many recently abandoned winter dwellings, suggests a general reduction of population by the early nineteenth century. Between 1818 and 1860, a succession of European visitors to the Thule region remarked on the signs of famine and impoverishment in the Aboriginal population. For example, in April 1855, Elisha Kent Kane reported that the lack of food resources had obliged the Inughuit on Northumberland Island to kill all but 20 of their dogs. He also commented on their high death rate; according to Kane, five of 140 residents at eight settlements had died in the preceding two years. Another serious limiting factor was the recurrent presence of infectious disease epidemics, precipitated by contact with Europeans, throughout the nineteenth century. On the basis of such observations, Kane and other European observers of the period concluded that the Inughuit were then on the brink of extinction.[13]

As with other Aboriginal peoples occupying or visiting Ellesmere Island, Inughuit culture was organized around hunting, fishing, and gathering.[14] The requirements of the hunt determined the location and form of their settlements, their seasonal rounds of activity, migrational patterns, and daily movements. The great majority of their material needs, including food, clothing, and tools were supplied by products obtained from hunting, supplemented by the ancillary activities of fishing and netting birds. Of necessity, the Inughuit were a conserving society, utilizing as much of the procured carcasses as possible. For example, narwhal meat was used as food for both humans and dogs. Practically the entire skin, or *mattaq*, including the tail and flippers, was eaten as a delicacy, while the sinews of the back were split and dried for use as thread. Narwhal blubber provided the Inughuit with the principal source of fuel for blubber lamps, essential for heating dugout dwellings, boiling meat, and drying skins, clothes, and boots.[15]

Inughuit diet in 1850 consisted almost exclusively of the flesh of marine mammals, supplemented by birds and their eggs, and, to a lesser extent, fish and crustaceans. Mammalian game resources were quite varied and included pinnipeds (seals, particularly ringed seals, and walrus), narwhal, polar bear, fox, and hare. The only kind of fish utilized was arctic charr, and even these were caught only "accidentally, the use of the fish hook being unknown to them," according to Dr. Emil Bessels, who visited them while with C.F. Hall's expedition of 1871.[16] More importantly, lack of driftwood and whalebone contributed to the loss of kayak technology, which severely constrained opportunities to hunt larger game animals.

Inughuit settlement patterns reflected a complex of factors, including the seasonal cycle, migration patterns of game animals, physiography, proximity to leads of sea ice, and the existing technology of the group. It was considered particularly important to select sites where smooth and firm ice formed to facilitate access to the sea and for safe sledging. Other requirements included finding sea ice that would not be covered with snow that was too soft or deep and ice that would persist in all seasons. Fresh water was another necessity, and since all land-locked waters were frozen solid in the winter, the Inughuit often preferred to settle near grounded icebergs, from which they could hack off pieces to melt for drinking. Other considerations bearing on the selection of sites included the presence of shelter from the region's heavy winds and snowfall and exposure to sunlight early in the spring and late in the fall. The optimal sites for settlement were therefore in the fiords, sounds, and inlets of northwestern Greenland or other areas of the Arctic Archipelago where smooth ice formed, and with accessibility to fresh water.

Generally, the small population of Inughuit was spread out along a broad expanse of coastline between Cape York on the southern shores of the Hayes Peninsula to Etah, the most northerly settlement, located on the Greenland side of Smith Sound about 50 km across the water from Ellesmere Island. This represented a vast expanse of more than 800 km of coastline. Each wintering settlement consisted of from three to seven families, while summer settlements were more dispersed and oriented to individual families. In the spring, the Inughuit also grouped in more temporary settlements adjacent to the floe edge of the North Water for the annual walrus hunt, an activity which required co-operation by several hunters.

We must avoid speaking of the Inughuit as if they were a monolithic people. Depending on the locality and its environmental characteristics, there were significant differences in the hunting regimens of different families and communities, reflected in varying settlement patterns. In the First World War era, the Inughuit themselves classified their people according to types of wind, indicative of different localities within Avanersuaq, the Thule District, i.e., *Nigerdlit* (those who live nearest the southwest wind), *Akunarmiut* (those who live between the winds), *Orqordlit* (those who live in the lee of the southwest wind), and *Avangnardlit* (those who live next to the north wind).[17]

For the *Nigerdlit* in the area of Cape York, the relative absence of open water rendered hunting from kayaks difficult or ineffective. Compensating for the comparative lack of seals, the mountains surrounding this locality were home to innumerable "sea-kings," or auks, which the hunters captured with nets rigged to poles. In 1818, when Captain John Ross led the first documented European expedition to the region, he found the Inughuit of this area relied on seals and narwhal ("sea-unicorn") as the mainstays of their diet, supplemented by foxes and hares secured in traps.[18] Around Thule, on the other hand, the mainstay of the *Akunarmiut* was the walrus, supplemented by considerable numbers of seals and narwhals. Here, it was important that the sea ice settle evenly in late October or early November, in order that the walrus remain in the area for the winter. The *Oqordlit,* ranging around the Inglefield Gulf, enjoyed some of the best hunting in the Thule district and had a large number of hunting camps. In addition to walrus, they obtained narwal and beluga whales in relative abundance. With a drier climate than the settlements to the south, this group generally enjoyed a longer hunting season. The *Avangnardlit*, with camps at Etah and Anoritooq, had access to a large population of walrus. At Etah, these game animals were supplemented by sea-king birds from a nearby mountain, while at Anoritooq, narwhals were available.[19]

Inughuit settlement patterns show a lack of territoriality among this group; typically, they came together to share the harvest of natural resources, as in the annual walrus hunt off Pitoraarfik (Peterahwik) on Smith Sound (Figure 10). Remarking on their use of this "favourite hunting ground" in the 1850s, Isaac Israel Hayes noted a close relationship between Inughuit settlement patterns, the seasons, and accessibility to open water for hunting sea mammals. In winter, when the gradually widening belt of sea ice along the coast made the distances between winter communities and the floe edge "inconveniently great," the Inughuit moved up to the cape to establish temporary hunting settlements on the coast or on the ice.[20]

In the 1890s, Robert Peary also remarked on Inughuit temporary settlements near Pitoraarfik and suggested some additional factors bearing on their selection of habitation sites. These included the Inughuit's co-operative approach to walrus hunting and its influence on their settlement patterns. In addition to general proximity to the North Water, the morphology, siting, and architectural forms of the settlements were influenced by the availability of suitable snow for dwelling construction and accessibility to the ice foot for a travelling surface. Peary wrote:

> The precise position of the settlement of Peterahwik depends upon the particular season and condition of the ice. In 1894, the snow igloos, over forty in number, were located under the bluffs close by the glacier, some two miles east of the point of the cape, and over two-thirds of the entire tribe were assembled here. At the time of my visit now, the majority of the igloos were located on the ice-foot on the southern side of the trap dyke, at

Figure 10: "Walrus hunt off Pikantlik," 1850s. Illustration from Elisha Kent Kane, *Arctic Explorations*, Vol. II, Plate between pp. 214-15.

its very extremity, where a long drift of compact snow furnished suitable material for construction purposes. Other igloos in groups of twos and threes were located at various points along the coast, for a distance of twelve miles.

The igloos at the cape were arranged in a regular line with their backs to the dyke, their entrances to the south, and about fifty feet from the ice-foot, the level upper surface of which formed a wide, smooth street in front of them. These igloos were on an average twenty-five feet apart, and though varying somewhat in size, according to the number of occupants, were all built on one pattern.[21]

The fact that the Inughuit congregated at these settlements for the winter was a necessity tied directly to their procurement activities and the characteristics of the animals being hunted. In this case, hunting of seals at breathing holes determined both the number of hunters and co-operation in hunting. Since the seals maintained various breathing holes in the ice over a wide area, many hunters were needed to watch continually at the holes, so that seals could be harpooned when surfacing to breathe (Figure 11).[22]

At the beginning of the period of perpetual daylight, in late April or early May, the Inughuit moved out of their winter dwellings. During the brief summers, they dispersed into much smaller family units and travelled to their summer hunting locations, where they lived in sealskin tents. These were fashioned from the same skins used for bedding in the winter dwellings. Families might set up temporary quarters by themselves, but typically settled in small groups as mutual assistance by hunters was required in hunting narwhals or walruses. Benjamin Hoppin, who accompanied Robert Peary on his Greenland

Figure 11: Hunter with two killed seals, Flagler Bay, Ellesmere Island, 1923–25. Credit: The Peary-MacMillan Arctic Museum, Bowdoin College (Brunswick, Maine), Negative no. NG-600.

expedition in 1896, described several small summer communities in the Thule district visited by the relief vessel, the *Kite*, that August, which give an indication of the size of settlements in this season. At Uummannaq (Omenak) in North Star Bay, they found both a winter grouping of seven stone dwellings (*igloo*) and a summer collection of four tents (*tupik*) about a hundred yards away. The residents of this village also possessed four sledges and a large number of dogs, which they housed in small stone shelters with roofs. At Kiketarsuak on Saunders Island, Hoppin's party found the community situated on a promontory, presumably to aid in accessing the sea ice or open water to hunter travel. This settlement consisted of five tents, five "meat houses," or caches, four "columns for drying meat," and one column of wood. Several stone winter dwellings (*igloo*) belonging to this group were also located nearby.[23]

While Inughuit forms of shelter and settlement patterns represented a successful adaptation to the physical environment, they cannot explain the apparent resiliency of this people to the psychological stresses of living in this region. As French ethnologist Marcel Mauss observed nearly 100 years ago, Inuit forms of shelter are not reducible solely to environmental considerations, but also incorporate important principles of social organization and group interaction.[24] Anthropologist Kwang-Chih Chang has proposed a very useful distinction between the terms "settlement patterns" and "community patterns" as they relate to circumpolar societies. In Chang's typology, such responses to the physical environment as siting in relation to topography or natural resources, seasons of occupation, and subsistence activities fall under settlement patterns. On the other hand, positioning dwellings in a settlement in terms of social or cultural ties collectively define the community pattern.[25]

In Inughuit winter settlements, clustering dwellings functioned to ameliorate the insecurity and scarcity of the dark period. For example, winter visiting enabled sharing food resources during the period of greatest scarcity. In his diary, Dr. T.S. Dedrick, who was at Etah during the winter of 1899-1900, described both communal sharing of food and the active social life in a small *igloo*: "I was in Tungwee's [Torngi's] igloo at village today. Assayah [Asiajuk] & wife were visiting there. That made three couples, besides the two children and myself. They were eating some deer meat, but principally little auks which had been packed in seal skin bags in the summer."[26]

Inughuit banding together not only facilitated communal sharing of food resources, but occasioned the group's participation in shamanistic activities, feasts, and sharing sexuality. In the wintering context, family ties were supplemented and to a degree supplanted by obligations to the larger body, the community.[27] The communalistic character of such villages was also reflected in the spatial arrangement of individual dwellings, which showed an absence of hierarchy among constituent families.

The Inughuit themselves, as well as ethnologists and visitors to the Thule region, remarked on the importance of social interaction in winter to this group. In the early 1900s, Mâsangguaq (Maisanguaq), a young man of about 30, informed Knud Rasmussen that "during the Long Dark, people do not go out fishing; they only pay visits to one another and sing drum-songs."[28] Norwegian Eivind Astrup, who participated in two of Robert E. Peary's expeditions to northern Greenland in the 1890s, wrote that "a chief reason which makes it possible for the Esquimaux at Smith's Sound to endure the long winter nights of four months is their social disposition." He went on to observe that young people "generally occupy more of the time of darkness in visits to relatives and friends than they do at home."[29] In the same era, T.S. Dedrick described the atmosphere of the *igloo* he was visiting as one of "chatter and laughter," and remarked that "a palace could not have held happier people."[30] French anthropogeographer Jean Malaurie, who spent a year with the Inughuit in the early 1950s, reported on the winter practice of visiting and communal drum dancing, often extending far into the night.[31] Mauss attributed to such winter activities the vital role of renewing group solidarity in all Inuit societies.[32] In the High Arctic, confronted with recurrent risks of famine, hunting accidents, and other dangers, the Inughuit developed community patterns that seemed admirably suited to preserving the psychological health of the group. It was a strategy whose survival value was demonstrated by their persistence over many generations.

Inughuit society was characterized by flexible social arrangements, loosely organized around patterns of natural resource use. The basic unit of Inughuit social structure was the family. In most cases families were headed by male hunter and a female partner who looked after all domestic functions and rearing children. Gender roles were clearly differentiated, although women often took on the role of procuring smaller game, through such techniques as setting and monitoring stone fox traps (see Figure 12), and ice fishing for arctic charr with traditional spears, an activity also carried out by men and boys (Figure 94).

Families often banded together with a few other families for pragmatic reasons, including the need for a larger group to hunt particular species, such as caribou, muskoxen, and walrus. When several men departed on longer hunting trips, it was also important to leave a male to continue to procure game for the families remaining at the settlement. Communities were loosely organized, without a formalized leadership structure. On the trail, however, the "most successful" hunter of the group generally assumed responsibility for determining when the settlements should go travelling, where to go hunting, and so on. Knud Rasmussen noted that it was the best hunters, "men who are already in a position to command the respect of their fellows" who often also became *angakut* or shamans.[33] These men used their powers to conjure up helping spirits and visions to lead the group to game animals.[34] Two generations later, Malaurie made further observations regarding the leadership structure of the Inughuit in the early 1950s. According to Malaurie, community leaders or *naalagaq* were individuals who not only had acquired extensive experience and knowledge of the environment, but also possessed the necessary wisdom and judgment to guarantee the safety and well-being of the group.[35]

Visitors to the Thule region in the nineteenth century found the Inughuit were a communitarian society, characterized by mutual assistance and sharing resources. Hunters and their families might amass a quantity of meat, but if others were in need, they were expected to share the food equally. Often the hunt itself was a mutual undertaking, as in the case of walrus, bear, or caribou hunting, and its products were divided among the families according to custom. Housing, too, was frequently shared. Even in the case of more substantial dwell-

Figure 12: Mother showing her daughter how to set a fox trap, Etah, northern Greenland, 1923-25. Credit: The Peary-MacMillan Arctic Museum, Bowdoin College (Brunswick, Maine), Photograph no. NG-335.

ings, families might build and occupy a stone *igloo* for a winter or two, but others were free to use them in their absence.

This is not to say that families did not own their own belongings, whether hunting or domestic tools, or items such as clothing, skins, and various accessories. But these few possessions were the materials of necessity and survival, rather than surplus. European visitors to the Thule region in the early contact period were amazed at the Spartan character of their material culture, as in the comment of Dr. Emil Bessels:

> Among the Inuit the communistic mode of life is so pronounced that the dower scarcely comes into consideration. A sledge, a team of dogs and the rude weapons are essentially the total personal property of the man, while the woman owns a lamp, a cooking pot, a knife and a few needles. In addition to this we may mention the scanty wardrobe.[36]

To European observers such as Bessels, whose own culture tended to measure progress in terms of material accumulation, the apparently meagre possessions of the Inughuit signified poverty and backwardness. From another perspective, the small number and portability of their materials showed an effective adaptation to a region where scattered resources required a high degree of mobility among its inhabitants. Likewise, the "communistic mode of life" was a pragmatic response to frequent scarcity in the harsh High Arctic environment, where group survival demanded sharing resources.

Notions of private property with regard to land, sea, and resources were said to be alien to Inughuit thought and practice. In his 1899 diary at Etah, while serving as surgeon on one of Robert Peary's Greenland expeditions, Dr. T.S. Dedrick reported an incident illustrating a strong rejection of private ownership of land and resources. One evening, several Inughuit were in Dedrick's winter dwelling, where they were examining a magazine. He showed them a photograph portraying a poacher whom the landowner had caught in the act of stealing a hare. Dedrick recorded their reaction: "Looking intently, suddenly one of the women shook her fist at the landowner and said 'Ad'a nuck shah,' or 'Confound you!'"[37]

As in other circumpolar societies, the role of Inughuit women was fundamental to the development and persistence of their culture and society. Beyond their roles in nurturing and supporting families, women performed at least half the labour in the community. While many of their roles reflected a clear-cut cultural division of labour, women also carried out non-gender-specific work. For example, in describing building stone winter *igloos* at an Inughuit settlement in 1895, Robert Peary remarked: "The construction of the igloos falls very largely upon the women, and in an emergency they even assist in bringing stones."[38] Women also played an important role in food procurement. In the warmer months, they fished for charr in the small lakes that hugged the coast. Both women and children netted large numbers of auks that nested on the small islands of Smith Sound (Figures 13 and 91).[39] After killing the netted birds they stored as many as 700-800 in a sealskin bag, which was placed under rocks, the cache to be retrieved in winter.[40] Other birds were procured for consumption in the spring and to be fed to the dogs. Prior to contact, the women also collected and prepared the dovekie skins for the manufacture of children's undergarments.[41] While on the island rookeries to catch birds, they also took the time to collect the eggs of eider ducks.

Much of women's labour revolved around household tasks and raising children. In mild weather during the summer, their work included cooking, preparing and stretching skins, which were performed outside. Generally, the women tended to leave their sewing for poorer weather, so that they could perform the tasks that were best done outside while the weather was favourable.[42] Inughuit children assisted their mothers in various tasks around the camp. Girls helped in the preparation of skins for use in clothing, while boys learned to make stone fox traps, which they set along the beach.[43]

In the winter, a vital responsibility of the women was maintaining the blubber lamps for warmth, light, and for use in cooking. The only method of cooking was boiling; in the confines of their small dwellings,

Figure 13: "Catching little auks," Etah, northern Greenland. Credit: American Museum of Natural History, Donald B. MacMillan Collection, Crocker Land, 1913-17, Negative no. 231708. ," Etah, northern Greenland

other methods were impracticable, and in any case they lacked the requisite fuel. Winter was also devoted to such tasks as sewing clothes and repairing skins. Another important responsibility of the women was to dry and repair their husbands' kamiks and to chew them to keep them soft and pliable — essential to preventing frozen feet. Indeed, they chewed all of the family's leather garments to keep them in good condition.[44]

For the Inughuit, sewing was not merely a desirable skill, but essential for survival of the family and group. In the often severe climatic conditions of the region, all outer garments needed to be impervious to wind and snow. But it was especially important that footwear be sewn carefully to avoid frozen feet, which could spell disaster for the entire family if the hunter was so stricken. Therefore, the women performed exacting stitch work to make kamiks as water-resistant as possible (Figure 14). For travelling in very cold weather, fur outer shoes needed to be perfectly shaped so as not to loosen and insoles prepared and inserted under the stockings.

In the generally cold climate of the region, it was important for all garments to be warm. Since the Inughuit economy required people to be outdoors and on the trail so much of the time, the clothes also needed to be durable. Materials for clothing were obtained from a variety of sources, principally the skins of game animals, as is illustrated in a watercolour drawing of "Ervick," an Inughuaq man involved in the first encounter with Ross's party in 1818 (Figure 15). As staple game animals, seals provided the skins used for many items, such as boots, mittens, summer coats and pants. Double boots (*kamik*) were made from sealskin, with the hair scraped off the outer boots and the fur turned inside in the inner pair, both sewed with the dried tendons of narwhal skin.[45] Men's winter pants were sewn from polar bear fur, chosen not only for its warmth, but also its capacity to shed snow and ice.[46] Men's and women's winter jackets (*qulittaq*) were made from blue fox and caribou, said to be the warmest of skins (Figure 16).[47] Underwear was fashioned from skins of birds such as dovekies, murrs, and eiders.[48] The skins of hares were used in making stockings. Caribou skins were used to fashion mittens, sleeping bags, and bed covers for the *igloo*, *iglooyah*, or *tupiq*. All these items were sewn with strips of sinew from the hides of narwhal or the flanks of caribou. Sinew had the important characteristic of swelling when wet, making well-prepared seams impervious to water.

While not an article of clothing, the sleeping bag was another sewn article of importance, as it protected hunters on extended trips away from the settlement. In the period after 1900, the Inughuit preferred to use caribou skins for their sleeping bags, but sometimes muskox or bear skins were used as well. Using two or three caribou skins, the seamstress sewed them lengthwise, with the hair side turned inwards, and sewed an additional flap to be laid on the under side (Figure 17). In cold weather, the wearer would draw this flap over his head, leaving only a small opening through which to breathe. To avert perspiration and problems of dampness, all the clothes were removed when crawling into the sleeping bag.[49]

The Seasonal Cycle

Following Marcel Mauss, various writers have attempted to explain arctic Aboriginal cultures in relation to their physical environments, especially the climate and seasonality.[50] Roughly speaking, the rhythm of life varied according to a number of seasonal factors, including the

Figure 14: "Inah-loo [Inaluk] sewing skin kamik, Etah, northern Greenland." Credit: American Museum of Natural History, Donald B. MacMillan Collection, Crocker Land, 1913-17, Negative No. 233531.

extended hours of daylight in the spring, summer, and autumn; the protracted darkness of winter; the melting or freezing of the sea ice; and the availability of game animals in the different seasons.

Generally, an accelerated pace of activity filled the months of continuous daylight, as hunters and their families moved quickly to secure as much game as possible in preparation for winter scarcity. For the Inughuit in the nineteenth century, the busiest periods were spring, summer, and fall. During this period, they travelled over extensive tracts to maximize utilization of the region's resources. For example, in 1818 at Cape York, an Inughuit man named Meigack related to John Ross that in the summer his family moved from Petowack [Pitoraarfik?] to

Figure 15: "Arctic Highlander — Ervick, a native of Prince Regents Bay," 1818. Water colour, pen and ink over pencil drawing by John Ross, ca 1819, National Archives of Canada Photo no. C-119394.

Cape York, where they hunted seals and narwhal and procured iron, before departing again when the sun disappeared.[51] Travel in the summer was complicated by the melting of the sea ice; by the nineteenth century, the Inughuit had lost the knowledge or skills of boat building and their mobility was severely curtailed. This made travel to good hunting locations all the more imperative during the spring months from March to June and the fall months of September and October. In the 1850s, extended hunting trips away from the settlements continued throughout the fall, including stalking the breathing holes of pinnipeds.[52]

Winter was probably a time of reduced productivity in all periods of Inughuit history, as the complete lack of daylight, particularly when moonlight was at low ebb, made hunting and procurement very diffi-

Figure 16: "A northernmost man and his wife, Me-coo-sha [Meqqusaaq] and Ah-ma, standing next to sledge, two Inuits [Inughuit] who served as helpers to Frederick Cook during his expedition to the North Pole," 1907. Library of Congress (Washington, D.C.) Reproduction No. LC-USZ62-103152.

cult. Hunting was also inhibited by the freezing of leads of water near the shore, necessitating travelling farther afield to find seals, which was difficult in reduced light. Even so, Inughuit could sometimes find open cracks in the ice where wildlife congregated, enabling a continuation of procurement activities. In 1854, Kane observed at one such lead: "To these spots, the seal, walrus, and the early birds crowd in numbers. One which kept open, as we find from the Esquimaux, at Littleton island, only forty miles from us, sustained three families last winter until the opening of the North Water."[53] When confined to the settlement Inughuit men were kept busy preparing for spring hunting through such activities as mending harness, preparing harpoon lines, and making bird nets, while women maintained boot soles and bird skins by chewing, and sewed numerous articles of clothing during the dark period.[54]

In early February, before the sun had returned, men from the nearest Inughuit community sent out scouts to the floe edge of the North

Figure 17: Inughuit sleeping bags, in use on Ellesmere Island, 1910. Photo from
Harry Whitney, *Hunting with the Eskimos* (1910), p. 175.

Water. If they heard the sounds of walrus, these men returned to their
community to convey the information, whereupon other couriers carried the news to the other settlements. Each family gathered and packed
its belongings and set out for the cape, where they built an *iglooyah* or
snow house. By the end of February "half or two thirds" of the entire
group might congregate at this snow-house village. Group hunting of
walrus was interrupted by periodic trips to transport walrus meat back
to caches on Robertson Bay. This work continued until well into the
spring, when the widening North Water dissolved the fast ice as far as
the cape. To avoid being stranded by the melting ice foot, their escape
route, the Inughuit departed hurriedly to the east, where, collecting
their meat, they separated into smaller groupings for the summer.[55]

In the 1850s, the Inughuit practised a distinctive form of sealing or
walrus hunting according to their existing technology, a method described by various European visitors to the region, beginning with
John Ross in 1818.[56] Known as *utoq* hunting (*utoq* meaning an animal
lying on the ice), this form of hunting lasted as long as the ice was
safe to walk on and was only practicable on calm, clear days, which
predominated until early summer. By this method, the hunter hunted
the animal by open leads or holes in the ice maintained by the walrus
or seal for breathing. Carrying a harpoon and flensing knife, the hunter
sometimes crouched behind a screen of stretched membrane, mounted
on a pair of runners, to conceal his presence. Typically the runners
were shod with bearskin to muffle the scraping sound produced by

pushing the screen over the snow or ice.[57] Keeping still for an extended period, the hunter listened for the faint sound of a seal's breathing, before again advancing another hundred paces or so. If hunting without a screen, the hunter wore bearskin soles on his kamiks with the hairs turned outward to muffle the sound of his steps. Very carefully he lifted his feet straight up and down to avoid making any noise. On hearing the sounds of a seal breathing, the hunter knew that it would breathe about 20-30 times before diving to catch fish, only to return again to the breathing hole after about 10 minutes. After the animal submerged, the hunter again moved toward the breathing hole very carefully, approaching from against the wind if there was a breeze. When the animal again poked its head out of the water, the hunter quickly harpooned it through the ice and immediately pulled it out on the surface to be dispatched with his killing iron (Figure 18).[58]

This technique required great skill, both to insert the harpoon and to hold the line to restrain the animal. Frequently, hunters lost their harpoons in the struggle.[59] This method was practised throughout the winter, but particularly after the onset of daylight in February. The most productive time for seal hunting was in late April or early May, when the seals were beginning to come up through holes in the ice to bask on the surface in the warm sunshine. The hunting of walrus was necessarily a co-operative activity involving several hunters, partly due to the dangerous nature of the undertaking, and also because of the great weight of these animals, requiring a team effort to haul the carcass out on the ice. In the 1850s, Kane observed a "clever contrivance" used to land one of these animals. Cutting two pairs of incisions in the thick hide at the back of the walrus's neck, a hunter inserted a strip of animal skin through one of these bands. He then drew the strip back to a stick driven into the ice, where it was passed through a loop, drawn back to the animal and passed through the second band, creating a "double purchase" to enable the men of the hunting party to winch the carcass out for butchering.[60]

Beyond the seasonal round of travel to areas rich in particular game animals, the Inughuit practised longer-term migrational patterns to enable fuller exploitation of the region's resources. Peter Freuchen, who managed the trading store at Thule after 1910, remarked on the Inughuit practice of periodic travel to obtain necessary materials. He noted that in only three places in the district were they able to obtain soapstone for use in carving lamps and pots. Knives were constructed with meteorite iron at Salve Island near Cape York at the southern periphery of the region. Yet, before they could exploit this resource, they needed to

Figure 18: "Holding with toque," Etah, Greenland. Credit: American Museum of Natural History, Donald B. MacMillan Collection, Collection, Crocker Land, 1913–17, Negative no. 231661.

go far to the north, to the region around Humboldt Glacier to gather an agate that was suitable for chipping away the chunks of iron. Freuchen argued that the necessity of frequent movements over long distances obliged the Inughuit "to develop superior travelling methods, which in turn enabled them to perform their long distance migrations."[61]

Jean Malaurie, who spent a year with the Inughuit around 1950, identified a tri-annual cycle of activity then being followed in the Thule region. While recorded in the modern era, it presumably was analogous to earlier trends in the rotation of resource use. Malaurie argued that these cyclical patterns of activity enabled the Inughuit to maximize returns from areas rich in particular resources, including:

> "bears in Melville Bay; walruses in Neqi (Neqe) Fiord; seals in Savigssivik (Savissivik); walruses and foxes in Thule; stones for oil lamps north of Neqi (Neqe); birds and seals in Siorapaluk; sharks in Kangerlussuaq; birds in Etah and on Saunders, Herbert and Northumberland islands, whose surrounding waters are rich in walruses; reindeer in Inuarfissuaq; and bears on the Humboldt Glacier."[62]

In 1851 Kallihirua, also known as Erasmus York, an interpreter with the British ship HMS *Assistance*, drew a map of the Thule District, which noted Inughuit place names and locations of various resources then being utilized by the people. He recorded hares in abundance near

Kaugarsuk (Cape Athol), caribou in the country to the east of Uummannaq, flint stones at Ignoi on Northumberland Island, and charr in a small lake at Akaluq, near Cape Alexander on Smith Sound.[63] Other materials offered by the region included iron for knife edges and spear points, obtained from the meteorites at Savissivik; soapstone for use in making cooking pots and lamps, obtained from a supply between Cape York and Cape Atholl; dried grass, used to line their boots, collected from below the dovekie colonies southwest of Cape Atholl; and iron pyrites from south of Booth Sound, used in igniting fire.[64]

Inughuit Material Culture at the Time of Contact

At the time of initial contact, Inughuit material culture represented an ingenious maximization of use of the limited range of materials available in this region of sparse resources. For the most part, materials consisted of the products of game animals, such as bone, skins, and organ membranes, and driftwood. In 1818, Sir John Ross observed that the Inughuit lacked wood and readily accessible iron, though he admired their ability to improvise with the few materials that were available. For example, he found that their spears and sledge runners were made from the tusks of narwhals, while the sledge framework was fashioned from seal bones, and tied together with sealskin thongs.[65] After the arrival of European whalers around 1820, these basic materials began to be supplemented by wood and iron or steel, although the supply remained very limited until well into the twentieth century. A scarce commodity, wood was carefully conserved and handed down from one generation to the next. In 1900, for example, the Inughuaq Patdloq (Pooblah) related that he had made his first kayak two years before with wood passed on to him by his uncle.[66]

In 1818, Ross's blacksmith examined knives traded by the Inughuit and was told that they had obtained the metal from nails attached to a piece of driftwood.[67] Clements Markham, who accompanied a British voyage to the region in the early 1850s, described some of the tools then used by the people:

> Their weapons are a lance of narwhal ivory, or sometimes of two bear thigh-bones lashed together, tipped with steel since their intercourse with whalers, and a harpoon. They also have a knife made from some old drifted cask hoop, which they conceal in the boot. The lance is used in their gallant encounters with bears, and in securing a walrus or seal on the ice, when its retreat has been cut off; the harpoon for the far more dangerous battles with the walrus in his own element. They have bird-nets, with which they catch the little auks and guillemots that breed in myriads on the perpendicular crags.[68]

Part of the difficulty in reconstructing hunting tools from early in the contact era is that many European visitors were less engaged by Inughuit procurement strategies than more exotic aspects of their existence. However, Hans Hendrik, a Greenlander from the Prøven district who was hired by several expeditions as a dog driver and hunter, took great interest in Inughuit hunting tools and practices, and his observations were subsequently recorded by ethnographer Dr. Henrik Rink. Hendrik reported that, in the 1850s, the Inughuit hunted beluga whales from the floe edge. They attached five hunting bladder floats to one line; while only one bladder was used on the "big ice." Walrus, on the other hand, were also pursued from the ice with the aid of two harpoons on opposite ends of a hunting line. A *toq* or chisel was affixed to the opposite end of a spear shaft, and after impaling the walrus with one harpoon, as soon as the line was tightened, the hunters plunged the other spear's chisel end into the ice to secure the animal (Figure 18).[69] Hans also remembered that in the 1850s, the Inughuit hunted polar bears with spears, using their dogs first to pursue the bears and hold them at bay. Foxes were trapped in traps of four different types of design, while hares were secured with nets made of sealskin thongs.[70]

During the First World War period, American Donald MacMillan also recorded Inughuit hunters' descriptions of a number of tools used by their ancestors prior to European contact. They included the harpoon, traditionally made from narwhal tusks and the penis bones of the walrus. His informant, Majak (Myak), reported that each hunter constructed a harpoon equal to his height, from eyebrow level to the ground.[71] He recalled that two types of *toq*, or holding iron, were used traditionally. One served solely as a holding device, while the other functioned both as a holding iron and a killing iron, with a lance fitted on the opposite end of the shaft.[72] Majak's description indicated that the form of this tool had changed little since Hans Hendrik observed these weapons in the 1850s. In the 1850s, Kane observed that narwhal tusks were also used in fashioning holders for bird nets, while the purse receptacle was made with sealskin.[73] Inughuit sledges were fashioned from an assortment of materials from game animals, as follows:

> The sledges were made up of small fragments of porous bone, admirably knit together by thongs of hide; the runners, which glistened like burnished steel, were of highly-polished ivory, obtained from the tusks of walrus ... their lances, which were lashed to the sledges, were quite a formidable weapon. The staff was of the horn of the narwhal, or else of the thigh-bones of the bear, two lashed together, or sometimes the mirabilis of the walrus, three or four of them united. This last was a favourite material also for the cross-bars of their sledges. They had no wood.[74]

When some wood subsequently became available during the Peary era, the Inughuit applied their customary ingenuity in assembling any available pieces into serviceable tools. An example was an Inughuit kayak paddle examined by a passenger on Peary's supply vessel, the *Erik*, in 1905. It was fashioned from many pieces of wood lashed together with strips of walrus hide.[75]

Even before the introduction of European materials and technology, the material culture of the Inughuit was in flux in the late nineteenth century. An example was the umiak, the so-called "woman's boat," a large vessel which was still part of the material culture of the Inughuit when Qitlaq and his party from Baffin Island arrived around 1860. By the First World War era, American explorer Donald B. MacMillan noted its abandonment and offered several explanations, including: i) the loss of population in villages, leaving inadequate numbers of people to operate the boats; ii) the amount of wood and skins required to build these boats; iii) the fact that Inughuit kayaks were adequate for hunting narwhals and seals; iv) women were needed at home for various household duties during the summer season, including dressing skins, catching auks, making garments, attending and feeding dogs; and v) umiaks were too large to be transported from place to place on the spring hunting trips of the Inughuit.[76]

In the contact era, the Inughuit built three principal types of dwelling structures. Two of these, the *igloo* and the *kangmah*, were quasi-permanent winter habitations, while the *iglooyah*, or snow house, functioned as a more temporary shelter. The *igloo* was an oblong shelter constructed almost entirely of stone. To enable this length to be spanned, it was roofed over with a corbelled stone arch supported in part by cantilevered slabs anchored by stone weights.[77] Typically, the Inughuit took advantage of natural topography to build these structures into the side of a rise of land. The gradient facilitated the excavation of partially subterranean units and also reduced the extent of exposed surfaces. Raised ground also enabled the builders to dig long entrance passages into the slope to serve as a buffer from the outside cold. The entrance tunnel, called a *tossut*, measured about three metres long.[78] It was also lined and roofed with stones, and the whole banked in with an insulating layer of sod and turf. A space for a window was left over the tunnel entrance, which was covered with the translucent membrane of seal intestine. In the autumn snow banking provided an additional insulating layer, and blocks were cut from hard drifted snow to construct a domed outer entrance vestibule.[79] As well, on the interior, the Inughuit lined the *igloo* with seal skins with the fur turned toward the wall. Inside the dwelling, the principal features were the raised bed platform at the rear, and two side ledges used by the women to support their seal-oil lamps and for food preparation.[80] A subsequent adaptation of the *igloo*, reflecting the impact of manufactured lumber following European contact, is shown in Figure 19.

These small dwellings, measuring about three metres in diameter and less than two metres high, not only housed one or two families but an array of material objects essential to their winter survival. These included men's and women's tools, their clothing, skins for bedding, and oil lamps, the principal source of heat. Isaac Israel Hayes, who was invited into an *igloo* in the 1850s, described the assorted objects he saw:

> The hole of entrance in the floor was close to the front wall, and was covered with a piece of seal-skin. The walls were lined with seal or fox-skins, stretched to dry. In the cracks between the stones were thrust whipstocks, and bone-pegs, on which hung coils of harpoon lines. On one side of me, at the edge of the "breck," sat an old woman, and on the other side a young one, each busily engaged in attending to a smoky, greasy lamp. A third woman sat in a corner, similarly occupied. The lamps were made of soapstone, and in shape much resembled a clam-shell, being about eight inches in diameter. The cavity was filled with oil, and on the straight edge a flame was burning quite brilliantly. The wick, which supplied fuel to the flame, was of moss. The only business of the women seemed to be, to prevent the lamps from smoking, and to keep them supplied with blubber, large pieces of which were placed in them, the heat of the flame trying out the oil. About three inches above the flame, hung, suspended from the ceiling, an oblong square pot of the same material as the lamp, in which something was slowly simmering. Over this was suspended a rack, made of bare rib-bones lashed together crosswise, on which were placed to dry, stockings, mittens, pantaloons, and other articles of clothing.[81]

Hayes counted 18 persons crowded into this tiny space, including 13 members of the three resident families, and several visitors. One of the families was represented by three generations.[82]

Such modest structures served as the families' dwellings during the sunless winter between mid-October and mid-February and on into the late spring. Inughuit wintering dwellings had not always been so small, as their ancestors had occupied larger dwellings for which driftwood and whale ribs, used as ceiling supports, enabled a broader span. By the nineteenth century, however, the use of the cantilevered-arch technique was made necessary by the absence of driftwood, occasioned by the colder climatic regime, in which increased drift ice levels prevented driftwood from reaching northwest Greenland. In these circumstances, the residential capacity of the dwelling was increased by building ancillary domed wings for supplementary sleeping quarters.[83]

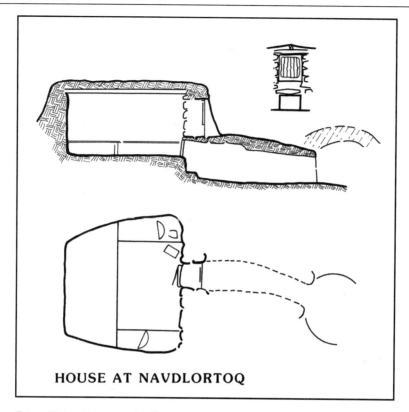

HOUSE AT NAVDLORTOQ

Figure 19: Inughuit winter dwelling at Navdlortoq, ca 1960. The illustration depicts a subterranean tunnel entranceway built lower than the sleeping platform of the house, with a snow-domed vestibule indicated on the right. Erik Holtved, "Contributions to Polar Eskimo Ethnography," *Meddelelser om Grønland*, Vol. 82, No. 2 (1967), Fig. 9, p. 17.

The third form of dwelling, the *iglooyah* or snow house, was not limited to a particular season, but used as a temporary shelter during hunting trips. Hard, frozen snow of the right consistency was required to build these arch-domed structures (Figure 20). Around May, when the snow was less suitable, the Inughuit hunters tended to build only a low snow wall, which they roofed over with a folded skin tent. Sometimes, this makeshift roof might be dispensed with, and the wall used only as a windbreak (Figure 21).[84] On the trail, having built a windbreak, Inughuit often slept on their komatiks, or sledges, in the open air (Figure 17).[85]

With the return of milder weather in the late spring, the Inughuit set up skin tents (*tupiq*), which provided adequate shelter until the return of snowfall in the autumn. Hugh J. Lee, who accompanied Peary on an

Figure 20: Inughuit men building an *iglooyah* at Eureka Sound, during Donald B. MacMillan's Crocker land Expedition, 1913-17. Credit: American Museum of Natural History, Donald B. MacMillan Collection, Crocker Land, 1913–17, Negative no. 233531.

Figure 21: Building a snow-block wind break on the trail. From Harry Whitney, *Hunting with the Eskimos* (1910), p. 288.

85

expedition to northern Greenland in the mid-1890s, left a description of the construction of these highly portable dwellings:

> In the summer time the native lives in a tent (too-pik) made of seal skin. The framework consists of two upright poles about two feet apart with a short piece lashed across the top and this is the front with the door between the two uprights. Then a longer pole reaches from the short cross piece down to the centre of the back. Then there are as many more poles as the man owns radiating from the centre at the top.[86]

The interior consisted of a platform about eight inches or a foot high, with a place for the fire. On this platform, "all sleep side by side between deer skins and all stark naked."

Larger tents could consist of as many as 50 or 60 skins, but usually a smaller number was used. At times, the tents had two layers, with an inner tent as the principal shelter, and an outer fly to be drawn over during storms or with the approach of cold weather. As in the winter dwellings, the rear half of the tents was taken up by a bed platform, with smaller platforms for food preparation on either side of the entrance. W. Elmer Ekblaw, a member of the MacMillan "Crocker Land" expedition of 1913-17, described these bed platforms as flat sandstone blocks fitted together to a height of 8 to 10 cm. For cushioning, a layer of dried grass was spread over the stones and covered with sealskins or caribou hides. Bed covers of caribou hides, or heavier polar bear or muskox skins for colder weather, were stacked at the back of the tent.[87] Slabs of food such as seal or strips of blubber might hang from the uprights adjacent to the entrance of the tent (Figure 22).[88]

Prior to contact, a factor limiting Inughuit travel was the scarcity of suitable materials with which to construct komatiks, or sledges. As with the induced disappearance of boat-building skills, climatic deterioration had imposed severe constraints on material culture. The increased sea ice levels that prevented both driftwood and whales from reaching the Thule region had curtailed the available stock of materials for sledge construction as well as boats. In these circumstances, the Inughuit improvised by lashing together lengths of ivory or bone, limiting the sleds to a small size, no more than two metres long. Given the absence of replacement parts, the existing stock of materials needed to be continually repaired and reused. The Inughuit showed their characteristic adaptability in fashioning a motley array of materials into serviceable komatiks. Isaac Israel Hayes marvelled at the skills revealed in one of these makeshift sledges, which he judged to be "almost without exception, the most ingeniously contrived specimen of the mechanical art that I have ever seen."[89] He described the component parts:

Figure 22: "Native skin tents at Bache Detachment, Ellesmere Island, NWT, ca 1926." National Archives of Canada, Photo no. PA-102670.

It was made wholly of bone and leather. The runners, which were square behind and rounded upward in front, and about five feet long, seven inches high, and three-fourths of an inch thick, were slabs of bone; not solid, but composed of a number of pieces, of various shapes and sizes, cunningly fitted and tightly lashed together. Some of these were not larger than one's two fingers, some were three or four inches square, others were triangular, the size of one's hand; while others, were several inches long and two or three broad. These pieces were all fitted together as neatly as the blocks of a Chinese puzzle. Near their margins were rows of little holes, through which were run strings of seal-skins, by which the blocks were fastened together, making a slab almost as firm as a board.[90]

After flattening the bones, the komatik maker painstakingly cut them into the desired shape with stones before they were carefully lashed together. Turning over the specimen he was examining, Hayes discovered that the runners were shod with walrus ivory. These, too, had been ground flat and the corners squared with stones. Typically, Inughuit secured the shoes to the runners with sealskin thongs recessed into the ivory to avoid friction.[91] The cross pieces were fashioned from an assortment of available bones: a bear's femur, caribou antlers, and ribs from a narwhal. For the uprights, two walrus ribs were lashed and braced by a piece of caribou antler secured across the top. A pre-contact Thule komatik, photographed by Adolphus Greely in the 1880s (Figure 8), closely matched the descriptions of Inughuit sledges in the mid-nineteenth century. Given the considerable time required to build them, Hayes observed that such sleds were valuable "family heirlooms," passed on from one generation to the next.[92] Despite their makeshift appearance, these sledges were perfectly suited to travel in the High Arctic. In admiring their design, Kane observed that Inughuit komatiks were easily righted if rolled over, while the whalebone runners could withstand the heavy punishment of sledging over the rough ice.[93]

If, at mid-century, the Inughuit lacked such technologies as the kayak and the bow and arrow, they nevertheless retained the techniques of dog sledge travel and the training of dogs to work as draught animals. The use of dogs for motive power in sledging was one of the cardinal features of all Inuit cultures and their ancestors, the Thule people. Perhaps more than any other single factor, the development of dog teams and associated technologies of sledging and suitable sled designs enabled the rapid spread of the Thule culture across the circumpolar region. Dogs were particularly important in the High Arctic, where food resources and materials for tools were often scarce and scattered, necessitating frequent and extensive travel.[94] For the Inughuit in the nineteenth century, the use of sled dogs took on even greater significance, due to the loss of their capacity for building boats.

At the time of initial contact, the draught animals used by the Inughuit were a strain of grey-black Husky dogs. Ethnographer W. Elmer Ekblaw, who lived and worked with the Inughuit for four years during MacMillan's expeditions of 1913-17, described their dogs as "the Eskimo's chief asset."[95] This was particularly true in the nineteenth century, before contact with Inuit immigrants from Baffin Island enabled the Inughuit to develop boat building skills to supplement their modes of land transportation.

In the Thule region, Inughuit practices of dog raising and driving approached the complexity and devotion of an art form and were an important part of a complex of folk traditions within this group. Skills in dog handling were acquired through practice over many years of experience. The development of good sled dogs began in earnest with their training from the age of four months. At this time, pups were harnessed for the first time and worked in progressively long training runs. The young dogs learned to respond both to the whip and to oral commands and were socialized to run with the other dogs in the team. Dogs that were too weak to withstand the pace or too fractious were killed and the others put in permanent harness from the age of seven months.[96]

Sled dogs were kept tied at all times. They were restrained for the safety of the community—in particular, the children—and for efficiency in assembling them for sledging (Figure 23). To reduce the risk of the

Figure 23: "Eskimos matching their dogs,"Etah, ca 1920s. Credit: American Museum of Natural History, Donald B. MacMillan Collection, Crocker Land, 1913–17, Negative No. 232625.

dogs biting through their harness straps, the Inughuit crushed their carnassial molars with a stone while they were still puppies.[97] Occasionally, women sewed boots of skin for the dogs to wear during the spring, to protect their paws from the sharp edges of sea ice.[98] After the re-introduction of kayak technology in the 1870s, the Inughuit were able to set their dogs loose on nearby islands, where they were fed regularly. Prior to this, they were obliged to keep the dogs tied even during the warm months,[99] to prevent them from robbing food caches or breaking into their dwellings. If stopping for the night on the trail, while crossing a glacier or sea ice, the Inughuit tied the dogs' traces to a stake driven into the ice.[100]

In the 1850s and since, the mode of harnessing dogs in the Thule District was the fan hitch, in which all the traces radiated out from the same loop or "eye" attached to the sledge.[101] This form, as opposed to the tandem hitch of Inuit groups farther south, was made necessary by the rugged condition of pack ice in the region, where pressure ridges presented ubiquitous obstacles to sledging. Use of the fan hitch enabled each dog to find its own way over the rough ridges, facilitating the forward movement of the sledge. Traces were usually about 5.5 to 6 m long, and the dogs fanned into a semi-circle in front of the sledge. They were constructed of bearded seal thongs or strips of walrus skin, cut to a thickness of approximately 1 cm.[102]

Dogs were guided by a combination of oral commands and the skilful use of the driver's whip. Commands might include the utterance "Huk, Huk," accompanied by a crack of the whip over the dogs' heads to start them running, with other commands to guide them to the right or left. Skilful manipulation of the whip enabled the driver to impel greater efforts from lagging dogs by grazing their ears with a crack of the lash. On the trail, dogs were normally fed every third day. During hunting trips men would feed their dogs from meat secured on the trail. Where possible the dogs would be fed fresh meat to repletion, rested for ten or twelve hours, and then fed a second smaller meal than before, before departing again. When travelling through areas where game was scarce, hunters were obliged to load large pieces of walrus meat on the sledge for dog food. Every third or fourth day, hunters would hack pieces from these frozen slabs. Since the dogs could not eat frozen meat without their carnassial teeth, hunters were obliged to thaw it or cut it into bite-sized chunks.[103] While based in the village, dogs were fed according to the amount of sledging performed, usually either seal or walrus meat and blubber.[104] During the summer they were fed infrequently and often turned loose to fend for themselves.

Handling the whip to control dogs on the trail was a demanding activity, requiring great manual dexterity. The dog driver had to throw a six-metre-long length of hide with accuracy and to do so with sufficient force to produce a loud crack. In the 1850s, Elisha Kent Kane wrote that it required the dog driver to make an arc from the shoulder, with stiff elbow, with both the hand and wrist engaged to jerk the whip to produce the crack. To conserve energy, Inughuit drivers travelled in pairs, with one sledge following the other. Since the second team of dogs would automatically follow the first, the drivers "take turns in guiding the lead team, enabling the other driver to rest his arm."[105] Specialized training was required for dogs used in hunting particular mammals. When released after the hunter had spotted a polar bear, the dogs were trained to pursue and surround the bear, keeping it at bay until the hunter arrived to dispatch it.[106]

Inughuit Intellectual Culture and World Views

At the time of contact, the Inughuit embraced a shamanistic belief structure which guided their approach to cultural and material life. Their shared set of beliefs represented their relationships to one another, to the natural environment and its animal resources, and particularly to spirits that symbolically represented these relationships. In giving expression to these relationships, they were assisted by shamans or *angakut*, in whom were invested special powers to communicate with spirits. Using their capacities to draw on the supernatural powers of these spirits, the *angakut* were in a position to mediate between the Inughuit and the forces affecting their existence, in the process influencing these forces for the benefit of the group.

Only certain members of the community had the capacity to serve as shamans. Among the men, the best hunters tended to become *angakut*.[107] They already commanded the respect of the community and had highly developed knowledge of the animals from whose spirits the shaman needed to be able to draw strength. Women, too, served as shamans. As with the men, they were individuals possessing remarkable abilities to communicate with the spirit world and to harness its forces to work for the well-being and survival of the group.

Knud Rasmussen, who witnessed several shamanistic ceremonies when staying with the Inughuit in 1903-04, described these happenings:

> The incantations take place in the winter in the houses, with lamps turned low, and in the summer in tents, by daylight. The pretext of a conjuration of spirits is either illness, continuous bad weather, or a bad fishing and hunting season.
>
> When an Angákok becomes "inspired," he groans, as if he were near fainting, begins to tremble all over from head to foot, and then suddenly springs out on the floor and strikes up the monotonous spirit-song, to a text which he improvises to fit the special case that he has to treat. He sings the chant loudly and more loudly, and gradually, as the conjuration progresses, he grows more and more unrestrained in his antics and his cries. He sighs and groans, as if invisible powers were pulling at him, and he often makes it appear as if he were being vanquished by a strong power.
>
> But further than this, the auditors see nothing of the spirits. The Angákut themselves declare that they suffer agonies in every limb while the spirits communicate their prophecies to them. And, during the song, which is accompanied by beats on a little round drum, they sometimes work themselves up into a peculiar state of ecstasy, during which, with their closed eyes, long floating hair, and anguished expression, they sometimes produce an overwhelming effect on their auditors.[108]

Among the more important functions of the *angakut* was the ability to be able to predict the weather and to know where to find game animals, for which they enlisted the assistance of helping spirits. At other times, they were called upon to heal the sick and to drive away evil spirits that were threatening the settlement. One of the principal vehicles for connecting with and harnessing the supernatural forces was through a group seance. In leading these ceremonies, the shaman demonstrated his or her powers, while enlisting the assistance of community members in establishing contact with the spirit world. The group's participation was expressed through the singing of drum songs and rhythmic dancing. Meanwhile, the shaman, using incantations and other techniques, achieved the right conditions for out-of-body journeys to obtain the desired knowledge or control of the relevant spiritual forces.[109]

Another of the shaman's roles was the enforcement of a complex of taboos guiding Inughuit social and economic behaviour. The extent to which these taboos fulfilled cultural imperatives or may have represented an adaptive response to ecological conditions remains the subject of debate.[110] Several taboos appear to have had a connection to ecology, as in the case of the hunting and food taboos regulating the species that could be procured or eaten at various times. By restricting hunting particular species to particular seasons, they were a kind of institutionalized restriction on overhunting or methods of resource exploitation considered to endanger animal populations.

A further inference would be that prohibitions on the consumption of specific foods by women or young people might have functioned to help ensure an optimal allocation of high-protein foods to the hunters on whose efforts the survival of the entire group depended. In the nineteenth and early twentieth centuries, American explorers observed that women were generally forbidden to consume the meat of bears, foxes, or rough seals. Young people were proscribed from eating young rough seals, eggs, entrails, heart, lungs, liver, narwhals, and the flesh of small animals such as hares and birds such as ptarmigan. Young men could eat these types of meat only after they had first captured an animal of each of the species, while women could eat them only after having given birth to five children.[111] Further proscriptions of food consumption applied to women who had been widowed for a year after the loss of their spouses. Such women were forbidden to eat various high-protein parts of caribou, including the legs, marrow, brains, heart, liver, or tongue.[112]

In the contact era, other Inughuit taboos may have functioned to prevent the spread of contagious diseases. Knud Rasmussen, who wintered with this group in 1903-04, reported that the *angakut* were then insisting that each person should wear his or her own clothing; for example, the *angakoq* Alattuq urged two brothers not to borrow one another's kamiks. Similarly, the shamans instructed that people should not share drinking vessels. Young people, in particular, were forbidden to drink from the cups of the elderly.[113] Whatever the ideological function of such practices, they seem to have been well designed to curtail the transmission of infectious pathogens in an era of devastating, recurrent epidemics.

Even the myths and legends of the group often suggested an ecological connection. One myth in particular, a creation story reported by Rasmussen in the early 1900s, is a case in point. Describing a world in which there was no death, the myth related the problems that ensued:

> But the people who did not know how to die grew too many; they overfilled the earth — and then there came a mighty flood. Many men were drowned, and men grew fewer. The traces of this flood are to be found on the tops of the high hills, where you often find shells.
>
> Then when men had grown fewer, two old women began one day to talk to each other. 'Let us do without the daylight, if at the same time we can be without Death!' said the one; doubtless she was afraid of death. "Nay!" said the other, "we will have both Light and Death." And as the old woman said those words, it was so—Light came and with it Death.
>
> It is said that when the first man died, they covered up the corpse with stones. But the body came back; it did not properly understand how to die. It stuck its head up from the stone sleeping-place and tried to get up. But an old woman pushed it back.
>
> "We have enough to drag about with us and our sledges are small!" They were, you must know, just about to start on a seal-catching expedition.
>
> And so the corpse had to return to its stone grave.
>
> As men by this had light, they could go on long seal-hunting expeditions, and no longer needed to eat the soil. And with Death came the Sun, the Moon, and the Stars.
>
> For when men die, they go up to Heaven and grow luminous.[114]

Whatever else the myth might signify, it expresses a concern with maintaining a sustainable population, and an acceptance of death as part of a self-regulating natural cycle.

A key function of Inughuit shamanism was its contribution to the psychological health of individuals and the group. Despite their hunters' expertise, the lives of the Inughuit were made perpetually insecure by characteristic fluctuations in the population and spatial distribution of game animals. For example, under the difficult climatic regime after 1800, famine was a continuing threat, particularly during the dark winter months. Compounding the insecurity of life were the ever-present risks of death to hunters from capsizing kayaks, falling off cliffs when netting auks, breaking through the sea ice, and other dangers. In this context, shamanism was an essential means of renewing group solidarity and faith in its own survival. Its importance to the group was well expressed by an Inughuit man to Knud Rasmussen around 1900:

> We believe our Angákut, our magicians, and we believe them because we wish to live long, and because we do not want to expose ourselves to the danger of famine and starvation. We believe, in order to make our lives and our food secure. If we did not believe the magicians, the animals we hunt would make themselves invisible to us; if we did not follow their advice, we should fall ill and die.[115]

Other important aspects of Inughuit culture included their concepts of time and space that expressed a distinctive way of responding to the natural environment of the High Arctic region. Time and space were relational concepts marked by environmental reference points and defined by recurrent patterns of resource use. Time was cyclical, regulated by daily and seasonal rhythms. Apart from the period of 24-hour light, the Inughuit divided the year according to the moons, each of which was assigned a name. As well, time was marked according to the migrations of animals and birds. Further temporal bearings were provided by reference to landmark events in a person's life.[116]

Time was also measured by reference to natural signs. Kane noted in the 1850s that Inughuit were "careful observers of the heavenly bodies." When interpreter Johan Petersen was at Tessieusak in November 1854, he tried to hasten his party's departure but was prevented by one of his guides. The Inughuaq asserted that only when a particular star had moved to a point no higher in the sky than another star would it be the time to harness his dogs. Wrote Kane: "Petersen was astounded; but he went out the next day and verified the sidereal fact."[117]

In 1909, Danish ethnographer H.P. Steensby studied the Inughuit during a brief summer field season. He wrote:

> The Polar Eskimos have very little notion of time. No one knows his own age. Even the age of the children can only be given by the parents after they have sat down and calculated how many winters have passed since the child was born.[118]

He hastened to add that these measures were given in response to his questions; "for the Polar Eskimos themselves, the reckoning of time has not the slightest importance."[119]

As with time, space was regarded as a dynamic rather than a static entity and hence the Inughuit had no precise measures for spatial relations.[120] Space was conceptualized in such terms as the amount of time spent to travel between places within areas of natural resource use. Distances were typically marked by the number of times the person had slept during the journey. Longer trips were marked by the number of moons' travel separating two places. Shorter periods of time were marked by the distance travelled by the sun across the sky.

At the same time, Inughuit space was defined experientially. According to the conjuncture of various factors, including weather conditions, time of year, and available technology, the Inughuit revised their notions of space to accommodate the immediate situation. In his article "Space Concepts of the Aivilik Eskimos," anthropologist Edmund Carpenter argued that for Inuit "the distance between camps can only be understood in relation to climate."[121] In the often precarious conditions in this environment, a precise knowledge of weather, its signs, and their interrelationships was essential to the hunters' survival. Reading a wide variety of environmental signs in combination enabled arctic Aboriginal travellers to traverse terrain that continually defied European attempts to find bearings. Inuit bearings were established partly through the observation of relationships between environmental signs: the nature of the snow and its contours, wind, and leads in the pack ice, "supplemented by a few available natural landmarks or constructed stone piles or inukshuks."[122] In the Thule district the 1850s, Elisha Kent Kane noted how the Inughuit found their way by reference to the most innocuous landmarks: "Every rock has its name, every hill its significance; and a cache of meat deposited anywhere in this harsh wilderness can be recovered by the youngest hunter in the nation."[123] In 1855, when Kane requested directions to the village of Netelik, his Inughuit companions gave him "in their own style, a complete itinerary of this region."[124]

Aboriginal spatial concepts were also revealed in the maps they drew for Western explorers in the nineteenth century. As Renée Fossett has observed, the important point about their approach to mapping was that it was rooted in oral tradition. They did not have a cartographic tradition in the Western sense. They drew maps in the snow or sand to aid in communicating routes to their compatriots, but did not produce maps as a permanent reference of the land. Rather, such routes were stored in memory.[125] European visitors sometimes viewed Inuit maps as erroneous in their lack of Western scientific precision, but the place names they gave to particular landmarks were the key to the preparation of their own maps of these lands.[126]

In summing up the spatial orientation of the Aivilik Inuit, Carpenter identified three characteristics of their approach: "i) Aivilik do not conceptually separate space and time; ii) their acute observation of details; and iii) their concept of space, not as static enclosure such as a room with sides or boundaries, but as direction, in operation."[127] This characterization of Canadian Inuit might equally be applied to the Inughuit in the nineteenth century and since.

Inughuit Environmental Knowledge and Adaptability

In manifold ways, the Inughuit, like other arctic peoples, reduced the risks of life through careful observation and experience of their environment. Their expertise included detailed knowledge of the characteristics, behaviour, migration patterns, and daily movements of arctic animals. Given the sparse distribution of the animals, it was essential that hunters be able to predict the best hunting locations, in each of the seasons, to maximize their efforts.[128] Techniques such as the periodic alteration of hunting areas and modulation of the numbers and types of animals taken were characteristically practised. To protect themselves from disaster, hunters needed to learn a myriad of environmental data, such as how to read the thickness of the sea ice, where to find snow suitable for snow-house construction, or how to predict the weather.

In 1854, Kane remarked on the depth of Inughuit knowledge of their homelands. He wrote: "Every movement of the ice or wind or season is noted; and they predict its influence upon the course of the birds of passage with the same sagacity that has taught them the habits of the resident animals." He related that the Inughuit had advised him in advance of the precise extent of open water in Smith Sound off Cape Alexander between September and December of that year. They also accurately predicted an unusually heavy snowfall would occur in the area, divining these conditions from the presence of open water.[129]

Since arctic animal populations were observed to fluctuate dramatically over time, possibly due to climatic fluctuations,[130] the Inughuit needed to be quite flexible in their hunting and survival strategies. Due to the lack of predictability of food resources, they harvested as wide a range of game animals as the region afforded, itself an adaptive strategy.[131] As stocks of particular species diminished, they needed to make rapid pragmatic shifts to the utilization of alternative species. Such changes demanded an alertness to changing migration patterns and available technology, as well as an intimate environmental knowledge to enable successful exploitation of alternative resources.

The writings of Europeans visiting the Thule District in the mid-nineteenth century abound with stories attesting to Inughuit environmental expertise. Kane provided one such example when he recounted a sledge journey to Anoritooq (Anoatok) in the month of October in the 1850s. While on the trail, the usual sources of running streams on shore had frozen solid and Kane's dogs were suffering for lack of water. His Inughuit companion, Myouk, climbed a succession of ice hills, which he tapped with his ice-pole, occasionally listening with his ear. On the fourth attempt, he called out "Water!" On inspecting the spot, Kane could not detect any liquid, but after a few minutes' digging, he reached a small reservoir of drinkable water.[132]

Kane related another anecdote that further illustrated the importance of environmental knowledge to survival. During a mid-winter famine at Etah, two Inughuit men, Awahtok and Myouk (Majak), decided to hunt walrus on the open ice in stormy weather. Despite the risk, they reckoned that it was a sounder strategy than sacrificing their dogs, which were essential to future survival. After killing a large walrus, they were attempting to return, when the wind broke up the pack ice, and they were stranded on an ice floe. Kane noted that "the impulse of a European would have been to seek the land," but the Inughuit men knew that the drift would be most dangerous near the coast. Instead, they drove their teams toward the nearest iceberg. Reaching the iceberg with difficulty, they managed to land their teams and the walrus carcass. In near total darkness and in the middle of a violent storm, they tied the dogs to chunks of ice, and lay prostrate to avoid being blown off by the wind. Splashed by the freezing water, they climbed up to gain a higher toehold on the iceberg, where they clung to this perch until the winds drove the iceberg to a point where they could make their way to land.[133] Stories such as this one may help explain how the Inughuit persisted in this difficult environment even through the stringencies of the Little Ice Age.

Yet, Inughuit survival through dramatic changes in the arctic environment cannot be explained solely by reference to their accumulated knowledge. Confronting frequently changing animal populations, migration patterns, and unpredictability in the availability of materials, they needed to be able to improvise according to unexpected circumstances. In these situations, Inughuit displayed a capacity to adapt and solve problems for which there were no pre-existing models or templates. An example from the post-contact period may serve as illustration. In 1925, the American teenager Kenneth Rawson served as cabin-boy on the explorer Donald MacMillan's expedition to northern Greenland and Ellesmere Island. Observing the daily activities of the Inughuit, he remarked:

> "They are never at a loss and never 'stumped.' Once someone was repairing a sledge, and he could not find a drill. An Eskimo stepped forward and shot a hole through the runner. They are like that in everything, always alert, always on the job."[134]

What Rawson attributed to "innate skill and ingenuity" might more accurately be considered a learned culture of adaptability. While it relates to the twentieth century, this seemingly innocuous episode displayed the pragmatic approaches of problem solving that sustained the Inughuit throughout their history.

The Inughuit at the point of contact were living in very strained circumstances, obliged to operate in the context of both climatic stress and the loss of key skills from their repertoire. With few materials at their disposal, they managed to make the most of their reduced repertoire to persist even during the Little Ice Age, one of the most inhospitable climatic episodes in the human history of the High Arctic. Like all adapting peoples, they were nevertheless eager to exploit opportunities to improve their life chances. With the arrival of both Inuit newcomers from Baffin Island and explorers from Europe and North America in the nineteenth century, the Inughuit quickly perceived an opportunity to develop new relationships to enhance their utilization of this difficult environment.

4

The Inuit on Ellesmere Island
and Exchanges with Inughuit
in the Nineteenth Century

Qitdlarssuaq's Great Journey
from Northern Baffin Island to Thule in the 1850s

Perhaps no single episode of Inuit exploration in the post-contact period has attracted so much attention as the migration of Qitlaq and a band of followers from northern Baffin Island to northwestern Greenland in the 1850s. Renowned in both Inuit folklore and in the documentary histories of European historians of the High Arctic, this journey was remarkable both in terms of distance travelled and duration. Yet this migration was probably not unique in the sense that Inuit groups, and their predecessor, the Thule culture, have always been travelling peoples. In the previous chapter it was noted that the Inughuit needed to move over large tracts of the Thule District to hunt animals in different seasons and also travelled in winter to trade or to visit for social reasons. Clearly, these patterns formed part of a much broader complex of movements by Aboriginal peoples over vast areas of the High Arctic. Often, more extensive travels by families and larger groups lasted for years at a time.

Several first-hand narratives of the Qitlaq migration were recorded by Western visitors to the Thule District and have survived in their writings. While at Cape York in the early 1900s, Rasmussen interviewed Meqqusaaq (Figure 16), one of the original 38 travellers with Qitlaq, who provided a narrated version of their travels.[1] Panippak, another survivor of the journey, related his version of the story to American Donald MacMillan during his "Crocker Land" expedition of 1913-17.[2] In addition, Itussaarssuaq, the granddaughter of Piuaitsoq, who was Qitlaq's brother-in-law, narrated the story of Qitlaq in 1936-37 to the Inughuit historian Inuutersuaq Ulloriaq.[3] Thanks to the translation of Kenn and Navarana Harper, this version of the journey, based on oral tradition, is now available in English. Combined with the documentary and oral history research of the historian Guy Mary-Rousselière[4] and an article by Robert Peterson,[5] these accounts enable a reconstruction of the epic story.

Qitlaq was a shaman in the area of Pond Inlet at the time of departure. Also known as Qitdlarssuaq, meaning "the great Qitlaq," he was known as a strong leader with reputed magical powers.[6] He is thought to have been living in east-central Baffin Island where he was alleged to have been involved with a murder. Reportedly, he moved to northern Baffin Island to escape retribution by the Inuit group associated with the man who had been killed.[7] Various reasons have been given for Qitlaq's subsequent travels from Pond Inlet to northern Greenland. According to oral tradition, during a shamanistic seance he envisioned the presence of Inuit much farther north.[8] Later, these magical premonitions were confirmed by contact with European whalers, who had visited the region of the Inughuit and brought news to Canadian Inuit of the existence of their counterparts in Greenland.[9] When Qitlaq's group departed Pond Inlet, without a map, to head for northerly lands, they must at least have been aware of earlier Inuit travels to and use of such islands as Devon and Ellesmere. Presumably, oral tradition of these lands and their game resources persisted in the collective memory of the Igluligmiut, whether or not members of this group were still visiting these regions in Qitlaq's era.

Around 1850, six families, consisting of 38 men, women, and children started their journey with 10 dog sledges and supplies. According to Meqqusaaq, the group left Pond Inlet in winter, after the return of the sun. Their sledges were built long, more than six metres, to enable them to carry their kayaks. Later, their numbers were increased by the addition of several Inuit who joined the party on the trail.[10] The movements of this group followed a somewhat circuitous path to Greenland, suggesting that the ultimate destination was not established before they left Baffin Island. Travelling as far as possible before the melting of the sea ice, they camped and hunted walrus and beluga whales to stockpile provisions for the coming winter. After two years, the party divided into two, with 15 people continuing on to reach northern Greenland in the third year, and the other party returning to their home territory.

While Meqqusaaq did not describe the initial leg of the journey, scholars Robert Peterson and Guy-Mary Rousselière and Inughuit historian Inuuterssuaq Uvdloriaq reconstructed the itinerary from interviews with descendants in both Greenland and northern Baffin Island. Leaving the vicinity of Arctic Bay, Qitlaq's party crossed Admiralty Inlet and traversed the Brodeur Peninsula to reach the Baffin Island shores bordering Prince Regent Inlet. From there, they crossed to Somerset Island, following its northern coast to the Barrow Strait. This, apparently, was the "large strait which never freezes over because the water is always moving," described by Ittussaarssuaq to Inuuterssuaq Ulloriaq.[11] Waiting until April, when the ice was almost frozen fast, they crossed at the narrowest point to Cornwallis Island.

Turning now to the east, they crossed to Devon Island and travelled along the northern shores of Lancaster Sound, where they hunted seals from the floe edge. No longer feeling under threat, they camped here for a while, fishing and hunting to build up their stores of provisions. It was during this leg of the journey that Qitlaq's brother-in-law Piuaitsoq was carried away by the ice, a story that illustrates the resourcefulness that enabled Inuit to survive in this often dangerous environment. Inuuterssuaq Ulloriaq related how Piuaitsoq improvised to secure a basic subsistence, while marooned on an ice floe and equipped with only a knife.[12] He caught various birds in an ingenious manner; after building a small snow house, he formed a small hole in the roof, just large enough for a gull, and laid out some food to attract the birds. When a gull landed on the snow house, he grabbed its feet from below and pulled it inside. At other times, he subsisted on partially eaten seals that had been killed by polar bears. Finally, near the end of summer, the current carried him to the island's shores far to the west, near the Grinnell Peninsula.

Piuaitsoq's trials were far from over. His kamiks were in tatters, and food was difficult to find along this stretch of coast. Sleeping at night under rocks, he eventually came across a stone house that entombed the bodies of its former inhabitants. Apparently, all had recently starved to death, but the materials they left behind were of use to him. Finding a needle and thread, he fashioned stockings from one of the caribou hides in the *igloo*; these he inserted into a pair of kamiks, which were still in "excellent condition." Piuaitsoq also found a bow and arrow, which was serviceable once repaired. At last he had the means to secure food again.

Preparing to retire, Piuaitsoq heard a polar bear outside the shelter. Apparently picking up his scent, the bear stuck its head inside the dwelling's window opening and proceeded to prowl around the outside. Drawing his bow, the Inuk waited beside the window-space for the right moment. When the bear passed broadside in front of him, he released the arrow, shooting it in the side. Afraid of being attacked by the bear, he waited until morning and departed the *igloo* cautiously. In the twilight, he followed a trail of bloody pawprints to the shore, where he found the bear dead. He had shot it through the heart. Now he had a large store of food; after eating, he packed sufficient provisions for the balance of the journey. Meanwhile, Qitlaq, knowing that his brother-in-law "would try with all his effort to save himself and to return," had decided to winter at their summer hunting place on Devon Island, in hopes he would be able to catch up. His expectations were fulfilled when Piuaitsoq returned near the onset of the dark winter.[13]

According to Guy Mary-Rousselière, it was while camped at this location on Devon Island that Qitlaq obtained specific knowledge of the Inughuit. In 1854, he reportedly met members of the ship's company of British Naval Commander E.A. Inglefield at Dundas Harbour. Inglefield was then on his last voyage with the *Phoenix*. Having encountered the Inughuit in the Thule district earlier, Inglefield's companions may have informed Qitlaq of the presence of Aboriginal people to the north, living in northwestern Greenland across from Ellesmere Island.[14] The party then proceeded along Devon Island's southern coast to the mouth of Lancaster Sound, making periodic excursions to the interior of the island to hunt both muskox and caribou to supplement their catch of seals along the coast. With the arrival of colder weather, they built stone wintering dwellings, which they roofed with turf and occupied during the dark period.[15]

Qitlaq and his band were still living on Devon Island when they were next encountered by a European expedition in July 1858. While approaching De Ros Islet, a small island off the eastern coast of Devon Island near Cape Horsburgh, Sir Leopold McClintock's crew of the *Fox* was hailed by a small band of Inuit on the shore. Anchoring the ship to the fast ice, McClintock welcomed three Inuit men, three women, and two children on board, while four Inuit remained on shore. Wrote McClintock:

> The old chief Kal-lek is remarkable amongst Eskimaux for having a bald head. He inquired by name for his friend Captain Englefield. The above three families have spent the past two years upon this coast, between Cape Horsburgh and Croker Bay. Their knowledge does not extend further in either direction. They are natives of more southern lands, and crossed the ice in Lancaster Sound with dog sledges. Since the visit of the *Phoenix* in '54 they have seen no ships, nor have any wrecks drifted upon their shores. They seemed very fat and healthy, but complained that all the reindeer had gone away, and asked if we could tell where they had gone to. Our presents of wood, knives, and needles were eagerly received.[16]

With the remaining 14 persons, Qitlaq pressed on to the north, crossing the mouth of Jones Sound to Coburg Island, thence across to Ellesmere Island's southeastern shores. Mary-Rousselière has suggested that during several years of occupation of the Queen Elizabeth Islands, Qitlaq's group had become completely "acclimatized" to their new territory. Throughout their journey, they exploited a variety of available resources. These may have included the rich repository of birds and eggs on Coburg Island, a short detour of 20 km from Ellesmere's southeastern coast. Inuuterssuaq Uvdloriaq related that on a low-lying island called Pikiuliq, where eider ducks build their nests, Qitlaq's party harpooned several walruses, which they hauled up on shore.[17]

From their temporary base on the southeast shore of Ellesmere Island, the party continued their travels along the coast to the north. According to Meqqusaaq, after crossing two large fiords (perhaps Makinson and Talbot inlets), they came to a place where the sea closed to a narrow channel. This was Smith Sound, where the Ellesmere–Greenland channel closes to only 50 km across. Qitlaq's group travelled from near Bedford Pim Island off Ellesemere Island's western coast to a place in northern Greenland known to the Inughuit as Ingiirsarfik, near Easter Island. Here, dissension arose between Qitlaq and Oqe, another of the elders. As a result, they split into two groups, each numbering 25 to 30 people. Oqe and 24 others, intending to return to Baffin Island, turned back with five of the sledges.[18]

Qitlaq, however, remained convinced that there were people on the other side. Pitching camp, he conjured spirits for guidance as to where to go next. With his body in a lifeless state, his soul travelled across the sea to confirm the presence of the people they were to meet. Accordingly, the smaller party crossed over the frozen pack ice from Ellesmere Island to Greenland, where they found the remains of Native dwellings, but no inhabitants. To replenish their food supplies, they first established a base camp, from which the men hunted an abundance of caribou in the interior. It was during one of these hunting excursions that they first came into contact with Inughuit who were then living at the small settlement of Etah.[19] According to Donald MacMillan, Panippak told him that the first people they encountered were Ah-go-ta, a man with a wooden leg, and Ahng-ee-na, a younger man.[20] The itinerary of Qitlaq's party is illustrated in Figure 24.

Having established contact, Qitlaq's party remained with the Inughuit at Etah for six years. Then, deciding to return to Baffin Island, Qitlaq and 15 other Inuit packed their belongings and departed for Ellesmere Island with four dog teams and sledges, accompanied by Eré, an Inughuit hunter, his wife, and child. Experiencing great difficulty in procuring food, several of this party died on the trail; the others were obliged to resort to cannibalism. In 1873, five years after their departure, two Inuit families led by Qumangâpik and Meqqusaaq returned to the Thule District. They remained there permanently and were absorbed through marriage into the Inughuit population.[21]

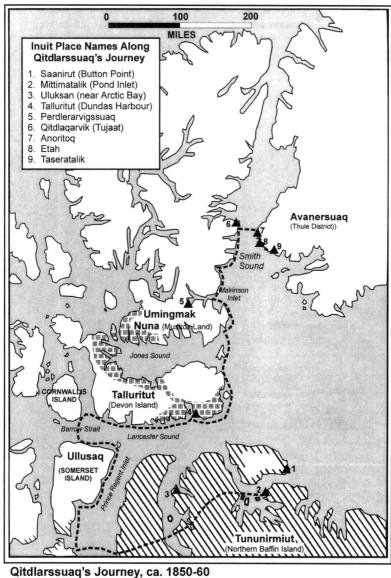

Qitdlarssuaq's Journey, ca. 1850-60

- - - - - - - - - - -   Itinerary

\\\\\\\\\   Area of recurrent land use by Canadian Inuit in the 19th century

≣ⅲ≡ⅲ≡ⅲ≡ⅲ≡ⅲ   Areas of occasional land use in the High Arctic by Canadian Inuit in the 19th century.
(After Freeman (1976))

Figure 24: Route of Qitdlarsuaq's Journey, ca. 1850-60

Thus ended one of the most remarkable journeys recorded in the history of the High Arctic. While not different in character from Aboriginal migrations of earlier and later eras, the diverging approaches of Qitlaq's people and European explorers of the same period underscored what was remarkable about Inuit movements in the region. First, Qitlaq's trek consisted of travel by whole families, demonstrating the importance of women and the family unit to group survival when moving through remote areas. Second, the party had the necessary environmental knowledge, technical skills, and way of life to live off the land indefinitely. They pragmatically made use of the available resources in each of the areas they passed through, including a variety of animals for food and skins and such materials as stone and turf for building wintering shelters. With their knowledge of the region's seasons and the resources associated with each season, they could adjust to its rhythms, accumulating food in the relative abundance of the warmer months to prepare for the scarcity of the dark, forbidding winters.

For the Inughuit in the nineteenth century, the arrival of Qitlaq's party in the 1860s was a critical event, enhancing their material repertoire at a time when they badly needed to expand their range of natural resource procurement activities. It may be noted that cultural exchanges had been occurring across the High Arctic long before the nineteenth century. For example, the Thule people in both what is now Canada and Greenland were fashioning tools from meteorite iron 800 to 1,000 years before the present. Tools whose materials are traceable to the Cape York meteorites in northwestern Greenland have been identified in many archaeological sites from Smith Sound to Silumiut on the northwestern coast of Hudson Bay, some 2,500 km away. The broad distribution of iron artifacts is evidence of an extensive Arctic trading network centuries before Westerners presumed to introduce trade, commerce, and the "Iron Age" to the Indigenous populations in the High Arctic.[22]

Qitdlarssuaq's migration was of particular importance because it helped the Inughuit overcome various material deficiencies occasioned by the loss of key skills from their repertoire. In some cases, the Baffin Islanders could be said to have reintroduced the techniques, since ancestors of the Inughuit had formerly practised these skills, but the knowledge had been lost.[23] One of the more important of the newcomers' innovations was the introduction of superior techniques for snow-house construction, including building long, low entrance passages from below the dwelling. This technique enabled the passage to effectively buffer the dwelling from the intrusion of cold air, while warmed air remained trapped in the igloo. Allowing heat conservation, the cold-air trap lessened energy needs and the need to hunt as many animals.[24]

Another useful technology imparted was the knowledge of kayak construction and associated techniques for hunting from these boats. Inughuit legends recorded the former use of kayaks but the knowledge of how to build them was lost when an epidemic killed all the elders of the group. The younger men had not yet learned the skills from their elders before their deaths. In the 1890s, Eivind Astrup reported having met Kommanapek (Qumangâpik) and Mektascha (Meqqusaaq), two members of Qitlaq's party who had taught their Inughuit hosts how to build kayaks.[25] Ethnographer Rolf Gilberg has described the particular type of kayak brought by the Baffin Island immigrants as a "clumsy one with a triangular man hole."[26] This meant that the kayaker's jacket could not be tied over this opening, leaving the boat liable to the intrusion of water. If this kayak type was inferior to its counterparts in West Greenland, its reintroduction nevertheless represented the first time in several generations that boat technology was available to the Thule group. By the 1890s, the Inughuit had successfully resumed hunting narwhals from kayaks, a demanding activity requiring the co-operation of several kayakers to finish off the harpooned animal and to haul the carcass back to shore.[27] Owing to the great weight of these animals, the assistance of the entire community was needed to haul the carcass out on the ice (Figure 90).

Among the hunting tools which the immigrants taught their hosts to construct and use were the bow and arrow (Figure 25). This technology had been lost in part because of the increased emphasis on the summer muskox hunt in the first half of the nineteenth century. Since the grazing areas of the two species tended to be in different places, the Inughuit were obliged to abandon the caribou hunt, and the skills of constructing and using the required tools diminished accordingly. Other reasons cited for the disappearance of these skills include the loss of knowledge due to disease epidemics and lack of suitable materials, such as driftwood, made scarce due to increased pack ice following climatic deterioration. Thus, the reintroduction of the bow and arrow had an immediate impact, enabling the Inughuit to successfully hunt caribou resources in their region. Access to this largely unexploited resource helped them to garner larger quantities of food resources for the winter and also to expand their collections of skins for clothing and bedding.[28]

The introduction of Igluligmiut techniques of spear fishing and its principal tool, the three-pronged spear,[29] also enhanced the Inughuit capacity to more fully exploit the food resources of their environment. In 1855, Elisha Kent Kane noted, while camped at a lake near Etah, that "the lake abounds in fish, apparently the salmon-trout [charr]; but the natives have not the art of fishing."[30] Previously able to catch charr

Figure 25: "Ka-ko-chee-ah with bow and arrow," Etah, northern Greenland, Credit: American Museum of Natural History (New York City), Donald B. MacMillan Collection, Crocker Land Expedition, 1913–17, Negative no. 230920.

only "accidentally," the Inughuit applied the introduced technology to make greater use of this resource. When interviewed by the Danish ethnographer Ludwig Mylius-Erichsen around 1903, Meqqusaaq gave an account of how this technique was carried out at that time: "On a strong line we fix small pieces of narwhal's teeth or walrus teeth, then drop it into the water and pull it up and down until we catch the salmon, which we land with a two-pronged fork."[31] Within only a few years, the Inughuit incorporated Western metal into their fishing tools, although the technique was unchanged. Writing in 1910, the explorer Robert E. Peary described the procedure and technology of Inughuit spear fishing following the introduction of the new skills:

> The Eskimo method of fishing is interesting. The fish in that region will not rise to bait; they are captured by cutting a hole in the ice and dropping in a piece of ivory carved in the shape of a small fish. When the fish rises to examine this visitor, a spear is thrust into it. The Eskimo fish spear has a central shaft with a sharp piece of steel, usually an old nail, set in the end. On each side is a piece of deer antler pointing downward, lashed onto the shaft with a fine line, and sharp nails, pointing inward, are set in the two fragments of antler. When this spear is thrust down on the fish, the antlers spread as they strike the fish's back; he is impaled by the sharp point above him, and the sharp points on either side keep him from getting away (Figure 94).[32]

While the techniques introduced by the Igluligmiut immigrants would have a decisive and beneficial impact on the lives of the Inughuit, their adoption was not immediate. Emil Bessels, who was in the Etah region in 1871, claimed that, at that time, residents still lacked the use of boats and only one hunter, a Baffin Island immigrant, was then using a bow and arrows. Bessels' description of his set illustrated both the scarcity of suitable materials and Inuit resourcefulness in utilizing the few materials that were available for constructing hunting tools:

> They had frequently been mended, and were in a rather dilapidated condition. The bow was made of four pieces of reindeer horn lashed together with sinew, and was but slightly curved. Its length was thirty-three inches. The bow string was four-ply and made of the cervical ligament of the reindeer. It was fastened around two neatly carved bear-heads at either end of the bow. The arrows, of which he had only three, were provided with iron points. Their shafts were made of splinters of wood lashed together and feathered with raven quills. Including the point their length was from eighteen to twenty inches."[33]

By the 1880s, several Inughuit hunters had sufficiently mastered the new technology to expand their range of game resources during the summer, alleviating their long-term dependence on netting auks in this season. A collection of Inughuit ethnographic specimens obtained by Peary in 1891-92 includes both Baffin-type bows and arrows and a two-pronged fishing spear.[34]

For their part, the Baffin Island immigrants adopted the Inughuit sledge and method of hitching dogs. The newcomers found the uprights on the Inughuit sledge ideally suited for manoeuvring over the rugged pressure ice surfaces of the High Arctic. Similarly, the Greenlanders' fan hitch with traces of equal length facilitated sledge travel as it enabled each dog to find its own way over the jagged pack ice.[35] Beyond the exchange of Aboriginal technologies, historian Robert Peterson and anthropologist James VanStone have suggested that the Baffin Island immigrants may have provided the Inughuit with much-needed wood and iron materials that they could utilize for the balance of the nineteenth century.[36]

Even so, the pace of diffusion of technological change appears to have been rather slow within the territory of the Inughuit. Limiting factors included lack of accessibility of sufficient quantities of wood to enable the construction of many kayaks or even bows. While the Inughuit living in the vicinity of Cape York, the southernmost settlement in Avanersuaq, came into more frequent contact with European whalers, contact was much more limited for the Inughuit living to the north of Inglefield Gulf.

When American Robert N. Keely Jr. accompanied Robert Peary to the Whale Sound region in the early 1890s, he found the Inughuit in possession of only "a couple of kajaks, and a few bows and arrows."[37]

Other Inuit Migrations to Ellesmere Island in the Nineteenth Century

While Qitdlarssuaq's odyssey was the most dramatic and best-documented example, evidence suggests that it was not the only journey by Canadian Inuit to Ellesmere Island in the nineteenth century. Much later, in the 1920s, Panippak, who was born on the trail during Qitlaq's trip northward, told RCMP officers at Craig Harbour that other Baffin Island families had travelled north to Etah in this period.[38] On another occasion in the early 1900s, Panippak related to Knud Rasmussen a tradition among the Inughuit that caribou hunters who had crossed to "Akalineq, the country on the other side of the sea"—presumably, Ellesmere Island—had encountered strange-looking people living there.[39]

Intriguing reports of Inuit living on Ellesmere Island in the late nineteenth century are found in the official narrative of American Charles Francis Hall's North Polar expedition of 1871-73. While at Etah in 1873, in a conversation with Captain Budington of the *Polaris*, a man from the Qitlaq group named "Jimmy" reported that there were many Inuit living at Cape Isabella and "all along the coast of Ellesmere Land." He stated that his father-in-law lived there and in winter he and others on the Greenland side crossed the pack ice of Smith Sound to visit their relatives. Jimmy described Ellesmere as an island, which the Inuit immigrants to Greenland referred to as *Uming-mak* [Muskox] Island after the large number of muskoxen living there,[40] He reported that he had been around it several times, leading Budington to infer, correctly, that Ellesmere Land and Grinnell Land were the same land mass.[41]

Meanwhile, Ellesmere Island apparently continued to be visited by Canadian Inuit from the south. In 1885, ethnographer Franz Boas reported interviewing several Baffin Island Inuit who had crossed Lancaster and Jones Sounds to live on Ellesmere Island. His principal informant was a woman from Iglulik who described travelling with a party to Devon Island around 1870. Traversing the island by sledge, the group reached a long, narrow peninsula—presumably, the Grinnell Peninsula—which they followed to a narrow ocean passage with a strong tidal current. These straits connected, through a series of islands, to a land which they, too, called *Umingmak Nuna,* meaning "Muskox Land."[42] Boas deduced that his informant had described Cardigan Strait and Hell Gate between the Grinnell Peninsula and North Kent and Ellesmere islands. After crossing to Ellesmere, they met another small group of Inuit on the shore, with whom they lived for a period to hunt the region's abundant supply of seals, apparently in the Jones Sound region.[43]

Boas also wrote of travel by North Baffin Islanders to Devon Island and their contacts with Ellesmere Island Inuit in his book *The Central Eskimo*. Here he reported that "in favourable winters" the Iglulik hunters wintered on the eastern half of Devon and "while here they keep up some intercourse with the inhabitants of *Umingmak Nuna* (Ellesmere Land),"[44] meaning "Muskox Land." These travellers presumably also crossed the pack ice of the eastern edge of Jones Sound, via Lady Ann Strait and Coburg Island, to reach Ellesmere Island.

The suggestion of continuing migrations by Canadian Inuit after Qitlaq was also implied in a 1964 RCMP patrol report at Grise Fiord on the southern coast of Ellesmere Island. The writer, Constable T.C. Smith, reported that Grise Fiord Inuit had learned ten years earlier of good charr fishing at a lake near the southwest point of Makinson Inlet, on Ellesmere Island's eastern coast. Their informant was "an old Greenland Eskimo woman, Pudloo [Patdloq?]," whom they had met: "She stated that when she was a child, her people, before moving to Greenland, were migrating up the eastern Ellesmere Island coast, starving when they came upon this lake with its fish."[45] Since the woman conveyed this information in the mid-1950s, it is entirely possible that the referred-to migration occurred well before 1900.

In the same period as Boas, scientist Emil Bessels, who had accompanied C.F. Hall on the voyage of the *Polaris* in 1871, wrote of "Eskimos inhabiting the region of Ellesmere Land near Cape Isabella," facing Smith Sound.[46] Bessels also stated that Inughuit hunters occasionally crossed the straits to visit the Ellesmere coast. Presumably, the crossings were influenced by the recent arrival of Canadian Inuit newcomers via this route and their stories of game animals and other resources on the Ellesmere side. These trips were reportedly infrequent, given the fact that high winds tended to inhibit the formation of a continuous sea ice surface in the straits. When it did form, the extremely rough character of the pack ice in Smith Sound was an impediment to such crossings.[47]

In his narrative of the Hall expedition, Bessels reported that Ittukusuk, who had immigrated from Baffin Island to the Thule region via Smith Sound, had found the Ellesmere coast in this area inhabited by Inuit, and it was here that he met his future wife, Ivalu.[48] Captain George Nares, commander of the British Arctic Expedition of 1875–76, writing of their brief sojourn at Cape Isabella, referred to the "Eskimo who are said to wander round the shores of Ellesmere Land."[49]

Bessels pointed to the evidence of Nares, who reported having found three umiaks, or skin boats at Lifeboat Cove, the wintering site of part of the *Polaris* crew in 1872-73. Nares found the *Polaris* caches had been pillaged, leading Bessels to suspect that Aboriginal people had visited the site in the intervening period, although he acknowledged that "none of the objects it contained could have been of the least service to the Eskimos." Noting that the Inughuit on the Greenland side did not have any vessels at this time, he concluded that the skin boats "belonged to some of the Western Eskimos," meaning the Baffin Islanders who were then visiting their Inughuit counterparts.[50] In 1899, on the Ellesmere Island coast bordering Kane Basin, the American Robert Peary also reported having examined evidence of abandoned Thule boats. Then based at Cape D'Urville, Peary wrote in his diary that Ahngodagipsu and Asiajuk (Ahsayoo), two of his Inughuit companions, had discovered the remains of three kayaks on the shore just south of Carl Ritter Bay. Arranged in a line and covered with gravel, the kayaks had been constructed with long strips of wood, with bone and ivory fittings.[51] The Inughuit believed that the owners of the kayaks were travelling south when they cached the boats, although their reasons for thinking so are not provided. The kayaks were very long and narrow, suggesting that they did not belong to migrating Igluligmiut or Baffin Island Inuit, who utilized a wider prototype in building their boats,[52] although the survival of organic materials suggested that these boats may have been of comparatively recent vintage at the time Peary viewed them.

Further indications of prior Inuit occupation of Ellesmere Island also appeared in the writings of Isaac Israel Hayes, who mounted an expedition to northern Greenland in 1860-61. During this trip, Hayes sledged across Smith Sound and up Ellesmere's eastern coast as far as 81° 35' N. lat. On his return to Etah, Greenland, the Inughuit leader Kalatunah asked him if he had encountered any Aboriginal people during the excursion. Kalatunah related a "well-established tradition of the tribe" that Inuit had lived on Ellesmere Island, both to the north and to the south of Smith Sound. While they had been prevented by deteriorating environmental conditions from communicating with these people, he believed they were still living on Ellesmere Island "in both directions." Hayes had not met any Inuit on Ellesmere Island, but the absence of contact did not satisfy Kalatunah, who suggested that he had simply not gone far enough. Hayes provided a translated version of Kalatunah's comments: "There are good hunting-grounds at the north, plenty of musk-ox (oomemak), and wherever there are good hunting-grounds, there the Esquimaux will be found."[53]

Danish interpreter Johan Petersen, who served on Elisha Kent Kane's Second Grinnell Expedition, reported a conversation with Inughuit informants in 1854 which suggests that they not only designated Ellesmere Island as the place where muskoxen abounded, but were also aware of the presence of other game animals on the island. He related:

> They told us that directly north of the ship was found a sound which was supposed to lead to more open water, in which a large island was said to be situated. This island they called *Omimasuk*, or isle of the musk-ox. I asked them whether animals of this kind were found on the island; but about this they could give no explanation; yet they related that large numbers of moose [caribou] or walrus were found there.[54]

Despite their apparent familiarity with Ellesmere Island, the Inughuit do not appear to have made the crossing of Smith Sound during the early contact era. We might speculate that the loss of boat-building techniques, coupled with the presence of open water in this period, may have inhibited such crossings, but this is only conjecture. By the 1890s, however, Inughuit from the Hayes Peninsula were reported to be making periodic trips to Ellesmere Island to hunt muskoxen with traditional weapons. During Peary's 1893-95 expedition to northern Greenland, his designated zoologist George H. Clark wrote: "It is not an unusual thing for the Whale Sound natives to cross to this island [Ellesmere Island], and only a few years ago some of them killed muskoxen there with their lances...."[55] In the autumn of 1898, Inughuit hunters serving with Peary at Cape D'Urville on the Ellesmere side of Kane Basin, were again reported to be hunting muskoxen. As soon as Peary selected the site of his wintering camp, Merktoshar [Meqqusaaq], spokesperson for the Inughuit, proposed leaving the women and children on board ship while the men went on land to hunt muskoxen. Meqqusaaq had been a member of Qitlaq's party almost 40 years earlier and had first-hand knowledge of the muskox resources of the island. After hunting in the fiords for several days, they returned, having killed twenty muskoxen and four polar bears.[56] As will be discussed in Chapter 6, it was a practice that would increase exponentially with the intensification of exploration activity after 1900.

Until recently, it was believed that the Thule culture had completely abandoned the High Arctic after the onset of the Little Ice Age around AD 1450. Archaeologist Moreau Maxwell, who carried out extensive excavations in northern Ellesmere from 1957 on, found no pre-contact Native artifacts that could be dated later than the fifteenth century. He also noted at the time of contact, the Inughuit had no legends of their own travels to the region and surmised that the region may have acquired a reputation as a dangerous place, contributing to its abandonment. Maxwell based this inference partly on the observations of American Adolphus Greely, who visited the area in the 1880s. Finding a large number of abandoned Native sledges—eight in all—Greely argued that these artifacts signified earlier disasters, since Inughuit would not have scuttled their sledges except in dire circumstances.[57]

At the same time, Maxwell suggested that even during the cooler climatic episode of the Little Ice Age, ca. AD 1450 to 1850, small groups of Thule and later, post-contact Inuit people, who normally wintered in more southerly locations, may have occasionally ventured to northern Ellesmere Island in the spring in search of muskoxen and caribou. Sledging across the pack ice of Kennedy Channel and along the ice foot of the east coast of Ellesmere, or alternatively up the west coast of Greenland, they would have arrived in the region of Lady Franklin Bay between late April and early June. Hunting seals that were basking on the ice during these warm months or at their breathing holes, the families would have also secured game at inland meadows in the vicinity. By late June, some of the families then would have sledged to Lake Hazen to take advantage of the rich muskox resources of the interior. As the men sought the larger animals, the women and children would have killed smaller game, such as hares, or fished for charr. Maxwell goes on to reconstruct a scenario in which a few families may have remained at Lake Hazen for two or three years, housing themselves in stone wintering dwellings. The others would return to the coast in late September, establishing temporary lodgings in semi-subterranean shelters or in substantial tents before returning to the south along the coastal ice foot, which would be sufficiently frozen by late October to support their sledges.[58]

In more recent investigations of Aboriginal sites in northern Ellesmere and Axel Heiberg Islands, Patricia Sutherland unearthed evidence of a comparatively small number of corbelled-arch stone dwellings coexisting with more numerous tent rings. Her work on the Eureka Upland led Sutherland to conclude that, even after AD 1700, the Thule-Inughuit might have continued to make use of the region's resources, albeit on a more limited basis than prior to climatic cooling.[59] These conclusions are compatible with interpretations by Peter Schledermann, who viewed the former inhabitants of the Smith Sound area as the principal resident Thule population on Ellesmere Island. From their permanent settlements and a comparatively secure resource base adjacent to Ellesmere Island's polynyas, the Thule could stage seasonal forays to the north. Small parties of hunters, perhaps unaccompanied by their families, might have travelled to northern Ellesmere to hunt, and returned within the same season, that is, between April and June. They would necessarily have turned back before the ice foot melted and became unstable, or they would be stranded until it formed again in the fall. These men would not necessarily have used tents, but could have slept on their sledges over which they rigged a tent covering on cooler nights. Such short-term seasonal patterns of resource use could explain the lack of archaeological resources, since the hunters would have camped on the ice, and any traces of their presence would have disappeared with its melting.

Documented migrations to and across Ellesmere Island in the nineteenth century provide an insight as to how Inuit, Inughuit, and their predecessors managed to travel over such vast stretches of the circumpolar region. They show the scope of Aboriginal knowledge of the region's geography and natural resources and their need to move in accordance with animal migrations in order to exploit their environment effectively. They also show that Aboriginal groups were effectively exploring the High Arctic region and exchanging technology and skills well before the arrival of Europeans.

5
European Cultures in the High Arctic, 1818–1940

European cultures were the other major group participating in the contact experience. Beginning with a visit by British naval officer John Ross in 1818 and followed by Scottish whalers, Europeans attained the northern far reaches of Baffin Bay and first encountered the long-isolated Inughuit of northwestern Greenland. More extensive interactions commenced in the 1850s, when a series of British parties made summer forays to the area of Smith Sound, and three American expeditions wintered there between 1853 and 1872. The appearance of Europeans in northern Baffin Bay in this period initiated a sporadic, but continuing presence in the High Arctic. It apparently marked the first contact between European and Aboriginal cultures in the region since the era of Norse settlement on Greenland between ca. AD 1000 to 1400.

To understand more fully why the Europeans responded to the arctic environment and its peoples in particular ways, I propose to sketch some of the relevant ideologies, cultural imperatives, and material repertoire of the explorers. An overview of aspects of Inughuit culture at the point of contact was provided in Chapter 3. In this chapter, the culture of the exploring countries will be treated as it relates to their activities in this region, responses to the natural environment, and relationships with Aboriginal inhabitants. Among the more interesting aspects of the European experience of the Arctic were the technologies they brought to the region. Their successes and failures highlighted in stark relief both the advantages and limitations of the application of Western technology to the problems of travel, clothing, sustenance, and shelter in the extraordinary conditions of the region. Western historians have long assumed that the technological prowess of Europe enabled it to conquer and dominate Indigenous societies around the globe. For example, Fernand Braudel has distinguished between "civilizations," which extended their dominance around the world through advances in such fields as oceanography and artillery, and "cultures" or "immature civilizations," which "collapsed in the face of a small number of men."[1] Yet, the process of technological diffusion and adoption is never entirely directed or determined by the group exporting its culture. What is missing from this analysis is a treatment of how Indigenous populations actually received and applied the technologies brought by Westerners. As Robin Ridington has noted with regard to Aboriginal technologies, it may be more pertinent to enquire into the world views animating the use of technology, rather than viewing the technologies themselves as autonomous historical forces.[2]

The interest of European and North American countries in the High Arctic in this period derived from the geopolitical and expansionist imperatives of the participating nation-states. Their exploratory goals had an overriding economic dimension, linked to a continual search for resources and markets throughout the nineteenth century.[3] As the first great power to explore the region in this era, Great Britain's interest coincided with its rise as the world's pre-eminent economic and military nation.[4] Its quest to map the globe accompanied a great expansion in its overseas trade,[5] buttressed by naval power and geographical knowledge generated by explorers.

A specific impetus to arctic exploration was provided by a core of arctic enthusiasts in the British Navy who, after 1800, revived the long-standing search for a Northwest Passage to markets in Asia. The navy's motivation was partly defensive, as by the early 1800s its leading officers feared that if they did not pursue the Passage, Russia might beat them to it, resulting in a serious loss of national prestige constructed on a foundation of naval pre-eminence.[6] Led by Sir John Barrow, First Secretary of the Admiralty for 40 years after 1804, the Royal Navy embarked on an ambitious program of exploration in the Arctic Archipelago, beginning with the voyage of John Ross in 1818.[7] Beyond the Northwest Passage, Barrow was an enthusiastic supporter of reviving the eighteenth century search for the North Pole. He wrote: "The North Pole is the only thing in the world about which we know nothing; and that want of all knowledge ought to operate as a spur to adopt the means of wiping that stain of ignorance from this enlightened age."[8]

At mid-century, a major competitor had emerged in the United States, whose aggressive expansion across the North American continent was already well underway.[9] By this time the focus of arctic exploration had shifted from the Northwest Passage to a competition to be the first to reach the North Pole. For the United States, the race for the pole offered an opportunity to continue the imperial expansion that characterized much of American history in the nineteenth century.[10] By the late nineteenth century, the federal union had consolidated its control over the continental United States, and American expansionists were in search of new fields to conquer.

Indeed, competition and the prospect of rewards to the victor, whether prestige or money, was at the root of much exploration activity by the Europeans in the High Arctic. The Arctic was only one of several regions whose exploration was contested by European nations. Other examples included earlier campaigns to find the heart of Africa and the race to be the first to reach the South Pole after 1900. In the 1850s, the decade in which High Arctic exploration began in earnest, the competing powers were staging international exhibitions to showcase their technological prowess.[11] As the search for resources and new markets intensified, competition took on a nationalistic tone in this period.[12]

In the United States, promoters of the major arctic expeditions pointed to the perceived benefits to American resource industries, shipping, and trade. In a 1878 report, the U.S. House of Representatives recommended Congressional support for an expedition to Lady Franklin Bay. Its author noted the loss of a whaling fleet of six vessels in arctic seas, due to a "lack of proper knowledge of climatic and tidal influences," representing a loss of half a million dollars. The report added that such scientific work was supported by boards of trade and chambers of commerce in the United States.[13] In approving funding for the expedition, Congress added to the original scientific justification a clause directing this party to search for new whaling grounds.

This latter objective had been promoted by prominent American scientists. Professor Matthew Maury, the leading American oceanographer at Yale University, claimed that "within this Polar area the whales have their nursery."[14] Writing to the president of the American Geographical Society, Louis Agassiz asserted that whale fishing would be "one of the most important results" of the projected discovery of open water around the North Pole.[15] Supporting Captain Henry Howgate's plan for an expedition to Ellesmere Island, Professor Elias Loomis of Yale College argued that the commercial benefits from Arctic expeditions "are more than equal to all the money which has been expended on these enterprises."[16]

This is not to suggest that all promoters of arctic exploration were animated by economic goals, but to obtain government support for their expeditions they often needed to convince their compatriots of the potential economic or strategic spinoffs from this activity. Even scientific objectives were justified on commercial and military grounds. Civilian and military supporters of the Greely expedition pointed to its expected contribution to better and more comprehensive weather information. The Smithsonian Institution had long advocated an integrated continental system of weather observation to Congress and its secretary, Joseph Henry, argued that improved weather data would provide an important boost to shipping.[17]

Economic motives help explain the competing countries' initial interest in the High Arctic. But to understand why they persisted in supporting expensive expeditions, it is also important to appreciate the ideological functions of these voyages. In long-established nations such as Great Britain, expeditions to the Arctic, Africa, and other regions in the nineteenth century functioned symbolically to shape and maintain a national consensus in support of its political institutions and the Capitalist system, then the new economic order. The strength of the British Empire depended on its real or imagined influence in all of the world's regions. Whatever their economic fruits, polar expeditions helped consolidate support for their leaders' expansionary political and economic policies.

For newly emerging powers such as the United States, the High Arctic and other far-flung regions of the globe assumed a pivotal role in nation-building efforts. The American union had only recently conquered or purchased much of its continental land base and was beginning to populate it with immigrants. It required major symbols of national endeavour to help forge a unitary state from its diverse ethnic and regional populations. Such objectives are alluded to in Isaac Israel Hayes's justification of his own expeditions as contributing to the American "national character."[18] Typical definitions of the elusive "national character" in this period framed it in terms of struggle and triumph over the environment. *Hampton's Magazine*, which serialized Peary's narrative of his last polar expedition, played up its potential to inculcate values of capitalism, progress, and national greatness in America's young people: "What has made America great? The power of will. What has made America rich? The triumph of spirit over matter. And no man ever put up such a fight with material conditions as Peary did; no man ever proved more conclusively the power of will."[19]

A new development in arctic exploration in the late nineteenth century was the emergence of the individual, private explorer.[20] Governments continued to contribute to several of the private expeditions, particularly when they perceived national objectives to coincide with those of the explorer. By this time, a large portion of the high costs of exploration were raised through subscriptions from wealthy businessmen, sometimes in conjunction with support from scientific organizations and museums, such as the American Museum of Natural History in New York City.

The Arctic afforded opportunities for the ascendant business classes of the United States to enhance their prestige. Where exploration had previously depended on governments for financing, the emergence of a wealthy and powerful business class afforded new possibilities for private sponsorship of expeditions. Early American sponsors of the polar quest included Henry Grinnell, a wealthy businessmen from New York City, who backed Elisha Kent Kane's voyages in the 1850s. His involvement reflected that city's emerging status as the leading city of the United States, in terms of wealth. It was also from this city's business leaders that Robert Peary enlisted the member patrons of the Peary Arctic Club, led by Peary's long-term sponsor Morris Jesup. In other cases, sponsors of polar expeditions were the owners of less legitimate enterprises, such as John R. Bradley, proprietor of a number of casinos,[21] who aspired to a degree of respectability by funding the expedition of Frederick Cook.

Another source of funding in this period appeared with the developing mass media. By the late nineteenth century the reading public had developed a taste for real-life adventure stories serialized in popular magazines and newspapers.[22] After the enormous success of his commissioning Henry Morton Stanley to find the British explorer Livingstone in Africa, publisher James Gordon Bennett sought more glamorous expeditions to sponsor. In the 1870s, Bennett underwrote the entire cost of the polar voyage of the *Jeanette* to generate newspaper sales.[23] While the expedition ended in failure, Bennett proved the power of the mass media to generate and feed the public's appetite for polar adventure.[24]

By 1900, competition to become the first to reach the North Pole had given it the character of an athletic contest, a "race for the pole." This was explicitly asserted by Dr. Frederick Cook in his book *My Attainment of the Pole*:

> The attaining of the North Pole meant at the time simply accomplishing a splendid, unprecedented feat — a feat of brain and muscle in which I should, if successful, signally surpass other men. In this I was not any more inordinately vain or seekful of glory than one who seeks preeminence in baseball, running tournaments, or any other form of athletics or sport.[25]

Even when individualized in this way, the polar quest expressed the larger cultural objectives of the dominant groups in Euro-American society, an allegory for competition in the free market, with attendant rewards to the victor.

More than anyone else, Robert Peary personified the shift in exploration to an individual quest for fame and fortune. During a period of more than 20 years, from 1886 to 1909, Peary staged a succession of widely publicized expeditions to northern Greenland and Ellesmere Island, aimed at furthering his career-long obsession with reaching the North Pole. He obtained the backing of the New York businessman Morris K. Jesup and institutions such as the American Museum of Natural History. In addition, Peary was also able to obtain long-term leave from the military and official American support for the pursuit of his goals. In his polar quest, personal and national ambitions converged. Writing to Peary in 1903, Charles H. Darling, Acting Secretary of the

United States Navy, expressed the official U.S. government objectives in granting Peary a leave of absence to continue his polar explorations:

> The attainment of the Pole should be your main object. Nothing short will suffice. The discovery of the poles is all that remains to complete the map of the world. That map should be completed in our generation and by our countrymen. If it is claimed that the enterprise is fraught with danger and privation, the answer is that geographical discovery in all ages has been purchased at the price of heroic courage and noble sacrifice. Our national pride is involved in the undertaking, and this department expects that you will accomplish your purpose and bring further distinction to a service of illustrious traditions.[26]

What was noteworthy in Darling's statement was the omission of any reference to science. Science would henceforth be subordinate to the primary objective of national aggrandizement, to be advanced through the personal ambitions of the explorer-as-hero. For both nation and explorer the overriding goal was now, as Peary put it, "to secure the North Pole as an American trophy."[27]

European Concepts of Time and Space in the Nineteenth Century

By the mid-nineteenth century, a characteristic of European approaches to the environment was the "annihilation of time and space." Examples were the rapid advances in transportation and communications systems in this period. With the advent of train and railroad technology, European countries had essentially triumphed over the space enclosed within their national boundaries.[28] In North America, railroad and telegraph development enabled the United States to expand across the continent, a process duplicated in the late nineteenth century in the northern half of the continent by the new Dominion of Canada after 1867. Comparable advances in overcoming space occurred in shipping, as steam power rapidly supplanted sailing after 1860.

Time was the other variable driving explorers in the Arctic. Time was measured against the time taken by competitors, in terms of who reached the goal first, summed up in the phrase "race for the pole." Given the exigencies of travel in this environment, it was often a race against time, a struggle to reach a geographical destination before beset by ice or weather conditions. The newcomers' activities were regulated by such devices as clocks, calendars, written orders, and deadlines.[29] Clocks, indeed, were at the heart of the imperial imperative.[30] They represented a new, mechanistic approach to the external world, regulated and controlled by precise Western time.[31]

By the Peary era, the reliance on timepieces had become not only part of the repertoire of arctic explorers; these instruments were now considered essential to success in exploration. In a commercial endorsement following his final attempt on the North Pole, Peary wrote that watches were distributed to each of his support parties for synchronization of their efforts. He reported that Ross Marvin, the leader of one of the support parties, had taken five watches with him, so that they "might give us absolute certainty of correctness of our time."[32] For Peary, a descendant of an old New England family, the preoccupation with time may have had deeper cultural roots, as it echoed his Puritan ancestors' obsession with making every moment count.[33]

To the introduction of mechanical timepieces, we should add the introduction of text-based approaches to the planning and execution of polar voyages and expeditions. Military orders, written in the south, prescribed the actions to be taken under particular circumstances, and the timetable. Necessarily, such directives involved an element of abstraction from actual circumstances.

Spatially, the explorers were guided by navigational devices, i.e., sextants, compasses, and astrolabes. Maps also comprised a key component in strategies to claim the High Arctic by European and North American nation-states. As geographer D.W. Meinig has written about map-making by the European powers competing in the colonial era for control of the continental United States: "The very lines on the map exhibited this imperial power and process because they had been imposed on the continent with little reference to indigenous peoples, and indeed in many places with little reference to the land itself. The invaders parcelled the continent among themselves in designs reflective of their own complex rivalries and relative power."[34]

The mapping of formerly uncharted terrain constituted both a contribution to knowledge and an expression of empire, extension of dominion, and competitive superiority for the countries participating in the polar quest.[35] The importance of maps in staking claim to the Arctic was acknowledged during the 1920s, when Canada's sovereignty over the Arctic Archipelago was challenged by Denmark. At this time, a Public Archives of Canada official pointed out the problem for Canada that an 1887 map, entitled "Dominion of Canada," which did not extend farther north than northern Labrador, might be used as evidence against Canada's claim, "in such a case as the Ellesmere Land dispute."[36]

By and large, Europeans viewed space in linear terms, as terrain to be traversed, or obstacles to be overcome. Their conquest of space was asserted by erecting cairns, raising national flags, and assigning place names to natural landmarks they believed they had discovered; by these actions they presumed to assert their country's sovereignty. Assigning place names often involved rewriting history, as successive interlopers renamed places earlier marked by other nationals. An example was the northernmost point of Axel Heiberg Island. It was named Cape Svartevoeg by Norwegian explorer Axel Heiberg, when he sighted it in 1900.[37] When Peary arrived at this spot in an overland journey in 1906, he renamed it Cape Thomas Hubbard, after the President of the American Geographical Society. Later, in 1929, following a visit to this location by Constable Stallworthy and Nukappiannguaq, in search of the missing Krüger expedition, the Canadian government renamed the site Cape Stallworthy, which it has remained to the present.

Military Cultures in the Arctic — Discipline and Masculinity

The particular approach of Euro-American explorers to social organization while in the region was military. In contrast to the flexible, egalitarian character of Inuit social organization, Euro-North American expedition parties in the nineteenth century tended to be structured into rigid hierarchies. This was especially the case in the military expeditions sent by Britain and the United States to Ellesmere Island late in the nineteenth century. Even Robert Peary, whose expeditions were privately sponsored, was a lieutenant of the American Navy, and given leave for missions viewed by the United States government as important to American national interests.

The hierarchical organization of these parties was illustrated by the separation of living quarters on the Nares and Greely expeditions. As was customary in the British Navy, the men of the British Arctic Expedition were segregated in terms of living space aboard ship. The commanding officer, in this case, the captain, occupied a wardroom at the after end of the quarterdeck, below which the lieutenants, surgeon, and engineer were housed in the officers' wardroom, while the lower decks were occupied by lower ranks of seamen.[38]

During the American Army's Lady Franklin Bay Expedition, all members were housed in the large expedition house, but the internal organization of space by rank defined and reinforced the class divisions in the United States Army. Enlisted men were quartered in one large room filled with bunk beds, doubled to save space. This room was separated by a central kitchen/galley from the officers' quarters, designed to house the three lieutenants and surgeon of the expedition. Each of these officer class members had his own area, with bed, desk, and table, and could achieve a degree of privacy by drawing heavy curtains between his area and the space of the other officers (Figure 44).[39]

Promoters and organizers of polar expeditions in both countries believed that in so stressful an environment as the High Arctic, large parties required military discipline to avoid anarchy. Yet severe discipline could only be sustained so long as those in command could demonstrate they had the necessary knowledge and judgment to back up their orders.

There are no reports of open conflict during the British Arctic Expedition of 1875–76. The major sledging expeditions were not sent out before the spring of 1876, and it was only on the trail that problems with scurvy and sickness emerged. The expedition departed within a year after arrival in northern Ellesmere Island, well before unrest might have developed. The expedition was also mounted in a period of rigid discipline in the British Navy, when, despite reforms, corporal punishments of flogging, caning, and birching were still widely practised.[40] If disaffection arose, these penalties would presumably have served to suppress open expressions of unrest.

European military expeditions also brought notions of the virtues of arduous effort to their arctic activities, combined with strict adherence to written orders. On the sledging excursions of the Nares expedition, the leaders exhorted their men to "ten, eleven, sometimes twelve hours' steady marching."[41] It was a case of mind over matter. Committed to achieving predetermined goals, the Europeans followed the plan, even when weather conditions might have dictated otherwise. A case in point was a sledge journey mounted in March 1876. Nares ordered a party from the *Alert* to travel 160 km across land to Lady Franklin Bay to communicate with the crew of the *Discovery* before the departure of the spring sledging excursions. This trip was delayed for several days due to very low temperatures, but the team of three men departed on 12 March when a daytime high of –30° F was recorded, still very low for safe sledging. Soon after their departure, the temperature plunged again; within three days the sledgers returned with Peterson, the dog driver suffering from severe frostbite; he died two months later. He had followed orders, literally, to the death.

The drawbacks of the military command structure were highlighted in sharp relief during the U.S. Army's Lady Franklin Bay expedition of 1881-84. From the outset, the army determined to exercise rigid discipline at the party's wintering station, as illustrated by the following passage from the expedition plan:

> "The station should be kept under the strictest discipline and to this end should be formally enrolled in the military service, save perhaps the strictly scientific members. By discipline only can such control be exercised as will be indispensable to the successful prosecution of the work."[42]

In his book on the Lady Franklin Bay expedition, Lieutenant Greely expressed his own view that for arctic service only men and officers "of thorough military qualities" should be selected, "among which subordination is by no means of secondary importance."[43] During the expedition, it was not long before he put these notions of discipline into practice. Within days of their arrival at Fort Conger in August 1881, Greely relieved Lieutenant Kislingbury, whom he considered insubordinate, of his responsibilities. The commander continued to exercise his authority throughout their tenure at Fort Conger, not always wisely. In February 1883, according to expedition surgeon Dr. Octave Pavy, he upbraided a group of men for laxity in taking scientific observations: "This evening at 8 o'cl[ock] he grossly insults the observers Jewell, Ralston and Gardiner (because of errors in their table). He is enraged and says to Jewell, the man who did his duty 'There is not in the service any work more disreputable than yours.'" Pavy commented on Greely's display of temper: "If this should be true, why alienate the men [?]"[44]

Despite his advances in the area of material culture, Robert Peary also brought military concepts of social organization to the High Arctic. Peary held up his use of smaller expedition parties as a model of flexible expedition organization.[45] But as a naval lieutenant, Peary, too, was committed to a hierarchical command structure. While there is no evidence of a breakdown of authority, Peary's rather authoritarian approach may have contributed to early departures by both Americans and Inughuit from his employ during his expeditions of 1898–1902 and 1905–06.[46] A striking example of his assumptions is contained in notes Peary wrote in preparation for a conversation with Matthew Henson, an African-American who had served as his long-term assistant, while they were at Fort Conger in northern Ellesmere Island. Peary wrote:

> "Am old enough now & you have been in my service long enough to show me more respect in small things. Have a right to expect you will say sir to me always. That you will pay attention when I am talking to you & show that you hear the directions I give you by saying yes, sir, or all right sir. Have no fault to find when we are alone together but when D[octo]r or number of Eskimos present or we are on board ship you are very different. Will give you memorandum of this."[47]

Similar notions of hierarchy and discipline continued with military personnel recruited for service on arctic expeditions following Peary's last voyage in 1909. One of the members of Donald B. MacMillan's Crocker Land expedition in 1913 was Fitzhugh Green, a young ensign of the U.S. Navy, described by MacMillan's biographer as an adherent of "strict discipline."[48] An article on the personnel of this expedition commented on Green: "His experience in the navy has already taught him how to command as well as to obey."[49] Green also brought to the Arctic notions of superiority toward the Inughuit; he was said to be "conscious of the great intellectual abyss between Smith Sound and the Naval Academy, and had no such faith in the natives."[50] When these notions of hierarchy and discipline were put to the test in a situation of perceived crisis, the result was the death of Piugaattoq in 1914, discussed in Chapter 11.

A further dimension of the culture of nineteenth century military settlements on Ellesmere Island was that, before Peary, these were all-male communities. In the range of behaviour allowed or proscribed at these outposts they displayed the exaggerated models of masculinity prevalent in Anglo-American societies, particularly in the military cultures of this era. Both the explorers and their backers shared a view of the arctic as a proving ground to demonstrate manliness. Historian Lisa Bloom explained that by the early 1900s, "an increasing number of Americans thought the survival of white masculinity depended upon contact with the wilderness and strenuous physical work."[51] The assumed virtue of pitting men against the wilderness was commonly expressed in the explorers' writings. During the Lady Franklin Bay Expedition, Greely refused to direct his men to focus on fuel collection rather than further exploration feats, saying that such notions were "dishonorable and unmanly."[52] Writing of his own expeditions, Robert Peary remarked that spending a season in the polar regions would quickly show "the true calibre of a man," in particular "whether he is a cur, or has a yellow streak."[53] In 1899, Peary wrote that he was pursuing the North Pole because "it has value as a test of intelligence, persistence, endurance, determined will, and, perhaps, courage, qualities characteristic of the highest type of manhood."[54]

Heightened notions of masculinity also represented the ideological aspirations of the expedition sponsors, themselves exclusively male. Discussing the contributions of Robert Peary, former U.S. president Theodore Roosevelt wrote of his "great physical hardihood and endurance, iron will and unflinching courage," among other qualities that produced a successful arctic explorer.[55] Roosevelt lauded Peary's "admirable work for America [by] setting an example to the young of our day which we need to have set amid the softening tendencies of our time."[56] The exaggerated emphasis on masculinity persisted during the tenure of the Royal Canadian Mounted Police at its detachments on Ellesmere Island in the 1920s and 1930s. In the 1930s, RCMP Commissioner J.H. MacBrien wrote that, in selecting personnel for arctic work, the force looked for "handy men who are robust, reliant, resourceful and self-reliant and not temperamental."[57] In a recent article, Steve Hewitt argued that service in the force in this period was an amalgam of "manly and masculine values, such as order, patriotism, militarism and physicality."[58] For the Mounties, as for the British Navy and the American Army, the culture of manliness also involved unflinching adherence to orders in carrying out their duty, even in the context of objective danger. A further dimension to the culture of polar masculinity was its patriarchal character, discussed in Chapter 11, which came into play during Peary's expeditions as he was the first to include Aboriginal women among expedition personnel.

Nineteenth-century notions of Euro-American masculinity on polar expeditions represented more than an approach to polar exploration. It was integral to the ethos of nation building,[59] as hardy explorers assumed the role of symbols of national endeavour and achievement. From the British Navy through the U.S. Army to the Canadian RCMP, the succession of European explorers not only carried their countries' banners to the Arctic, they embodied their aspirations to forge or reinforce their respective national identities through allegories of struggle with and triumph over the wilderness.

Ships and Navigation in the Arctic

In the field of navigation, the stage for the age of arctic exploration was set by European mariners over several centuries. Mastery of the oceans and their water routes, more than any other factor, explains the European rise to world supremacy.[60] Partly due to developing technical capacity and knowledge, explorers were able to reach the High Arctic by the early seventeenth century. In 1616, Robert Bylot and William Baffin explored the waters between Greenland and Baffin Island and apparently came within sight of Ellesmere Island and the Hayes Peninsula.[61] Yet, the Europeans' faith in the navigational expertise to conquer any of the globe's uncharted seas sometimes exceeded their capacities.

The age of polar exploration took place well after the scientific revolution in navigation. Many of the technological devices employed by the arctic expeditions had been in place since the seventeenth century. By 1600, navigation manuals had appeared, including one authored by arctic explorer John Davis. By 1700, English navigational charts covered much of the known world. The practice of measuring latitude had become widespread by this time, as well as the use of latitude in keeping a ship's course. An English school of cartography developed in this era, through which the value of measurements and mathematical projections came into general use.[62]

Several navigational techniques employed by expeditions to the High Arctic were developed over the century preceding the race for the North Pole. For example, in 1764, British inventor John Harrison developed a chronometer, or timekeeper, which enabled mariners to keep the time of the prime meridian.[63] By the early nineteenth century, the navigational repertoire of arctic expeditions included such instruments as compasses for ascertaining direction, chronometers, or timepieces, and astronomical charts, used in determining latitude.[64] Yet, magnetic compasses, oriented to the north magnetic pole rather than the geographic pole, began to lose their usefulness in high latitudes. For these reasons, nineteenth century expeditions increasingly relied on such devices as azimuth compasses, useful in determining distance through triangulation calculations. Used in combination with astronomical telescopes, they proved more reliable than magnetic compasses in the Arctic.[65]

By the mid-nineteenth century, the newly discovered Sumner method of navigation signalled a breakthrough in astronomical navigation. By this method, the navigator established the altitude of the sun and the longitude by assuming two different latitudes. Both positions were then plotted on a chart and joined by a position line, which defined the course of the ship. The advantage of this method was that readings could be taken at any time during the day or at twilight, whenever two stars could be observed.[66] In this era, another technology used in establishing latitude and longitude was the theodolite.[67] On several occasions, professional scientists engaged by European expeditions brought specific expertise to optimize the results of observations taken with these instruments. An example was August Sonntag, an astronomer engaged by both Elisha Kent Kane and Isaac Israel Hayes, who established meridians by observations of moon culminations, eclipses, and osculations.[68]

Barometers were used in establishing and predicting weather conditions,[69] hydrometers for measuring the specific gravity of ocean waters, and hygrometers, to measure the humidity.[70] Self-registering thermometers were used to gauge water temperatures at various depths. Both the Kane and Hayes expeditions employed a variety of thermometers, including spirit, mercury, and metallic versions.[71] Readings from all these instruments were taken at regular intervals and recorded in the ship's log. For depth soundings, the ancient method of using lead and lines was generally applied.

Nevertheless, nineteenth century navigators to the High Arctic confronted formidable challenges in negotiating ocean waters previously unknown to Europeans. Prior to Inglefield's foray into Kane Basin in 1852, no European ships are known definitively to have penetrated the ice dam of Smith Sound.[72] They therefore had little reliable data indicating a probable range of dates within which shipping in Nares Strait was possible. Without experience or knowledge of the particular sailing conditions of the Ellesmere–Greenland channel, ship commanders were virtually obliged to learn their way by trial and error.

The ice-clogged waters of the region posed particular challenges to European mariners. These problems were magnified in the treacherous areas of the High Arctic, especially in Nares Strait, where colliding ocean currents could drive floes together with tremendous force, crushing ships caught between ice masses. In this context, the dimensions of large objects such as icebergs were determined through trigonometric observations.[73]

It was not until the twentieth century that shipping in this high latitude region was made safer by advances in navigational technology and the development of specialized knowledge of the waters and sea-ice conditions of the Arctic Archipelago. Eventually, the acquisition of data over several decades indicated the problematic character of sea-ice conditions in the channel, and their sensitivity to short-term climatic changes. For example, the earliest recorded date by which a sailing ship reached the North Water was 25 June, reported in 1834, but the average date of access for such ships has since been computed as the last week of July.[74] At best, shipping was feasible for a few months in the late summer and early fall and then only during periods when the sea ice in Davis Strait melted sufficiently to permit ocean-going vessels to penetrate to Baffin Bay.

Ships were the sole means of transportation by which Europeans and North Americans reached the High Arctic in the nineteenth century. In the waters of this region, they confronted hazardous ice conditions that mariners had never before encountered. Early attempts to refit ships for arctic service involved minor adjustments to vessels designed for navigation in more southerly waters. For Ross's expedition of 1818, the bows, keel, and sides of the *Isabella* and *Alexander* were strengthened, and large beams were stretched below the lower decks, to reinforce the ships from the pressure of compacting ice floes.[75] Immediately after this expedition, during which Ross and his crew noted the presence of large number of whales in northern Baffin Bay,[76] whaling vessels from various countries appeared in these waters the following year. Here, in the North Water, they confronted the dilemmas of navigating High Arctic seas, especially the complexities of negotiating vessels through the pack ice, as driven by wind and ocean currents.

Arctic whalers were the first mariners to make a serious attempt to refit sailing vessels to deal with the dangerous conditions of icy arctic waters. In the early nineteenth century, whalers were building ships with double hulls, reinforced by iron plates fitted around the bow.[77]

However, the shortcomings of traditional European sailing ships in the extraordinary conditions of the High Arctic were demonstrated by a series of disasters befalling the British whaling fleet in the early nineteenth century. In 1819, 14 whaling ships were "smashed to pieces" by colliding floes of moving pack ice in northern Baffin Bay. In 1821, 11 ships were lost, in 1822, seven vessels, and in the worst year, 1830, 19 ships were completely destroyed. A retrospective account by Sir Clements Markham reconstructed the scene: "In a quarter of an hour several fine ships were converted into shattered fragments; the ice, with a loud grinding noise, tore open their sides, masts were seen falling in all directions, great ships were squeezed flat and thrown broadside onto the ice, and one whaler, the 'Rattler,' was literally turned inside out."[78]

Following these heavy losses, whalers in the 1830s began to provide greater reinforcement for the ships' hulls to enable them to better withstand the extraordinary conditions of the polar ice pack. Techniques common to arctic whaling vessels by this time included the strengthening of exposed surfaces with two or three layers of timbers. These surfaces were fortified with iron plates, while on the interior they were braced with stanchions and crossbars. Internal trusses serve to distribute the pressure on any one part so that it was borne by the entire vessel. Whaling entrepreneurs generally opted for ships of at least 350 tonnes.[79]

While European whalers developed valuable experience in arctic waters, expeditions following the Franklin disappearance pushed to everhigher latitudes, with sea-ice conditions never before encountered by ships. Navigation in the Ellesmere–Greenland channel became associated with a series of experiments in the technology of ship construction, addressing the particular challenges of negotiating sea ice in these straits. In the 1850s, Henry Grinnell, sponsor of Elisha Kent Kane's Franklin search expeditions, selected two small sailing ships, the 89-tonne *Rescue* and the 142-tonne *Advance*, because he believed they would better withstand the pressure of heavy sea ice than larger vessels. Kane and his associate Edwin J. DeHaven undertook to fit the ships for arctic service by ordering a double sheathing of the hulls with oak, buttressing with timber and iron reinforcement of the bows, and provision of additional supports throughout the hull. As an extra precaution, the hull was lined with cork and tarred felt inserted between the double planking of the decks.[80]

In 1861–62, Israel Hayes employed traditional sailing technology, more from reasons of economy than preference. For his expedition, Hayes had hoped to use two ships — a steamer to be taken out under sail and powered by steam in icy waters and a sailing vessel for use as a store ship. Financial stringency obliged him to abandon these plans in favour of refitting a single, small fore-and-aft schooner of 131 tonnes, which he converted to a fore-topsail vessel and renamed the *United States*. As with the Grinnell ships, Hayes sheathed the ship by spiking two-and-one-half inch oak planking to its sides and casing the bow and stern with iron plates. Within the hold the vessel was buttressed with heavy timbers below the water line and further braced with diagonal supports.[81] During his expedition in 1873, Charles Francis Hall was obliged to rely on a 361-tonne steam tug, christened the *Polaris*, which the U.S. Navy refitted for the purpose.[82] While this ship was obviously much more powerful than Hayes's *United States*, it proved unable to negotiate the congested ice in the northern reaches of the Nares Strait. Its forward momentum arrested, the ship's shortcomings were revealed when the southward current in the channel carried it to the south, where it was ultimately crushed in the ice, and sank.[83]

In the same decade, the British Arctic Expedition led by Captain George S. Nares partially reverted to the earlier practice of sending sailing ships to the region. The *Alert*, a 17-gun sloop, was converted for arctic service by overhauling the hull with new timbers and encasing it with a 15-cm sheathing of teak, tapered at the ends. Lengthwise, a heavy beam was placed between the shelf-piece and the lower deck and bound and strapped to the ship's entire structure. To brace the hull from the pressure of ice, iron knees were added and the stem fortified with thick iron plates, while the bow was reinforced with diagonal beams and dead wood. The smaller *Discovery* was a steam vessel,[84] built by a shipyard in Dundee for use in whaling and sealing. This ship had been employed in sealing off Newfoundland before being acquired for the British expedition.[85]

By the 1880s, steam power technology had sufficiently advanced to improve the capacity of ships to navigate in frequently ice-clogged channels. However, several disasters occurred before improvements in ship design after 1900 demonstrably reduced the risks of sailing in these hazardous seas. In 1881, the ship commissioned to transport Adolphus Greely's United States Army expedition to Lady Franklin Bay was the *Proteus*, an oak-hulled barkentine-rigged sailing steamer, built only seven years earlier in Dundee, Scotland (Figure 26). Based in St. John's, Newfoundland, the ship was used by sealers in the ice-congested waters off the Newfoundland and Labrador coasts. Powered by two compound engines totalling 110 horsepower, this heavy ship weighed 460 tonnes. To withstand the stress of sea ice the *Proteus* was sheathed with a belt of ironwood from above the water line to below the bilge, while its prow was reinforced with iron buttresses.[86]

In the favourable sea ice conditions of 1881, the *Proteus* was able to negotiate the waters of the Ellesmere–Greenland channel successfully,

Figure 26: The *Proteus* in the ice at the entrance to Discovery Harbour, August 1881. Credit: US National Archives, RG 27, Lady Franklin Bay Expedition Records (Washington, DC), Box No. 17. Photographer: George W. Rice.

and it delivered Greely's men, supplies, and equipment to Discovery Harbour without incident. But, the following year, a similar ship engaged to resupply the party was unable to penetrate the ice dam in Smith Sound to reach its destination. In 1883 the *Proteus* was again commissioned, but it was crushed in the ice of Kane Basin and sank.[87] Despite 60 years of navigation in High Arctic waters, Europeans had still not mastered the exigencies of navigation in this difficult, remote region.

Following the loss of the *Proteus* and the disastrous conclusion to the Greely expedition, polar explorers turned their attention to revamping ship design to address the specific challenges posed by arctic navigation. Between 1898 and 1900, Norwegian explorer Otto Sverdrup explored the icy channels of the Queen Elizabeth Islands. For his expedition vessel, he borrowed the *Fram*, an auxiliary steam ship designed by his compatriot Fridtjof Nansen for polar exploration. In 1890, Nansen secured the backing of the government of Norway to build a vessel for his proposed drift across the Arctic Ocean toward the North Pole. Realizing that no ship could resist the force of ice driven by winds or tides, he sketched out a plan for a ship that could effectively counter the crushing pressure of the ice. The solution was an oval hull whose curved shape would effectively deflect the ice by sliding out of the way when caught between colliding floes. A further innovation in the design of the hull was the provision of wells recessed in the stern for withdrawing the propeller and rudder in heavy ice conditions.[88]

The Norwegians rigged the *Fram* as a three-masted fore-and-aft schooner, enabling it to be staffed with a minimum crew.[89] Powered by a 200-horsepower reciprocal steam engine, it consumed three tonnes of coal propelling the *Fram* forward at six knots an hour. The ship's lighting was powered by a collapsible windmill.[90] Two 30-cm timbers of elm were used to build the keel, while 44-cm timbers, closely spaced, provided the framing members. The intermediate spaces were filled with a mixture of coal tar, pitch, and sawdust. Both the bow and the stern were built of oak to a thickness of 1.2 metres. The hull was sheathed with three layers of planking, including an outer skin of hard South American laurel, a wood commonly used in whaling ships to deflect the ice. An inner skin of pine was fitted over 450 pine knees, or L-shaped timbers, and diagonally braced for further reinforcement. Finally, the hull was wrapped in iron straps and painted.[91]

The influence of Nansen's design for the *Fram* was evident in the expedition ship commissioned by Robert E. Peary after 1900. When his supply ship, the *Windward*, proved unable to advance through Nares Strait to Fort Conger in 1899, Peary concluded that the North Pole was unattainable unless a suitable ship could be developed to enable expedition quarters to be established on Ellesmere Island's northern coasts. In 1904, with the backing of Morris K. Jesup and the Peary Arctic Club, Peary commissioned the building of the *Roosevelt*, a specially designed steam-powered icebreaker for his polar voyages of 1905–06 and 1908–09. Where his predecessors had relied on ships with full sail power, backed up by auxiliary steam engines, Peary reversed previous practice by developing a powerful steam ship with auxiliary sail power.[92] Studying the design of sailing craft then in use in polar regions, Peary noted that the Scottish whaling fleet had narrower, sleeker ships than their Norwegian or American counterparts. "It has been said by one writer that the American whalers use their steam to keep out of the ice, while the Scotch use theirs to get into and through it."[93]

For the *Roosevelt*, Peary opted for a rounded, egg-shaped hull, apparently using the *Fram* as prototype. Weighing 1476 tonnes,[94] the *Roosevelt* featured a steel-clad bow and heavily reinforced sides. Its engines also generated far greater power than had previously been seen in High Arctic ships.[95] The ship was built with a valve-operated bypass that allowed steam from its boilers to be diverted into a large cylinder. In emergency situations, this enabled the ship's power to be increased for short periods. It bore a very heavy shaft and propellor.[96]

Peary noted that many ships lost in arctic waters were characterized by heavy draught. He therefore sought a design that would enable the ship to be raised out of the ice in the event of pressure from ice floes

Figure 27: "The Roosevelt lies trapped among rough ice floes off the barren coast of Ellesmere Island. Members of the crew can be seen standing on the ice near the bow of the ship." Credit: National Geographic Society (Washington, DC), Robert E. Peary Collection, Project No. 02116, Consecutive No. 3159, Picture Id. No. 123658A, Picture Rec. Id. No. 132029.

(Figure 27). Another feature was its "stubby" shape, measuring 56 m long by 11 m wide. Broadside, it appeared "as trim and rakish as a yacht;" viewed head-on, it gave more the impression of a "battleship" and a "battering-ram." Such proportions permitted the ship to manoeuvre readily in the ice, while its rounded hull enabled the boat to be lifted by the pack ice without damage to the hull. Thus equipped, Peary's parties were able to pass through Nares Strait successfully in both of his last two expeditions and to reach his intended wintering site at Cape Sheridan on Ellesmere's northern coast. Building the *Roosevelt* therefore marked the first successful adaptation of shipping technology to High Arctic conditions.

Beyond the development of suitable vessels, the heavy sea-ice conditions of the High Arctic posed daunting technical challenges for which European mariners were ill prepared. When trapped in the ice—a frequent occurrence—they needed to find ready ways to extricate themselves. During the search for Franklin, relief expeditions developed a standard toolkit to deal with these situations, which was identified by historian W. Gillies Ross. The tools included: ice-saws, ice-anchors, tracking harnesses, blasting powder and canisters, and sleds for hauling ice and water.[97] A corresponding repertoire of techniques was developed by

133

whaling ships obliged to work their way through the icy waters of Baffin Bay. No set of techniques in the pack ice was foolproof, however, and mariners found they confronted situations where they were obliged to improvise, as Sir Edward Belcher noted:

> we discovered, even with three masters in each vessel,... that there is always much to learn, and moreover,... that method is imperatively required. Our [ice] docks, constructed in haste, and without previous organization, were imperfect.[98]

European Man-Hauled Sledging

Beyond reliance on sailing vessels to reach the region, exploration in the High Arctic involved travel over the pack ice, rocky coastlines and a variety of other challenging surfaces, including glaciers, rivers, and tundra, encountered while penetrating to the interior of northern Ellesmere Island. Travel over the generally rugged terrain was complicated by snow, melted water, and pressure ridges that formed in the ocean channels. In contrast to Inughuit or Inuit use of sled dogs, most European sledge parties of the early contact period relied on humans for motive power. An exception was the American explorer Elisha Kent Kane, who travelled in part by dog team. Kane brought 20 Husky dogs which he procured in West Greenland, as well as nine Newfoundland dogs "in the supposition that they might be drilled to sledge driving."[99] Kane was also the first to introduce man-hauled sledging to the High Arctic. During his Second Grinnell Expedition in the mid-1850s, Kane reported obtaining a freight sledge from the British Admiralty for transporting provisions to distant cache sites. This particular sledge was apparently modelled after Inuit prototypes in the Central Arctic and had earlier been tested by Leopold McClintock in journeys in the Lancaster Sound region. Kane made some adjustments to the height and width of the runners to strengthen it and prevent it from sinking too far into the snow. Loading the sledge with its 640-kg cargo, Kane assigned nine men to pull Manilla rope traces of varying lengths. When hauling, the men wore shoulder belts attached to varying lengths of rope to allow them to pull without running into one another.[100]

By the second winter, finding the man-hauling method excessively arduous, Kane began to emulate Inughuit methods of dog-sledging. He also followed their practice of reducing sled gear and provisions to "the Eskimaux ultimatum of simplicity,—raw meat and a fur bag."[101] Referring to his sledge loads of the succeeding year, he wrote: "Compare it with similar sledge-outfits of last winter, and you will see that

Figure 28: One of the sledging parties of the HMS *Discovery*, prior to their departure to explore the coast of Lady Franklin Bay, 1876. The sledge weights were as much as 450 kg. National Archives of Canada, Photograph no. C-52571.

we are now more than half Esquimaux."[102] In the 1860s, Isaac Israel Hayes, who had served with Kane in the previous decade, returned to the High Arctic and continued to rely on dogs to power his own sledging excursions.[103]

Despite the prior experience of Americans with sled dogs, the British Arctic Expedition of 1875–76 reverted to the earlier practice of man-hauled sledging. Historian Michael Pearson described their approach as "a caricature of British exploits of the Franklin era."[104] The principal advocate of this outmoded practice was Sir Clements Markham, a venerable arctic enthusiast, the dominant personality in the Royal Geographical Society, and father of Commander A.H. Markham, second only to Captain George Nares in the chain of command on this expedition. One student of this tradition concluded that the elder Markham, swept away by the romance of man-hauled sledging, became disdainful of the American preference for dogs.[105]

The British sledges, made of oak, shod with steel runners, and weighing 65 kg before loaded, were both heavy and unwieldy (Figure 28). When loaded with trail gear, the sledges weighed 500 kg or more, and their weight was increased by frozen tents and sleeping bags, which had to be packed before they had dried. To add to their difficulties, the men had inadequate footwear, as no snowshoes had been issued.[106] Encountering deep stretches of wet snow, the hapless sledgers sank into it knee-deep or up to their waists.[107] Commander A.H. Markham's report of his excursion across the polar ice pack in April 1876 details the enormous difficulties his party encountered in making even minimal progress in these conditions. Surface obstacles obliged him to deploy his entire force of men to pull each sledge through snowy stretches, before backtracking to pull the next sledge forward. Since this practice involved several journeys over the same route, the sledgers travelled five miles (8 km) for each mile they advanced the party. When crossing the ocean pack ice, they were forced to use picks and shovels to cut a path through the jagged hummocks, which rose as high as 13 m. Often, travel was even more arduous between hummocks, where snow drifted to great heights.[108]

In a retrospective address on arctic sledge travelling, Markham described the miserable conditions endured by these parties:

> The snow over and through which the sledges had to be dragged was generally over the men's knees, and frequently up to their waists. It was of such a consistency, the upper layer or crust being slightly frozen, that they were unable to force their legs through it, and were therefore compelled to lift them straight out of the holes before they could be either advanced or extricated. This was very exhausting; walking for an hour through this description of snow being infinitely more tiring than dragging a heavy sledge for the whole day. On several occasions the men found it not only easier, but they could make better progress whilst dragging the sledges, by crawling on their hands and knees, than by dragging in the more orthodox manner, on their feet.[109]

The exhausting experience of hauling heavy loads in such arduous conditions was later cited as a contributing factor, along with the lack of adequate nutrition, in the general outbreak of scurvy that afflicted all the major sledging excursions of this expedition.

Between 1881 and 1883, the Greely expedition also relied heavily on man-hauled sledging for exploratory work, and its personnel experienced difficulties similar to their predecessors. During Lieutenant Lockwood's trip along Greenland's northern coast in April 1882, two Hudson Bay sledges were soon wrecked and had to be abandoned. In their place, the men improvised by fashioning a sled from old runners and planks left behind by the Nares expedition at the site. Their progress was slowed by rough surface conditions, obliging them to divide the sledge loads and pull half the packs before retracing their steps to retrieve the remaining gear and provisions. The field notes of Sergeant David Brainard, a member of this party, attested to the great hardships they encountered, as he wrote: "to add to our discomforts, aside from the severe strain of tramping through snow knee-deep and more, there was a high wind with the snow blowing directly in our faces... Besides, the crust breaks just as we put our weight on the drag ropes for a strong pull; this taxes the strength severely, and will soon break down the hard workers."[110] Both the Nares and Greely expeditions brought Native dog drivers from Greenland, along with their sleds and dog teams, but they made only limited use of Aboriginal techniques while in the Arctic.

European Approaches to Shelter in the High Arctic

Nowhere were the problems inherent in imposing nineteenth century European material culture on High Arctic life more apparent than in the crucial area of shelter. At the beginning of the post-Franklin period, expedition sponsors in the expansionist nations of Europe and the continental United States had accumulated comparatively little experience with arctic environmental conditions. That the Franklin ships were missing was evidence of the dangers and difficulties of travelling and living in the region, but Europeans and Americans continued to mount expeditions ill-prepared in equipment, environmental knowledge, and techniques for addressing its challenges.

Through trial and error, improvements in methodologies for both short-term and wintering shelter eventually occurred over the half-century between Kane's expeditions of the 1850s and Peary's Greenland expedition of 1898–1902. At the same time, enhanced understanding did not occur in a linear progression, as every advance seemed to be followed by a retreat, and hard-won wisdom repeatedly gave way to folly. As late as the 1880s, Europeans were continuing to employ inappropriate approaches to human habitation, sometimes with disastrous consequences.

Euro-North American naïveté in polar shelter was well represented by the Nares and Greely expeditions to northern Ellesmere Island in 1875–76 and 1881–84. Ironically, expeditions staged in part to advance the scientific knowledge of polar regions showed little awareness of the applied science of High Arctic survival. The approach of the British Arctic Expedition was perhaps the most outmoded, as it conformed to practices whose suitability was already in doubt during the Franklin era. Specifically, the British wintered aboard ship at both Discovery Harbour, where HMS *Discovery* was stationed, and at Floeberg Beach, the base of operations for the *Alert*. At both sites, the crews hauled the vessels to safe positions by the shore where they were anchored and frozen into the ice in the autumn (Figure 29). They undertook a number of steps to insulate the ships by mounding snow up to the channels or holes in the gunwales for the rigging,[111] and by spreading snow over the top deck. In an attempt to insulate the hatch entrances from the intru-

Figure 29: The *Discovery* anchored at Lady Franklin Bay, with the depot and observatories on shore, September 1875. National Archives of Canada, Photograph no. C-25921.

sion of cold air, the crews constructed snow block porches over the hatches (Figures 30 and 38).[112]

Despite the porches, the hatch doors defied the axioms of gravity by which warm air rises and cold air falls. These axioms were the most fundamental principles of Thule-Inuit architecture, but in the case of the British ships, each entrance to or exit from the hold was accompanied by a cascade of freezing air.[113] To make matters worse, the snow porches, receiving the heated air from below, melted frequently, necessitating frequent repairs. At the same time the insulating layer of snow over the deck melted and froze into a slippery layer of ice.[114]

Below decks, problems developed with excessive condensation, poor ventilation, and oscillations in temperature. The ship's quarters were not conducive to the development of proper up-takes and down-takes of air, while moisture forming continually on the beams produced a constant drip. Moreover, the *Discovery*'s coal-burning stoves were unable to maintain a consistent interior temperature, as wild fluctuations between –6° and 20° C were reported.[115] In a subsequent report on the health of the party, Dr. Thomas Colan, expedition surgeon, cited both the dampness and the extreme changes of temperature as predisposing factors to the outbreak of scurvy suffered by the men. These tragedies were the subject of a parliamentary investigation on the expedition's premature return to Britain in 1876.[116]

Figure 30: "Lat. 81° 44' N. The people who did not leave the ship in the early spring sledding season. A discarded face protector on snow bank, 1876." Photograph by Thomas Mitchell, National Archives of Canada, Photo No. C-4588.

Only six years later, the United States Army's Lady Franklin Bay Expedition established a base camp, which they named Fort Conger, on the wintering site of the *Discovery*. This time, the wintering headquarters were established on land, as the expedition ship was not retained for the winter. The *Proteus* departed after unloading men, supplies, and pre-cut lengths of lumber for the prefabricated expedition house. The house was patterned after trading houses of the Hudson's Bay Company in northern Canada. A board organized by the Signal Office to develop specifications for the expedition concluded that such a structure was "assumed to be suitable, both as to size, style, and comfort."[117] For the sledge parties, four wall tents and 12 "A" tents were provided for shelter away from the station.

Assembled within a few days, the expedition house measured 18 m long by 5.5 m wide, and featured 3-metre-high ceilings and a steeply-pitched gable roof with intervening loft space used for storage (Figure 31). Its double walls consisted of outside vertical boards, battened with tarpaper and separated by an airspace from the tongued and grooved inner walls, which were also lined with tarpaper. Tarpaper was also used to line the ceiling and roof boards. Inside, the structure was partitioned into three rooms: a central entrance and cook house, an officer's quarters, and a men's room.[118]

Figure 31: The expedition house at Fort Conger under construction. Note the vertical board-and-batten siding, high ceiling and extensive attic space. Photograph by George Rice. Credit: US National Archives (Washington, DC), RG 27, Lady Franklin Bay Expedition Records Box No. 17.

Greely's house was of questionable suitability for a High Arctic environment as its considerable size and extent of exposed surfaces imposed heavy energy demands. For example, during September 1881, the first complete month of occupancy, the house stoves consumed five tons of coal, "nearly double the proper amount" in Greely's opinion. The heavy energy demands obliged Greely to send men to the coal seam in the vicinity to mine and haul coal on virtually a daily basis. More significant, perhaps were the effects of heavy burning of coal on the air quality of the expedition house. In May 1883, Dr. Pavy wrote in his diary "Today the mess has been burned blacker than ever since we are at Fort Conger."[119] The men were exposed to coal fumes continuously throughout much of the year, a probable contributing factor to the respiratory illness that visited the party the first year at the station.

Nor did the expedition demonstrate an adequate knowledge of banking techniques for insulating purposes. The house was partially banked with sod but inexplicably mounded only to a height of two metres (Figure 32).[120] For the second winter the banking was improved by carrying it up to the eaves, but the roof, through which most of the heat escaped, was left uncovered. Even after improved banking, Dr. Pavy's diaries revealed the continuing need to assign one or two men to haul coal for fuel.[121]

Figure 32: The completed house at Fort Conger, showing canvas additions. Note that the banking of sod has only been brought part way up the walls. Photograph by George Rice. Credit: US National Archives (Washington, DC), RG 27, Lady Franklin Bay Expedition Records, Box No. 17.

Moreover, such features as the building's height, large exposed surface areas, and extended roof overhang were poorly designed to withstand the ferocious winds that often characterize this region. Without emergency shelters to accommodate the men, the party would have met certain disaster in the event of destruction of the house from either fire or tempest. Writing about a severe storm in January 1882, Greely recorded his belief that they came close to losing the roof, with potentially catastrophic consequences :

> The wind was then blowing a hurricane, the air full of snow, and the house shook and creaked in an alarming and ominous manner. Every instant I expected that the roof would be twisted or torn off, and the whole building blown into the open harbor. Such a catastrophe would have left us in desperate straits, and would probably have proved fatal to some of our party. The violence of the wind for over an hour kept us in a state of suspense as to what would be our fate.[122]

Despite its unwieldiness and energy inefficiency, the big house was evidently an improvement on Nares's shipboard wintering arrangements. But after Greely led his men into a premature retreat following the failure of supply ships to reach them in 1882 and 1883, the perils of polar unpreparedness were visited on the ill-fated party. Reaching the southern part of Kane Basin by late September, Greely's party became marooned on Pim Island off Bache Peninsula. At Camp Clay, they again set up wintering quarters in what was to become a dismal starvation camp.[123]

Here, Greely's ignorance of Aboriginal techniques was demonstrated in the makeshift shelter his men constructed for their winter habitation. After selecting a site, the men hauled rocks to build a low rectangular wall about a metre high on which they inverted the hull of a whaleboat to serve as a roof. At the sides the boat was supported by oar blades inserted into holes cut into the gunwales anchored in the ends of the wall, and the whole was covered with canvas. Snow blocks were stacked outside the stone walls and also fashioned into a passageway and storehouse.[124] Yet no attempt seems to have been made to cover the roof with either sod or snow. How suitable this makeshift shelter was for High Arctic accommodation soon became apparent. In early November, Greely wrote:

> Our sleeping-bags and clothing were already frozen to the ground and their interiors were thawed only by the heat of our bodies, and froze solidly on quitting them. The roof and walls speedily gathered frost and ice, as did every other article in our wretched hut."[125] Not only did the roof allow most of the shelter's heat to escape to the outside, Greely reported that, on 1 December, a violent storm caused drifting snow to blow through the roof, further lowering the interior temperature. Continuing storms unroofed the passageway and repeatedly filled it and the storehouse with snow.[126]

Both the Nares and Greely parties experienced further difficulties in shelter on the trail during their respective sledging excursions. The British sledgers were housed in tents fashioned from "duck," an untwilled cotton fabric used in making small sails, lined with holland to a height of 60 cm across the rear and sides of the tent.[127] Clements Markham, the venerable promoter of arctic expeditions and advisor to the expedition, recommended using these tents when the temperature was –30° F or higher. In the event the temperature fell below this level, he advised building snow huts, "they being very much better and warmer than tents." For smaller excursions, it was a relatively simple matter to erect a small snow shelter, but for larger parties it was a more difficult proposition owing to the size of dome required to house the men; consequently, tents were the norm.[128]

When actually on the trail the British sledgers suffered from inadequate protection while housed in their flimsy canvas shelters. A.H. Markham wrote that the British brought very lightweight tents to reduce the sledge weights, but these offered little protection from "the furious onslaughts of a biting wind, always accompanied by a blinding snowdrift." An anonymous document, copied into the expedition journal of Captain Nares, graphically depicted the hardships experienced by these men. The writer wrote that "very few can possibly realize the utter wretchedness undergone by young men in the utmost health & strength when imprisoned by a heavy gale of wind within a small light tent" in temperatures of –20° to –30° F. Conditions were worsened by the cramped quarters in the tents:

> What then must be the feelings of anyone compelled to remain lying down at full length cramped up in a contracted space having 30 to 32 inches across for *yourself and companion*—for one or two and even three consecutive days—packed in order to economize space—heads and tails alternately like preserved sardines amongst your fellows in the oily tins—where if your blanket bag allowed you to kick it most necessarily be at the risk of striking your next neighbour's nose.[129]

Adding further to their discomfort, the tents filled with drifts of fine snow, driven by the high winds of the autumn season. Members of the sledging parties of both the Nares and Greely expeditions suffered from severe exposure and frostbite, contributing to amputations of toes, deteriorating health and, eventually, to several deaths.[130]

European Clothing and Provisions in the Arctic

Clothing was another aspect of material culture in which European goods were initially inadequate to the conditions of High Arctic work. For example, the Nares expedition equipped its men with moccasins, lined with a double layer of blanket flannel, with gaiters drawn over the tops of the moccasin. On the trail, they found such footwear to be poorly suited to travel over jagged, icy surfaces. By Christmas, the winter cloth boots were already "very much the worse for wear," forcing the men to be confined to the ship and "the shoemakers are continually kept employed."[131]

The problems in their gear were particularly pronounced during the spring sledging excursions of 1875-76. Lieutenant Pelham Aldrich, the leader of one of the sledging crews, compiled an extensive list of the articles of clothing worn by his party. While the men employed around the ship wore fur garments, the sledgers' clothing, apart from their outer caps, included no fur or skin articles. Headgear consisted of: 1) a skull cap; 2) "Eugénies," or woolen head covers worn over the skull cap; 3) sealskin caps, sometimes worn over the Eugénie, considered by

Aldrich to be heavy and cumbersome; and finally, 4) "duck" caps, which he found to fit better over the ears and forehead. Undergarments included Guernsey shirts, heavy-duty Good and Doidge drawers, and grey boot hose. Overgarments were duffle trousers and duffle jumpers, over which an outer suit was drawn to repel the snow. For hand coverings, sledgers wore Shetland and grey mitts; the former shrank immediately, while the latter were awkward to use (Figure 30).[132]

Members of A.H. Markham's sledging party found their Guernseys wore out quickly.[133] Even the Victorian facial hair of the men proved an impediment, as they found that their breath quickly froze to beards and moustaches. After two hours' exposure, a fringe of icicles had grown to the point that the mustachioed men found they were unable to drink from their tumblers. Their beards froze to their scarves, and since these could not be thawed in the unheated tents, they were obliged to cut off their beards close to the skin.[134] Constrained by the need to reduce sledge weights, the men of the sledging parties wore only what was considered the minimum required apparel. They did not bring a change of clothes, so that when their garments became wet, they suffered from exposure and frostbite. It was on these sledging excursions that the intense cold of the High Arctic was most severely felt, as the *Alert*'s surgeon Dr. Edward Moss observed: "its miseries can hardly be exaggerated."[135]

Sleeping bags were another essential covering for sledgers in the Arctic. During the Nares Expedition, Commander A.H. Markham led a fall sledging excursion along the northern coastline of Ellesmere Island in October 1875 to establish a cache of provisions and sledge boats. Once out in the field, he found his party was poorly outfitted with bed coverings with which to withstand the very low temperatures they encountered. On these occasions "the night clothing seems hardly sufficient, the cold being so intense as to effectually banish sleep. The duffle of the jumpers and sleeping bags, and also the coverlets and lower robes are made of, does not keep out the cold that would be imagined from its composition." As well, the waterproof floor cloths, intended to protect the sleeping sledgers from surface moisture and cold, proved to be a "total failure."[136] Later, during the Greely Expedition, Sergeant David Brainard later wrote that the best bag was made of caribou skins, while an outer layer of oil-tanned sealskin made the bag impervious to water. However, the Greely party's sleeping bags were actually made of buffalo hides without a protective outer layer. Only a single rubber blanket separated the bags and their occupants from the snow. Brainard wrote that frequently two or three men shared the same bag to keep warm, with the drawback that any shifting in position disturbed the rest of one's companions.[137]

Early European wintering expeditions to northern Ellesmere Island exploited the game resources of the region only to a very limited degree. Their principal food sources were dried or tinned foods which they brought with them from Europe or North America, occasionally supplemented by the meat of local animals. They had neither a good understanding of the characteristics and movements of High Arctic animals, nor more than a superficial knowledge of Aboriginal hunting techniques. As a result, fresh game occupied a marginal place in meeting their overall food requirements.

A case in point was the Nares expedition of 1875–76, whose members were only able to supplement their diet with fresh meat on a limited basis during their year in northern Ellesmere Island. Dr. Thomas Colan, Fleet Surgeon for the expedition, later reported that from the establishment of wintering quarters, the *Alert*'s crew consumed only 14 days' fresh meat, and this included some mutton they had brought from England. More significantly, the extended sledge parties, who had the greatest need of foods rich in protein and vitamins, were unable to secure any game at all.[138]

Explaining the general outbreak of scurvy among the men, Colan noted the expedition's lack of fresh vegetables, and he surmised that the lack of fresh meat might have been a "remote cause." Regarding the sledging parties, he acknowledged that the absence of fresh meat, vegetables, and lime juice "tended to detrimental results." He also cited additional contributing factors to the outbreak:

> Any one or more of the following may have acted as a predisposing cause or causes: —our long and difficult winter, the confinement between decks in a damp atmosphere for the long period I have mentioned, the extreme changes of temperature undergone during the prevalence of the great cold. The exciting cause I can only attribute to the heavy physical work undergone during the prevalence of the great cold.[139]

The diet aboard the *Discovery* was better balanced, due to the greater success of crew members in shooting 44 muskoxen and 139 hares during the winter.[140] However, even these stores of fresh meat were insufficient to forestall the onset of scurvy during the spring sledging excursions by the personnel of this ship.

During the first half century of Euro-North American exploration in the High Arctic, most Western visitors failed to approach this region on its own terms. Typically, they regarded the environment as a hostile wilderness to be overcome, rather than accommodated, and early attempts to impose European techniques of travel, provisioning, and shelter often enough yielded disastrous results. Their refusal to embrace Inuit or Inughuit techniques of survival can largely be explained by reference to the mindset they brought to early encounters with the Aboriginal inhabitants of the region. Nineteenth-century Europeans tended to consign its inhabitants to the "primitive" races whose way of life was no match for the onslaught of superior Western technology and culture. The fact that the Inughuit appeared to be in difficult circumstances at the time seemed to confirm this prejudicial assessment, as in Kane's characterization of the Inughuit as "improvident" in the 1850s.[141] Some Western visitors viewed the Inughuit as curiosities providing interesting material for their expedition reports, while others saw economic potential in initiating a fur trade. Few understood or appreciated the extent of this Aboriginal people's knowledge of their environment or their manifold and successful adaptations to it. The notion that Western newcomers might learn important principles and techniques of arctic survival from the Aboriginal people was alien to the self-image of newly ascendant European cultures in this period. In the nineteenth century, Western science and technology had produced levels of economic growth and mastery of nature unparalleled in human history. Through most of the century, Europeans and Americans persisted in the belief that their technological prowess could not fail to conquer the Arctic as it had so many other regions of the globe.

Continuities in High Arctic History: A Preliminary Perspective

With the introduction of European cultures into the High Arctic, the major continuities of the post-contact history of the region were in place. The natural environment and its elements of physiography, climate and ecology established the physical opportunities and constraints of the region with which all humans in this area had to contend. Aboriginal cultures, in particular Inughuit and Inuit from the Arctic Archipelago, operated within a cultural framework of world views, technology, natural resource use, and social organization, adapted to the environment and developed over hundreds of years. The European explorers brought their own ideologies, technology, and cultural imperatives of comparable duration, developed through the expansion of European exploration and commerce since at least the seventeenth century. The interaction of the forces of nature and culture circumscribed the range of options within which humans would operate over the succeeding two centuries.

This is not to say that any of these continuities of history operated as monolithic forces. The arctic climate and ecosystems, both closely interrelated, were dynamic factors, in recurrant flux throughout High

Arctic history. The oscillations of the physical environment presented a highly variable set of influences within which the various occupants of the High Arctic were obliged to function. Nor should the human cultures be viewed as static entities. From the time of the early Independence cultures, Aboriginal peoples in this region were involved in a continual process of cultural adaptation to changing climate and resources, necessitating periodic migrations, acquisition of new knowledge, and adjustments to technology to address new challenges. For European cultures, perpetual change was integral to the expansionist forces that first brought their representatives to North America and ultimately to the Arctic. Given the pre-existing cultural frameworks of European newcomers, some individuals, at least, had the potential to learn from their encounters with Aboriginal cultures and the environment and to apply this knowledge to arctic survival. With these important caveats, the continuities of culture and nature could not fail to influence the decisions, actions, and, ultimately, the fates of the respective actors throughout the balance of High Arctic history.

PART II

CIRCUMSTANCE

History of Events on
Ellesmere Island,
1850–1940

Part II focusses on the narrative history of Ellesmere Island in the exploration era. The term "narrative history" is used to refer to the presentation of human history as a succession of events in chronological sequence. Familiar in Anglo-American writing, this form of historical writing is typically concerned with the role of individuals in history, the factor of personality, and the play of chance. Out of the myriad of reported happenings in the past, historians customarily choose to highlight as "events" those incidents considered to have importance, i.e. to have either changed the course of human history or which belong to a series of occurrences connected to historical change. In the case of the post-contact era of the High Arctic, these works have largely focussed on the explorers' successive quests for the Northwest Passage and the North Pole. From Clements Markham to Pierre Berton, innumerable exploration narratives and biographies of arctic explorers have represented the region's history as a contest between individuals and nations, or between humans and the environment, to the greater glory of the sponsoring countries. Typically, these books have highlighted the stirring exploits of intrepid European heroes and reproduced the explorers' own perspectives regarding their expeditions and place in history. Referring to historical subjects in another place and era—the Mediterranean region in the sixteenth century—Fernand Braudel has noted that participants' own perceptions of significance must be acknowledged:

> As spectators and actors, ... they felt, rightly or wrongly, that they were participating in a mighty drama which they regarded above all as personal to them. But this illusion, this feeling of being an eye-witness of a universal spectacle, helped to give meaning to their lives.[1]

Few historical developments seem so well suited to charting linear history than the race to reach the North Pole. For more than half a century after 1850, a succession of explorers followed more or less the same route toward the same goal. Their expeditions followed in chronological sequence, each spurred to try to exceed the previous farthest north, as they measured success by attaining a meagre degree or a few minutes north latitude beyond their predecessors, before being turned back by the unsparing polar environment. Yet, the quest for the Pole was less a linear than a circuitous process. Far from a progression from one triumph to the next, it involved many false starts, missteps, reversals, and retreats. Notwithstanding the apparently methodical preparations of several exploration parties, both the successful and disastrous conclusions to expeditions owed much to the factor of individual personalities in interplay with pre-existing cultural frameworks and the environment.

In the mindsets of the Anglo-American exploring countries, individual agency was the decisive factor impelling their parties to new discoveries. Benjamin Disraeli, Prime Minister of Great Britain during the British Arctic Expedition of 1875-76, wrote: "Man is not the creature of circumstances, circumstances are the creatures of men. We are free agents, and man is more powerful than matter."[2] Disraeli's belief in free agents well expressed the individualistic ethos of his class and culture in this period. On the other hand, Herodotus, the father of Western historiography, gave the opposite advice that "men are at the mercy of circumstances, which never bend to human will."[3] Which of these two sages should we listen to? The examination of the narrative history of arctic exploration occasions an opportunity for a renewed enquiry into the factors of individual agency and circumstance as they pertain to High Arctic history.

Previously, the narrative history of polar exploration has largely focussed on the leaders of European or Euro-American expeditions to the High Arctic in the period 1818 to 1940, while the roles of other members of these parties have received scant attention. Similarly, Aboriginal members of these parties have been accorded little credit for their contributions. In some cases, their omission reflects the history, as parties such as the Nares and Greely expeditions largely bypassed the Inughuit in their advance to the north and retreat to the south. In other instances, the omission of significant references to Inughuit reveals the explorers' cultural presuppositions that they alone were responsible for any achievements or discoveries, and their inability to acknowledge the indispensable role of their Aboriginal companions. For the majority of expeditions to the region, it should be recalled that two cultures were involved in the undertakings. These cultures were not monolithic entities, but were groups of individuals, each individual bringing his or her own personality to the encounters. At the same time, differences in power within the parties ensured that the voices of some individuals were heard and others ignored. To give due credit to these actors, it is necessary to delve beneath the official record to note the subtle ways these participants communicate their presence, even in the narratives in which they form an invisible backdrop to the feats of European heroes.

6

Early Exploration of the High Arctic by Europeans, 1818–90

Ross, Parry and the Opening of Whaling in Northern Baffin Bay, 1818

Following the conclusion of the Napoleonic Wars, Britain emerged as the most powerful economic and military power in the world, supported by its undisputed pre-eminence as a naval power.[1] Its maritime hegemony confirmed, Britain soon renewed its search for the Northwest Passage to Asia. The specific impetus for the resumption of the search in northern Baffin Bay was the announcement by William Scoresby, Junior, a whaler, in 1817, that the ice in these waters had recently receded, and he had penetrated Baffin Bay near the Greenland coast to 74° N. latitude.[2] Soon after, Sir Joseph Banks, president of the Royal Society, supported by John Barrow, second secretary of the British Admiralty, proposed a revival of the quest for the Northwest Passage via the North Pole. It was quickly endorsed by the First Lord of the Admiralty and approved by the Prime Minister. In an anonymous review published in October 1817, Barrow announced plans to send ships to the Arctic—two to Baffin Bay and the other two north of Spitsbergen. He wrote that reports of a southerly ocean current in the Davis Strait, accompanied by driftwood, implied an opening in the ocean waters to the north. In his assessment, these ocean currents themselves were evidence that the Arctic Ocean to the north was in perpetual motion and unlikely to be frozen over at any time. This was a revival of a long-standing hypothesis in polar exploration, the idea of an "open polar sea."

For the voyage to Baffin Bay, the British navy sent two ships to the region, the *Isabella* commanded by John Ross and the *Alexander* under William Parry. Reaching northern Baffin Bay by late July, the British observed "an immense number of whales."[3] Encountering heavy ice floes, carried by a surprisingly strong southerly current, Ross was encouraged to continue the journey to the north. On 9 August, while anchored to an ice floe by an island at the entrance to Wolstenholme Sound (75° 55′ N. lat., 65° 75′ W. long.), the ships' company spotted three sledges drawn by dog teams, carrying a total of four persons.

The ships had made very little progress, when we were surprised by the appearance of several men on the ice, who were hallooing, as we imagined, to the ships; the first impression was, that they were ship-wrecked sailors, probably belonging to some vessel that had followed us, and had been crushed in the late gale; we therefore tacked, hoisted out colours, and stood in for the shore. On approaching the ice, we discovered them to be natives, drawn on rudely-fashioned sledges, by dogs, which they continued to drive backwards and forwards with wonderful rapidity. When we arrived within hail, Sackheuse called out to them, in his own language; some words were heard in return, to which a reply was again made in the Eskimaux, but neither party appeared to be in the least degree intelligible to the other.[4]

The people on the shore departed but they returned the following day in greater numbers and met the British on the ice near the ship, enticed by an offering of gifts by the crew. They were the Inughuit, and this meeting was the first documented encounter between these people and Europeans. Members of this Aboriginal group were amazed to encounter the strange people who had arrived in the ships. Observing that these people "seemed to be altogether in a state of nature," a member of the crew of the *Alexander* stated that they were "perfectly ignorant ... of whatever belongs to every part of the globe."[5] In the days that followed, Ross's party traded a number of items, including knives, glass articles, and beads in exchange for Inughuit knives, narwhal horns, and "sea-horse teeth" (Figure 33). It was the beginning of a pattern of cultural exchange that continued, with significant interruptions, throughout the contact era.[6]

Few explorers followed immediately into upper Baffin Bay, but Ross's voyage showed the potential for whaling in these remote waters. The following year, British whalers returned and initiated a resource extraction industry that set a pattern for future use of the region by Europeans over the next century. However, in 1830, the whalers experienced the first of a series of disasters that demonstrated the continuing power of the natural environment. In that year 22 ships caught in the pressure ice were crushed and had to be abandoned.[7] It was the first of a series of misfortunes befalling the British whaling fleet in the 1830s. In 1835 and 1836, 230 deaths among the crews of seven Scottish whaling ships were reported in arctic seas.[8] As a result of these and other losses, the numbers of ships dispatched to Davis Strait and Baffin Bay dwindled considerably. An average of slightly more than 15 whalers operated in these waters between 1840 and 1849.[9] There is no evidence that any of these ships sailed beyond the northern parts of the Bay, although they reportedly stopped periodically to trade with Inughuit at Cape York and Saunders Island.[10]

Figure 33: "First Communication with the Natives of Prince Regents Bay as Drawn by John Sackheouse and Presented to Captain Ross, August 10, 1818." National Archives of Canada, Photograph no. C-119412. Handcoloured aquatint by John Sackeuse, 1818-19. Plate originally published in John Ross, *A Voyage of Discovery, Made under the Orders of the Admiralty, in His Majesty's Ships Isabella and Alexander, for the Purpose of Exploring Baffin's Bay and Inquiring into the Probability of a North-West Passage*, Vol. I (1819).

The Search for Franklin and Penetration of Smith Sound, 1848–52

The impetus to renewed exploration in the region was the search for the missing expedition of Sir John Franklin in the late 1840s. A byproduct of the search was the discovery of arctic regions previously unknown to Europeans. While the focus of activity was in the area of Lancaster Sound, several voyages looked for traces of the missing expedition in the northern reaches of Baffin Bay. In the process, they intensified contact with the Inughuit, while extending the world's awareness of the region.

Even before the abandonment of the Franklin Search it began to give way to a renewal of efforts to be the first to reach the North Pole. The emphasis gradually shifted from a humanitarian undertaking to an open preoccupation—and ultimately, obsession—with attaining the Pole and the honours expected to accrue to its conquerors. By the 1870s, the search for the Pole became the overriding justification for continued exploration of the region. During the third quarter of the nineteenth century, European High Arctic exploration culminated in a succession of high-profile wintering expeditions to northern Ellesmere Island, previously one of its least-known regions. At the cost of many lives, they provided Western societies with first-hand knowledge of one of the world's most remote regions. In the course of their explorations, the assorted explorers also initiated a long-term association with the region and its Aboriginal inhabitants.

Expedition of Edwin DeHaven, 1850–51

The initial impetus for American involvement in north polar exploration came from outside the United States, in the appeal from England for assistance in locating the members of the expedition of Sir John Franklin. In 1850, Lady Franklin wrote to U.S. President Zachary Taylor to request the assistance of the American government. In particular, she requested that American whaling crews be enlisted in looking for traces of her husband's expedition. Taylor passed the request to Secretary of State John M. Clayton, who responded by implicitly promising to send a search party.[11] Concurrently, Silas Burrows, owner of a ship-building firm in New York, wrote to the secretary of state to advocate sending a U.S. expedition in search of Franklin. President Taylor sent this correspondence to Congress, but in the meantime, Henry Grinnell, a wealthy ship owner and merchant from New York, took up the cause. Grinnell offered to purchase two ships and to refit them for arctic work if the U.S. Navy would staff the vessels and provide provisions and scientific instruments.[12]

Pending congressional approval, Grinnell pursued the matter with Lieutenant Matthew Maury of the Naval Observatory and Hydrographic Office, who selected Lieutenant Edwin J. DeHaven to assume the role of expedition leader. Together, Grinnell and DeHaven selected two ships: a 90-tonne schooner, which was strengthened and re-rigged as a brigantine and renamed the *Rescue*, and a larger brig of 142 tonnes, the *Advance*. Following approval by the U.S. Senate, the Secretary of the Navy, in consultation with Maury, drew up official instructions to the expedition. This document revealed Maury's emphasis on obtaining scientific information about the region, as much as addressing the official goal of searching for Franklin. The *Advance* and the *Rescue* were instructed to search various channels in the Canadian archipelago but, if unable to penetrate the Barrow Strait, to attempt to push northward through Jones Sound or Smith Sound. These instructions reflected the still-current belief in the "open polar sea" to the north.[13]

Departing from the United States in May 1850, the expedition's two ships encountered heavy ice in Baffin Bay. After being caught in the ice for three weeks, they sought refuge in the more protected waters of Melville Bay before working their way westward across the North Water. En route, they stopped near Cape York and landed twice south of Cape Athol, where they made contact with the Inughuit of that area.[14] It was the first encounter between Americans and the Aboriginal people of northern Greenland who would play such an important role in future expeditions from the United States.

DeHaven's party then proceeded to Lancaster Sound, where, along with other ships involved in the Franklin search, they visited a wintering site of the missing expedition on Beechey Island. At a meeting with the commanders of British ships involved in the search, they agreed that William Penny would continue their efforts to the west, John Ross would proceed into Prince Regent Inlet, while DeHaven would attempt to press north through Wellington Channel. Stopped by the ice at 75° 24' N. lat., their ship was frozen into the ice and commenced a drift that would ultimately take them back out into Davis Strait; they were only able to extricate themselves the following summer, returning to New York on 30 September 1851.[15]

Voyage of Commander E.A. Inglefield, 1852

In 1852, British Commander E.A. Inglefield demonstrated both the existence of a salt water channel beyond Smith Sound and the possibility of navigating through its ice dam. Inglefield commanded the *Isabel*, one of several Royal Navy ships then in the region in search of the missing Franklin expedition. After departing Peterhead, England on 10 July 1852, the *Isabel* followed the west coast of Greenland to the Thule District, reaching Cape York by 20 July.[16] Stopping briefly to trade with the Inughuit, the *Isabel* continued toward Cape Alexander, northern Greenland, at the far northern end of Baffin Bay, and passed through Smith Sound on 26 July. Inglefield later wrote of his excitement at this point at the possibility of reaching either the North Pole or the Northwest Passage; his mention of Franklin's party seemed almost an afterthought:

> We were entering the Polar Sea, and wild thoughts of getting to the Pole — of finding our way to Behring Strait — and most of all, of reaching Franklin and giving him help, rushed rapidly through my brain. A few hours and we should either be secure in our winter quarters, or else plying onward in the unfreezing Polar Basin.[17]

Proceeding into Kane Basin, Inglefield observed the Greenland coast to comprise a table land "broken up by vast glaciers." Two prominent headlands flanked the entrance to the basin; he named the one on the Ellesmere Island side after Prince Albert. The ship reached a north latitude of 78° 28'21", surpassing by 210 km the farthest north attained by previous sailings to Baffin Bay.[18] His party witnessed the widening of the channel, giving rise to the belief that they had reached the shores of the polar sea. Inglefield named the next bay to the north after the Princess Marie, Duchess of Hamilton. He directed his men to manoeuvre toward Ellesmere Island's central coast to erect a cairn and hoist the British flag, but they were forced back by the grinding pack ice of the basin.[19] On the return voyage, Inglefield explored parts of Jones Sound and the southern coast of Ellesmere Island until turned back by increasingly heavy fog.[20] Having skirted both the southeast and southern coasts of this large land mass to the west of Greenland, he sketched out the beginnings of geographical knowledge of a new land mass, which the British subsequently named Ellesmere Land after the vice-president of the Royal Geographical Society.

Expedition of Elisha Kent Kane, 1853–55

Following DeHaven's return, a member of his party, Elisha Kent Kane, was soon formulating plans with Grinnell for a second arctic expedition.[21] The specific impetus was the news of Inglefield's successful foray to the Smith Sound region, as Kane became alarmed that the following year the British might return to the region and reach the "open polar sea" before the Americans. He announced his own plans to return to the region in a presentation to the American Geographical Society in New York in December 1852.[22] Officially justifying an expedition in terms of the search for Franklin, Kane persuaded his American backers of his conviction that the Franklin party had reached the presumed open sea and had been marooned there by ice.

While Grinnell was apparently motivated by humanitarian impulses, the prospect of making new geographical discoveries, in particular the North Pole, was prominent in Kane's thought.[23] Kane therefore proposed to John Pendelton Kennedy, Secretary of the Navy, that his orders be worded to read "at the request of Lady Franklin, for the purpose of taking an Overland Journey from the upper waters of Baffin's Bay to the Shores of the Polar Sea,"[24] leaving him plenty of scope to pursue his overriding ambitions. In his book on his expedition, Kane subsequently recounted his plans to sail up Baffin Bay

> "to the most northern attainable point, and thence, pressing on toward the Pole as far as boats or sledges could carry us, examine the coastlines for vestiges of the lost party."[25]

Preoccupied with vanquishing his British rivals, Kane pointed out that, on his ship's initial approach, they reached the headland of Smith Sound and "passed the highest point attained by our predecessor, Captain Inglefield, R.N."[26] Later, when Kane was planning his sledge excursions, his crew member Johan Petersen observed: "Dr. Kane wanted to outdo the English."[27]

In the spring of 1854, two of Kane's parties undertook sledge journeys which led the way for future Euro-North American exploration to the far reaches of Nares Strait and northern Ellesmere Island. For the first journey, Dr. Isaac Israel Hayes and William Godfrey were charged with exploring the northwest coast of Smith Sound, i.e., the central coast of Ellesmere Island.[28] On 20 May they departed from Kane's ship with a light sledge, seven dogs, 10 days' provisions, and trail gear. For two days they made rapid progress, before rugged pressure ice in the straits presented severe difficulties to their forward advance. By 27 May, with most of their provisions gone, they reached the Ellesmere coast. Here, Hayes planted a flag at the summit of Cape Fraser and bestowed the name "Grinnell Land"[29] on the terrain named Ellesmere Land by Inglefield just two years before. Proceeding along the coast of Kane Basin, Hayes and Godfrey found sledging along the ice foot much easier than the difficult crossing of the pack ice in the channel. On 28 May, they reached their maximum northerly point at 79°42' 9" N. lat., which Hayes estimated to be 240 to 320 km farther northeast than was attained by previous expeditions. At this point, they turned to the southwest and entered Dobbin Bay on the Ellesmere side of the channel. Hayes and Godfrey then followed the Ellesmere coastline back to Cape Sabine, where they crossed the sound to return to the ship on 1 June.[30]

The other notable sledge journey was by William Morton, accompanied by the West Greenlander Hans Hendrik and two other Americans, who sledged in July up the Greenland coast of Kane Basin and Kennedy Channel as far as Cape Constitution on Hall Basin, only about 50 km across from the mouth of Lady Franklin Bay. From a vantage point he estimated to be about 100 m above sea level, Morton viewed a succession of physical features on Ellesmere Island across the channel. Beyond the coastal cliffs, which he traced to a distance of up to 80 km, he sighted a distant range of mountains.[31] Morton may have spotted the United States Mountains, the dominant range in northern Ellesmere Island. As well, he discerned a widening of the channel into a "boundless, iceless sea," considered by his companions to be confirmation of the presumed "open polar sea."[32] To assert U.S. territoriality, Morton temporarily converted his walking pole into a flag pole, to which he affixed the Grinnell flag of the ship *Antarctic*. Wrote Kane: "It was now its strange destiny to float over the highest northern land, not only of America but of our globe."[33]

Kane's expedition was hampered by an outbreak of scurvy and the effective loss of his ship which was frozen into the ice and could not be extricated. After using much of the ship's lumber for fuel and exhausting their provisions, the party was saved from starvation by the Inughuit who shared their food with them.[34] In the fall of 1854 the Inughuit brought them bear meat, seal, walrus, fox, and ptarmigan. The following summer, they brought the Americans birds on a daily basis and facilitated their retreat by carrying their provisions and stores to the floe edge, prior to their departure for the south.[35] In May 1855, the party began its crossing of Melville Bay in three small boats, reaching Upernavik on 6 August. While confining most of his activity to the Greenland coast, Kane had charted the length of much of Nares Strait and had given names to many features along Ellesmere Island's eastern coast (Figure 34).

The expedition's principal claim to geographical discovery—Morton's reported sighting of land on Ellesmere Island north of Cape Constitution—was challenged in Kane's own era. Danish folklorist and historian Henrik Rink, who carried out field work with the Inughuit at Etah in this period, doubted Morton's claims regarding the reported land north of the Humboldt Glacier. British naval officer Captain Richard Collinson, a veteran of the Franklin search, subsequently calculated that Kane's positioning of Cape Constitution was 50 to 75 km farther south than the American had reckoned.[36] William Godfrey, a disaffected member of Kane's expedition, later expressed his own belief that the mountains reported by Morton were a hallucination.[37]

While Kane's expedition received only modest financial support from the federal government, the U.S. Congress did appropriate $150,000 to send two relief vessels when Kane's party did not return after the first year.[38] These ships missed encountering Kane's party, which had already commenced its retreat across Melville Bay to the south in whaleboats. Nevertheless, the appropriation for the relief expedition set a precedent for American official sponsorship of polar expeditions and affirmed the commitment of the United States to the extension of its national influence even to the most remote regions of the continent.

Perhaps Kane's principal achievement was to lead the first non-Aboriginal party to overwinter in this remote region of the High Arctic since the possible arrival of Norsemen from southern Greenland in the Middle Ages. Kane's expedition occasioned more intensive contact with the Inughuit than previous encounters. He was a pioneer among Western explorers in his reliance on Aboriginal guides and material culture, including the use of Inughuit dog teams, sledges, and skin clothing.[39] Another noteworthy aspect of Kane's voyages was the impact of his books on readers in both the United States and Britain. In three books on his expeditions,[40] Kane captured the excitement and exotic fascination of this remote land, previously largely unknown in both countries.

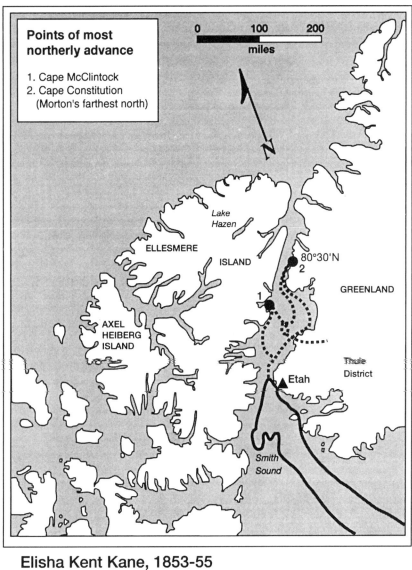

Points of most northerly advance

1. Cape McClintock
2. Cape Constitution
   (Morton's farthest north)

Elisha Kent Kane, 1853-55

••••••••••• Dog sledging excursions ━━━━━━ Ship

Figure 34: Map of the route of the expedition of Elisha Kent Kane, 1853–55

His gripping narratives, accompanied by the surreal engravings of arctic scenes by Van Ingen and Snyder, inspired a generation of adventurers, from Hayes to Peary, to continue in his path. Simultaneously, the
immense popular appeal of Kane's books sparked an enduring fascination with the region, generating the necessary popular support to sustain the polar quest.

Expedition of Isaac Israel Hayes, 1860–61

In 1860, Isaac Israel Hayes, who had served with Kane in 1853–55,
organized his own private expedition to the region to continue the
search for "an open sea within the Arctic Ocean."[41] His specific objectives were

> to complete the survey of the north coasts of Greenland and Grinnell
> Land, and to make such explorations as I might find practicable in the
> direction of the North Pole.[42]

Hayes also stated that he expected to contribute knowledge to the field
of climatology, anthropology, and natural history.[43] For this expedition,
Hayes intended to establish his base of operations on Ellesmere Island.
His plan was to sail through Nares Strait to about 80° N. latitude, then
haul a smaller boat by dog team over the pack ice adjacent to the coast
to what he expected was an open polar sea beyond. Then, if possible,
he would launch his boat northward toward the Pole.[44]

Unable to secure more than token government support for his expedition, Hayes nevertheless succeeded in raising $20,000 from pri-
vate donations.[45] He used the money to purchase a 135-tonne schooner,
re-christened it the *United States,* and recruited a small party of three
scientific personnel, eight merchant marine officers, and four other volunteers.[46] Hayes's plans to sail to 80°N. lat. were thwarted by heavy ice
conditions in Smith Sound, and with his ship damaged, he was obliged
to set up wintering quarters in Port Foulke, Greenland, just south of
Etah. Engaging the services of several Inughuit families, Hayes secured
adequate stores of food and fur garments prepared by the women. Prior
to departing on his principal excursion to the north, Hayes and his colleagues made a number of sledging trips. These included Hayes's eastward traverse 150 km across the Greenland ice cap, when Hayes lost all
his dogs, and a trip by August Sonntag, Hayes's second in command,
with his Greenland companion Hans Hendrik, to Whale Sound. Their
orders were to bring presents to lure the Inughuit to the ship as Hayes
wished to obtain the use of their dogs. During the journey between

Figure 35: View of Cape Louis Napoleon, US National Archives (Washington, DC), RG 401, Series XPX-1898-8892-2.

Sutherland and Northumberland Islands, Sonntag fell through the ice and froze to death. His death dealt a heavy blow to the expedition.[47]

With the objective of reaching the most northerly latitude possible on Ellesmere Island, Hayes set out on 4 April 1861 with his remaining men and dogs on the principal sledging trip. Proceeding north along the Greenland coast to Rensselaer Harbour, they struck out across the pack ice of Kane Basin toward Ellesmere. Out on the pressure ice of Nares Strait, his party met extremely rough sledging conditions.[48] On 28 April, with his exhausted party suffering from such ailments as an injured back, a sprained toe, and gastritis,[49] Hayes was obliged to send back most of his men, retaining only three companions for the balance of the traverse. Eventually reaching the Ellesmere coast on 1 May near Cape Louis Napoleon (Figure 35), they pressed on to the north. Travelling over the pack ice, the little party climbed up onto the ice foot. Hayes described the coast:

> great wall-sided cliffs rising at our left, and a jagged ridge of crushed ice at our right, forming a white fringe, as it were, on the dark rocks. We were, in truth, journeying along a winding gorge or valley, formed

by the land on one side and the ice on the other; for this ice-fringe rose about fifty feet above our heads, and, except here and there where a cleft gave us an outlook upon the sea, we were as completely hemmed in as if in a canyon of the Cordilleras.[50]

Within three days, they discovered a prominent headland, to the north of which a broad inlet stretched far into the interior of Ellesmere Island. While attempting to traverse this body of water, the party's further advance was arrested by rotten ice. In an attempt to circumvent the impassable ice, they made a brief foray out into the ocean, to no avail. Returning to the shore, Hayes climbed a cliff, where he observed the coast stretching to the north, culminating in a lofty promontory, which he named Cape Union. The ocean extended to the northeast, and the blue sky beyond it seemed to signify the presence of a large open body of water, in Hayes's mind, the open polar sea. According to Hayes's calculations, they had reached latitude 81° 35' N. lat. At this place, where he believed Kennedy Channel opened to the Polar Basin, he erected a cairn, hoisted two flags, and deposited a record in a glass vial.[51]

While it was long believed that Hayes had arrived at the mouth of Lady Franklin Bay, researchers now believe he probably reached Cape Joseph Good or perhaps Cape Lawrence at 80° 11' N. lat., 100 km to the south[52] (Figure 36). His attempt to negotiate the eastern coast of Ellesmere Island with dogs and Inughuit sledges, a continuation of methods followed by prior Native travellers to Ellesmere Island and his former colleague William Morton on the opposite side of Nares Strait in the 1850s, anticipated the methods of transport employed to greater effect a generation later by Robert E. Peary.

Expedition of Charles Francis Hall, 1871–73

Even before the conclusion of Hayes's expedition to Smith Sound, the Civil War had broken out between the northern and southern United States and the young American republic was drawn into the most violent episode of domestic U.S. history. The North's victory in 1865 left the nation exhausted and consumed in the reconstruction effort. And yet, the late 1860s were simultaneously a period of revived expansionist sentiment, as American imperialists clamoured for the annexation of the new Dominion of Canada to the American union.[53]

The revival of expansionist sentiment also provided a favourable ideological climate for the renewal of American interest in arctic exploration, as promoted by C.F. Hall. In the 1860s, Hall had led two expeditions to the Canadian Arctic, nominally as part of the efforts to find the Franklin party, which provided material for two bestselling books. On

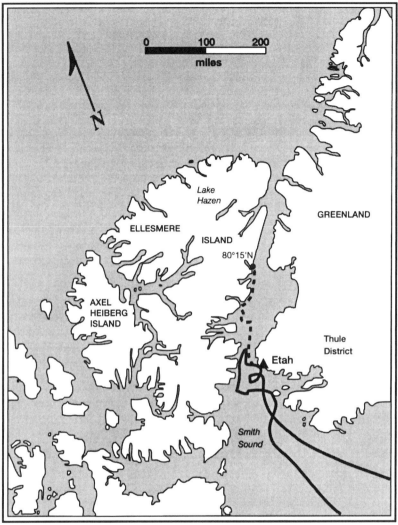

Isaac Israel Hayes, 1860-61

▪ ▪ ▪ ▪ ▪ ▪ ▪ Sledging excursions (dog sledging)

▬▬▬▬▬▬ Ship

● Cape Joseph Good, Hayes's probable farthest north

Figure 36: Map of the route of the expedition of Isacc Israel Hayes, 1860–61

his return to the United States, he devoted much of the period from late 1869 to early 1871 to lobbying influential members of the United States Congress and President Ulysses S. Grant for government support for the expedition. In February 1870, Hall visited the president at the White House and enlisted his support for another foray to the Arctic. A short time later, he delivered a lecture at Lincoln Hall, with the president and influential members of Congress in attendance. Their support translated into bills passed by both houses of Congress to authorize and appropriate $50,000 to fund an expedition to the North Pole.[54]

In June 1871, Secretary of the Navy George Robeson issued his instructions to Hall. He ordered that, after proceeding across Melville Bay to Cape Dudley Digges,

> you will make all possible progress, with vessels, boats and sledges, toward the North Pole, using your own judgement as to the route or routes to be pursued, and the locality for each winter's quarters.[55]

For an expedition ship, the navy refitted the *Periwinkle*, a 381-tonne steam tug, which Hall renamed the *Polaris*. The crew was to consist of 25 officers and seamen, three scientists, the Inuit couple Ebierbing and Tookoolito, who had served with Hall before, and their child. It was also prearranged that, on the way to Smith Sound, the ship would stop at Prøven in Western Greenland to pick up Hans Hendrik, another experienced hunter and guide, his wife, and their three children.[56]

Thus, in 1871 the seasoned polar explorer departed for one last hurrah in the High Arctic with the straightforward objective of becoming the first person to reach the North Pole. Hall was so intent on reaching the Pole that he decided, if all else failed, to simply ask the U.S. Navy to drop him ashore on Ellesmere Island as far north as possible. From there he would attempt to make his way north toward his goal, although if implemented, this desperate plan would have been tantamount to suicide.[57]

Departing from New York City on 29 June 1871, the *Polaris* made several stops on the western coast of Greenland before reaching Smith Sound on 27 August. Within 24 hours, the ship passed through the length of Kane Basin and entered the narrows of Kennedy Channel. Good sailing conditions enabled the party to continue past the previous Euro-American farthest norths registered by Kane and Hayes into the widened section of Nares Strait, now known as Hall Basin, and through the narrows of Robeson Channel to its northern mouth opening out onto the Arctic Ocean. On 30 August, at latitude 82° 11' N. lat., the ship encountered an impenetrable ice barrier which stopped its forward movement, while

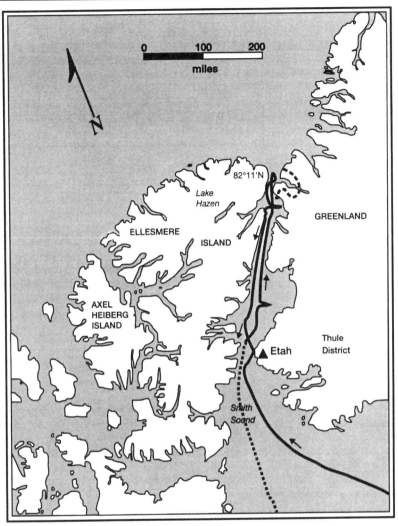

Charles Francis Hall, 1871-73

—————— Ship

▪ ▪ ▪ ▪ ▪ ▪ ▪ ▪ Sledging excursions (dog sledging)

▪ ▪ ▪ ▪ ▪ ▪ ▪ ▪ ▪ ▪ Drift on the ice floe

Figure 37: Map of the route of the expedition of Charles Francis Hall, 1871–73

the strong current in the channel caused it to drift to the south (Figure 37). Hall took a boat ashore on the Greenland side of the channel to search for a wintering harbour. Failing to find a suitable site, he raised the American flag at Repulse Harbour, the most northerly site to that date and claimed the territory for the United States.[58]

Returning to the ship, Hall decided to sail west toward northern Ellesmere Island, which he named Grant Land after the U.S. president. He had hoped to find open water by the shore affording a path to the north but, within a short time, the *Polaris* became trapped in the ice floes. Faced with the danger that the ship would be crushed in the ice, Hall ordered his crew to unload their provisions on the ice. After being driven to the south by a floe, the ship was freed, and its captain was able to work it over to a sheltered bay south of Cape Lupton. Hall's relief at finding what he believed to be a safe refuge was expressed in the name he gave it—Thank God Harbour.

Preparing to winter there, Hall endeavoured to explore the land to the north along the eastern side of Hall Basin and Robeson Channel. Soon after undertaking a reconnaissance mission to the northwest, to 83° 5' N. lat.,[59] he was stricken by a series of severe seizures and died on 8 November. On 21 November, the ship was torn loose from its moorings in the ice but again became lodged on a floe. On this frozen anchorage the crew established wintering quarters aboard ship. With the hull rising and falling with the tides, the Aboriginal guides and their families left the ship and set up their winter quarters ashore.[60]

Despite the ice barrier that the expedition encountered earlier in Robeson Channel, the new expedition commander, Captain Budington, decided to continue seeking the Pole by means of small boats the following summer. The first of these was crushed in the ice, while one of the other two boats found enough open leads to sail around Cape Lupton. Meanwhile, in August 1872, the *Polaris* became free from the ice, but efforts to sail to the north met with little success, and it began to drift again to the south. With the ship leaking and seriously weakened by the pressure of the ice, the party began to make preparations to abandon ship and set up quarters on the ice floe. While this work was in progress, the ship broke free and the 15 persons on board drifted helplessly to the south, while the other 19 were marooned on the floe. Meanwhile the *Polaris* subsequently drifted to the north, where Captain Sidney Budington and the remaining ship's company were able to bring the disabled vessel to land on the shore of northern Greenland near Etah. Building a hut with the ship's timbers and canvas, they were able to survive the winter there with the aid of food provided by the Inughuit. The ship itself was caught in the ice and sank, but in the spring the party fashioned a boat from panelling they had salvaged from the *Polaris* to enable a retreat across Melville Bay similar to Kane's retreat in the 1850s.[61]

Adrift on an Ice Floe

It was to be the fate of Hall's last expedition that it is remembered not for the explorer's "farthest north" but the remarkable story of the other group's protracted drift to the south on a slowly melting ice floe. The heroes of this strange conclusion to Hall's dreams of glory were the Inuit men and women whose skills enabled the entire group to survive the ordeal. Soon after being stranded on the ice floe, this group of Hall's party set up their quarters. For shelter and food, they relied on the knowledge and skills of their Inuit guides from Baffin Island. Four snow-domed houses were built from snow blocks cut by the Inuk Joe Ebierbing—one for each family and the others for the ship's officers and crew. In the crew's shelter, the tent canvas and a muskox skin were thrown over the floor, and another skin served as an over-covering. A small amount of heat was generated by two makeshift oil lamps fashioned from two used pemmican tins.[62] The igloos were connected by snow-domed passages that branched off from a shared entrance vestibule, while the officers and crew's quarters shared a common entrance.[63] Soon after building the shelters, the Aboriginal hunters shot three seals, which provided the group with both fuel oil for the Inuit lamps and two meals a day for each person.[64] As well, Joe Ebierbing spotted a drifting expedition boat, which they recovered with its contents of 365 kg of provisions, further enhancing their chances to survive while marooned in the polar seas.

By 13 March 1873, the floe had drifted far to the south, to 64°32' N. lat., adjacent to Cumberland Sound in Davis Strait.[65] The party spent the month of April in extremely perilous circumstances, as the disintegrating ice floe became increasingly unstable. By 30 April, they were successful in signalling their presence to the Newfoundland sealing steamer, the *Tigress*, which rescued the stranded party. They were at this point south of 53° 30' N. lat., having drifted more than 3,000 km over the six-and-a-half-month period of the drift.

Apart from the fleeting glimpses of northern Ellesmere and the farthest north attained on the initial approach, the expedition achieved little of lasting significance to arctic science. Nevertheless, the dramatic story of the ice floe drift, highlighted during a subsequent investigation of the expedition, underscored the value of Aboriginal environmental knowledge to survival in the unpredictable conditions of the High Arctic region.

Pomp and Circumstance: The British Arctic Expedition of 1875-76

The British Arctic Expedition of 1875–76 was the first European party to land and winter in northern Ellesmere Island and one of the first wintering groups to visit this remote region since members of the Thule culture finally abandoned multi-year occupation of the region after ca. AD 1700 in the wake of climatic deterioration. While proponents of this expedition espoused differing objectives, it was ultimately the national competition with the United States for polar honours that won the day. Between 1865 and 1874, when plans for the expedition were finalized, a core of North Pole enthusiasts within the British Admiralty succeeded in promoting the concept sufficiently with the public to enlist the support of the government. In particular, Clements Markham, editor of the new journal *Geographical Magazine*, proved a tireless advocate of an expedition, although he was dismayed to discover that his intended focus on science was swept away by the senior naval officers' imperial objectives. In a retrospective account Markham recalled that, in the 12 years leading up to the announcement, the Royal Geographical Society had been urging the British government to support an expedition on scientific grounds. Once the undertaking had passed into the hands of the Admiralty, however, these arguments were disregarded. "It was announced that the main object of the expedition was to attain the highest latitude and if possible, to reach the North Pole!"[66]

As well, by 1874 Benjamin Disraeli had returned to power and the new Prime Minister's concerns with enhancing national prestige helped tip the balance in favour of approving a party with geographical exploration as its primary object.[67] Endorsing the Arctic Expedition, Disraeli hailed both the scientific advantages and "the importance of encouraging that spirit of maritime enterprise which has ever distinguished the English people."[68] Beyond the lofty sentiments, British authorities, particularly the influential core of senior officers within the Admiralty, were also concerned about the extension of American influence in the Smith Sound region, most recently through the Hall expedition of 1871. Their overriding objective for the expedition was to send a party to be the first to reach the North Pole.[69] Only two days before the departure of the expedition, the venerable arctic explorer Dr. John Rae wrote to the *London Times* to express his expectation that the party had a good chance of attaining the prize. If the preceding winter had not worsened the sea-ice conditions, Rae thought that both ships should be able to reach the point where C.F. Hall wintered, perhaps even the place 48 km farther north where Hall had advanced with sledges and found a navigable ocean and "water sky" to the north. He wrote:

If this sea be navigable for 200 miles [320 km] further, the leading ship might advance within 300 miles of the Pole, and would have a fair prospect of arriving there, either on sledges in the spring, or by sledge and boat operations in the summer of 1876.[70]

Behind the avowed desire to attain the North Pole, a number of underlying geopolitical motives may also explain the British government's decision to send the expedition. The American historian Beau Riffenburgh has argued that the government wished to reinforce the rights of its whaling industry to the resources of Baffin Bay. As well, the Royal Navy was beginning to lose its expertise in arctic navigation, and the Admiralty recognized the need to burnish its skills. Further, following the Austro-Hungarian Exploring Expedition in 1872–74, Britain had experienced a loss of prestige as the pre-eminent exploring power in polar regions and needed a renewed demonstration of its polar achievements. For all of these diverse purposes, an arctic expedition could serve to re-assert British presence in the region.[71]

With expedition personnel of 61 officers, seamen, and marines aboard HMS *Alert*, and a similar crew of 59 men on HMS *Discovery*, the expedition's two ships set sail from Portsmouth on 29 May 1875. As was by now common practice with polar expeditions, they stopped en route at Prøven to hire two Greenlanders to serve as hunters and guides. They were Christian Peterson, who was to serve as an interpreter, and the "Esquimaux" Hans Hendrik, by now a seasoned High Arctic explorer who had served with three previous wintering expeditions. Making additional stops to purchase sealskins for overboots and hire 55 husky dogs for the winter,[72] the ships passed through Smith Sound in late July and negotiated the narrow passage through Kennedy Channel to arrive off Lady Franklin Bay off Ellesmere Island's northeast coast in late August. Leaving HMS *Discovery* under Captain George Stephenson to winter in the protected harbour that bears its name, Nares sailed on in the *Alert* through the narrow straits of Robeson Channel to the edge of the Arctic Ocean. Before establishing his own base at Floeberg Beach on the northeastern tip of Ellesmere Island, Nares's party landed a cache of 1,000 rations for subsequent sledging parties and then sailed as far north as the pack ice would allow, to mark a new farthest north of 82° 24' N. latitude.[73]

After securing the ships by the shore to serve as their respective wintering quarters (Figure 38), the commanders sent parties to various locations along the coast to lay caches for the sledging excursions scheduled for the following spring. During these fall forays the men had their first taste of the difficulties of man-hauled sledging that would later bring the expedition to a premature conclusion. One observer who re-

Figure 38: The HMS *Discovery* in wintering quarters, Lady Franklin Bay, 1875–76. National Archives of Canada, Photograph no. C-52573.

corded his experiences was Reginald Fulford, a junior officer who accompanied an eight-man sledge team on an overland excursion in early October to lay caches along the western coast of Robeson Channel. In vain, his party struggled for two days to pull their 365-kg sledge load over rough terrain and deep snow. Concluding that further efforts would be futile, Fulford wrote in his diary: "I further consider overland travelling at present is utterly impracticable while the snow is soft."[74] Fulford also asserted his view that the rations provided to the men were inadequate and that the breakfast allotment should be increased by one-fourth. He expressed the view that their eight-man sledge should be reduced to a party of five, presumably charged with a lighter load. Fulford apparently felt strongly enough to send a letter along these lines to the captains. However, the military character of the expedition may have prevented a completely frank exchange, as he revised its text according to the order of his superior officer and his apparent regret over the appearance of insubordination. He wrote:

> My letter of the 7th inst, to the Capt. Is being sent in today altered by his wish & my intense disgust but fear it cannot be helped as in a rash moment I decided I would feel bound to stick to it, conscious it teaches me a lesson as no more will![75]

In any case, there is no evidence that the difficulties reported by Fulford and the other leaders of sledging crews had any impact on the commanders' plans to resume man-hauled sledging in the spring.

Following the fall sledging excursions, the men were engaged in various labours at the wintering sites of both the *Alert* and the *Discovery*. These included the additional precautions of burying of heavy anchors on the shore to provide a secure berth for the ships and the landing of large quantities of provisions on the shore. The offloading of stores was an insurance measure against unforeseen destruction of the ships from fire, or, in the case of the *Alert*, by moving pack ice. At Floeberg Beach, the men constructed a house of packing cases and casks of sufficient size that it could house the entire party of 60 men in the event of disaster. Christened "Markham Hall," this structure measured 15 metres long, 3.7 metres wide, and 3 metres high, and was roofed over with the mainsail of the ship. Here, the crews also constructed a number of other temporary structures on the land, such as the snow-block houses used to house their magnetic instruments, food stores, and a munitions depot.[76] A further labour requirement was the shovelling and maintenance of paths between these structures, described by the surgeon Edward Moss as "a whole system of catacomb-like passages."[77] At Discovery Harbour the crew of that ship also built a number of structures on the shore, illustrated in Figure 38.

The officers were of the view that successfully passing the polar winter depended on "strict discipline." Daily life at Floeberg Beach and Discovery Harbour was organized into a routine for all members of the expedition. Both Captain Nares and Dr. Edward Moss, the expedition surgeon, left descriptions of a typical winter day at the ships. Rising in the early morning, the men lit the oil lamps and the wardroom stove. After performing their ablutions, the enlisted men had breakfast at 7:30 a.m. An hour later, the officers gathered at their mess table, where cocoa, hot rolls, and lime juice, mixed with warm water, were consumed. All hands then gathered on deck for inspection at 10 a.m. Next, the chaplain conducted a brief service and led the men in prayers, after which they were assigned their work of the day.[78] For some men, the tasks to be carried out included cutting ice from the top of a floeberg with picks and drawing it by sledge back to the ship to be melted for drinking, cooking, and washing. Other teams were charged with transporting provisions on a large working sledge from "Markham Hall" to the ship. Meanwhile, the blacksmith and his assistants set to work on repairing the shovels for use in cutting snow for snow-block construction. In the event of snowdrift in the night, a party would be assigned the task of digging out the structures on shore such as the declinometer house.

At 1 p.m. the men re-assembled on board for dinner, after which they returned to labour outdoors until 4 p.m. Meanwhile, the officers' dinner followed at 2:15 p.m. Their fare consisted of such items as salt meat, either mutton or beef, preserved onions or carrots, and two glasses of sherry. Quiet time was scheduled after dinner to enable the officers to write in their diaries, to read, or to work on scientific observations or experiments. Tea followed at 6 or 7 p.m. This was a light meal, followed by instructional courses for the enlisted men, led by the officers on the lower deck until 9 p.m.[79] The evening concluded with a game of chess or card games.[80]

A preoccupation of the officers was keeping the men sufficiently occupied to resist the psychological effects of the long winter night. Their prescription was a healthy dose of "strict discipline." As the *Alert* surgeon Edward Moss explained:

> Routine must extend to the smallest domestic affairs. Some men would never go to bed, and others would never get up if there was nothing special to make them; and constant darkness is so enervating that few, if any, would keep up a steady, healthful amount of exercise without routine.[81]

During the dark winter months of mid-October to early March, the men were generally occupied with outside work at least five hours each day. In addition to the regular work regimen, schedules were drawn up for the monthly lashing up of hammocks and the airing of bedding; a washing day was arranged once a fortnight for each mess to wash their dirty laundry and to take a bath.

Captain Nares was a believer in maintaining recreation throughout the long winter darkness. To help boost morale at the *Alert*, regular live entertainment was scheduled on Thursday evenings at 7:30. The fare alternated between "pops programs of mixed songs, lectures, and readings, magic lantern programs, and burlesques staged by the Royal Arctic Theatre."[82] Much care was devoted to the making of costumes, including the use of muskox skins for wigs, and eiderdown quilts "converted into the robes of a lovely oriental princess."[83] For both ships in his command, Nares also provided a variety of sporting equipment and games, including footballs, chess and backgammon boards, boxing gloves, single sticks with baskets, foils and masks for fencing, lawn tennis sets, and race horse games. For musical entertainment and amusement, 12 fifes and 6 concertinas were provided to each ship.[84] At the *Discovery*, Reginald Fulford recorded having played frequent games of pool on a billiard table during the evenings between December and February.[85] With the return of daylight in late February, the evening recreational activities ceased as the men focussed on preparations for their forthcoming overland excursions.[86]

The spring sledging parties, which were to be the focus of the expedition's work, departed in early April. From the *Alert* at Floeberg Beach, Nares sent out two parties with man-hauled sledges, and two others were sent from the *Discovery*. Issuing instructions to the sledging parties, Nares acknowledged that the task would "undoubtedly be a very arduous and irksome one, and monotonous in the extreme," but he exhorted his men "to show that we possess the high quality of resolute perseverence to overcome whatever obstacles are before us."[87] Despite the difficulties encountered during the fall excursions, Captain N.F. Stephenson of the *Discovery* wrote on 28 March that

> the greatest enthusiasm exists on board about sledging and all think that if they do not have an opportunity, they will never be able to face their friends in England."

Stephenson was only too happy to oblige his men: "I have promised each and all a belly full of it, and no doubt they will get it before we have done."[88]

The party under the command of Lieutenant Pelham Aldrich was charged with exploring the northern coast of Ellesmere to the west. The northern party under Commander A.H. Markham was instructed to set out across the pack ice of the Arctic Ocean in search of a new "farthest north," and "to ascertain the possibility of a more fully equipped expedition reaching the North Pole."[89] While both excursions were to venture into uncharted regions, Markham's journey in particular represented a new departure. No European had ever before attempted to cross the polar ice pack. Much of its surface consisted of rugged pressure ridges formed when large ice floes were driven together, presenting an extremely difficult surface to cross. Moreover, the ice pack, in motion for much of the year, was highly unpredictable.

Markham's party began with four sledges, led by the "Marco Polo," a 12-man sledge hauling 1,075 kg and three other 8-man sledges hauling an average of 670 kg.[90] For the first leg of the journey the party travelled over the relatively level surface of the fast-ice adjacent to Ellesmere Island's northern coast, yet even here they experienced considerable difficulty. Edward Moss, the leader of HM Sledge "Bulldog" in the northern party, reported that his group immediately experienced great difficulty in pulling their sledge even over the first mile. The heavy sledges frequently became stuck; "it took a united effort with a 'one, two, three, haul!' to start it forward again." One of the men said that it was "like a plough with a cart-load on it."[91] These problems were magnified once the men attempted to strike out over the pack ice beyond Cape Joseph Henry. On 19 April, Markham reported that great exertion had advanced the largest sledge a mere 400 metres and he felt obliged to abandon it. It was no easier for the men hauling the smaller sledges, as they encountered great difficulty in moving their loads over the jagged pressure ridges and perpendicular drops between adjacent ice floes.[92]

Markham had planned for easier sledging once the loads were lightened by the consumption of provisions. Within weeks, however, his men began to suffer from such complaints as shortness of breath, loss of appetite, swollen ankles, and stiff legs, and the weights increased rather than diminished, as the sick individuals had to be placed on the sledges. By 8 May, Markham came to the realization that his men were suffering from scurvy.[93] On 10 May, with five of his party incapacitated and five others showing signs of scurvy, Markham "reluctantly" concluded that further efforts would place the entire party in peril and ordered a halt to their forward advance. Overall, they had travelled a distance of over 800 km to reach a new farthest north about 160 km to the north of Ellesmere Island at 83° 20' 26" N. lat.. They had reached a point about 640 km from the North Pole (Figure 39). To commemorate the achievement, the exhausted sledgers raised five flags, including the Union Jack, a white ensign, and three officers' standards. They gave three cheers, cheered the captain, and sang the "Union Jack of Old England," the grand Sledging Chorus, and concluded with "God Save the Queen."[94]

The coastal parties encountered difficulties similar to Markham's journey over the rugged pack ice when obliged to traverse ocean channels or to cross the mouths of numerous inlets and fiords while following the island's irregular coastline. Even when travelling along the preferred ice-foot surface, progress was difficult in areas where ice floes had been driven against the coastal belt, mounding the crushed ice to considerable heights. In these situations the men resorted to the use of pickaxes and shovels to hew a path, while drifting snow around the hummocks caused them to flounder up to their waists, resulting in "snail-like progress."[95]

With instructions to explore the "largest extent of land possible," to leave records at prominent headlands along the route, and to construct a "conspicuous cairn" at the farthest position attained,[96] Lieutenant Aldrich's party departed on 3 April. The sledge crews followed the northern coast of Ellesmere as far as Alert Point on the western side of Yelverton Bay. Travelling conditions were favourable on the outward trip and they made rapid progress. But by the end of May, several of these men, too, were beginning to show the signs of scurvy, forcing

Figure 39: "Lat. 81° 44' N., at Cape Beechey. The Nip. Cutting away the top of a grounded floeberg to enable it to float way and release the ship, August 1876." National Archives of Canada, Photograph no. C-52565.

Aldrich to order a retreat. Within a week their condition deteriorated, the men suffering from shortness of breath and others becoming completely incapacitated. For those remaining at their posts, the reduced numbers of men hauling imposed a heavy burden. By 18 June, he wrote that "all of the men nearly were only fit to be dragged on the sledge" but he exhorted them to incredible efforts to reach View Point, from which he intended to send for help from the ship.[97] In the meantime, Nares had already sent out a rescue party from the *Alert*. Using a dog team and sledge the men labouriously transported the stricken men back to the ship, a task that took a week to accomplish.

The most serious effects of scurvy were felt by the Eastern Sledge Party sent by Captain Stephenson from the *Discovery*. Under the command of Lieutenant L.A. Beaumont, this party was given orders to cross Robeson Channel and to explore the coasts of Greenland to the north and east. Two of its specific objectives were to reach Polaris Bay, the most northerly position reached by C.F. Hall on land, and to erect "a conspicuous cairn" at the farthest north attained by Beaumont's party, underlining the expedition's overriding objective of besting the Americans in geographical discovery.[98] Beaumont's group departed Discovery Harbour on 6 April. Separate reports by Beaumont and Lieutenant Reginald Fulford, the leader of one of his sledging crews, document the many difficulties and suffering experienced by these men. On the trail, they encountered both heavy sledging and severely cold temperatures, which hindered their ability to sleep. By May, they reached the Black Horn Cliffs of northern Greenland, where they were forced to negotiate treacherous scree slopes. Not only was the sledging extremely slow and arduous, the rugged terrain took its toll on the sledges, one of which was damaged and rendered useless by travel over this stretch. One of the crew, James J. Hand, displaying the signs of scurvy, became very ill. He died as soon as the party reached Polaris Bay on 3 June. By 25 June, Beaumont described four others as "now utterly prostrate sick"; of these, two were in critical condition,[99] including William Paul, who died on 29 June.

Through renewed hunting efforts, Greenlander Hans Hendrik was able to secure seal meat, which helped mitigate the effects of scurvy for the other stricken sledgers. On 12 July, Fulford and two other men headed back to the *Discovery* to enlist a relief party to come to the aid of their stricken compatriots.[100] When the larger party finally returned to the ship on 14 August, physician R.W. Coppinger wrote that, with two exceptions, the afflicted sledgers had been restored to health. He credited Hendrik with having saved many lives. He wrote:

> So fertile was he in expedients, so keen in appreciating the require-ments of the sick, and so skillful in hunting, without his aid we might have had to deplore a larger mortality.[101]

His commendation was echoed in the report of Fulford, who wrote:

> Hans Hendrick (Esquimaux) I beg leave to bring to your most favour-able consideration. His untiring energy, his ability in managing the dogs, and his unceasing efforts to procure game merits the highest approbation.[102]

Nevertheless, with half his expedition personnel suffering from scurvy and most of the remaining members in poor condition, Nares wrote on 16 June that "it was with the greatest regret I felt it my duty to give up the very interesting further examination of the northern coast of Green-land."[103] His previous orders provided that, following the release of the ships by the melting ice, the expedition party should retreat to the south to Port Foulke, "where we know that fresh meat can be obtained in great abundance." Nares intended that one ship would then return to England, while the other would remain in Smith Sound to explore

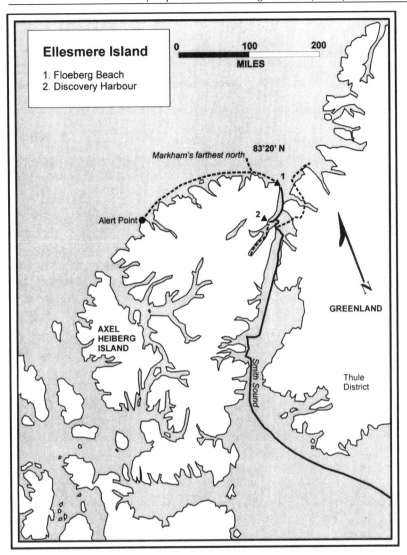

George Nares, 1875-76

————— Ship

---------- Sledging excursions, 1876 (man-hauled)

Figure 40: Map of the route of the expedition of George S. Nares, 1875–76

Hayes Sound, the only unexplored area of the region, before returning to England the following spring. The condition of his men had so deteriorated by mid-summer that he determined to bring back both the *Alert* and *Discovery* to England a year earlier than expected. Due to the buildup of sea ice in adjacent waters during the winter and spring, the crew of the *Alert* was only able to extricate this ship from its anchorage at Floeberg Beach in mid-August to sail to Discovery Harbour. There, on 20 August, the two ships' crews succeeded in dislodging their vessels from the ice to enable them to negotiate a narrow clearance back to the Nares Strait to make their way south (Figure 40). Following their return to England, the scurvy outbreak, which had contributed to three of four deaths during the expedition, was the subject of a Parliamentary investigation.[104] The Committee of Enquiry concluded that Nares had erred in not providing his men adequately with lime juice; however, a more recent paper on the issue has argued that a greater use of Ellesmere Island's game resources by the expedition members would have been needed to avoid the disease of scurvy altogether.[105]

Despite the errors that hampered the expedition and precipitated its early return, the British Arctic Expedition was hailed by some contemporary observers in Britain as a resounding success. In a historical narrative on exploration published only one year after its return, the English writer D. Murray Smith enumerated what he viewed as its major accomplishments:

> Captain Nares carried his ships to a higher latitude than had ever previously been reached by ships; he demonstrated the fact that Europeans may winter safely in a climate in which the most intense degree of atmospheric cold known prevails. He discovered that the Polar ocean is apparently a 'Sea of Ancient Ice,' and is certainly not an 'open sea;' his sledges reached a point within 400 miles [640 km] of the Pole itself — a point much farther than had ever before been reached; he explored the fringe of the frozen ocean over fifty degrees of longitude, and has thus added vastly to our knowledge of the heart of the Arctic region; and he has above all demonstrated that the skill and heroism of Englishmen, which have already won for England so many triumphs in the northern seas, remain unimpaired.[106]

In a subsequent publication, expedition member A.H. Markham tallied 12 additional achievements of Nares's party relating to scientific and geographical discovery.[107]

These positive assessments were countered by Nares's detractors in the naval community, who clamoured for an investigation from the moment of his return to England in 1876. Among other charges, an article in a prominent naval periodical castigated the commanding officer for alleged negligence in not personally leading the sledging crews but rather leaving the work to inexperienced men; for "unnecessarily risking the life and health of the men under his command" by the neglect of proper "sanitary arrangements" (meaning, the lack of adequate diet to prevent scurvy); and most galling to naval prestige, for "absence of zeal and determination in abandoning the objective of the expedition," the attainment of the North Pole.[108]

Whatever the accomplishments or failures of the British Arctic Expedition, it would be this country's last exploit in the great age of High Arctic exploration. Polar enthusiasts such as Clements Markham continued to press for a British presence in the Arctic, but with little tangible progress in securing either the economic benefits of a Northwest Passage or the symbolic prize of the North Pole, public support for continued investment in polar exploration waned. In 1880, Britain transferred the arctic islands to Canada; thereafter the young Dominion assumed responsibility for managing this vast, yet little-understood outpost of the British Empire.

Renewal of American Interest in the North Pole, 1868–1880

The Nares expedition's return to England in 1876 coincided with the opening of the Centennial Exposition in Philadelphia, a national exhibition of American culture, economy, and technology to celebrate the centenary of the founding of the republic. Including displays and artifacts from all regions of the globe, the exposition announced the United States' emerging status as a major power, intent on expanding its influence throughout the world.[109] In this imperialistic era, a prevailing frontier ethos of pitting heroes against a savage wilderness continued to animate the Anglo-American self-image even in the context of rapid population increase, industrialization and technological change.[110] Yet, the defeat of Custer at the Little Big Horn on 16 June shook the aura of invincibility promoted at Philadelphia.[111] The republic badly needed victories to reinforce its shaken convictions in continuous progress and American ascendancy. Over the next five years, the underlying ideological forces of expansionism and aspirations to national greatness, combined with a developing need for symbols of triumph over a hostile environment, provided fertile ground on which to sow the seeds of renewed arctic exploration.

The eventual American expedition to the same site on Discovery Harbour where the *Discovery* had wintered was the realization of a concept that developed currency in the United States over a period of nearly 20 years. The first American to propose establishing a colony on Ellesmere Island was Isaac Israel Hayes, who initially advanced the idea only a few years after returning from the High Arctic in 1862. In an address to the American Geographical and Statistical Society in 1868, Hayes elaborated on his proposal. Emphasizing the importance of arctic science in this flowery speech, Hayes nevertheless appealed to nationalistic and imperial sentiment, as he rhetorically asked:

> Shall the victory remain with the sea, or shall it remain with us? Shall we not make one more effort to plant over it the standard of our science, to wave over it the flag of our country?"[112]

In arguing for the efficacy of the Smith Sound route, Hayes presented a deceptively simple formula for an assault on the North Pole. In his view, the two essentials were the establishment of a base of operations on a polar land mass and "the opportunity to colonize a party of hunters and natives as a permanent support."[113] Hayes's talk was also noteworthy for his identification of Ellesmere Island as an appropriate land base for North Pole exploration. The viability of the overall concept of establishing a settlement on Ellesmere Island with Aboriginal hunters for permanent support was eventually demonstrated by Robert E. Peary in his expeditions around 1900 and later by the Royal Canadian Mounted Police detachments established in the 1920s.

Conditions were not yet ripe for Hayes's appeal to nationalism, but within a decade, promoters of arctic science were able to strike a responsive chord with the public and the federal government. The impetus for a science-based expedition to Ellesmere Island developed in the U.S. Army, within whose ranks the country's first weather service was organized in the nineteenth century. The importance of acquiring comprehensive weather information had long been recognized by the United States military, and arctic weather data were increasingly being viewed as essential to accurate forecasting.[114] From 1870, responsibility for the co-ordination of weather data was assigned to the Signal Office of the U.S. Army. Its head, Colonel Albert J. Meyer, energetically promoted its standing in United States government circles through extensive entertaining of Washington notables.[115] Only two years later, Congress expanded the scope of the Signal Office's meteorological operations to encompass the entire nation to provide "for such additional stations, reports and signals as may be found necessary for the benefit of Agricultural and Commercial interests."[116]

The return of the Nares expedition in 1876 was the specific catalyst for renewal of American participation in the North Pole quest. At this time, Captain Henry Howgate of the Signal Office delivered a series of addresses and publications to advance his own proposal to send an American party to the same area as the British party. The diverse character of his audiences—comprising both scientific and political groups—reflected the mixed objectives he was promoting. Lack of congressional support for funding army operations presented a continuing impediment to the Signal Office's ambitions,[117] but, in 1877, Howgate persuaded some members of Congress to sponsor a bill

> to authorize the President to fit out an expedition to the North Pole, and to establish a temporary colony for purposes of exploration and equip an expedition to the Arctic.[118]

Appended to the bill were various testimonials in support of the expedition, including one from Isaac Israel Hayes, who elaborated on his earlier concept, which had further evolved in the decade since his address of 1868. Interestingly, Hayes now favoured establishing a colony or base of operations in northern Greenland, accompanied by a network of caches along the coast of Ellesmere Island to the north. If the ice were too congested in Smith Sound,

> I would still have secured my object, for, with a provision depot now within six hundred miles of the pole, with the colony at my back, and in the winter readily accessible, with dogs breeding there, and with furs and provisions accumulating, I would have overcome the obstacles which embarrassed me in 1860 and 1861, and which had embarrassed Dr. Kane before me. Once in this favourable situation I would have brought up all my available strength from the colony, and, in the early spring, put out depots of provisions along the line of Grinnell Land, and following them up on a boat mounted on runners, I would then have sought the open water and the pole.[119]

In almost every major detail, Hayes anticipated the approach of Robert Peary during his expedition of 1898–1902 to northern Greenland.

The Signal Office, however, remained wedded to the notion of establishing its arctic station in northern Ellesmere Island, rather than the Thule District of Greenland 400 km to the south. According to the Howgate plan, expedition personnel would consist of 50 Army servicemen, three commissioned officers, two surgeons, an astronomer, and two or more naturalists, while one or more of the staff were to be competent to take meteorological observations. While sufficient supplies and provisions should be provided for three years, Howgate proposed that in addition the colony should be re-supplied annually with fresh food, and its diet supplemented by hunting game in the vicinity of the colony. An annual visit would also enable an exchange of personnel and information with the outside world, which he thought "would do much to alleviate the discomforts of the long arctic night and the feeling of isolation so graphically described by arctic explorers."[120] For shelter, Howgate proposed the transport of a few "strong, substantial buildings" on shipboard; he argued that special arctic accommodations were not required. Howgate cited the example of polar explorer C.F. Hall, who, he asserted, had found himself better able each year to withstand the severe climate. Likewise, "the colony would...become acclimatised, and eventually succeed in accomplishing the long-sought end."[121]

In 1878, Lieutenant Adolphus Greely of the Signal Corps presented Howgate's paper "Plan for the Exploration of the Arctic Regions" to the American Geographical Society of New York.[122] He would later assume the leadership of the Lady Franklin Bay expedition that was eventually sent in 1881 to fulfill Howgate's plan. By this time the concept had crystallized into the establishment of a colony at Discovery Harbour near the coal seam identified by the Nares expedition. Meanwhile, Congressman Benjamin Willis, representing the Committee of Naval Affairs of the U.S. House of Representatives, presented a Congressional report in 1878 proposing an "expedition to the Arctic Seas." In it he revived the clarion cry of competition with other nations, whose exploratory activities he viewed as threats to U.S. national prestige. He wrote:

> Other nations are already there or getting in readiness to be there. The way through Smith's Sound, where de Haven, Kane, Hall, and Hayes, by their heroic researches, have given immortal glory to America, seems to be the fittest field for Americans in this race for conquest and discovery.[123]

Howgate had in fact accurately detailed many of the key features of the eventual U.S. Army expedition, although when the expedition was finally staged in 1881, the plan had undergone several changes. Where Howgate had recommended a party of 50 men, the Greely expedition comprised a smaller party of 25. Howgate had also recommended that several Aboriginal men should be included to serve as hunters and guides and "an ample number" of Inuit dogs provided for sledging. By the time of the expedition, Greely as expedition commander scaled down this aspect of the proposal to a token complement of Greenlanders and dog teams.

Howgate was not without detractors. Dr. Emil Bessels, scientist with the Hall expedition of 1871 to northern Greenland, wrote that

> the valuable parts of [the plan] are based on the work of Hayes and Weyprecht; the rest, emanating from the brain of Lieutenant Henry W.

Howgate, bears testimony that the originator of the Howgate Plan was not familiar with even the rudiments of Arctic exploration....[124]

Bessels also enlisted the comments of Commander A.H. Markham of the Royal British Navy, who had travelled to Smith Sound in 1873 and served with the Nares expedition to northern Ellesmere Island in 1875–76. Markham was even more severe in his assessment of Howgate's proposal, as he wrote:

> It all reads and sounds very well, and perhaps may delude the inexperienced public; but speaking as an arctic man myself, I must confess that the scheme is utterly impracticable, and one that could only emanate from the brain of a conceited man desirous of notoriety, who has compiled his pamphlet from the works of others and brings it out as his own originality.[125]

Pending the departure of the party, the U.S. Congress approved Howgate's proposal to send a small ship to the Arctic "for the purpose of collecting such supplies during the winter as might be useful for the main expedition of 1878."[126] In the summer of 1877 the *Florence* sailed from Provincetown, Massachusetts under the command of Captain George Tyson, who had been with C.F. Hall's North Pole party in 1871–73. Tyson's instructions were to stop at Cumberland Sound on Baffin Island, recruit 10 Inuit families willing to travel to establish a colony on northern Ellesmere Island, and collect at least 25 dogs, "mostly females, and selected for their docility, training, strength and endurance," two sledges, and enough clothing to supply 50 persons for three years. The clothing was to be "carefully selected, of choice furs and skins, and all made up by native women."[127] After wintering in Cumberland Sound, the Inuit and their supplies were to be transported to Disco in Western Greenland, where they would meet and be transferred to the main expedition ship of 1878 to sail to Ellesmere Island. In the event, the *Florence* did winter in Cumberland Sound and recruited several families of Canadian Inuit, but the principal expedition plans foundered, and the Inuit were returned to their homelands around Cumberland Sound.

The Howgate plan might never have come to fruition but for the International Arctic Congress convened only three years later. At this meeting of meteorologists in Rome in 1879, General Albert J. Meyer, Chief Signal Officer of the U.S. Army, met Lieutenant Charles Weyprecht of the Austrian Navy, who proposed a co-ordinated plan to establish polar stations across the Arctic. The result was the first International Polar Year, an effort by the participating nations to undertake simultaneous scientific measurements at various locations within the Arctic

Circle. The United States undertook to send two parties to establish scientific research stations at Barrow, Alaska, and Lady Franklin Bay in northern Ellesmere Island. Areas of particular emphasis would be the study of meteorology, aurora, and earth magnetism, considered at the time to be the fields with the greatest gaps in scientific knowledge of the circumpolar regions.[128]

In 1880, as a result of these and other initiatives, the Secretary of War upgraded the Signal Office to the Signal Corps and promoted Meyer to brevet brigadier general, although he died within a few months of his promotion. Meyer's successor, Brigadier General William B. Hazen, vigorously promoted both scientific research and publication by his staff and reinforced the American commitment to send a Signal Corps expedition to the High Arctic. Most importantly, Hazen also had allies in the Congress, without whose approval expedition funding could not be obtained.

While the Signal Corps emphasized the scientific aspects, Congressional approval reflected a mix of objectives, motives, and ambitions. Presenting its report to the full House of Representatives in March 1880, the Congressional Committee on Naval Affairs recommended authorization and appropriations to equip an expedition along the lines of the Howgate plan and justified its recommendation on the grounds of "expected and hoped-for results—scientific, philosophic, and economic."[129] The report also emphasized the potential of the expedition to attain the North Pole. The committee identified Lady Franklin Bay as the preferred site for the wintering station largely for its strategic location as a staging point in this quest:

> To get farther north, or to reach the Pole, prompt advantage must be taken of such favouring circumstances [winds and temperatures] and to do this with the greatest certainty and with the least expenditure of time, money, and human life, it is essential that the exploring party be on the ground at the very time the ice gives way and opens the gateway to the long-sought prize, fully prepared to improve every opportunity that offers.[130]

The Congressional Committee accepted the argument that the British Arctic Expedition's failure to reach the Pole was due largely to "the abnormally cold season" and "the exceptional character of the winds" encountered by the British in 1876. Animated more by earnest hopefulness than science, the committee asserted that the American Army's expedition would master the forces of nature in attaining its geographical objective:

> It is reasonable to suppose, from past meteorological records, that these unusual conditions will not exist during the present season, and, in-

deed, may not occur again for several years. Instead of discouraging further effort, the result of Nares' expedition, from the causes named, should stimulate fresh endeavours and hold out a fair prospect of success. In any event, the little station on Lady Franklin Bay, during their three years' residence, besides having the opportunity of selecting an open season and becoming thoroughly hardened and acclimatised, would have their work narrowed down to a common focus — the pathway due north.[131]

In its buoyant assessment of the safety of the overall plan the Congressional Committee was matched by the optimism of the Signal Office Board charged with detailed planning of the expedition. Noting that the *Polaris* crew of C.F. Hall's expedition had left "abundant stores" only 48 to 56 km away from Lady Franklin Bay on the Greenland coast and the Nares expedition had left a "large quantity of biscuit at Cape York," the Board asserted: "there is little reason to anticipate any danger to the permanent station; it is to be provisioned for two years or more."[132] In one important respect the planned expedition differed from Howgate's earlier concept—rather than enlist a significant number of Inuit families to assist, the Signal Office now proposed to hire only one or two Aboriginal hunters, to be engaged when the expedition ship stopped at western Greenland on its way to Ellesmere Island. With such extensive provisions at their disposal, it was assumed, there would be no need for Indigenous hunting expertise.

The unbridled optimism of the Signal Office and its Congressional backers was echoed by the bullish predictions of the American exploration community. In May 1880, Reverend Benjamin Franklin Da Costa, a U.S. writer and proponent of expansionism, spoke on the forthcoming expedition in a talk on "Arctic Exploration" to the American Geographical Society in New York City. Focussing on the potential of the expedition to reach the North Pole, he reduced the issue to a straightforward question of technology: "the question of reaching the pole is now resolved into one of equipment." Asserting that by establishing a permanent colony at Lady Franklin Bay, the United States would readily reduce the dangers of polar exploration, he argued that "such work can no longer be objected to on the ground of its risk." Da Costa concluded with a rousing appeal to patriotism: "with prudence, courage and perseverance, the dream of the middle ages will be realized and the American flag will be planted at the Pole."[133]

The eventual Act to authorize and equip the expedition, approved by the U.S. Senate in April 1880, restated the three main objectives of the undertaking as "scientific observation and exploration, and to develop or discover new whaling grounds."[134] However, only a month later, the pro-

Figure 41: Personnel of the Lady Franklin Bay expedition. Plate from Adolphus Greely, *Three Years of Arctic Service*, Vol. I, p. 40.

ceedings of a board convened by the Signal Corps to organize the expedition confirmed that whaling discoveries were actually peripheral to their plans: "It is understood by the Board that the discovery and development of new whaling grounds would be incidental to the duties of exploration."[135] Geographical discovery, alongside science, would be paramount.

The U.S. Army's Lady Franklin Bay (Greely) Expedition, 1881–84

In July 1881 the United States Army's Lady Franklin Bay Expedition, under Greely's leadership, departed from St. John's, Newfoundland aboard the *Proteus*, a wooden Barkentine-rigged sailing steamer, which the expedition had commissioned to transport men, equipment, and building materials to Lady Franklin Bay off Ellesmere Island's northeastern coast. The ship was under the command of Captain Richard Pike, a seasoned Newfoundland seaman with experience navigating ice-congested waters off Labrador during the annual seal hunt.[136]

While officially focussing on scientific investigation of this remote region, expedition personnel, like the U.S. Congressional Committee sponsoring their activities, tended to view the expedition in terms of a competition with other countries for international honours. In this regard, they shared with the Nares expedition an unofficial objective of achieving a new "farthest north." In 1883, expedition surgeon Dr. Pavy wrote of his commanding officer, Lieutenant Greely:

Figure 42: "Ship and part of Fort Conger, 17 August 1881." US National Archives (Washington, DC), Photograph by George Rice. RG 27, Lady Franklin Bay Expedition Records, Box No. 17.

When he looks to the accumulation of documents, it is not for the interest of science, but to be able to boast, like a child making a collection of postage stamps, to say that it has more than Harry, 'we have beaten the English.'[137]

The Greely expedition personnel consisted of three officers, a surgeon, and 19 enlisted men (Figure 41), with two Greenlanders hired as dog drivers and hunters. The Greenlanders' services were enlisted when the ship stopped at Upernavik en route to Ellesmere Island. Skin clothing for the sledging parties was obtained at Prøven. In addition, at Godhavn, Greenland, Greely purchased a team of twelve dogs, dog food, and sealskins for outfitting exploratory parties on excursions away from the intended base camp on Ellesmere Island.

Cutting through the heavy ice-congested waters of Nares Strait to reach the wintering site of the *Discovery*, the *Proteus* arrived at Discovery Harbour off Lady Franklin Bay on 12 August. The party spent the next two days unloading the cargo, which included equipment, provisions for two years, and lumber components of a prefabricated frame expedition house (Figures 42-43). Plans for the building had been drafted in Washington "after the model of those used in the Hudson Bay Territory by the Company," which the Signal Corps had "assumed to be suitable, both [sic] as to size, style, and comfort."[138] Work on assembling the house began immediately; a photograph taken on 17 August shows that the frame of the structure was in place by this date and

Figure 43: "Fort Conger four days old — 16 August 1881." US National Archives (Washington, DC), Photograph by George Rice. RG 27, Lady Franklin Bay Expedition Records, Box No. 17.

work on the lumber siding in progress (Figure 42). When completed sufficiently for occupancy by the end of the month, the house measured 18 m long by 5.5 m wide, with 3-m-high ceilings. The structure was divided into three rooms: an officer's quarters (Figure 44), an enlisted men's room, and in between, an entranceway and galley.[139] Greely named the station Fort Conger after a United States senator who had supported the project.[140]

Even before the departure of the *Proteus*, an open rupture developed in Greely's relationship with Lieutenant Kislingbury, one of his three officers, whom he summarily relieved of his command. In a letter to be conveyed by the departing ship to the Chief Signal Officer, Greely requested that a replacement be sent with the intended resupply vessel the following year, along with three sergeants to replace any men "invalided or who are found to be unfit otherwise for the work." In the event the vessel could not reach Lady Franklin Bay, he specified the desired items and location of caches of provisions in the region of Kane Basin and Smith Sound. If the ship could not reach the northern part of the island, he also specified contingency plans for another ship to be sent in 1883.[141]

Figure 44: Lieutenant Greely's corner in the big house at Fort Conger. Credit: US National Archives (Washington, DC), RG 27, Lady Franklin Bay Expedition Records, Box No. 17; original held by US National Archives, US Signal Corps Photo No. 111 SC-91240.

Fall work included initial exploratory forays, including a sledge journey by Dr. Pavy, Corporal Rice, and Greenlander Jens Edward along the Ellesmere coastal ice foot to Cape Union, where Robeson Channel opens on to Lincoln Sea in the Arctic Ocean (Figure 45). Also in September, Greely led a reconnaissance trip to the west of the station, during which Lieutenant Lockwood explored the Bellows, a valley subsequently found to lead to Lake Hazen. On this excursion, the group shot 18 muskoxen, which they cached for subsequent transport to Fort Conger. Another party led by Sergeant Brainard established a depot of 900 kg of provisions and supplies at Cape Beechey on the Ellesmere coast of Robeson Channel, in preparation for subsequent sledging parties. Meanwhile, at Fort Conger, the other personnel were constructing observatories for meteorological, magnetic, and astronomical observations. They constructed the magnetic observatory about 200 m north of the house. In October Lockwood led another party in an attempt to cross Robeson Channel to Thank God Harbour, the unhappy refuge of C.F. Hall in 1871 on the Greenland side of the channel. In mid-crossing they were stopped by rapidly drifting ice floes and a large open lead of water, which forced their early return to Fort Conger.[142]

Figure 45: "Making Ready for a Sledge Journey from Fort Conger," ca. 1881. Photograph by George Rice. US National Archives (Washington, DC), RG 27, Lady Franklin Bay Expedition Records, Box No. 17. The man on the left is probably Jens Edward. Note the contrast between his skin clothing and the woolen garments of the Americans.

By late October, the sun had disappeared and extended excursions away from the base were discontinued until the return of daylight in late February. Now the men confronted the problems of adjusting to the monotony of perpetual darkness. The commanding officer ordered his men to maintain a regular work regimen, but there were reports that several men, including officers, were both retiring early and sleeping in during the long winter night. Lieutenant Lockwood described a typical winter day:

> My daily routine is somewhat as follows: Breakfast at half-past seven, with scarcely a word spoken by any one. Then I smoke, standing by the stove in the cook's room. Afterward, tailoring, or some other work. At noon, a walk to Proteus Point if possible. Afterward, read or sleep till dinner at four. Again, smoke as before. Then a few games of chess with Lieutenant Greely or checkers with the Esquimaux. Then read a little French or a good deal of whatever I find most interesting. Then to my army-bunk, to sleep till next morning, when the same routine is repeated.[143]

During the first winter at Fort Conger, several men were beginning to express open disaffection within the expedition. At least, this is the implication of several entries in the diary of Dr. Octave Pavy, the expedition surgeon. On 22 January 1882, Pavy wrote:

I hear the men speak. They say and express loudly, that they came here only to make a stake. That they have no desire and interest to make discoveries and that, if they could return the next year, they will do so.[144]

Nevertheless, such sentiments appear to have dissipated by late winter as the men geared up for spring sledging parties.

One of the principal objectives of the expedition was the exploration of the northern coast of Greenland. Reconnaissance missions in preparation for the spring sledging party began on 19 February, when Lieutenant Lockwood, Sergeant Brainard, and Greenlander Frederick Christiansen travelled with one dog team to inspect depot "B" at Cape Beechy and to determine ice conditions in Robeson Channel. They established that beyond a narrow belt of rough pressure ice, the channel ice consisted of fairly level floes, suitable for sledging. Returning to Fort Conger, these three, with Sergeant Jewell, again departed from Fort Conger on 1 March for further reconnaissance work. Their trail gear consisted of a tent, a four-man sleeping bag, and ten days' rations, a total weight of about 150 kg. After spending the night at Depot "B," they crossed over the pack ice of Robeson Channel, visited Thank God Harbour, and took inventory of its provisions and supplies. Visiting the graves of Hand and Paul, the English sledgers who had perished during the Nares expedition's Greenland sledging excursions, Lockwood's party collected the carved wooden memorial boards to bring them back to Fort Conger.

On 3 April, Lockwood departed on the major exploratory mission to Greenland with a party of 10 men, including Greenlander Frederick Christiansen. Their equipment initially comprised a dog sledge and team, which carried the largest share of provisions and five sacks of dog pemmican, totalling 450 kg, including the weight of the sledge, and four man-hauled sledges, including two of the Hudson Bay variety. These sledges carried weights of 70 kg each.[145] For the Greenland excursion, the party limited trail gear to an extra 22 kg per man, comprising their sleeping bags, extra socks, mittens, and jumpers. With the exception of a minority of the party who wore skin outer garments, the clothing they wore consisted largely of woolen articles, with light duck suits worn on the outside to keep the snow from contact with the wool.

On reaching Cape Beechey, they loaded additional provisions from the cache laid the previous month. Forced to camp for two days in their sleeping bags on the pack ice of Robeson Channel, they reached the *Polaris* boat camp, where they were again weather-bound by heavy storms. Departing two days later, they were obliged to abandon two of the Hudson Bay sledges which had been wrecked and in their place

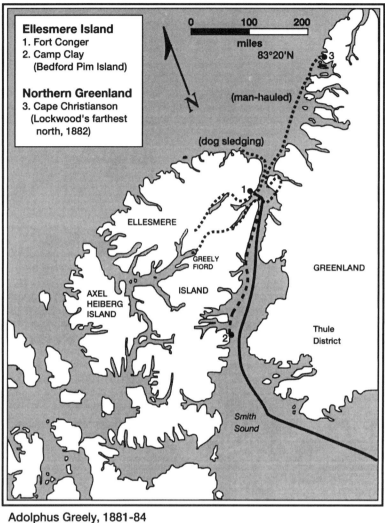

Adolphus Greely, 1881-84

▬▬▬▬▬ Ship   ▪ ▪ ▪ ▪ ▪ ▪ . Retreat by whaleboat,1883

▪▪▪▪▪▪▪▪▪▪ Sledging excursions, 1882-83 (man-hauled and dog)

Figure 46: Map of the route of the expedition of Adolphus Greely, 1881–84

take a sled improvised from old runners and planks left behind by the Nares expedition at the site.

Lockwood reported that while en route to Cape Brevoort, his men were obliged to retrace their steps five times over the same stretch.[146] When one of the sledge runners broke, the party needed to take a runner from the improvised sled, which then had to be abandoned. Finding 75 rations cached by the Beaumont sledge party of the Nares expedition, Lockwood's party transported them to Cape Bryant, about 125 km from the boat camp. At this place they made a cache of provisions, and Lockwood sent back the supporting party with the only man-hauled sledge in acceptable condition to be used on the return trip. Lockwood, Brainard, and Frederick Christiansen, who drove the dog team, pressed on for the balance of the mission, and achieved their farthest north on 13 May when they reached 83° 23' 8" N. lat. near Cape Washington, slightly surpassing the previous farthest north of 83° 20' 26" N. lat. set by Commander Markham of the Nares expedition in 1876 (Figure 46). Brainard wrote:

> We have reached a higher latitude than ever before reached by mortal man, and on a land farther north than was supposed by many to exist. We unfurled the glorious Stars and Stripes to the exhilarating northern breezes with an exultation impossible to describe.[147]

When notified of their achievement, Greely wrote: "For three centuries England had held the honours of the farthest north. Now Lockwood, profiting by their labours and experiences, surpassed their efforts of three centuries by land and ocean."[148]

Another of Greely's exploration objectives was to investigate the interior of northern Ellesmere Island. As groundwork for his initial foray, two of his men made an excursion between 19 and 22 April 1882 to lay caches along the fiord system to the west of Fort Conger. With three men and two man-hauled sledges, Greely departed from Fort Conger late in the month and proceeded westward along the length of Discovery Harbour and to the southwest along the rock-strewn ice foot of Conybeare Fiord. Following this fragile footing beneath the fiord's desolate cliffs and scree slopes, they reached a tributary inlet (subsequently named Chandler Fiord) angling to the northwest.

Proceeding northward to the head of Chandler Fiord, Greely's party found what at first appeared to be a glacier snout. It turned out to be a large ice dam, nearly 2 km in width and 8 m in height, formed by the freezing over of a fresh water stream that emptied into the fiord. Naming this stream Ruggles River, Greely found its smooth ice a good surface for sledging, and the party proceeded along its winding course through a deeply incised valley which angled generally to the northeast. On the evening of 30 April they came within view of a remarkable scene, which Greely described in evocative terms:

> a sharp turn brought in sight a scene which we all shall remember to our dying day. Before us was an immense, ice-bound lake. Its snowy covering reflected "diamond dust," from the midnight sun, and at our feet was a broad pool of open blue water which fed the river. To the northward some eight or ten miles—its base at the northern edge of the lake [Hazen]—a partly snow-clad range of high hills [Garfield Range] appeared, behind and above which the hogback, snow-clad summits of the United States mountains rose with their stern, unchanging splendour ... The scene was one of great beauty and impressiveness.[149]

They had sighted Lake Hazen, the largest freshwater lake north of the Arctic Circle and the source of Ruggles River. Camping at its mouth, they observed a wide variety of birds and animals, including arctic wolf, fox, lemming, hare, muskox, and ptarmigan.

Continuing westward along the lakeshore, Greely and company discerned an immense glacier spilling out through the Garfield Range, and they crossed over the lake ice to inspect it. Naming it Henrietta Nesmith Glacier after his wife, Greely had his men construct a stone cairn about 3 km from its toe to mark the occasion.[150] This was on 4 May. With temperatures rising fast, Greely became concerned about the possible breakup of the ice on the Ruggles River, which would present serious difficulties for the return trip. Accordingly, they headed across the lake on a direct line to the mouth of the Ruggles, a traverse of 35 to 40 km, and reached it in a state of exhaustion eight hours later. From this point, they returned to Fort Conger by forced marches in three days.

Greely soon determined to lead a second, larger excursion to explore the interior of northern Ellesmere Island. After sending out several preliminary parties in May to do reconnaissance work in the region of the Bellows and Black Rock Vale to the west of Fort Conger, Greely decided to seek an alternative route to Lake Hazen via one of these valleys.[151] Departing Fort Conger on 24 June, Greely's party moved down the valley of Black Rock Vale, passing a series of lakes including Lake Heintzelman, before reaching Lake Hazen three days later. At the mouth of the Ruggles on the southern shore of the lake, Greely discovered three Thule culture stone wintering dwellings, which were dug into a bank facing the river.[152] Of cantilevered-arch construction, the houses had been built to take advantage of natural topography to utilize the slope for the rear wall of the structures and for protection from the wind. Greely appropriated various archaeological artifacts, including whalebone fish hooks, walrus ivory combs, an ivory shoe for a sledge runner, and other items. On crossing the river, they found two other abandoned structures of similar construction. From these sites, they took about 40 artifacts of wood and worked bone including: narwhal horns, walrus ivory toggles for dog traces, an arrow head, two bone handles, a skinning knife with a bone handle and iron blade, a bear's tooth, whalebone shoes for the runners of two sledges, and a wooden sledge upstander with a bone top (Figure 8).[153]

Proceeding to the western end of the lake, the party continued up the Very River Valley to the river's source at the base of Mount Arthur. Ascending this mountain, whose summit afforded an expansive panorama, Greely viewed another chain of mountains, which he named the Conger Range, a westward extension of the Garfield Range. To the north of these ranges were "a confused mass of hog-back mountains, all snow-clad," which he correctly inferred to be part of the United States Range. He noted that this higher range pressed closely behind the Garfield Mountains, which presented the only barrier to the glacial ice caps overflowing the country to the south. Far to the south of his vantage point, Greely saw another range of snow-clad mountains, revealed by a depression in the hills, which he estimated to be at least 125 km distant. He wrote: "I cannot but think that this depression drains the western country into a channel or strait between the near hills and the distant mountains and that the range is situated on a separate land."[154] While he had to turn back before confirming its presence, Greely had in fact discerned the presence of Tanquary Fiord, the northern arm of Greely Fiord, the major salt water channel system linking northern Ellesmere Island to the island's west coast.

Returning along the same route, Greely's party reached Ruggles River on 7 July and collected about 65 to 90 kg of Native artifacts remaining from the Thule wintering dwellings they had excavated on the trip out. However, after encountering great difficulty in crossing the Ruggles with only a portion of the objects, Greely decided not to risk another crossing and abandoned the remaining artifacts. This was only the beginning of his party's hardships on the return trip. Their problems were compounded by wet clothing, lowering temperatures, and high winds. On a march to Lake Heintzelman, Greely's men met with a "violent dust-storm," which obliged them to take cover under a high bank. Dogged by recurring high winds, they abandoned virtually all sledge loads apart from the Aboriginal artifacts. Crossing the swollen river waters of Black Rock Vale on 9 July and reaching the coast the following day, they travelled labouriously along the rotten ice foot and a series of dangerous crossings of unsafe harbour ice before arriving at Fort Conger that evening.[155] Also in 1883, two sledging excursions headed by Lockwood were staged, including a return trip to the Greenland coast in March, 1883, in which he was accompanied by two enlisted men, the two West Greenlanders and their dog teams; and an overland excursion in April and May to the west to the head of Archer Fiord and thence to the head of Greely Fiord.

Despite the extensive sledging regimen and assorted scientific tasks, it is apparent from the assorted expedition journals and diaries that all was not well with the expedition. A competitive ethos prevailed, with little evidence of camaraderie or mutual support. Following his landmark expedition to northern Greenland in the spring of 1882, Lieutenant Lockwood returned to a cool reception from apparently jealous colleagues. Of his companions in the officers' quarters, he wrote:

> I find the social relations of our room not improved—rather worse than better. Dr. P[avy], though he shook hands and asked me several questions as to my trip, relapsed into silence, which he seldom breaks. Lieutenant K[islingbury] had but one question to ask. I often contrast ours with the pleasant relations of the English officers when here, and think how much happier we should be in following their example. As it is, I soon relapse into *ennui* and apathy. A sledge-journey, with all its trials, is preferable to this. I view those ahead of us with indifference, as it will rid me of this forced association. Another winter would render me a maniac, or put me under a cairn.[156]

With the failure of a resupply ship to appear in 1882, the lack of team spirit mutated into overt friction, as culture, circumstance, and character interacted to produce a volatile mixture. In this context of anxiety and uncertainty, petty conflicts, formerly suppressed by military discipline, came to the fore. By the spring of 1883, Pavy commented:

> I have for nearly 2 years lived in a circle that even the genius of Dante could not have created for the most guilty souls of his inferno. What a contrast with other expeditions, Nares, Nordenskiold, Weyprecht and the Germans at their worst moments.[157]

When the first intended relief vessel failed to appear by September 1882, Greely began to make contingency plans in the event a second relief effort failed the following summer. In the meantime, the commanding officer pressed forward with his plans for continued exploration activity in the spring of 1883. Two additional sledging excursions headed by Lockwood were planned, including a return trip to the Greenland coast in March 1883 and an excursion in April and May to the west to the head of Archer Fiord across land to the head of Greely Fiord.

On 8 March, prior to Lockwood's departure for Greenland, Dr. Pavy, as expedition physician, wrote to Greely to urge him to abandon plans for these trips to conserve the health of the men. In response to Greely's avowed intention to order a general retreat in the event the supply ship failed to arrive, Pavy stated his desire "to influence the chances of success in a retreat that you consider inevitable." The physician suggested that in the event of a serious accident, the patients would probably not have recuperated by August, "becoming then an encumbrance, threatening to compromise the safety of all, by rendering the departure impracticable." Invoking the prior risks of spring sledging experienced by the Kane and Nares expeditions, Pavy wrote: "I should *earnestly* [Pavy's emphasis] recommend that no work entailing exposure of more than a night or two in the field should be undertaken during the month of March."[158] Pavy also drew attention to the lack of coal reserves. He argued that it would be injurious to the health of the party, especially in the event of sickness, if they were left without fuel in the months leading up to their departure. In his view, there was still time to mine and stockpile the coal if the men were directed to those activities rather than continued exploration.

In his reply of 9 March, Greely scoffed at Pavy's concerns as hypothetical and unfounded. He chided the physician for placing human safety above the potential for new discoveries and greater national glory, as he wrote:

> This expedition was planned and fitted out solely for the purpose of increasing our knowledge of the Arctic regions. While I have the honor to command it, I shall continue to pursue the object in view.
>
> In assuming charge of this work I considered it important and dangerous. As an American soldier I have yet to learn than any prospective dangers or accident should deter a man from pursuing to his utmost any end which is in the line of our duty, and instead, prepare for a possible retreat.
>
> To practically abandon it and think only of personal safety, especially at a time when there seem possible discoveries which would be valued by the world and creditable to my country, would be difficult for me even under the most adverse circumstances, but now — under favorable circumstances — would appear dishonorable and unmanly.[159]

By August 1883, when a second intended resupply mission did not appear, Greely determined, over the objections of several members of the party, to proceed with his plans to abandon Fort Conger and he

Figure 47: Artist's version of the retreat from Fort Conger in the steam launch. Plate from Adolphus Greely, *Three Years of Arctic Service*, Vol. II, between pp. 84 -85.

ordered a general retreat from Fort Conger to Smith Sound to increase the likelihood of encountering a ship. The party departed on 10 August in haste, with the men distributed between the steam launch *Lady Greely* and three other small vessels it was towing—a whaleboat, an iceboat scavenged from the items left behind by the Nares expedition, and a jolly-boat (Figure 47). Both the men and rations for 40 days were divided among the boats. On the first day the excitable Greely snapped at the men. As they proceeded into the channel, encountering turbulent waters, Greely again lost his temper and became abusive toward Sergeant Cross, while barking orders to the others.[160] When the launch became grounded at Carl Ritter Bay on a falling tide, the men offloaded the cargo to lighten the hull to extricate it. Blaming Sergeant Cross for the mishap, Greely acknowledged that "with profane language I ordered him out and threatened to shoot him if he refused," while other members of the party recalled an even starker exchange.[161]

Within three days, they had covered a third of the distance to Smith Sound, only to be driven back by southerly winds, forcing them to take refuge in Carl Ritter Bay, at 80° 44' N. lat. Southerly winds impeded their progress and even began to push the boats to the north. With this change of fortune, tensions in the party increased. On 15 August, Kislingbury commented in his diary on the abusive conduct by Greely, including "threatening to shoot Cross without the slightest reason the other day and swearing to the men on other occasions." He wrote that during the retreat the commander carried around a self-cocking pistol, which he characterized as "ridiculous." As the men had "behaved without exception, so unexceptionally good throughout the whole expedition there is not the slightest excuse for such intimidation."[162]

Another change of direction in the wind, now blowing from the southwest, cleared a patch of open water adjacent to the Ellesmere coast but also drove them farther out into Kane Basin. Adjacent to Cape Collinson at 79° 22' N. lat., the party was frozen into the ice, then helplessly buffeted by winds, tides, and the driving ice pack. At this point, Greely prevaricated. His inclination was to head for the Greenland coast, but in deference to his officers, put off his decision until the drift carried them too far to attempt it. Some men favoured abandoning the boats in favour of leaping from floe to floe, but Greely again postponed making a decision. Over the next week, morale faded quickly among the men along with their confidence in their commander.[163]

In a retrospective account, Lieutenant David Brainard recalled the dramatic tension that gripped the party during the difficult retreat from Fort Conger. From the time of their departure from Fort Conger, Greely "kept the men in a state of great anxiety," owing to the commander's repeatedly expressed desire to abandon the steam launch and all but 20 days' provisions, then haul the whale boats onto an ice floe "and trust to Providence to accomplish our Salvation" by drifting southward toward Littleton Island. In Brainard's view, "such an act would be little short of madness, and everyone, except Greely, realized the dangers that would result from such a course, and fought hard to discourage it."[164] At this point, three senior expedition members approached Brainard with "an extraordinary proposition." They proposed that Pavy, as the expedition's physician would examine Greely and "pronounce him insane and therefore incapable of maintaining longer the leadership of the expedition." Pavy asserted that such action would not be difficult to defend, as Greely's "frequent outbursts of passion ... evinced insanity of an emotional type if not more serious...." With Greely stripped of his command, Kislingbury would replace him because of his rank, and he would then order the party to return to Fort Conger to pass the winter. In the spring, the party would then retreat on sledges along Ellesmere Island's eastern coast to meet a relief party or to wait at Cape Sabine for its arrival. Despite his own personal premonition of disaster during the party's retreat from Fort Conger, Brainard flatly refused to join the incipient mutiny. His resistance apparently nipped the rebellion in the bud, although he reported that the conspirators "never quite gave up the idea." Brainard wrote that he had not mentioned the proposed mutiny to Greely as "I well knew his obstinate nature and feared he would immediately put in execution the plans we all wished to prevent—that of drifting helplessly on the Polar pack!"[165]

Greely's rationale for scuttling most of the provisions and striking out across the pack ice for the Greenland shore, was that by jettisoning the supplies, they could haul everything without retracing their steps, thus making three times the distance as with the extra weight. He believed that the Inughuit at Etah comprised "the only quarter where positive relief could be expected," while there were no certain prospects at Cape Sabine. "Owing to the unanimous opinion" of his officers, he decided to wait another day to determine the speed of the drift but remained resolved to move toward the Greenland coast on 20 August, "unless remarkable changes resulted from our drift in the meantime."[166] Abandoning the launch, the men hauled the two remaining whaleboats over the rugged pack ice with difficulty as they attempted to work their way toward Smith Sound. But winds moved the ice floes away from the intended destination, and the party watched helplessly as they drifted to the north, then to the east, before being pushed to the southwest, within striking range of Ellesmere Island. Trekking over the ice floes, on 30 September, they went ashore near Eskimo Point, south of the intended destination of Cape Sabine.

At this site, to provide winter shelter, Greely divided the party into three groups, each charged with building its own dwelling. On 3 October, the men began erecting their huts, consisting of low stone walls, to be lined with snow and ice after the onset of winter and roofed over with a canvas.[167] On 9 October, Jens Edward and Sergeant Rice returned from a trip to the cape where they found 1300 rations, along with the abandoned whaleboat at Payer Harbour and news that the relief vessel,

Figure 48: Artist's version of the interior of the hut at Camp Clay, 1883. Plate from Adolphus Greely, *Three Years of Arctic Service*, Vol. II, between pp. 206-7.

the *Proteus*, had sunk in the ice of the straits during the resupply attempt. Considering Cape Sabine to be a more promising location at which to encounter a ship, Greely ordered the group to again strike camp and undertake the trek 33 km to the north, where, on Bedford Pim Island, they would remain for the balance of the expedition.

The party's wintering quarters on Pim Island, became a doleful refuge (Figure 48). Greely named Camp Clay after Henry Clay, an intended member of the expedition who had abandoned it in its first days because he and Pavy "could no longer remain friends"[168] and returned to the United States on the *Proteus* in August 1881. The tribulations of the Greely party at this site have been often recounted,[169] although most accounts bypass the most disturbing details of the last few months of this party in the High Arctic. An exception is the recent book *Ghosts of Cape Sabine* by Len Guttridge,[170] which is an insightful treatment of the personality conflicts, psychological corrosion, and suffering that characterized life at this camp. In addition, I have carried out my own research in the extant diaries of expedition members at the U.S. National Archives, which further illuminate the interpersonal dynamics of the expedition. The conflicts revealed in these documents point to the shortcomings of the expedition's military command structure in an emergency situation, when combined with an unstable leader and an unruly command.

Once again the men set to work hauling rocks to build a wintering shelter, this time a larger structure to house the entire party of 25 men.

This primitive dwelling, roofed over with a whaleboat and lengths of canvas, is described in Chapter 5. They spent an extremely difficult winter, finding little protection from the extreme cold of that season, and nourished by a few game animals secured by Greenlander Jens Edward.[171] By spring the rations had virtually run out, and the men were subsisting on whatever shrimps and seaweed they were able to catch or gather in the water off the beach[172] and the thongs of sealskins, which they boiled to extract a meagre nourishment. In early April, a polar bear killed by Jens and Long was retrieved, skinned, cooked, and eaten.[173] It came too late for several men who died over the following weeks, but may have provided enough sustenance to enable the surviving members to stay alive until the appearance of a relief party. With the advent of spring, by June they were able to collect reindeer moss, saxifrage, and lichens, which Greely described as "very palatable and nutritious."[174]

Meanwhile, relations between various members of the party continued to deteriorate, as periods of calm were punctuated by increasingly acrimonious exchanges. On 24 September, Greely reported that Dr. Pavy "was very strong in his language to Schneider, swearing at him."[175] On 2 October, following his order to move their camp to Cape Sabine, Greely wrote that Corporal Elison had made "mutinous" remarks criticizing this decision. Despite the corporal's reported contrition, Greely "reprimanded him very severely in the presence of the whole party."[176] The next day, Greely wrote of "grumbling and growling" by Connell, and he vowed to himself "to reduce him," but he would wait before announcing the demotion. "I expect to try him for language on the floe and his reduction will refer to language and deportment since landing."[177]

On 11 May, Private Bender wrote that "Lt. Greely acted the man for once in his life and spoke to Lt. Kislingbury and asked him to forgive him for not putting him on duty sooner." Yet only the next day, Bender reported that Greely and Kislingbury were again "on the war path."[178] On 11 May, Private Henry wrote of alleged threats by the commanding officer to shoot members of the party: "Cowardly action in G[reely] in wanting to shoot Dr. P[avy], also drew rifle on Bender. Calls Kis[lingbury] a liar and apologizes to enlisted men."[179] At least part of Henry's account was corroborated by Lieutenant Kislingbury, who on 12 May wrote what would be the last words in his diary. He related a discussion with Greely in which he requested an order to place him back on active duty, which he said Greely had previously agreed to:

> I was obliged to commence reminding him of this when he cut me short, flew into a passion and called me, in loud, insulting (highly so) manner, 'a Liar'—God help me! I had to take this. Too weak to write any more tonight."[180]

Private Jacob Bender corroborated Greely's outburst in his own diary.[181]

Soon Private Henry would be singled out for disciplinary action. At issue were allegations of stolen food; he was accused of stealing seal thongs and other scarce edibles in defiance of strict orders. Greely wrote that he confronted the enlisted man on 5 June and he admitted having stolen food. Greely then "cautioned him of his coming to grief if he did not act properly."[182] Later, on questioning Henry, he wrote that the private again acknowledged stealing seal thongs and the commander ordered that he be summarily executed.[183] Suspecting "complicity on the part of several [others]" in the alleged thefts of food, Greely ordered "three of the most reliable men to form the firing squad."[184] He signed the following order, which he addressed to Sergeant Brainard, and privates Long, and Frederick:

> Notwithstanding promises given by Private C.B. Henry yesterday he has since, as acknowledged to me having tampered with seal-thongs, if not other food at the old camp. This pertinacity and audacity is the destruction of the party, if not at once ended. Private Henry will be shot today, all care being taken to prevent his injuring anyone as his physical strength is greater than that of any two men. Decide the manner of death by two ball and one blank cartridge. This order is *imperative* and *absolutely necessary* for *any chance* [Greely's emphasis] of life.[185]

The reference to the reliability of the men selected to carry out the execution confirmed Greely's serious doubts regarding the party's loyalty, a fact underscored by his decision to keep the order confidential until after the execution had been carried out. Around 2 p.m., a gun shot was heard, as Henry was put to death with a single bullet. Afterward, Greely ordered Sergeant Brainard to hand the signed execution order to Private Henry Biederbick, who was instructed to read it aloud to the group.[186]

If guilty, Henry apparently was not the only offender. In his journal, Greely wrote on 9 and 10 April, that Pavy had taken Corporal Elison's bread and was also hoarding several cans of beef extract.[187] Brainard recorded in his dairy that he had extracted a confession from Private Roderick Schneider that Schneider, Henry, and Bender had eaten "large quantities of seal skin clothing in their [sleeping] bags at night after the others retired."[188] For his part, Greely told Biederbick

> confidentially, that after hearing from Dr. Pavy the weak condition of Lt. Kislingbury and after a great deal of mental worry, he [Greely] had allowed himself an extra allowance of a small quantity of pemmican and hard bread, as he saw the necessity of keeping himself up for the well [sic] of the party...[189]

Through this act of altruism, Greely may have ensured his own survival while his men, undernourished and suffering also from frostbite, exposure, and respiratory diseases, began to die.

During this period interpersonal conflicts resumed, including the long-standing feud between Greely and Kislingbury. They had been at loggerheads since the first day at Fort Conger. In his diary, Kislingbury recorded his harsh assessments of both Dr. Pavy and Greely:

> "The doctor is irascible and has made himself mean and disagreeable and has done me great injury in various ways, yet I cannot tolerate backbiting, sneaky, underhanded, such low minded cowardly work on the part of an officer and especially a Commanding Officer, and shall note everything of the kind for future information."[190]

Following Kislingbury's death on 1 June 1884 Private Maurice Connell wrote what he believed would be his last letter to a Captain Johnson:

> This is the last you will ever hear from me. I am laying helpless in a starving condition at this point without any hope of recovery. 12 of our number has died of starvation since Jan. 17. Lieut. Kislingbury died at 3 p.m. today and I feel it my turn next, the other 13 are helpless. It is the blunders of the heads of this expedition ... who are to blame for our misfortunes and it ought to be a warning to the United States to keep fools and incompetent people at home. If there is to be fools it is better they should meddle in little things than in great. I hold Lieut. Greely personally responsible for the lives of this party. All this has been pointed out to him but it was of no avail, he rushed into where he was not able and it is well that he should not be made a martyr of and if he ever returns to the U.S. he ought to be tried and hung for murder...[191]

It should be noted that Kislingbury, Connell, and Pavy were among Greely's principal adversaries during the expedition[192] and could not be considered objective observers. I have included these quotations, not to endorse the sentiments of the writers, but rather to illustrate the heightened rancour of interpersonal conflicts in the context of physical and psychological stress, set off by desperate circumstances of exposure, starvation, and dwindling resources. When a rescue ship finally appeared on 22 June, only seven of the original party of 25, including Greely, were still alive. Poignantly, his survival and legacy at stake, the weakened commander managed to blurt out a boast to his rescuers: "Did what I came to do—beat the best record."[193]

The circumstances of the deaths at Camp Clay were clouded by the condition of the bodies of several dead soldiers at the end of this tragic drama. When the relief expedition led by Commander W.S. Schley arrived at Camp Clay in June 1884, Schley reported that the six exposed bodies were fully clothed and initially appeared intact. However, when preparing the bodies, it was found that this was not so.[194] In his official report, Schley summarized the condition of the bodies and offered a rationalization: "In preparing the bodies of the dead for transportation in alcohol to St. John's, Newfoundland, it was found that six of them (Lieutenant Kislingbury, Sergeants Jewell and Ralston, Privates Henry, Whisler, and Ellis) had been cut and the fleshy parts removed to a greater or less extent with a view no doubt to use as shrimp bait. All the other bodies were found intact."[195]

However, not all the other bodies were found. The situation was complicated by the fact that four of the men who had died at the starvation camp—Nicholas Salor, Jacob Bender, Octave Pavy, and Hampden Gardiner—had been buried "in the sea,"[196] so potential evidence that might confirm possible depredations was missing. As well, the Greenlander Jens Edward had drowned on 29 April while hunting in his kayak and so his body, too, was not recovered.

On returning to the United States, the survivors endured the mortification of allegations in the press of cannibalism at Camp Clay. The sensational headline of the *New York Times* tells the story:

> "HORRORS OF CAMP SABINE—Terrible Story of Greely's Dreary Camp— Brave men, Crazed by Starvation and Bitter Cold, Feeding on the Dead Bodies of Their Comrades—HOW PRIVATE HENRY DIED—The Awful results of an Official Blunder."[197]

As other newspapers picked up the story, the possibility that bodies of men who had died from starvation had been scavenged became inflated into suggestions that men had been killed for food. According to the newspapers, one of the survivors had become hysterical and begged rescuers not to be shot and eaten, "as they did poor Henry." In the midst of such extravagant allegations, others were drawn into the fray to defend the survivors, including the venerable British explorer Sir Clements Markham, who asserted: "The accusation of murder and cannibalism made against the Greely party is a disgrace to American journalism."[198]

Prompted by the explosive allegations in the press, the relatives of deceased expedition members doubted official statements about the deaths of their loves ones and determined to find out the truth of the matter. One such sceptic was Lilla Pavy, widow of Octave Pavy, who made a series of attempts to secure her husband's expedition papers following the return of the *Thetis* in 1884. In February 1885, her mother, Mrs. M. Stone of New Orleans, wrote a letter to General A.J. Warner of the U.S. Army, in which she referred to an accusation made in a

Rochester, New York newspaper that her son-in-law had been "shot with four or five others for food, by orders of the commander."[199] That fall, Lilla Pavy wrote to the Secretary of War to protest what she regarded as the "unlawful withholding" of her husband's papers by the Signal Office. She alleged that, in reviewing the small number of her husband's papers forwarded by the Army, "doubtless hundreds [of] others are missing," including absent diary entries for three years. Because of the missing papers she insisted:

> The fact that these mysteries exist, and that more than one [of these accounts] have been given me regarding Dr. Pavy's last hours, death and burial is quite strange and melancholy enough to justify me in demanding not only an investigation of the Signal Office and the Greely effects, and the properties held by different parties who survived or were among the rescuers, but that I should demand a thorough investigation before the American people.[200]

The Lady Franklin Bay Expedition papers also include a file with a document bearing a fragmentary series of notations on the alleged manner of death of various individuals. Apparently prepared by M. Stone, Pavy's father-in-law, these notes apparently were purported to represent comments by survivors of the Camp Clay ordeal on the alleged causes of death for several expedition members:

> Body dropped between the ice cracks—"survivor"
> Body laid on an ice floe where the tide water washed it away in six hours—"survivor"
> Died of starvation alone "survivor, enlisted man"
> Died of an overdose of ergot taken by mistake for iron. Dr. Pavy insane three days before death—"Greely"
> Drowned (like the Eskimo, accidentally)
> Committed suicide by running into the sea, and drowning, when pursued by a comrade or comrades of the party.
> Ran toward the sea to drown himself when trying to escape those who threatened his life, but fell before reaching the water, and the body was cut before it was cold....
> Without doubt Dr. Pavy died by the use of the knife.
> That Dr. Pavy was shot by the same order as caused the execution of Henry or a similar one.[201]

Greely resolutely denied all allegations. As he wrote in his book on the expedition, "I know of no law, human or divine, which was broken at Sabine, and do not feel called on as an officer or as a man to dwell longer on such a painful topic."[202] It must be stated that none of the accusations of wanton violence at Camp Clay ever received first-hand corroboration by any of the surviving members of the expedition, nor are these allegations supported by the extant documentary record. At the same time, there can be little doubt that the men ate the flesh of their deceased compatriots. Following the return of the relief expedition, at the insistence of the relatives, the bodies of both Kislingbury and Private Whisler were exhumed and inspected by doctors. In the case of Kislingbury, they concluded that "the flesh was cut away with some sharp instrument," while observers of the Whisler exhumation stated that "all the flesh had been cut from the shoulders and the limbs as if by an expert."[203]

The full story of the last few weeks in that desperate starvation camp may never be known. While most of the participants perished in the Arctic, the survivors were not only the purveyors of the prevailing version of events but also guardians of the records that were brought back to the United States. Writer Leonard Guttridge has recently written that, in the period, some diaries were said to have been either mutilated or scuttled on the way back to the United States.[204] As well, Dr. Pavy's original diary was apparently not retained, although a transcribed version appeared in the records of the Lady Franklin Bay Expedition at the U.S. National Archives. If a faithful transcription, Pavy's diary reveals a level of distrust and dislike of Greely bordering on paranoia throughout the expedition's tenure in northern Ellesmere Island.[205] For his part, Greely's official account of the expedition was written in a detached manner in marked contrast to his apparently overwrought mental state during their retreat from Fort Conger and bleak tenure at Cape Sabine.[206]

The implications of Greely's decision to retreat from Fort Conger in 1884 have been the subject of considerable debate in his own era and since. Agonizing over the tragic loss of 17 of the 25 men during the retreat, Sergeant David Brainard recalled the unsuccessful mutiny he had been asked to join. He speculated:

> Had their [the conspirators'] plan been consummated, it would be interesting now to note what a great change such action would have made on the history of the expedition. It is not at all improbable that every man would have escaped with his life.[207]

It was a poignant conclusion regarding the consequences of blind adherence to orders. Whether or not Brainard was justified in his hypothetical reasoning, the disastrous conclusion to the Greely expedition would occasion the complete rethinking of polar exploration. The era of the large military expedition was over.

Following their rescue by the U.S. Navy, Greely and the other survivors had to endure yet a further ordeal, this one orchestrated by their rescuers. Exhibiting the traditional rivalry between the American armed services, the Navy organized a reception for the survivors immediately on their return to the United States, to be convened at Portsmouth, New Hampshire, on 1 and 4 August 1884. Indeed, naval orders were issued to sail directly to Portsmouth from Saint John's, Newfoundland, where they had been detained for several days on the return voyage. On arrival, the survivors were greeted by the North Atlantic squadron, accompanied by a flotilla of training ships and school ships from the Naval Academy at Annapolis, "a greater amount of material for such an occasion than had ever been at one time in this port, from which was furnished the most imposing part of the display." Numerous public buildings and residences were festooned, with crowds estimated at ten to fifteen thousand people. An elaborate procession was organized, incorporating various naval branches, including marines, cadets, and apprentices, as the Navy paraded the Camp Clay survivors as trophies through the city. Numerous dignitaries, including Governor Hale of New Hampshire, members of Congress who had supported the relief expedition, and senior naval officers were assembled on a large stand at the reception chaired by William E. Chandler, the Secretary of the Navy. He talked at length about the elaborate preparations for the relief expedition and how the decision "that the force should be wholly naval" had been vindicated, as he congratulated the officers and men of the relief expedition "upon the brilliant success of their efforts."[208]

Notwithstanding the humiliation of seeing the rescued Army party paraded by the Navy before the assembled throng, General Benjamin Butler of the Army tried to make the best of a bad situation. Speaking from the stand, he declared his support for sending another party to the High Arctic for an even longer stay, so that "our children or our children's children will see the North Pole belonging to us (tremendous applause), not by right of discovery but because we shall own all the intervening territory between Portsmouth and there." Suggesting that Canada to the north and Mexico and central America to the south would soon be absorbed into the United States, he stated: "It is the manifest destiny of this country."[209]

Butler also invoked the competition for national prestige between nations when he expounded on his goal:

> The subjects of monarchy had planted the Red Cross of Saint George farther up towards the Pole than any other nation, and the young people, the free American citizens of the nation determined to plant the

Stars and Stripes farther on still, until that glorious banner, as it waves in the Arctic seas, will be mistaken by the wandering Esquimaux for the aurora borealis (great applause).[210]

General Butler's Army may have been upstaged by the Navy in the official welcome of the Greely party, but his speech revived the overriding spirit of competition between countries. His nationalistic appeal for the United States to realize its destiny by annexing Canada and its arctic territories, heartily endorsed by his audience, announced the arrival of a new era of imperialism in polar exploration history.

A year and a half after the survivors' return to the United States, Adolphus Greely, now a major with the U.S. Army, was in England to deliver a lecture, entitled "Arctic Exploration, with special reference to Grinnell Land." His audience was the Royal Geographical Society, and in the crowd were several famous British explorers, including his rival Captain Sir George Nares.[211] In his lecture, Greely acknowledged the geographical discoveries of earlier explorers to the Smith Sound region, before bestowing his most generous praise on his own achievements in exploration: his "good, honest, and proper work" in sending Lockwood to the north and, with regard to the 1882 trip to the interior of northern Ellesmere Island: "we succeeded in making on foot one of the most remarkable inland voyages of Arctic exploration."

Following a discussion of scientific issues, Greely finally referred obliquely to the tragedies of the expedition. Dealing pre-emptively with anticipated criticism, he justified decisions for which he was already the target of censure in the United States, including his decision not to attempt a crossing of Smith Sound to the Greenland side during the retreat from Fort Conger in 1883. He made no reference to the dissension and conflict precipitated by that decision and others that succeeded it.

Greely concluded with an anecdote to pay tribute to the courage of his party. In the interests of science, the commander had considered it important to carry back a bulky scientific pendulum on the retreat from Fort Conger. Greely related that he had said to his men: "Whenever anyone speaks the word the pendulum shall go, and afterwards such instruments as you think fit." According to Greely, despite the fact that this instrument weighed down the party, no one advocated scuttling the pendulum, and some indicated their willingness to go the bottom of the sea with it. He stated:

I can say with regard to that pendulum that when the Relief Squadron came on the 22nd June, the first sight that any American had of the signs of us was that pendulum, standing there and pointing to the heavens as an indication that we had done our work and had come to the place we had promised, in order that our work might live after us even if we died.[212]

With this lofty panegyric, Greely banished all remembrance of his party's internecine strife as he evoked an image of collective heroism for posterity.

Perhaps the most interesting part of the event was the exchange with British explorers following the formal address. Greely's talk elicited kind remarks by the deans of British arctic exploration, many of whom were in attendance, including Admiral Sir Leopold McClintock, Captain Sir George Nares, and Captain A.H. Markham. Nevertheless, the old rivalries resurfaced with Nares's comment regarding the Americans' attainment of the highest north latitude. "Although it was only three or four miles farther than Markham's farthest, still they [the Americans] carried off the palm, but he hoped that one day England would wrest it from them."[213]

In 1886 Greely published his two-volume book on the Lady Franklin Bay Expedition, in which he expounded on what he regarded as his expedition's greatest achievement:

> For three centuries England had held the honours of the farthest north. Now Lockwood, profiting by their labours and experiences, surpassed their efforts of three centuries by land and ocean. And with Lockwood's name should be associated that of his inseparable sledge companion Brainard, without whose efficient aid and restless energy, as Lockwood said, the work could not have been accomplished. So, with proper pride, they looked to that day from the vantage-ground of the farthest north [Lockwood Island] to the desolate cape which until surpassed in coming ages, may well bear the grand name of Washington.[214]

Imperatives of national destiny again overrode any thought of sharing the credit for this geographical milestone. The names of Frederick Christiansen, the Greenlander who had driven the dog team that took Lockwood and Brainard to their farthest north in 1882, and Jens Edward, who had drowned while hunting for the party at Camp Clay, were omitted in his triumphal tribute to American supremacy.

The Nares and Greely Expeditions: Post-Mortem

What conclusions can be drawn from the Nares and Greely expeditions? Can historical patterns be isolated to explain the fatal consequences of these pioneering forays into the arctic wilderness? Depending on the viewer, the outcomes of these expeditions may be viewed as the product of environmental, cultural, or circumstantial factors. Adherents of any of these models would not have difficulty in finding evidence supporting their interpretations.

An environmental historian would presumably note a sequence of physical occurrences relating to the historical role of climate, beginning with the fact that the sea-ice levels in Nares Strait in 1875 and 1876 were sufficiently low that the ships of the British Arctic Expedition were able to negotiate these potential barriers with relative ease. Both access to and egress from the northern waters of the Ellesmere–Greenland channel could help account for the lower levels of mortality experienced by this expedition, relative to its American counterpart. Conversely, the Greely expedition, while initially transported successfully by the *Proteus* through the ice of the Nares Strait in 1881, was subsequently imperilled by increased sea-ice levels in Nares Strait in successive years in 1882 and 1883, preventing relief vessels from successfully resupplying the expedition. The key factor here seems to be a short-term cooling trend resulting in the build-up of sea ice in these years. At the same time, following his retreat from Fort Conger, Greely selected a wintering site on Pim Island, whose shores are typically separated from Greenland by open water for much of the year. Comprising the northern edge of the North Water, Smith Sound is recurrently kept ice-free by the ice dam that forms to its north as moving pack ice wedges together in the southern part of Kane Basin. When, in early 1884, Greely ordered two of his men to traverse Smith Sound to reach a cache of provisions at Littleton Island off the Greenland coast, they encountered open water and were thwarted in the attempt. Greely could not have known that a successful crossing would have required a wide swing to the north to find a frozen surface on which to make the crossing.[215] Better knowledge of local environmental conditions might have helped save some lives during the critical period of Greely's retreat to Smith Sound, although the unpredictable character of sea ice in this area could make a crossing to Greenland a problematic undertaking even for seasoned Aboriginal travellers in any era.[216]

A cultural historian might try to explain the deaths suffered by the Nares and Greely expeditions by referring to the overweening confidence, even arrogance of the exploring nations of this era, as exemplified in the explorers' belief in the superiority of Western technology over "primitive" forms. Such an explanation could be applied to the failure of its organizers to employ more than a token complement of Aboriginal employees and to eschew Native material culture and know-how, despite the extensive lack of arctic environmental knowledge among the expedition's Euro-American personnel. On another level, a cultural historian might note the ingrained organizational cultures of the British Navy and the U.S. Army in this period, their hierarchical structures, and the premium placed on obedience to written and verbal orders and on military discipline generally. This approach might take into account the role of exaggerated notions of masculinity and devotion to duty in the practice of man-hauled sledging long after it was considered outmoded by experienced arctic travellers. A cultural historian might equally note the almost total lack of naval or maritime experience in Greely's Army command, a shortcoming of major proportions when the party retreated by steam launch in 1883, or assess the consequences of rivalry between different factions of this military party, itself in part the product of a competitive and aggressive culture.

On the other hand, a historian inclined to seek explanations in the role of circumstance would likely gravitate toward a more traditional approach of narrative history, in which precedence would be placed on the personalities of the major players, their virtues of character or vices, skills or ineptitude. Such a historian might examine such factors as the insecurities of Adolphus Greely, his apparently rigid and authoritarian bent, lack of judgment, and refusal to accept advice on key questions affecting the safety and well-being of his command. Practitioners of this approach would presumably also consider the role of personality traits and behaviour of the other men interacting with Greely. Among other characteristics, they might treat the apparent paranoia of Pavy, the contentiousness of Lieutenant Kislingbury, or the presumed larceny of Henry. Other pertinent personal factors might include the role of ambition in figures such as Greely and Brainard, who went on to attain the rank of major general and brigadier, respectively, in the U.S. Army. Greely's aspirations could not accommodate the appearance of weakness and could be considered a factor in his obsession with maintaining the appearance of military decorum. Brainard, whatever his lack of confidence in Greely's judgment, could not afford to appear insubordinate. Having participated in a mutiny, if he survived to return to the United States, he would undoubtedly have faced a court-martial and been severely punished, his career in ruins. The prospect of such sanctions might account for his fateful decision not to join the mutiny, when a return to Fort Conger might have saved the party from disaster.

Which explanation from this menu of explanatory options would we wish to adopt? Perhaps the soundest approach would be to refuse to choose, to acknowledge the multi-faceted and complex nature of historical causation, and to leave the door open to both these and other interpretations and perspectives omitted in the respective narratives.

Two Expedition Failures in the 1890s: Björling and Stein

After the major military undertakings of the Nares and Greely expeditions, the structure of High Arctic expeditions returned to smaller, civilian undertakings in the following decade. In principle, smaller groups had the advantage of greater flexibility to meet unanticipated challenges and could be undertaken without the strict military discipline that eroded morale during the Greely expedition. Like the larger parties, they certainly also required adequate resources, extensive experience with Arctic conditions, and carefully arranged contingency plans to meet unforeseen difficulties. Remarkably, despite the well-documented logistical problems of the Nares and Greely expeditions, Europeans continued to stage ill-equipped expeditions to the High Arctic, with predictable consequences.

One tragic example was the expedition undertaken by young Swedes Alfred Björling and E.G. Kallstenius in 1892–93. A botanist, Björling was only 21 years old when he decided in 1892 to attempt to explore the southern coastal regions of Ellesmere Island. His only first-hand experience of the North American Arctic was during a trip to Greenland in 1891, when he accompanied several West Greenlanders on a summer voyage in an *umiak* along the coast of Melville Bay as far north as the Devil's Thumb in the region of Thule.[217] But if Björling had little prior experience of High Arctic conditions, his companion, Evald Gustaf Kallstenius, a 24-year old zoology student at the time, had none at all.

The would-be explorers' original plan was to obtain passage on a whaling ship sailing from St. John's, Newfoundland, which they intended to drop them off at Cape Sabine on the Ellesmere side of Smith Sound. Arriving after the whaler had departed, Björling quickly changed his plans and purchased the *Ripple*, a small schooner. He also added another three crew members, before sailing north. The boat was poorly provisioned, and Björling was obliged to obtain additional supplies at Godhavn, Greenland. He apparently was attempting to take additional provisions from a cache left by the Nares expedition at the Carey Islands, in northern Baffin Bay, when the *Ripple* was wrecked on 17 August 1892. After an abortive attempt to reach Foulke Fiord in an open boat, the party returned to the Carey Islands in October. In the meantime, one member of the party died. In late October, Björling and his remaining colleagues departed the Carey Islands in the small boat, apparently bound for Ellesmere Island's eastern coast. They probably never reached their destination as they disappeared without a trace and were never heard from again.[218] When American Henry Bryant arrived at Southeast Carey Island in 1894, he discovered a scatter of various objects left behind by Björling's departing party, including a silver watch, zoological notebook, and a botanical press—"memorials of the brave but fool-hardy adventurers."[219]

After the pathos of Björling, the inept foray of Robert Stein into the region was a farcical interlude in the saga of the polar quest. Stein was a German immigrant to the United States who, while working with the American Geological Survey and as a translator, developed plans to mount an expedition to the High Arctic. He proposed to explore the triangular area between the south coast of Devon Island and eastern and western coasts of Ellesmere, much of the uncharted portion of the Queen Elizabeth Islands.[220] Stein's first Arctic foray was to hitch a ride with Robert E. Peary on his 1897 voyage to the Thule region to retrieve the Cape York meteorites for the American Museum of Natural History. After this trial trip, Stein made a series of unsuccessful attempts to persuade Peary to transport him and two companions to Cape Sabine on Ellesmere Island, near Smith Sound.

Finally, in 1899, Stein was able to make arrangements with Herbert Bridgeman, secretary of the Peary Arctic Club, to transport him, two colleagues, and equipment to Ellesmere Island, including 10 tonnes of coal, 5 tonnes of lumber for the construction of an expedition house, provisions for 15 months, and such items as boats, hardware, guns, and tools.[221] Incredibly, Stein seems to have expected Peary to share his own supplies, without having secured such a commitment in advance. Offloaded by the *Diana* at Payer Harbour, Pim Island in early August, the little party constructed the frame wintering structure, which they named Fort Magnesia. Stein, his colleagues Julian Warmbath and Dr. Leopold Kann, and several Inughuit passed an uneventful winter there. Lacking adequate dogs and provisions, Stein was unable to proceed with his plans to explore parts of southern Ellesmere Island the following spring. In the summer of 1900, Kann abandoned the expedition and crossed Smith Sound to secure passage on a whaler back to Scotland. Waiting in vain for Peary to free up supplies to enable them to explore the Sverdrup Pass region, Stein and Warmbath did not venture very far from Fort Magnesia for the duration of their uneventful sojourn on Ellesmere Island. After a second sedentary year, they returned to the United States on one of Robert Peary's supply ships in August 1901, having accomplished nothing of scientific value in two years on Ellesmere Island.[222]

Even if Stein had proceeded with his exploration plans, they would have been redundant, as Norwegian Otto Sverdrup had already charted areas on Ellesmere's western coast where he intended to carry out geographical investigations. The expeditions of Stein, Björling and Kallstenius underlined the absurdity of venturing into the Arctic with inadequate funding and preparation.

Otto Sverdrup Expedition, 1898–1902

In 1896, with the encouragement of the famous explorer Fridjof Nansen and approval of funding by the Norwegian government, Otto Sverdup agreed to lead an expedition to the High Arctic. The Norwegians intended that Sverdrup sail in the *Fram* through Nares Strait to winter on the northern coast of Greenland, which he would explore before returning via its eastern coast. Departing from Norway in June 1898, he and 15 others reached the North Water and attempted to sail along Ellesmere Island's east coast before they were stopped by pack ice off Cape Sabine, just north of Smith Sound. The *Fram* wintered in Fram Havn, a sheltered cove on Ellesmere's eastern coast in the northern part of Rice Strait. The following spring, Sverdrup and three others proceeded by foot across the island via the Sverdrup Pass between Hayes and Bay Fiords.[223] At the head of Bay Fiord on Ellesmere's western coast, they sighted Axel Heiberg Island across Eureka Sound. Returning to the ship, Sverdrup again attempted to sail north into Kane Basin. Impeded by heavy ice conditions and a storm, he got no farther than a point adjacent to Cape Hawkes before being forced to turn back.

At this point, Sverdrup changed his expedition plans and proceeded south to Greenland's Northumberland Islands to hunt seals for winter provisions, before sailing across Baffin Bay to Lady Anne Strait at the mouth of Jones Sound. The party explored Ellesmere's southern coast before wintering in Harbour Fiord. That fall, Sverdrup's party undertook a series of hunting excursions in the Jones Sound region, surveying the coastline of various fiords and bays on Ellesmere and Devon Island across the sound. The following spring, Sverdrup and nine others proceeded by dog team with extreme difficulty past the treacherous waters of Hell Gate along a narrow ice foot adjacent to the Simmons Peninsula. At the mouth of Baumann Fiord, five men turned back with their dog teams to replenish their provisions. The remaining four men pushed out across Norwegian Bay and along Axel Heiberg's western coast. Isachsen and Hassel split off to explore lands they had sighted to the west, while Sverdrup and Fosheim continued as far north as 80° 55' N. lat.[224]

When the *Fram* proved unable to penetrate the ice-clogged waters of Cardigan Strait at the western end of Jones Sound, the party wintered on the southern shores of Ellesmere Island for the balance of the expedition, this time in Goose Fiord. From this base, the Norwegians undertook extensive sledging expeditions over the next two years to various islands in the Sverdrup group, including Amund Ringnes, Ellef Ringnes, and Cornwall Islands, while filling in much of the map of Ellesmere and Axel Heiberg Islands. The most far-ranging sledge excursions were reserved for the spring of 1902. After spending the first part of the winter hunting, Sverdrup and Schei sledged along the ice foot of the Ellesmere side of Eureka Sound to Greely Fiord. Crossing the fiord, they attempted to penetrate Hare Fiord in northern Ellesmere Island, but their progress was blocked by heavy snow. Returning to the fiord's mouth, they proceeded up the length of Nansen Sound to Kleybolte Island (81° 40' N. lat.) at the northwestern extremity of Ellesmere Island. From here, they crossed the mouth of the sound and reached the northern tip of Axel Heiberg Island on 10 May, before retracing their steps back to the ship on 16 June. Departing Goose Fiord after the *Fram* dislodged from the ice in early August 1902, Sverdrup's party arrived back in Norway on 19 September.

While its work generated few headlines, the judgment of history has ranked Sverdrup's expedition highly in terms of its contributions to geographical knowledge. In four years the Norwegians identified several islands previously unknown to Europeans, including Axel Heiberg Island, the two Ringnes islands, and Prince Christian Island. As well, they mapped the entire western coast of Ellesmere Island, with the exception of Greely and Tanquary fiords. Overall, they charted 2,800 km of coastline, in addition to scientific observations.[225] Summing up its work, geographer Andrew Taylor wrote: "No expedition operating within the area of the Queen Elizabeth Islands has contributed so much to its exploration as did Sverdrup's, at least, not since the days of Parry." Its contributions included opening up the entire area to the north of the Parry group of islands, apart from the north and east coasts of Ellesmere Island, and the western islands later explored by Stefansson.[226]

In 1894, Sir Clements Markham delivered the presidential address to the Royal Geographical Society. Taking stock of the state of polar exploration, Markham expressed his own view that, in itself, the race for the North Pole had little redeeming merit: "The Council has always consistently maintained that merely to reach the North Pole, or to attain a higher latitude than some one else, were objects unworthy of support."[227] In his address, Markham paid tribute to the exploratory work then being carried out by American Robert E. Peary in northern Greenland. Already at this early date, Peary's skills in planning and equipping his parties and developing appropriate approaches to arctic shelter had attracted the notice of the polar fraternity. Markham added: "in all Peary's operations there is the evidence of capacity and skill."[228] Markham also noted Peary's plans to cross over the Greenland ice cap to the far north of the island, where he intended to surpass Lockwood's farthest north. He wrote: "But it appears that Peary is also bitten with the 'beating the best record' mania, and thinks of pushing due north with the object of reaching the highest latitude attainable. It is to be hoped that this fancy will not be allowed to mar the real work of the expedition, which is to complete the outline of Greenland." But if Markham imagined that Peary's interest in achieving a new farthest north was a passing fancy, he was mistaken. A new breed of explorer had emerged, utterly devoted to attaining the North Pole, with a personality the likes of which the Arctic had never seen.

.

"*Mine* at Last"
Robert E. Peary's Polar Expeditions,
1890–1909

Few episodes of exploration have inspired so much writing as the succession of High Arctic expeditions by American Robert E. Peary around 1900. Much of the credit for this proliferation of texts must go to the explorer himself, who saw the potential to generate a wide audience through the burgeoning popular culture of the era. In numerous books and innumerable articles and speeches in the United States and Europe, Peary went to great lengths to leave a voluminous official record of his explorations.[1] His version has been faithfully reproduced in countless biographies and accounts of North Pole exploration by his family, colleagues, friends, admirers, and institutional supporters,[2] while Peary has been elevated to the status of a national icon in the United States.

Peary has also been a controversial figure, in his own era and since. Despite a voluminous literature on this explorer, he remains an enigma (Figure 49). From the time of the exploration era, he has been both lionized as a hero and vilified as a villain, with supporters and opponents represented in roughly equal measure. During the first decades after his presumed North Pole triumph, most books on Peary presented his case favourably, although even then he was not without detractors. For example, H.P. Steensby, a Danish ethnographer of the Inughuit in Peary's day, characterized his approach as "brutal and inconsiderate."[3] In recent years, other books and articles have begun to debunk the achievements of the legendary explorer, presenting him as highly exploitative of his employees and the environment.[4]

What drove Peary in his polar endeavours? In an article published in 1899 during his first major North Pole expedition, his official justification framed his goal partly as a personal test and partly in terms of the prestige that would accrue to the country sponsoring a successful assault. He wrote:

> I am after the Pole because it *is* the Pole: because it has a value as a test of intelligence, persistence, endurance, determined will, and, perhaps, courage, qualities characteristic of the highest type of manhood; because I am confident that it can be reached; and because I regard it as a great prize which it is peculiarly fit and appropriate that an American can win.[5]

Figure 49: Photograph of Robert E. Peary wearing Inughuit-styled fur garments, 1910. Peary Arctic Expedition, 1908-09. Credit: National Geographic Society (Washington, DC), Robert E. Peary Collection, Project No. 02116, Consecutive no. 3947, Picture Id. No. 124691A, Picture Record No. 132817.

Peary's unpublished writings suggest that the prospect of money and honours were also prominent in his thoughts. During the winter of 1900–01 at Fort Conger, Peary scribbled notes to himself for future reference. Written at a melancholy time for all members of his party, the explorer turned his thoughts to the recognition and rewards he felt had so far eluded him:

> Look up the honors (peerages, knighthoods, etc. bestowed by England on her Arctic Explorers. Look up also pecuniary rewards.
> Note rewards to American explorers Melville and Schley, Chiefs of Bureaus, Greely excessive promotion & a soft snap for life.
> Look up opinions expressed by Gov't officials themselves (Robeson & Kennedy, particularly, perhaps) on the importance of Arctic work. Compare Greely's geographical work with mine.[6]

For the present study, our interest in Peary derives from fact that it was during his expeditions that full-fledged contact was initiated between Euro-American and Aboriginal peoples in the High Arctic. Other expeditions had employed small numbers of Aboriginal guides and hunters, but Peary was the first to employ large numbers of Inughuit, including whole families, for service in the far north. As noted in chapters 6 and 9, the contact experience occasioned an extensive exchange of material culture and also had a major impact on the human ecology of the region.

Peary staged several expeditions to the High Arctic in the 1880s and early 1890s, while he developed his knowledge of the region and advanced its geographic exploration. From virtually the outset, he decided on Nares Strait between Ellesmere Island and Greenland as the focus of his activities. In a diary written in 1885, he explained his rationale:

> Smith Sound is preeminently the American route. Almost the entire shores from C[ape] Sabine & Cairn P[oin]t N[orth] on both sides have been mapped by our expeditions & now we are farthest north on this same road. Let the English, the Germans, the Austrians, have Spitsbergen & Franz Joseph [Land] & all the other routes, but let us stick to Smith S[ound] & fight it out on this line all winter.[7]

Following the disaster of the Lady Franklin Bay Expedition, Peary was calling for a new approach. "The time has arrived now," he wrote, "for an entire change in the expeditionary organization of arctic research parties." The old approach, involving large parties and several ships "has been run into the ground & almost every American authority at least is beginning to see the necessity of a new departure." With the exception of failed explorers whose objectivity he questioned, Peary asserted that arctic authorities were now "leaning to the side of smaller parties." He added, "the new plan of a small party depending largely on native assistance, inaugurated by Schwatka, deserves to be regarded as the American plan & another successful expedition will make it prominently such and put us far ahead in the race."[8]

In the same diary, Peary sketched out his plan to succeed where others failed. Surmising that success would come "to the patient waiter and the persistent devil," he vowed to be both. He then sketched out the composition of the ideal exploration party, which would consist of the explorer, "two [American] companions, a Danish or half-breed driver & interpreter, & three natives & their wives." With such a party, Peary vowed to "settle down on the shore of the northern ocean till the secret is wrested from the ice or I have my life."[9]

Apart from the size of the party, Peary's envisioned expedition structure departed from earlier European expeditions in two major respects. First, he proposed to involve more than a token complement of Aboriginal men as hunters. Second, he foresaw the value of employing Aboriginal women as well as men on these excursions. He wrote:

If colonization is to be a success, in Polar regions, let white men take with them native wives. Then, from that union may spring a race combining the hardiness of the mother with the intelligence & energy of the Father. Such a race would reach the Pole if their fathers did not succeed in doing it.

In choosing the Euro-American members of his expeditions, Peary looked for a mix of physical and mental characteristics that he thought were optimal qualities in the rigorous context of polar exploration. For example, he specified that his prospective expedition personnel should be of slight, yet robust build. He explained his rationale:

Small, wiry men have a great advantage over large ones in polar work ...The latter require more material for their clothing and usually eat more. Large men take up more space than small ones, necessitating the building of larger snow igloos. Every pound in weight beyond the maximum requirement tends to lessen a man's agility; in fact, renders him clumsy and more apt to break his equipment. And the decided disadvantage which a large man is under in crossing new ice is apparent.[10]

In another publication, Peary wrote that, for his Greenland expedition of 1895-96, he had selected only young men in their twenties who, "in addition to possessing a first-class physique and perfect health, are men of education and attainments." He wrote:

I believe this to be the type of man best fitted to endure with minimum effect the ordeal of the Arctic winter, and to effectively execute a two or three months' dash on sledges, where intelligent will-power, elasticity, and enthusiasm are at a premium over the stolid endurance of muscles hardened by years of work.[11]

Peary also elaborated on the desired attributes when searching for a surgeon for his 1898–1902 expedition. He wrote that he wanted a person who was dependable, intelligent and ambitious, with a positive disposition, self-reliant, and possessing a good knowledge of surgery, as well as botany or geology. Further, all prospective expedition employees needed to be men who were not publicity-seekers, smokers, or drinkers.[12]

Finally, Peary outlined a specific strategy for attaining his goal. Proposing to sail through Smith Sound as far north as Thank God Harbour or farther, he would mark the route by building "permanent stone huts or stations at convenient distances which shall always contain supplies & always afford shelter. Then, even if I fail I shall have left permanent assistance to my successors."[13] While a number of details were to be modified in the course of his actual expeditions, such as the replacement of stone shelters by the more flexible snow *iglooyah*, it was remarkable how well he had anticipated his eventual North Polar plan, decades before it was actualized.

Peary's success in enlisting large numbers of Inughuit to devote themselves to his service can be explained in large measure by the fact that they needed Western goods, and he was the sole source of supply. Engaging a system of barter, he paid the Inughuit with guns, ammunition, and discarded pieces of wood or metal. Aware of the scarcity of materials available to them, the explorer cannily exploited this fact. He carefully rationed trading goods to provide incentives for performance of labour, but not in such quantities that his employees would become independent. For example, in 1900, he wrote a series of instructions to Matthew Henson regarding the sledge journeys to Fort Conger that winter. He directed Henson to pay each Inughuaq with 10 boxes of revolver cartridges, a barrel, some old clothing, and "some not too valuable pieces of wood."[14] During the 1908–09 expedition, Peary paid each of his male Inughuit employees a .44 Winchester rifle for the services of their entire families for a year.[15]

Overall, Peary espoused an instrumentalist view of expedition organization, in which his employees functioned as cogs or moving parts in a machine designed and controlled by the explorer. He explained:

> The designs for this expedition may not improperly be called a work of mechanical engineering, in which the component fractions were human brains and bodies, dogs, sledges, ice craft, Arctic experience, and perishable supplies, with the indomitable will of man for driving power.[16]

Peary's Greenland Expedition, 1898–1902

Despite the vast extent of writing on much of Peary's Arctic career, the events of his first North Pole expedition of 1898-1902 have never been fully detailed by Peary or analysed by others. Before Peary's papers were opened to general research, historians suggested that Peary's irregular diaries might hinder the historical reconstruction of this expedition, and that many questions might have to go unanswered.[17] An examination of the extensive records of this expedition in the U.S. National Archives shows that this is not the case; in addition to Peary's own diaries and other writings, his papers contain the notes and diaries of Dr. T.S. Dedrick, the expedition surgeon, and some rare letters by Matthew Henson, Peary's long-term assistant. A more likely explanation for the historical neglect of this period is Peary's failure to mount a serious attempt on the North Pole during this expedition. Despite considerable fanfare and the investment of much time and expense, Peary made little progress toward his cherished goal, obliging him and his supporters to downplay the entire enterprise.

Still, Peary's 1898–1902 expedition is of particular interest for the study of Ellesmere Island history, since it was during this trip that he first visited the northern regions of the island and wintered there. It also marked Peary's first experiment with moving entire families of Inughuit to the far north to establish new settlements to support his polar quest. Peary had not previously set foot on Ellesmere Island, although members of his 1893–95 expedition to northern Greenland made a brief foray to the island in 1894. They were accompanied by Henry Bryant, commander of an auxiliary expedition to provide relief if Peary's party were unable to evacuate from Anniversary Lodge in Inglefield Gulf. Departing Greenland on 4 August 1894, this group managed to penetrate the pack ice of Smith Sound to land at Cape Faraday on 7 August. Erecting two cairns on prominent points of land, Bryant believed, erroneously, that they were the first Europeans to land on this coast. Apparently, he had not read Kane's *Arctic Explorations*, which showed that all the major headlands of Ellesmere's central coast were already mapped in the 1850s.[18]

In 1897, already a seasoned High Arctic traveller, Peary proposed to the American Geographical Society his plan for a four-year expedition to Greenland and Ellesmere Island. During the 1890s, he had undertaken a series of explorations in the region, capped by a dramatic sledge trip across the Greenland ice cap to the island's northern coast.[19] He now determined to continue in the tradition of Kane, Hayes, Hall, Nares, and Greely, to push through the Ellesmere–Greenland channel to the Arctic Ocean and to the North Pole. In studying the history of these earlier expeditions, Peary concluded that they were seriously flawed in their reliance on European methods of exploration and survival. In his address to the Society, Peary outlined the essentials of his plan, including the following steps:

> raise a fund sufficient to insure the continuation of the work of exploration for ten years, if necessary, say $150,000, and deposit it in a trust company; purchase a ship, give her a minimum crew, load with concentrated provisions; proceed to Whale Sound; take on board several picked families of my faithful Eskimos, with their tents, canoes, dogs, etc.; force a way through Robeson Channel to Sherard Osborn Fjord or farther, and land people and stores; then send the ship back.[20]

Before the ship's return, Peary intended that it would sail north as far as the ice would permit, before crossing to the western side of Kane Basin, then sail north along the eastern coast of Ellesmere Island, landing small caches of supplies along the way. The caches would serve as emergency provisions in the event disaster befell the ship and would facilitate winter communication by sledge between his base in northern Ellesmere Island and the Inughuit homeland at Whale Sound.

After establishing a wintering site at Etah on Smith Sound, Peary intended to set in motion the next phase of activity, the transshipment of provisions and materials along Ellesmere Island's coast toward the far north, where he would set up a polar base camp at Fort Conger. As soon as the great fiords on Ellesmere Island's eastern coast had frozen sufficiently to permit surface travel, sledge parties would first be organized to break the trail, move small quantities of supplies, and construct snow houses to shelter the main freighting groups that would follow. To help ensure rapid progress, these trips would be made with small parties and light loads. Upon reaching an intermediate destination, the party would leave a cache and then continue on to the next goal. On the trail, the sledgers would subsist on local game and shelter themselves by building snow houses, which would also serve as shelters for the succession of parties moving northward or returning to the south to reload supplies.[21]

The next stage in the plan was to send a series of more heavily loaded sledge trains along this route until the departure of the sun, when these forays were to continue during each period of moonlight. By spring, Peary hoped to have his party and most of its supplies "at the northern tip of the North Greenland archipelago...with caches behind it at each prominent headland." Then, with a selection of the best dogs, the lightest equipment, and "two of the best of the Eskimos" he would attempt to reach the North Pole, "with strong possibilities of a successful termination."[22]

With the announcement of these plans, Peary signalled a major departure from previous expeditions to the region. The expeditions led by Nares and Greely relied exclusively on ships to move their men and supplies to the north and, from these advanced points, surface exploratory excursions were then staged. However, following the disastrous conclusion of the Greely expedition, Peary realized the riskiness of depending on an ice-free corridor through Nares Strait. As an alternative, he chose two mutually reinforcing strategies of penetrating to the northern reaches of Ellesmere Island and Greenland. Travel by ship would be complemented by a co-ordinated system of freighting labourers and supplies over the surface of the sea ice.

The lynchpin of the enterprise was Peary's intended reliance on the labour of Inughuit families, who had provided the lion's share of work on his three previous expeditions to northern Greenland. Other explorers had employed individual Greenlanders as hunters and sledge drivers, but they were given a minor role on these expeditions. As well, these men had been separated from their families, who remained in Greenland. Having observed Inughuit society during earlier wintering expeditions to the Thule district, Peary understood the importance of women's labour, especially their skills in manufacturing fur clothing, to the success of polar parties.

In the spring of 1898, Peary organized the Peary Arctic Club to raise money for the expedition; several friends of his, all wealthy businessmen, served as its nucleus. Peary himself was indefatigable in raising additional resources through the lecture circuit. Over a period of 96 days he delivered 168 lectures, raising $13,000. He sold letters to the *New York Sun* for $2,000, while his wife Josephine Peary wrote a book whose proceeds she devoted to the expedition.[23] That May saw the arrival of the schooner yacht *Windward*, the British steam ship he had commissioned for the expedition. Due to a machinists' strike, new engines had not been installed as planned, and it was essentially limited to use as a sailing ship.

The specific catalyst for Peary's return to the High Arctic apparently was Norway's announcement of the impending Sverdrup expedition to the region of Smith Sound and Ellesmere Island. Fearing that Sverdrup would establish the right to use "my route towards the Pole" if he arrived there before him, Peary quickly stepped up his own plans to ensure an earlier arrival. Securing additional credit for the expedition, he chartered a small ship, the Newfoundland vessel *Hope*, to carry coal for the *Windward*, which would enable his main expedition ship to hurry toward its destination at full speed.[24]

First, however, it was essential to line up a supply of labour for this ambitious undertaking. In the summer of 1897, a year before his expedition was scheduled to commence, Peary sailed to northwestern Greenland to alert the Inughuit of his forthcoming plan and to ask them to begin to hunt to stockpile a large supply of meat and skins for his use.[25] The following year the expedition got underway when the schooner yacht *Windward* departed from New York harbour on 4 July, 1898. Three days later, departing from Sydney harbour on Cape Breton Island, Peary sailed on the *Hope*, an auxiliary ship he had commissioned for the northern trip. On his arrival at Whale Sound in northwestern Greenland, Peary's ship effected a rendezvous of the ships at Etah in August, after which he sent back the *Hope* to the United States. Loading several Inughuit men and women (Figure 50) along with their stockpiled meat and skins, the *Windward* continued on to the Ellesmere Island coast of Smith Sound and Kane Basin in search of a wintering

Figure 50: Photograph of Peary's party, including Matthew Henson, Inughuit women and men aboard the *Windward*, 1898. U.S. National Archives (Washington, DC), RG 401(1)(A), Papers Relating to Arctic Expeditions, 1886-1909, Greenland- Ellesmere Island, 1898–1902, Photograph No. 401-1/ 1898/ 455, "Deck of the *Windward*, 1898."

location. Moving between the fixed ice of Princess Marie Bay and the heavy moving pack ice in Kane Basin, the ship threaded its way to a small area of open water off Cape D'Urville, where a large grounded ice floe thwarted their further forward advance. After undertaking several reconnaissance forays by sledge, Peary decided to set up autumn quarters on this coast. He ordered the offloading of one third of his supplies; his Inughuit employees proceeded to sledge loads of 300 to 450 kg over the young ice to the shore.

Peary's intention was to move supplies during the winter moons to Fort Conger, where he intended to move his entire party by February. He and the Inughuit spent the balance of the fall and early winter hunting muskoxen and walrus to build up their stocks of meat in preparation for the journey to the north.[26] After the onset of the long winter night, this work was performed during periods of moonlight, while, during the dark periods, the Inughuit were occupied with such tasks as making and repairing sledges and bringing in meat from caches.

During this period, Peary experimented with the caching system he learned from arctic Aboriginal people and for which he was to become famous. At convenient intervals, beginning with Cape Fraser, a series of snow-domed shelters (*iglooyah*) were constructed to house future sledging parties. For example, during the moonlight period in late November, two sledging parties transported 1,500 kg of supplies and stocks of dog food to Cape Wilkes on the north side of Richardson Bay, about 100 km north of Cape D'Urville. Peary's plan was to attempt to reach Fort Conger during the January moonlight. As the sledges had been wrecked by very rough surface travelling conditions, the Inughuit men took advantage of the dark interval of late November and early December for repairs on the runners, while the women were engaged in sewing and repairing the party's traditional animal-skin garments, before again pressing on toward Fort Conger.

In a contemporary publication, Peary described the rigours of striking out from the ice foot to the pack ice when traversing bays or fiords, necessitated by the rugged and irregular shoreline of Ellesmere Island's eastern coasts:

> As there is always a descent from the headquarters camp to the ice-foot, and another from the ice-foot to the sea ice, usually along a narrow, tortuous path, previously cut through the ice blocks with pickaxe and axe, the first one or two hundred yards of the start is as lively work as any man can desire.[27]

If the ice foot was rendered impassable by pressure mounds, it was often necessary to resort to the perilous negotiation of a narrow ice strip along its face:

> Here at the sliding joint, between the face of the ice-foot and the pack ice, which rises and falls at every tide, a little water is forced up at each rising tide and, freezing, forms a very narrow, tortuous ribbon of glare ice, frequently interrupted and sometimes lacking entirely for several hundred feet."[28]

In these places, dogs had to be detached from the sledges, which were lowered one at time from one tentative foothold to the next. Readers are referred to Figure 97, an exploration-era photograph by Donald MacMillan of two Inughuit men hauling a komatik over a rough stretch of the ice foot on Ellesmere Island's eastern coast, which illustrates the hazardous nature of this activity.

On 20 December, Peary departed from Cape D'Urville with his surgeon, Dr. T.S. Dedrick, his long-term assistant Matthew Henson, four Inughuit men, and 30 dogs with light sledges. Apart from moonlight, this was the period of near-total darkness. Utilizing the six snow-block shelters constructed earlier along the route, the group was housed in relative comfort. However, the rough condition of the ice foot north of Cape Lawrence made for extremely arduous sledging, and severe northerly winds stopped their forward advance. Peary left two of the Inughuit and several dogs near Cape Defosse. With their food gone and moonlight rapidly waning, his group stumbled across the rugged sea ice to Cape Baird, where they slept for a few hours in a burrow hollowed out of the snow, before pressing on across the jagged pack ice of Lady Franklin Bay.

Arriving on the northern shores of the bay 18 hours later, they killed a dog for food and abandoned nine others in an exhausted state along with a wrecked sledge. The group continued to grope its way over difficult stretches of ice foot to what proved to be the entrance to Discovery Harbour. At midnight on 6 January 1899, they arrived at Fort Conger, which Peary found in good condition, albeit showing the signs of its chaotic abandonment by Greely's party more than 15 years earlier. He described the scene:

> Forcing an entrance and lighting our oil stove, [I] found the interior presenting the utmost confusion. Floor of both officers' and men's quarters and kitchen blocked and littered with boxes, packed and empty, pieces of fur, cast-off clothing, rubbish of all descriptions. In the kitchen, partially consumed tins of provisions, tea, coffee, etc., were scattered about, their contents spilled on table and floor. In the men's quarters dishes remained on the table just as left after lunch or dinner on the day the fort was deserted. Biscuits scattered in every direction, overturned cups, etc., seemed to give indications of a hasty departure....[29]

Noteworthy Incidents: The Case of the Missing Toes

To Peary's dismay, his arrival at Fort Conger coincided with the discovery that his toes were frozen. His injury represented more than a personal misfortune. It was to become the basis for one of the most famous anecdotes in the annals of arctic exploration. Numerous writers have chosen to interpret this episode as a demonstration of the explorer's unshakeable courage, the essential ingredient without which he could never have reached the North Pole. For example, J. Gordon Hayes used the incident as a demonstration of Peary's "iron will": "He could stand any amount of physical pain, and stumped about for weeks, after losing nearly all his toes, with eight open wounds on his feet!"[30] In *The Arctic Grail*, Pierre Berton saluted the explorer's legendary perseverence:

The adjective "indomitable" has been used to describe more than one polar hero, but it fits no other so neatly as it does this single-minded and desperately driven forty-two-year-old American, who would for the rest of his life hobble on the stumps of his feet, yet feel it a small price to pay for the fulfilment of a dream.[31]

William Henry Hobbs, Peary's official biographer, further added to the drama of the incident by writing that, while confined to his bed in the dead of winter at Fort Conger, he scratched a quotation from Seneca on the walls of Greely's house: *inveniet viam, aut faciet* ("find a way or make one").[32] The story of the inscription, too, has become a staple of exploration literature, reproduced by Berton and numerous other narrators of this heroic tale.

Given its attributed significance, the story of the toes warrants closer examination. Berton's version is one of the most recent, and certainly among the most vivid reconstructions of this incident. In narrating the story of the party's arrival at Fort Conger, Berton wrote:

> While he was sipping Greely's coffee, Peary became aware of a wooden feeling in his feet. When Henson ripped off the sealskin boots he saw that the explorer's legs were bloodless white to the knee. As he tore off the undershoes, two or three toes from each foot clung to the hide and snapped off at the joint.
>
> "My God, Lieutenant!" he cried. "Why didn't you tell me your feet were frozen?"
>
> "There's no time to pamper sick men on the trail," Peary told him, and added, "besides, a few toes aren't much to give to achieve the Pole."[33]

For this account, Berton evidently relied on Bradley Robinson's biography of Matthew Henson,[34] a book filled with colourful dialogue. Robinson himself provided no footnotes. While he credited Henson for his "earnest and cooperative" assistance, the book was published nearly 50 years after the frozen toes incident, long after an authentic reconstruction of verbatim conversations could be considered feasible or credible.

The only primary versions of the incident dating from the 1899 visit to Conger were separate diary notes by Peary and his surgeon, Dedrick, neither of which reports any dialogue.[35] Peary wrote that Angutdluk (Ahngoodloo), rather than Henson, helped him take off his kamiks. There is no indication that the toes snapped off at the joint; Dedrick reported that after working to get the frost out of them, he removed some dead tissue from the toes on both feet. Moreover, in his or Dedrick's diaries there is no evidence that Peary responded so cavalierly to the prospective loss of his toes; understandably, his own account suggests that he was extremely concerned about the consequences of this misfortune. Further, the apocryphal story of Peary's supposed inscription of "Find a way or make one" on the walls of Fort Conger is not mentioned in the primary accounts. His biographer William Henry Hobbs, who first reported the story, also failed to provide a footnote. However, John Edward Weems, a more recent biographer of Peary, may have found the source of the story. He noticed that the same inscription can be found on the inside cover of Peary's diary beginning 4 April 1901. The Latin phrase is in the third person and can be translated as: "He will find a way or make one."[36]

An examination of the available primary sources, then, suggests that the drama associated with the missing toes has been constructed more in the imaginations of the writers than from the documentary record. It is acknowledged that the colourful "facts" do fulfil a necessary function in the narratives to set off the heroic character and indomitable spirit attributed to the protagonist. We may deduce that the prime suspect in this case is the impulse to impart moral lessons, so integral to the construction of epic narratives and national mythologies.

Notwithstanding the pain and disability caused by his frozen feet, Peary recognized the advantage of finding the Fort Conger house in good condition. Well stocked with furniture, materials, and provisions and other supplies which Greely's party had abandoned in haste when they retreated in 1883, the fort proved a virtual emporium of goods for Peary for the balance of the expedition and during his succeeding polar forays of 1905–06 and 1908–09. After six weeks of confinement to his bed, Peary decided to return to the ship to have his toes amputated. In mid-February his men lashed him to a sledge to begin the arduous 450 km trip back along the rough ice foot to Cape D'Urville. This they accomplished in 11 marches averaging about 40 km a day. Following the amputations, Peary returned to Fort Conger twice that spring as he endeavoured to transport the necessary provisions and equipment to support the attempt on the North Pole he had promised his benefactors in the Peary Arctic Club. After making the last of these trips to Fort Conger in six days, between 23 and 29 May, his party returned to Etah on the Greenland side of Smith Sound, to winter. From this base, his men spent the month of January sledging supplies over the pack ice of Smith Sound to Payer Harbour, where they established a depot of provisions, to be transshipped to Fort Conger. Beginning with Henson's party, which left on 19 February, they then utilized the remaining winter moons to move the supplies in forced marches up to Conger.[37]

To move goods from Smith Sound to northern Ellesmere Island, Peary organized sledge "trains" or relays to advance supplies and dog food in stages to strategic locations along the ice foot to the north. On 4 March 1900, he reported having organized two relay trains, the first bound for Fort Conger consisting of six Inughuit drivers, each with seven to nine dogs, and a second train of four sledges, two bound for Cape D'Urville, another for Anoritooq in northern Greeland, and the fourth apparently assisting the others. Peary indicated that he would ride on Torngi's (Tungwee's) sledge and Angutdluk's (Ahngoodloo's) wife would ride with her husband.[38]

In addition to their labour, Peary relied on the Inughuit for the manufacture of all harness and traces for the dog teams and the construction of the sledges. In 1900, he indicated his specifications for the sledges, which he instructed should be between 2.45 and 2.90 metres in length, and 2.15 metres high, not including the width of the shoeing, with ivory from walrus tusks used in building the shoes.[39] Constructing and repairing the sledges proved to be a continuous responsibility, as Peary demanded that his sledgers continue through frequently difficult weather conditions over the rugged ice surfaces of the ice foot and the polar pack. For example, on 25 March he reported that two sledges had been broken.[40] The sledge trains also took their toll on the travellers. Peary, already suffering from amputations of his frozen toes, complained of torn tendons and muscles and callousing of his toe stumps.[41] Once again, the principal route of travel was along the coastal ice foot, which provided a relatively flat surface, contrasting with the ice pack, an extremely rough surface of pressure ridges and recurrent leads of open water.

By the spring of 1900, Peary and his party were established at Fort Conger with the ultimate objective of staging a serious attempt on the North Pole. Before the explorer's arrival, the Inughuit had already shot 21 muskoxen nearby. Less than two weeks later, Peary, Henson, and five Inuit departed from Conger on an excursion across Robeson Channel to Greenland and up its northwestern coast. It was on this trip that Peary first experimented with his system of using supporting sledge parties when food supplies could not be assured in the area in which he was travelling. Under this system the entire party was provisioned by the cargo of a single sled or group of sleds. After helping advance the party part of the way, some members of the group would be sent back with only enough food to enable them to return to the base camp. Subsequently, more men and sledges would be dismissed, leaving only a small core to complete the journey. Peary would retain only the best drivers, dogs, and the bulk of the food for the final leg of the trip.[42]

Figure 51: "Muskox at Bay." Photograph from Harry Whitney, *Hunting with the Eskimos* (1910), p. 293.

This was the essence of the system he later employed in his last attempt on the North Pole in 1909.

During Peary's absence, Dedrick and several Inughuit were engaged in a number of hunting excursions in the vicinity of the fort where they obtained 30 muskoxen and 10 seals. In July, Dedrick was again in the field to the west of Fort Conger with several young Inughuit hunters at Black Rock Vale and Lake Hazen. On these trips, they reported using Aboriginal hunting methods to conserve ammunition.[43] Meanwhile, other Inughuit at Conger were engaged in hunting seals, while two Inughuit men constructed two kayaks for use in sealing. For kayak frames they utilized pieces of scrap wood found scattered around the Greely house, over which they stretched the skins of newly-slaughtered seals.

During the brief period of open water, the Inughuit also hunted walrus from the edge of the sea ice near Fort Conger.[44] To attract the walruses, the men imitated the bellow of the bull leader. When the animals were within 6 m of the floe edge, the hunters selected one, harpooned, and secured it. This was accomplished by tying the harpoon line around an ice pinnacle or a harpoon iron which they drove into the ice to provide an effective anchor. When thus secured it was relatively easy to kill the animal with a lance. Seals and walruses taken along the coast were supplemented by a larger kill of muskoxen in the interior. In addition to the meat, muskox skins were used in making clothing, covering the surface of sleeping platforms, and coverings in cold weather.[45]

By August, Peary decided to winter his party at Fort Conger in shelters they would construct from the lumber of Greely's house and other materials abandoned by the American and British expeditions to the site. One of his biographers described his decision to winter and "live off the country" in northern Ellesmere Island in 1900–01 as "daring."[46] It might more accurately be described as a pragmatic response to an emergency situation. Peary had planned to winter aboard the *Windward*, whose commander he had instructed to sail the ship to Fort Conger in the summer of 1900. When it failed to appear by August, he was obliged to fall back on contingency plans, which involved building a complex of wintering shelters on shore after Inughuit and Inuit prototypes. According to this plan, his party began digging the foundations of these semi-subterranean structures, which were largely completed within three weeks. A full discussion of the design of the complex and its antecedents in Inuit settlement patterns and architectural principles is provided in Chapter 10.

Here again, Peary's legendary skill in planning came into play. In June 1900, knowing the uncertain character of navigation in Nares Strait, he instructed his surgeon, Dr. Dedrick, and several Inughuit to spend three weeks in the interior hunting to feed the dogs and "cache meat for Fall use in case of non-arrival" of the *Windward*. Perhaps recalling the lack of readiness of the Greely party, Peary intended to be prepared for any eventuality.[47] In early September, Peary's party was engaged in work in the vicinity of Fort Conger, principally hunting land or sea mammals, especially muskoxen, hare, and seals, and fishing for charr in nearby streams or lakes. With winter fast approaching, another important task was procuring coal for fuel, which they obtained from a nearby coal seam, perhaps the one mined earlier by the Nares and Greely expeditions. Peary's diary entry for 14 September gives an indication of some of the activities: "Ahngmaloktok & Ootah went to Sun Peninsula & brought in 2 hares & 1 foreshoulder Drs bull [muskox], also Pooblah's seal...Ahngoodloo & Pooblah went to Dutch I [Island] to bring in remainder of coal there & look for seal. Ahngoodloo shot a seal in the water & secured him. We[ight] 100 lbs."[48]

By this time, Peary and his hunters were also making preparations for the fall hunting trip to the interior. His diary account reveals much about the organization and activity structure of these excursions. Like his Inughuit companions, Peary planned these trips to exploit as many hunting areas and different kinds of game animals and fish as could feasibly be included in the itinerary. Where he differed from their customary practice was in the scale of the slaughter. On 16 September he left Fort Conger with Matthew Henson and four male Inughuit hunters—Angutdluk, Sipsu, Uutaaq (Ootah), and Patdloq (Pooblah). They took four sledges, 20 dogs, and five pups. Scouring the interior from the Bellows and Black Rock Vale in the east, along the southern shores of Lake Hazen to the Very River Valley in the west, Peary's party had killed 92 muskoxen by the time they returned to Fort Conger on 22 October. Most of these animals were taken in a period of less than three weeks.[49] Figure 51 shows a muskox cornered by Husky dogs during a contemporary muskox hunt on Ellesmere Island by American Harry Whitney.

Despite their success in securing an abundant supply of game, Peary insisted that his men continue to hunt throughout the winter. His objective was to amass even larger stockpiles of meat to support an intended attempt on the North Pole the following spring. All members of the expedition spent an extremely difficult winter in 1900–01. They had constructed warm, relatively comfortable dwellings at Fort Conger, but most of the time were living in more rudimentary shelters in the interior, such as two *kangmahs* built by Angutdluk of rocks and skins at the western and eastern ends of Lake Hazen,[50] and even in snow shelters on the trail. The sites of these dwellings also served as collection areas for meat,[51] which was cached under rocks.

The field notes kept by Dr. Dedrick provide extensive evidence of the day-to-day activities and logistics of these interior hunting parties during the dark months. His notes confirm Peary's obsession with surplus meat collection; Dedrick clearly felt under pressure to report continued hunting successes. As large quantities of the muskox meat were consumed by the sled dogs, the intended stockpile was reduced accordingly. Dedrick also reported extreme weather conditions, including severe temperatures and violent storms, and expressed concerns that his personnel were at risk of developing scurvy.[52]

Indeed, during that winter in northern Ellesmere Island, both Peary and his expedition surgeon reported a general malaise among the American members of the party. For example, on 21 February 1901, housed in a stone dwelling at Lake Hazen, Dr. Dedrick wrote to Peary of the material difficulties of life for the hunting parties in the interior. Lamenting the crowded and uncomfortable conditions in these more rudimentary shelters, he wrote: "The circumstances which have compelled the party to live in such igloos so continuously are a great misfortune." He suggested that the stresses of having such a large party in the field and "living so nearly from hand to mouth" had taken its toll on the group's psychological health. Particularly affected was Matthew Henson. Dedrick reported he was giving him some pure spirits, that is, rum, whisky, brandy, or wine, to be administered in the evening "in times of mental depression."[53]

Peary was convinced that maintaining an intensive winter regimen was essential to the psychological health of his party. However, both his and Dedrick's diaries reveal that depression and malaise were widespread among the group, even affecting the normally indefatigable explorer. Following the difficult winter at Fort Conger, Peary prepared plans for an attempt on the North Pole the following spring. He was not well positioned for this risky journey. Disheartened by the extreme winter conditions of northern Ellesmere Island, the Inughuit members indicated their unwillingness to follow Peary in his risky plans for an attempt on the North Pole that spring. Peary's first biographer, Fitzhugh Green, wrote that they designated a spokesperson to tell Peary that they would not accompany him but would return to Smith Sound with the arrival of spring.[54] Only one young Inughuit man, Angutdluk, agreed to join Peary and Henson for the journey to the north.

Peary's small party departed on 5 April. Reaching Lincoln Bay on the Arctic Ocean on 9 April, they confronted very rugged sea-ice conditions.[55] Peary's diary pages for the next four days are empty but, on 13 April, he reported that they were "busy getting things in readiness for trip south," confirming that they were about to turn back. If this was an attempt on the Pole, it was at best a half-hearted effort, a symbolic "demonstration to his backers"[56] that he had not abandoned the overriding goal for which they had financed the expedition. Within days of their return to Fort Conger, his small party retreated to the south.

Peary had already decided to re-establish wintering quarters at Payer Harbour off Ellesmere's eastern coast. By September, several Inughuit in his company were stricken with serious cases of influenza. Meanwhile, a full-scale rift had opened between Peary and his surgeon Dr. Dedrick, who had established his own wintering quarters at Etah, Greenland, across Smith Sound. Dedrick wrote to offer medical assistance, but Peary declined. One by one, the ailing Inughuit began to die and, by November, six individuals had succumbed to the epidemic.[57] In his diary, Peary reported that he was attending to the afflicted Inughuit, but pondered whether these "misfortunes" did not represent a hidden purpose, as he wrote: "Is it possible that my compulsory landing at Erik H[arbour], followed by this epidemic among my people has been a means of Providence to keep me from wasting my strength in work to the westward this Fall?"[58]

With little to show for his efforts over the previous three years, Peary determined to make another attempt on the North Pole the following spring. This time, he had to contend with heightened fears precipitated by the epidemic and deaths of Inughuit in his employ. In his field notes at Cape D'Urville, Peary reported that Henson had related Ootooniaksoah's statement that "so many of the natives have died that he and the others are afraid." He also recorded his own skeptical reaction: "perhaps they are conscience stricken at looting my things at Etah."

Despite their fears, Peary wrote that some Inughuit were still prepared to accompany him. "Ahsayoo [Asiajuk] is not only willing but anxious to go to Conger and beyond, if only Annahwee [Annowgwe], who is now sick can remain here [Cape D'Urville] while he is away." Peary also stated that Atangana (Ootooniaksoah) wanted to return to Conger, adding: "in view of their misfortunes I shall let bygones be bygones with those who have been on my blacklist."[59]

By late February, Peary had assembled a sledge train to the north with Henson and six Inughuit men. As with previous relays, he sent the men ahead to build snow houses and lay caches, before embarking himself after the ground had been prepared. After a month of arduous travel in temperatures ranging from –35° to –57° F, Peary arrived at Cape Hecla on the shores of the Arctic Ocean. On 6 April they struck out over the rugged ice pack, floundering first in heavy snow, then zigzagging their way over smoother patches of young ice to avoid the difficult pressure ridges, before again being stymied by soft snow. By 12 April, they encountered a large expanse of open water, the "Big Lead" that figured prominently in all his forays over the Arctic Ocean. Movements in the pack ice closed the lead within two days but produced heavy pressure ridges, which stretched in three directions. Combined with deep soft snow, the pressure ice prevented further progress. By 21 April, with his men exhausted and their supplies of pemmican running out, Peary was ready to give up. He wrote: "I have made a good fight but I cannot accomplish the impossible."[60] He reckoned he had reached 84° 17'27",[61] a new farthest north for the Western Hemisphere, but a bitter disappointment nevertheless (Figure 52).

Peary's 1905–06 Expedition

Despite his lack of success in attaining the Pole, Peary refused to abandon his cherished long-term goal. For his next expedition, in 1905, Peary drew on the lessons he learned from the four frustrating years spent on his Greenland excursion of 1898–1902. His experiences convinced him that a serious attempt on the North Pole could not be staged from Etah. The logistical difficulties of moving his party and supplies across Smith Sound and along 320 km of rugged coastline to Fort Conger were daunting. Having arrived at Conger, they would still be nearly 960 km distant from the Pole. Peary concluded that only by penetrating the ice-clogged Nares Strait to establish a base on the Arctic Ocean could he realistically position himself to succeed in reaching the Pole. This meant that he would need a ship capable of both navigating the channel and providing wintering quarters, enabling an assault on the Pole with the return of daylight and improved weather in the spring.

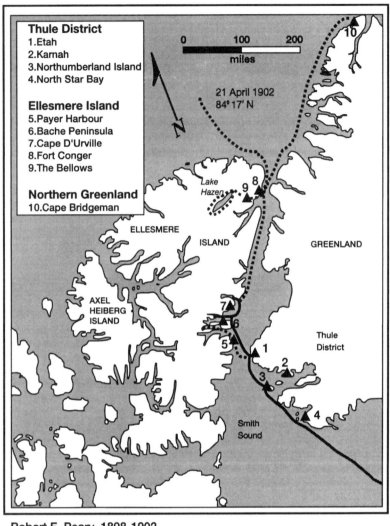

Robert E. Peary, 1898-1902

············· Dog sledging excursions ━━━━━━ Ship

Figure 52: Map of the route of Peary's 1898-1902 expedition

Such a plan required a large infusion of capital to finance it. For this expedition, Peary persuaded two wealthy backers, Thomas Hubbard and Morris K. Jesup, to contribute $50,000 each for the building of his custom-designed arctic vessel, the *Roosevelt*, while George Crocker pledged another $50,000 to underwrite the costs of the voyage.[62] Other members of the Peary Arctic Club contributed smaller amounts, while Peary himself borrowed money to the limit of his credit. The cost of the voyage has been estimated at more than $500,000.

Peary also devoted considerable thought to assembling an optimal team for the expedition. To captain the ship, he recruited Robert Bartlett, at 30 already a seasoned Newfoundland mariner with arctic experience, having served as the mate of Peary's ship the *Windward* in 1898–99. This time, his second cousin Moses Bartlett, former mate of the *Neptune*, "one of the best Newfoundland ice-pilots," would serve as mate.[63] The other Americans were a mix of arctic veterans, including Peary's long-term assistant Matthew Henson, and younger men chosen for their physical condition and potential for arctic work. As on previous expeditions, he intended to rely heavily on Inughuit labour throughout the expedition.

Peary's party departed New York in the *Roosevelt* on 6 July, 1905.[64] En route, the ship made a series of stops at Inughuit settlements throughout the district of Avanersuaq, where Peary recruited hunters and their entire families for service on the expedition. For the 1905 expedition, Peary reportedly selected "only men upon whom he can rely," including 23 hunters, their female partners (seven of these with infant children), several boys aged 14–18 years, and "one or two young widows," totalling about 60 individuals.[65] In addition, Peary undertook to hire the use of 213 Husky dogs for the expedition, which were housed in the centre of the top deck. A passenger on the companion supply vessel observed: "the usual howling, barking, and fighting were worse than any time before, owing to the increased number of dogs and the narrowness of the space assigned to them."[66]

Prior to their departure, Peary directed his party to hunt walrus for food for his Inughuit companions and their dogs during the trip toward his intended wintering base on Ellesmere Island's northern coast. On the *Erik*, 17 dead walruses were hauled up on deck to be slaughtered by the Inughuit boys. Nicholas Senn, a passenger, described the scene as one of virtual mayhem:

> As the young butchers proceeded with their work, the deck became flooded with grease and steaming blood. The boys, in their sealskin boots, were ankle deep in the slippery mixture. The more than a hundred

snarling, fighting dogs dragged the entrails in all directions, each of them determined to get his liberal share of this, to them, their greatest delicacy. Men, women and children waded through pools of blood and scattered it all over the deck. The dogs were smeared with blood, and this, together with the thirty tons of coal still on deck, will give some idea of the discomforts of deck-life during this part of our trip.[67]

After the walrus meat was loaded on the *Roosevelt*, the party proceeded from Greenland toward Smith Sound and the rugged journey through the ice-congested Nares Strait. In his unpublished narrative of the expedition, Robert Bartlett later related the difficulties they confronted in negotiating the treacherous floes of the channel en route to their destination. Hugging the shoreline, Bartlett took advantage of any opportunities presented by clear stretches of water to move forward, while quickly manoeuvring the ship into protected bays or fiords with the approach of ice floes from the north. "It was a waiting and a watching game, eternal vigilance was the price of safety and success and keeping the vessel afloat so that we would slip into the bays that lined the Ellesmere shore, and let the ice pass along...." At times, such as the stretch between Cape Joseph Good and Rawlings Bay, he steered the ship very close to the ice foot. Bartlett remarked:

> In some cases, one can get a friendly niche where he can secure his ship against the onrush of the oncoming ice, which hurled itself relentlessly and with tremendous force against the face of the ice foot. Should a ship be caught outside of the friendly niche, she would be crushed as easily as a steam hammer would crush an egg.

While close vigilance was essential, Bartlett acknowledged that "even luck plays a great part of the game."[68] After anxious moments during which he zig-zagged across the channel, he eventually found a narrow ribbon of water adjacent to the Greenland shore, affording a route to the north. Several further close calls ensued, in which the *Roosevelt* was lifted right out of the water by the pack ice. At one point the *Roosevelt* "was like a billiard ball at the end of a cue... She was beyond our control and we were at the mercy of the ice, and it looked pretty bad, we were hurled against the ice foot before the ice could jam us, we slipped by into a friendly nitch [niche], which seemed to be made there for us."[69] With difficulty, Bartlett and his crew finally managed to make their way to the Lincoln Sea on the edge of the Arctic Ocean, arriving at Cape Sheridan, near the wintering site of the *Alert* in 1875–76, on 5 September.[70]

Here, Peary's men began to prepare the site to serve as his wintering base. One of the principal roles of the Inughuit men was to hunt and fish to provide most of the expedition's provisions. While still aboard ship they were already engaged in the manufacture and repair of harness and preliminary work on sledge construction. For their part, the Inughuit women were engaged during the voyage and for much of the winter in sewing fur clothing for all members of the party in preparation for Peary's planned assault on the Pole the following spring.[71] After arrival at Cape Sheridan, the men completed the sledges and harnesses, in addition to general tasks such as cutting a bed in the ice to accommodate the ship for winter quarters.[72]

Within days the hunting parties departed for such distant localities as Clements Markham Inlet, Rowan Bay, and Porter Bay in search of muskoxen.[73] During these excursions, Inughuit hunters killed large numbers of muskoxen and caribou, the meat of which they cached or transported back to the ship. Once again, the Lake Hazen area would be a focus of hunting. On 14 September, Peary sent the first of several Inughuit hunting parties on a hundred-mile trek to the interior. By 15 October, four hunting groups returned to Cape Sheridan, bringing news that they had taken 144 muskoxen and caribou.[74] Shortly after their return, 80 dogs died from eating poisoned whale meat and Peary was obliged to discard several tons of the stores of dog food. To make up the shortfall, in late October he sent 26 Inughuit inland with 102 dogs to Lake Hazen, with orders to accelerate their procurement activities. He instructed that they return to the ship every full moon with fresh stores of meat and fish, before returning to the interior to repeat the cycle.[75] On 8 November, the families who had occupied *igloos* at the Ruggles River, returned with the news that they had secured 75 muskoxen, some hare, fox, and a "large number" of arctic charr from Lake Hazen.[76] Guided by their Inughuit drivers, the dog teams hauled muskox meat back to the ship on a continuous basis throughout the autumn and winter. After unloading their cargo, the men loaded provisions such as tea, coffee, sugar, and biscuits to bring back to their families, along with No. 10 shotguns loaded with buckshot for continued hunting of muskox.[77]

Peary wrote that his hunters occupied "settlements" at three locations in the Hazen region. The largest was on the southern slopes of the United States Mountains north of Lake Hazen. Another was located "at the head of Lake Hazen," possibly the corbelled-arch stone Inughuit dwelling whose remains have been identified near the mouth of the Turnabout River.[78] The third settlement was situated near the entrance to the Ruggles River. These more substantial shelters were supplemented by snow *iglooyahs* built between the settlements and Cape Sheridan,[79] enabling them to seek shelter and sleep while traversing the large distances between these nodes. Using the stone *kangmah* shelters as a base, the hunters and their families hunted mammals throughout the dark winter months, using periods of moonlight to haul the meat back to the ship. Then, with the sledges refitted, a new party of Inughuit families would then depart for the interior, before returning with a fresh load of meat with the succeeding moon.

Peary's assistant Matthew Henson, who accompanied the Inughuit parties on several hunting excursions to the interior, left a written account of one of these trips. Accompanied by four men—Inuutersuaq Ulloriaq (Ooblooyah), Akpudingwah, Kudlah, and Iggiannguaq (Egingwah)—Henson left the *Roosevelt* on 6 November, with the objective of feeding the dog teams and hunting muskoxen during the December moon. After feeding the dogs from a cache near the ship, they were confined to one of the temporary *iglooyahs* by a storm that lasted three days. When the storm abated, the hunters began hauling in various loads of cached meat from other locations to feed the dogs again to repletion in preparation for renewed hunting efforts scheduled for the December moon. During this interim period of darkness, Henson travelled extensively in the interior to convey instructions to the Inuit to haul in loads of slaughtered meat from various locations, such as Salmon Lake and Divide Lake, to his base camp west of Lake Hazen. From this base, the meat was to be transshipped to Cape Sheridan. Hunting began in earnest during the moonlight of early December, when Henson reported 13 muskoxen and two caribou killed. Noting that on 12 December another gale had "cut the igloo to pieces," Henson reported that his party broke camp on 13 December, and arrived back at the ship on the morning of 16 December.[80]

In addition to larger game animals, the Inughuit also hunted foxes and hares. Both men and women fished charr from the lake during the autumn.[81] Beyond hunting to provide the majority of the expedition's food, the Inughuit contributed much of the manual labour at the base camp. For example, soon after the ship's arrival at Cape Sheridan, the men were engaged in hauling supplies from the hold. When the ship was in danger of being crushed by the driving pack ice, the Inughuit men, women, and children worked alongside the Americans for 36 hours to unload much of the coal and bring all supplies and equipment ashore.[82] They also performed such tasks as constructing the snow-block wind barriers protecting the crew's wintering quarters in the deckhouse of the *Roosevelt*,[83] and digging snow for drinking water.

Having acquired the clothing, meat, and labour required for his polar attempt, Peary dismissed most of the Inughuit for the balance of the season, saying that they "could either stay about the ship, or go in to

Lake Hazen, or to Fort Conger with their families."[84] Retaining only the best Inughuit sledge driver, Peary soon departed on his prospective attempt on the Pole with a small party, sledges, and dogs. The remaining hunters and families were left behind to fend for themselves.

By the middle of February 1906, Peary's men set out along the north coast of Ellesmere on the first leg of his polar attempt. Using the relay system, they transported equipment and provisions to a base camp at the foot of Cape Sheridan, the most northerly point of land on Ellesmere Island, some 680 km across the Arctic Ocean from the North Pole. Peary's plan for his attempt on the Pole was an experiment in using relay teams to advance men and materiel across the polar pack ice , a practice he would later perfect on his last expedition in 1909. The concept was to establish a base on the ice, 400 to 480 km north from Cape Moss, from which the final assault would be staged. Two parties would proceed across the ice, the first breaking the trail, and the main party following several days behind it. These parties would be further subdivided into five smaller units, each consisting of an American and two or three Inughuit, which would drop out at intervals of 80 km as they advanced.[85] After reaching their goal and dropping their loads, these parties would retrace their steps to pick up supplies left by the previous relay team, before again heading north again with the new load. By thus ensuring the transshipment and replenishment of provisions, Peary would be able to sustain his base camp at such a remote location, within striking distance of the Pole.[86]

On 6 March 1906, Peary's division struck out across the ice pack. In the early stages, they were hampered by ice movements, which capsized their snow shelters and shifted the travellers to the west. On the trail, Peary's men also confronted the unpredictable and dangerous character of the polar ice pack, set in motion by heavy northwest winds and high tides.[87] By 4 April, he reckoned that he was near 85° N. lat. Here, he was encountering occasional smooth sledging amidst frequently difficult conditions:

> The rest of the way heavy old floes, some of the blue hummock kind, on which the going was good, interrupted by old ruptures and belts of rubble ice over which the going was very bad. These places serve as nets to catch all the snow blown off the level places, and there it lies soft and deep.[88]

Peary acknowledged the skills of his Inughuit companions in negotiating the rough pressure ice; he wrote: "It is going that would discourage two, three, or four white men, but my little brown children of the ice cheerfully toil their sledges through it with the skill borne of life-long experience and habit." Yet, over the next six days his party was virtually stymied by a severe wind storm. Peary wrote from his *iglooyah* erected on the ice:

> Another day, the 6th of this interminable gale. Will it never end? Wind and drift continue with unabated violence. For some three hours today I pushed, and butted, and at times almost crawled on hands and knees, back and forth across the small floe on which we are camped.[89]

Eventually, the storm cleared and, following a further series of marches, he attained a new farthest north, at 87°6', 51 km beyond Cagni's record, on 21 April (Figure 53). At this point, his dogs close to starvation and the men suffering from exhaustion, Peary ordered a general retreat. Returning via the Greenland coast, Peary's party was fortunate to escape human fatalities; only 41 of their initial 120 dogs survived the journey,[90] many of which were killed for consumption by men and dogs.

The continuing role of the natural environment was further demonstrated on the expedition's return voyage to the United States. No sooner had the ship been released from the ice at Cape Sheridan than the moving pack ice drove it against the ice foot, wrecking the rudder and breaking the skeg (an extension of the keel to which the rudder was attached). Peary made provisional plans for spending another winter on Ellesmere Island, while Captain Bartlett and his men made a series of attempts to manoeuvre the ship into the Lincoln Bay. By 6 August, they were able to carve a path through the pack ice toward Thank God Harbour on the Greenland coast. However, the driving pack ice forced the ship back to the Ellesmere coast and into Lady Franklin Bay. There, the ship remained marooned for 18 days.

According to Bartlett, it was during this period of uncertainty that eight Inughuit families left his ship at Fort Conger, reportedly in a dispute over reductions in their rations.[91] Their departure also occurred shortly after the *Roosevelt* was heavily knocked about by the pack ice in Nares Strait.[92] Whatever the reasons for their departure, their winter was described as a "hard one."[93] The Inughuit wintered in the interior at Lake Hazen, but, according to Malaurie, they nearly died from starvation. The group arrived at Etah eight months later on foot, most of their dogs having perished en route.[94]

On 24 August the ship made its way into Nares Strait and headed for Cape Tyson on the Greenland coast. Eventually open water was found, enabling the *Roosevelt* to sail to the south until stopped by heavy ice east of Hayes Point on Kane Basin, where the ship was again detained by the ice from 29 August to 5 September,[95] before it was finally extricated. Experiencing stormy seas and other harrowing adventures on

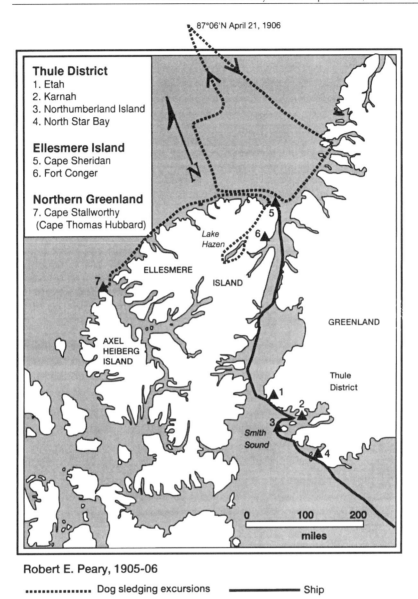

Robert E. Peary, 1905-06

················· Dog sledging excursions ━━━━━━ Ship

Figure 53: Map of the route of Peary's 1905–06 expedition

the return trip, the ship arrived back in New York City nearly four months later, on Christmas Eve, 1906.

Despite this setback, Peary remained preoccupied with achieving his own place in history. Among his many published statements articulating a continuing obsession with honours and supremacy was the following excerpt from his book on the 1905–06 expedition:

> A day's march beyond Aldrich's 'Farthest,' and what I saw before me in all its splendid, sunlit savageness was *mine* [Peary's emphasis], mine by the right of discovery, to be credited to me, and associated with my name, generations after I have ceased to be.[96]

Expedition of Dr. Frederick Cook, 1907-08

The narrative digresses here to include a brief account of the North Pole expedition of Frederick Cook in this chapter, as it occurred between Peary's last two expeditions and is inextricably linked to the story of Peary's polar attempts. Cook first came to the High Arctic while serving as surgeon on Peary's expedition of 1893–95 to northern Greenland. In 1906, he led a party that claimed to have ascended Mount McKinley in Alaska, establishing his reputation as a leading explorer in the United States.[97] In 1907, he turned his attention back to the Arctic and unveiled his strategy to John R. Bradley, the owner of several casinos in Florida, Louisiana, and Texas, whose patronage he was seeking. Taking note of the difficulties Peary encountered the previous year with heavy ice conditions in Nares Strait, Cook developed an alternative itinerary that would bypass the so-called "American route" altogether. To reach the pole, he proposed to cross Smith Sound, traverse Ellesmere Island to Eureka Sound, and then travel to the northern tip of Axel Heiberg Island, whence he would strike out over the ice pack toward his destination. He also advanced a theory that the currents of the Arctic Ocean divided into two northwest of Ellesmere Island, and that this would leave an area of relative calm between the two streams, facilitating sledge travel toward the Pole. By taking this route, he reasoned, he could stage an attempt on the Pole with a much smaller party, at less expense than Peary's expeditions.

With this plan in place, Bradley purchased a fishing schooner in Gloucester, Massachusetts, which he had reinforced with heavy oak strakes for added strength in pressure ice. Captain Moses Bartlett of Newfoundland, a relative of Robert Bartlett, was engaged as commander, and the ship was loaded with equipment for the polar foray, including several light sledges.[98] Thus equipped, the *John R. Bradley* sailed in the summer of 1907 from Gloucester to the Thule district. Here, Cook established quarters at the tiny Inughuit village of Anoritooq with the objective of making an attempt on the North Pole in the late winter. The only other American to stay with Cook was Rudolph Francke, the steward of the ship, who agreed to accompany him on his polar attempt. Applying skills he had learned while serving with Peary, Cook spent the winter months between October and February hunting with the Inughuit to secure meat for his polar foray. The men repaired sledges while the women made skin garments for Cook and his party.

On 19 February 1908, Cook traversed Smith Sound with Francke and nine Inughuit men, each driving a sledge, their komatiks pulled by 105 dogs. By the time they made the crossing to Bache Peninsula, Ellesmere Island, air temperatures had dropped to -64° F, and most members of his party suffered frostbite on the face.[99] Proceeding along Buchanan Bay, they travelled over the ice cap along the spine of the island, and down to Bay Fiord on the western coast of the island. Proceeding from Eureka Sound to the north, they entered Nansen Sound and continued to Cape Svartevoeg at the northern end of Axel Heiberg Island, where they established a camp of several snow shelters. Previously, he had arranged for Pualuna, an Inughuaq who also served with Peary, to lay a cache of provisions at this location to support his North Pole excursion.[100]

On 18 March, Cook and two young Inughuit companions, Ittukusuk and Aapilaq (Figure 54), struck out over the ice pack of the Arctic Ocean with two komatiks and 26 dogs. They had loaded on the sledges 109 kg of pemmican for the men and 218 kg for the dogs; Cook planned to kill the dogs for food as they began to fatigue, leaving them with six dogs by the time they returned to land. Other provisions included 59 kg of walrus meat, 22 kg of muskox meat, and 211 kg of tallow. According to Cook, within four days they travelled nearly 160 km from the coast, when they encountered the open water of the Big Lead. Waiting for black ice to form, they then succeeded in crossing this dangerous stretch and by 26 March progressed to 84° 26' N. lat, about 300 km from their camp at Cape Svartevoeg. Then, experiencing a severe storm, during which they narrowly escaped rupture of the ice floe on which they were camped, Cook's party continued to 84° 26' N. lat. (Figure 55). Cook thought he saw land lying to the west, a coastline running parallel to their course, which he named Bradley Land after his sponsor. Like Peary's mythical "Crocker Land," no such island existed, although some scientists have speculated that Cook saw an ice island, an enormous chunk of ice that had calved from one of the ice shelves off Ellesmere Island's northern coast.

Figure 54: Ittukusuk and Aapilaq, companions of Frederick Cook on his North Polar expedition, of 1908–09. Photo taken ca 1907. Library of Congress (Washington, DC) Reproduction no. LC-USZ62-103160.

On 11 April, Cook asserted, they reached 87° 20' N. lat., 95° 19' long., having covered 480 km across the Arctic Ocean in 24 days.[101] By this time the spirits of his Inughuit companions were at a low ebb. We do not have their direct testimony, but Cook's version of what they said. According to him, the Inughuit made the following statements:

> *Noona-terronga, neuliarongita, ootah–peterongito* (land is gone; loved ones are lost; signs of life have vanished).
> *Tig-ilay-waongacedla–nellu ikah-amisua* (Return will I, the sky and weather I do not understand. It is very cold), said Ah-we-lah...
> *Sikinut-nellu* (The sun I do not understand) said E-tuk-ishuk.[102]

If Cook's rendition of their dialogue is accurate, the despair of Ittukusuk and Aapilak related to their remote position, isolation from their own people, and the fact that they were in a place where they could not

Figure 55: "Latitude 84 degrees North," 1908. US National Archives, RG 401 Series
    XPX, Photograph No. 401-XPX-1989-8884-2.

read the environmental signs. They wanted to turn back. Cook stated
that he was able to overcome their resistance to continuing by promising his companions that they would reach the "Big Nail" within five
days, and then return to their territory within two moons. Continuing
in steady marches, Cook reported that they reached the North Pole on
21 April. Retrospectively, he recorded his reaction:

> We had reached our destination. My relief was indescribable. The prize
> of an international marathon was ours. Pinning the Stars and Stripes to
> a tent-pole, I asserted the achievement in the name of the ninety mil-
> lions of countrymen who swear fealty to that flag.[103]

If Cook reached the Pole, his problems were only beginning. Now he
and his guides confronted the problem of making a 800-km return journey to Cape Svartevoeg and nearly 1,600 km to the Thule District. The
balance of his book described the difficult retreat back to the Arctic
Archipelago. On 13 June, he wrote in his diary that he had sighted land
to the south and east, which he presumed to be Axel Heiberg Island

and the Ringnes Islands; he and his companions had been carried by currents to the west, but could not return to Axel Heiberg due to open water and thin ice. His last diary entry recorded that they would head south with the 10 remaining dogs and a small amount of pemmican, enough on which to survive for 20 days.[104] His remaining records were notes written on loose pieces of paper which were left with Harry Whitney after their eventual return to Etah, buried in a cache, and never recovered. Therefore, we are obliged to rely on the explorer's two published accounts of his expedition,[105] neither of which can now be corroborated by other evidence other than second-hand versions of interviews with his Inughuit companions.

Exhausted and hungry, Cook's little party made its way across the Queen Elizabeth Islands to the south. This leg of their excursion was remarkable, as Theon Wright has observed:

> The saga of this journey during the fall and winter of 1908, the struggle of three men making their way across one of the most desolate regions on the face of the earth and surviving to tell the tale was in itself enough to rank Cook among the immortal explorers of the Arctic, with Greely, Nansen, Sverdrup, and Peary himself.[106]

Between Ellef Ringnes and Amund Ringnes islands, Aapilaq saved them and their dogs from starvation by shooting a polar bear. They struggled constantly with hunger as they made their way south, subsisting on muskoxen, caribou, seals, hare, and lemmings along the way. Cook hoped to reach Lancaster Sound, where they might encounter a whaling ship, but on inspecting the ice conditions in Norwegian Bay, decided to turn to the east.[107] Abandoning their remaining dogs on Devon Island, they cut the komatik in half, stowed the lumber and continued in the canvas boat Cook had carried on the journey. Reaching Jones Sound, they constructed a subterranean dwelling at Cape Sparbo on the northern coast of Devon Island and spent the winter there before returning to Etah via the eastern coast of Ellesmere Island in the spring. Figure 56 is a photograph by Cook of his two Inughuit companions spearing a muskox near their encampment at this site. Using only stones to drive the muskox into an enclosed area where they could kill it with spears, Ittukusuk and Aapilak drew on Inughuit traditional knowledge, overcoming their lack of numbers or firearms.[108]

Whether Cook had actually reached the Pole is another issue; he did not prepare a reliable set of observations or have the support of witnesses who might verify his putative achievement. In 1984, ethnographer Rolf Gilberg published a reconstruction of Cook's itinerary written by Inuuterssuaq Ulloriaq, historian of the Inughuit, who discussed Cook's

Figure 56: Ittukusuk and Aapilaq hunting a muskox at Cape Sparbo on the northern coast of Devon Island, 1908. Library of Congress (Washington, DC) Reproduction No. LC-USZ62-103157.

journey with both of his companions and members of their families. Ulloriaq himself was familiar with the geography of the region, having travelled to Ellesmere and Axel Heiberg Islands with Christian Vibe during the van Hauen Expedition of 1939-40. According to this version, Ittukusuk and Aapilaq, when shown a map of the presumed itinerary to the Pole, had scoffed at the notion that they had travelled such a distance from land.[109] Yet, in other respects Ulloriaq's reconstruction closely approximates Cook's version of their travel across the archipelago in *My Attainment of the Pole*.[110] Some writers have accepted Cook's claims as valid,[111] authors in the Peary camp have taken pains to debunk his asserted achievement,[112] while several have rejected the claims of both Peary and Cook.[113] Others have concluded that these questions are ultimately unanswerable, although Peary is usually credited with having come far closer to the Pole than Cook.[114]

Peary's Last Polar Voyage, 1908–09

Thwarted in his second major attempt on the North Pole, Peary returned to the United States determined to mount one last effort to reach his goal. By the spring of 1907, the explorer enlisted his navigator Robert Bartlett to help in efforts to raise money for a third polar voyage. Their target for contributions was a list of American political leaders and prominent businessmen.[115] While initially unsuccessful, Peary generated some money with the publication of *Nearest the Pole*, a new book on the 1905–6 expedition. The book opened with an announcement by Morris K. Jesup, President of the Peary Arctic Club, that Peary would soon launch a final attempt to reach the North Pole. Peary confirmed these plans in an address to the National Geographic Society later that year. After being presented with the society's Hubbard Gold Medal by United States President Theodore Roosevelt, the explorer made public his intentions.[116] Backed in part by Jesup and long-term supporters in the Peary Arctic Club, Peary's fundraising campaign failed to generate enough money to underwrite the entire expedition, and so he decided to proceed on "faith, hope, and credit." In Bartlett's assessment, "Success would bring millions of dollars from the lecture circuit. Failure would mean financial ruin. It was the gamble of a lifetime."[117]

On 6 July 1908, Peary and a crew of 21 Americans departed New York Harbour aboard the *Roosevelt* on what was to be his last expedition in search of the North Pole. As with his 1905 expedition, he directed the ship to stop at various points in the Thule district to pick up Inughuit families engaged to work for the expedition. In all, 69 Inughuit men, women, and children were assembed for the voyage.[118] The names of most of the men were identified in one enumeration; they included Uutaaq (Ootah), Ukkujaaq (Ooqueah), Sigluk (Seegloo), Iggiannguaq (Egingwah), Panippak (Panikpah), Kudlah, Qaajuuttaq (Kyutah), Aleqasinnguag (Keshungwah), Inuutersuaq Ulloriaq (Ooblooyah), Inukittoq (Inighito), Inawahhos, Kridtluktoq (Kudlooktooh), Equ (Arco), Uisaakassak (Wesharkoopsi), Karka (see Figure 96), Pualuna (Poodlaloonah), Qulutana (Koolatinah), and Toocumma.[119] This tabulation is not completely accurate, as Uisaakassak did not actually accompany Peary to the north but remained in Greenland.[120] Regrettably, as with so many other expeditions in this patriarchal era, nearly all of the 41 Inughuit women who travelled with Peary remain anonymous, as their names are usually not given other than in references to exotic behaviour such as "pibloktoq," discussed in Chapter 11.

For his last polar voyage, Peary once again established wintering quarters at Cape Sheridan on the northern coast of Ellesmere Island. After reaching Cape Sheridan on 8 September 1908, the members of the expedition set about their autumn work. The Inughuit men began to prepare for fall hunting and sledging parties by repairing harness and building sledges.[121] The women set fox traps along the shore and made fishing excursions to lakes in the vicinity.[122] As on previous expeditions, the Inughuit also served as general labourers at the base camp, cutting and hauling ice and whatever other manual tasks were assigned to them (Figure 95). By early October, 21 of these men had left with the autumn sledging parties.[123] As in 1905–06, the Lake Hazen region was a focus of hunting activity.[124] Other hunting excursions were undertaken along the northern coast. While on these trips, Peary's men built a series of snow houses that they would later use when moving supplies to Cape Columbia. A major supporting sledge excursion was undertaken by Donald MacMillan, George Borup, and five Inughuit assistants to Cape Morris Jesup on the north coast of Greenland. Peary instructed this party to cache meat at this remote location in the event that the prevailing currents drove the pack ice and his party eastward, as they had in 1906.[125]

While still based at Cape Sheridan, several Inughuit men expressed their unwillingness to accompany Peary on his foray over the pack ice and the Big Lead. Danish ethnographer H.P. Steensby subsequently explained their reluctance. The pack ice "to them...was half feared for its dangers, and looked upon as absurd and useless, because they knew that it was in itself (*per se*) a barren place with no prospect for hunting."[126] Interpreting their reticence as blackmail, Peary responded with bribery. On 14 February, he placed on the messroom table a number of items and covered them with a blanket. Calling for the Inughuit, Peary explained to them his plans for the polar foray, and then unveiled the display of coveted articles, including a "Winchester repeating rifle, shotgun, ammunition reloading outfit, knives, hatchet, lance heads, a box of tobacco and pipes." The explorer then promised that similar articles would be given to each of the four Inughuit who proved the best on the march and who would accompany him all the way to the North Pole. As well, he would give them a whaleboat, wood for sledges, oil, and provisions. According to the Euro-Americans, the prospect of these rewards helped overcome the resistance of most Inughuit men to embarking on this last, most dangerous mission.[127]

As in 1906, Peary planned to spend the winter moving supplies from Cape Sheridan to Cape Columbia, from where his parties would strike out across the ice pack of the Arctic Ocean toward the North Pole in late winter or early spring. From Cape Columbia, he would rely on a co-ordinated relay system to move men and supplies to an advance base camp on the ice. This time, he determined that the rear base camp would be established north of the Big Lead, so that the progress of the relay teams would not be stymied by open water.

In February, Peary's men were occupied in sledging equipment and provisions, as well as hunting for additional meat, along Ellesmere Island's northern coast. Dr. John Goodsell, his expedition surgeon, estimated that many of Peary's men travelled at least 1,600 km in this period.[128] En route, they utilized snow houses such as the ones erected by Bartlett at Parr Bay and Cape Colan. In analysing the siting of these camps, archaeologist Caroline Phillips has established that the sledge camps were located adjacent to the ice foot and spaced according to the distance covered in one day's sledging, while depot sites were spaced apart at intervals equivalent to several days' sledging.[129] On 26 February, Peary's teams reached Camp Crane, or "Crane City," on the coast near Cape Columbia, where they established their land base from which to stage the polar assault, consisting of nine *iglooyahs*, or snow shelters, to house men and supplies.

Peary knew that the arctic environment provided only a brief window of opportunity in which to make an attempt on the North Pole. While leads or open cracks in the pack ice of the Arctic Ocean could appear throughout the year, the cold winter temperatures caused many leads to freeze over by February, making a crossing viable. In May, increased temperatures were liable to re-open the leads, meaning that any group making a foray over the pack ice would need to have returned to terra firma on Ellesmere Island by the beginning of that month.[130]

Before commencing the relays across the ice pack, Peary worked out the logistics of the planned advance in minute detail. He divided the group into seven divisions of four men, including four support parties, each consisting of several sledges driven either by experienced Inughuit employees or Matthew Henson. At the outset, the teams consisted of seven Americans, 19 Inughuit, 28 sledges, and 133 dogs. Each division, supported by the provisions on one sledge, would advance the provisions carried on their other sledges to support the next team in the relay. The healthiest members from each of relay teams would be selected for the next leg of the polar assault, while the injured or less effective members would be sent back. As he assumed that the return journey would be easier than the outbound foray because of the marked trail, Peary calculated that these retreating parties would require less food, enabling most of their provision loads to be transferred to those who would continue to the north.[131]

To reduce the sledge weights, Peary worked out a minimal allocation of fuel and food for each of the relay parties. Each division was allowed only a single stove and an allowance of 170 grams of oil per day for drying clothes and kamiks and melting ice for drinking water. One hundred and seventy grams of alcohol were allotted twice a day for boiling tea. Provisions for each division were limited to a daily ration of 1.8 kg of pemmican, 450 grams of condensed milk, and 450 grams of compressed tea, comprising a ration of slightly more than a kilogram for each person.[132] For the huskies, 5.4 kg of pemmican per day were allocated for each team of seven dogs. To conserve the dog pemmican, Peary also instructed that the 26 dogs brought back by the parties of MacMillan and Goodsell were all to be shot except the two strongest animals.

Peary's diaries provide only a perfunctory treatment of the actual advance across the polar ice to the north. Fortunately, Robert Bartlett, Dr. John Goodsell, and Matthew Henson, who served on the relay divisions, filled in some of the missing details in their own accounts of the polar excursion. The campaign began with the departure of two advance parties led by Bartlett and George Borup. Bartlett broke trail for five days, before waiting for Peary and the other five divisions to catch up. Borup led a support party that closely followed Bartlett for three days, then offloaded provisions to Bartlett, before returning to a cache at Cape Aldrich to pick up additional supplies, which they brought up to the expedition through forced marches. The advance parties were also charged with building two snow shelters per day while travelling over the ice pack, to be utilized by the divisions that followed. Before the departure of the main party, Ross Marvin, Donald MacMillan, and Goodsell then formed an "advance pickax brigade." Sledging out on to the pack ice, these parties began to hack a trail over the hummocky surface to facilitate the forward advance of Peary, who departed a day later. However, on the second day they encountered heavy conditions with high pressure ridges, beyond which there was open water, necessitating a delay while they waited for the lead to freeze over. By 4 March the parties had reached the Big Lead, where a 1.5 km wide gap of water had opened, stretching for kilometres to the east or west.

Despite the advance work, the rear divisions encountered craggy ice ridges as soon as they departed the coastal ice foot. Sledges were frequently damaged by travel over the jagged hillocks of ice, necessitating repairs on a daily basis. In his book on the expedition, Matthew Henson described the difficulties of work in the frigid conditions they encountered on the ice pack. In severe wind and cold, he was periodically obliged to undo the lashings of his komatik, remove its load, and retrieve the brace and bit to bore new holes in the wood. This work had to be done slowly and deliberately, owing to the risk of the steel bit breaking. With ungloved hands he attempted to thread the sealskin thongs through the hole. By this time his fingers were frozen and needed to be pulled into his fur clothing to be thawed. When he felt his fingers burning, he knew that they were thawed and he could begin to work again on the repairs. But, by this time, the following party had passed his group and Henson had to hurry to retake the lead, "as orders are orders."[133]

While camped on the edge of the Big Lead, two Inughuit men, Pualuna and Panippak, complained of illness and indicated their inability to cross the water. Peary was skeptical: "I have had enough experience to know a sick Eskimo when I see one, and the excuses of Pooadlonah and Panikpah did not convince me."[134] On 7 March, "in order to impress the other Eskimos on the consequence of malingering or disobedience," he sent them back to the *Roosevelt*. He instructed the two Inughuit men to carry a note to the ship's mate; in his message he gave orders to provide these men and their families with some provisions and dismiss them from the ship. They and their families, including a baby girl born on 8 March, would be forced to make their own way back from Cape Sheridan to Etah, a distance of 480 km over rugged terrain and sea ice.[135] Meanwhile, for those who remained at the Big Lead, the continuing impasse was psychologically trying for the expedition members, compounding the physiological stresses they were enduring. According to Robert Bartlett: "We could not read, we could not sleep, all we could do was walk about. It was plain, pure, unadulterated Hell."[136]

By 10 March, the temperature had fallen and the lead closed and the parties crossed over the "black water" of newly formed ice. Further difficulties were encountered with other leads and hummocky pressure ridges. By 14 March, Peary reckoned they had reached approximately 84° 29' N. lat., about 131 km north of the Ellesmere coast. By this time, the temperature had fallen to −59° F and the men were experiencing severe discomfort. In Goodsell's judgment, if they had carried more caribou and muskox skins for sleeping covers, the disabled members of the parties would have been able to recover more readily and they would have conserved heat, reducing their energy expenditure. However, Peary refused to allow these skins to be used by the sledgers, as there were higher priorities than the health of the crew. The skins, which remained on the ship, had been prepared for mounting and sale to scientific institutions.[137] At this point, Goodsell turned back, according to Peary's plan, followed by MacMillan, while the others pressed on in the direction of the Pole. Suffering from frostbite, swollen limbs and other ailments caused by excessive exposure, they crossed the black water of the Big Lead before arriving back at Crane City.

Meanwhile, Peary's remaining divisions advanced toward their goal. On 1 April, at 87° 48' Bartlett was sent back. Peary continued with five others: Henson, Uutaaq, Iggiannguaq, Ukkujaaq, and Sigluk. By his calculations, he was now only 212 km from the North Pole, a distance Peary believed he could traverse in five marches. With sledges loaded to capacity, they pressed on. Peary's diary entries, spotty through the entire march, became increasingly cryptic. As his four colleagues on the last march toward the pole did not write diaries, historians have been obliged to rely generally on Peary's retrospective account of this last leg of his polar assault, written after his return to Cape Sheridan. In his subsequent recounting of the trek, Peary related that his party encountered unusually level ice surfaces, enabling rapid progress toward their goal, while a succession of narrow leads could be bridged by his longer sledges. By 5 April, Peary calculated that they had reached 89° 25' N. lat., only 55 km from the Pole. The following day he reported that they were at 89° 57' N. lat. Observing Peary unloading his sledge to retrieve his silk flag of the United States, Matthew Henson later recounted his feelings at that moment:

> A thrill of patriotism ran through me and I raised my voice to cheer the starry emblem of my native land. The Eskimos gathered around and, taking the time from Commander Peary, three hearty cheers rang out on the still, frosty air, our dumb dogs looking on in surprise.[138]

In his diary, Peary scribbled his own reaction:

> The Pole at last!!! The prize of 3 centuries, my dream and ambition for 23 years. *Mine* at last. I cannot bring myself to realize it. It all seems so simple and common place, as Bartlett said 'just like every other day.' I wish Jo could be here with me to share my feelings. I have drunk her health and that of the kids from the Benedictine flask she sent me.[139]

He apparently had travelled 660 km in 37 days. Proceeding 21 km toward the sun in an attempt to confirm his position, Peary assembled his small party for a group photograph (Figure 57), planted the American flag on an ice hummock and deposited a record in a bottle, before commencing the return trip back to Cape Columbia. Peary's reported route to the North Pole is shown in Figure 58. On returning to the north coast of Ellesmere, he memorialized his achievement with a further annotation in his diary:

> April 23. CAPE COLUMBIA. My life work is accomplished. The thing which it was intended from the beginning that I should do, I have done. I have got the North Pole out of my system. After 23 years of effort, hardships, privations, more or less suffering, and some risks, I have won the last great geographical prize, the North Pole, for the credit of the United States, the Service to which I belong, myself and my family. My work is the finish, the cap and the climax, of 300 years of effort, loss of life and expenditure of millions, by some of the best men of the civilized nations of the world, and it has been accomplished with a clean cut dash, spirit, and I believe, thoroughness, characteristically American. I am content.[140]

Figure 57: "Peary Sledge Party and Flags at the Pole," U.S. National Archives (Washington, DC), RG 401, Series XPS, Photograph No., NWDNS-401-XPS-17(11).

His contentment was to be short-lived. Peary returned to the United States to learn that his professed achievement was already enveloped by controversy. Expecting a hero's welcome, the explorer was dismayed to discover his prize had already been claimed by his rival Frederick Cook, who had astonished the explorers' community with assertions of having reached the Pole almost a year earlier. The bitterness of the Peary camp is palpable in the notes of his assistant Donald MacMillan, recorded shortly after the expedition sailed into New York harbour:

> Arr'd New York... Anchored under Sandy Hook quietly. No flags, no recognition, no civic reception, no address of welcome home. The *Attainment of the Pole* by Dr. Frederick Cook fill the newspapers, especially the *New York Herald*, owned by James Gordon Bennett, who has purchased Cook's story for, it is said, $24,000![141]

His legacy in jeopardy, Peary's compatriots set in motion a massive coordinated attack on Cook. This fierce campaign set a standard of ruthlessness that few could rival. Among other activities, Peary's supporters published assorted articles, letters to newspapers, and gave press

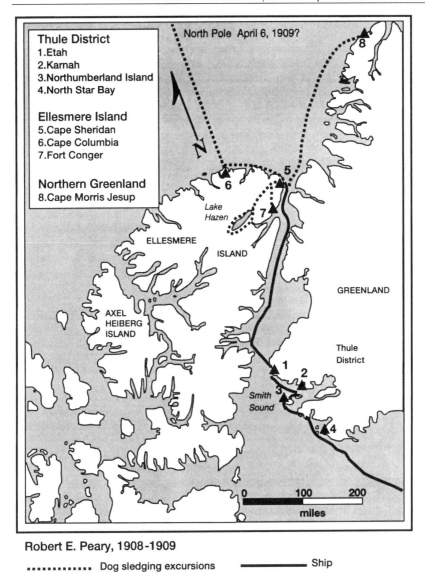

Thule District
1.Etah
2.Karnah
3.Northumberland Island
4.North Star Bay

Ellesmere Island
5.Cape Sheridan
6.Cape Columbia
7.Fort Conger

Northern Greenland
8.Cape Morris Jesup

North Pole April 6, 1909?

N

Lake
Hazen

ELLESMERE

ISLAND

GREENLAND

AXEL
HEIBERG
ISLAND

Thule
District

Smith
Sound

0   100   200
miles

Robert E. Peary, 1908-1909

·········· Dog sledging excursions ——————— Ship

Figure 58: Map of the route of Robert Peary's 1908-09 expedition

interviews in which they attacked Cook's character, challenged the specifics of his readings, and even provided their own version of his itinerary, in which they asserted that he had turned back only a few miles north of Cape Svartevoeg. As sources, they referred to an interview conducted by Donald MacMillan with Cook's companions in Etah on the way back from Cape Sheridan in August 1909. It is not clear from MacMillan's diary account of this interview whether he spoke directly with both Ittukusuk and Aapilaq. MacMillan wrote:

> Have questioned nearly all of the men who were with Dr. Cook on the ice. They are all agreed upon this one point that they were never out of sight of land and did not spend more than three nights on the sea ice. They did discover two islands to the southwest of Cape Thomas Hubbard.[142]

MacMillan was hardly a disinterested observer, and we do not have the unfiltered testimony of Ittukusuk and Aapilaq regarding these interviews.

Almost immediately, a rival literature emerged in books seeking to debunk Peary's claims to polar supremacy.[143] I will not revisit the controversy over whether Peary or Cook, or both, or neither reached the North Pole. The literature on the controversy is voluminous. In addition to congressional examinations and testimonies, it includes innumerable journalistic treatments,[144] academic analyses,[145] biographies by Peary's colleagues and admirers,[146] and monographs analysing the evidence and providing comparative reconstructions of Peary's and Cook's possible itineraries.[147] Few observers have been able to resist the urge to pronounce judgment for or against. What seems certain is that the controversy will be with us for some time to come.

Attainment of the North Pole: An Event of Consequence?

Peary's problematic triumph invites reflections on the nature and significance of historical events. His claim to have attained the North Pole was one of the most famous reported occurrences of the twentieth century. It seemed to vindicate the preceding 60 years of effort by numerous American expeditions to out-do the Europeans, confirming the status of the United States in the pantheon of exploring nations. Yet, mirroring the explorer himself, the significance of his achievement remains an enigma. Its significance has been obscured, rather than clarified, by the inordinate emphasis of historical writings attempting to resolve the question as to whether or not Peary actually reached the North Pole.

No consensus on this issue appears achievable. Peary's accomplishments provoked both admiration and skepticism in his own day and since. Some powerful interests, including the National Geographic Society and prominent U.S. naval personnel, have continued to endorse the explorer's claims and have provided detailed arguments to support their position.[148] Others have critiqued Peary's assertions from the standpoint of logic or the dissection of the explorer's own evidence. For example, writer Dennis Rawlins and others have asserted that Peary did not assemble sufficient credible scientific documentation to enable his own assertions to be verified.[149] Probably far too much has already been written on this topic, and I do not wish to clutter the debate with yet another pronouncement.

For this discussion, the discovery of the North Pole is of interest only as it relates to the significance of this event for the societies participating in the contact of cultures during High Arctic exploration. If Peary did reach the Pole, it seems pertinent to ask a series of questions. What was accomplished? Who was affected by its discovery? Was it a national or a personal achievement? Should it be viewed as a breakthrough in science and planning, courage and determination, or some other benchmark of accomplishment? What, if any, was its long-term impact? Further questions could be addressed to the hundreds of writers who either burnished the Peary legend or sought to tarnish it. Why has the issue of who first reached the North Pole so captivated journalists, historians, and armchair explorers for the past century? Wherein lies the enduring fascination of this event—or non-event—depending on the observer?

In the Arctic, the actual event of Peary's North Polar foray was of little consequence. The trek across the polar pack ice was never to be repeated by the Inughuit — it was a dangerous undertaking that produced no side benefits in terms of new knowledge of resources or hunting grounds. In 1950–51, Jean Malaurie interviewed Pualuna, the brother of Uutaaq, who accompanied Peary on his last expedition and raised the American flag on what they believed was the North Pole. Regarding the attainment of the landmark, Pualuna's response was perhaps representative of his compatriots: "North Pole or not ... that's the white man's business!"[150] If, on the other hand, we consider the larger effects of contact precipitated by Peary's expeditions, he clearly exerted a significant impact on the Inughuit within his own era. This impact is detailed in Part III of this book. Peary also influenced the approaches of several subsequent expeditions to Greenland and Ellesmere Island, many of which followed his practice of relying on the labour of the Inughuit, as well as their material culture and techniques of living in the High Arctic. Peary might be viewed more as a conduit for disseminating Aboriginal knowledge than an innovator, but he can be credited as the first

Western explorer in the High Arctic to extensively integrate Inuit and Inughuit strategies into a program of arctic survival.

Regarding his own society, the impact of Peary's asserted discovery of the North Pole will continue to be debated, but few could doubt his prominence as a historical figure. In his own era, his exploits generated a plethora of newspaper headlines, commentaries, and public discussion. The question of whether he reached the North Pole was the subject of a protracted debate in the U.S. Congress.[151] Whether considered famous or notorious, his name was known in virtually every household in the United States. Peary was fêted by monarchs in Europe and celebrated by presidents of his own country. He was an undisputed star at the very beginning of the phenomenon of celebrity popular culture.

Much of the credit for Peary's fame and success must go to the explorer himself. A master of organization and planning, Peary seized every opportunity to promote his expeditions and to raise money to underwrite them. He appeared on the scene at a time when mass circulation newspapers and burgeoning popular culture established the preconditions for his remarkable public relations campaign. In his shrewd use of media in this period, he was perhaps rivalled only by Theodore Roosevelt himself before and after his famed 1898 charge at St. Juan Hill, Cuba, during the Spanish-American War.[152] Peary was one of the first individuals to recognize the power of the popular press to shape public opinion and he wrote voluminously on polar exploration for all forms of publication. Endlessly retold in popular literature, the explorer's exploits provided ready material with which to inculcate generations of Americans in the virtues of courage, endurance and determination, as well as the business ethos of competition. The continuing fascination of his polar attempts demonstrated the enduring capacity of culture to shape public consciousness, particularly when constructed around a national icon or legend. In the early twentieth century, the United States required a triumphant hero to represent its self-image as an emerging world power, and Peary obliged his country's need by providing both a polar victory and a narrative to support it. In fulfilling the larger master narrative of his country's triumphal ascendency, his influence may have been largely symbolic, but the symbolism of his North Pole conquest resonated long after this pivotal moment in the construction of American national identity.

In at least one other respect the explorer was an undisputed pioneer, in the nascent field of commercial product endorsements. Raised by his polar endeavours to the status of a national icon, he discerned the potential to trade on his celebrity, and product endorsements commenced even before his last polar expedition. During Peary's serialized publication of the story of his last polar voyage in *Hampton's Magazine*, a variety of advertisements appeared, including "Schering's Formula, the Ideal Disinfectant and Deodorant," "Triscuit, the Shredded Wheat Wafer," "Waltham Watches," "Norfolk and New Brunswick Hosiery," the "Rubberset Shaving Brush," and Dupont Sporting Powders," a rifle powder.[153] At the Peary-MacMillan Arctic Museum in Brunswick, Maine, a tobacco tin for North Pole Smoking Tobacco bears Peary's testimonial, which asserts: "This tobacco was most highly prized by both members of the party and the Eskimos, and assisted materially in passing many an hour of the long, dark winter night at Cape Sheridan." Six years later, the endorsement was contradicted by the explorer in his book *Secrets of Polar Travel*, when he stated that "I have always selected men for my parties who used neither tobacco nor spirits. Describing tobacco as "objectionable,"' he elaborated:

> It affects the wind endurance of a man, particularly in low temperatures, adds an extra and entirely unnecessary article to the outfit, vitiates the atmosphere of the tent or igloo, and, when the supply gives out, renders the user a nuisance to himself and those about him.[154]

Whatever the extent of Peary's exploration accomplishments, the North Pole had become a marketable commodity, the first of many athletic tests in the twentieth century to generate wealth for the sponsors alongside the honours to the victors.

8
Assertion of Canadian Sovereignty over the High Arctic, 1895–1940

In the heyday of nineteenth century imperialism, the mighty powers of Great Britain and the United States focussed their imperial gaze on the High Arctic. By 1900, it was Canada's turn to direct its attentions to this remote region, part of its own dominion after Britain transferred the Arctic Islands to Canadian jurisdiction in 1880. During the first 20 years, Canada's only significant action was to define the boundaries of its Arctic territories by orders-in-council in 1895 and 1897.[1] A byproduct of the Peary expeditions was that they prompted the Government of Canada to awareness that control of its Arctic Archipelago required action beyond adding the Queen Elizabeth Islands to a map of Canada's dominions. After his apparent discovery of the North Pole in 1909, Robert Peary expressed his view that "nothing can stop the ultimate destiny of this country [United States] to occupy that portion of the western hemisphere lying between the Panama Canal and the North Pole,"[2] an implicit challenge to Canada's sovereignty and control of these lands. Responding to what they now regarded as the unauthorized use of this territory by foreign nationals, Canadian authorities perceived a need to assert sovereignty over the Arctic Islands. Their initial motivation was defensive. Alarmed by the incursions of other nations into the area, they concluded that unless an effective presence were demonstrated, other nations then exploring the High Arctic might establish a claim to this vast territory.

Peary's activities prompted concern beyond a potential American challenge to Canadian jurisdiction. By introducing Greenland Inughuit to Ellesmere's extensive wildlife resources, Peary unwittingly also contributed to a possible Danish claim to the island. According to international conventions, sovereignty could not merely be asserted; it needed to be demonstrated through effective occupation of the land.[3] Canadian authorities belatedly came to the conclusion that they would have to send official representatives to Ellesmere and other islands or forever forfeit their sovereignty over the region.

Following Peary's Greenland expedition of 1898–1902, the Government of Canada responded by approving its own expedition to the High Arctic, to be led by A.P. Low, accompanied by Superintendent J.D. Moodie of the Royal North-West Mounted Police. The instructions of Colonel Fred

White, Controller of the RNWMP, to Moodie explicitly defined the objectives of the expedition. White wrote:

> The Government of Canada having decided that the time has arrived when some system of supervision and control should be established over the coast and the islands in the northern part of the Dominion, a vessel has been selected and is now being equipped for the purpose of patrolling, exploring and establishing the authority of the Government of Canada in the waters and islands of Hudson's [sic] Bay and north thereof.[4]

In addition to the ship's crew, the party comprised representatives of the Geological Survey of Canada, the Survey Branch of the Department of the Interior, the Department of Marine and Fisheries, the North-West Mounted Police, and other federal agencies. If the specific objective of the Low expedition was to assert sovereignty through enforcement of Canadian laws in the region,[5] it was also intended to make a symbolic statement of Canadian presence. In this regard, a crude, albeit straightforward approach was to plant the Canadian ensign at strategic sites in the High Arctic, particularly Ellesmere Island, the pivotal land mass at the northern extremity of the Arctic Archipelago. In the summer of 1903, the expedition sailed in the *Neptune* to the north, reaching the eastern coast of Ellesmere Island in late July. At Cape Herschel, adjacent to Smith Sound, Low's party went ashore and formally took possession of the island by reading a document in the name of King Edward VII, which they deposited in a large rock cairn. After raising and saluting the Canadian flag, the party returned to the ship, which quickly retreated to the south to avoid the "heavy, dangerous ice" of the sound.[6] Low's brief foray set the tone for a succession of symbolic actions by Canada to reinforce its sovereignty over the Arctic Archipelago.

After the announcement of Peary's polar expedition of 1905, the Dominion government engaged Quebec mariner J.E. Bernier to lead three expeditions to the Arctic Islands between 1906 and 1910 to wave the flag and exercise sovereignty in other symbolic ways. Federal authorities were concerned that no representative of Canada had ever set foot on the islands to the west of Ellesmere, which had been visited and named by the Norwegian Sverdrup expedition of 1898–1902. Bernier later wrote that during his expedition of 1906–07, he had instructed the second officer of the CGS *Arctic* to prepare a record to formally declare possession of these lands and place it on land at King Edward Point near Craig Harbour. They included "Lincoln Land, Grinnell land, Grant Land, Ellesmere Land, Axel Heiberg Island, Amund Ringnes Island, Ellef Ringnes Island, North Cornwall, Findlay Island, Graham Land,

Table Island, also all adjacent islands to Ellesmere Land."[7] Canadian authorities did not realize at the time that Grinnell Land and Grant Land were both part of Ellesmere Island.

At the time of the expedition, federal authorities were divided regarding the wisdom or legitimacy of claiming lands through symbolic gestures. Officials in the Department of the Interior favoured the sector approach to sovereignty, according to which the planting of a flag in the region would enable a country to assert its rights to all lands lying in that geographical sector on a line to the North Pole. However, officials of the Departments of Justice and External Affairs took a contrary view that only through demonstrating effective occupation would Canada's claim be upheld in international circles. While Commander Inglefield had named Ellesmere Island in 1852, effectively claiming its lands for Britain (and later, Canada), he skirted only the southeastern coastline during his voyage. The majority of subsequent expeditions to the central and northern areas of the island were sent by the United States, while Sverdrup's party mapped the bulk of Ellesmere's extensive coastline. The federal government retroactively accepted Bernier's gesture but over time came to the realization that sovereignty over the Arctic Archipelago could not merely be asserted, but would need to be demonstrated through year-round occupation.[8]

During Bernier's 1909 voyage, he encountered the American sport hunter Harry Whitney at Clyde River, Baffin Island. Whitney was returning from a hunting excursion to Ellesmere Island, where he and his Inughuit guides had taken a number of muskoxen and polar bears. Bernier described their exchange:

> I informed Mr. Whitney that I was patrolling Canadian waters, and, as he had on board his vessel a motor whaleboat, it would be necessary for him to take out a fishery license, and that I would issue it. He stated that if it was a regulation, he would pay the legal fee of $50, and take the license. I accordingly issued the license and received the fee. We exchanged a quarter of musk ox meat for some magazines furnished by Mr. Whitney.[9]

The exchange of muskox meat with the American big game hunter was ironic, as the protection of this animal soon became the vehicle for Canadian efforts to assert its sovereignty in response to perceived incursions by American explorers. By 1910, Peary's slaughter of muskoxen was already an issue of concern to Canada. In his book on the voyages of the *Arctic*, Bernier remarked on the large numbers of muskoxen taken by the explorers; he estimated that Peary's parties and other American expeditions had taken 800 muskoxen over the preceding 27 years,

Sverdrup's expedition had killed 200 on Ellesmere and adjacent islands to the west, while he reckoned that Cook had taken 100 muskoxen during his polar foray. Bernier wrote that he thought that Canada would not object to the hunting for food in the case of expeditions devoted to science, but he advocated adopting regulations "to prevent numbers of Eskimo natives of foreign countries exploiting Canadian territory, and destroying valuable hunting and fishing grounds."[10]

Donald MacMillan's "Crocker Land" Expedition, 1913–1917, and Canada's Response

The specific impetus to Canadian action was the expedition led by the American Donald B. MacMillan in 1913. Only four years after the conclusion of Peary's last Polar expedition, MacMillan embarked on an expedition in search of "Crocker Land," the land Peary thought he saw to the northwest while standing on a peak near Cape Thomas Hubbard on the northernmost point of Axel Heiberg Island in 1906.[11] The official objectives of the "Crocker Land" expedition, later summarized in the preamble to an article on the undertaking, included the following:

> Actually visiting, reconnoitring, and mapping Crocker Land or the sea ice at or about its supposed vicinity; Scientific exploration of the region between Flagler Bay [on Ellesmere Island] and Cape Thomas Hubbard [on Axel Heiberg Island] and of the Ellesmere Land interior; The attainment of the Greenland Ice Cap east of Cape York; The collecting of data and specimens along all scientific lines as far as practicable, including ethnology, geology, botany, seismology, ornithology, geophysics, terrestrial magnetism, meteorology, oceanography, and chemistry; Cooperation with the U.S. Weather Bureau for practical as well as research purposes, through wireless connection with a Canadian station which was to have been erected in the Hudson Bay district the summer the expedition sailed.[12]

MacMillan had served as an assistant to Peary in 1908–09 and was to become one of the most experienced Euro-American travellers on Ellesmere Island after Peary. Following in his mentor's footsteps, he planned to live off the resources of the country and to press Inughuit men and women into service to achieve these goals. Assembling a party of six Americans, MacMillan sailed to Northwestern Greenland, arriving in late August 1913. Enlisting the services of three Inughuit families at Cape York, the party proceeded to Etah, where MacMillan engaged additional assistance from the resident families there. In all, he hired 12 Inughuit guides, their spouses, 19 dog teams and sledges.

To build up their provisions, they spent the fall and early winter hunting walrus, rabbits, ducks, and collecting duck eggs.[13] Some Americans and Inughuit women tended fox traps; the women also spent the fall making fur garments for the Americans. By February, each man had been outfitted with a complete outfit of fur clothing, including a caribou skin coat or kooletah, bearskin pants, seal, caribou and bearskin kamiks or boots, and hare skin stockings.[14] In addition, MacMillan asked the seamstresses to make them shirts and coats of sheepskin that the Americans had brought with them from the United States.[15] One concession to Western dress was the addition of a light undergarment of wool to prevent chafing and absorb perspiration.[16]

In February 1914, MacMillan embarked on the principal exploratory work of the expedition, a sledging excursion to ascertain the existence of "Crocker Land" and to discover new lands to the north of Axel Heiberg Island. His party's itinerary was to cross Smith Sound and traverse Ellesmere Island toward Eureka Sound. Temporarily halted by an outbreak of influenza and measles among his Inughuit guides, he was forced to retrace his steps to take his sick companions back to Etah. Departing once again on 10 March, with Fitzhugh Green, Ittukusuk, and Piugaattoq, MacMillan crossed Smith Sound and Beistad Fiord, and ascended the Ellesmere Island icecap to its summit before descending to the west coast by 28 March. Proceeding along Eureka and Nansen Sounds to the northwest, they arrived at Cape Svartevoeg, on the northern tip of Axel Heiberg Island, on 14 April. On 21 April, the two Americans thought they saw the snow-covered hills and valleys of Crocker Land; however, their Inughuit companions said it was mist. From there, MacMillan struck out over the pack ice of the Arctic Ocean in search of the elusive land which Peary claimed lay to the northwest. After 10 days, and travelling 275 km to the northwest, MacMillan concluded that "Crocker Land" was a mirage and turned back. On his return, he spent several days searching for Sverdrup's records left at Cape Svartevoeg and then crossed Nansen Sound to retrieve Peary's record at Land's Lokk on Ellesmere Island.

Meanwhile, Fitzhugh Green, the expedition's physicist, departed with his Inughuit guide, Piugaattoq, to complete the survey of northwestern Axel Heiberg Island. During their absence, a blizzard struck and lasted a week. Returning unaccompanied six days later, he announced to the group that Piugaattoq was dead, asserting that he had been buried in an avalanche. To MacMillan, the agitated Green revealed the shocking truth— he had killed Piugaattoq with two shots from his rifle. A more complete account of this tragic incident is provided in Chapter 11. The remaining members of the party returned via Bay Fiord and a traverse of

Ellesmere Island, arriving at Etah on 19 May, having covered 2,250 km in 10 weeks.

The other major sledging excursion of this expedition was led by eth-nographer Walter Ekblaw to northern Ellesmere Island in 1915. Accom-panied by Issingguak (Esayoo) and Ittukusuk (Etook-a-shoo), who had been with Cook in 1907–08, Ekblaw also received support from several other sledgers who advanced his supplies as far as Eureka Sound. After departing Etah on 26 March, they crossed to Ellesmere Island and camped at Cape Sabine for two days so that the dogs could be fed to repletion with meat previously cached at that location. Proceeding westward via Flagler Fiord, Ekblaw followed Eureka Sound to the north; reaching Greely Fiord, he turned to the east. Proceeding along Greely Fiord to its head, he retraced the 1883 route of Lockwood and Brainard of the Greely expe-dition when they traversed northern Ellesmere Island. Crossing the Hazen Plateau, he followed the Ruggles River to the coast, reaching Fort Conger at the end of May. In early June they crossed to Greenland and followed the coast back to Etah.[17] Ekblaw's intention was to support the excur-sion with game resources encountered en route, and he placed a major emphasis on securing muskox meat for the dogs as well as human consumption. In all, 60 muskoxen were recorded killed on this trip, including one at Flagler Fiord in early April, 25 muskoxen in two hunt-ing excursions at Bay Fiord on 7 April, 21 taken at the mouth of Greely Fiord on 15 April, 2 muskoxen killed farther up Greely Fiord, and 11 killed at the head of Discovery Harbour on 30 May. However, the overall tally was apparently greater, as Ekblaw also recorded killing another entire herd on Greely Fiord in mid-April 1915, the number unspecified.[18] In his published account of the excursion, Ekblaw praised his "good companions, true fellows of the trail, gentlemen unafraid" with the following tribute:

> To old Esayoo [Issingguak] I am glad to give the lion's share of the credit. Throughout the trip he had been cheerful, interested; his good sense and judgement had kept us out of trouble...To E-took-a-shoo [Ittukusuk] I wish to give due credit, too. His unfailing good humour, his rare hunting ability, and his excellent driving, all had contributed immeasurably to our success.[19]

In subsequent excursions to Ellesmere Island, MacMillan focussed on geographical survey work, including mapping Ellesmere Island's eastern coasts; his major contribution was to map 42 glaciers between Cape Sabine and Clarence Head in 1917. Meanwhile, his Inughuit as-sistants continued to hunt animals on Ellesmere Island and trap furs in Greenland for the explorer to sell in the United States. By the summer of 1917, with 200 boxes of furs and specimens packed, MacMillan and his party departed in the *Neptune*, skippered by Robert Bartlett, arriving at Sydney, Nova Scotia, on 24 August 1917.[20]

Canada's Response to MacMillan's Incursions, 1917–21

In 1917, apparently in response to the continuing destruction of muskoxen in Canada's arctic by MacMillan's party, the government of Canada initiated conservation legislation to protect the species. A new clause was written into the Northwest Game Act, stating that muskoxen "shall not be hunted, trapped, taken, killed, shot at, wounded, injured, or molested at any time, except in such zones and during such period as the Governor in Council may prescribe." The only permitted exception was the hunting of muskoxen by Aboriginal inhabitants of the Territories "when they are actually in need of the meat of such musk ox to prevent starvation."[21] The addition of the muskox amendment to the Northwest Territories game regulations signified Canada's intention to enforce its laws in the territories. Government officials perceived the passage of this measure to be a key step in asserting Canadian sovereignty over the region. Yet, sovereignty could not merely be asserted; it needed to be demonstrated. In the absence of any actual capacity to ensure compliance to Canadian laws, approval of the ordinance and other laws would constitute little more than a symbolic gesture.

Canadian efforts to assert sovereignty over the Arctic Islands after the First World War were spurred in part by concerns that other nations were then planning to occupy these lands. Denmark, in particular, had insisted that Greenland Inughuit had a stronger claim than Canadians to the Queen Elizabeth Islands, based on the belief that these lands were within their traditional hunting territories. Danish scientist Knud Rasmussen, who established the Thule trading station in 1910, wrote to Vilhjalmur Stefansson in the period: "It is well known that the territory of the Polar Eskimos falls within the region designated as 'no man's land'"[22]—meaning, Ellesmere Island.

Several specific factors converged around this time to hasten federal government action. One such catalyst was a letter sent by an American, George Comer, who had been with MacMillan's Crocker Land Expedition, to Vilhjalmur Stefansson in May 1919. He was responding to Stefansson's proposal to capture muskoxen on Ellesmere Island to develop herds on the Arctic mainland to be raised domestically. Comer wrote that while he was at Etah during the winter of 1916–17, the Inughuit took about 150 muskox skins on Ellesmere Island. He surmised that such hunting would persist until the muskoxen on the island became scarce. Comer also reported his belief that Donald MacMillan, representing a fur company, was about to go up to the Smith Sound region to set up a post from which to engage Inughuit to hunt on Ellesmere Island.[23] Clearly concerned by Comer's letter, Deputy Minister of the Interior W.W. Cory wrote to the RCMP that "these two matters suggest the necessity of the location of a police post to adequately patrol the outlet from Ellesmere and contiguous islands."[24]

In 1919, amidst reports that Denmark was in the process of laying claim to Ellesmere Island, the Dominion government organized a Technical Advisory Board from a core of senior civil servants, who were charged with the addressing the entire issue of Canadian sovereignty over the Arctic Islands. The Board considered sending an expedition to Ellesmere in 1920 but postponed it when it became clear that there was no prospect of reaching the destination before the fall freeze-up. In the event of further evidence of Danish encroachment, the Board proposed sending an airship or dirigible to Ellesmere Island during the winter to establish effective occupation. If carried out, this proposal would have involved sending an airship from northern Scotland to Ellesmere and dropping RCMP officers and supplies by parachute. The Board calculated that the distance involved was only about 2,200 miles (4,000 km), and that such an operation could be staged in January after the presumed return of daylight.[25] Apart from the inherent risk in such an escapade, it was fortunate that this idea was never pursued. Ellesmere Island does not receive daylight until well into February.

In 1920, Canada's concerns over activity by non-Canadians in the Queen Elizabeth Islands quickly turned to alarm with the announcement of Knud Rasmussen's plans to undertake a major expedition across the archipelago. Reportedly, he intended to establish trading stations and to colonize the region with Inughuit from Greenland. After receiving instructions from J.B. Harkin, Dominion Commissioner of Parks, that the expedition must not hunt muskoxen, Rasmussen had replied that: "There is no question of our breaking Canadian Game Laws because we are not coming into Canada but a part farther north. It is not under Canadian jurisdiction."[26]

The following year, Harkin wrote that Canada must curtail muskox hunting on Ellesmere Island by Inughuit if Canadian sovereignty was to be preserved. Without such a tangible demonstration of Canada's preparedness to enforce its laws, Canada would be shown to be incapable of demonstrating effective presence or control.[27] He recommended to the deputy minister of the Department of Interior:

> that Canada should in the first place take a very strong stand in regard
> to its exclusive ownership of and authority over Ellesmere Land; that

the Danish Government should be advised that a continuance of the slaughter of musk ox in Ellesmere Land cannot be tolerated because it inevitably will mean the early extermination of the musk ox; that if Denmark will not immediately agree to entirely stop this slaughter Canada should establish a Mounted Police post in Ellesmere land for the purpose of stopping the slaughter and asserting Canadian authority.[28]

During a meeting with the Technical Advisory Board that fall, explorer Vilhjalmur Stefansson argued that Canada could best assure territorial jurisdiction by establishing a Mounted Police detachment or a revenue cutter service "to enforce the game laws, or whatever other Canadian laws need to be enforced up there." Second, he argued that exploration of the island and region was necessary "to show what it is good for; to show our intentions; and then get commercial companies to establish trading posts there. That amounts to occupation."[29]

In 1921, Harkin referred to the "great danger" posed by possible possession of these lands by foreign countries. Such occupation "would always have been undesirable but it would be particularly so now in view of the development of aircraft and submarines." His belief that the new technologies brought military risks anticipated future concerns of post-Second World War military planners regarding the strategic significance of the High Arctic.[30] Harkin warned that if the United States "realized how incomplete the Canadian title is," it might "make an attempt to wrest the northern islands from Britain." Noting the hostility of Americans of German and Irish ancestry toward Great Britain, he predicted that the Hearst newspaper chain might succeed through propaganda in forcing the U.S. government to seize the islands. For these reasons, he justified the prospective expedition as a way of strengthening Canada's "inchoate title" to the region.[31]

A further rationale was the potential economic benefits of sovereignty; Harkin pointed to the example of Alaska as an unexpected windfall to the United States:

> I know Ellesmere Land is valuable, certainly from the muskox and caribou standpoint and for fur resources generally. There is coal on Ellesmere Land; I do not know how much.... What it will be worth in the future is a matter of uncertainty, but it is altogether likely it will be valuable."[32]

Harkin argued that if Canada was serious in its desire to keep the Arctic Islands, it would need to take action to support its claim. He concluded that effective occupation was the only way that this could be accomplished and suggested that Ellesmere Island was the strategic land mass on which such occupation should be established.[33]

In the same period, a position paper prepared for Canada's Technical Advisory Board also argued for the potential economic benefits of occupying Ellesmere Island. The paper proposed that an intensive investigation of the occupied islands be undertaken with a view to establishing their "mineral and other wealth." It was hoped that occupation of the islands could be justified on grounds other than "simple assertion of sovereignty." The authors added that "any examination of the country should be made not simply from a scientific standpoint but chiefly from a commercial standpoint."

Of interest was the suggestion that, if important "natural resources" were identified—presumably, game animals—the government "should transfer Eskimos from other Canadian areas to establish small centres of population" and also "induce trading companies to extend their operations to the islands or establish trading posts of its own."[34] This proposal closely conformed to Harkin's recommendation that, following the establishment of two or three police posts, Canada should initiate "the transfer of some Canadian Eskimos to the Island" and that "steps should be taken to encourage the Hudson's Bay Co. or other traders to extend their operations northward."[35] These were apparently the first references to the idea of relocating Canadian Inuit to Ellesmere Island, a proposal which was eventually carried out in the 1950s. Finally, Harkin asserted the desirability of exploration by the police of Ellesmere and adjoining islands.[36]

After 1920, federal officials determined that the most effective vehicle for demonstrating a Canadian presence would be the establishment of RCMP posts in the region. In 1921 a secret internal document spelled out the government's objectives in staging an expedition to establish a series of RCMP detachments in the High Arctic, which included:

> establish effective occupation and administration, with the subsidiary objects of controlling the natives, enforcing law and order, protecting animal life, exploring and protecting the country, and in general bringing it within the scope of civilization.[37]

Technically, sovereignty was to be asserted through the administration of Canadian laws, including customs regulations, issuance of scientific and archaeological research permits, and administration of game and muskox ordinances. Regarding law enforcement, officers were also appointed coroners and justices of the peace.[38] In terms of science, they were expected to keep meteorological records and collect animal and bird specimens for various government departments. Also important to sovereignty assertion were the frequent patrols made by detachment personnel throughout the Queen Elizabeth Islands, although the

Police argued that usually these journeys had an exploratory function and added to geographical and physical knowledge of the region.[39] Other government functions, largely symbolic, included the establishment of post offices at the High Arctic detachments. Letters posted at the detachment were to be picked up once a year by the resupply ship on the eastern Arctic Patrol for delivery to the south.

Establishment of the Craig Harbour Detachment, 1922

The plan for RCMP occupation of the High Arctic Islands called for the establishment of four detachments: two on Ellesmere Island on its eastern and southern coasts, one on Devon Island, and another on Bylot Island. Each of the detachments was to be staffed by a sergeant, two constables, and an interpreter, with two other officers stationed at the central detachment; these were the inspector in charge of the entire operation and an acting assistant surgeon. Each detachment was to have four frame structures: one barrack hut (5 m x 13 m), a store hut (5 m x 10 m), a blubber house, and an outhouse.[40] The total projected cost of $106,572.59 included approximately $38,000 for salaries, $20,000 for provisions, $20,900 for buildings, $3,600 for dogs, sleds and harness, and $5,900 for "trade supplies for services rendered by Eskimos."[41]

In July 1922, the *Arctic*, skippered by Captain Bernier and led by expedition commander J.D. Craig, departed Quebec City with instructions to establish a RCMP detachment on Ellesmere Island. To deter hunting by Inughuit on the island, the RCMP intended to set up the post on Ellesmere's eastern coast as close to the crossing of Smith Sound as possible. Due to heavy ice conditions,[42] they were obliged to find a site on the southern coast. Accordingly, the first detachment on Ellesmere Island was established at Craig Harbour, a site with a number of location drawbacks but which was protected from moving pack ice by Smith Island.[43] As well, its siting near the mouth of Jones Sound gave it presumed navigational accessibility for re-supply operations.

For the expedition house at Craig Harbour and later at Bache Peninsula after 1927, the RCMP approach to shelter on Ellesmere Island was similar to the approach of the Greely expedition 40 years earlier. In this case, the Department of Public Works prepared designs for prefabricated buildings, and the structures were constructed in the south according to specifications. Disassembled for transport, the various lengths of lumber and other building materials were loaded onto the transport ship, dropped off at the destination, and reassembled on site (Figure 59). As with the first Fort Conger station house erected more than 40 years earlier, the RCMP buildings were of wood frame construction, rectan-

Figure 59: The RCMP buildings at Craig Harbour, 1925. National Archives of Canada
Photo No. PA 100771.

gular and gable-roofed, with no provision for insulation.[44] The design reflected the Force's belief in the principle of utilizing a dead air space as an insulating layer between double walls, an outmoded notion dating to the era of the Greely expedition; its utility for High Arctic shelter was refuted by Peary in *Secrets of Polar Travel*, published in 1917. At Craig Harbour, the sole concession to insulation was a thin covering of canvas burlap tacked to the inside walls and ceiling of the detachment house.

The drawbacks of this approach to shelter emerged early, in March 1923 during the first winter at Craig Harbour, when the barracks building burned down. The fire started during a blizzard when the burlap inner lining of the ceiling was set ablaze by the heat from one of the stoves. Attempting to utilize the fire extinguishers, the men found them frozen and useless. The only available water for dousing the flames was the contents of a half-empty slop bucket. In vain, they attempted to suppress the fire from outside the building before concluding that it was hopeless. Efforts switched to salvaging whatever articles they could from within, including bedding, sleeping bags, rifles, ammunition, and other items, which were hurled out the windows. Constable Herbert Lee, one of the officers stationed at the detachment, credited the Inuit special constables with heroic efforts to save these items, as they suffered frostbite in the process. The men took refuge in the blubber house, a small structure 3 m by 3.5 m, which was the only available shelter (Figure 59, centre).[45] At the time of the fire, the air temperature was –51° F, with high winds blowing.[46]

During the Mounties' tenure at Craig Harbour, their Aboriginal employees were housed in a makeshift hut constructed of packing crates. In 1925, two families occupied one of these dwellings, before Panippak and his family moved out following the return of the sun in late February. He constructed a snow *iglooyah*, with two entrance porches, on which he threw water to form a wind-proof barrier of ice, and lined the interior with old canvas. A window was fashioned from a sheet of fresh water ice. According to policeman Herbert Patrick Lee, this *iglooyah* was divided into two sleeping platforms; on one side, Attsoongwah kept a seal-oil lamp and cooking apparatus, and on the other, Innocushia (Inoqusiaq) kept a lamp and a few belongings.[47] Three Inughuit who served the Mounties at Craig Harbour in 1923–24, the male Qisuk, and females Inoqusiaq and Padlunga, are portrayed in Figure 60. During the summers, the Inughuit residents moved into traditional skin tents, like the tents in a photograph at Bache Peninsula in the 1920s (Figure 22).

In 1923, the Eastern Arctic Patrol Expedition under Craig returned to Ellesmere Island with materials to rebuild the barracks buildings and provisions to resupply the detachment at Craig Harbour and they also intended to make a second attempt to establish a more northerly detachment at Cape Sabine, a continuing priority. Canadian officials were also responding to a rumour that Knud Rasmussen's former post at North Star Bay had been taken over by the Danish Government. If true, they believed this might lead to the establishment of a third hunting inspectorate in Greenland, with headquarters probably located at Etah, directly opposite Cape Sabine, "with a consequent increase in hunting and trapping activities in that district. There is no doubt that the presence of the police at Cape Sabine would discourage, if not entirely prevent, poaching by Greenlanders on Canadian territory."[48] The ship stopped at Etah on 8 August, and RCMP officers disembarked to persuade two Inughuit families to accompany them to serve at the Ellesmere Island detachments.

As in 1922, the *Arctic* encountered heavy ice conditions in Smith Sound and was unable to reach the intended destination of Cape Sabine. Craig related that he wanted to wait another 24 hours but Captain Bernier, realizing the peril of their position, advised an immediate retreat:

> As a matter of fact we had penetrated the ice field to what the captain designated the "key position." In drifting south the large ice fields are retarded on either side by their contact with the coast, and consequently revolve like immense wheels with one edge "rolling" along the coast and the other drifting at double speed down mid-channel. Where the channel contracts, as it does, just beyond or abreast of Cape Sabine, the two series of rotating ice masses come together like the jaws of an immense crusher, separating again where the channel widens.[49]

Figure 60: "Padlunga, Klishook [Qisuk] and Inacosea [Inoqusiaq]—Arctic Highlanders who spent the winter 1923-1924 at Craig Harbour, Ellesmere Island, NWT." National Archives of Canada Photo no. PA-102279.

Bernier stated that he had no desire to be caught in the "jaws of the crusher," in which the light construction of the *Arctic* would be readily smashed to pieces in the vice of the compacting floes. In light of the disastrous fate of the *Proteus* in these waters in 1884, his caution was warranted.

The MacMillan-Byrd Expedition of 1925

By the mid-1920s, unveiling plans for two expeditions to Ellesmere Island sparked renewed federal concerns over possible challenges to Canadian sovereignty in the region. The first involved American explorers Donald B. MacMillan and Lieutenant Commander Richard E. Byrd, who announced plans for an ambitious air expedition to Ellesmere and Axel Heiberg Islands. The other party generating anxiety for the Canadian government was led by Hans Krüger, a German geologist. Justifying his expedition to the Department of the Interior on scientific grounds, Krüger indicated his plans to proceed to northern Greenland

and cross over to Ellesmere Island, where he hoped to spend a winter. From there, he would proceed to Axel Heiberg Island. His intended party was to include two other Europeans and a complement of Inughuit families, sledge dogs, and equipment. Noting that Krüger intended to "live off the country," O.S. Finnie stated that this made Canadian officials "naturally uneasy" about this party's potential impact on Ellesmere's game animals, particularly muskoxen. He warned: "If three white men, with many Eskimos and dogs, live off the country, for a period of three or four years, as Krüger contemplates, there will not be a muskox left."[50]

MacMillan's activities in the region had been a source of concern among federal administrators for some time. In 1924, Danish explorer Knud Rasmussen alleged that MacMillan and three Inughuit companions killed 12 muskoxen in northwestern Ellesmere Island that spring. When questioned by officials regarding Rasmussen's testimony, MacMillan flatly denied killing any animals in "Canadian Territory."[51] Later that year, Finnie wrote that he had received information that, while based in Greenland, MacMillan had

> made several excursions to Canadian territory—Ellesmere Island—and killed our musk-ox. He has denied this, but nevertheless he goes into our country without our knowledge or consent and what he does, is a closed book as far as the Canadian government is concerned.[52]

Indeed, an examination of MacMillan's unpublished journals contradicts the explorer's denials, as his diary of a sledge excursion to Ellesmere Island during this expedition records his Inughuit companions having killed muskoxen.[53] The Inughuit utilized the meat, but the skins were reserved for MacMillan for export as specimens. On the party's return to Greenland, he wrote: "The Eskimos are all busy on my musk-ox, wolf, and young musk-ox skins, cleaning and pegging them out on the ground."[54] During one of these trips MacMillan also erected a bronze plaque at the site of Greely's 1883–84 wintering habitation at Camp Clay on Bedford Pim Island (Figure 89), although no prior authorization was sought in this case as well.

In late 1924, Finnie again remarked on MacMillan's failure to secure a hunting or trapping license for his 1923 expedition to Greenland and Ellesmere Island. Finnie wrote to MacMillan before his departure, but the American explorer had not bothered to reply to his letter. "There is sometimes a doubt whether the real object is scientific or something else altogether. I have always thought that the Canadian Government should be advised of these explorations and permission given before the parties proceed to the North country."[55] At Finnie's suggestion, the federal government added a clause to Section 8 of the Northwest Territories Act, giving the NWT Council authority to issue licenses to scientists or explorers as a precondition of approval to enter the territories, which was passed in 1925.[56]

Following passage of the amendments, the federal government drafted a list of procedures to be followed by explorers in the Canadian Arctic. Among other requirements, this document re-asserted the need for expeditions to adhere strictly to the regulations of the North West Game Act as they related to muskoxen; as well, permits were required for hunting migratory birds. The document indicated that Canada would not permit any flags to be hoisted in Canadian territory other than the British flag.[57] This new requirement apparently responded to MacMillan's statements that, in 1923, he had hoisted the stars and stripes at Camp Clay on Bedford Pim Island, the site of Greely's starvation camp in 1883–84, but had made no attempt to seek authorization from Canada.

Apart from the specific challenges posed by MacMillan and Krüger, the Dominion was concerned about a potential Danish challenge to Canadian sovereignty posed by continuing hunting by Greenland Inughuit on Ellesmere Island. During the Peary era, the Inughuit had reincorporated Ellesmere and other islands to its west within their hunting range. After Peary's final departure in 1909, they continued to hunt the comparatively rich resources of polar bear, seals, and walrus off Ellesmere's coasts, as well as muskox, caribou, and other smaller mammals in the interior. As well, the Inughuit made annual hunting expeditions into Canadian territory in search of polar bears for use in making their hunting pants. Typically, they crossed Smith Sound in March to hunt bears along Ellesmere's eastern coast or on the adjacent sea ice of Kane Basin. These were areas of polynyas where large seals maintained breathing holes in the ice, and polar bears congregated to prey on them.[58]

In 1925, MacMillan proceeded with plans to stage a return expedition to Greenland and Ellesmere Island. Enlisting support from the National Geographic Society and Zenith Radio Corporation, he was initially unspecific about his goals for the undertaking. In a published article he referred to the need to collect data on the amount of open water in the High Arctic in the summer months. However, he also revealed his intentions to continue exploration of the region west and north of Axel Heiberg Island.[59] As well, MacMillan also indicated his desire to utilize the new technology of fixed-wing aircraft for travel in the region, and he approached the U.S. Navy with a request to use its seaplanes.[60] To his patrons in the Navy, he was more explicit in his objectives. He and E.F. McDonald, the president of the Zenith Corporation, spoke of their desire to chart the lands of the archipelago by air, to find new lands for air-base sites, and to fly over the North Pole.[61]

Byrd was not part of MacMillan's original plans. A retired administrator with the U.S. Navy, he had worked with Robert Bartlett to develop a concept to stage an aerial assault on the North Pole and approached the navy independently with his own request for the use of their planes on his polar flight.[62] Asserting that air travel across the Arctic Ocean would become more important in the future,[63] Byrd promoted the notion that any lands discovered in the process should be "claimed for the United States."[64] MacMillan concurred that any new discoveries would belong to the American republic. Quoted in the *New York Times* in April 1925, he stated: "If we are the first to raise the American flag there, I believe it vests the title to the territory in this country for a given period of time, during which it must be revisited or the title lapses."[65]

With only three planes available, the Navy proposed that the two expeditions join together. They would lend MacMillan three airplanes and eight officers, mechanics, and pilots, but the personnel would be placed under Byrd's command.[66] As Byrd was a retired naval officer, the Navy could take credit for any aeronautical achievements realized by the expedition.[67] Accordingly, Byrd and MacMillan announced their intention to establish two air bases on Canadian territory, including one on Ellesmere Island, on the western side of Kennedy Channel, and the other on the northern coast of Axel Heiberg. In Canada, noting that MacMillan's ship would be partly supplied by the United States Navy, O.S. Finnie, Director, Northwest Territories and Yukon with the Department of the Interior, reported: "it can reasonably be supposed to be official or semi-official in its nature and that if new land is discovered it will be taken possession of under the 'Stars and Stripes.'"[68]

The expedition departed Wiscassett, Maine, on 20 June 1925. It was soon hampered by personality conflicts. Byrd reportedly bristled at MacMillan's refusal to place him second in command, and his diaries indicate his unhappiness with MacMillan's denial of authorization for several flights he proposed, including one along the coast.[69] On 8 August, the three expedition planes piloted by Byrd and two other pilots departed form Etah on a first attempt to find a landing base on Ellesmere Island. Crossing Smith Sound, they flew over the Greely camp on Pim Island, before traversing Ellesmere on a flight path toward Cañon Fiord. They searched in vain for a level landing surface but found only rugged mountainous terrain. With clouds rolling in, Byrd was obliged to order the planes to return to Etah. They attempted several further flights in the following days but encountered continuing poor weather. One plane continued on to Eureka Sound, where it identified a landing place. Byrd and his companions again took off and tried to reach an intermediate landing spot at Beistandt Fiord, but were prevented from landing by a heavy cross wind. On 14 August two planes departed Etah to establish a cache at Flagler Fiord, where Byrd had spotted open water. They landed and deposited 90 kg of food, 379 litres of gasoline, and other articles of equipment on the beach. However, by the following day they discovered that this landing place had become unusable due to the buildup of pressure ice in the fiord.[70]

By 30 August, with opportunities for further discovery fading fast, Byrd and another pilot indicated their readiness to fly to the limit of their cruising radius and, if possible, to make an attempt on the Pole. MacMillan refused as they had been able to establish only two caches within 160 km of Etah, and their use was doubtful. He ordered the return of the expedition before they were beset by ice and forced to remain in Etah for another winter.[71]

MacMillan and Byrd returned to the United States with different conclusions regarding the suitability for fixed-wing aircraft for High Arctic travel. MacMillan believed that the expedition showed that airplanes were not suitable, as landing places were not guaranteed and caches of food and gas could not be relied upon. Byrd, on the other hand, was reinforced in his belief that aviation would "conquer the arctic." In an article published in *National Geographic Magazine*, he pointed out the fact that the expedition's three planes had flown more than 9,500 km. He wrote: "This work will not end until all the wonderful records made by the dog sledges have been surpassed and the heart of the great unexplored area reached."[72]

The controversy precipitated by the MacMillan-Byrd expedition had evidently caused sufficient concern in diplomatic circles that the State Department decided to comply with Canadian laws in this matter. According to historian Nancy Fogelson, to "avoid an embarrassing diplomatic situation," the U.S. State Department conveyed orders to MacMillan to obtain the necessary explorers' licences from Canada.[73] This indicated a significant change in heart within the American administration. In an interview in 1927, MacMillan stated that, in 1925, he had asked the U.S. Bureau of Aeronautics to secure a permit for him to fly over Ellesmere Island. They refused on the ground that the application would constitute de facto acknowledgment of Canadian sovereignty in the region.[74] At that time, within the U.S. State Department, there was still sentiment in favour of applying the Monroe Doctrine with regard to the High Arctic. Believing Bolsheviks to be the root of problems with the Mexican government, some State Department officials believed that an extension of Canadian sovereignty in the Arctic Archipelago might also constitute a challenge to American pre-eminence, as they viewed it as an extension of British influence in North America.[75]

Establishment of the Bache Peninsula Detachment, 1926

When, in 1925, MacMillan announced his intention to establish the air bases on Canadian territory, federal officials took action. They realized that sovereignty might be asserted but could not be enforced without a presence in the immediate vicinity of exploration activity. Since the Craig Harbour detachment was more than 320 km from Byrd and MacMillan's proposed base of operations, O.S. Finnie, Director of the Northwest Territories Branch, proposed to RCMP Commissioner Cortlandt Starnes that a more northerly detachment be established on Ellesmere Island, at least for a period of a few years. With sovereignty as the justification, Finnie suggested a site opposite Etah on Ellesmere Island's eastern coast, from which Canadian territorial integrity could be more readily policed:

> If these men would make a yearly patrol to Axel Heiberg and other is-lands in these latitudes, it would help very materially in definitely estab-lishing Canadian sovereignty. It looks as if we should try and establish a post on Bache Peninsula. I understand Cape Sabine is not a favourable location, but that Bache Peninsula offers better possibilities.[76]

Accordingly, while much of the campaign was being waged on the diplomatic front, the government made hasty arrangements for the es-tablishment of a new detachment at Bache Peninsula to replace the detachment at Craig Harbour, which would be simultaneously de-staffed. Canadian authorities were also aware of the difficulty of penetrating the pack ice to reach Ellesmere Island's eastern coast. They first ex-plored alternative ways of setting up the detachment, writing to the Danish government to request permission to land material at Etah for a detachment house, which would subsequently be transported across to Cape Sabine on Ellesmere Island.[77] This idea was not pursued; instead, the RCMP on the *Arctic* tried once again to penetrate the ice in Kane Basin to reach Bache Peninsula, to no avail.[78] As a provisional step, they directed Inspector C.E. Wilcox aboard the *Arctic* to visit MacMillan at Etah to monitor his activities. While at Etah, Commander Byrd asked if any Canadians had ever been to Axel Heiberg Island, prompting a decision to send a patrol to the island the following spring. In the fol-lowing years the federal government secured the *Beothic*, a steel-hulled 2,660-tonne steamship to replace the antique *Arctic* and was finally able to penetrate the ice of Kane Basin on 6 August 1926 to unload men

Figure 61: "New detachment at Bache Peninsula, Ellesmere Island, NWT," 1926. Photograph by L.D. Livingston. National Archives of Canada Photo no. PA-111799.

and supplies to establish the new Bache Peninsula detachment. Located above 79° N. lat., it was probably the most northerly police post in the world (Figure 61).[79]

On the legislative front, in 1926, the federal cabinet established the Arctic Islands Game Preserve by order-in-council, requiring trading companies to obtain the consent of the Commissioner of the Northwest Territories before establishing trading posts anywhere in this territory. The rationale for the game preserve was dual; it was established in part to protect arctic mammal species, but also to support effective sovereignty in the region, as a contemporary report of the Department of External Affairs made clear: "The creation of this preserve and its appearance on our maps serves to notify the world that the area between the 60th and 141st meridians right up to the Pole is under Canadian sovereignty."[80] As with its earlier gestures of sovereignty following the Peary expeditions, fear of American "spread-eagleism" was the principal factor impelling the federal government to respond.[81]

RCMP staffing plans for the Eastern Arctic detachments called for the appointment of a non-commissioned officer in charge of each post, with two or three constables for general duty and patrols. Staffing the Ellesmere detachments was necessarily "the matter of much careful thought."[82] Apart from annual resupply visits by the Eastern Arctic Patrol ships, the detachments were completely cut off from the south. In such isolated circumstances, it was essential to find independent, self-sufficient individuals capable of undertaking a wide range of tasks demanded by these postings. In this objective the RCMP was successful in recruiting officers who proved to be among the outstanding High Arctic travellers of the twentieth century, especially Inspector A.H. Joy[83] and Sergeant Harry Stallworthy, both serving at Bache Peninsula between 1927 and 1933.

In addition to Euro-Canadians, the Mounties proposed to engage Inughuit to work at the detachments and serve as guides, interpreters, and dog-drivers on the lengthy patrols carried out to assert Canadian presence in the region.[84] These "special constables" would be assigned responsibilities to hunt for the detachments, primarily for dog food, and to perform much of the manual labour around the post. The Inughuit men would also tend to such tasks as repairing their own dwellings, building and maintaining komatiks and kayaks, cutting up sealskin for dog harnesses and traces, making harpoons, floats, and other tools, and feeding the dogs.[85] Figure 62 shows the Inughuaq Qisuk (Klishook) bundling muskox skins at the Craig Harbour detachment around 1924. In addition to the services of the men, the RCMP hoped to benefit from the labour of Inughuit women, whose preparation of hides and sewing skills would provide suitable skin clothing for all detachment personnel.

Finding Aboriginal men and women who were both willing and able to work at the detachments was not a straightforward proposition. The RCMP needed to find people with extensive knowledge of the region and its resources, experience with High Arctic conditions, and the capability of hunting and travelling during the dark winters of this far northerly latitude. Since there were then no Inuit living on Ellesmere Island, they would need to be recruited elsewhere and transported long distances from their homelands.

For the first year at Craig Harbour in 1922, the plan was to engage two Inuit families from northern Baffin Island for service at the Ellesmere Island detachments. Stopping at Pond Inlet en route to Craig Harbour, the Eastern Arctic Patrol vessel picked up the family headed by an Inuk, Kakto, and his spouse Oo-ar-loo. However, they were unable to secure the services of any other Inuit, as all available labourers had already been engaged by the Hudson's Bay Company at Pond Inlet.[86] During their tenure both Kakto and Oo-ar-loo performed essential labour for the detachment. Kakto hunted to provide the detachment sledge dogs with food and accompanied all its patrols designed to assert sovereignty over the region. Oo-ar-loo sewed all the detachment's skin clothing for these excursions and commenced these duties even on the ship en route to Ellesmere Island. A year later, Inspector Wilcox, the officer in charge at

Figure 62: "Klishook [Qisuk]–Arctic Highlander at Craig Harbour, Ellesmere Island, NWT, ca 1924. " National Archives of Canada Photo no. PA-102279. Photographer: T. Tash.

Figure 63: "Noo-ka-ping-wa [Nukappiannguaq] and dead square flipper seal, Off Cairn Point." Photo courtesy of the Peary-MacMillan Arctic Museum, Bowdoin College (Brunswick, Maine), Photograph no. 285.

Craig Harbour, stated that the Inuit from Pond Inlet were "perfectly satisfied with their treatment at Craig Harbour and very pleased to have been fortunate enough to have spent a winter with us."[87]

However, the difficulties of life in such a remote location were compounded by tragedies befalling the special constable's family. In July 1923, Oo-ar-loo and Kakto suffered a severe blow when their two young children died, apparently from influenza.[88] Inspector Wilcox noted: "life no doubt has been rather lonely for them on Ellesmere Island, with no native company and the loss of two young children this year is bound to have its affect [sic] in their desire to return home." He also observed that "the climate too, is far more severe than Baffin land, colder and darker in winter, making hunting conditions far different from Pond Inlet."[89] The commander of the Eastern Arctic Patrol reported that the Inuit family was "most anxious to return to their old haunts at Pond Inlet, having found the much longer winter night of the more northerly point most depressing."[90] In consequence, the Inuit boarded the *Arctic* to return to their home after only one year.[91]

Thereafter, all special constables recruited for the Ellesmere detachments up to their closure in 1940 were Inughuit hunters and their families from Northwestern Greenland. Recruitment of Greenland employees followed the pattern of the earlier British and American expeditions to the island. Prior to heading for the detachments, the Eastern Arctic Patrol vessel, the CGS *Arctic*, made a call at Inughuit settlements to enable the RCMP to try to enlist workers for the posts. For example, in 1925, the ship sailed to Etah Harbour, where two families were engaged for the year. One Inughuit man's equipment was stored at his camp 30 km farther north, but a futile attempt by the ship to penetrate the ice pack obliged them to depart for Ellesmere Island without his equipment. On this occasion the new special constables included an older man and his wife, who had previous experience at the Craig Harbour detachment, and a younger couple.[92] In his report on the 1923 expedition, J.D. Craig wrote that the two Inughuit families from Etah

> were well pleased at the prospect of a winter so far to the south, and in addition, having lost so many of their friends and relatives from the 'flu' epidemic of last winter, were apparently glad of a new home where they would be beyond the power of the 'devil' who is after them at Etah.[93]

The special constables were paid a nominal salary in the form of cash credits, which they could apply to the purchase of various goods from the RCMP. For example, in the year between 2 August 1926 and 31 July 1927, both Nukappianguaq and Aqioq (Ahkeeoo) were paid 50 cents a day or $182 in salary. In addition, they were paid for the hire of their dog teams on the patrol to King Christian Island from March to May 1927 at the rate of one dollar a day, totalling $54 each. Further, Nukappiannguaq and Aqioq were paid wolf bounties, totalling $60 and $30 respectively.[94] After being paid approximately $200 each in trade goods, the special constables were left with surplus credits that they could carry over the following year. For example, in January 1927 Nukappiannguaq obtained four oak boards, a length of Khaki duffle fabric, and 4.5 kg of rope to use building a new komatik.[95] Other trade items included such Western foodstuffs as butter, flour, baking powder, sugar, tea, jam, and biscuits.[96] Western clothing and fabrics were also much desired items. On 12 January 1927, in addition to various foods, Nukappiannguaq purchased a pair of drawers, an undershirt, an overshirt, three metres of print fabric, and four spools of thread. Other trade goods obtained on this occasion included an axe handle, 227 grams of Players cut tobacco, and 570 grams of Old Virginia plug tobacco.[97] The accounting system represented a formalization of the cash economy introduced a generation earlier by Peary and Rasmussen. The influence of Western trade goods is revealed in Figure 64, a 1926 view of an Inughuit man and woman at Bache Peninsula, which shows them wearing shirts of woven fabric in combination with traditional skin leggings and boots.

Nukappiannguaq was probably the most famous special constable at the Ellesmere Island detachments (Figure 63). He was the most experienced High Arctic traveller of his day, and reputed to be "the best hunter in north Greenland."[98] A hunter and guide with Donald MacMillan's "Crocker Land" Expedition of 1913–17,[99] he also worked as a dog driver and hunter on Lauge Koch's Danish Jubilee Expedition from 1920–23.[100] On these occasions he travelled to the far northern regions of Ellesmere Island and Greenland, visiting Fort Conger during both expeditions. First engaged by the Craig Harbour detachment in 1925, Nukappiannguaq applied his knowledge of the land and ecology of the region in RCMP patrols over a vast territory. He participated in most of the major RCMP patrols in the Arctic Islands in the 1920s and 1930s, including excursions to Axel Heiberg Island, Devon Island, and along the coastline and interior passes of Ellesmere Island. No other Aboriginal constable was as knowledgeable of the lands and seas of the High Arctic in his own era or since, or served so long with the Mounties at Ellesmere Island posts. For his exploits with the Force, he has been lionized in Mountie folklore.[101]

At the same time, Nukappiannguaq's tenure at the detachments was far from the unproblematic story presented in RCMP folklore. Acknowledging that he was a "good hunter and has a lot of experience on long patrols," Stallworthy reported that he was not popular with the other Inughuit. He recommended his discharge, "if he can be replaced."[102] The previous year, Stallworthy had made a similar complaint about him, although he provided an interesting explanation for Nuk-appiannguaq's behaviour. He wrote: "At times last winter he appeared to be sullen, perhaps this was on account of the absence of his children, also not having a partner to hunt with, however, he has many good points which would outweigh this."[103] In any case, Nuk-appiannguaq was not replaced. There were no further complaints in the RCMP files, and he served the Mounties in almost every year until the Craig Harbour detachment was closed in 1940.

At the Ellesmere Island detachments Inughuit women played important roles in the Mounties' ongoing occupation of the High Arctic, analogous to women's contributions to American expeditions in this region. Their work in food preparation, curing and sewing of skins, and child rearing enabled their male spouses to accompany the RCMP on extended patrols away from the detachments. In addition to all the customary tasks of maintaining their own families' households, these women provided important services to the Euro-Canadian Mounties, particularly by sewing fur garments.[104] Their labour began on the voyage to Ellesmere Island, long before arrival at their destination. On the initial voyage of the *Arctic* to establish Craig Harbour detachment in 1922, the partner of special constable Kakto was said to be "busily making boots for several members of the expedition out of sealskin."[105] In addition to work around the detachment, women sometimes also assisted on the trail in the procurement of game. In May 1927, a RCMP officer recorded in the Bache Peninsula detachment diary that "Eskimo Akoonadingwak and wife left post in p.m. for a few days hunting."[106]

Daily Life and the Seasonal Round at the Ellesmere Island Detachments

Established to assert sovereignty, the Ellesmere Island RCMP detachments could be sustained only through accommodations to the natural environment, which soon assumed the character of long-term cycles of life in this remote region. With negligible contact with the outside world and few responsibilities other than keeping the premises in reasonable order, activities gravitated toward hunting and procurement to meet the needs for maintaining the dog teams and to supplement the diet of the detachment population. In his report for 1929–30, Constable N. McLean of the Bache Peninsula detachment provided an account of the seasonal round at this post.[107] Supplemented by the two surviving detachment diaries for 1927 and 1928, this report gives a good indication of the range of typical tasks undertaken by its personnel.

In August, following the arrival of the annual supply ship with the Eastern Arctic Patrol and unloading supplies, detachment members turned their attention to hunting walruses and bearded seals (*oojook*) for the balance of the open water season. These animals were pursued in the detachment motorboat and whaleboat,[108] and the meat obtained from the hunt was stockpiled for dog food. In this season, the Inughuit also hunted from their kayaks as well as a rowboat, and secured both bearded seals and narwhals.[109] When the ice formed in late September, the constable instructed three Inughuit hunters to form a sledge train for a trip to hunt caribou for skins and fresh meat. Two of these men, Nukappiannguaq and Kahkacho, were sent to the west coast of the island, while Kahdi accompanied them as far as Flagler Bay, where he hunted for hares, required for making their winter socks. On 27 October, Nukappiannguaq and Kahkacho returned from the west, having killed seven caribou and one wolf. The caribou skins were needed for the preparation of *qulittaq* or parkas. Meanwhile, seals were hunted in Flagler Bay, and the meat was cached for subsequent transport to the detachment. By this time, detachment members also needed to provide as much insulation as feasible for the forthcoming winter. By mid-October in 1927, Constable Anstead was reportedly building a snow wall around the expedition house, while Nukappiannguaq was erecting a similar barrier around his own dwelling.[110]

During the dark period, 18 October to 23 February, the Inughuit and European members of the detachment were preoccupied hauling meat from the caches of walrus, seal and narwhal meat for the dogs, as about 90 dogs needed to be fed at this time. Most of the caches were within 32 km of the post, but some of the caches were made at Cocked Hat Island near Rice Strait, a round trip of 112 km. Due to heavy snow conditions, they were obliged to keep the sledge loads light, necessitating many trips. McLean observed that this work kept all members of the detachment in good physical condition. He added that the work "was also a benefit to the members of the detachment in that there was an objective and a good reason to get out and travel in the winter, this accounted for a lot of mileage and many sleeps away from the detachment." Work activities ceased on Christmas Day, when a good dinner was prepared and gifts exchanged between the European and Inughuit employees.

Hunting and related tasks resumed in January, as the Inughuit men caught seals at Flagler and Hayes fiords and hauled the meat back to the detachment. By February, as usual, the weather had become considerably colder. In 1930, McLean reported that he had sent the Inughuit hunters to hunt for additional dog food so that the remaining stockpiles of meat could be preserved for the patrols. As seals had become "very scarce" in Flagler Fiord, they hunted at small patches of open water using the *utoq* method. For the duration of the winter, throughout the months of March and April, the detachment was kept busy in preparations for search patrols planned for the missing Krüger expedition. The Inughuit men were engaged in making sledges, dog harness, clothing and "a lot of native equipment." In this period, they also made large quantities of pemmican and prepared dog food for the patrols.[111]

With the return of extensive daylight in May and June, longer trips away from the detachment were feasible. In addition to departing on patrols, the men also made longer hunting excursions to areas along the floe edge of Kane Basin, and trips back to Etah, Greenland, on the other side of Smith Sound, to obtain such goods as sealskin lines for dog traces and hare skins for stockings.[112] Inughuit women accompanied their partners on some of these hunting trips, but they were not permitted to join them on patrol. The special constables who stayed at the detachment were engaged in a variety of tasks, including hunting in nearby Flagler Fiord and Hayes Sound, repairing equipment, and fashioning harpoons.[113] The Euro-Canadian officers also made short hunting trips, in addition to work around the detachment, such as paperwork on accounts and patrol reports, hauling ice for fresh water, hauling coal, cooking, cleaning equipment, repairing the banking around the detachment buildings, hauling gravel to fill in holes around the detachment buildings, and making repairs to the structures.[114] In July 1927, the detachment diary reports that Constables Garnett and Bain were painting the detachment house, storehouse, and blubber shed.[115] In these accounts the Inughuit women of the detachment are seldom mentioned, although clearly they were occupied with traditional tasks maintaining their households, including child rearing, food preparation, making and repairing clothing, preparing skins, and numerous other tasks (Figures 60 and 64).

Other pragmatic strategies involved reusing equipment and supplies left behind by earlier explorers. Just as Peary had liberally availed himself of the materials at Fort Conger, so the Mounties made use of various items left behind by Peary. In 1927, for example, the officer in charge at Bache Peninsula sent Nukappiannguaq and Aqioq to Victoria Cape to pick up a cook stove and several bags of coal abandoned by the American explorer.[116]

With the need to feed a large number of sled dogs at the detachment and on the trail, as well as provide meat for personnel, hunting

Figure 64: "Eskimo man and woman at Bache Peninsula, Ellesmere Island,
NWT," late 1920s. National Archives of Canada Photo no. PA-102650.

became the major preoccupation for the Ellesmere detachments. For
dog food, Inughuit employees hunted walrus, narwhal, and seals.[117]
Despite the ban on muskox hunting, in the first few years, RCMP
officers also hunted muskoxen for food. Herbert Patrick Lee, who was
at Craig Harbour in 1923–24, subsequently related he participated in
various hunting trips by detachment officers to secure muskox meat,
when as many as ten animals were killed at a time.[118] Constable P.
Dersch, in a report on a 1925 patrol from Craig Harbour to northern
Devon Island, wrote that he and Nukappiannguaq had killed five
muskoxen for the meat and hides.[119]

Hunting of all major game animals continued at Bache Peninsula when
that detachment was in operation between 1926 and 1932. By this time,
however, the policy was to hunt muskoxen only in case of emergency. In
1929, Constable Anstead and Aqioq killed two bull muskoxen near the
head of Bay Fiord, while on the return journey, Constable Beatty killed
two others in the same area.[120] On 23 July 1927, an officer reported in
the detachment diary that the Inughuit were "crating muskox and deer
[caribou] skins."[121] While at the Bjorne Peninsula on patrol in 1930 Constable N. McLean and his companions shot two muskoxen for dog food.[122]

In 1932 Constable R.W. Hamilton wrote that on patrol that spring he and his Inughuit companions "reluctantly" killed three muskoxen for dog food when their supplies ran out; "had we not killed these animals I am sure that we would have lost more of our dogs."[123] Polar bears were more commonly killed on these patrols for dog food;[124] the skins apparently were either retained by the Inughuit guides or brought back to the detachment for subsequent preparation of bearskin pants for the officers. In 1931 Constable Stallworthy reported that their hunters had killed eight polar bears south of Pim Island; the meat was fed to the sled dogs and the skins brought back to the detachment for use in making winter pants and dog harness.[125]

Some RCMP officers were also reportedly involved in a thriving trade in fox furs at the Ellesmere Island detachments. In 1925 Inspector Joy wrote to Governor Rosendahl of Northern Greenland to request the right to hire two families of Inughuit for detachment service. He referred the matter to Knud Rasmussen, who requested assurances that the RCMP would not try to persuade Inughuit to live at the Ellesmere detachments or to initiate a fur trade with them in competition with the Thule trading store.[126] To allay concerns that the Mounties might try to compete with the Thule station, A.H. Joy gave assurances that RCMP staff were "forbidden to trade fur, or to transact business with the Eskimos in any manner for personal gain, so that you or any person engaged in business in Greenland will have no cause for concern in this regard."[127] The trade in fox furs reportedly continued nevertheless. In 1932, an official with the Eastern Arctic Patrol recommended that employment of Inughuit from Greenland should cease, in his view, as "trapping foxes for the detachment" had become the "prime motive" for employing Inughuit at the Ellesmere posts. He had come to these conclusions "particularly in view of the trading and trafficking in furs that has been rampant on the *Beothic* and with the Government employees in the Eastern Arctic."[128] A 1932 government report on Craig Harbour stated that one of the detachment officers there told Inspector T.V. Sandys-Wunsch that he earned $5,000 from fox pelts in one year alone.[129]

Bache Peninsula was the most remote RCMP posting and one of the most isolated sites of the High Arctic. It could not reliably be reached by ship and, at its high latitude, experienced four months of continuous darkness during the polar winter. Due to recurrent sea-ice obstruction in Kane Basin, resupply of the detachment proved a problematic undertaking throughout the five years it was in operation. For example, in early August 1928, the resupply vessel *Beothic* attempted to negotiate Rice Strait but was stopped by a large pan of ice stretching from Cape Sabine to the mainland. Unable to make progress within two days, the ship was obliged to retreat to Fram Havn, where supplies for the post were offloaded for storage in a police cache for subsequent transshipment to Bache Peninsula.[130] This created its own difficulties, as continuing turbulence in the movement of sea ice created hazardous conditions for those attempting to retrieve the contents of the cache. The officer in charge wrote that "on several occasions we narrowly averted being crushed." In September they attempted to reach the cache by boat; he described the scene:

> Whilst off Cape Rutherford a thick fog descended so that we could see only a few yards ahead. Between Cocked Hat Island and the mainland we became jumbled up in a veritable maze of swirling, grinding, heavy ice, which was continually moving, and whichever way we turned we could not find an outlet.

Finally, they reached land but were stranded for two days. With great difficulty, they chopped and moved the new ice out of the way as they inched their way back to the detachment. The officer commanding wrote: "We were exceedingly lucky we did not lose the boat on this trip, as it is about one of the worst spots in this district."[131] A comparable image of resupply of the Craig Harbour detachment by boat in 1925 is shown in Figure 65.

Detachment personnel had better luck the following year when, after being stopped by pack ice in Rice Strait and Buchanan Bay, the ship was able to proceed to Cape Rutherford, where the stores were landed.[132] Problems resurfaced in 1930 when supplies had to be unloaded at Rice Strait and brought to the detachment in small boats and by komatik. As most of the personnel were away from the past on patrol, fortunately the presence of a hunting party of Inughuit provided an alternative labour pool for hauling the supplies. The officer in charge engaged 10 Inughuit dog drivers and their teams for transshipment of the cargo.[133]

Nevertheless, life at Bache was difficult and, with resupply always uncertain, an unsettling experience for many officers. In 1928, Constable E. Anstead reported that he had "lived solely on a diet of seal and walrus meat all winter."[134] Professional medical or dental assistance was out of the question. In 1928, the constable in command reported that Constable Makinson had nicked his thumb while cutting up a seal for dog food. The wound quickly developed into blood poisoning. While medical assistance was administered, his arm was rendered useless, putting him out of service for five weeks.[135] Also in 1928, the Inughuaq Qulutana (Coolitanga) was injured on patrol. While crossing some very rough ice near Clarence Head on the eastern coast, his komatik fell on him, "spraining his leg so badly that he could not walk."[136] After resting his leg for a day, Qulutana

Figure 65: "Landing supplies at RCMP Detachment, Craig Harbour, Ellesmere Island, NWT, August 1925." National Archives of Canada Photo no. PA-102444.

continued for the balance of the patrol despite the injury. In 1930, Constable N. McLean reported that he had experienced ptomaine poisoning from eating a tin of kippered herring, while Constable Beatty suffered from an ear ailment, which seriously affected his hearing.[137] In 1931, the annual report for the detachment noted that Constable Fraser had experienced "considerable trouble with his teeth," causing difficulty with his left eye in the cold months. As well, during the winter, Constable Stallworthy slipped on the shore ice while hauling walrus meat and injured his elbow. The injury continued to plague him when he needed to use his whip continuously on long patrols.[138]

The sense of isolation must have been particularly pronounced during the long, dark winters. The Mounties' sole link to the outside world was via radio signals, with very limited results in the pre-satellite age. On 2 February 1927, a policeman recorded that he was able to tune in many stations "but [the] speech was so badly distorted, I could not get names of any of them up to 10:45 p.m." Two days later, he wrote that many signals were heard, but the reception was poor "until KDKA and WPG were heard a few minutes before midnight." On 5 February, they successfully tuned in radio station WGN in Chicago between 7 and 8 p.m., while on the next day, they listened to a concert broadcast from Lincoln, Nebraska and a church service over the station WPG.[139] A few weeks earlier they succeeded in tuning a music program on an unidentified station: "The orchestra was very good but the announcer must have been eating his lunch by the sound of him. I could not understand a word he said."[140]

Problems of isolation at the Ellesmere Island detachments were particularly pronounced for Inughuit women, who were usually left behind
during patrols that took their partners away for periods of up to six
weeks or longer. There were occasional exceptions. At Craig Harbour, a
1934 report stated that Killecktee's spouse and two children had accompanied the party on a short patrol to Grise Fiord: "Killecktee's wife was
glad of the opportunity of a trip, after being cooped up all winter."[141]

In these isolated conditions, it was perhaps not surprising that interpersonal conflicts periodically emerged. In the 1929–30 annual report,
the constable in charge wrote of fisticuffs with one of his colleagues at
this place:

> It is with regret that I have to report the conduct of Cst. F—. During the
> hunting last fall Cst. F—was forever grumbling about the way the na-
> tives were hunting, so knowing that this man had no idea of hunting
> in this country I told him to never mind the natives and pay attention
> to his own affairs, immediately he invited me to take off my hat and
> fight, but I refrained from this method as long as possible, but in
> December he carried it into personal affairs and it came to blows.[142]

In other cases, conflicts arose between Euro-Canadian officers and
Inughuit employees. In 1929 N. McLean, the constable commanding
the Bache Peninsula detachment reported that he had dismissed one
of the Inughuit employees who had been employed at the detachment since its inception. He wrote:

> I decided to let him go for he was becoming very Independent and told
> me on two occasions that Insp. Joy was the only one who could dis-
> miss him, he did not want his wife to do any sewing for the members
> of the Detachment and during the dark period he went to one of the
> cashes [sic] of meat. This cash [sic] consisted of eight narwhals, and
> [he] cashed it elsewhere for his own use, we were finding small cashes
> all over the place during the sealing season.[143]

Other reports were much more positive. In 1931, Corporal H.W.
Stallworthy, the officer in charge of the Bache Peninsula detachment
commented favourably on the service of Nukappiannguaq. Previously
critical of his attitude, Stallworthy paid tribute to his skills; he wrote:

> native Nookapingwa in my opinion is a valuable native to have as sen-
> ior native, particularly with his experience in these regions on long pa-
> trols. At times last winter he appeared to be sullen, perhaps this was on
> account of the absence of his children also not having a partner to hunt
> with, however, he has many good points that would outweigh this.[144]

RCMP Patrols over the High Arctic

A major focus of activity at the Ellesmere Island detachments was patrols carried out by police personnel between 1922 and 1940. In staging the patrols, the RCMP hoped to demonstrate their capacity and willingness to administer the laws of Canada over the Arctic Islands. The patrols substantially fulfilled the vision of J.B. Harkin, who had originally recommended such tangible demonstrations of sovereignty and effective occupation in 1920. Nevertheless, the patrols following the MacMillan-Byrd affair of 1925 far exceeded the earlier excursions in terms of distances travelled (Figure 66), the product, in part, of hypersensitivity within the federal government on the sovereignty issue. Historian William Morrison has noted that in 1925 Commander Richard Byrd met G.P. Mackenzie, leader of the party on the Eastern Arctic Patrol at Etah. Byrd asked whether any Canadian had ever been to Axel Heiberg Island. Since no Canadian national had in fact visited this territory, Mackenzie, Inspector C.E. Wilcox and Staff-Sergeant Joy decided on the spot to send a patrol from Bache Peninsula to Axel Heiberg Island the following year to redress the situation.[145]

In 1926, Joy himself led the patrol to Axel Heiberg, the first of several outstanding patrols by the RCMP in the High Arctic. Following an itinerary along the southern coast of Ellesmere Island to Hell Gate, Joy's party followed the west coast of Ellesmere to Axel Heiberg Island, before returning to the detachment, having covered 1,560 km in 40 days.[146] Joy was gracious in acknowledging the assistance of his guide Nukappiannguaq:

> I would like to express my appreciation of the splendid assistance rendered by Nookapeeungwak on this patrol. He is an Eskimo from North Greenland, and bears the reputation of being one of the best hunters in that district. I found him on this journey to be all that is said of him, and in addition to being a first-class hunter, he is a capable and energetic traveller.[147]

The following year, accompanied by Constable Garnett, Nukappiannguaq, Aqioq, and Uutaaq, with four sledges pulled by 11, 14, 12, and 15 dogs respectively, Joy carried out an extended patrol over much of the Queen Elizabeth archipelago. The party departed Bache Peninsula on 26 March 1927, followed Flagler Fiord to its head, travelled over the Sverdrup Pass to Bay Fiord, and along Ellesmere Island's west coast, crossing Eureka Sound to Skaare Fiord on Axel Heiberg Island. The party then proceeded to Cape Southwest, turned southwest to the northern coast of Cornwall Island, crossed Hendriksen Strait to

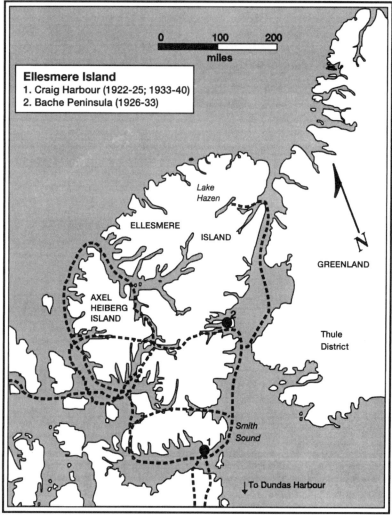

Major R.C.M.P. Patrol Routes, 1922-40
(after Taylor (1955), p. 128, and NAC, RG85, Vol. 268, File 1003-G[1])

■ ■ ■■ ■ ■■■ ■■■ Dog sledging excursions

Figure 66: Routes of RCMP Patrols on Ellesmere Island and adjacent islands, 1922–1940

Amund Ringnes Island, turned to the west to the southern point of Ellef Ringnes Island, and continued on to King Christian Island. From there, they returned to Cornwall Island, went south to Graham Island, and then on to Great Bear Cape on the Bjorne Peninsula on Ellesmere Island's west coast. They travelled northwest to Axel Heiberg, continued along its southeast coast as far as Storoen, then crossed Eureka Sound to Ellesmere's west coast. They again crossed Eureka Sound to Axel Heiberg, continuing north before returning to Ellesmere at Bay Fiord, retracing their steps across the island to Bache Peninsula. In 54 days they had covered 2,100 km. Reporting on the journey, Joy paid tribute to his Inughuit companions; he wrote:

> I would like to express my appreciation of the splendid manner in which the Eskimos Nookapeeungwak and Ahkeeoo behaved on this trip. They worked very hard at times; were always willing and cheerful, and I found them to be first-class travellers.[148]

In 1929, Joy undertook what RCMP Commissioner J.H. MacBrien called "probably the most outstanding patrol in the history of the Eastern Arctic."[149] This patrol began at Dundas Harbour on Devon Island and involved sledge travel through most of the major islands in the Queen Elizabeth group, including Melville, Ringnes, Axel Heiberg, and Ellesmere islands, before finally concluding at Bache Peninsula. The party travelled 2,720 km between 12 March and 31 May.[150] By these extended and difficult excursions, publicized in press releases and books by RCMP officers and retired personnel, Canada hoped to demonstrate that it was serious about maintaining an effective presence in the High Arctic.

The disappearance of German scientist Dr. H.K.E. Krüger in 1929 inspired a series of patrols in search of his missing party, which also served as tangible gestures of sovereignty. In March 1929, Dr. H.K.E. Krüger, R.A. Bjare, and the Inughuaq Aqioq departed Bache Peninsula on an expedition to the areas explored by Sverdrup. Planning to live off the country, they carried inadequate ammunition with them, and Krüger was already suffering from meat poisoning when they left the post.[151] With no word as to their whereabouts a year later, the RCMP incorporated a search for the lost expedition into their 1930 patrols in the southern part of Ellesmere Island. In addition to the longer patrols, the RCMP sent Nukappiannguaq on a journey back to Robertson Bay, Greenland, to enlist the services of another Inughuaq to work with him. Absent during the coldest weather of the winter, he was obliged to hunt at the floe edge in Smith Sound to secure two walruses to feed his dogs.[152]

When these excursions failed to turn up any evidence of the missing party, the police determined to make a major search effort the following year. As planned by Sergeant Joy, the police recruited some of the most seasoned Inughuit guides, including Nukappiannguaq and Kahkacho, who were already in the employ of the Bache Peninsula detachment, and crossed Smith Sound to enlist the services of Ittukusuk.[153]

In 1932, two parties departed from the Bache Peninsula detachment in search of Krüger on 20 March 1932. Officially led by Corporal Stallworthy and Constable R.W. Hamilton, these patrols included seven Inughuit and 124 dogs. At Bay Fiord, the party divided, with Stallworthy heading north and Hamilton toward the west. Hamilton's party reached Cape South-West on 3 April with no sign of the missing explorers. One of the Inughuit was severely injured by a wounded bear. They persisted and reached Baumann Fiord on 22 April and crossed overland to Smith Sound, returning to Bache Peninsula on 7 May. They had travelled 1,500 km while experiencing blizzards, difficult sledging through deep snow, and the loss of 17 dogs en route.[154]

Stallworthy and his team proceeded north to Eureka Sound where, their dogs suffering from malnutrition, they shot six bull muskoxen for dog food. They scoured the shoreline and found no trace of the missing expedition until they reached Lands Lokk at the north tip of Axel Heiberg Island. There, they found a record, written in German and signed by all members of the Krüger party, which indicated that they had reached this point by 24 April 1930 and were then departing for Meighen Island. Proceeding to the southwest in pursuit, Stallworthy's group was short of food and headed for a cache at Cape South-West. On 6 April, they killed six dogs to feed to the others. On 26 April, seven Peary caribou were killed and also fed to the dogs, but on reaching Eureka Sound six more dogs had to be killed. Returning via Bay and Flagler Fiords, Stallworthy's party reached the detachment on 23 May, having spent 65 days on the trail, covering 2,250 km.[155]

Patrolling carried an element of danger, as in the case of a patrol in 1932, when Nukappiannguaq, attacked by a polar bear, suffered a "severe wound" in his right hip before he was able to kill the bear with a second shot.[156] Crossing glaciers and sea ice also had inherent risks. While traversing a glacier on a patrol north of Makinson Inlet in 1931, Constable Stallworthy fell down a crevasse, his body jamming at nine metres below the surface. Fortunately for him, his Inughuit companions heard his cries for help before he passed out. Standing astride the crevasse, they were able to haul him out with a harpoon line.[157] On another patrol from Craig Harbour in 1925, one of the sled dogs fell into a crevasse to a depth of 23 metres. The other men formed a long rope by tying together lengths of line and lowered Nukappiannguaq into the crevasse; he succeeded in rescuing the dog.[158] In 1928, Constable Anstead attempted to lead a party over one of Ellesmere Island's great ice caps en route to Lake Hazen. Ascending from Sawyer Bay on Ellesmere Island's eastern coast, his party was thwarted by crevasses, into which the sledge dogs fell at an increasing rate. Removed from the coast and its environmental signs, the Inughuit guides were uncertain that they were on the right glacier, and the party was obliged to retreat.[159]

Patrols were major undertakings and could not have been successfully carried out without the Inughuit guides' considerable knowledge of the country, skills in dog driving, and hunting prowess. The Inughuit had already acquired extensive experience of Canada's High Arctic while serving with American and Danish expeditions to Ellesmere and Axel Heiberg Islands. As well, the Mounties relied heavily on their guides' knowledge of environmental signs, as in a 1931 patrol along the southern coast of Ellesmere Island near Glacier Strait. On this occasion Nukappiannguaq advised against travelling around the foot of a large glacier as the wind was blowing from the east, suggesting the likelihood of encountering thin ice and possibly open water. The party built a snow shelter and camped until a change of wind.[160]

In agreeing to undertake the many patrols with the RCMP, the Inughuit guides had their own objectives, which did not always coincide with those of their Euro-Canadian employers. As has been noted, from the standpoint of the RCMP, the sole purpose of the patrols was to demonstrate effective Canadian presence in the High Arctic. With sovereignty uppermost in their thinking, the Mounties sometimes embarked on extended trips across dangerous or unproductive terrain. To the Inughuit, such travel was mystifying. Their pragmatic modes of thought told them it made sense only if it enabled them to hunt game or to learn more about the resources and opportunities for future utilization. A case in point was a patrol carried out between Bache Peninsula and the west coast of Ellesmere Island in 1928. Constable Anstead, the officer in charge, wanted to circumnavigate Axel Heiberg Island. According to Anstead, his companions, Aqioq and Nukappiannguaq, were unwilling to go that far, "owing to tales of hardship they heard from natives who had travelled with Dr. Cook on his supposed trip to the pole, and also because they wanted to hunt bears."[161]

Accusing his companions of wanting the bears only to sell the skins to passengers aboard the Eastern Arctic Patrol, Anstead wrote that he "quickly knocked [the idea] on the head." Later, he wrote of his suspicions that the Inughuit had deliberately allowed his supplies of oil, stowed on his komatik, to leak, forcing him to abandon the remote destinations of the patrol. It is possible that interpersonal conflicts were also at play. Anstead complained throughout his patrol report of passive-aggressive behaviour on the part of Nukappiannguaq, apparently precipitated by continual criticism from the Mountie. He wrote:

> The conduct of the native Nookapeeungwah on this patrol was bad. On several occasions I reprimanded him for various things, and he would then sulk and do things just the opposite to what I wanted, knowing that it would annoy me.[162]

On another occasion Anstead placed an Inughuit man in a dangerous situation, and he encountered similar resistance. While on patrol on the eastern coast of Axel Heiberg Island,

> native Ahkeeoo became sick, vomiting, dizzy, and having a temperature...Ahkeeoo was so bad that he remained in bed for four days and did not wish to eat anything; practically had to force him to eat a little broth and biscuits sopped in milk.[163]

Yet, despite Aqioq's diminished capacity, Anstead refused to allow him to accompany Constable Beatty and Akkamalingwah back to Bache Peninsula; instead he insisted that they continue on to Lake Hazen. "Although he was still weak and complained of dizziness, I decided to move on." He wrote: "Ahkeeoo refused to proceed to Lake Hazen, although I tried to persuade him and finally threatened him with dismissal, but all to no purpose."[164] While the RCMP officer was obliged to back down, his own words signified that patterns of military discipline still governed European–Aboriginal relations in the High Arctic.

With the outbreak of the Second World War in 1939, the Canadian government turned its attention to the European war effort and marshalling resources to meet this new challenge. The Craig Harbour detachment was closed in 1940 and would not be re-opened for more than a decade. This detachment and its counterpart at Bache Peninsula had substantially achieved Canada's objectives of demonstrating its effective sovereignty over the region, both through establishing the detachments and carrying out extensive symbolic patrols across the Queen Elizabeth Islands.

Canadian assertion of effective sovereignty over the High Arctic followed a familiar pattern for at least 75 years after it acquired the region in 1880. Long periods of benign neglect were punctuated by brief episodes of frenetic activity in response to perceived incursions into Canadian sovereignty. After responding to the perceived challenge, federal officials lapsed again into complacency. Concerned with keeping down costs, the Dominion did the minimum it considered necessary to maintain sovereignty, and no more.

The Ellesmere Island RCMP detachments represented the first attempt to establish an effective Canadian presence in the High Arctic since the transfer of the Arctic Islands from Britain to Canada in 1880. The detachments could more appropriately be termed "colonies," rather than "settlements," since they were little more than tentative footholds. Nevertheless, the establishment of installations with year-round occupation by law-enforcement officials signified that Canada was serious about maintaining its sovereignty over its Arctic Archipelago. While largely symbolic, the RCMP presence went far to meet the basic international conventions regarding the maintenance of effective occupation. The establishment of the High Arctic RCMP detachments also initiated an extended interaction between Euro-Canadians and Native peoples of the region. At the Ellesmere Island detachments, RCMP constables and Inughuit were brought into daily contact, commencing a process of cultural exchange that would be revived with Canadian Inuit after the Second World War. The relationship with Inughuit was sufficiently strong that Mounties at Bache Peninsula even went hunting with visiting members of this group who were not employed at the detachment.[165] Employment of Greenlanders unwittingly contributed to later concerns that their presence might support a possible claim to sovereignty over the Queen Elizabeth Islands. While perceived to be essential to the Ellesmere Island detachments between the wars, by the end of the period, federal authorities came to regard their employment as a mistake, as it reinforced the Greenlanders' perception that the Queen Elizabeth Islands were within their traditional hunting territories.

In his quasi-official history of the RCMP in the region, Harwood Steele depicted the Force's activities in the region in terms of "conquest" and the "subjection" of a part of the British Empire, as he wrote:

> This story of Arctic conquest is a very important one, not only to Canada and the British Empire, but to the world at large. Any story which deals with the gradual subjection of almost half a continent in the teeth of difficulties which our forefathers found practically insurmountable, obviously is of more than merely national interest.[166]

It may have been a gentler form of conquest than the High Arctic had previously experienced, but as Steele's account made clear, an imperial endeavour nevertheless.

9

Adventurers, Big-Game Hunters, and Scientists on Ellesmere Island, 1934–40

The Oxford University Ellesmere Land Expedition, 1934–35

With the conclusion of the era of polar and scientific exploration by Americans and Scandinavians around 1920, human activity in the remote northerly areas of Ellesmere Island ceased for more than 10 years. While the RCMP patrolled much of the Queen Elizabeth archipelago in the period between the wars, it did not visit the most northerly part of the region until 1935. The catalyst was a party of young British students from Oxford University in 1934–35, which also provided an impetus to other British expeditions to Ellesmere Island in the late 1930s.[1] While these expeditions were of minor importance to Arctic science, they illustrated something of the character of romantic adventure seeking during the twilight of the British Empire.

Following its establishment in 1928, the Oxford University Exploration Club, like its counterpart at Cambridge, sponsored a large number of expeditions in the 1930s. The emphasis was on polar exploration in both the Arctic and Antarctic regions. The Oxford Club was essentially an undergraduate organization, but more senior and experienced members were customarily included to instill discipline and encourage the publication of findings.[2] It was logical that Britain's two leading universities took the initiative in university-sponsored exploration in this period. Upper-class traditions of grooming the younger generation and inculcating responsibility through physical challenges, whether mountain climbing or exploration in remote areas, were well entrenched from the heyday of "Muscular Christianity" in the mid-nineteenth century. The specific goal of an expedition was not so important as its role in building character and training future members of Britain's ruling class to assume leadership roles in the more serious spheres of politics, commerce, and society. More general motivations are suggested by the Oxford party's depiction of Ellesmere Island as "the most northerly part of the British Empire."[3] The expeditions helped maintain an illusion of Anglo-Saxon pre-eminence around the globe in a period of Britain's rapidly declining influence.

The driving force behind the Oxford University Ellesmere Land Expedition was Edward Shackleton, a 21-year-old Oxford undergraduate and son of the veteran Antarctic explorer, Sir Ernest Shackleton. His only apparent experience in exploration was a recent Oxford expedition to

Borneo, for which he had served as surveyor. In 1933, he obtained the necessary approvals for the Ellesmere expedition, first from the Royal Geographical Society and then the Canadian government. He also met with Major-General Sir James MacBrien, Commissioner of the RCMP, who pledged his strong support and offered the loan of an officer experienced in Arctic travel.[4]

Shackleton's British companions included four other men, Dr. Noel Humphreys, a 48-year-old physician and botanist; A.W. Moore, a 21-year-old student who had served as an assistant biologist on the Oxford expedition to Borneo; Robert Bentham, a geologist; and David Haig-Thomas, another student assigned the role of ornithologist for the party.[5] Shackleton also recruited two Inughuit guides and their families by obtaining permission from the Danish government to have Aboriginal employees engaged at the RCMP detachments on Ellesmere reassigned to work for his expedition instead. They included the hunters Nukappiannguaq and Inuatuk and their spouses Enalunguak and Natuk.[6]

The general plan was to winter on Ellesmere Island, carry out geographical exploration, and make a crossing of northern Grant Land, the region between Lake Hazen and the Arctic Ocean,[7] the main objective of the expedition. Shackleton justified these objectives in that little geological work had been done in Ellesmere, and "scarcely any survey further than the coast." He added that an attempt would be made to form "some conception of the resources of the unknown interior of Grant and Ellesmere Land." The survey work was an assessment of muskox and caribou populations depleted by Peary and an investigation of the mineral resources of the country.

The RCMP first expressed an interest in visiting northern Ellesmere Island in the 1920s when Sergeant Joy, then based at Craig Harbour, sketched out a plan for a patrol to the northern part of the island.[8] However, the patrol never materialized. The officer assigned to accompany the expedition was Sergeant Harry Stallworthy, a seasoned Arctic traveller, who travelled to England to accompany the party on its outward voyage to northwest Greenland. From England, Stallworthy wrote to RCMP headquarters that the plan at that point was to base operations at Bache Peninsula, but if ice conditions were particularly favourable, the headquarters would be established farther north, possibly even at Fort Conger. Due to congested ice conditions, the party was unable to advance through Smith Sound to establish the intended base at Fort Conger and was obliged to winter at Etah, with the revised plan of making a 500-km sledge journey to the north in the spring. It was eventually decided that only the most experienced sledge travellers would make this trip: Stallworthy, Moore, and Nukappiannguaq and Inuatuk, the two Inughuit guides.

During the autumn of 1934 at Etah, members of the expedition engaged in illegal hunting of walrus. They shot several animals with firearms without first harpooning them, an infraction under the game laws of the region. Stallworthy reported that the Inughuit guides offered to harpoon any walrus before the commencement of shooting, but were ignored by the British hunters: "since Dr. Humphreys and other members of the expedition, led by Haig-Thomas, continued to shoot at every opportunity, three Eskimos joined in with their rifles, more to prevent the wounded ones from slipping off the ice-pans into the water."[9] Alarmed at the display of "indiscriminate shooting," Stallworthy handed Humphreys a handbook of the North Greenland Game Laws, to no avail. In February, both Humphreys and Haig-Thomas were summoned to appear before a Danish official and Inughuit council at Thule to face charges of shooting and wounding walrus without first securing them by harpoon. Humphreys pled ignorance and charges against him were dismissed. For his part, Haig-Thomas also "defeated the charge" by claiming that in each case, walrus were shot for emergency food, a false explanation.[10]

During the winter, the British men were preoccupied with laying caches of walrus meat for the forthcoming spring sledging party. Meanwhile the Inughuit women sewed such articles of clothing as sealskin mitts and kamiks, while the men used bearded seal strips to construct dog lines, harness, and lashes.[11] With the approach of spring, plans for the Ellesmere leg of the expedition began to change. It was by now apparent that the expedition was not sufficiently prepared to send a large party to northern Ellesmere. The British students had little experience in High Arctic travel and handling dogs; they experienced particular difficulty in learning to handle the nine metre dog whips.[12] To complicate matters, their dogs were in poor condition, having spent a bitterly cold winter at Etah. In an attempt to assert himself as the leader, Haig-Thomas tried to interest the Inughuit guides in accompanying him to Meighan Island to search for the missing Krüger party of 1929, but they declined.[13] The members eventually decided to split into three groups, with only the most experienced travellers making the more difficult sledge journey to northern Ellesmere Island. Robert Bentham was to proceed with Shackleton to the Bache Peninsula area and focus on the geological survey of south-central Ellesmere, while Humphreys and Haig-Thomas would cross Grinnell Land (central Ellesmere Island) to do survey and exploration work.

In early April 1935, expedition parties bound for destinations in central and southern Ellesmere Island set out from Etah across the pack ice of Smith Sound. Bentham's group included the Inughuit Anauka and

Rasmus, supported by two others—Sakius and Macheto—and 55 dogs. Haig-Thomas and Humphreys were accompanied by guides Kuuttiktittoq and Kakutiak, a support party of Uutaaq and Kakachinguaq, and 59 dogs.[14] The northern party, consisting of Nukappiannguaq, Inuatuk, Stallworthy, and Moore, proceeded up the Greenland coast, supported by another party of two Inughuit men and a total of 59 dogs. The sledge train included two komatiks loaded with dog food, supplemented by a cache of pemmican established to the north of Etah the previous autumn. Their intended route was to cross the northern section of Kane Basin to Ellesmere Island. Poor sea ice conditions obliged them to proceed farther north before crossing the northern section of Kennedy Channel.

Nukappiannguaq's experience in High Arctic travel proved of great value to the party, particularly when crossing the pack ice in Kane Basin, where his keen navigational skills enabled the party to locate smooth stretches of ice for sledging. He was the only member of the group who knew the terrain of northern Ellesmere Island, having travelled there previously with both the American "Crocker Land" (1913–17) and Danish Bicentenary Jubilee (1920–23) expeditions. Moore described his prowess as a navigator:

> Often Nookapingwa would suddenly whip up his dogs and gallop ahead to some distant iceberg. There he would sit motionless on top, with the glasses glued to his eyes for what seemed to us ages. As we drove up he would descend, and once more gallop ahead into the lead, the route for the next few hours carefully locked in his brain.[15]

In his approach to sledging Nukappiannguaq also demonstrated his adaptability to the particular circumstances of a given situation. During the search for Krüger, a particularly long and gruelling journey for both dogs and men, he increased the number of sled dogs to 21, double the number normally utilized on patrols.[16]

Arriving at Fort Conger, the party set up temporary quarters in Peary's shelters, where they remained for two days. Stallworthy and Moore occupied the former Dedrick shelter, and Nukappiannguaq and Inuatuk slept in Henson's hut. Here, they were able to dry out their clothing and sleeping bags, a necessity for High Arctic travel. The men were also fortunate to find a cache of pemmican in sufficiently good condition to supplement their dwindling resources of dog food. It had been left at Fort Conger in 1919 by Godfred Hansen for Roald Amundsen to support his fateful attempt to reach the North Pole by airship. To assert British presence, Moore raised the Union Jack.[17]

After some quick repairs on their equipment, the men struck out for Lake Hazen via Black Rock Vale. They arrived in two days after an arduous trip, their progress hampered by severe cold and frequent rocky surfaces swept clear of snow by the wind. Finding the lake ice only about 1.5 m thick, they bored holes 35 cm thick and began to haul out charr. Their method of fishing was the traditional Inughuit technique of lowering a baited hook on a line into the water and to jig the line until a fish was secured. After five days' effort produced only fish of disappointingly small size, they were obliged to change their plans again. With only three days' rations of dog food at Fort Conger and two other caches on the return route, they were forced to conclude that only two members of the party could be sent on to northern Grant Land. Accordingly, Stallworthy and Inuatuk remained at Lake Hazen to continue fishing charr for dog food, while the other two continued the trek.[18]

On 29 April, Nukappiannguaq and Moore struck out across Lake Hazen with 17 dogs and pemmican for eight feeds, arriving at the Gilman Glacier on the second day. This long glacial tongue provided an access route to the United States Range and the Grant Land Ice Cap. Travel was made much easier by the smooth surface of the glacier. At 1,000 m Nukappiannguaq built a rough snow block wall on the windward side and they slept in the open in their sleeping bags.[19] Reaching 82° 25' N. lat., they climbed the highest nunatak within view, from which they sighted two additional ranges of mountains to the north. After descending to their camp for the night, they again ascended the summit, where Nukappiannguaq pointed out through their binoculars the sea ice of Markham Inlet on the northern coast of Ellesmere. After christening the high mountains to the north the "British Empire Range" and flying the Union Jack, Moore descended with Nukappiannguaq to make the return journey. After setting up camp at the toe of the Gilman Glacier, Nukappiannguaq scouted the area for game and shot three caribou, on which the men and their dogs feasted heartily. They proceeded to rejoin Stallworthy and Inuatuk, who had fished continuously for the dogs since their departure.[20]

Returning to Fort Conger, the party rested for two days before embarking on the long sledge journey south. Having run short of dog food, they abandoned one komatik and consolidated their dogs into two large teams to speed up their return to sealing grounds to the south. Stallworthy and Nukappiannguaq shared one sledge; Moore and Inuatuk the other. Crossing to Greenland, they utilized the caches left on the way up. Progressing down the middle of Kennedy Channel, they reached Cape Calhoun, where the Inughuit secured several seals, enabling them to feed their half-starved dogs and complete their return without incident.

On his return to England, Shackleton embarked on the lecture circuit in Britain and Canada to memorialize the expedition. His presentations ranged in nature from the assertion of the British imperial presence to expositions on the potential of the region's natural resources, to speculations on the value of Arctic science. In St. John, he spoke of the difficulties and dangers faced and overcome and described how his party had planted the King's gift of a silken Union Jack within sight of the Arctic Ocean.[21] In a Montreal talk, entitled "Exploring the Unknown Canadian Arctic," Shackleton pronounced the Arctic an important future source of "raw materials."[22] His views of the significance of their activities appeared in an article in the *Manchester Evening News* in 1937. Characterizing it as an essentially scientific undertaking, he contrasted its focus with other expeditions said to be animated by purely personal motives. He described the expedition's geological and archaeological collections as of great value[23] and extolled the potential of Arctic science to advance humanitarian and commercial objectives. However, in terms of relating the actual accomplishments of his own party to these lofty ideals, he was short on specifics.[24]

Shackleton's Plans for a Second Expedition to Ellesmere Island, 1936

Only a year after the Oxford University party's return to England, Edward Shackleton was already formulating plans for a much more ambitious expedition to northern Ellesmere Island. He defined the proposed expedition's objectives in terms of completing the exploration of "Ellesmere Land" north of 79° N. lat., carrying out detailed geological and topographical survey work in this area, and conducting flights over the Arctic Ocean, northwest of Ellesmere Island, to the "Pole of Inaccessibility."[25]

Shackleton's high-flown plans went far beyond the scale of the Oxford University expedition. First, he envisioned the establishment of an initial wintering base in the district of Robertson Bay at the northern mouth of Inglefield Gulf in northwestern Greenland. He chose this area for its accessibility by ship every year, for the comparative absence of wind, and because it was within range of all the settlements of the "Smith Sound Tribe," on whom he proposed to rely for labour, particularly in the area of the base.[26] Personnel in the advance party of four would be a leader in charge of the base camp and three others serving dual roles: a doctor/biologist, physicist/meteorologist, and wireless operator/engineer. The main party, in addition to the organizer and leader, would be four pilots, four assistant pilots and mechanics, three geologists, three surveyors, a wireless operator, a photographer, a doctor/biologist, and possibly an archaeologist or ornithologist.

Shackleton's plans specified that the advance party leave London on 20 June 1937 in a ship of 300 gross tonnage, carrying the following supplies for the main expedition: 98 tonnes of petroleum, 47 tonnes of food supplies, 34 tonnes of coal, and assorted equipment, including lumber for huts and an airplane hangar, and smaller items of camp equipment, including a wireless, motor boat, and airplane spare parts. The main party would depart England by ship for Ivigtut, southwest Greenland, in early 1938. Shackleton intended that the expedition's airplanes be loaded aboard ship, including two large two- or three-engine models, each capable of carrying a load of four to five tonnes and equipped with skis, floats or wheels and two smaller twin-engined airplanes, each with three seats. These planes were to carry the 19 members of the main party from Ivigtut to the main base at Robertson Bay, making stops en route, if necessary, at Godhavn and Upernivik. Meanwhile, an advance party would be sent to Lake Hazen to reconnoitre a landing strip. Shackleton projected that the first of five flights between the base camp and Lake Hazen would take place in April. From this base, sledge parties would carry out geological and ornithological investigations and set control points for an aerial survey of northern Ellesmere Island. The Lake Hazen personnel would be divided into a base party, consisting of an expedition leader, a wireless operator, a doctor/biologist, and two Inughuit, equipped with 20 dogs, tents, sledges, a small hut, and wireless equipment powerful enough to transmit to Robertson Bay, and three sledge parties, each to consist of a geologist, a surveyor, and two Inughuit.[27]

Shackleton made no detailed estimates of the cost of the proposed expedition, but surmised that the greatest expenditure would be for the purchase and maintenance of the airplanes. Apart from the aircraft, he thought the expedition's cost would not exceed $100,000, "the bulk of which it should be possible to raise from outside sources, such as the press, films, books, etc." Estimating that an overall guarantee of between $250,000 to $500,000 would be required, he sought both financial assistance and the backing of such a guarantee from the Canadian government. He also claimed that "the mere fact that the expedition will be operating in unexplored country will open up funds and sources of money which would otherwise not be available."[28]

In November 1937, Shackleton requested an audience with the Northwest Territories Council to present his expensive, albeit sketchy plans for a large-scale expedition to northern Ellesmere. Acknowledging that the principal object was not scientific investigation but, rather, a search for new land to the north and west of Ellesmere, Shackleton asserted that the maintenance of British sovereignty in the region was of paramount importance. However, the Commissioner replied that before Canada could support such an expedition, there would have to be a clear and definite statement of the results to be achieved. As well, his Deputy expressed the view that the development of social services among the Inuit would achieve more in the assertion of sovereignty than aerial or other expeditions.[29]

The Council decided to refer the proposal to an interdepartmental committee, which subsequently recommended its rejection. It is not surprising that Canadian officials balked at supporting such an expensive proposal by a non-resident of Canada. Nevertheless, to a remarkable degree, Shackleton's plans anticipated the logistical arrangements followed for the program of scientific research carried out by the Defence Research Board in northern Ellesmere Island two decades later.[30]

David Haig-Thomas and Big-Game Hunting on Ellesmere, 1938

In 1936, the Royal Geographical Society again approached the Canadian government to obtain permission for another expedition to Ellesmere Island under its auspices. This time, David Haig-Thomas, a former member of the 1934–35 Oxford University Ellesmere Land expedition, sought approval to cross Smith Sound in March 1938 and to travel from Flagler Fiord to Bay Fiord. From there, he proposed to continue to Cañon Fiord and map the interior of the Fosheim Peninsula and Grinnell Land, before returning to Greenland in June. Haig-Thomas requested permission to bring a few Inughuit and to shoot six "old bull Muskox," which he claimed were very numerous on the western coast of Ellesmere Island when he was there two years earlier. He also sought permission to use petroleum and biscuits from a cache at Framhaven and the authorities' approval to collect birds and archaeological remains of "old Eskimo settlements" on Ellesmere Island.[31]

When asked to comment on Haig-Thomas's proposed expedition, Sergeant Stallworthy responded that he knew Haig-Thomas "intimately" through their association on the 1934–35 Oxford University Ellesmere Land Expedition, when they wintered in northern Greenland, and added:

> I doubt very much whether his personal objective in another expedition is in the interests of science. His chief interest in the OUEL expedition was undoubtedly big game hunting, which hobby he has pursued in other parts of the world.[32]

Stallworthy related that, in 1934, Haig-Thomas and another member of the Oxford University expedition had been charged with slaughtering walrus contrary to the game laws of Greenland. He stated that the Inughuit had told him of Haig-Thomas's attempts to engage them to search for Krüger's party or to go to Lake Hazen to spend the summer.

He asked them to mark muskox grazing areas in western Ellesmere Island, Axel Heiberg Island, and the region of Greely Fiord on a map, suggesting his overriding interest in hunting this animal. Overall, Stallworthy stated that he was "not impressed with his [Haig-Thomas's] ability as a Northern man, particularly where manual labour, care of dogs, cooking, etc. were concerned."[33]

Concerned over Haig-Thomas's plans to use its facilities at Craig Harbour for three months in the spring of 1938, the RCMP extracted a commitment from the Royal Geographical Society that Haig-Thomas would not make "any unnecessary demands upon the accommodation and supplies" at this detachment.[34] In addition, the explorer was obliged to sign a letter in which he promised that he and his two companions would abide by the game laws of the Northwest Territories.[35] Despite resistance from the RCMP, Haig-Thomas found an important ally in Colonel Georges Vanier, Secretary to Canada's High Commissioner in London. After a lecture by members of the Oxford expedition in London in November 1935, Vanier expressed his view that when they returned to Ellesmere, they would have the full support of the Canadian government, and promised to help them obtain permission "to shoot a few muskox."[36]

Haig-Thomas also found little difficulty in lining up backers in England. Writing to prospective sponsors on "flashy notepaper" with the letterhead "British Arctic Expedition 1937," he received several immediate offers of free supplies. Then, he wrote, "I put on the old school tie, brushed my hair, and went round visiting publicity managers of firms." He perceived, somewhat cynically, that talk about "polar bears, ice, seals, and Eskimos" offered the public relations officers a respite from their mundane daily routines: "Many of the people I met wished they were coming too. They reminded me of overgrown schoolboys who had never satisfied their desires for Red Indians and stories of the wild and woolly West."[37]

Haig-Thomas sailed with two British companions, John Wright and Richard Hamilton, from Denmark to Disco, Greenland, in June 1937. On arrival, he was told that the Greenlanders had experienced a difficult winter. Seals were very scarce, he wrote, "owing to their ruthless slaughter by foreign seal hunters."[38] Proceeding to Robertson Bay, Haig-Thomas enlisted the services of Nukappianguaq as his guide for the trip to Ellesmere Island. They moved their equipment by motorboat to Etah in two trips.

During a second boat trip with Wright, Haig-Thomas revealed both his ignorance of High Arctic survival techniques and a continuing contempt for its ecology. Blown off course by a storm, they drifted toward the Ellesmere side of Smith Sound, where they were stopped by the ice a few miles from the coast. Fearing they would be stranded on Ellesmere until the spring, they began to concoct plans to survive the winter. Haig-Thomas envisaged building a low snow-block wall on which they would invert their boat, a hypothetical structure remarkably similar to Greely's hapless shelter at Camp Clay (see Chapter 5). The English adventurers also decided that they would need to hunt walruses for food and fuel, and then lay over the snow walls the "moist walrus hides, letting them freeze solid." Assuming the need to kill at least three walruses, they steered their boat toward a nearby walrus herd. Without securing them by harpoon, they shot four or five walruses, most of which disappeared under the sea.[39] This episode occurred only three years after Haig-Thomas's initial prosecution for shooting walrus without the use of a harpoon. Fortunately for the Englishmen, the congested ice began to drift to the south, and they were able to make their way back to Greenland. Given their lack of preparation, had they been forced to remain on Ellesmere Island, they would almost certainly not have survived the winter.

Back at Etah, Haig-Thomas whimsically abandoned his approved plans before departing on the spring sledge trip. A more interesting opportunity had presented itself. Aapilaq (Ahpellah), who had visited the Ringnes islands with Dr. Cook in 1908–09, told him he had seen the bones of "great animals" there.[40] Haig-Thomas decided to head for the Ringnes Islands to look for these bones, while Wright and Hamilton focussed on a survey of the Ellesmere coast between Fram Havn and Makinson Inlet.[41] In March 1938, Haig-Thomas and Nukappiannguaq crossed the ice of southern Kane Basin to Ellesmere Island. Traversing the island to Eureka Sound, they crossed to Axel Heiberg Island and followed its coastline south before striking out across the pack ice to the south coast of Amund Ringnes Island and sledging in a northeasterly direction across the island. Returning along the eastern coast, they perceived the outline of an island "in the shape of a large banana" to the east. However, they carried out no survey work. From this point, Haig-Thomas returned to Greenland along roughly the same route as the outbound journey. While he accomplished little for arctic science, he had acquired enough anecdotal material to build a reputation among Arctic enthusiasts.

On returning to Britain, Haig-Thomas quickly produced a book and several popular articles on his journey, in which he highlighted his "discovery" of a new island off Amund Ringnes Island's eastern coast.[42] He estimated its mass to be about 500 square kilometres in area, but since no surveying work had been done, the island remained unmapped. His claims of new land inspired a flurry of enquiries from skeptical Arctic scientists, as the region had been extensively surveyed by Sverdrup's party in 1900 and Vilhjalmur Stefansson in 1916, but neither explorer had mentioned the presence of any land in the identified area.

To clear up the question of the new discovery, Major D.L. McKeand of the Department of Mines and Resources suggested that the RCMP question Nukappiannguaq, who had returned to their employ at Craig Harbour, about the journey.[43] Nukappiannguaq denied that they had found a new island, but he also gave a very different account of their hunting experiences than Haig-Thomas reported in his book. The Police provided a translated transcript of the Inughuaq's sworn statement:

> On arriving at Ulvingan Island we saw lots and lots of muskoxen. Davy said 'I would like some muskoxen' and asked me if I would talk, and I said 'Yes, the Police will know,' Davy then said 'I want three muskoxen, you will not talk, I am your boss, you will not even talk to the Eskimo, you will not talk to the Police,' I said 'No, I am afraid, I worked for the Police before and they will be angry.' Davy said 'I want Muskoxen, you will go and shoot them.' I went with my gun and shot three male muskoxen. We brought them from the land and skinned them on the ice. Davy helped with the skinning. Davy said 'We will skin them on the ice so the Police will not find out.'[44]

Nukappiannguaq also asserted that they were not "in dire need of food" at the time, the only allowable excuse for disregarding the ban on muskox hunting.[45] In addition to the muskoxen, he had shot three polar bears, and each of the travellers had killed a caribou. He also stated that Haig-Thomas rode on the komatik for the entire trip, even when the Inughuaq was attempting to steer the sledge through rough ice.[46]

Operating through the High Commissioner's office, the Canadian government lodged a formal complaint with the Royal Geographical Society. The Society's Council interviewed Haig-Thomas, who denied all the allegations. Without attempting to corroborate his testimony, the RGS affirmed its support for his version of events, while expressing concern that the Canadian government could believe that a "solemn undertaking given to its Council and transmitted to it had been broken."[47]

The zeal with which the RCMP assembled the evidence against Haig-Thomas suggests the Police were also very concerned about maintaining their reputation in the Arctic, in light of the explorer's assertions relating to muskox hunting by its members. In 1939, Commissioner S.T. Wood wrote that Haig-Thomas had libelled well-known Inspector A.H. Joy, "a distinguished Officer who is dead and who is no longer able to answer."[48] Wood was referring to Haig-Thomas's assertion in his book that Joy had killed muskoxen on Ellesmere Island contrary to game regulations. It was true that this allegation was uncorroborated, although other evidence suggests that the RCMP were hunting muskoxen on Ellesmere Island in this period, discussed previously in Chapter 9.

The RCMP was also irritated that Haig-Thomas was claiming to have discovered an island in an area formerly patrolled by the police. R.W. Hamilton, the officer in charge at the Craig Harbour detachment, wrote to Haig-Thomas to express skepticism regarding his alleged discovery:

> I would respectfully point out to you, that the district referred to in your letter has been patrolled by members of the force, stationed at Bache Peninsula for number of years, and if such island did ever exist, it would have been discovered before now.[49]

Subsequent survey work in fact confirmed the existence of a small island off the west coast of Amund Ringnes Island, although it is considerably smaller than the one Haig-Thomas described. It was subsequently named Haig-Thomas Island.

Most provocative were Haig-Thomas's critical comments on Canada's establishment of a RCMP detachment at Bache Peninsula, coming as they did from a person who had not been shy about using either the detachment facilities or its cached stores. He wrote:

> I thought how foolish it was of the Canadian Government to waste so much money in building a police station here—a station which had been occupied for only a year or two and then abandoned. Outside lay motor boats and masses of equipment to rot and splinter and warp in the dry Arctic air. Most of the small useful things had been carried off by the Eskimos, for, as they said, the white men didn't want them, and there was no point in leaving them.[50]

When RCMP officers visited the Bache Peninsula detachment the following year, they found the facilities in a sorry state. Despite his commitment not to make undue use of the RCMP facilities or caches, during a three-day stay the previous year, Haig-Thomas had liberally used its supplies, opened boxes and cases without afterwards securing them, and generally left the house in a mess. Reporting in 1939 on the condition of the facilities, Inspector D.J. Martin stated that the British explorer had used it, alternately, as a dwelling, repair shop, and slaughterhouse:

> During the time that Mr. Thomas stayed at Bache every pot, pan, bucket and other utensil to be found was used for cooking and other purposes, these were left lying about the floor uncleaned and are practi-

cally ruined. The office which had been used as a repair shop was merely untidy and unswept as was the living room. The kitchen in which a walrus had been cached the previous summer and where it was cut up during the winter was filthy beyond description. It would appear that this man was careless and absolutely indifferent as to the safety of Government Property, to such an extent that ashes removed from the ash pit were dumped under the stove together with the other rubbish accumulated over the period of their stay there.[51]

Haig-Thomas's own book confirms his having slaughtered and cached the walrus meat in the detachment building at Bache Peninsula.[52] Thus ended the story of a "scientific" expedition whose actual purpose was recreational, in which the collection of data took a back seat to the acquisition of animal trophies.

The MacGregor Expedition, 1938

In 1938, Clifford G. MacGregor, an American Army captain, announced plans to lead a private scientific expedition to Fort Conger to collect data on meteorology, solar radiation, terrestrial magnetism, geology, and the aurora borealis. Specifically, he stated that his main objective was "to study weather and earth currents and the effect of the aurora borealis on magnetism and radio reception."[53] As a meteorologist with the U.S. Weather Bureau, MacGregor had led the Second International Polar Year Expedition to Point Barrow, Alaska in 1932–33. Writing to Prime Minister King in 1937, MacGregor indicated his intention to leave the United States on 27 June 1937 and return in the fall of 1938. His 11-person party would sail to the north in a 33.5-m-long three-masted schooner, the *General A.W. Greely*, named in honour of the commander of the U.S. Lady Franklin Bay Expedition of 1881–84.[54] In a letter to Charles Camsell, Commissioner of the Northwest Territories, MacGregor stated that he had arranged to carry "ample provisions" for two years, along with emergency rations for a third year, if necessary.[55]

Reporting on the expedition in October 1938 MacGregor stated that due to adverse ice conditions his party was unable to advance beyond Smith Sound and could not reach Fort Conger. The Americans were obliged to winter near Etah, Greenland. They did make a sledge trip across Smith Sound to Pim Island to make magnetic observations. As well, Lt. Commander I. Schlossbach made a flight over Ellesmere Island, crossing Grinnell Land (central Ellesmere Island) and Nansen Sound, flying to 115° West long., 84° N. lat., and then to the south to 112° West long., 82° N. lat., before returning to Greenland. MacGregor stated that the purpose of this flight was to ascertain whether or not

Robert Peary's "Crocker Land" existed.[56] He apparently was not aware that Donald MacMillan's sledge excursion to Axel Heiberg Island in 1914 and Byrd's flight over this region in 1925 had already definitively established that "Crocker Land" was a figment of Peary's imagination. Nevertheless, MacGregor stated that his full program of weather, magnetic, and aurora observations had been successfully carried out, "with excellent results."[57] As well, MacGregor was successful in transmitting radio messages from Etah on a daily basis, attracting "a huge international following of short wave bugs," according to *The Detroit Free Press*.[58]

MacGregor's prowess in radio transmission served him in good stead when, on the return voyage, he sent out several appeals for help when his ship was caught in the ice in Rice Strait and was reported to be in danger of being crushed in the ice. In his messages, MacGregor also reported that his party was running short of food at that point. Robert Bartlett's ship, the *Morrisey*, was contacted and moved to within 160 km of the marooned ship. Fortunately, the crew of the *General A.W. Greely* managed to extricate the ship from its predicament and it was able to continue its voyage back to the United States.[59]

The Van Hauen Expedition, 1939–1940

In 1939 a small Danish party embarked on a scientific expedition to Northwestern Greenland and Ellesmere Island. Led by James van Hauen, the party included Niels Rasmussen, photographer and son of Knud Rasmussen, botanist M.G. Thorlaksson, geologist J. Troelsen, and zoologist Christian Vibe. Their plan was to travel to Inglefield Land, where they would build an expedition hut before travelling to Ellesmere Island in the spring. The itinerary would take them via Flagler Fiord and Bay Fiord to Eureka Sound, where they would split into two parties. One would proceed south to the Raanes Peninsula and Baumann Fiord, while the other would proceed north to Greely Fiord and Lake Hazen and back via Washington Land on the Greenland side of the Nares Strait. Essentially, the itinerary of the northern party would almost exactly retrace the path of Elmer Ekblaw with MacMillan's Crocker Land Expedition in 1915.[60]

Van Hauen was a professional hunter who had been living in East Greenland and working for the Nanok hunting company; he was also described as "an expert in dog sleigh driving."[61] In a request channelled through the Danish consul, he applied to Canada for permission to visit Ellesmere Island and to shoot "up to five muskoxen for scientific purposes."[62] Approving the explorer's permit, the federal government also denied his request to hunt muskoxen on the grounds that it had "made it clear to the natives that muskoxen are not to be slaughtered and no exceptions can be made." A precis on the expedition prepared for the Northwest Territories Council elaborated: "The closed season was essential to prevent the extermination of the few remaining animals." A subsequent book on the expedition by Christian Vibe reported that its members had killed various seals, polar bears, caribou, and arctic hares but observed the requirement not to hunt muskoxen.[63]

As with so many other expeditions to the region, the van Hauen expedition plans had to be revised according to sea-ice conditions. Encountering congested pack ice in Kane Basin, they were obliged to establish their winter base at Neqe, a small settlement just south of Cape Alexander. Here, they built an expedition house with the assistance of the four Inughuit families then living at the village. On 20 March, several sledges carried supplies across Smith Sound and deposited them at various points along the route. Reaching Bache Peninsula on 26 March, they crossed Ellesmere Island, arriving at Bay Fiord on 1 April. At this point, the last support sledges and drivers were sent back and the party divided into two. Van Hauen, Troelsen, and Rasmussen, supported by four Inughuit, headed north. Their Inughuit assistants included Kakutiak and his spouse, Patdlok, Magsianginah, and Baadsmanot [?].[64] The party travelled through Greely Fiord, over land to Archer Fiord, around Cape Baird, and south through Kennedy Channel to Washington Land and Inglefield Land. In addition to its Danish members, the western party included three Inughuit guides and their dog teams. This group travelled south along Eureka Sound to Cape Southwest on Axel Heiberg Island, and then on to the area of Baumann Fiord, before returning via the same route (Figure 67).[65]

Van Hauen's party accomplished little in terms of geographical discovery,[66] although it confirmed a number of details of topography and coastline that had earlier been mapped out by Sverdrup and other explorers. Their scientific work was cut short when van Hauen suffered an internal rupture, hastening the retreat of the northern party from northern Ellesmere Island.[67] Nevertheless, the expedition introduced two scientists, Christian Vibe and J. Troelsen, to the region. Vibe's subsequent monographs on arctic terrestrial and marine mammals were landmark studies in their era,[68] while Troelsen contributed several pioneering works on the geology of the region.[69] In this regard, the expedition anticipated the much more extensive scientific research program coordinated by Canada's Defence Research Board in northern Ellesmere Island, beginning in the early 1950s.

The European and American expeditions to Ellesmere Island in the 1930s were a brief interlude between the geographical discoveries of

Figure 67: "View taken from a point about 81° W. between Bay Fiord and Flagler Fiord [Ellesmere Island] (taken towards south)."Photograph by Christian Vibe, Van Hauen Expedition, May 1940. National Archives of Canada Photo no. C-137056.

the exploration era and the serious interdisciplinary research of the post-Second World War period. They were not the last European adventure seekers on Ellesmere Island, but there was an anachronistic character to these parties. Their intended exploits recall the age of adventure, but they occurred well after the conclusion of British imperial expansion. The excursions added little to the pre-existing base of geographical knowledge. These explorers relied on Inughuit guides such as Nukappiannguaq and others, who once again demonstrated the importance of their environmental knowledge and skills to successful exploration and travel in the High Arctic.

Events and High Arctic History

With the conclusion of the van Hauen Expedition, the great age of exploration of the High Arctic came to an end. Between 1898 and 1902, Sverdrup surveyed much of the coastline of Ellesmere and Axel Heiberg islands and mapped most of the remaining Queen Elizabeth islands to the west. If we assume that Peary sledged to the North Pole in 1909 and Byrd flew to the North Pole in 1926, all landmark geographical discoveries in the region had been achieved by 1940. In 1915, MacMillan's sledge foray from Cape Thomas Hubbard suggested that Peary's "Crocker Land" had been a mirage. Flying from Etah in 1925,

Byrd confirmed that neither "Crocker Land" nor Cook's "Bradley Land" existed. Between 1926 and 1932, the major patrols of Sergeant Joy and other RCM policemen on Ellesmere Island effectively completed the exploration of the region. By 1940, the coastlines and interior of Ellesmere Island had been extensively travelled, and the geographical survey of the Canadian High Arctic, essentially unknown to Europeans before 1850, was largely complete. North Pole exploration, largely a combination of ocean navigation in Western ships and surface travel with Aboriginal sledges, would soon be superseded by the advancing technology of fixed wing aircraft. The romantic age of the High Arctic passed into history.

The attainment of the goals of polar exploration also meant that the era of territorial assertion by Western powers was drawing to a close. The apparent triumphs of Peary and Byrd in reaching the North Pole by surface travel and aerial flight provided the United States with triumphal symbolism for its developing metanarrative of national greatness. MacMillan sought to continue the quest for new arctic lands but, after Peary's 1908–09 voyage, he was fighting an uphill battle against shifting public attention and interest. For Britain, the Oxford University Ellesmere Land Expedition of 1934–35 was a last gesture toward its former arctic glories and not to be repeated. Finally, having confirmed its sovereignty over the Arctic Archipelago by 1930, Canada found itself engaging more pressing priorities by the end of the decade. With the outbreak of the Second World War in 1939, Canada turned its attention to the European war effort and focussing its efforts to address this new challenge. The Craig Harbour detachment was closed in 1940, and RCMP staff carried out the last patrols that spring. The RCMP had substantially achieved its principal objective of maintaining Canadian sovereignty through effective occupation, both by establishing detachments on Ellesmere Island and carrying out extensive patrols across the Queen Elizabeth Islands. While wildlife hunting continued despite the RCMP presence, Canada had demonstrated its intention to enforce its laws, to the eventual benefit of ecological preservation.

The history of exploration is essentially a European story and the narrative form in which this story is presented tends to focus our attention, perhaps inordinately, on the European or American individuals who led these expeditions. From the unpublished diaries and journals of the explorers, it is clear that they relied heavily on the knowledge and assistance of Aboriginal people throughout the period. However, in books on High Arctic exploration or the Mounties' occupation and patrols, the Aboriginal participants fade into the background, relegated to the generic category of anonymous "Eskimos," without names or identities. The few outstanding travellers who are mentioned, such as Uutaaq in Peary's day and

Nukappiannguaq in the era of the Mounties, are the exceptions that prove the rule. Yet, the participation of Aboriginal guides often represented the difference between success or failure for the European parties.

Similarly, the narratives of arctic exploration reduce the American or European members of these expeditions to an ancillary role, subordinate to the triumphs of the explorer-as-hero. Christy Collis has noted these hierarchies in various explorers' journals, including references to Franklin and his "party," Kane and his "crew," and Maguire and "the people on the lower deck," in which the only characters represented as autonomous individuals are the explorers themselves.[70] As Collis writes:

> If the reader is to take the journals' first-person narratives literally, she or he will have to accept that Franklin and Kane accomplished both the physical and mental rigours of their voyages single-handedly, while their hapless 'men' bumbled along behind them in various states of ignorance and temerity.[71]

What was the long-term significance of the events of European and American exploration in the High Arctic? Depending on individual perspective, any number of interpretations can be drawn from these complex occurrences. Some observers, perhaps searching for a retrospective vindication of the suffering and loss of life associated with the expeditions, have chosen to view them as supreme examples of the human spirit. For example, the Nares and Greely expeditions have recently been described as "heroic examples of the courage, integrity, and sacrifice made by man in his first efforts to discover northern Ellesmere Island and Greenland."[72] Innumerable superlatives have also given a retrospective meaning to—and justification for—the chimeric quests of individuals from Elisha Kane to Edward Shackleton.

Yet, in retrospect, it is apparent that these events were the product of historical forces of which the explorers themselves could hardly have been aware. A survey of the last 200 years of European activity in the High Arctic enables the identification of long-term trends that are not apparent at the level of day-to-day occurrences. In terms of culture, each of the exploring countries was in an expansionist political mode during its respective phase of arctic activity. Great Britain, which dominated the field between 1818 and 1875, sent its expeditions at the height of its imperial power. Its search for the Northwest Passage was part of a process of global expansion, reinforced by British economic and maritime supremacy. By the 1880s, the United States' consolidation of its continental land base freed that country to turn its own imperial attentions to the larger hemisphere. During Peary's North Polar expeditions, the United States was emerging as a global power in its own right, reflected in the expansionist foreign policy of President Theodore Roosevelt, who, coincidentally, was one of Peary's greatest backers. By the 1920s, the young Dominion of Canada, whose identity as a self-governing country had crystallized during the First World War, focussed its own attentions on the Arctic by sponsoring the Eastern Arctic patrol and the establishment of RCMP detachments in the High Arctic. While these countries differed in specific goals and the intensity with which they pursued them, their political cultures displayed a common view of the Arctic as a vehicle for promoting their respective national identities. In this light, the role of individual agency begins to pale in comparison to long-term national agendas of imperialism as determining factors in the evolution of European involvement in the High Arctic.

The heyday of High Arctic exploration coincided with the great expansion of the popular press in the nineteenth century and the capacity of the media to generate enormous public interest and support for the polar quest. In the United States, it caught the imagination of the American public, especially powerful and influential individuals such as Theodore Roosevelt and Morris Jesup. While Canada's Dominion government was perhaps less successful in inspiring the imaginations of Canadians, federal officials intended that the High Arctic assume a similar role in the nation-building appeals of the 1920s and 1930s. If the short-term exploits of the explorers and Mounties were too brief to have produced many lasting impacts on the High Arctic, they nevertheless inspired an enduring legacy of didactic heroism for readers on all continents.

Another important factor was the institutional culture and ideology of the groups that carried out many of the expeditions to Ellesmere Island. Many of these parties were characterized by devotion to discipline, hierarchy, concentration of power in the commanding officer, and a rigid command structure. European concepts of time and space brought by the explorers to the region often prevented them from coming to terms with the High Arctic environment. Their shortcomings were not limited to their material repertoire, but also reflected their unpreparedness to learn from the mistakes of their predecessors. The Nares and Greely parties, in particular, having locked into predetermined plans and strategies, lacked the flexibility and resourcefulness to revise their plans to respond to changing circumstances. The European explorers also applied the technology of their societies to exploration in the High Arctic. Yet, the technology which the explorers brought with them had generally been developed for application in more southerly climates and contexts. In their approaches to clothing, shelter, land and sea transport, and provisioning, the expeditions adhered to techniques largely untested in polar contexts.

Finally, the natural environment should not be overlooked as a factor influencing even day-to-day occurrences, as the rugged physical geography and rigorous climate of the Arctic imposed further constraints on human action in the post-contact era. Several events of the exploration era, usually explained in terms of human agency, can be seen from an environmental perspective as heavily influenced by the climatic conditions prevailing at particular moments in time. In a fascinating analysis of the arctic climate over the past 200 years, a Canadian interdisciplinary team of scientists has reconstructed several variables bearing on the long-term viability of shipping in this region. Their tabulations show that the loss of the Franklin expedition in the mid-1840s coincided with the culmination of a period of lower than average summer temperatures in the Arctic Archipelago.[73] Short-term cooling climatic episodes correlated with the build-up of sea ice and restriction of navigational opportunities during the period of the Kane and Hayes expeditions of 1853–55 and 1860–61. By the late 1860s, the effects of a warm cycle, which commenced in the late 1850s, were apparent. The resulting relief of sea ice congestion allowed the ships of the British Arctic Expedition to successfully navigate Nares Strait to reach the Arctic Ocean. Warmer conditions continued into the early 1880s, when the *Proteus* was able to penetrate the ice-strewn waters of the Kane Basin to deliver the Greely party to Lady Franklin Bay. However, by 1882–83, when supply vessels again attempted to negotiate these waters, summer temperatures had dropped to average levels and the relief ships were unable to penetrate beyond lower Kane Basin, leaving the Greely party stranded. By 1900, average summer temperatures had begun to warm again, a trend that continued throughout Peary's three major expeditions, which may have enabled the *Roosevelt* to reach Cape Sheridan in both 1905 and 1908. Overall, of the numerous attempts made between 1850 and 1940 to navigate Nares Strait, only five vessels succeeded in reaching Kennedy Channel north of Kane Basin.[74] These were the *Polaris* under C.F. Hall, the *Alert* and the *Discovery* under Nares, and Peary's two sailings in the *Roosevelt*, captained by Robert Bartlett in 1905 and 1908. While more research of this nature is required, it is reasonable to infer that the climate may have played as significant a role in the explorers' successes or failures as their levels of knowledge or personal attributes of character and determination.

If it is assumed that men and women "make history," a few important caveats are in order. Individuals make history not in the sense that they are free agents but players operating within particular socio-cultural and environmental constraints. An individual's freedom to act is also subject to the imperatives of circumstance, including the political context, the interaction of personalities, and chance. Occasionally, an individual such as Robert Peary appears with the insight, skills, and drive to make a breakthrough. Whatever his obsessions with personal greatness, Peary also recognized the need to accommodate the forces of environment and circumstance. Whether he reached the North Pole or not, his powers of planning and organization were unequalled by any of his contemporaries. He also operated within a nineteenth century mindset that ultimately limited his impact on the very region he devoted so much time to exploring. Like many of his contemporaries, Peary assumed that the Inughuit belonged to an "inferior race"[75] and that their most useful contribution was to assist in his own achievements. The implications of the cultural baggage brought to the Arctic by Peary and his contemporaries are the subject of the next part of this book, dealing with the changes brought about by the contact experience.

PART III

CHANGE

The Interplay of Cultures
and the Environment, 1850–1940

From the continuities of nature and culture and the drama of circumstance, it remains to chart historical change over time. To identify changes affecting entire societies, historians are obliged to identify periods of sufficient duration in which to measure progress or decline, or to discern the impact of ideas, cultural practices, and technological innovations. Yet, any division of history into a particular time frame seems arbitrary and raises new questions as to why a given era has been selected over periods of longer or shorter duration.

Here again, Fernand Braudel's example is instructive. In addressing the issue of historical change, Braudel selected periods of approximately 50–100 years for analysis. These eras were long enough to record fluctuations of economic growth or contraction, or the advance or decline of a social group in its milieu. Such intervals also provided a sufficient period of time to measure changes in material culture, social structure, and the impact of the interface of different cultural groups.[1] Braudel cautioned that historians must also be open to the possibility that, within such periods, changes can be neutralized or undone. Swinging first in one direction, then in another, the pendulum of socio-economic history has often advanced and then reversed the fortunes of human societies.[2] For this reason, the study of medium-term time also needs to be accompanied by a parallel understanding of long-term trends such as the continuities of culture and nature, as outlined in Part I. The study of the different registers of time in combination can enable us to discern enduring trends in human history.

The selection of periods of 50–100 years' duration also affords opportunities to chart changes in the ecology of a region through the study of the interplay of cultures and the environment. Such an approach represents a refinement of Braudel's model in that, today, the natural environment is regarded as much more dynamic than it was viewed in Braudel's own era. Various recent works of environmental history have shown that human societies can exert dramatic effects on ecosystems within a very short period of time, with attendant effects on both the human and animal populations operating within them. In addition to assessing the material and cultural implications of Aboriginal–

European contact, this section will attempt to address the impact of contact on the ecology of Ellesmere Island in the medium term, as well as its long-term significance for the High Arctic environment.

For a group confronted with intercultural exchange, several historical questions arise. What were the economic and material constraints on life prior to these interactions? How does a culture accommodate new technologies in its existing patterns of life? What are the social effects of rapid economic or technological change? Do these changes result in material advancement or an enhanced quality of life for a society's members or a decline in their economic position, however that might be defined? Regarding the environment, what are the ecological effects of cultural contact? What are the net benefits and costs of such exchanges?

10
Material and Technological Adaptations
of the Contact Era

Within the brief span of 70 years—1850 to 1920—contact between Europeans and Inughuit produced significant effects on both these cultures operating in the High Arctic. A significant dimension to relations between these groups was the series of exchanges of goods, technology, and knowledge occasioned by contact. These exchanges were not the first to occur in the region. The spread of Greenland meteorite iron across the Arctic confirms that communication and exchange links between arctic peoples had occurred periodically over hundreds of years. As well, evidence of Norse chain mail and many other artifacts identified by the archaeological program of Peter Schledermann and associates at Bache Peninsula, Ellesmere Island, showed that the Thule culture in this area had acquired European goods as early as the thirteenth century. Whether this evidence proves direct contact between Vikings and Inughuit is not yet certain, but at least it confirms that the region's Aboriginal groups, like other Greenlandic branches of the Thule culture, encountered Norse artifacts centuries before the European voyages of the nineteenth century.

Accepting that there were possible encounters during the era of Norse occupation on Greenland, cross-cultural exchanges between Europeans and Inuit in the nineteenth century represented a new phenomenon. As with the contact of cultures farther south, European contact after 1800 involved a significant intrusion of Western technology and face-to-face interactions within the territory of the Inughuit groups. Geographer Donald Meinig has noted that such an intrusion could be expected to have both a profound and asymmetrical effect on the Aboriginal participants in this exchange.[1] These radically different cultures, each with little prior knowledge of the other, were brought into increasing contact over time in the context of polar exploration. What they brought to these encounters, how they responded to one another, and what they took away from these exchanges could be expected to have significant implications for both groups.

This chapter focusses particularly on the material dimensions of the exchange and attempts an assessment of the significance of the transactions for both parties. In assessing the consequences of interfaces between two cultural systems, it is suggested that technology per se is not the principal issue so much as the social organization of technology and the goals to which it is applied. When technology begins to have a quantitative impact on the relations of the ecosystem, i.e., in terms of exploitation of the natural environment or of one group of humans by another, "positive feedback" results and leads to either qualitative changes or to destruction.[2] The disruptive effects of technology transfer thus do not derive from the actual technology, but rather from its application, as guided by particular ideological imperatives and world views.

Early Bartering Exchange between Europeans and Inughuit, 1818–90

Europeans eventually exerted a significant impact on the lives of the Inughuit in the nineteenth and twentieth centuries, commensurate with increasing levels of contact between the two groups. Unlike Qitlaq's band of newcomers from Baffin Island, the Europeans had few useful living skills to offer the Inughuit, but their technology and goods offered them access to an expanded repertoire of materials. For much of the early contact era, the Inughuit did not use European goods and materials to change their culture so much as they pragmatically incorporated these items into pre-existing patterns of technology and use of the physical environment.

Initially, the European trade items most sought after by Inughuit were wooden and metal objects that could be used in constructing kayak or sled frames and in making hunting and domestic tools. Inviting several Inughuit aboard ship in 1818, Captain John Ross wrote that "they proceeded both to beg and to steal, laying hands on every small piece of wood they met with, and pocketing every nail they could find about the ship."[3] In return, the Inughuit offered a sled, knives, and a piece of narwhal flesh. Other specific items that Ross suggested could be traded with the Inughuit included knives, harpoon heads, pieces of iron, crockery, and "various cheap and useful utensils and tools" (Figure 33).[4]

Historians have drawn different conclusions about the scale of trade between whalers and Inughuit in the nineteenth century. Relying on oral testimony Inughuit historian Inuuterssuaq Ulloriaq has written that in the mid-nineteenth century, whalers "returned every year" in June to trade with the local population at Ivnaanganeq.[5] However, British historian Richard Vaughan, who consulted the logbooks of several whaling ships, suggested that this trade occurred only intermittently. Whalers did not overwinter in the region and were often in a hurry to cross to the western side of Baffin Bay; nevertheless, they occasionally traded knives and other items in exchange for narwhal ivory. Vaughan has suggested that detailed research in whaling records in Dundee,

Scotland is required to determine the extent of whalers' trade with Inughuit for ivory and furs in the nineteenth century.[6] Whalers were said to have acquired principles of harpoon construction from Canadian Inuit. Using Inuit harpoons as prototypes, they commissioned the manufacture of industrial models with Western iron and used these harpoons during their excursions to northern Baffin Bay after 1818.[7]

During the Franklin search expeditions in the late 1840s and 1850s, a greater range and quantity of Western goods became available in the region. Assessing the extent of contact between British exploration vessels and Inughuit in this period, Clements Markham counted 10 ships that had some degree of exchange with this population between 1849 and 1858.[8] For example, when Captain Sherard Osborn visited Cape York in 1850, he presented the Inughuit there with a boathook staff and a piece of wood 3.7 metres long. He wrote: "They danced, shouted, and laughed again with astonishment at possessing such a prize. Wood was evidently with them a scarce article; they had it not even to construct sledges with."[9] In 1851, William S. Lovell visited an Inughuit village about 19 km south of Cape Alexander on Smith Sound. Its residents showed him a number of items which they said Elisha Kent Kane had given them: "a bake-pan, a galley spoon, pemmican cans, preserved meat cans." The Inughuit inhabitants wore articles of Western clothing, including a white shirt and "guernsey frocks," and were living in canvas tents with tent poles of pinewood. Lovell recalled that when in service on the *Advance*, the ship's mainsail was made of the same fabric.[10] When British Commander E.A. Inglefield met the most northerly Inughuit near Petowik (Pitoraarfik) on Smith Sound in 1852, he inspected several tupiks for "articles of European manufacture." He found a knife blade, stamped "B. Wilson, cast steel," a dilapidated tin canister, and some small pieces of steel which had been inserted into a piece of bone to form a continuous blade. He inferred that these articles may have been acquired through trade with the Inughuit to the south who had encountered whaling ships.[11] The British captain added to the group's small number of metal materials when he traded files, spears, knives, and other objects in exchange for a Native stone pot.[12]

Occasional shipwrecks also deposited useful European materials in the region. While at Petowik (Pitoraarfik), Inglefield also noticed a piece of rope, which he thought might have originated on a whaler and drifted on a shore.[13] Lieutenant Parker Snow, who sailed to Baffin Bay in 1848, reported finding a wooden mallet branded with the words "Alfred No. 6" in an Inughuit habitation in northern Greenland. The name was found to correspond to a whaling vessel abandoned in the area a few years earlier.[14] In 1876, Commander Allen Young described several wooden articles possessed by a resident family at Northumberland Island, all of which, according to the family, had been washed up on shore by the tide. They included wooden sticks used for tent poles, a ship's bucket, a west Greenlander's kayak paddle, and a piece of a deal case marked "Limejuice, Leith."[15]

The scale of trade increased during the expeditions of Kane, 1853–55, and Hayes, 1860–61, when these parties overwintered in the Thule District. According to Kane, the principal goods exchanged were familiar items, such as needles, files, knives, and lengths of wood.[16] After these expeditions departed, the explorers' abandoned base camps also provided the Inughuit with a ready source of materials, especially wood and metal. Other explorers in this era stopped occasionally at Cape York, including Captain Leopold McClintock, who arrived in 1858 and presented the Inughuit with presents of knives and needles.[17]

The Nares and Greely expeditions to northern Ellesmere Island followed in 1875–76 and 1881–84, but both of these parties engaged Aboriginal hunters from the Upernavik area of West Greenland and the Greely expedition bypassed the Thule district and its people altogether. In 1875 Nares did stop briefly near Cape York in an attempt to engage the services of Hans Hendrik's brother-in-law, and presented a small group of Inughuit with matches, biscuits and knives "which appeared to please them greatly."[18] As well, Nares's relief vessel, the *Pandora*, stopped in the district in 1876. While anchored at Bardin Bay on the south shore of Northumberland Island, Commander Allen Young encountered an extended Inughuit family and presented its members with six knives, a large saw, a gimlet, and a wooden oar and plank, suitable for use in making spears. The ships' officers also gave the women in this group some packets of needles and thread, combs, and scissors.[19] Despite the careful conservation of scarce metal articles, these materials were eventually exhausted. As both whaling and exploration activity dwindled in the latter part of the nineteenth century, access to European goods slowed to a trickle by the 1880s. Occasionally, whalers visited in the late nineteenth century and traded small articles, including tobacco and pipes among the typical items.[20]

Trade and Material Change in the Peary Era

During the extensive contact of the Peary era, 1890–1909, intermittent exchanges with whalers expanded to frequent trade of Western manufactured goods for skins, labour, and other commodities. While Peary's relief vessel in 1892 brought the Inughuit gifts of lumber, hardware and cooking utensils donated by residents of Philadelphia and West Chester, this episode of charity was an anomaly overshadowed by mercenary trade of goods in exchange for services.[21] Employing Inughuit for extended periods, Peary developed a barter system, according to which he paid individuals with rifles, shells, and other materials considered useful by this group. The articles Peary traded were rationed out precisely. He gave his American assistants strict instructions not to exceed the quantities of goods he had established in exchange for services or to trade items that were of use to him. For example, in early 1900 Peary employed Inughuit men to form a succession of sled dog trains to transport his equipment from Etah to Fort Conger. He gave instructions to Matthew Henson to pay each driver the following materials left behind by Greely: "10 boxes of revolver cartridges, a barrel, and some old clothing, and some not too valuable pieces of wood."[22] In April 1899, he wrote a memorandum to Henson, who was about to depart for Fort Conger with five Inughuit: "Give each of the natives 100 of the revolver cartridges, such barrel staves or other similar pieces of wood as they may want, and a shirt apiece. They are not to have any of the buffalo coats or other clothing or any material that is likely to be of use to us in the future."[23]

According to Danish ethnographer H. P. Steensby, the most useful trade good from the standpoint of the Inughuit around 1910 was a steel file. They used such tools to hone walrus and narwhal teeth into harpoon points and foreshafts, and to fashion ivory pieces into the shoes of sledge runners. Iron saws were also desired items, as they ground the back of the saw to a sharp edge for use in hewing and chopping food. Steel knives were used in cutting up animals and scraping the skins and bones. While the Inughuit continued to use traditional drills with bone mouth pieces, by this date the points were always made of metal, as were harpoon points.[24]

Peary knew that the material privations of life in such a remote location placed the Inughuit in an inherently disadvantageous trade position. Without a ready supply of wood or manufactured iron, the Inughuit were anxious to secure even scrap items that could be used in fashioning weapons, such as spear points and sledges, while such simple tools as needles were much sought after by the women. In these circumstances, they were prepared to trade valuable items, which had consumed many hours of productive labour, for articles of little value to their Euro-American counterparts. As Peary himself acknowledged: "A man offered me his dogs and sledge and all his furs for a bit of board as long as himself; another offered me his wife and two children for a shining knife, and a woman offered me everything she had for a needle."[25] The potential for the Euro-Americans to abuse their position of comparative power and wealth was apparent (Figure 68).

Figure 68: "Robert Edwin Peary, full-length portrait, standing on deck of ship or dock, facing left, distributing gifts to Eskimos, Greenland." Library of Congress (Washington, DC), Photo no. LC-USZC4-7505

Peary's barter system was followed by other Americans in his parties. In the fall of 1901, following an acrimonious falling out with Peary, his surgeon Dr. T.S. Dedrick established winter quarters at Anoritooq on Smith Sound. Dedrick recorded frequent exchange of small quantities of trade items, which he carefully dispensed in exchange for reciprocal goods or services, as follows:

Panikpah—seal liver for carrying my pkge—12 gun caps
Panikpah, carrying pkg [from] E[tah] to A[nortok]—7 needles & 12 gun caps
Ootunusuah—Kane relic (turned in to expedition)—25 gun caps
Cudlah, carrying pkg [from] E[tah] to A[nortok]—5 needles & 5 gun caps
Panikpah—last year small tent [in exchange for], knife, two boxes matches
Merkashah, for a hare & wife cooking several hare—3 gun caps
Inuita, for errands, grass for bed, etc.—5 gun caps
Various natives for red harpoon points, etc.—10 needles
Obloyah, to hunt hare with—6 gun caps[26]

Following the Peary era, American Donald MacMillan continued the practice of barter with Inughuit on his expeditions. In 1916, for example, after sending several hunters to hunt caribou, he reported providing the hunter Ka-bloo-nar-ding-we with a shotgun and 50 shells "on condition that he gives me half of all killed."[27]

Between 1890 and 1909, Peary introduced the technology of firearms and mechanical traps to this group, which radically altered Inughuit procurement strategies. They had previously been exposed to firearms, as American William Lovell wrote in 1851 that the Inughuit put their hands to their ears when an officer raised a rifle to fire,[28] but no members of the group appear to have possessed a rifle at that time. Later in the century, a few Inughuit men reportedly possessed guns. In 1873, a passenger on a Dundee whaler observed Inughuit men with two American government rifles, perhaps obtained from the U.S. naval vessel, the *Polaris*, after it was abandoned by C.F. Hall and his crew. Indeed, when the *Pandora*, a British relief vessel, visited Hall's deserted camp on Littleton Island in 1879, Captain Sir Allen Young found four gun barrels cut in half "as if to make pistols," in the midst of many Aboriginal arrows and spears.[29] In the early 1890s, Eivind Astrup, a Norwegian member of Peary's parties on two expeditions, observed that a young man, Akpalia, had obtained a gun by bartering a "considerable quantity of ivory" with whalers.[30] However, without bullets and only a few charges of powder, he was obliged to shoot pebbles; the barrel's bursting caused its foreshortening. The lack of replacement firearms or ammunition was itself evidence that guns were not readily available or in general use at this time.

All this changed with Peary. However proficient the Inughuit had been with bow and arrow and spear, their weapons were no match for the speed and sureness of a rifle. The change occurred early in Peary's tenure. Astrup observed:

> When we first arrived on these coasts in 1891, the chase [of caribou] was still carried on with the bow and arrow; at our departure in 1894 these were put away on the shelf; and the time is not far distant when they will be on view only in the glass cases of a few collectors.[31]

By the time of Peary's final voyage in 1909–10, guns had completely superseded the bow and arrow in the Thule District in everyday use.[32]

Beyond revolutionizing their capacity to hunt land mammals, combined with associated camouflage, netting and other European materials, the rifle was responsible for important changes in techniques for procuring several marine mammals, including seals. One such method was the *utoq* method of hunting seals; a hunter proceeded by rigging a white sail camouflage to a small sledge that he pushed in front of him. Where, previously, Inughuit hunters relied on spears, after the introduction of firearms they mounted a rifle on the sledge, which protruded through a hole cut in the screen (Figure 69). After spotting a seal from a distance, the hunter was able to approach it stealthily while remaining behind the screen of this apparatus, always approaching from the leeward side. A hunter armed with a spear was obliged to emerge from behind cover at the decisive moment, risking alerting the seal to his presence, but a hunter with a rifle could remain behind the screen while he took aim and fired.[33] As was the case when using a spear, hunters still needed to be very quick to harpoon the killed animal before it sank,[34] but they were nevertheless able to maximize procurement opportunities by incorporating this new technology into their repertoire.

The introduction of guns also occasioned a change to the Inughuit method of hunting ringed seals from kayaks during the summer months of July and August. Where formerly they speared the seals, hunters began to kill them with a rifle shot through the head. Since seals were low in blubber in summer, the hunter needed to paddle in quickly to harpoon the felled seal before it sank. It therefore seems probable that more seals were wasted through sinking after the introduction of firearms than previously. Occasionally, sealers still harpooned seals directly, but only in the case of young seals who were not yet wary enough of approaching hunters.[35]

The introduction of European steel traps greatly increased the capacity of Aboriginal hunters to procure animals to trade the skins. Hunters were previously limited to game animals they could obtain while on the trail, or that could be secured by building and setting traditional stone traps. However, building these traps consumed considerable labour and they lacked versatility as they could not be moved. The mechanical traps enabled hunters to place many more devices across their territory, greatly increasing the product of their labours.

The introduction of mechanical traps also initiated a major economic shift from hunting for subsistence to commercial trapping. From the time of initial contact, Europeans saw the potential to encourage the Inughuit to hunt for trading purposes. At the first recorded meeting of Europeans with the Inughuit in 1818, Captain John Ross concluded that Western trade goods could be used to induce them to trap foxes for export to Europe. Commercial trapping was slow to develop in northwest Greenland, and Peary's diversion of the bulk of Inughuit labour to his polar expeditions delayed it further until after his final departure in

Figure 69: "Eskimo with kometaho," Credit: American Museum of Natural History (New York City), Donald B. MacMillan Collection, Crocker Land, 1913-17, Negative no. 231657.

1909. Peary's interest in furs was ancillary to his polar exploration objectives and fur trade occurred sporadically according to his need to raise money to underwrite his expeditions. It was not until the establishment of the Thule trading station in the year following his final departure from the region in 1909 that the fur trade was initiated on a consistent basis.

So long as Peary remained the principal supplier, the flow of guns into the Thule District remained irregular, and access to ammunition was unreliable. Peary traded guns for furs, but after his departure for the United States following each voyage, the Inughuit were left without a source of supply of firearms and replacement parts for damaged guns. With the decline in the whale stocks in Baffin Bay, Scottish whalers ceased to visit the Thule District. At this point, according to Knud Rasmussen, "the small Eskimo tribe was threatened with a catastrophe, no more being able to procure guns and ammunition."

Rasmussen, who had been in the district with ethnographer Ludwig Mylius-Erichsen in 1902-04 and during an expedition in 1906–07, responded to the Inughuit's plight by establishing a trading store at Thule in 1910.[36] His partner in this venture was Peter Freuchen.[37] It was at this point that firearm technology introduced by Peary took on particular significance for the Inughuit, as Rasmussen's store assured ongoing access to these goods and thus rifles became incorporated into every hunter's toolkit.[38]

Europeans profited financially from the trade. In addition to fox skins, walrus and narwhal tusks were attractive items for the consumer market in the United States. Beyond commercial sales, Peary, and later Donald MacMillan, acquired a variety of animal skins and manufactured items from the Inughuit commissioned by sponsoring institutions such as the Museum of Natural History in New York City. Some writers have characterized these exchanges as exploitative; Jean Malaurie, who spent a winter with the Inughuit in 1950–51, has asserted that there was "considerable profiteering" by Americans in the fox trade. In one season alone, in 1907–08, a small number of Inughuit hunters secured about 200 fox skins for explorer Frederick Cook; he estimated their value at $10,000.[39] Even after the Second World War, the Inughuit were still receiving only a small portion of the sale price for their furs.[40]

The Peary and Cook expeditions also appear to have had a decisive impact by greatly expanding the range of hunting by Inughuit throughout the northern Queen Elizabeth Islands. In Chapter 2, it was noted that, prior to contact, and perhaps into the nineteenth century, the Inughuit and Canadian Inuit made periodic use of hunting territories along the east coast of Ellesmere Island. By the early twentieth century, the hunting territories of the Inughuit had expanded to include muskox grazing grounds in the Sverdrup Pass and Lake Hazen regions of Ellesmere Island and areas of Axel Heiberg, Ellef Ringnes, and Amund Ringnes islands; and polar bear and seal hunting areas along Ellesmere's eastern and western coasts, and the southeastern shores of Axel Heiberg Island. Evidently they had become reacquainted with these more westerly regions and their stocks of muskoxen and other animals when several male hunters accompanied American explorer Frederick Cook on his unsuccessful polar attempt.[41] In the late 1930s, Aapilaq, who had travelled with Cook in 1908–09, told English adventurer David Haig-Thomas that he and Ittukusuk had crossed "Muskoxland" (Ellesmere Island) and the island to the west of it (Axel Heiberg), "until we found new lands beyond."[42]

In the immediate aftermath of the polar expeditions of Peary and Cook, the Inughuit continued to cross Smith Sound to hunt on Ellesmere Island. Knud Rasmussen later wrote that between 1910 and 1914, at least 20 hunters were carrying out an annual muskox hunt on Ellesmere and Axel Heiberg islands.[43] Explorer Donald B. MacMillan, testifying before Canada's Muskox Commission, later reported that, in 1911, several Inughuit spent a year in the region of Eureka Sound. They told him they wintered there because of the available muskox and caribou resources, and the ready presence of coal seams, which they mined for fuel. The Inughuit burned the coal in makeshift stoves of tin biscuit boxes. The substitution of coal for blubber was not a happy one. MacMillan reported: "One man told me he built a fire of coal in his igloo, set fire to it, his wife died and his boy was nearly suffocated. That scared him and he went back home." The other Inughuit also returned to Greenland. They had become "very lonesome"; they preferred living in their own houses and in larger communities, "if they can get food."[44]

Other Euro-Americans who accompanied the Inughuit on subsequent hunting trips to Ellesmere and other islands have left accounts of these excursions to the Canadian islands to the west.[45] Harry Whitney, who was at Etah in 1908–09, detailed his own muskox hunting trip with Inughuit guides to the Sverdrup Pass region in central Ellesmere Island. Knud Rasmussen, who lived with them in 1902–04 and later established the Thule trading store in 1910, reported annual hunting expeditions in this period through Ellesmere to Axel Heiberg Island in April, long enough to enable the men to obtain enough meat and skins to accommodate their annual needs. Rasmussen reported that these hunting parties normally comprised 20 men, who secured an estimated 300 muskoxen during the trip. While he deplored what he regarded as a lack of conservation on their part, he thought that the muskoxen were not in any immediate danger of extinction in this period, as "certain flocks in these regions number upwards of two hundred animals, which make a big mountain look quite alive—an impressive sight never to be forgotten by one who has seen it."[46] Evidently the muskox hunting trips could last longer than the spring season. Writing of the same era, Peter Freuchen reported that one Inughuit party, who had gone muskox hunting on Ellesmere Island, did not return until a year later.[47]

Captain George Comer, who wintered at Etah with MacMillan's "Crocker Land" Expedition in 1916–17, later reported that the Inughuit had brought back 150 muskox skins from Ellesmere Island during the season. He stated that this had not been their prior practice, but surmised that since they had now found that crossing Smith Sound was not so dangerous, "they no doubt will continue to do this until the Musk Ox become scarce."[48] On 29 May 1917, MacMillan wrote that an Inughuit hunting party had arrived at Etah. He described the haul of game: "They bring some good specimens, among which are two small muskox calves, a six-legged muskox; and a baby bearded seal. Only one bear to their credit, but muskox galore. Their sledges were piled high with skins and meat."[49] Despite the large numbers of muskox taken, in 1920 Rasmussen argued that the annual kill of various species was within sustainable limits. He wrote: "It must, however, be observed that Esquimaux expeditions have never had the extensive or destructive effect on the breed [muskox] which marked the systematically planned American expeditions."[50]

Muskoxen were not the only mammal species on Ellesmere attracting the attention of Greenlanders. Peter Freuchen also reported that, in the era of the First World War, he had accompanied Inughuit on various long trips across Smith Sound to Ellesmere Island. On these occasions the principal objective was to obtain snow hares, whose soft furs were used in making stockings. According to Freuchen, the richer vegetation on Ellesmere supported a much larger population of hares, which is why the trips were made. These excursions in themselves were necessitated by changes in the resource base of the Inughuit, especially the depletion of caribou herds in northwestern Greenland, which deprived them of a source of materials for leggings.[51] The elimination of caribou in northern Greenland was itself caused by overhunting for American parties, possibly in concert with climatic change. In other cases, polar bear skins were the principal object. Every spring in the years after Cook's expedition, according to Rasmussen, particular hunters "who lived outside the bear districts so-called"[52] crossed to the west side of Ellesmere Island in search of bear skins for manufacturing their pants.

Hunting trips to Ellesmere Island were a regular occurrence by this time. In a retrospective account of his "Crocker Land" expedition, MacMillan reported coming across the stone cairn of A.P. Low at Cape Herschel on Ellesmere Island's eastern coast in 1917. Low had been sent by Canada's Dominion government to assert sovereignty in 1903–04. MacMillan found the cairn demolished and its record removed, "without a doubt the work of Eskimos [Inughuit], who are in the habit now of visiting this coast annually in search of polar bear."[53]

By the 1930s, Inughuit were not only exploiting the land mammal populations of Ellesmere, but also the marine mammal resources in the channels to the west of the island. Danish zoologist Christian Vibe, who spent two years with the Inughuit from 1939 to 1941, wrote that the ringed seals caught west of Ellesmere Island were "very large" on the average, much larger than the seals on Ellesmere's west coast.[54] Hunting in the fiords and sounds of Axel Heiberg Island and western Ellesmere Island was made easier by smaller variations in tidal levels, enabling smoother passage from the coastal ice foot to the pack ice.[55] Observing the Inughuit between 1939 and 1941, Vibe placed the excursions to Ellesmere Island between the months of March and May.[56] One of the reasons for the sealing excursions was the size of the seals that could be obtained off Ellesmere Island. In a subsequent publication, Vibe reported that the ringed seals found along Ellesmere's east coast and in the far north of Kane Basin were also much larger than those that had migrated to the outer coasts of the Thule district. These were older seals that were able to maintain breathing holes in the heavier ice conditions in these areas, while younger seals were forced out to places where stronger currents produced more open water. The polar bears stayed where the larger prey congregated.[57]

Indeed, Inughuit hunting of mammals along Ellesmere Island's coast and interior continued well into the modern era, a worrisome fact for Canadian officials who saw the trips as an implicit threat to Canadian sovereignty. Following the re-establishment of the detachment at Craig Harbour and Alexandra Fiord in the 1950s, the RCMP reported a succession of such episodes in the 1950s and 1960s. For example, in 1968, three Inughuit arrived at Grise Fiord with their dog teams. When asked if they had done any hunting, they replied that they had shot several seals along the eastern coast of Ellesmere Island and nine polar bears near Coburg Island.[58] One of the men was a direct descendent of Robert Peary. These hunting trips were said to continue as late as the 1980s, including periodic excursions to the Ellesmere coast of Kane Basin in search of polar bears for skins.[59]

The excursions to Ellesmere Island also helped the Inughuit become acquainted with other useful resources of these lands, enabling more effective exploitation of interior regions formerly considered out of reach. For example, after the Second World War, Danish geologist Troelsen reported that the Inughuit had told him of using tar-like substances found at Lake Hazen while hunting there in former years.[60] The availability of this alternative source of fuel for fires, and knowledge of its usefulness, freed them of dependence on seal blubber and the need to stay near the coast.

In addition to the natural resources, abandoned camps from Ellesmere Island's exploration era provided the Inughuit with a storehouse of materials left behind by various European expeditions. These abandoned camps offered a continuing source of scarce materials such as wood, useful in constructing sledge runners, and iron, which could be refashioned into projectile points and bullets, and used in building larger tools. For example, while stopping at the north Greenland village of Etah in 1875, Captain Nares noted the presence of "many relics" of C.F. Hall's *Polaris* expedition, including pieces of books, ice chisels, fish hooks, and bottles.[61] Much later, in 1917, the Inughuit woman Inaluk related to Donald MacMillan that her compatriots had visited Life Boat Cove in 1873. Among the items left behind by the Americans was a box with a glass cover filled with books. Wrote MacMillan: "The Eskimos broke the glass into pieces and divided it to be used as windows for their snow houses and igloos."[62] Peter Freuchen recalled that shortly after his arrival at Thule in 1910, the Inughuit had already dismantled part of Peary's wintering house of 1901–02 at Payer Harbour on Pim Island.[63] In the same period, in 1914, Donald MacMillan visited this site. Confirming that it was then missing its floorboards and windows, he asserted that since 1902, "various and numerous Eskimos have had it as their home." Among its periodic occupants were Sipsu and Aapilaq (Ahpellah), who spent a year at this site while waiting for the arrival of MacMillan's party in 1913.[64]

After Peary reintroduced various Inughuit to Ellesmere Island between 1899 and 1909, more remote destinations, especially Fort Conger, became favoured destinations. Owing to the large scale of the Lady Franklin Bay Expedition, Fort Conger was particularly endowed with desirable items, including both objects and provisions. Situated near the northern margins of sea mammal migrations, Fort Conger became a logical terminus for spring hunting expeditions to Ellesmere Island. Typically, in late March or early April, hunters crossed the ice dam above Smith Sound or farther north across Kane Basin to hunt polar bears at various small polynyas along the Ellesmere coast. Reaching Fort Conger by May, they loaded selected items before retracing their steps on the return journey.

An indication of the kinds of articles salvaged can be gleaned from the period texts of Europeans visiting the region. Harry Whitney, an American big-game hunter, wrote that "Ilabrado," an Inughuit man, had given him "a highly prized relic—a little china gravy bowl picked up at Fort Conger."[65] Writing of Peary's 1905–06 expedition, Robert Bartlett stated that the ship picked up an Inughuit family who had just visited Fort Conger. He wrote: "The little girl was wearing a pair of long kid gloves. Anahwe [Annowgwe] had a small trunk full of shirts and ties and clothing of many colours, while Asayu [Asiajuk] had copper bolts and iron in different shapes and sizes."[66] Several years later, Meqqusaaq (Figure 16), already seasoned from his early journeys with Qitlaq, reportedly travelled alone to Fort Conger. Among other items, he collected a large box of granulated sugar for his daughter.[67] Thus, within only a few years after their reintroduction to Ellesmere Island, the Inughuit had effectively incorporated its lands, waters, and abandoned European camps and materials into their range of resource use.

Aboriginal Impacts on European Exploration, 1850–1920

For nearly 50 years after contact, most Europeans in the Arctic failed to appreciate the potential importance of Inughuit guides and hunters to successful travel and subsistence in the High Arctic. Several expeditions employed Aboriginal people, but in small numbers, perhaps two or three men, and never accompanied by their families. The men hired for these expeditions were not Inughuit but rather West Greenlanders from farther south. Typically, the expedition ship would stop at Prøven or Upernavik in the northern part of Western Greenland, and its commander would request the governor's assistance in finding suitable hunters or dog drivers for hire. These men were accomplished hunters in their own localities, but they lacked experience of the regions to be explored. When Inughuit were employed on these expeditions, the expedition leaders did not always make optimal use of their skills, especially their prowess in hunting and dog driving, where they could have been of greater assistance. For example, the Hayes expedition of 1860 employed four Inughuit, but only one of these was engaged in hunting. The others were employed aboard ship in general labour or carpentry work.[68]

The guides engaged by the Nares and Greely expeditions had no prior knowledge of the High Arctic—its topography, snow conditions, the character of its sea ice, or where to find animals. Reviewing the tragic conclusion to the Greely expedition, John Edwards Caswell noted a number of shortcomings in hunting technique by West Greenlanders in these parties, reflected in reports of seals or walruses lost. They did not utilize harpoons and floats and apparently also failed to employ the extended stalking method in hunting seals. Relying heavily on guns, they lacked the more sophisticated hunting skills of the Inughuit.[69] In Caswell's interpretation, the West Greenlanders' lack of High Arctic experience yielded meagre returns from hunting for the Greely party while marooned on Pim Island.

Despite these limitations, West Greenlanders and Canadian Inuit were nevertheless useful to the large military expeditions of the 1870s and 1880s and particularly effective on the trail. During the Greely expedition, Dr. Octave Pavy observed about Jens Edward that:

> his services cannot be too much praised ... I will further say, that according to my belief, the Eskimos are indispensable for extended sledge journeys. Their experience in managing dogs and the apparent facility with which they can drive at once over difficulties where the best of their inexperienced Caucasian pupils will fail—or labor for long hours,—put the usefulness of their services out of the question. Moreover, their endurance to cold will allow them to perform the many duties of a driver with bare hands and in half of the time that it would take to freeze ours.[70]

Before the Peary era the most experienced, and hence, effective of the Aboriginal expedition guides was Hans Hendrik (Figure 75). While he was a West Greenlander, Hendrik lived with the Inughuit for extended periods during these expeditions and married an Inughuit woman. His memoirs indicate he paid close attention to the life skills and techniques of the Inughuit, which he then applied in the far north. During service on three major expeditions to the region, he amassed considerable knowledge of Ellesmere Island's coastal areas and their animal resources, perhaps comparable only to the hunters of Qitlaq's party in the nineteenth century.

Hendrik's expertise was particularly evident on the well-known excursion of William Morton to the Kennedy Channel during the Kane expedition of 1853–55 and the sledging parties of the British Arctic Expedition of 1875–76. During Lieutenant Beaumont's excursion to northern Greenland in 1876, Hendrik's capture of seals was credited with saving the life of George Bryant and possibly others who were then suffering from scurvy.[71] RW. Coppinger, a Royal Navy surgeon with the HMS *Discovery*, was effusive in his praise of Hans Hendrik's role on the 1876 sledging parties. He wrote:

> I must express my sense of the invaluable nature of the services which the Esquimaux, Hans Hendrik, has rendered to the sick, as well as of the unflagging zeal and energy with which he has performed every duty entrusted to him. So fertile was he in expedients, so keen in appreciating the requirements of the sick, and so skilful in hunting, without his aid we might have had to deplore a larger mortality.[72]

Hans Hendrik and even his less experienced counterparts with the Greely expedition aided the Europeans by providing them with fresh game. These hunters also provided seasoned leadership on the trail and offered aid to Europeans in distress. In Chapter 6, I commented on the role of Tookoolito and other Inuit in hunting and building snow shelters to help ensure the survival of Hall's survivors during the ice floe drift of 1872–73. Even so, neither the Nares nor the Greely expeditions made an optimal use of their Native employees. Despite an awareness of extensive numbers of muskoxen in the northern Ellesmere Island, Greely did not direct his hunters to take full advantage of this prime food resource. His journal and diaries also make clear that he did not share Pavy's views regarding the Greenlanders' value to the expedition and gave them only a very limited role in his expedition.

In addition to the labour of Aboriginal employees, the Europeans' eventual adoption of Inughuit and Inuit dog sledge technology decisively improved their capacity to travel and survive over great stretches of the High Arctic. As early as the 1860s, the British explorer Sir Leopold McClintock made extensive use of dogs in expeditions in search of the Franklin party.[73] The Hayes and Kane expeditions, which wintered at Smith Sound in the 1850s and 1860s, also learned basic survival skills and useful travel techniques from their Inughuit hosts. By the second winter, Kane admitted his debt to the Inughuit in his adoption of their use of dogs, their sledge type, and an economical approach to outfitting, reducing the load to the absolute minimum:

> It requires some suggestive incident to show us how we have gradually become assimilated in our habits to the necessities of our peculiar life. Such an incident I find in my equipment. Compare it with similar sledge-outfits of last winter, and you will see that we are now more than half Esquimaux. It consists of—
> 1. One small sledge, five feet six by two.
> 2. An extra jumper and sack-pants for sleeping.
> 3. A ball of raw walrus-meat—This is all.[74]

Nevertheless, it was not until 1900 that Europeans began to take full advantage of the use of dogs. The importance of the adoption of sled-dog techniques was far from self-evident to Peary's contemporaries, which is demonstrated by such anomalies as the British explorers' use of ponies as draught animals in the Antarctic during the race to the South Pole after 1900.[75] A mercenary justification for using dogs rather than ponies was that, in the event of the death of a pony, its meat could be eaten by the men of the party but the other ponies would reject it, whereas if a dog expired, both men and dogs would eat the flesh.[76]

Earlier explorers made sporadic use of dogs, but it was Peary's innovation to fully integrate dogs in a comprehensive program of transportation, hunting, and survival in the region. Having observed the unreliability of shipping in Nares Strait, Peary developed the use of sled dogs for hunting and exploratory excursions, as well as transporting large quantities of food and equipment over long distances. The successful use of dogs depended on applying an overall program of environmental adaptation, including an extensive and varied hunting regime necessary to sustain dogs while on the trail.

Peary and his Norwegian contemporary Otto Sverdrup learned several ancillary techniques from the Inughuit, enabling the effective use of dogs. Dr. John Svendsen, a member of Sverdrup's party, reported that Inughuaq Qulutana (Kulutinguah) had shown him "an easy and practical" way of securing both dogs and tents when camping on the ice:

> He hacked small loops or rings in it [ice] with his knife, and to these
> the traces were attached. This method is also very practical for fasten-
> ing the guy-ropes of the tents; the loops are quickly hacked, and it is not
> at all difficult, for the first time I tried it I was completely successful.[77]

For his sledges, Peary adopted the general design of the Inughuit komatik, but modified for his own purposes. Bringing planks from the United States for the purpose, he specified the construction of much longer models than their Aboriginal counterparts. To increase manoeuverability in pressure ice conditions, he incorporated rocker runners into the design.[78] As well, the shoes were shod with a specific form of steel, "soft enough that I could drill it in the field, yet hard enough so that the constant use would not too quickly wear it through."[79] Obviously, the Inughuit themselves and their Thule forerunners should be credited with the development of arctic dog-sledge travel. However, Peary was wise enough to learn the importance of this and other techniques from them, which proved crucial to the success of his overall project.

It could be stated with accuracy that Peary could not have reached the North Pole without the remarkable skills and exertions on his behalf of his Inughuit companions. The explorer acknowledged as much, in his familiar egocentric manner, when he remarked: "From the very beginning of my polar work I believed that these most northerly human beings in the world [Inughuit] could afford me invaluable assistance in my plans for exploration. Later I had a fatalistic feeling that the Almighty had put the little tribe in this particular place for the express purpose of assisting [me] to win the pole."[80] On his last two polar expeditions, as many as one third of the entire Inughuit population was engaged in his service. While his specific hunting techniques and supporting material culture, such as shelters and caches, were derivative of Inuit or Inughuit practice, Peary's strategy and organizational approach to hunting was distinctly Western. His overriding objectives in hunting involved the indiscriminate slaughter of animals to stockpile huge surpluses to support his larger goal of reaching the North Pole. In this, Peary diverged sharply from the Inughuit's emphasis on accumulating a surplus only for group subsistence during the winter months of scarcity.

With Peary, European approaches to provisioning shifted dramatically from dependency on imported Western foodstuffs to reliance on hunting mammals in the region or "living off the country."[81] Beyond these essentials, Peary developed a systematic plan for procuring wild game in each of the seasons and structured his hunting parties and their itineraries around such factors as the presence of moonlight during the dark winter months, and the likelihood of finding game animals in various areas at particular points in time. While admitting that twice his hunting parties were close to starvation when they were saved by muskoxen, he asserted that the discovery of the animals was not due to luck or accident. Rather, it "was the result of careful, intelligent search in suitable localities, examining every slope and valley and rock within range of field-glasses, carried for that special purpose, and as much a part of the hunting equipment as the rifle."[82] Peary's methodical approach could not be doubted, although the thorough scouring of the countryside for game animals had been practised by Aboriginal hunters long before the arrival of the Americans.

One of Peary's innovations in provisioning, which proved both effective and influential, was his adaptation of pemmican, long a staple of Plains Aboriginal cultures, to arctic use. Peary developed his own recipe for pemmican in the Arctic, consisting of dried pulverized meat and fat, wheat flour, dried vegetables, sugar and raisins. This mixture provided a relatively lightweight, concentrated food that gave his sledgers all their vitamin and energy requirements. It could readily be thawed and would keep indefinitely, ideal for use on the trail. Given the need to minimize sledge weights, Peary considered it the only food sufficiently compact to enable a serious attempt on the Pole.[83] Peary also developed a pemmican mixture for dog food, which was similar to the pemmican for humans, minus the raisins and sugar. The quality of Peary's form of pemmican was such that Danish explorers of the era used it as the basis for their own food preparation.[84]

Peary's reliance on Inughuit skin clothing represented another major departure from previous expeditions. Unlike the Nares expedition's sledgers, whose sole concession to Native clothing was in the area of footwear, or the Greely party, which relied entirely on Western clothing, Peary engaged Inughuit women to make a full range of clothing for use in each of the seasons. Here again, his larger project, which involved hunting by Aboriginal employees, produced large quantities of skins for use in making the clothes.

A basic principle of Inughuit garments was the use of animal skins with effective insulating properties. These garments utilized the chimney or venting effect enabled by cutting the various shirts or coats with wide necks so that they could be pulled away from the body to release excess heat and moisture. Generally, the parkas made for Peary's party followed the Inughuit practice of making pullover outer garments without shoulder seams (Figure 70). Collars were made wide, with the winter jacket designed to overlap the top of the trousers only slightly, while there was a similar small overlap of the boots by the trousers. These features enabled the wearer to readily let off excess heat and moisture

Figure 70: "Peary on the main deck of steamship *Roosevelt.*" Library of Congress (Washington, DC), Photo No. LC-USZC4-7507.

readily when necessary.[85] The loose cut of the Inughuit *qulittaq* or parka also enabled individuals to place their arms and hands next to their torsos for additional warmth, as required.[86] Lightweight skin kamiks or boots were impervious to water and had the added advantage of being readily turned out to dry while resting on the trail. Keeping feet dry during the extended exposure to cold on the trail, perhaps more than any factor, enabled the wearer to survive the extreme conditions encountered in travel in the High Arctic.[87]

During Peary's expedition of 1905–06, Matthew Henson recorded a list of garments and clothing materials he had obtained for use on the polar assault the following spring, including kamiks with deerskin soles, sealskin mittens, a deerskin short, a birdskin shirt, hare skins for stockings, and flannel for lining trousers, presumably bearskin pants.[88] In his book *Secrets of Polar Travel*, Peary described his men's garments on his last expedition in 1908–09. They included a skin-tight shirt of flannel, Inughuit bearskin trousers, a deerskin hooded coat with a

Figure 71: "Matt Henson (of Peary's crew) in Arctic costume on deck of the *Roosevelt* on arrival at Sydney, Nova Scotia." Library of Congress (Washington, DC), Photo no. LC-USZC4-7506.

binding of tanned sealskin with bands of fur along the bottom and at the wrists, and a hood ringed with bearskin, "partly to protect the face from the wind, partly to serve as a packing, as at the wrists and bottom, to prevent the entrance of cold air or the escape of warm...Worn ordinarily turned up down like a coat-collar, in bitter winds, this bearskin roll can be turned like a collar to form a wind-guard for the eyes and face"[89] (Figure 71).

Peary was the first Euro-American in the High Arctic to integrate Inughuit techniques of sledge travel and shelter into a transportation system for polar discovery. When his ship, the *Windward* was ice-bound in Kane Basin in 1899, he ordered his employees to set caches and stage relays along the route to advance his supplies up the rugged eastern coast of Ellesmere Island to Fort Conger. The effectiveness of this approach probably influenced his development of the Peary relay system which he later employed in moving men, equipment, and provisions across the pack ice of the Arctic Ocean during his two major attempts on the North Pole in 1906 and 1909. Peary probably also drew on prior Western experience and sources for his ideas. Half a century earlier, August Sonntag, astronomer with Elisha Kent Kane, proposed the use of advance parties to set caches on the arctic pack ice to support attempts on the North Pole. He proposed sending a party out in the late winter or early spring to establish "depositories of provisions" 160 km out before the departure of the main party.[90] His proposal accurately anticipated the approach Peary would adopt 50 years later.

Peary also relied on Inughuit precedent in developing a system of temporary snow shelters (*iglooyah*) or quasi-permanent stone dwellings (*kangmah* or *igloo*) in the interior to maximize his use of animal resources. These shelters were placed at strategic locations to serve as bases for hunting operations. While on a hunting trip to Lake Hazen in 1900, he reported that his Inughuit assistant Angutdluk built a *kangmah* there for his party; he described it as "roughly roofed with skins."[91]

The shelters were supplemented by a network of meat caches. The practice of caching was also a vital component of Peary's subsistence strategies, as he utilized this practice to optimize procurement of meat for his polar forays. Recently, Abraham Pijamini, a senior hunter at Grise Fiord, has asserted that, more than any other factor, caching enabled Inuit to survive on Ellesmere Island since the 1950s.[92] For Peary's hunting parties, caching meat freed hunting parties to continue hunting even after shooting large numbers of animals. In the case of muskoxen, hunters immediately removed the heart, liver, and kidneys, laid them out to be frozen, and cached them under rocks as protection from dogs, wolves, or foxes. The remaining internal organs were then fed to the sled dogs. Next, the major bones were cut out, cracked, and the marrow consumed by the hunters. Finally, the large sections of meat, such as hams, foreshoulders, neck, and ribs were roughly butchered, frozen, and cached.[93] Subsequently, arrangements could be made to haul the meat to Fort Conger, while the hunters were in a position to continue pursuing the herds until they had met Peary's objective of killing the maximum number of animals. During the cold months, the meat was frozen, assuming it was well cached; therefore, the hunters could leave it in place for several months before reclaiming it.

While hunting excursions usually focussed on the search for major game staples, particularly muskoxen, Peary learned from his Inughuit companions to exploit secondary game resources while on the hunt. Ancillary animals and fish were worthwhile supplements to a staple diet of muskox or seal, and were often vital sources of food for the hunting party in the absence of success with the larger animals. Among these smaller animal resources were birds (auks, Brunich's guillemot, eider-duck, long-tailed duck, brant, and king-eider); land mammals (arctic hare); and fish (grayling and arctic charr).[94] As an example of their importance, Peary related how, in September 1900, his party of six men and 23 dogs subsisted for 10 days on charr alone.[95]

For his major polar expeditions of 1898–1902, 1905–06, and 1908–09, Peary secured his supplies of muskoxen from a wide range of locations in northern Ellesmere Island, generally within a 150 km radius of his wintering quarters. Among the areas hunted by his men were the Discovery Harbour area and Black Rock Vale, St. Patrick's Bay, Black Cape, near Floeberg Beach, and the rich muskox region of Lake Hazen and its tributaries. An excerpt from Peary's book on his 1905–06 expedition gives an indication of how productive his hunters' efforts were in the field. Referring to a party of four Inughuit families who had returned on 8 November 1905, he wrote:

> They have been in the field twenty-seven days and have secured some seventy-five musk-oxen, thirty to forty hare and twenty to twenty-five foxes. Besides musk-ox meat they brought in some hundred pounds of the peerless salmon trout from Lake Hazen.[96]

An important lesson Peary learned from the Greely disaster and other ill-fated arctic forays was the value of small parties to the expedition's ultimate success. As early as the 1890s, after several years' experience in northern Greenland exploration, he wrote:

> My experience has strongly accentuated my belief in small parties for Arctic work. The results obtained by Graah, Rae, Hall, Schwatka, Greely, and others, were obtained by parties of two or three. Many of the sad disasters, which form a part of Arctic history, would have been avoided had the parties been small. It is a popular fallacy that there is safety in large parties.[97]

Peary believed that the optimal size for a field party was three men, exactly the number that could be accommodated easily in a temporary snow house. Beyond the advantage of being easily erected, these small shelters facilitated conservation of warmth when fuel resources were low. The wisdom of this principle was proven during Frederick Cook's polar expedition, when he and two Inughuit guides survived an extended sojourn in the area to the west of Ellesmere Island, in part because of their ability to build such temporary shelters along the way. Peary's expeditions in 1905–06 and 1908–09 involved larger numbers of people, but the majority were Inughuit, who were largely self-sufficient in providing for their own needs. The hunting and sledging parties formed during these expeditions remained small, achieving the desired nimbleness and flexibility.

Peary also placed considerable importance on engaging the services of only the best people for polar work. Whether choosing American or Inughuit employees, he claimed to know the "capabilities and characteristics" of each expedition member. In an article in 1899, he referred to the example of the Inughuaq Sipsu:

> Sipsu I met for the first time one brilliant but bitter cold April day six years ago, in Inglefield Gulf, besides the Hurlbut Glacier. He was only a boy but active as a steel trap. Already he had a record of several deer killed with his rude bow...The next year he brought me as a trophy an eight-foot narwhal horn, the wearer of which he had himself harpooned and killed. In 1895 he was among the most successful of the numerous walrus hunters at Peterahwick.[98]

It was only with Peary's wintering occupations that Euro-North American approaches to High Arctic shelter can be said to have achieved a degree of maturity. The key was Peary's emulation of Inuit and Inughuit architectural principles and settlement patterns in designing wintering complexes. Nowhere are these principles better illustrated or documented than in the surviving shelters built by his party at Fort Conger in 1900. Peary's design for this complex was the outcome of years of careful study and experimentation. Prior to his arrival in the Arctic, Peary was familiar with earlier explorers' accounts of Inuit snow villages of interconnected dwellings and ancillary structures, particularly among the Netsilik and Iglulik Inuit.[99] During his own expeditions from the 1880s on, he also had numerous opportunities to examine the Greenlanders' techniques of insulating wintering dwellings with sod embankments, as well as their use of dugout entrance tunnels to conserve heat. To these techniques he added his own ideas, which, combined with particular circumstances and available materials, produced an unorthodox, highly distinctive approach to arctic building.

At his wintering quarters at Etah, northern Greenland in 1898, Peary began to experiment with the application of several principles of Inuit and Inughuit domestic architecture, including the interconnection of small, low-lying dwellings, banked with sod and insulated with snow. A photograph by Peary of this complex, taken in 1898, shows its grouped structures and the practice of sod banking (Figure 72). It was apparently a prototype for the wintering complex Peary's party constructed at Fort Conger two years later. In 1899, at Cape D'Urville on the Ellesmere Island side of Kane Basin, Peary constructed another low-

Figure 72: "Etah, 1898." Photograph showing the interconnected complex of structures at Peary's wintering complex in 1898. U.S. National Archives, RG 401(1)(A), Papers Relating to Arctic Expeditions, 1886–1909, Greenland - Ellesmere Island, 1898–1902, Photograph No. 401-1/1898/ 8985, "Etah, 1898."

lying wintering complex from wooden boxes and packing crates, which he double-roofed with canvas and banked with gravel. After the onset of snow in the autumn, the central structure was connected to individual snow-block dwellings of Peary's Inughuit employees. In a published paper on the expedition, Peary later described these accommodations as "comfortable."[100] Subsequently, at Cape Sheridan in 1905-06, Peary took advantage of the presence of his ship, the *Roosevelt*, to improve on the land-based wintering arrangements of Fort Conger. His plan consisted of applying Aboriginal techniques to shelter his crew aboard ship and constructing emergency quarters on the shore in the event disaster struck the ship.[101]

The complex constructed at Fort Conger in 1900 was the most fully realized of Peary's wintering settlements. Even before his first arrival at the site in early January 1899, Peary had planned to establish his principal northern base of operations at Fort Conger, the site abandoned by the Lady Franklin Bay Expedition only 15 years earlier. Peary found the house largely intact and initially tried to use the structure for accommodation, while making some adjustments to conserve fuel. During this first trip, his party refitted the officers' quarters by nailing up the outside door and entering through the kitchen, averting loss of heat through direct exposure to the outside air.[102] Further improvisations on succeeding sledging excursions to the site included the refitting of the central kitchen/galley by doubling the walls and insulating the room with any available materials, including rags and old clothes, covering the partition surfaces on both sides with battened tar paper,[103] and adding a further insulating layer of blankets and canvas on the inside walls.[104]

Returning to Etah for the winter of 1899–1900, Peary developed plans to spend the following winter at Fort Conger prior to a planned assault on the North Pole the following spring. He reasoned that, by wintering at such a northerly latitude, he would be positioned to stage an assault on the Pole the following spring. However, after returning to Fort Conger in the spring of 1900, Peary concluded that Greely's big house was unsuited to his needs for High Arctic shelter. As he later wrote in his book *Secrets of Polar Travel*:

> This great barn of a structure, sixty feet long by 30 feet wide, was grotesque in its utter unfitness and unsuitableness for polar winter quarters. With its great size, its light construction, and its high-posted rooms, nine or ten feet from floor to ceiling, it embodied about everything that should not be found in winter quarters.[105]

While he rejected the notion of using the big house for accommodation, it was not his preferred choice to build a completely new wintering complex at this site, as he intended to rely on his supply ship, the *Windward*, for shelter. When it became apparent by August that the ship was unable to penetrate the ice of Nares Strait, Peary's contingency plans came into play. Knowing that the warm weather season during which the ground could be readily worked would last only a few weeks, he ordered his Inughuit and American employees to commence digging the foundations for their prospective dwellings.[106]

At Fort Conger, the igloo-sized shelters, which measured between 3 and 2.5 m long and 2.15 to 2.8 m wide, were of simple frame construction and partially constructed of wood from the Greely expedition's packing crates and barrel staves.[107] Archaeological analysis has revealed that there were six layers of protection or insulation. They consisted, first, of a layer of tar paper tacked to the face of the outer wall of boards. This wall was separated by a layer of silt and gravel from the inner wall of lumber, the outside of which was also covered with tar paper. Finally, the inside face of the wall was lined with various types of paper, principally star charts and asbestos paper found in the Greely house.[108] Peary's diaries indicate that two additional layers should be added to this list: banking the structures with earth and turf, and, after the onset of snow in the fall, a final layer of drifted snow.[109] To provide sheltered access between the huts, tunnels were dug and banked to connect, Inughuit-style, to low-lying doorways (Figure 73). These, in turn, were roofed over with canvas and muskox skins and after the onset of snow and its hardening by wind, with snow-block domes. [110]

The settlement pattern of Peary's complex closely paralleled Aboriginal principles of siting and grouping dwelling units. Low-lying structures dug into a rise and mounded over with earth and sod, they would have functioned well to deflect the high winds that characterize this region.[111] The semi-subterranean character of the dwellings and their small size, clustering, and interconnectedness enabled an adequate degree of warmth for a minimal expenditure of fuel. Peary later reported that, on returning to Conger from his fall hunting trips he could "warm the interior of my tent to a comfortable temperature by the judicious burning of a yard of tar roofing paper in my sheet iron stove."[112] Similarly, his employees experienced few problems heating the shelters; on 20 December 1900, he wrote of the dwelling of Dr. Dedrick, his expedition surgeon, that "very little coal keeps his house so warm now that he goes naked to the waist practically all the time, and some of the time entirely nude."[113]

For his own dwelling unit at Fort Conger, Peary opted for a highly unorthodox shelter, which he built around the nucleus of an army tent he had scavenged for use as his summer domicile. His rationale for his approach was "partly to economize the lumber, partly as a practical experiment, and partly to furnish occupation and amusement" for himself.[114] Peary's process of construction revealed a fascinating blend of Western structural practice and Aboriginal-inspired improvisation.[115] To winterize the tent, he began by driving four posts into the gravel to define a rectangle 2.5 m by 3.5 m, and connected the tops with 6 cm by 8 cm joists. The tent poles were then set into the ground, braced diagonally, and the tent stretched over this framework. With the installation of a floor of old boards from a Fort Conger lean-to, an inner window sash from the Conger big house that he set into the south wall of the tent, and a door from Greely's magnetic observatory, the shell of his residence was in place.[116]

Covering the tent with a large tarpaulin that formerly covered Greely's biscuit barrels, Peary heaped gravel on the ends until the tent was banked to the height of the wall.[117] With the arrival of cold weather, he blanketed the sides of the wall with the remaining mattresses from Greely's

Figure 73: Aerial view of Fort Conger in 1979, showing the outlines of the surviving shelters of Peary's wintering complex of 1900. The outline of Peary's wintering tent and its passageway to Dr. Dedrick's shelter are visible on the left side of the complex, while on the other side of Dedrick's dwelling the remains of the former tunnel connection to the Inughuit shelter are visible. The depression in the right centre is the site of the former kitchen, which the outlines of Greely's big house of 1881 appear in the upper right corner of the photograph. Parks Canada, Western Canada Service Centre, Cultural Resource Services, Winnipeg.

house and sewed these together. He then covered the gravel with a layer of turf and erected an additional wind barrier of turf 25 cm wide, rising 25 to 50 cm above the embankment. In late October, he built a snow-block wall around the ensemble, filled in the space between the wall and the mattresses with loose snow, and threw water on it until it became a solid envelope, impervious to wind.[118]

Peary's insulated tent was connected to the other structures of the complex by a canvas passageway linking it to the shelter of his surgeon, Dr. T.S. Dedrick. When hardened snow became available, they added a domed snow-block vestibule with a curtained door to act as an additional buffer. Peary also reported the presence of a shared snow-block entrance to Dedrick's and Matthew Henson's shelters, which apparently connected both to the tunnel passageway between their shelters and a tunnel connecting the dwellings of Dedrick and the Inughuit members of the expedition party (Figure 74).[119] This complex served as the core wintering settlement of Peary's party in 1900–01. It was sufficiently well constructed that it continued to serve as an ancillary base for his subsequent arctic expeditions in 1905–06 and 1908–09. After the Peary era, the buildings provided shelter to American, Danish, and British expeditions to northern Ellesmere Island in 1914, 1921, and 1935.[120]

The culmination of years of study and experimentation, Peary's complex embodied an admirable synthesis of European technology and Aboriginal ecological knowledge. Where Peary appeared to fall short was in his failure to recognize that Inughuit community patterns were as important to their long-term survival as their settlement patterns. Whereas the Inughuit were concerned with subsistence to foster group goals, Peary was preoccupied with generating a surplus to support his individual exploration objectives. During the winter of 1900–01, Peary was determined to secure large quantities of game—principally muskox meat—in preparation for an intended assault on the North Pole the following spring. To this end, he sent parties to the interior on long hunting trips throughout the winter; this regimen separated family members and friends for extended periods. Such separations were not without psychological consequences, as his expedition surgeon T.S. Dedrick noted: "Soundah does poorly when Pooblah is gone, is listless, eats little and sleeps all the time."[121] Whatever the comfort level of the shelters at Fort Conger, when working in the interior for much of the winter, Peary's employees were housed in crowded conditions in more rudimentary igloos. In a letter to Peary in February 1901, Dedrick complained: "The circumstances which have compelled the party to live in such igloos so continuously are a great misfortune."[122] Back at Fort Conger, Inughuit winter patterns of group interaction were effectively thwarted by Peary's imposition of a 10 p.m. noise curfew, and while no set time was imposed for retiring, each person was expected to rise to work a full day.[123] Peary viewed such a work routine throughout the year as essential to the well-being of his party, but his and Dedrick's diaries reveal a tendency of all its members, including the Inughuit, to experience depression and malaise during the dark period.

Perhaps Peary's notions of military hierarchy came into play here, negating some of the advantages of his adaptive approach. If it is true, as Claude Lévi-Strauss has argued, that "spatial configuration seems to be almost a projective representation of the social structure,"[124] then the arrangement of the Fort Conger shelters is suggestive of its own distinctive social organization. Peary's tent connected directly to only one other dwelling—the shelter of Dedrick, his second in command. In turn, the dwelling of Dedrick, who was charged with communicating Peary's orders to the other members of the party, was linked to the shelters of his subordinates, Matthew Henson and the Inughuit, by the tunnel passageways between them. The complex was therefore organized to maintain a degree of social distance and to reinforce its underlying military command structure (Figure 74) .

Peary's shelters at Fort Conger demonstrated that if explorers could not conquer the High Arctic with Western methods, they could survive in this region by studying and emulating Inughuit settlement patterns, architectural principles, and adaptive ingenuity. At the same time, while Peary's settlement pattern was well-designed for physical survival, his accompanying community pattern and activity structure seem to have represented a less successful adaptation to the psychological stresses of the dark High Arctic winters. Like many aspects of Peary's system, his approach to High Arctic shelter was adequate for a period of one or two winters, but in the long run was not sustainable. Beyond considerations of physical survival, successful long-term adaptation to the Arctic required a holistic approach to living in the region, in which the social, cultural, and psychological needs of the people could be accommodated.

Between 1850 and 1920, the experience of contact brought about significant changes in material culture for both Europeans visitors and Inughuit inhabitants of this region. For the Inughuit, greater access to European materials, such as wood and metal, did not initially lead to changes in technology, as they applied these materials to the manufacture of pre-existing Aboriginal tools and traditional techniques. In the Peary era, more extensive contact contributed to more wide-ranging changes in their economy and material culture. By introducing firearms and mechanical traps and hiring Inughuit to hunt to supply the materials for expedition provisions and clothing, museum specimens, and animal trophies, Peary and his successors brought about major changes in the nature of Aboriginal hunting. They thereby hastened the participation of the Inughuit in the international market economy, a process which intensified after the establishment of the American air base at Thule around 1950.

In Peary's day, Danish ethnographer H.P. Steensby asserted that Peary contributed to the impoverishment of the Inughuit by "buying up in great quantities the tribes' costly products, fox and bear skins."[125] In exchange, Peary traded guns and bullets, increasing the dependency of the Inughuit on Western technology. A further result of Peary's expeditions was his removal of the best hunters and dog teams for service on his expeditions, leaving behind the less well-provided families in difficult straits, an inference for which there appears to be considerable evidence. For those Inughuit who accompanied him to northern Ellesmere Island, life was at least as difficult as it was for those who

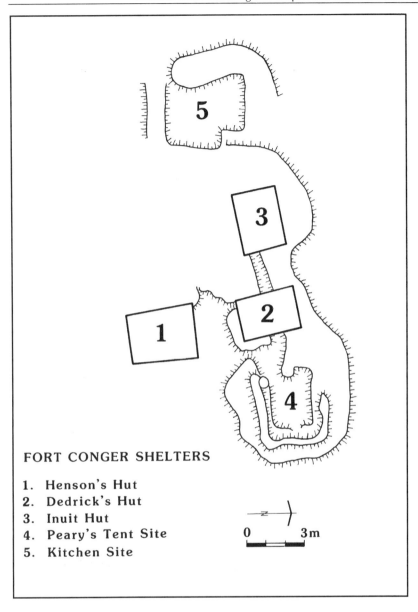

FORT CONGER SHELTERS

1. Henson's Hut
2. Dedrick's Hut
3. Inuit Hut
4. Peary's Tent Site
5. Kitchen Site

0   3m

Figure 74: Plan of Peary's wintering complex at Fort Conger, showing the spatial relationships of its constituent structures.

remained in the Thule District. Peary drove his Aboriginal employees to incredible efforts on his behalf. Steensby wrote that Peary exhausted the labour of the Inughuit for the benefit of his own polar expeditions.[126] In this light, the advantages of Peary's introduction of European technology and material goods to the Inughuit must be weighed against the toll exacted by these exchanges.

Euro-American explorers probably benefited the most from the material exchanges with Inughuit. Explorers often brought with them a limited understanding of the High Arctic environment, and their material approaches equipped them poorly to withstand the rigours of the region. Those who were astute enough to study Aboriginal lifeways and material culture learned valuable skills that enabled them to survive, if not thrive, in this region. More perceptive visitors, such as Peary, observed that the Inughuit already possessed both a sophisticated ecological knowledge and an array of material strategies to enable successful adaptation to this region. Peary recognized the importance of acquiring comprehensive knowledge of the High Arctic environment, especially northern Ellesmere Island, and employed large numbers of Inughuit hunters to exploit its resources. Aware of the importance of Inughuit women to the Native hunting economy, he engaged entire families to serve on his expeditions and incorporated their methods in a comprehensive strategy for survival and resource use. His integration of a range of Inughuit techniques for shelter, clothing, sledge travel, and hunting enabled him to succeed in exploration where others before him had failed, although in the process he exacted a heavy price from this group, who went to great lengths to support his polar endeavours.

11
Intercultural Relations in the Contact Era

In the High Arctic, the interface of European and Aboriginal peoples produced an entirely new dynamic in social relations. Previously, as in the encounters of Qitlaq's party and the Inughuit, cultural exchanges had been between similar Aboriginal groups with common approaches to living in this region. With the arrival of Europeans, representatives of very different cultures, each with a particular set of goals, form of social organization, and approach to human interaction, were brought together for extended periods. Inughuit, Inuit, and West Greenlanders responded in distinctive ways to the cultural, interpersonal, and environmental stresses of contact, while European explorers struggled to comprehend the diverging reactions of their western compatriots and Aboriginal companions. A further complicating factor was that each member of these parties was an individual who brought a particular personality and repertoire of experience to intercultural relations in this period.

The most dramatic effects of contact occurred during the Peary era. Peary was responsible for the first European-initiated relocations of large numbers of Inughuit to the remote northern regions of Ellesmere Island. These and other experiments in Native relocation in the exploration era had many important and unexpected consequences, both for the people who accompanied the Europeans and their compatriots who remained in Greenland. The wholesale removal of large numbers of Inughuit disrupted customary patterns of social organization and land use. Relations between Inughuit and Europeans were complicated by the Europeans' attempts to impose a military command structure on all members of their expeditions and power imbalances implicit in the relationship of these groups. The explorers held most of the cards in exchanges with the traditional societies they co-opted in their expeditions.[1]

The day-to-day interactions of Europeans and Greenlanders brought different and sometimes conflicting cultural imperatives into stark relief. Most of the expeditions to Ellesmere Island in the nineteenth century were staffed by members of the army or navy of the exploring nations, supplemented by a few Native hunters and guides from Western Greenland. I remarked on the general imposition of military discipline on these expeditions. Both the hierarchical command structure of the military and its penalties of corporal punishment and imprisonment were alien to the experience of the Greenlanders. Considerable evidence suggests that Inughuit and other Aboriginal members of these expeditions feared the Europeans who held most of the power in their various transactions.

In his *Memoirs*, Hans Hendrik (Figure 75) recalled having been threatened with a lashing or even more severe punishment. In April 1855, while leading the Second Grinnell Expedition, the American Elisha Kent Kane began a sledging excursion north toward Kennedy Channel with Hendrik and two other Aboriginal guides. Within 24 hours, the trip foundered when the guides left the trail to hunt polar bears. Using Hendrik as an interpreter, Kane demanded that they stop hunting and return to the trail, to which the Greenlanders "declared that this could not be done because the snow was lying too deep in that region."[2] The incensed Kane threatened to have them executed. Following this incident, Hans Hendrik abandoned Kane's employ and headed for the Inughuit settlement of Etah. In his *Memoirs* he related how Kane had also threatened to have him killed for removing a caribou head from a skin he had procured:

> A pity it was that our master behaved with haughtiness towards his crew. Also, once he treated me in a similar way. The occasion was as follows:—I had cut the head off a reindeer-skin of my own catch, intending it for a sledge seat. I went to the Kavdlunak [Dane], who was just taking a walk, and said to him: "The Master intends to shoot me for having cut the head from a reindeer-skin; that is the only reason." The Kavdlunak replied: "Don't be afraid, he will never shoot thee, I am going to say to him: we have another king [of Denmark]." While he repaired to the ship, I stayed upon the ice, expecting I should be fired at, but perceived nothing at all. This Kavdlunak, on coming out again, said: "There is no reason for you to be afraid, only remain with us, I will be your protector."[3]

The Dane referred to in Hendrik's account was Johan Petersen, who substantially corroborated these stories in his own memoirs of this expedition. He recalled:

> Dr. Kane, upon arrival at the ship, ordered me to announce to Hans the Greenlander that the commander of the Expedition had the right to order any man to be shot on the spot whenever he should attempt, without the permission of the Commander, either to abandon the ship or any expedition which he had sent off.

Kane made a similar threat to execute Petersen, whereupon the Dane advised him that since the expedition ship was now a wreck, his power as captain no longer applied; "it would hardly be advisable for him to attempt the execution of any Yankee Laws on a subject of Denmark, in

Figure 75: "Hans Hendrik, Esquimaux dog-driver, with his son and daughter, 1875."
National Archives of Canada Photo no. C-52497.

particular if the question were about capital punishment!"[4] Hendrik
was also threatened with death while serving on the expedition of Isaac
Israel Hayes in 1860–61. In addition to Hendrik, Hayes had engaged
Peter, another Greenlander, to serve as a guide for this party. Peter
disappeared on one occasion, having fled from the ship. Hayes presumed that Hendrik had influenced his compatriot to flee by arousing
false concerns over his safety. The American retaliated by being ver-
bally abusive toward Henrik and vowing to hang him.[5]

Perhaps the Greenlanders' feelings of insecurity were worsened by
language differences and the difficulty of communicating with the European crew members. Their sense of estrangement was probably also
heightened by expectations that they conform to European-style dress,
deportment, and social behaviour. In December 1881, Dr. Pavy, expedition surgeon at Fort Conger, reported that he had found the Greenlander
Jens wearing his "Esquimaux shoes, pants, and coat." Pavy wrote that
he "made Jens put on the garments which the expedition had given
him."[6] On these military expeditions, compliance with such orders was
mandatory. Other important sources of disquiet were the disruptions in
family and community life occasioned by the experience of serving on

the polar expeditions. When Greenlanders were engaged to work for these parties, they typically were taken away from their families and communities for a year or more at a time. Under such circumstances, it would not be surprising if isolation from family, kinfolk, and familiar environments contributed to recurrent stresses on their psychological health. A photograph of Hans Hendrik with his son and daughter, taken just prior to leaving his family in 1875 to travel north with the Nares Expedition, is shown in Figure 75.

The extremities of the High Arctic environment also contributed to the distress of the Aboriginal members of the expeditions, many of whom had never encountered conditions of winter darkness to a degree found in northern Ellesmere Island. Various reports of the exploration era indicate that these men exhibited symptoms of anxiety when first encountering the polar winter in these latitudes. Hans Hendrik reported his reactions:

> Then it really grew winter and dreadfully cold, and the sky speedily darkened. Never had I seen the dark season like this, to be sure it was awful, I thought we should have no daylight any more. I was seized with fright, and fell a-weeping, I never in my life saw such darkness, even at noon-time. As the darkness continued for three months, I really believed we should have no daylight more.[7]

With the arrival of the winter's perpetual darkness and the cessation of most hunting activities, the Greenlanders' feelings of loneliness welled up, accentuated by the slackening pace of work. Hans Hendrik is a case in point. While serving on several American and British expeditions to Nares Strait, on several occasions he was reported to be lonely and ready to leave the expeditions. For example, at his party's wintering quarters on 16 November 1853, Elisha Kent Kane wrote that "poor Hans has been severely homesick." Three days earlier the Native hunter had packed his clothes and rifle and bid the crew goodbye. Wrote Kane: "It turns out that besides his mother there is another one of the softer sex at Fiskernaes that the boy's heart is dreaming of. He looked as wretched as any lover of a milder clime."[8] Kane thought he had "treated his nostalgia successfully" by giving the Greenlander a dose of salts and assigning him greater responsibilities. While charging him with the tasks of harnessing dogs, building fox traps, and accompanying him on ice excursions, Kane relieved Hendrik of other duties. According to Kane, this seemed to help improve his state of mind.[9]

A recurring pattern on these expeditions was the flight of Aboriginal employees in response to fears of reprisals from the Europeans. During the Hayes expedition of 1860–61, Hendrik reported the departure of

Umarsuak, one of his Aboriginal companions, from the Americans' wintering camp:

> In the beginning of winter one of these natives turned a Kivigtok [fled from human society to live in the country]. We were unable to make out what might have induced him to do so. The only thing we remembered he had uttered was—"What does J—say when he whispers in passing by me?" When he asked me this, I answered—"I don't know at all." Also of the others he inquired in the same way, but we were quite ignorant of what he meant. Once, when the sea was frozen, he went outside towards tea-time, as we supposed, without any particular purpose. But fancy! All of a sudden he had run away.[10]

Hendrik related that he, too, had run away from an expedition, in his case, from the Nares party's wintering quarters at Floeberg Beach in northern Ellesmere Island in 1875–76. He related: "the sadness of my mind was increased by my having no business on account of the terrible darkness. So when I took a walk near the ship I used to fall a-weeping, remembering my wife and little children, especially that little son of mine who was so tenderly attached to me, that I could not be without him even when I was travelling with the transport boat."[11]

Hendrik stated that he felt stigmatized and isolated by the English members of the expedition. At one point, he thought he overheard several Englishmen plotting to kill him and fled the ship in fear of his life. Captain George Nares sent out a search party in pursuit, and on finding him, gave assurances that no one would harm him. Whether Henrik's fears were exaggerated, he perhaps correctly discerned hostile signals from the others. In his diary at the *Alert*, Reginald Fulford recorded the skepticism of his British colleagues following Hendrik's disappearance: "Of course any amount of yarns were started up how he was going to make away with himself &c, &c."[12] In his own notebooks of the expedition, British officer Albert Markham wrote disapprovingly of Hans, stating that he did not like his abrupt manner.[13] Other British expedition members appear to have harboured suspicions about him. During the expedition of Isaac Israel Hayes in the 1860s, Hendrik had been with explorer August Sonntag when he died mysteriously on a sledging trip. The journals of Lieutenant Pelham Aldrich indicate that the British sailors suspected foul play and blamed Hendrik for Sonntag's death.[14] Whether through fear or ignorance, they appear to have treated the Greenlander poorly.

Similar difficulties were reported during the Greely expedition in 1881–84. During the dark period at Fort Conger, Jens Edward and Thorlip Frederick Christiansen, two employees from West Greenland, reportedly were depressed and feeling estranged from their American companions. Their symptoms appeared only a few months after departure from their homes in the Upernavik district and their arrival in northern Ellesmere Island. On 6 December 1881, Dr. Pavy, the expedition surgeon, reported that Christiansen was "morose;"[15] the next day, he wrote that Jens Edward "has been cogitating."[16] In his published expedition report, Lieutenant Greely stated that, like Jens Edward, Frederick said that the men "intended to kill him." In his view, "the men always treated the Eskimo in the kindest and most considerate manner, carefully avoiding any pleasantries with or allusions to them."[17] Greely's unpublished journal confirms the distress of the Greenlanders; he wrote that Jens had "asked Sgt. Rice and Pvt. Biederbick either to kill him or beat him and wanted them to take all his little property as presents."[18] Pavy believed both of the Aboriginal men were being harassed by one of the Americans and identified Corporal Schneider as the perpetrator.[19]

Like Hans Hendrik, Jens Edward was also reported to be lonely for his family back in Greenland. On 8 December 1881, Greely wrote in his journal: "Jens particularly down hearted today. Gave him & Frederick a glass of wine & some figs. Jens says he thinks of his picanninies."[20] Pavy, reporting on this encounter, wrote: "Frederick remains always under the influence,"[21] implying that alcohol was either dispensed or self-administered recurrently to this man, perhaps to alleviate his sorrow. On 13 December, Greely reported that both of the Greenlanders had been depressed for a week or more. Despite showing him several "kindnesses," he wrote that Jens Edward "kept saying he did not deserve [them], that he was bad and I good. He has frequently asked Sgt. Rice or Pvt. Biederbick to kill him. I thought that he was improving."[22]

The next morning, Greely reported that Jens was missing. With torches and dog teams, a search party set out in pursuit. Eventually, they located Jens near Cape Collinson about 32 km from the ship. Sergeant Brainard, one of the searchers, described the scene:

> Riding and running alternately we made good time and in rounding a point about half a mile from the tent, at Cape Murchison, we caught sight of the runaway. He was running at the time but soon stopped after I called to him repeatedly, to assure him that no harm was intended. He appeared sullen and stubbornly refused to answer my question. The Dr. now arrived and addressed him kindly but he refused to say anything to him. He reluctantly accompanied us back to the station.[23]

The search took its toll on the pursuers, as Sergeant George Rice fell from an ice hummock and fractured his shoulder, while Private William Whisler was brought back delirious from the cold.[24] Greely wrote that he was "much vexed" with Jens "but cannot otherwise but feel a certain compassion for him." Surmising that "Spring will give other ideas to the Eskimo," he vowed to discharge both Greenlanders if the supply ship arrived before the next winter.

Only two days later Greely related another dramatic episode, this time concerning Frederick. He wrote:

> This evening Frederick came into my room in quite a state of excitement and said "Good-bye" to me and the Doctor. It was only by a great deal of effort that the Doctor succeeded in quieting him. He stated that he overheard the men planning to shoot him tonight. After all our efforts to reassure him, he remains in an unsettled frame of mind and I am quite in despair as to how he and Jens are to be managed.[25]

Greely's account was corroborated by Sergeant Brainard, who wrote on the same date that Frederick had also appeared in front of the officers "armed with a huge wooden cross, and said that the men were going to shoot him, and that he was going away to die." Brainard added that Pavy assured Frederick that no harm was intended by anyone and that he could remain there in safety. "He must have taken a common sense view of the case as he deferred his flight indefinitely."[26]

Despite his compatriots' skepticism, Greely himself had no doubts of the sincerity of the Greenlanders. He assured Frederick of his intention to care for him and assigned Jens the task of carrying a lantern for one of the men conducting scientific observations that day. Pavy arranged for the two Greenlanders to make a kayak for Greely. There were no further reports of flight by either of the Greenlanders, although Greely later recorded in his journal, in January 1883, that Jens was "somewhat blue," adding that Doctor Pavy "attributes his condition entirely to homesickness."[27] Discussing with Pavy this "strange proceeding on the part of the Esquimaux," Brainard related that the doctor offered another explanation. Since a flight into the polar wilderness in winter was tantamount to suicide, Brainard himself could not account for his behaviour. However, Pavy, "who passed the winter of 1880–81 among the settlements at Disco and Rittenbank [Greenland], says that this is a custom among all Greenlanders when they consider themselves wronged."[28]

"Pibloktoq" (Arctic Hysteria)

Around 1900, recurrent reports by explorers of hysteria among the Inughuit suggested a wide-ranging distress in the period of greatest contact with Euro-Americans. A remarkable phenomenon, reported by

Peary and many of his associates, was "pibloktoq," or so-called arctic hysteria, which they asserted was prevalent in this population, particularly among women. On the basis of these accounts, an extensive scientific literature developed in the United States, as "pibloktoq" became entrenched in cross-cultural psychiatry as a "culture-bound syndrome." Yet, the fact that most of the primary accounts of "pibloktoq" were confined to the Peary era opens the possibility that the phenomenon itself was a product of the contact experience.

Situational data recorded in exploration narratives present opportunities to illuminate the specific reports of arctic hysteria. To this end, the narratives of 40 case reports from the primary source records of the exploration era were compiled, which are appended to my article on the nature and origins of "pibloktoq."[29] A major source for the study of these cases is the collection of Robert E. Peary's unpublished papers at the U.S. National Archives. Of particular interest is the collection of documents relating to Peary's expedition in 1898–1902, when he spent nearly four years with the Inughuit. In addition to Peary's daily diaries, the papers include very detailed diaries and notebooks of Dr. T.S. Dedrick, the expedition's surgeon between 1898 and 1901. Many of Peary's and Dedrick's references to "pibloktoq" were written from various locations on Ellesmere Island, when the party established wintering quarters in the remote northern parts of the island at Fort Conger in 1900–01 or Cape Sheridan in 1905–06 and 1908–09. Caution must be used in the approach to these reports. Euro-American observers such as Peary and Dedrick apparently lumped all manner of behaviour under the catch-all category of "pibloktoq." Nevertheless, the details of these episodes are extremely interesting and bear on a number of issues in Euro-American and Inughuit relations in this period.

In 1900, Peary made his fourth trip to Fort Conger, the station of the ill-fated Greely expedition of 1881-84. Other personnel in his party included about 10 Inughuit men and women, Dedrick, and Peary's long-term assistant, Matthew Henson. It was the first leg of what Peary hoped would be a serious attempt on the North Pole. That spring, while on a sledging excursion to northern Greenland, Peary reported having witnessed a series of "pibloktoq" attacks. Assembling a party consisting of Henson, five Inughuit men, and seven dog teams, Peary departed from Fort Conger on 11 April. Reaching Greenland by 18 April the party camped at Polaris Boat Camp where they encountered "furious," "infernal," and "blinding" snow drift for several days in succession. On 21 April he reported a "very bad" ice foot (the belt of sea ice that freezes fast to the shore), channel pack ice broken up by numerous leads and pools, and a lane of open water three miles wide and extending right across to Ellesmere Island. This meant that the group was stymied, both from northward advance or retreat. Peary wrote: "My 2 Etah men are very down hearted. Have told them will keep them only 5 days longer."[30]

After putting Henson, Sipsu, Ahngmaloktok, and Uutaaq to work hewing a path in the mangled ice foot, Peary again set out on 23 April in a "furious wind and drift." He reported the ice foot to Repulse Harbour was "very trying to sledges and men, wrenching the latter, ripping off ivory shoes and capsizing all sledges repeatedly." When they arrived beside the Black Horn Cliffs, Peary reported, the cliffs were fronted by open water and vulnerable to moving pack ice "crushing against the ice foot where we build our igloo." From this precarious perch he wrote on 24 April that "this camp can well be named Camp Wolf."[31]

The next morning, on waking after a heavy snowfall and with every hole in the *iglooyah* sealed by the snow, Peary wrote, while drinking tea, "Pooblah had a fit and remaining Eskimos began to follow suit." Peary immediately kicked out the igloo door, sent two of the Inughuit men outside, and gave the others a drink of brandy, which "finally quieted them down." Nevertheless, the ominous grinding of the ice and other difficult conditions continued to affect their morale, as Peary wrote that "the open water, the groaning pack, bad weather, and their attack of this morning, has put them in a very timid frame of mind." Peary accordingly sent Sipsu and Asiajuk back to Fort Conger two days later and, on 4, sent two others back, retaining only Ahngmaloktok and Matthew Henson for the arduous balance of the trip.[32]

What did these episodes of "pibloktoq" signify? Clearly they occurred in the context of difficult sledging conditions and objective physical danger. From Peary's description, the camp on the ice foot at Black Horn Cliffs was liable to be crushed by ice floes driving against the shore, and the "groaning" ice pack was a constant reminder of his party's vulnerability to disaster, while the opening leads in Nares Strait threatened to leave them stranded at a site vulnerable to being swamped by waves or crushed by moving pack ice.

By July 1900, Peary and his party were back at Fort Conger, anxiously awaiting the arrival of the *Windward*. Peary was relying on the ship to provide wintering shelter and also to bring pemmican and other supplies in support of continued exploration. Since few alternative provisions had been secured, he sent Dedrick and several of his younger Inughuit employees on a series of hunting trips in the area of Black Rock Vale and the Bellows about 32–40 km west of Fort Conger. While on these trips away from Conger Dedrick reported a series of "piblockto" attacks suffered by Uutaaq (Oh-tah), who was about 25 years old at the time. These references are extremely interesting and warrant quoting at length:

Thursday, 5 July [1900]

After breakfast, Oh-tah had another attack. He came to me, wailing an Eskimo chant, which beat any dirge I ever heard. He was trembling & beating right hand against his breast

Saturday, 7 July

Oh-tah shook & hardly talked as we ate breakfast. I knew what was coming & tried to engage him into pleasant conversation, but he said he wanted no breakfast & he had headache. I could see his hand shake as he lay in his blanket. Pretty soon, out he went & began his wild song, walking straight from tent in stocking feet...He walked to the meat cache, took the calf head & came & buried it under his bed clothes, then went out & toward river at rapid gait...He cried: "The Eskimos, the Eskimos." I said "where?" "Over there," pointing toward river in front of B. Rock Vale...He came back, grabbing on way a muskox boot, which he took into tent, then he remained there, on hands & knees, singing & chanting about friends at Whale Sound...This was a hard attack. His cries & wailing are heart rending

Sunday 8 July

Boy still blue, with loss of appetite. He could not go with me to the bay to see about Pooblah. I forced him to feed the dogs and gave him two doses of opium.[33]

On 8 July, Dedrick encountered Patdloq (Pooblah), who reported that Angutdluk (Ahngoodloo) was experiencing attacks of "pibloktoq" at Fort Conger and that he, Patdloq, had a "slight attack" when he found that Dedrick and Uutaaq were not across the river where he expected to find them. Patdloq then accompanied Dedrick back to camp. Dedrick reported:

Sunday, 8 July

Oh-tah brightened up when the boy came in. I had a big meal & coffee. Then had them shoot at a box at 300 yards, which put them in high glee. I guess the piblockto will cease for a while. Pooblah tells vividly how he dreamed he heard the Eskimos saying "Huk. Huk" ("Get up") to their dogs & he could not convince himself that Eskimos were not near. A dozen times he has told me this dream.

Monday 9 July

Oh-tah had his usual morning crazy spell. Took the calf-head into tent & later a musk ox hoof—same as other day...He announced to me before attack came on that "he was going to like yesterday," in a deploring tone.

Dedrick's account of Uutaaq's attacks provides a sequential description of behaviour labelled as "pibloktoq" seldom available in the literature, enabling the correlation of various factors with the phenomenon. It reveals a number of intriguing details, especially the religious associations represented in Uutaaq's chanting and garnering animal parts as amulets. Jean Blodgett has pointed out that such amulets could be used not only to express relationships with animals, but also to establish connections with other humans.[34] In this case, Uutaaq's collection of a calf head was accompanied by the cry "the Eskimos, the Eskimos," and while picking up a muskox hoof he sang and chanted about "friends at Whale Sound." Whatever else this behaviour signified, there is an obvious implication that Uutaaq was feeling lonely for his friends and relatives back in Greenland. The same dynamic seems to be present in Patdloq's recurring dream about the Eskimos being nearby. Also of interest is the disappearance of Uutaaq's depression and "pibloktoq" with the arrival of Patdloq on July 8, only to return the following day after Patdloq went back to Fort Conger. Here again his "pibloktoq" appeared to be connected to his separation from his friend.

Heightened fears of physical illness, coupled with a breakdown in the effectiveness of shamanistic cures, might account for some of the anxiety expressed in "pibloktoq" attacks during this expedition. Jane M. Murphy, in her PhD thesis on the psychopathology of an Alaska Eskimo village on St. Lawrence Island, argued that for non-Western peoples, periods of waning shamanistic practice and beliefs were times of particular vulnerability in emotional and mental stability, especially before Western psychiatric therapy replaced its shamanistic antecedents.[35] At Fort Conger on 23 September 1900, Dedrick reported that a female angakoq was engaged in shamanic practice in an apparent attempt to cure the woman Elatu, who was then dying of "liver trouble." He wrote: "She started in piblockto while in the sick woman house, but ceased when I ordered to stop."[36]

Dedrick not only interfered with shamanistic healing practices, but encouraged the young Inughuit in his charge to break food taboos. While in the field on 26 August 1900, he reported that he, Patdloq, and Uutaaq had each killed a hare. Since they were immature animals, the two Inughuit were prohibited from eating them. However, Dedrick stated: "Now I am authority on these things, and I say it is all right for you to eat the hare." On this advice, they ate the meat. Evidently Patdloq felt uneasy doing this, as Dedrick heard him cry out to his dead father "a sort of prayer apology."[37] Dedrick's and Peary's diaries indicate additional stresses on the Inughuit that might be connected to the "pibloktoq" attacks at Fort Conger. One of their fundamental worries appears to have been hunger, or the fear of starvation. On 25 October 1900, Dedrick reported that while the Americans still had some meat for their own use, "dog meat & meat for Esk are all gone. One of the women had a crying spell this morning on account of being brought here & being so often on short rations."[38]

One of the most frequently cited episodes of "pibloktoq" occurred at Cape Sheridan and during Peary's last polar voyage in 1908–09. Beginning with the psychiatrist A.A. Brill, various scientists have uncritically reproduced Peary's and MacMillan's reports of endemic hysteria among the Inughuit women on this voyage. On one day, five of the 20 women were said to have suffered "fits."[39] Despite the fact that this report of epidemic hysteria departs significantly from the usual stories of individual attacks, little contextual information has been utilized to help explain this extraordinary event.

Perhaps the Cape Sheridan "pibloktoq" epidemic can be best understood as the culmination of a cumulative series of stresses, rather than the product of specific precipitating occurrences. Northern Ellesmere Island was a region that had anxious associations for the Inughuit. In 1906, during Peary's return from Cape Sheridan, eight Inughuit families left his ship at Fort Conger, ostensibly in a dispute over reductions in their rations. According to Malaurie, the actual reason was that "they found the monotony of life on board oppressive and its comforts upsetting."[40] Their departure also occurred shortly after the *Roosevelt* was heavily knocked about by the pack ice in Nares Strait.[41] Whatever their reasons for abandoning Peary's company, their winter was described as a "hard one."[42] The Inughuit wintered in the interior at Lake Hazen, according to Malaurie, they apparently came close to dying from hunger. The group arrived at Etah eight months later on foot, most of their dogs having perished en route.[43]

Only a year later, the Inughuit were back with Peary at Cape Sheridan. After reaching their destination on 8 September 1908, the members of the expedition set about their autumn work, the men preparing for various hunting and sledging parties, the women setting fox traps along the shore and making fishing excursions to lakes in the vicinity.[44] This was the period of rapid transition from autumn to winter; at Cape Sheridan's far northerly latitude, the sun completely disappears by October 12.[45] By early October, 21 of the expedition's 22 Inughuit men had left with autumn sledging parties. Within days of the departure of the last party, according to MacMillan, "pibylokto was now common among the women."[46]

While there are few specific details, several possible factors may be noted. The "pibloktoq" attacks occurred soon after the departure of the male hunters at a time of year that carried ominous associations for the Inughuit. This was the season during which a general melancholy has been observed by various visitors to the Thule District.[47] In this case, the women had been left behind on the edge of the Arctic Ocean on the cusp of the long polar night. Freuchen, who knew the Inughuit well, wrote that "if a woman happens to lose her husband during travel in desolate places, she frequently starves to death along with all her children."[48] At Cape Sheridan, the women were in unfamiliar surroundings in a region known to have brought hardships and death to Inughuit individuals during Peary's previous expeditions.[49]

The spatial distribution of "pibloktoq" episodes generates some noteworthy associations, confirming that the great majority of reported cases occurred while the Inughuit were on extended duty away from their homeland (Figure 76). Of the 40 assembled cases, 22 took place in the far northern reaches of the High Arctic, several hundred miles from the Thule District. Twenty-one were in northern Ellesmere Island, and one episode was reported in the extreme north of Greenland. Five other episodes occurred on the central Ellesmere coast, including three at Bache Peninsula, one at Payer Harbour, and one at Cape D'Urville. Despite several winters spent by the observers with the Inughuit in their homeland, the Thule District, only 13 episodes were reported in this area, including seven at or near Etah, three at North Star Bay on Wolstenholme Sound, one at Qaanaaq, and another on Northumberland Island. Interestingly, five of the cases at Etah occurred within two months after one third of the group's population had departed to serve on Peary's North Polar expedition of 1908–09. Four fifths of the episodes, then, took place after the removal of the Inughuit from familiar surroundings, or the artificial separation of many families for extended periods.

For some individuals, episodes of "pibloktoq" or other physiological symptoms of hysteria might well have expressed "indirect resistance to social and occupational demands for adequate performance"[50] in stressful situations. In some cases, the resort to "pibloktoq" appeared to represent an effort to equalize the relationship with the Euro-Americans who held power over them during these expeditions. At least, this might be inferred from the comment by Robert Bartlett, Peary's navigator in 1905, about an Inughuit woman's "pibloktoq": "I would diagnose it as pure cussedness. She wants her way and cannot get it."[51] Scripted behaviour is also suggested in Donald MacMillan's comment that, on the day after displaying "pibloktoq" at Cape Sheridan, an Inughuit woman told him "that she did not have piblokto, that she was only shamming."[52]

The assumption of sick roles in coercive contexts was apparently not limited to women. Peary and his American colleagues complained of Inughuit men feigning illness when placed in stressful situations. Acting out hysteria could have released these men from immediate demands, either through cessation of hunting or sledging or dismissal from the undesired tasks. This, at any rate, was Peary's view, as he recorded his skeptical reaction to Angutdluk's "spells" during a sledg-

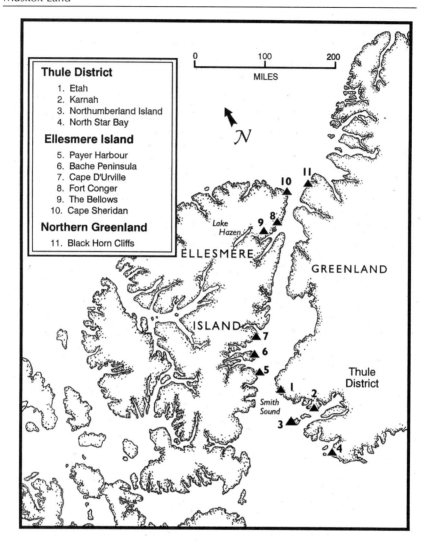

Figure 76: Map showing the spatial distribution of "pibloktoq" episodes on Ellesmere Island and northern Greenland

ing excursion along the ice foot of Robeson Channel in 1900. He wrote: "He walked off all right. I am disgusted with him."[53] Peary's skepticism was echoed by Bartlett when the same Inughuaq became "sick" and "lost his nerve" on a sledging excursion in 1905 along the north coast of Ellesmere Island.[54] Similarly, Dr. Louis Wolf wrote in 1906 that Inughuit men were shamming to shirk their responsibilities: "Angelo [Angutdluk], Ahletah, and Akpudingwah are all complaining of pains in various parts of their bodies, but, I am sure that the proposed sledging is the cause of the pains."[55]

Other socially disruptive aspects of the contact experience may have played a role in generating the distress labelled as "pibloktoq." Various observers have commented on the diversion of Inughuit hunting resources and productive effort from their own subsistence to aid Peary in his polar quest. Danish scientist H.P. Steensby, who visited the Thule District a year after Peary's final departure, wrote of Peary:

> He exhausts the Polar Eskimos' working power for the benefit of his expeditions towards the Pole, and he procures an economic advantage in buying up in great quantities the tribes' costly products, fox and bear skins.[56]

More recently, social scientist Rolf Gilberg also asserted that Peary hired the most skilful hunters and the best dog teams for his expeditions, in the process removing the "best manpower" from the Thule region for extended periods.[57] Finally, as is discussed in the next chapter, the Peary era was also characterized by recurrent infectious disease epidemics with high rates of mortality.

After the establishment of RCMP detachments on Ellesmere Island in the 1920s Inughuit women living at these posts also displayed symptoms similar to "pibloktoq." In March and early April 1928, one RCMP officer was left in charge of the Bache Peninsula post while the other officers and Native special constables were away on patrol. On 6 April 1928, he wrote:

> Native Coolitanga's [Qulutana's] wife went crazy this evening. She went some way out on the ice and tore off all her upper garments and created a great deal of noise. She had previously complained of dizziness for which I gave her medicine. She appears to be suffering with some lung complaint, which if contagious, is a menace to the natives living with her.[58]

In the same month, the detachment journal records that another woman, "Native Ahkeeoo's [Aqioq's] wife" was "suffering with unconsciousness."[59] Both reported episodes occurred after their spouses had departed on extended patrols away from the detachment.[60]

While it is difficult to establish a specific causal relationship, most of the episodes of "pibloktoq" appear to be connected to the psychological pressures imposed by contact with Europeans. For the Inughuit, the ever-present danger of infectious disease brought by the Europeans exerted a psychological toll in this period of uncertainty. A further source of anxiety was the breakdown in the effectiveness of shamanistic cures, undermining the community's faith in the capacity of their leaders to ensure their well-being. In the context of these stresses, "pibloktoq" appears to have been a catch-all rubric under which explorers lumped Inughuit anxiety reactions, symptoms of physical and sometimes feigned illness, and shamanistic practice. As is discussed in the next section, some cases of "pibloktoq" probably also represented expressions of resistance to patriarchy and sexual coercion. While the seasonal distribution of "pibloktoq" episodes, presented in Chapter 2, suggests that environmental factors played a role, arctic hysteria was principally the product of the stresses experienced by Inughuit on the polar expeditions. A reasonable conclusion is that "pibloktoq" cannot be separated from the contact situation or the role of Europeans in precipitating the behaviour they labelled as hysteria.[61] These conclusions have recently been supported in professional psychiatric scholarship by specialists who have accepted the argument that this phenomenon cannot be understood in abstraction from the social contexts of European–Inughuit contact implicated in historical occurrences of "pibloktoq."[62]

Gender Relations and Stresses in the Contact Situation

There seems to be little doubt that, during the peak of the exploration era, the lives of Inughuit women were dramatically changed by the contact experience. While in Peary's employ, they began to shift their productive labour from an exclusively family-oriented focus, to the production of food, garments, and other products for the American expeditions. Not only did their labour contribute to exploration successes, the women were engaged in trapping foxes for Peary, which he sold for profit in the United States. While the contact experience did not necessarily entail a change in the kinds of activities, the scale of production and orientation shifted from supporting a self-sufficient family unit and community to production for an external market. Evidence of disruption to gender relations within the Inughuit population suggest that the effects of the contact experience extended beyond economic change to significant impacts on society.

We lack specifics as to how the introduction of commercial hunting and employment may have affected the position of women in

Figure 77: Matthew Henson and unidentified Inughuit woman on the deck of the SS
   Roosevelt, 1908–09. National Geographic Society (Washington, DC), Robert E.
   Peary Collection, Project No. 02116, Consecutive No. 2105, Picture Id. No.
   122369A, Picture Record No. 130975.

Inughuit society. However, comparative evidence from other North
American contexts may be instructive. In a study of the impact of
contact on Plains Native cultures, anthropologist Alan M. Klein noted
a dramatic shift in power relations during the era of early trade. Not
only was the nature of their labour changed, the women of these
cultures were effectively shut out of the decision-making process by the
males, who assumed on their behalf the role of negotiators with European traders.[63]

Another significant change was in relations between the sexes in
Inughuit society. During Peary's expeditions, American members of his
party became involved in sexual relationships with Inughuit women.
While some of these relationships appear to have been consensual (Figure 77), they were complicated by differences in power between the
partners and sometimes also disrupted existing spousal relationships of
Inughuit men and women.

Peary's approach to the women of these expeditions was patriarchal;
he placed them at the bottom of a strict hierarchy organized along racial

and gender lines. In 1885, he articulated his vision of the ideal exploration party, which he likened to "the physical structure of a tough, hardy man." He wrote:

> Following this analogy, one intelligent white man would represent the head, two other white men selected solely for their courage, determination, physical strength, and devotion to the leader would represent the arms, and the driver and the natives the body and legs. The presence of women an absolute necessity to render the men contented.[64]

He went on to remark: "Feminine companionship not only causes greater contentment but as a matter of both physical and mental health and the retention of the top notch of manhood it is a necessity."[65]

Peary's instrumentalist view of the sexual role of Aboriginal females affords an insight into the pressures placed on the women who accompanied his expeditions to the north. Finding occasion to implement his plans, Peary assumed the role of patriarch, dispensing Inughuit women to his employees as if they were his personal property. At Fort Conger in 1900, he wrote in his diary about an exchange with Dr. Dedrick: "Dr. approached me on the woman question today. He wants to take Saune and have her live in with him permanently. I told him certainly, and that I knew he would be more contented and better physically and mentally for it."[66]

Peary's "philanthropy" extended to offering women in pre-existing conjugal relationships to other Inughuit men, as in the case of the spouse of Ittukusuk. After Ittukusuk had departed the Thule District as one of Dr. Frederick Cook's guides on his polar expedition of 1908–09, Peary took this man's female partner to Cape Columbia on Ellesmere's northern coast to serve as a seamstress for his own expedition. According to Peter Freuchen, Peary "gave the girl away to a young hunter in need of a wife."[67] Peary's interventions were reportedly extensive. On his return to Etah, Peary, used to exercising power over the Inughuit, "allowed all the Eskimos whose marriages he had arranged to keep their women forever."[68]

Further evidence of the treatment of Inughuit women as sexual objects can be found in Peary's book *Northward Over the Great Ice*, an account of his 1893–95 expedition to northern Greenland. Peary illustrated this two-volume book with numerous photographs of Inughuit, including several images of bare-breasted women. Ostensibly included for ethnological interest, at least two photographs presented unclad women in provocative poses staged, it appears, for the presumed delight of his Euro-American heterosexual male readers. These photographs are titled "An Arctic Bronze" and "Mother of the Seals."[69] In another image, Peary presented a larger Inughuit woman with the condescending caption: "Her curves were a trifle heavy."[70] Imbued with the attitudes of nineteenth century patriarchy, Peary and his readers were apparently unaware of the implicitly demeaning character of these images and commentaries.

Peary's actions apparently extended to the tacit approval of sexual harassment or coercion of Inughuit women by other Americans during the 1893–95 expedition. While based at the Anniversary Lodge at Etah, expedition member Evelyn Briggs Baldwin wrote of repeated attempts by four Americans to coerce Inughuit women into sexual relations. On 20 November 1893, he reported "Carr's boast that he would take 'a couple of the women to bed with him'" and "Vincent's remarking that he would take his turn later." He observed: "later developments almost confirmed me in the execution of their assertion." On the following evening, Baldwin reported:

> Two of them, Swain and Davidson...inveigled two of the young native women—mere girls—in with them and attempted to have them submit to their carnal desires. Neither would do so, however, one of them crying... "the Doctor cashany," "the Doctor cashany," meaning "the Doctor only," "the Doctor only," from which it would seem that the physician and surgeon of the Expedition has a monopoly on the poor woman's body.[71]

The indignant writer stated that he was on the verge of reporting these transgressions to Lieutenant Peary, when he recalled that Peary had already been informed and had not acted on this knowledge. He wrote that "the men, by various remarks, have intimated that the Lieutenant countenances the licentiousness practised by them." Further, a Mr. Stokes had informed him that Peary "considered it *necessary* [Baldwin's emphasis] for the men to do so and that it would not be long before all in the party would be 'at it,' etc., etc."[72]

Several of the Americans apparently continued to pursue Inughuit women, including those with Aboriginal spouses, with disruptive effects. On 28 November, Baldwin observed that Swain "attempted to persuade Ah-now-we [Annowgwe], wife of Ah-sha-yu [Asiajuk], to sleep with him, but her husband became very indignant and left the lodge in tears and started back to his igloo.... He took his faithless *koonah* with him." After this incident the diarist related that he "remarked openly that he objected to having the lodge converted to a whore-house." On 2 December, he wrote that two colleagues "are still unjustly [sic] incensed at the continued pollution of their quarters." Two weeks later, on 10 December, he reported that "some of the *careless* [Baldwin's emphasis] men gave cider to the natives in order to make them 'tipsy.'"[73]

Baldwin's observations provide a rare glimpse into a previously unexamined issue, the presence of sexual harassment or coercion on Peary's expeditions. The power imbalance in the sexual relationships between Americans and Inughuit women are apparent in these exchanges. Baldwin's diary entries suggests that several Americans' abuse of their position of power precipitated distress for several women, evidenced in reactions of hysteria or "pibloktoq." Two photographs taken during Peary's last polar voyage in 1908–09 are revealing; they show Alnayah, an Inughuit woman in distress, naked from the waist up and held by two smiling Americans as they posed for the camera in front of the *Roosevelt* at Cape Sheridan in northern Ellesmere Island.[74] Two other photographs show the Americans' remedy for this woman's hysteria. Their solution was to lash her to a wooden board in a kind of straitjacket, which they suspended from the boom of the ship's foremast. Enjoying a laugh together, the American men are shown gathered around to pose beside the tied-up woman, with the Inughuit men positioned slightly farther away. From the top deck, the Inughuit women look on, relegated to observer status by this show of Western male dominance (Figure 78).

Another source of strain was the frequent separation of Inughuit women from their spouses, as Peary assigned the men to extended hunting or reconnaissance trips away from the base camps. In February 1901, Dedrick observed that these separations had negative psychological consequences: "Soundah does poorly when Pooblah [Patdloq] is gone, is listless, eats little, and sleeps all the time."[75] That April, Peary, dividing a sledging party at Distant Cape on Robeson Channel, sent one woman's partner up the coast without her. He recorded her reaction: "Ionah, wife of Ahngmaloktok cried freely, poor girl, at parting from her husband, but I comforted her as best I could."[76] Also in this connection, two apparent episodes of "pibloktoq" reported by an RCMP officer at the Bache Peninsula Detachment on Ellesmere Island in 1928 occurred a week or more after the Aboriginal spouses of both women departed on extended patrols away from the detachment.[77]

Beyond the dynamics of male-female relationships on the expeditions, Peary's removal of hunters from Thule had an impact on the relationships of spouses separated by the voyages to the north. Peter Freuchen wrote that the Inughuaq Sigluk left his family to accompany Peary on his last expedition. He returned to find his spouse Aleqasinnguaq (Alakrasina) had been "abducted" during his absence by another hunter, Uisaakassak (Uvigsakavsik).[78] Another source of disruption was that, by his own admission, Peary took "only the best" Inughuit hunters with him on his extended trips to the north, increasing the vulnerability of the families left behind.[79]

Figure 78: "Alnayah having "Piblock-to" (Arctic hysteria), on board SS *Roosevelt*." Photo courtesy of the Peary-MacMillan Arctic Museum (Bowdoin College), Photograph no. NP-26.

Disruptions in gender relations continued during the tenure of the RCMP at its detachments on Ellesmere Island between 1922 and 1940. For many of the Inughuit women who accompanied their spouses to these remote locations, life at the remote Ellesmere Island posts was difficult. During their time at the RCMP detachments, the women must have experienced a high degree of isolation. To compound their difficulties, the Euro-Canadian policemen took the Inughuit men away from their families on extended patrols lasting as long as two months away from the station. Since Inughuit societies were organized around kinship as well as family relationships, their removal to isolated postings effectively cut them off from important social support networks. While we lack the women's testimony, occasional references to hysteria, reported in the Bache Peninsula detachment journal, are evidence of their distress.

The RCMP may also have unintentionally contributed to the breakup of Inughuit families serving at these posts. In 1925, Inspector C.E. Wilcox wrote that two Inughuit hunters had been recruited to serve at the Bache Peninsula detachment to be established in the following year. One of them was Nukappianguaq, selected apparently because "he is reputed to be the best hunter in north Greenland." Nukappianguaq was then living with a younger woman while his wife resided 100 km farther south. The young woman asked to accompany Nukappianguaq when he moved to Ellesmere Island, and Wilcox recommended grant-ing the request as "the elderly woman would not be capable of sewing for the two Eskimos and members of the detachment as well."[80]

Inughuit women serving on the American expeditions and later at the RCMP detachments were effectively shut out of a decision-making process organized along gender lines. While Inughuit men also lacked power in these interactions, they sometimes shared a degree of gender-based camaraderie with the Europeans or Americans. During Peary's expeditions, for example, bonds of friendship developed be-tween Inughuit and Matthew Henson. On the extended RCMP patrols, Aboriginal men necessarily assumed a leadership role based on their travelling and hunting skills. By contrast, the women often found them-selves without access even to limited forms of social interaction with the European bosses.

In the spring of 1928, Enalunguaq, the spouse of Nukappiannguaq, reportedly left the detachment and returned to Greenland while her husband was on patrol.[81] Two years later, Knud Rasmussen wrote to the Canadian government to advise them that, according to the laws of his home district, Nukappiannguaq was liable to pay alimony to sup-port his wife and children back in Greenland.[82] While we lack informa-tion on the specifics of this domestic breakup, it can be surmised that the isolation of the posting, coupled with frequent absences of the men on patrol away from the detachment, contributed to the stresses of interpersonal relationships at these posts.

Cultural Conflict: The Deaths of Marvin and Piugaattoq

Few events more dramatically illustrate the stresses of European-Inughuit contact than the deaths of Ross Marvin in 1909 and Piugaattoq in 1914. These events go to the root of many key issues: conflicting cultural values, the incompatibility of American hubris and Aboriginal con-cepts of survival, and the inherent problems in imposing a Euro-American command structure in a context requiring consensus-building.

In 1909, Ross Marvin was a member of Peary's last polar expedition. That spring, he and three Inughuit were charged with establishing food caches along the route of Peary's trek across the polar ice pack. The Inughuit members of the party included Kridtluktoq, one of Peary's best guides (see cover photograph), his younger cousin Inukittoq (Inukitsorkpaluk), and Aqioq, another experienced traveller. They accompanied Peary as far as 86° 38' N., before he sent them back on 26 March to rejoin the others at Floeberg Beach.[83] When the three Inughuit men arrived at the ship sev-eral weeks later, they related the grim news that Marvin was dead.

What happened on that fateful trip? On returning to the coast of Ellesmere Island, Marvin's Inughuit companions reported that during the return trip, he had fallen through the ice and perished in the freezing water. It was only much later, after the departure of the Americans, that a different story of Marvin's death began to emerge—according to this version he had been shot by an Inughuit member of his own sledge division.

After Peter Freuchen's arrival at Thule in 1910, two members of that party related to him their version of the sequence of events leading to the American's death.[84] It was consistent with Kridtluktoq's reported admission to the homicide when interviewed by Knud Rasmussen in 1926,[85] when the story was first reported to the general public by the *New York Times*.[86] Freuchen reported that there had been friction; Marvin and the Inughuit did not like one other. Marvin, they stated, could not understand their language. Whenever they talked among themselves, he demanded to know what they were saying or laughing about. The distrust evident in his behaviour increased as the trip progressed. When the small party encountered several wide leads covered with fresh ice, the Inughuit stopped, explaining that it would be best to wait until the ice had frozen more solidly. Marvin became angry, apparently, because he thought they were lazy; he ordered his companions to keep moving. The first time, he relented, but when they refused to cross a second patch of new ice, he charged forward and fell through the ice. His companions rescued him, but the following day, he again commanded them to cross a dangerous stretch of new ice. The impasse was only resolved when Kridtluktoq found a detour around the ice crack.

The conflict between Marvin and the Inughuit came to a head the next day, when Inukitsorkpaluk became ill, and Marvin ordered the others to abandon him in the snow house they had constructed on the ice. When Marvin began to load the sledge of the sick man, suggesting he was serious about abandoning Inukitsorkpaluk, Kridtluktoq retrieved his gun and shot the American through the head. The Inughuit decided to tell the Americans that, in ignorance, Marvin had tried to cross unsafe ice, had crashed through, and drowned. Since he had already fallen through the ice, this could have occurred in any case. After cutting a hole in the ice, they tied Marvin's gun and scientific instruments to his body and scuttled it. After resting perhaps two days in the *iglooyah* and eating a much larger meal than Marvin would have allowed, Inukitsorkpaluq recovered sufficiently to travel, and the three returned to the ship. The words of Inukittoq (Inukitsorkpaluk), nicknamed "Harrigan" by the Americans, if accurately translated, described and explained the sequence of events from his perspective:

As soon as he [Marvin] came up to us we saw that he was very excited and quite out of balance. He waved his clenched fist right up in my face and yelled at me. We stood silent and couldn't understand him. He was never that way before. He was like a sane man who for the moment was without the use of his faculties.

Suddenly he yelled that he couldn't bear to see me around any more. He would not have me in the party any longer. I must go my own way since I would not follow his tracks. He ordered that all my clothes should be left there. He undid the lashings on the sled and threw my clothes on the ice. But there were no provisions left for me.

Kudlooktoo [Kridtluktoq] told me later that Marvin kept on talking and yelling all the way. He said that I should not be allowed to come into the snow house when they camped, and that I should have nothing to eat and nothing to drink, even after we got to land.

Kudlooktoo understood, as he later told me, that if I didn't starve or freeze to death I would perish of thirst. Thirst is, as you know, the worst thing for us.

It was evident to Kudlooktoo that now Marvin didn't know what he was doing, and it was impossible to try to speak to him. Kudlooktoo was so distressed that he couldn't stand it, and his tears were running all the way as he drove the dogs.

I stood on the ice puzzled as to what I should do. All this had happened so suddenly. Part of my clothes that were left on the ice were wet, and because it was impossible for me to dry them I took with me only a pair of kamiks [boots]. The day was very cold and I couldn't stand still long on the ice.

Then I followed after the other two. During the afternoon, we came to a big lead [open water]. I saw that the sled was stopped there and Marvin and Kudlooktoo had gone ahead to find a place to get over. While they were away I reached the sled. I didn't dare go after them because I was afraid of Marvin. I just dropped down on the sled without thinking what next might happen.

While I was sitting there I saw Kudlooktoo on a big piece of rough ice and he yelled to me that I should bring him his rifle. He had seen a seal in the open water. I brought him his rifle and went back to the sled. I heard a shot a moment after and expected that Kudlooktoo had shot the seal. But right away he came over to me and told me what had happened. He had shot Marvin in order to save my life.[87]

Then, according to Inukitsorkpaluk, Kridtluktoq asked him not to reveal the actual circumstances of Marvin's death to the Americans. Fearing retribution, he invented an explanation that Marvin had drowned while trying to cross a lead, which was the story they presented to Peary's assistants on their return to Ellesmere Island.[88]

As soon as the news story broke, various arctic personalities began to impose their own interpretations as to what led to Marvin's death.

Fitzhugh Green, who shot an Inughuit man in another intense encounter on the trail in 1914, blamed Marvin's death on his own Inughuit guides. He asserted:

> I would reconstruct the scene as follows: The two men with Marvin realized their small party had little food left. They were, like other Eskimos, frightened at being left out on the Polar Sea. Marvin wanted to follow the old trail back to land. He refused to lighten his sledges by throwing away important scientific instruments and records. The natives finally went into one of their fits of despair that come under such circumstances and disposed of the white man, who was both the cause of their plight and, to their minds, the obstacle to their safe return.[89]

The Danish explorer Knud Rasmussen, who interrogated both Kridtluktoq and Inukitsoq and reported his findings to the Danish legation, came to a different conclusion. He wrote:

> The psychological explanation of this entire drama is close at hand, and in no single instance is there any reason to doubt that the reports of the Eskimos are truthful. An entire winter's fatiguing travel got the best of Marvin's nerves, and in a fit of anger he acted without thinking. He had hardly been in earnest in wanting to leave Inukitsoq behind, but the Eskimos looked upon his action as if he really meant it, and for this reason, I feel, they were fully justified in considering the situation dangerous. Furthermore, the close of Inukitsoq's report makes clear all the motives. As the matter stands now, I don't see how Kudlooktoo can in any way be held responsible for the sad outcome of the trouble.[90]

Readers will have to decide for themselves whether Green or Rasmussen more accurately reconstructed the dynamics of inter-group relations of that fateful party. It is not difficult to imagine that the extremely difficult conditions of these support parties exacted a physical and psychological toll on all members. With a member of their group ailing and encountering a string of ocean leads, they were evidently in a situation of objective danger. Robert Bartlett, who was also involved in sledging provisions across the ice pack, observed both physical illness and anxiety among his Native companions during the sledge relays across the Arctic ice pack:

> The Eskimos were beginning to get restless, and some spoke of returning to land. They did not say it in words, but they were gradually getting sick, or lame...On the 7th, Poodloona, my best man, went to Peary and told him he was very sick, Panikpak said that he was sick also, and that he wanted to go back to the ship."[91]

Marvin, too, was experiencing considerable physical distress on his foray over the ice pack. Bartlett later wrote of their last encounter on the trail. When he observed Marvin to be "lame," Bartlett enquired about his condition. His Inughuit guides informed him that the American was "badly hurt," suffering from frostbite to his heels and all his toes. Visiting Marvin in his snow shelter, Bartlett confirmed this report, as he found him dressing his feet. "All the skin was taken off of both heels and all his toes. He was in a sorry plight, but as far as I could see, it did not worry him in the least."[92]

Complicating the situation was the factor of time, as members of the relay parties raced against the clock. Peary, in three notes to Marvin within six days, repeatedly exhorted him to "hurry."[93] In one note, Peary insisted that they cross the Big Lead, emphasizing that "it is *vital* [Peary's emphasis] that you overtake us and give us fuel."[94] To meet Peary's expectations, Marvin in turn was obliged to make similar demands on his own party, in the process placing his employer's objectives ahead of their safety. When orders from Peary mutated into erratic and authoritarian demands on his assistants, Marvin pushed them beyond the limit.

An incident with many parallels to the Marvin affair, which also ended in tragedy, was the shooting of the Inughuit man Piugaattoq by American Fitzhugh Green during MacMillan's Crocker Land Expedition of 1913–17. Like the Marvin affair, this incident was not officially reported in the exploration era. It was later recounted in the books of Peter Freuchen, a Danish colleague of Knud Rasmussen, who lived with the Inughuit after 1910. More recently, an acknowledgment that the incident had occurred appeared in an extract from MacMillan's field notes, reproduced in a book by Harrison J. Hunt, the expedition's surgeon.[95]

The incident took place on a sledging excursion to northern Axel Heiberg Island in 1914. MacMillan and Green, supported by several Inughuit guides, were attempting to verify the existence of "Crocker Land," the land Peary thought he had sighted in 1906 to the northwest of Cape Thomas Hubbard (Cape Stallworthy). The excursion was a difficult one and most of the Inughuit guides turned back before they reached Axel Heiberg Island. With only two guides remaining, the party arrived at Cape Stallworthy at the northern tip of Axel Heiberg Island on 14 April. From here, MacMillan struck out over the pack ice of the Arctic Ocean in search of the elusive land which Peary claimed lay to the northwest. After 10 days and travelling 275 km, MacMillan turned back. On the return journey, Macmillan spent several days searching for Sverdrup's records left at Cape Stallworthy, then crossed Nansen Sound to retrieve Peary's record at Land's Lokk on Ellesmere Island.

Meanwhile, Fitzhugh Green, the expedition's physicist, departed with his Inughuit guide, Piugaattoq, to complete the survey of northwestern Axel Heiberg Island. Six days later, Green returned alone, driving Piugaattoq's dogs, "looking very pale and haggard and much worn"[96] and "like a ghost."[97] He announced that Piugaattoq was dead, having supposedly been buried in an avalanche. Drawing MacMillan aside, the agitated Green revealed the shocking truth: he had killed Piugaattoq with two shots from his rifle.

MacMillan attempted to reconstruct the incident from Green's verbal account. Green reported that he and Piugaattoq had been caught in a blizzard along the coast. After spending the night in a shelter dug out of snow, Piugaattoq reportedly "refused to proceed south when it partly cleared and said he was going home." Leaving Green's dogs and sledge behind, Piugaattoq and Green started out with only one komatik toward an intended rendezvous with MacMillan. Piugaattoq continued to drive his dogs hard, while Green, his feet freezing, could not keep up the pace. Twice, he claimed, his Native companion tried to get away from him, which would mean his own death. Seizing a rifle, Green ordered Piugaattoq to instead follow him, but Piugaattoq refused and moved in a different direction. Then occurred the tragic climax: "Green fired over his head first to warn him. He did not stop, so Green shot him twice, once in the body and once on the head, splitting it open." Green then carried the body to Cape Thomas Hubbard, where he left it on the ground.[98]

A more extensive and revealing account is provided in Green's own diary, which suggests a story of pre-existing distrust, deteriorating interpersonal relations, and intercultural conflicts. These conflicts were worsened by a situation of objective danger. During the blizzard on 30 April 1914, Green wrote, there had been a disagreement with Piugaattoq over the komatik and dogs. The dogs were tied at a distance from their snow house and Green feared they would be lost unless secured. According to Green, Piugaattoq told him that the dogs were fine where they were. Green wrote, bitterly: "Later we could do nothing to save [them]." He added that when Piugaattoq went out to build a second *iglooyah*, he tied his dogs in a different place without telling him.[99]

There were problems with their primus stove, which generated excessive smoke, and Piugaatoq refused to make a hole in the roof for an out-take. Green remarked: "In consequence the fumes made us both sick & P[ewahto] vomited several times." Piugaattoq complained that MacMillan's stoves were "no good." Then, according to Green, Piugaattoq commented that MacMillan, the expedition leader did not like him, and therefore had taken Ittukusuk with him instead. The

Inughuaq told Green that they could not take any skins back with them, as the American's dogs would not survive and the other teams were weak.

The next day, on 1 May, the blizzard abated. Green and Piugaattoq packed all their gear and provisions in the Inughuaq's komatik, and Green announced they would continue with their reconnaissance work along the coast. Piugaattoq disagreed, saying that MacMillan had specified that they should take "only one sleep down the coast & that Mac was 'Kashmu' (boss)." Green responded by asserting that he (Green) was in charge until they returned to MacMillan. In the meantime, the wind picked up and they were again confined to their snow house.

When the two men started again in the morning, the blizzard had worsened. Piugaattoq refused to go anywhere other than return to their *iglooyah* at Cape Thomas Hubbard. Green found it increasingly difficult to run, and he could not ride for fear of freezing his wet and cold feet. According to Green, Piugaatoq "said he was tired of the white man & that he was going back to Etah now. He said Mac had promised him a lot of things but that he didn't think he would get them."

The two men departed their camp with one sledge. Green related that Piugaattoq refused to proceed south and whipped the dogs to move as quickly as possible. Green could not keep up with him and demanded that he proceed more slowly. Piugaattoq then told Green to ride on the komatik, which he refused to do for fear of freezing his feet. Undeterred, Piugaattoq insisted on proceeding back to the *iglooyah* and invited Green to follow his trail, if he wished to walk. But Green found walking difficult and his visibility was poor in the wind and drifting snow. By his account, "Finally I grew desperate because I could not keep up." Piugaattoq kept whipping up his dogs and, according to Green, kept leaving the trail. Brandishing his rifle, the American ordered Piugaattoq to follow behind him; as he wrote in his diary: "I knew that I could make the point all right."[100] When Piugaattoq again left the trail, Green fired a shot over his head. The Inughuaq continued without stopping and Green fired twice, bringing him down.

It is impossible to know what thoughts raced through Green's mind at this juncture, but his subsequent actions suggest he was in a state of panic. He began to prepare a paper trail, perhaps with the intention of extricating himself from the difficult position in which he had placed himself. In his diary, apparently written that night, he wrote that, finding Piugaattoq "unconscious," he lashed him to the komatik and turned back for the little *iglooyah* they had recently departed. Then, after clearing out the snow and moving the stove and skins into the shelter, he wrote: "I had taken P[iugaattoq] in first & when I tried to do something for him found that he was dead."[101] Here, Green implied that, concerned about Piugaattoq's welfare, he had tried to render aid to a wounded man. This false implication is contradicted by MacMillan's diary reconstruction of Green's words to him on his return. According to MacMillan, Green told him that when Piugaattoq refused to comply with his orders: "He did not stop, so I shot him through the body. He fell back against the upstanders. As the dogs did not stop I thought that possibly he might be alive, so I shot again, splitting his head open so that his brains fell out."[102] MacMillan's version of his colleague's words indicates that Green intended to kill Piugaattoq and was under no illusions that he was alive after the second shot through the head. When Green encountered MacMillan and Ittukusuk (Etukashu) three days later, he reported that this man "took the news of his friend's death very complacently and was pleased with P[iugaattoq]'s kamiks, which I brought."[103]

In his biography of one of the expedition's guides, Kenn Harper has provided his own explanation of how the event might have occurred.[104] He suggested that Green completely misread Piugaattoq's behaviour and that the entire episode consisted of a succession of crossed signals, complicated by Green's aggressive attitude toward his Inughuit companion. When Piugaattoq insisted that they turn back and forced Green to walk, he did so because he knew Green's feet were wet, and a rapid march afforded the best chance for survival. Green also mistook Piugaattoq's zeal to move quickly as an attempt to abandon him, when he was actually trying to save the American's life. When Green picked up a rifle and shouted orders, Piugaattoq, fearing for his life, started to flee. Panicking at what appeared to him to be desertion, Green tried to assert his authority over his terrified guide by firing over his head. When his warning shot did not stop the Inughuaq, Green reestablished control over the situation in the only way he thought feasible, by killing his guide.

Harper's inferences are given credence by MacMillan's own brief summation of the incident in his book on the expedition: "Green, inexperienced in the handling of Eskimos, and failing to understand their motives and temperament, had felt it necessary to shoot his companion."[105] MacMillan and Green tried to conceal what had actually happened from Ittukusuk. MacMillan wrote: "Some explanation had to be made to Etookahshue so we told him that Pee-ah-wa-to had perished in a blizzard."[106] The story lacked credibility from the outset, as Ittukusuk knew that an experienced traveller like Piugaattoq was unlikely to have placed himself in such a situation. Moreover, Ittukusuk understood English and overheard the Americans' conversations; the true story of Piugaattoq's death travelled to Thule as fast as their fabrications. According to Peter Freuchen,

Ittukusuk advised other Inughuit that the Americans were easily angered and needed to be handled carefully.[107]

The homicide was apparently not reported to the Canadian authorities and, on their return to the United States, the members of the party downplayed it. In a popular article on the Crocker Land expedition published in 1928, Green briefly referred to the fact that he and Piugaattoq had sledged "down the unknown shores in the southwest [of Axel Heiberg Island]." He omitted any reference to the death, stating that "The rest of the trip, though long, was without noteworthy event."[108]

The story did not die and, in 1926, when the *New York Times* broke the news of the Marvin affair, Green's role in Piugaattoq's death was brought to the fore. Now a Commander with the U.S. Navy, Green was unrepentant when contacted by a *Times* reporter. He asserted that he had shot Piugaattoq "to save my own life":

> Pewahtoq tried to escape with our one can of pemmican and a can containing about a pint of oil, our only supplies. We had one rifle, which I lived and slept with because of Pewahtoq's singular behaviour when things looked so dark for us. With this I shot over his head to frighten him. But he only whipped up the dogs faster. As my feet were not in good shape, I could not hope to overtake him. Also the storm was coming on again. So I knelt and aimed at the back of his head.
>
> He was some distance away by this time, and the powdery snow had begun to smoke up with the wind again. Fortunately, I hit him. He toppled off the sledge dead.
>
> Alone I made my way westward.
>
> Under similar circumstances I would certainly do the same again.[109]

Apparently, Donald MacMillan did not agree with Green's justification of his actions. His biographer subsequently quoted MacMillan as saying:

> His [Green's] assertion that if he had permitted the Eskimo to escape with the sledge, dogs and food, he would have starved, is not a sufficient reasons for killing one of the best Eskimos I have ever known...It was, indeed, a long walk alone and without food, but Green knew perfectly well that I never would have left him to starve, that I would have been on my way in search of him immediately following Peeawahto's arrival at the dugout.[110]

However, there was no mention of the incident in MacMillan's official report on the expedition published a decade after their return to the United States. Referring to the rendezvous following the parting of the two groups on Axel Heiberg Island, MacMillan wrote: "He [Green] arrived on the fourth to relate that his experience in the storm had been similar to ours. His dogs were buried under the drift and were never seen after he had tied them for the night."[111] Where the lost dogs merited comment, Piugaattoq's fate had passed into historical oblivion.

Intercultural Relations in the Contact Era: Some Provisional Conclusions

In the misunderstandings and conflicts of the exploration era, it is possible to discern the complex character of historical process. While cultural differences were clearly a factor, the natural environment, individual personalities, and circumstance can also be seen to play significant roles. The convergence of these factors at particular points in time precipitated some of the most violent, and tragic, occurrences of the period.

Disruptive consequences of the contact experience followed from the hiring of Greenlanders to serve on the European expeditions to the Nares Strait region. Many of the Aboriginal guides experienced feelings of estrangement and isolation following their removal from their homes and families for extended service in the far north. These culminated in attempts by the Greenlanders Hans, Jens, and Frederick to abandon their expeditions or to commit suicide by fleeing into the wilderness. From the standpoint of the environment, these men were placed in a physical context unlike any they had previously experienced. While experienced in hunting arctic mammals, none of these men had previously hunted in the conditions of sparse animal populations of the High Arctic. The oppressive experience of nearly four months in the total darkness of arctic winter reportedly took its toll on each of these men and it was in the winter that their disaffection came to a head. Nineteenth-century Danish ethnographer Henrik Rink suggested that the decision by arctic Aboriginal people to flee to the wilderness represented a culturally-patterned response to stress.[112] Whether or not these incidents are illustrations of such a tradition, they do provide a glimpse of some of the difficulties encountered in intercultural relations with Euro-North Americans.

Disruptions to the Inughuit social fabric seem to have reached a peak during the Peary era. Peary's employment of a large proportion of the population appears to have had wide-ranging effects on the material and psychological well-being of this group. There is a strong likelihood that stresses of early contact with Euro-Americans contributed to many of the reported episodes of hysteria among the Inughuit. Service on Peary's expeditions represented dramatic, rapid change for this people, with disruptive effects. Subsistence in the High Arctic had always carried risks, but Peary dramatically increased the risks for all members of his parties. His single-minded pursuit of the North Pole, often in defiance of climate and the seasons, frequently placed himself and his employees in dangerous situations. On these expeditions, Peary imposed military notions of hierarchy and decision-making on a group accustomed to egalitarian forms of social organization by a hierarchical command structure.[113] What seems common to many episodes of "pibloktoq" is not merely the presence of stress, but the lack of power of people placed in these difficult situations.

The interplay of the different registers is particularly illustrated by the incidents of Marvin and Piugaattoq. In terms of environmental factors, both of these incidents occurred in the context of difficult weather conditions in an isolated environment. The individuals were on the trail, where the ever-changing environment presented continuous hazards and danger. In the case of Marvin, he and his companions were traversing the pack ice of the Arctic Ocean and had encountered many difficulties, including severe temperatures, rough pressure ridges, and leads of water that opened unexpectedly. One false step and immersion in the icy water would mean almost certain death. For their part, Piugaattoq and Green were on an isolated stretch of the coast of Axel Heiberg Island, with a storm fast approaching.

Pre-existing cultural differences were at play, reflecting the different concepts of time and space operative in the two cultures. Time was a key factor for both the Europeans and the Inughuit. In the context of travel, Inughuit notions of time centred on the strategies they had developed to make effective use of their environment. Travel was undertaken to procure resources for survival and was determined by the time required to reach particular destinations safely. Time and space were relative and shifted according to weather and travelling conditions. The Inughuit in Marvin's party sought to remain in their *iglooyah* on the pack ice until their compatriot had recovered sufficiently to resume the journey back to Ellesmere Island. In the case of Piugaattoq, his attempts to return to the *iglooyah* to ride out the storm reflected his awareness that he and Green would be in grave danger if they did not secure a refuge from the impending storm. In this case, time was measured in terms of the period required to reach safety.

For Europeans on the Peary and MacMillan expeditions, time and space were absolutes. Marvin had fixed goals for the distance he had to cover by particular points in time. No deviation from the predetermined plan could be entertained. With his feet wet and suffering from exposure, Green thought that if they did not stick to the original plan to proceed south to try to rejoin MacMillan, he would perish. For both men, their military training conditioned them to the hierarchical exercise of power. Accustomed to giving orders to those they considered their subordinates, these men seemed incapable of negotiation. Their dominance must be asserted or they might lose control of the situation altogether. Also at play were underlying assumptions of cultural superiority, evident in the words and deeds of both Americans. In his book *The North Pole*, Peary wrote patronizingly of the people on whose assistance he had relied: "I had come to regard them with a kindly and personal interest, which any man must feel with regard to the members of any inferior race who had been accustomed to respect and depend on him during the greater part of his adult life."[114]

By comparison, Inughuit culture was largely non-hierarchical. An individual who was an experienced hunter might exercise influence but not authority. Influence might be earned through the demonstration of skills on the land or sound judgment on the trail. But it could not be asserted as an empty expression of power or authority. A pragmatic orientation, perhaps the product of hundreds of years of adaptation to this difficult environment, had produced a relational approach to arctic survival.   Both of these incidents took place in a context of perceived crisis. In the Marvin affair, the Inughuit had been on the trail for days without sight of land. Prior to striking out over the pack ice, they indicated their reluctance to embark on this dangerous mission. Through a combination of threats and bribes, Peary had overcome their resistance. At the point of confrontation, however, one of their compatriots was incapacitated, and Marvin was showing preparedness to abandon the ailing Inughuaq on the ice pack, meaning certain death. In such a context of emergency, with no apparent potential for negotiation with the erratic American, it is not difficult to understand the rapid progression to violence.

The Marvin and Piugaattoq affairs illustrate the complexity of historical events. Personality characteristics, especially character flaws, played a role, along with accentuating environmental conditions and the clash of cultural backgrounds. Matters were brought to a head at moments of perceived emergency, when reactions of fear or panic erupted into two fatal episodes. These violent confrontations embodied some of the specific, problematic dimensions of contact that can easily be overlooked when only broad patterns of cultural exchange are examined.

Cultural Contact and High Arctic Ecology, 1818–1940

Enduring social or ecological change can usually be demonstrated conclusively only through scientific and, preferably quantitative measures. In previous chapters, qualitative evidence was presented to address material and intercultural issues of the contact experience. Yet without numerical data, can one say with certainty that change is enduring or fleeting? Without accurate indices of economic or social change over time, such as wealth accumulation or population growth, it is difficult to know with certainty how well a society is dealing with change. For this reason, scholars in the French Annales tradition, seeking to establish long-term trends in social history, have turned to demography to measure such basic indicators as the progress or decline of populations over extended periods.

This chapter addresses some of the larger issues of contact as they relate to ecological change of the High Arctic region. The specific ecological consequences of contact have never been comprehensively traced for either European and Aboriginal peoples in the region. Given that Inughuit territory was being colonized and their labour enlisted to support Europeans, it would be expected that this group experienced most of the change occasioned by contact. Therefore, the study of Inughuit population trends since extensive interchanges in the 1850s holds the potential to provide a more rounded picture of the impact of contact. As well, European contact could be expected to have exerted marked effects on animal populations. Explorers exploited the region's limited land and sea mammal stocks extensively to support their exploration objectives and to procure furs for southern clients, whether fox skins for fashion or specimens for museums.

Effects of Contact on Inughuit Demography, 1850–1940

The infectious disease epidemics of the period presented a serious challenge to the survival of the Inughuit people. With increased interaction between the groups, this long-isolated group was brought into more frequent contact with infectious disease pathogens, with devastating results. The impact was apparent very early in the contact era. In 1849, surgeon Robert Goodsir sailed with the Dundee whaler *Advice*, which stopped at Cape York. He wrote that a member of the crew, who had been with one of the ships lost in 1830, told him of a disaster befalling the Inughuit at that time. The stranded sailors approached and entered a tent in a small Inughuit summer village north of Cape York, where they discovered four or five frozen human bodies, fully clothed, but "stark and stiff."[1] An inspection of the interiors of two or three other tents yielded similar results, with the frozen bodies of entire families confirming the rapid demise of the entire community. The whalers ruled out starvation as a cause of death, as plenty of food was lying about. In the same period as Goodsir, the American Elisha Kent Kane also commented on this tragedy, surmising that the residents had been killed by either famine or an epidemic.[2]

During the era of the Franklin Search, ca. 1848–52, several expeditions visited the Thule District and reported the prevalence of infectious disease among the Inughuit. W. Parker Snow, who travelled with the yacht *Prince Albert* to Cape York in 1850, reported a visit by several Inughuit, from whom "we learned that sickness and disease had been playing sad havoc amongst them."[3] In the same period, Captain Sherard Osborn, who sailed to Cape York in 1850–51, related discussions with veterans of the whale fishery about "severe mortality" in the Inughuit population:

> Every whaler who has visited the coast northward of Cape York during late years reports deserted villages and dead bodies, as if some sudden epidemic had cut down men and women suddenly and in their prime. Our squadron found the same thing. The *Intrepid*'s people found in the huts of the natives which were situated close to the winter quarters of the *North Star* in Wolstenholme Sound, numerous corpses, unburied, indeed, as if the poor creatures had been suddenly cut off, and their brethren had fled from them."[4]

Osborn wrote that Erasmus York, his Inughuit guide, had identified his own brother among the dead, saying that they had all died of infectious respiratory illnesses.

During the polar expedition of Isaac Israel Hayes, Greenlander Hans Hendrik reported an epidemic among the Inughuit in the spring of 1861. Two Native men, who arrived at the ship "suffering from a swollen throat," related that "diseases of the throat and of the stomach" were raging among their people, several of whom had died. Following their departure, Hendrik's own mother-in-law, herself of Inughuit ethnicity, "fell sick, got still worse, and died."[5]

Transmission of the pathogens was swift and deadly. Their devastating impact is demonstrated in demographic statistics compiled in the late nineteenth and early twentieth centuries. In 1880, an epidemic struck at Cape York, a place of contact with Scottish whalers.[6] In 1895–96,

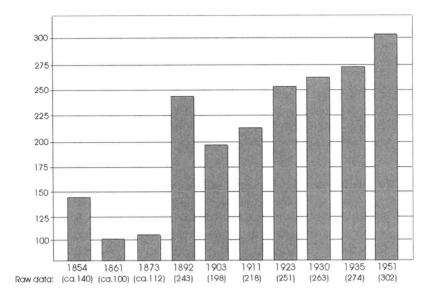

	1854	1861	1873	1892	1903	1911	1923	1930	1935	1951
Raw data:	(ca.140)	(ca.100)	(ca.112)	(243)	(198)	(218)	(251)	(263)	(274)	(302)

Figure 79: Population levels of the Inughuit since initial contact. Based on tabulations by Rolf Gilberg, "The Polar Eskimo Population, Thule District, North Greenland," (1976), p. 15.

29 Inughuit were estimated to have died from an unspecified infectious disease. This represented more than 10% of the 1895 population of 253. Over the following three years, according to Robert Peary, there were 29 additional deaths, many apparently from infectious disease.[7]

Only three years later, in 1901–02, 36 individuals died, including seven who were with Peary in the fall of 1901 at Payer Harbour on Pim Island off Ellesmere's eastern coast. They represented nearly 15% of the entire population of Inughuit at that time. Danish scholar Rolf Gilberg accepted speculation by ethnographer Ludwig Mylius-Erichsen that the epidemic, perhaps of typhoid fever, was transmitted by a Scottish whaler during a summer stop at Cape York, and the disease spread quickly thereafter.[8] In his diary, Peary surmised that gonorrhea was also present among the Inughuit, which, if true, was also transmitted by the Europeans.[9] In 1909–10, another epidemic of respiratory illness precipitated 13 deaths, including five members of missionaries' families. It was followed by a devastating epidemic of Spanish influenza in 1920–21, which killed

40 people, one sixth of the entire population. This disease had caused many deaths in Europe during the First World War; its arrival in the Thule district was perhaps delayed by the disruption of travel during the war.[10]

Even after the Peary period, continuing contact with Europeans brought new epidemics. Widespread loss of life forced the abandonment of many settlements on the Hayes Peninsula. In 1923, C.E. Wilcox, RCMP Inspector for the Ellesmere Island and Baffin Island detachments, and J.D. Craig, in charge of the expedition, separately reported a meeting with Donald MacMillan aboard the ship, the *Arctic* in Smith Sound. MacMillan related that an epidemic of influenza had recently "swept over North Greenland, wiping out a large number of natives, causing the remainder to commence a general migration in the direction of Cape York."[11] In 1925, a Canadian official on the Eastern Arctic Patrol mentioned in a wire that "epidemic whoop cough" had caused the deaths of seven Inughuit.[12] Only two years later, in 1927, an RCMP officer at Bache Peninsula recorded in the detachment diary that, on returning from Etah, Nukappiannguaq reported "much sickness amongst the Eskimos there and in the native settlements a few miles south."[13]

A historical survey of Inughuit demography confirms the devastation wrought by the diseases reported in these accounts.[14] Overall, between 1928 and 1938, half of Inughuit deaths were attributed to infectious disease, with 35.2% of deaths resulting from tuberculosis (including tuberculosis of the lungs, brain, bones, and internal organs) and 15% of deaths from pneumonia.[15] Ethnographer Rolf Gilberg reports that deaths were particularly concentrated in two years—1928–29, when a tuberculosis epidemic resulted in 12 deaths, and 1932, when 21 died of infectious disease, the majority from pneumonia and tuberculosis.[16] Another epidemic was reported in 1944-45, causing a further loss of population.

While both sexes were affected, there were important differences in the death rate between men and women. Noting a higher mortality rate for women, Rolf Gilberg attributed the greater immunity of males in part to their consumption at the hunting grounds of foods exceptionally rich in protein, which may have provided them with greater resistance to pathogens. As well, by virtue of spending more time in the crowded quarters of their small dwellings, women were more exposed than men to infections.[17]

Beyond the death toll, recurrent outbreaks of influenza and other diseases had debilitating effects on many Inughuit who were stricken with illness but did not die. In 1914, as he was preparing to depart Etah for Ellesmere island, Donald MacMillan noted that many Inughuit who were about to accompany him were ill:

Pee-ah-wah-to is not well tonight at all, has a headache and swollen testicles. This is without doubt a touch of the South Greenland influenza brought up some weeks ago. Many of the Innuits have it and are really not fit to go into the field at 50 below zero.[18]

Destructive as the epidemics were, did these losses tell the full story? If we were to rely solely on mortality rates, the contact experience would appear in hindsight to have been an unmitigated disaster for the Inughuit. Yet, if we look at the overall population trends for this group in the 120 years between 1850 and 1970, the picture appears much more positive. In his monograph on Inughuit demography, Rolf Gilberg reviewed the succession of censuses compiled by visitors to the Thule region in this era. Figure 79 presents a selection of these censuses in bar graph form, roughly organized into 10-year intervals.

Gilberg divided Inughuit demography into four periods of analysis. In the first phase, 1893–1903, the Inughuit benefited from the technological transfer attending the migration of Qitlaq and other Baffin Islanders in the 1860s, which enabled more effective utilization of their resource base. However, climatic deterioration in this period inhibited these gains by reducing the numbers of available game animals. The Inughuit population was also rapidly dropping in this period, due partly to epidemics brought by outsiders.

In the second phase, 1903–22, the Inughuit benefited from an improvement in the climate, as milder, drier conditions induced marine mammals to migrate farther north, where they could be hunted by this people. Their material advancement was inhibited by the excessive demands imposed by Peary's expeditions but, with Peary's departure, Rasmussen's establishment of the Thule trading store guaranteed the Inughuit access to desired Western technology on a regular basis. This enabled stabilization in their material circumstances, largely eliminating the risk of famine. As we have noted, introduced diseases, such as the devastating epidemic of Spanish influenza in the early 1920s, continued to inflict high levels of mortality in the context of a more general population advance.

The third phase, 1922–34, coinciding with warmer climatic conditions, was characterized by increased hunting opportunities, reflected by higher numbers of harp seals in the Thule region. The establishment of a hospital and physician at Thule provided professional health care, with a noticeable reduction in the mortality rate resulting from infectious diseases. In the fourth phase, 1934–53, improvements in hunting and administration were reflected in an almost continuous population increase of 1% to $1_{1/2}$% per year, with the population reaching almost 350 by the end of this period. Fatalities from the epidemic in 1944–45 represented a slight setback, but had little impact on the overall upward trend.

The fifth phase, 1953–69, corresponded to major changes in the lives of the Inughuit. With the advent of the Cold War, the United States established its Thule Air Base near the Uummannaq settlement, with the result that game animals were driven away from the area. The Inughuit were moved north to a new town established at the former village of Qaanaaq. They began to inhabit wooden houses heated by coal stoves. Dependence on imported goods increased as the Inughuit now settled in more permanent locations at places with stores. Once resettled, Inughuit had ready access to medical facilities, and most children were now born in the hospital. Population growth levels began a steep rise to one of the highest levels of increase in the world, an average of 2% annually. By 1969, more than half the population was under the age of 15, while older Inughuit were living longer than ever before. Overall, Gilberg tabulated a doubling of population in the 1950s from about 300 to 600 individuals.

The Inughuit population increases of the 1950s and 1960s were analogous to other demographic increases throughout the arctic regions of Canada, Alaska, and Greenland. By the 1960s, some sociologists and anthropologists working in the Arctic began to speak of overpopulation as a serious issue for these societies. Relating the human consumption of resources to the population levels of arctic animals, social scientists advanced the notion of sustainable human population levels, based on calculations of caloric requirements per capita, and the capacity of available arctic organisms to be used for food to maintain their populations. At the same time, Canadian anthropologist Milton Freeman suggested that technological changes since the 1960s call into question the notion of arctic overpopulation. With the advent of the snowmobile, arctic Aboriginal hunters were able to access territories previously beyond their capacity to reach with dogs on a regular basis. The new technology facilitated an expansion in their resource base, enabling larger populations to be sustained.[19]

In the sixth phase of Inughuit demography, 1969–73, concerns over the burgeoning birth rate were addressed by family planning programs, generating a rapid reduction in the rate of increase and general stabilizing of the population by the 1970s, as the rate of natural growth declined from 2.3% annually in 1970 to a rate of 1.1% by 1973.[20] In this rapid adjustment, the Inughuit demonstrated their continuing facility to adapt to new circumstances.

From a long-term perspective, then, the Inughuit appear to have emerged from the contact experience in a stronger position than prior to their encounters with Europeans. Notwithstanding the stressful aspects of interaction with Western cultures, they demonstrated the continuing capacity of their culture to adapt and survive, even through periods of adversity. This is not to make light of the difficulties imposed by contact or the suffering occasioned by the epidemics, which took a heavy toll on their population. At the same time, we cannot rule out the contribution of environmental factors to their enhanced well-being in the twentieth century. Christian Vibe and other scientists indicated that the climate of the High Arctic displayed a general warming trend in the twentieth century, improving the capacity of the Inughuit to exploit particular mammal species. Following service with Peary, which compromised their productive capacity for a generation, the Inughuit ultimately benefited from greater availability of animal resources, enhancing the health and vitality of the group as a whole. If these scientists are right, the most important recent factor in enhancing opportunities for the Inughuit was not the technology brought by cultural contact, but rather beneficial changes in the natural resource base caused by climatic change. However, this hypothesis cannot be definitively addressed here and bears further investigation.

Impact of Contact on Arctic Animal Populations

In the long term, the most damaging effects of European forays on the ecology of the High Arctic probably related to the depletion of arctic mammal populations from overhunting. At the same time, some caution in generalization is warranted. While we have reliable data to establish minimum numbers of mammal species taken, the lack of comprehensive data of the populations of these species prior to the exploration era makes it difficult, if not impossible, to assess these impacts definitively.

The first species to be affected by European exploitation of arctic wildlife were whales. According to statistics compiled by the Dutch, who kept extensive records, the slaughter was extensive even before the nineteenth century. Between 1669 and 1778, whaling enterprises in the Netherlands sent 14,167 ships to the seas around Greenland. In that period, they took 57,590 whales, generating 3,105,596 quardleelen of oil (roughly 12 billion hectolitres), and 42,266,000 kg of bone.[21] In Baffin Bay, the first species to be threatened by non-resident Europeans was the Greenland or Bowhead whale (*Balaena myticetus*). Harvesting Greenland whales in these most northerly waters began in earnest following Sir John Ross's voyage in 1818. Once it was demonstrated that these seas could be navigated, several British whaling fleets were dispatched

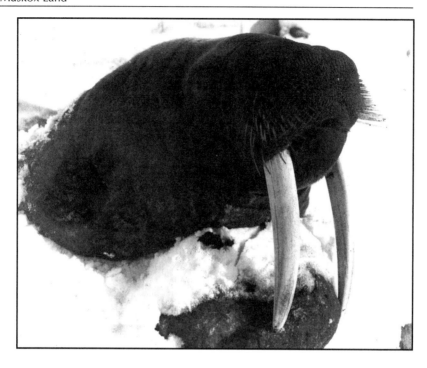

Figure 80: "Walrus Head." Credit: American Museum of Natural History, Donald B. MacMillan Collection, Crocker Land, 1913–17, Negative no. 231314.

the following year to the region. They began a harvest that continued relentlessly until the exhaustion of whale stocks 90 years later.

An indication of the scale of this fishery is provided in the returns for 1823. Statistics show that, in Davis Strait and Baffin Bay, a fleet of 17 ships from Hull, England, captured 469 whales producing 3,750 tonnes of oil. Another 14 ships from Aberdeen, Scotland, took 90 whales, producing 1205 tonnes of oil, while a single vessel, the *Bon Accord* under Captain Parker, returned with 34 whales, producing 256 tonnes of oil. Seven ships from the Dundee fleet killed 190 whales, making 1,500 tonnes of oil. In all, the British fleet numbered 62 ships,[22] while more than 700 whales were taken by British whalers in this one year alone.[23] The 1820s and 1830s marked the heyday of whaling in Baffin Bay, peaking in 1830, when 91 British whaling ships operated in these waters. Following a series of disasters in the 1830s, when many ships were lost in the pack ice,[24] the number of whalers dropped off considerably, although whaling continued until after 1900.[25]

Overall, W. Gillies Ross estimated that between 1814 and 1911, 2,575 British voyages to the Davis Strait fishery took 20,010 Greenland whales.[26] If the numbers taken by Dutch whalers in the eighteenth century are included, the kill figures rise to 29,966 whales taken in Davis Strait between 1719 and 1915.[27] Compilers of a more recent account of cetacean exploitation in the Eastern Arctic have suggested that Ross's figures may underestimate the total, as they omit whales killed and lost by the whalers from these tabulations. As well, in the case of ships carrying whale products which were lost en route, the animals rendered to produce the lost cargo have also been overlooked in the statistics.[28] Historian Richard Vaughan has tabulated a kill of at least 65,235 whales, mostly Greenland whales, taken by Dutch whalers in the north Atlantic between Spitsbergen and Greenland between 1661 and 1800.[29] These massive slaughters put enormous stress on arctic whale populations.

By the twentieth century, the Greenland whale had been virtually exterminated in northern Baffin Bay. By this time, whalers had turned their attention to other species in more southerly locations. The Dundee whaling fleet is a case in point. Late in the 1906 season, Captain Bernier reported that there were then five whalers from this fleet operating in Baffin Bay. Of these, one vessel, the *Scotia*, had captured four whales, the *Bellena* had taken a single whale, the *Windward* reported it had caught nothing, and the remaining ships had not yet appeared.[30] In 1909, the *Morning* under Captain Adams Jr., took only four Greenland whales and several narwhals in the region of the North Water and, in 1910, its catch was a mere five whales.[31] Moreover, the species has never recovered from the slaughter. It has been estimated that the population of this species in Davis Strait and Baffin Bay declined from about 11,000 whales in 1825 to fewer than 600 whales, less than five per cent of the baseline population, in the 1980s.[32]

During the polar exploration era, ca. 1850–1940, major impacts on smaller land or sea mammals was largely the work of American expeditions, particularly the explorers Robert E. Peary and his successor, Donald B. MacMillan, in the late nineteenth and early twentieth centuries. While other European and American explorers staged expeditions to Ellesmere Island after 1850, the repercussions of hunting on the island's ecology were minimal before Peary. For the most part, these expeditions relied on provisions imported from their home countries, while the numbers of game animals they secured remained small.

Peary's arrival in the Arctic represented a departure in the exploitation of animal resources. The explorer himself provided a clear statement of his approach:

> With the musk-ox, as with the walrus, in my later expeditions I hunted them on a large scale and in a systematic way, with careful attention to

details to secure the largest amount of meat and not waste an ounce. All hunting parties had detailed orders.[33]

Espousing a strategy of "living off the country,"[34] the explorer employed large numbers of Inughuit men as hunters, whom he charged with procuring unprecedented quantities of game. Various animal species were taken for provisioning his exploration parties and to feed his Husky dogs, the motive power for his sledging excursions. Beyond basic subsistence, Peary was preoccupied with stockpiling meat to support a series of attempts on the North Pole. In particular, his relay system of advancing provisions along the eastern and northern coasts of Ellesmere Island and sending staging parties across the pack ice of the Arctic Ocean demanded enormous quantities of caribou, muskox, and walrus meat.

The first species to be affected was the walrus (Figure 80). Danish scientist Christian Vibe has asserted that it was not until Peary commissioned an extensive slaughter of walrus in 1891 that these animals were hunted in large numbers.[35] Indeed, Peary described the "modus operandi of my big, systematic walrus hunts" in terms of securing "the maximum meat in the least time."[36] The Inughuit had hunted walrus before Peary, but their practice of hunting from kayaks or the floe edge, using such weapons such as spears and harpoons, did not pose a serious threat to the species.[37] Peary combined the Western technologies of firearms and whaleboats with Inughuit hunting techniques and knowledge of walrus feeding grounds to enable large-scale slaughter.

The explorer described how he organized walrus hunts to be carried out from whale boats painted white to present the illusion of a cake of ice. Assembling up to 50 of "the best [Inughuit] harpooners" with harpoons, floats, and drags, he deployed the men in three or four boats, each manned with six or eight "outfits." When walrus in herds were numerous, the boats would be launched simultaneously from the expedition ship in different directions. At other times, when the walruses were dispersed in smaller herds on the ice pans, the ship would drop whaling boats at intervals in proximity to the resting animals. The boats were then carefully rowed so as to approach as near as possible to the walrus, when the hunters would thrust their harpoons into the animal's side. Immediately, the line, float, and drag were thrown overboard. Once all the harpoons and lines were deployed, the boat was rowed toward the struggling animals, which were finished off with a rifle shot. The boats then headed for the ship and the dead animals were hoisted to the deck, where the older men and women skinned and butchered them. After particularly large hauls, "the deck was hidden under the huge, brown, shapeless forms, and the ship listed heavily to one side with the top-heavy load."[38]

A summer walrus hunt of this nature became a feature of each of Peary's subsequent arctic expeditions, in 1893–95, 1901, 1905–06, and 1908–09. Records are lacking for most of these hunts, but Peary's men reportedly killed 128 walruses on the central Ellesmere coast near Payer Harbour in July and early August 1901.[39] Extensive kills of walrus continued under the direction of American Donald B. MacMillan after Peary abandoned the region in 1909. Walrus populations were not protected from overhunting until Knud Rasmussen influenced the Inughuit to introduce a hunting regulation requiring that walruses be harpooned before they could be shot with a rifle.[40]

The principal terrestrial game species hunted during the High Arctic expeditions was the muskox. Its habit of forming a defensive circle when threatened, effective in fending off attacks by wolves, presented an easy target to human hunters armed with rifles. While it is difficult to reconstruct muskox populations on Ellesmere Island prior to contact, their numbers must have been considerable. The first European parties to winter on the island supplemented their diet with periodic hunting of muskoxen but did not take a systematic approach to its procurement. Muskox hunting by explorers was initiated by the Nares Expedition of 1875–76. The first kill occurred when, on the arrival of the ships at Discovery Harbour in northern Ellesmere Island in August 1875, a small herd was spotted. The ships dispatched a hunting party, which took nine animals.[41] Overall, the numbers killed remained fairly small, as the British party largely relied on tinned provisions. During the expedition's year in northern Ellesmere Island, the explorers aboard the HMS *Discovery* killed 44 muskoxen at various locations, while the crew of the *Alert* managed to bag only 18 animals.[42] Records of the Lady Franklin Bay Expedition indicate a greater reliance on the species, as its members killed 103 muskoxen between 1881 and 1883. Adolphus Greely, its leader, reported having seen 200 more and expressed the opinion that upwards of 300 animals were then "roaming about the fertile valleys of Grinnell Land [northern Ellesmere Island]."[43] Undoubtedly, this informal tally underestimated the total numbers. Other animals taken included 7 wolves, 7 foxes, 8 ermines, 8 lemmings, 19 seals, 44 king ducks, 53 long-tailed ducks, 30 eider ducks, 60 dovekies, 1 diver, 6 burgomaster gulls, 1 Sabine gull, 21 arctic terns, 178 sknas, 84 brent geese, 1 raven, 79 ptarmigan, 100 turnstones, 1 sandpiper, 1 sandling, 27 knots, 2 ringed plovers, 18 owls, 2 philaropes, and 1 walrus. Nevertheless, the scale of these hunts remained relatively small and in themselves, they were unlikely to have major effects on the resident wildlife populations.

Moderation in muskox hunting ended with Peary, who structured his procurement strategies around large-scale slaughters of the island's herds. The first major kill of this species took place during his four-year expedition to Greenland and Ellesmere Island in 1898–1902. His expedition report includes references to 250 muskoxen shot at various locations on Ellesmere Island during this expedition. In a single month, October 1900, Peary and a party of Inughuit and American hunters killed 92 muskoxen on a hunting trip to the interior of northern Ellesmere Island, most of them in a period of less than three weeks.[44] Peary's notekeeping was often sketchy, and unpublished records from this expedition indicate that his numbers underestimated the total kill.[45] For example, his tabulations omitted 18 muskoxen killed by an interior hunting party in February 1901, as reported by his expedition surgeon T.S. Dedrick.[46] He also missed 19 muskoxen killed at Distant Cape near Fort Conger recorded in Peary's diary in April 1901,[47] as well as 18 muskoxen taken by his hunters at Cape Sabine in the spring of 1902.[48]

In the same period, the men of Otto Sverdrup's Norwegian expedition of 1898–1902 also relied heavily on muskox meat to feed their dog teams. They killed at least 112 muskoxen, primarily at Baumann Fiord, Eureka Sound and the Schei Peninsula.[49] Sverdrup described one muskox hunt in which 20 animals were killed:

> It was not so horrible at first, when the big bulls out in the square made their furious attacks on their assailants; but as they were shot down one by one, and only the young animals were left standing alone in the middle of it, it was a dreadful sight to look on at. Round about them lay in heaps their friends and kin, while the blood spurted out steaming from their gaping wounds. The nearest of the fallen animals lay so close up to the survivors that the latter could hardly move. Terror was plainly written in their beautiful beseeching eyes, and every limb shook with fear, but to attempt to flee from their comrades—no; rather would they fall. There lay twenty animals in a heap—horrible riches that we had acquired all in a few minutes.[50]

Even larger numbers were taken in just one year on Peary's next polar expedition in 1905–06. En route to their winter quarters, while attempting to negotiate the icy waters of Nares Strait, Peary sent a party of Inughuit ashore at Wrangel Bay, where they secured six muskoxen.[51] After arriving at Cape Sheridan, he wrote that, by 1 October, his hunters had taken 73 muskoxen and 27 caribou at locations along the northern coast and the interior. According to Robert Bartlett, the captain of the *Roosevelt*, by 25 October 1905, the hunting parties from Lake Hazen returned with reports of taking an additional 144 muskoxen or caribou killed during that month.[52] On 8 November 1905, four families of Inughuit, who had been based at the source of Ruggles River on Lake Hazen, arrived with news of a further kill of 75 muskoxen,[53] a total revised by Matthew Henson to 74.[54] Henson and the Inughuit in the interior killed an additional 19 muskoxen between 26 November and 9 December 1905. William Barr has conservatively estimated that Peary's hunters killed 340 muskoxen on this expedition.[55]

Peary intended to follow a similar strategy of procurement on his last expedition in 1908-09, but by that time the stocks had been largely depleted. Even so, while based at Cape Sheridan, his hunters killed 15 muskoxen on the north coast, including five near Nares Inlet, five at Porter Bay, four at Cape Columbia, and one at James Ross Bay.[56] While based at Fort Conger, Peary's men took 13 muskoxen near Ruggles River in late May.[57] They made up for the shortfall by taking other animals in Greenland. On 19 May 1909, while assigned by Peary to hunt near Cape Morris Jesup in northernmost Greenland, Donald MacMillan wrote that his Inughuit hunters had killed 47 muskoxen, in addition to five others killed at other locations on this excursion.[58]

In his book *Secrets of Polar Travel*, Peary described how his parties slaughtered and utilized the muskox carcasses:

> Hearts, livers, and kidneys were removed, laid out to freeze solid, then stored under the rocks away from dogs, wolves, and foxes until sledged back to the ship. The remainder of the viscera was fed to the dogs on the spot. The heavy backbone, pelvis, and leg bones were cut out, the marrow bones cracked, and their contents eaten at the hunting camp. The others were thrown to the dogs to gnaw clean. The great brick-red hams, fore shoulders, and balls of meat from the neck and ribs, all frozen like granite, were then piled in a big stack, to be sledged to the ship from time to time during the winter. In this way, nothing was wasted; the bones and viscera were utilized on the spot, and only the clear solid meat had to be hauled over the arduous trails.[59]

Additional muskoxen were killed by ancillary parties loosely connected to Peary's North Pole expeditions. On his final voyage, Peary sold space on the *Roosevelt* to Harry Whitney, a wealthy American big-game hunter in search of trophies. In the spring of 1909, while Peary and his crew were in the far north, Whitney hired several Inughuit to accompany him on a hunting excursion to Ellesmere Island. At Flagler Fiord, he and his party killed 23 muskoxen, in addition to calves, and they killed another nine animals north of Victoria Head (Figure 81).[60]

During the winter of 1907–08, American Frederick Cook and his party killed an unspecified number of muskoxen. While Cook's account is

Figure 81: "Hauling muskox to camp." Photograph frm Harry Whitney, *Hunting with the Eskimos* (`910), p. 310.

very vague as to the locations of these muskox kills, they apparently included three killed approaching Bay Fiord, another seven on the southern coast of Bay Fiord, both in late February 1908, and a further 27 on the Schei Peninsula in early March 1908.[61] It is probable that Cook's recorded muskox kills were not comprehensive, as they killed various animals on their return journey. As well, any muskoxen taken by Inughuit hunters who turned back after escorting Cook as far as Cape Svartevoeg on Axel Heiberg Island would not be recorded in his account.

William Barr has estimated that during the Crocker Land Expedition of 1913–1917, American Donald MacMillan and his men killed perhaps 150 muskoxen, including 58 killed by Walter Ekblaw at Bay Fiord, Cañon Fiord, and Lady Franklin Bay in the spring of 1915, 77 taken by MacMillan in trips to Bay Fiord, Eureka Sound, and the Schei Peninsula in 1916–17, and a further 15 taken by Harrison Hunt in the area of Bay Fiord in 1915.[62] These numbers are incomplete, as Ekblaw's account records 60 muskoxen killed, in addition to an entire herd, the numbers unspecified, at Greely Fiord.[63] As well, during his excursion to Axel Heiberg Island in 1914, MacMillan reported that his party was sustaining itself through hunting en route: "We shall go on leisurely killing muskoxen whenever possible for ourselves and our dogs. With our limited supply of pemmican we must have meat on way to Cape Thomas Hubbard or fall short of our distance on Polar Sea."[64] Their kills included seven animals shot on 22 March by his Inughuit hunters near Hayes Sound on the central Ellesmere coast, and another 35 taken over the following week.[65] While MacMillan collected some of the skins for the University of Illinois and the meat from the slaughter "puts us on easy street for a while," he acknowledged that the kill was excessive: "It is a shame that the boys in their excitement killed so many. Magnificent heads, beautiful, soft warm skins, and juicy red meat will be left for the wolves and foxes."[66] In 1915, MacMillan led another party to Ellesmere Island in search of muskox skins for sleeping bags and igloo platforms; they reportedly killed at least 10 muskoxen in addition to wolves and other animals.[67]

MacMillan continued to engage Inughuit to hunt muskoxen on Ellesmere Island during his expeditions between 1923 and 1925, apparently in defiance of the amended North-West Territories Game Act. The explorer was primarily interested in collecting the skins of muskoxen, polar bears, and other mammals for museums with which he had contracted to deliver these products. In 1925, Danish explorer Knud Rasmussen asserted that MacMillan and three Inughuit companions had killed 12 muskoxen in northwestern Ellesmere Island the previous year.[68] MacMillan denied the allegation, but his own diary of a trip to Ellesmere Island in 1924 indicates that Inughuit in his employ had killed adult and immature muskoxen, as well as wolves, for the preparation of skins for export to the United States.[69]

In a tabulation of muskoxen killed by or for Europeans between 1875 and 1917, based on published sources, geographer William Barr estimated a minimum of 1,252 animals killed in this period,[70] but acknowledged that the totals could have been higher. Indeed, if we consider the muskox kills by Inughuit who returned regularly to Ellesmere Island following the American expeditions, the tally would be significantly increased.

The most damaging consequence of hunting during the American expeditions might well have been the depletion of the less abundant—and therefore more fragile—stocks of Peary caribou (*Rangifer tarandus pearyi*). The first caribou populations to be affected were herds of the Thule district of northwestern Greenland, which by the early 1900s became progressively scarcer in the Hayes Peninsula. In the 1860s, Isaac Israel Hayes counted 100 caribou grazing on the banks of Alida Lake at the head of the fiord near Etah. As late as 1901, Peary's assistant Clarence Wyckoff reported having seen "literally thousands" of caribou in this region. "It was as populated as an old Texas range."[71] However, by 1913, when the explorer Donald MacMillan came to this place to hunt caribou, he noted that it was then necessary to go 40 km inland to "to find any at all."[72]

What caused the rapid depletion of caribou populations in this period? In the opinion of Knud Rasmussen, the Inughuit "had not for long been possessors of American magazine-guns when the whole stock was exterminated."[73] Perhaps a fairer assessment would acknowledge the role of the American parties, not only in introducing guns, but in commissioning the slaughter of large numbers of caribou in northern Greenland in this period. In a retrospective account of hunting during his arctic expeditions, Peary described the populations in the vicinity of his wintering quarters at McCormick and Bowdoin Bays in 1891–93 and 1893-95 as "most plentiful."[74] Peary related that, during the winter and spring of 1891-92, his Inughuit hunting parties killed 36 caribou from various locations, including the plateau behind his Red Cliff House, the head of McCormick Bay, which they reached by boat, and on the northeast side of Five Glacier Valley. This figure may have been in addition to 34 caribou reportedly taken in the fall of 1891.[75] In 1893, Peary's hunters took 50 caribou on the northern side of Olricks Bay and another near Cape Athol. In January 1894, Peary's hunters took an additional 54 animals at Kangerlussuaq (Kangerdlooksoah).[76] In 1901, while based at Payer Harbour, Peary sent an American and Inughuit party into the interior of northern Greenland, with instructions to take 40 to 50 animals. Hunting in the area of Olrik Fjord, Inglefield Bredning, they returned within two days, having killed 46 animals.[77]

With the establishment of wintering quarters at Cape D'Urville in 1898–99, Fort Conger in 1900-01, and on Pim Island in 1901–02, Peary's slaughter of caribou continued on Ellesmere Island. In the spring of 1902, his hunters at Cape Sabine killed three caribou.[78] During the fall of 1905, when Peary's party was based at Cape Sheridan, he reported a net kill of about 75 Peary caribou in northeastern Ellesmere Island. The caribou had been secured over a large region including 11 on the north coast, seven from Porter Bay, seven from the Feilden Peninsula, and about 50 others in the region between Lake Hazen and Cape Hecla.[79] The caribou kill in northern Ellesmere Island continued during Peary's last polar expedition in 1908–09. In April 1909, Peary's Inughuit hunters shot 12 caribou around Black Cliff Bay.[80] Fourteen animals were taken at Porter Bay,[81] and a further 13 were killed by Dr. John Goodsell, Aleqasinnguaq (Allakasingwah), and Tautsiannguaq (Tawchingwah) in the area of Lake Hazen and Ruggles River in late May or early June.[82]

Peary's strategy was particularly effective—and devastating to the caribou as a species—as he employed experienced Inughuit men to do much of the hunting. Their traditional knowledge, employed in locating the animals and setting up the kill, added to European technology of firearms, proved a deadly combination. When hunting caribou, the explorer observed that Native hunters had a "magic call," taught to younger hunters by their elders. Similar to an extended hissing sound, this call would "cause a fleeing buck to stop instantly in its tracks, giving the desired shot."[83]

An even larger consumer of caribou skins in this era was American explorer Donald MacMillan, who spent most autumn and winter seasons in the district during his Crocker Land Expedition in 1913–17. In mid-October 1913, he reported that Inughuit hunters had returned from a single excursion to the north with 41 caribou carcasses. At that time, they reported "the hills covered with tracks."[84] Yet, within only three years, after MacMillan had commissioned a heavy kill each autumn, he reported diminished stocks. During the last such fall hunting season, the total kill had dropped to 45 caribou, "the smallest number in four years."[85] The long-term impact of such intensive hunting activity is difficult to determine. However, a survey of game animals on the Queen Elizabeth Islands carried out in 1963 concluded that perhaps only 200 caribou were then living on Ellesmere Island, a precariously small population even 50 years after the major polar expeditions.[86] During the Crocker Land and subsequent expeditions, MacMillan also travelled to Ellesmere Island with Inughuit hunters in search of polar bearskins for sale to museums and individuals in the United States. On one occasion alone, he reported that his party secured 20 bearskins.[87] MacMillan himself acknowledged the negative impacts of the American exploration activities on animal populations. Testifying before Canada's Muskox Commission in 1920, Donald MacMillan made the following observation about Inughuit hunting on Ellesmere Island: "It is little he takes anyway. It is the explorer who takes more."[88]

In 1920, Rasmussen provided an incisive analysis of the effects of Euro-American approaches to hunting the region's wildlife. Rasmussen had first wintered with the Inughuit in 1903–04 and after the establishment of his trading store at Thule in 1910. He knew the individual hunters and the extent of the catch of all mammal species in this era. Rasmussen was responding to official protests by Canada to Danish authorities regarding the hunting of muskoxen on Ellesmere Island. He asserted that the Inughuit had been obliged to make hunting excursions to Canadian territory because the stocks of Peary caribou in the Thule district had been exterminated following the Americans' introduction of firearms. Where hunters had formerly relied on the bow and arrow, the general use of the gun dramatically tipped the balance against this species in a very short period of time. According to Rasmussen, following the Peary era, ca. 1910–14, the Inughuit began hunting muskoxen in central and northern Ellesmere Island "on a grand scale," to provide meat for winter use. In addition to their meat requirements, they needed muskox skins for clothing and pallets or coverings for sleeping platforms and komatiks.[89] In this era, Rasmussen observed that "an average of a score of hunters" participated in the hunt on Ellesmere and Axel Heiberg islands every year, so "it would scarcely seem too high to estimate that about three hundred muskoxen yearly must bite the dust."[90]

Rasmussen recognized that conservation measures for the muskox and other species were doomed to ineffectiveness if they did not take into account the needs of the human populations of the region. If muskox were off-limits, an alternative supply of skins would need to be found. As a remedial step, he proposed importing reindeer hides into northern Greenland from Swedish Lappland, but thus far his proposal had not been approved. Failing such counter-balancing measures, he predicted disastrous consequences from the arbitrary imposition of a ban on hunting "within the immemorial grounds of the Esquimaux." He asserted: "The havoc wrought by white men should be made good by them. And it would be morally indefensible first to exterminate the reindeer and then to prohibit the hunting of the muskox."[91] In 1929, while serving as an administrator in the Thule district, Rasmussen introduced a law to prohibit shooting walrus before they had been first harpooned. This measure was designed to prevent wastage of animals that could sink if shot without first being secured. When Danish zoologist Christian Vibe spent two years in the district in 1939–41, he noted that the law on walrus hunting was strictly observed. He attributed to the conservation measure the apparent fact that the walrus population was then maintaining itself and not in decline.[92]

The contact experience brought major changes and imposed significant stresses on both the Inughuit population and the arctic animals on which they depended. The most serious threat was the introduction of infectious diseases, which for several decades caused considerable suffering and devastation to the small population. Two of the most destructive epidemics occurred in 1895–96 and in 1901–02, when 10% and 15% respectively of the entire Inughuit population succumbed to influenza and, in 1920–21, when an epidemic of Spanish Influenza took 40 lives. Nevertheless, when the overall demographic pattern of the twentieth century is considered, the picture is much more positive. Following the stresses of early contact, the adaptability of Inughuit positioned them to stabilize and increase their population by using enhanced access to materials and imported technologies to more fully exploit the resources of their homelands. As well, the climate continued to play an important role, as a succession of warming trends in the twentieth century generated largely positive effects of greater accessibility of marine mammal populations for this group.

In terms of the long-term effect of European resource procurement on arctic wildlife, it is not in dispute that whaling in Davis Strait and Baffin Bay dramatically diminished the populations of Greenland whales to the verge of extinction. The toll was such that the species has never recovered its population in these waters. Regarding other species, European contact precipitated the extinction of caribou in northwest Greenland and significantly diminished the numbers of muskoxen in northern Ellesmere Island. While it is difficult to definitively establish the numbers of various species killed during the North Pole exploration era, the foregoing tabulation of reported kills of muskoxen, caribou, and other species confirms both the indiscriminate character of the slaughter and the attendant risks imposed on the region's ecology.

Social and Ecological Change in the High Arctic, 1850-1940: Some Conclusions

What, then, were the major effects of contact in the High Arctic on the participating cultures? For this discussion, three areas of focus have been selected, specifically: changes to material life, including the exchange of technologies; sociocultural organization and relationships; and ecological changes. While these categories of analysis do not exhaust the possibilities, they lend themselves to empirical assessments, and, in the case of populations, to quantitative comparisons.

With regard to impacts on material life, the contact experience exerted a significant influence on the Inughuit in particular. Both positive and negative aspects of the exchange can be documented. The introduction of guns and steel traps increased the repertoire of Inughuit but tied them to market economies in a way that altered family labour. Inughuit men were increasingly tied to hunting for a southern market, while Inughuit women, formerly engaged in pursuits oriented to family production, were now heavily involved in preparing skins for export. The contact experience also reintroduced the Inughuit to Ellesmere Island, increasing their hunting range, which had been arrested by the loss of key skills by the early nineteenth century. As a result they were subsequently better positioned to more effectively exploit the marine mammal resources in this expanded territory. At the same time, Western firearms also posed a serious threat to the region's ecology, as the scale of hunting mammal populations increased exponentially during the contact era. Explorers like Peary commissioned unprecedented kills of muskoxen, caribou, and other species, which for a time placed into jeapardy both the High Arctic ecosystem and the well-being of the human cultures inhabiting it.

Increased opportunities and threats attending changes in technology and material capacity are not the only issues to be considered in assessing the effects of contact. Its impact on Aboriginal cultures, ways of life, and belief systems must also be factored into the equation. French anthropogeographer Jean Malaurie has described the contact era as a period of "psychological crisis" for the Inughuit people.[93] Among other issues, Malaurie was referring to the cultural confusion occasioned by the weakening of customary shamanistic belief structures. Such conclusions might also be inferred from periodic outbreaks of "pibloktoq" in this period. Many of these episodes appear to be related to stresses on gender relations imposed by American explorers, ranging from removal of hunters from their families for extended periods to sexual harassment and coercion of Inughuit women, as reported in Evelyn Briggs Baldwin's revealing account while on the 1893–95 Peary expedition to northern Greenland.

At a more fundamental level, i.e. the survival of the group, the contact experience appears not to have inflicted permanent damage on the Inughuit as a people. Whatever the stresses of the exploration era, their numbers, seriously threatened by periodic epidemics between 1850 and 1930, nevertheless increased throughout the twentieth century before stabilizing in recent decades. At the primary level of sustaining their population, the Inughuit demonstrated their resiliency throughout the dramatic changes of the past 150 years.

Assessing the impact of contact for Euro-Americans is perhaps a more difficult proposition. The contact experience directly involved only the Europeans, Americans, and Canadians who travelled to the region and typically spent only a few years there. Their brief presence in the Arctic was usually punctuated by much longer absences. While they were in the Arctic, the Inughuit carried out a myriad of tasks on their behalf, including preparatory work in advance, service in the field, and assistance to the Euro-American explorers after they came out of the field. The Inughuit carried out most of the scouting, hunting, butchering, skin preparation, sledge construction, and clothing production, as well as general labour required by these expeditions. On the trail, Inughuit men often saved the lives of the less experienced Americans. The more perceptive Westerners recognized that they could not have achieved their objectives without the assistance of Aboriginal people. Among the expeditions that engaged their services were those of Peary, MacMillan, Danish expeditions led by Knud Rasmussen, Lauge Koch, and James Van Hauen, and the British Oxford University Ellesmere Land Expedition. Norwegians made less use of the Inughuit, although Sverdrup traded with them in 1898–

1902 and, in 1919, Godfred Hansen engaged their services to accompany him on a journey to northern Ellesmere Island to lay caches for Roald Amundsen.[94]

It must be recognized that the great majority of people in the populous societies of North America and Europe were unaffected by exchanges with representatives of their societies who actually interacted with Inughuit and other arctic cultures. Therefore, it is perhaps inappropriate to speak of true cultural exchange, when only one of the cultures participated fully in the interchange. For Euro-Americans, the effects of contact in the High Arctic were experienced vicariously through the medium of popular culture. From the time of Kane in the 1850s, narratives of successive polar expeditions captured the imaginations of innumerable armchair explorers who would never visit the region. During the age of exploration, the High Arctic was invested with the values of struggle with and triumph over the environment, the site of innumerable allegories of character building and national symbolism. To his American backers, Peary's presumed attainment of the North Pole was a demonstration that the United States could be victorious in any field of endeavour, if they applied this explorer's qualities of courage and determination to the task at hand.

The High Arctic functioned in a similar way for the RCMP during its tenure at the detachments on Ellesmere Island and Dundas Harbour on Devon Island in the 1920s and 1930s. With the encouragement of the force and the federal government, the Mounties' work in the region was romanticized in the media and in official and popular works on the force.[95] For example, a 1928 newspaper article in the *Christian Science Monitor* was entitled "Romance Still Lives in the North with Canada's Royal Mounties."[96] This story and others played up the heroic efforts of the police to preserve law and order and stressed the courage displayed on many sledge patrols carried out across the Arctic. While the conduct of some members may have fallen short of the ideal, the heroic role attributed to the RCMP was integral to the construction of a Canadian national identity in this era. In this sense, while the High Arctic played no direct role in the daily lives of Canadians, the region did contribute to the construction of Canadian identity through intrepid tales of heroism and adventure.

Major cultural and economic differences of European and Inughuit societies in the Arctic must be acknowledged if we are to adequately explain the process of change in the post-contact era. In evaluating the impacts of contact, we are struck both by the unequal character of the power relationships of Europeans and Inughuit and the capacity of

Inughuit to turn an unfavourable situation to their own advantage. There is no doubt that the Inughuit contributed immeasurably to the success of European expeditions. They also took advantage of these exchanges to gain access to rare materials to improve their utilization of the region's resources.

In *The Mediterranean*,[97] Braudel wrote that "the mark of a living civilization is that it is capable of exporting itself, of spreading its culture to distant places." In *Capitalism and Material Life*, he extended his definition of a "culture" as "a civilization that has not yet achieved maturity, nor reached its greatest potential, nor consolidated its growth."[98] If these are the criteria, only Europeans exported their cultures in the context of contact. The Inughuit influence was apparent only in the emulation of their way of life by such explorers as Peary and his successors. While Peary and others failed to give them credit for their contributions, their impact can nevertheless be discerned in nearly every aspect of his adaptation to travel, shelter, hunting, clothing, and pragmatic adaptation to the High Arctic environment. Inughuit material culture and methods of survival became part of the standard repertoire of European and American visitors to the region, including the parties of Donald MacMillan, Knud Rasmussen, Lauge Koch, A.H. Joy, Harry Stallworthy, Edward Shackleton, and James Van Hauen, among others. Therefore, we are not dealing with the interface of a dominant "civilization" and a subordinate "culture," but rather with an exchange between two cultures of comparable stature, one populous and expanding, the other non-populous and indigenous, each endowed with a rich technological tradition to address its respective way of life. While these cultures remained solitudes for much of the contact era, it was the eventual synthesis of their two traditions, exemplified in part by Peary and more completely by Inughuit and Inuit people since 1950, that enabled further adaptations to life in the High Arctic.

PART IV

CIRCUMSTANCE, CHANGE, AND CONTINUITY

The Inuit on Ellesmere Island, 1951–2000

This last part of Ellesmere Island's post-contact history focusses on the re-occupation of the island by Canadian Inuit since the 1950s. It is a story that continues to the present day. With the more recent past, we encounter the uncertainties of history, when interpretations are necessarily provisional and contingent. Unlike the epic past of the exploration era, solidified by culture into an apparent bedrock of certainties, recent history flows inexorably into the present, with its numerous complexities, dilemmas, and diversity of perspectives.

Since its establishment in the 1950s, Grise Fiord, located on the southern coast of Ellesmere Island, has been Canada's most northerly community. The meteorological stations at Eureka and Alert and the Alert military base occupy sites at higher latitudes on the island, but these government installations are staffed by personnel from the south on limited assignments in the far north. They are completely dependent on provisions imported from the south. Only at Grise Fiord can one speak of actual settlement, in the sense of long-term occupation of the island. The Inuit there have maintained a community anchored in use of the region's wildlife and other natural resources. In so doing, they have revived a pattern of intermittent occupation and use of Canada's most northerly land mass by Aboriginal peoples for more than 4,000 years.

The community is probably best known to Canadians as a result of the recent public debate over the relocation of Inuit people to the High Arctic in the 1950s. This controversy generated a series of articles in journals and the popular press in Canada and the United States,[1] debates in the electronic media, reports by federal officials,[2] and academic monographs,[3] theses by university graduate students,[4] a report to the Canadian Human Rights Commission,[5] and a three-volume report issued by the Royal Commission on Aboriginal Peoples, including a synopsis of testimony at public hearings sponsored by the Commission.[6] Much of the debate has centred on the interpretation of the archival record of documents in various collections in the Government Archives Division of the National Archives of Canada and on the oral testimony of Inuit who were relocated and government officials involved in the relocations.

The purpose of this book is not to deal substantively with this controversy or to draw conclusions about the positions and motivations of the respective parties. Other authors have delved into the sources in great detail, debated the issues, and taken positions on the meaning and significance of the relocations. The issue was the subject of discussion and negotiation between the Minister of Indian and Northern Affairs and Inuit families who were relocated to Grise Fiord and Resolute Bay in the 1950s. This dialogue must speak for itself.

For the present study, it is considered more pertinent to focus on the aspects of the history of Grise Fiord that bear on the larger themes of this study—contact between European and Inuit cultures, and the relationships between culture, environment, and human agency in addressing the challenges of life in this remote region. As in earlier sections of this book, the material and technical exchanges between Inuit groups and adaptations to the physical environment and ecology will be examined. Grise Fiord's history, interesting in its own right, also connects to larger issues of historical process, including the relationships between forces of continuity and change, the multi-dimensional character of historical time, and contrasting concepts of space and time held by the Inuit and Europeans who participated in this story.

At the same time, the directed nature of Grise Fiord's origins requires that such issues as adaptation and cultural exchange be placed within the historical contexts of the community's establishment. Inevitably, such discussions lead us back to the political and social policy contexts within which the relocations first took place. When, in 1990–91, Parks Canada arranged an oral history project with former residents of Grise Fiord who had been returned to northern Quebec, the interviewees emphasized the relocations as an event of overriding significance in their lives. It is important to enable the people who were relocated to provide their own perspectives on the relocations, inasmuch as they are inseparable from the issues of adaptation, continuity, and change in the Arctic. Their versions, which often differ sharply from the official reports tendered by RCMP and other federal officers, are an authentic expression of their lived experience and perspectives regarding a very difficult period in their lives. Beyond the significance of the relocations to the people who were relocated, these events have an important bearing on the larger themes of circumstance, change, and continuity in High Arctic history.

Therefore, this section of the book briefly sketches some of the factors bearing on northern policy as it related to the relocation of Inuit people in this era, while enabling the voices of several Inuit to be heard on these issues. Care has been taken not to endorse, reject, or comment on interpretations or the specific reasons for decisions about the relocations, and readers are referred to the extensive literature on the topic, referenced in the notes.

13

Circumstance: Relocation of Inuit to the High Arctic, 1951-2000

Early Experiments in Inuit Relocation, 1934-47

The uprooting and resettlement of Canadian Inuit on the southern coast of Ellesmere Island in the 1950s was not the first experiment in Inuit relocation to the High Arctic. In 1934, the Hudson's Bay Company initiated a resettlement scheme to move Inuit to Dundas Harbour on Devon Island, the site of an RCMP detachment. The company's objective was to support the establishment of a new trading post, for which the Inuit would trap and hunt animals for trade. In August of that year, the company's vessel, the *Nascopie*, stopped at Cape Dorset on the southwestern tip of Baffin Island and collected 22 Inuit. Another 12 Inuit people were picked up at Pangnirtung on Cumberland Sound and a further 18 Inuit at Pond Inlet in northern Baffin Island; all were directly transported to Devon Island. The company had sought "volunteers" to trap furs for two years, after which they were promised safe passage back to their homes if dissatisfied with life on Devon Island.[1]

While the vicinity of Dundas Harbour was rich in marine mammals, such as seals, walrus, and belugas, the heavy pressure ice in this area hampered efforts to hunt these animals from boats. The rugged weather and ice conditions also hindered dog-sled travel along the coast to maintain fox traps. The HBC post manager at Dundas Harbour tried to mitigate these environmental obstacles by transporting the Inuit families by boat 50 km to the west, but there they encountered similar difficulties. In 1936, the HBC closed its post at Dundas Harbour, and again moved the Inuit, this time to Arctic Bay, after which two families from Pond Inlet were returned to their homes. Nevertheless, federal authorities were undaunted by the problems encountered at Dundas Harbour and continued to promote the idea of further relocations. In 1936, an official with the Department of the Interior wrote:

> From an administrative standpoint, it may be found desirable to move existing Police posts to new locations or close them altogether as in the case of Dundas Harbour. New trading posts are opened in areas where game is more abundant. The experiment of moving natives farther north is working out satisfactorily and might be extended in the near future."[2]

In 1937 the HBC moved the remaining families from Dundas Harbour yet again to Fort Ross on the southern shores of Somerset Island. In 1947, uncertain access due to congested ice conditions obliged closure of Fort Ross, and the odyssey continued, as the company moved the Inuit to Spence Bay, on the western coast of the Boothia Peninsula.[3]

The issue of whether the relocations to Dundas Harbour and other sites were undertaken voluntarily by the Inuit has been debated by several writers. In 1975, Farley Mowat wrote that the Inuit had been coerced into moving to these locations.[4] Subsequently, Ernie Lyall, a former Hudson's Bay Company employee at Pond Inlet, who had relayed the HBC's offer to take the Inuit north to Dundas Harbour, asserted that the families went willingly to this place and subsequent destinations.[5] Readers are referred to these books to form their own interpretations, although the lack of published oral history testimonies with members of the relocated families may hinder the development of definitive conclusions.

Sovereignty and "New Hunting Grounds"

Broadly, the re-establishment of RCMP detachments on Ellesmere Island and associated relocations of Inuit people after the Second World War took place at a time of renewed concern within the federal government over incursions into the Arctic Archipelago by non-Canadian nationals. A major source of Canada's concern was an increasing presence by the United States military in this region, which began with a major military build-up in the Northwest Territories during the Second World War and continued into the early Cold War era.[6]

In 1946, Senator Owen Brewster of Maine introduced a bill in the United States Senate to establish a network of joint Canadian-American weather stations in Canada's High Arctic. The plan had originated entirely within the U.S. military.[7] Alarmed by this unilateral initiative, Canada persuaded the United States to adjust its plans to place the weather stations under civilian authority, and six joint arctic weather stations were established under the dual sponsorship of the two countries.[8] Nevertheless, sensitivities persisted regarding the balance of personnel at these stations, and other symbolic issues related to sovereignty.[9]

By the early 1950s, American activity expanded to encompass the establishment of early warning stations across the Arctic. In addition, the United States announced plans to build airstrips at the Ellesmere Island weather stations at Alert and Eureka, capable of landing heavy jets and cargo planes. A 1952 memorandum prepared for the Minister by the Undersecretary of External Affairs drew attention to the increased

American presence and predicted that the number of U.S. citizens in the District of Franklin would substantially outnumber the population of "white Canadians." The writer proposed a "vigorous policy in all Canadian Arctic services," including communications, transportation, aids to navigation, meteorology, and police.[10]

Concurrently, a Privy Council Office memorandum predicted that if the airstrips were built, they "would probably assume the character of small U.S. bases, and Canadian control might well be lost." The memorandum also noted American requests to survey Ellesmere and Coburg islands for potential sites for radar stations, and remarked on the small number of Canadian personnel in the Arctic in relation to American counterparts. The document asserted:

> Any new U.S. activity is bound to change the delicate balance of manpower in the northern Arctic....Our experiences since 1943 have indicated the extreme care which we must exercise to preserve Canadian sovereignty where Canadians are outnumbered and outranked.[11]

At a meeting of the federal Cabinet in January 1953, Prime Minister Louis St. Laurent expressed the view that in succeeding years, "U.S. developments might be just about the only form of human activity in the vast wastelands of the Canadian Arctic"—a problem which needed to be addressed.[12] After reviewing a report by the Secretary of State for External Affairs on this issue, the Cabinet directed the Advisory Committee on Northern Development to consider and report on "all phases of development of the Canadian Arctic and the means which might be employed to preserve or develop the political, administrative, scientific and defence interests of Canada in that area."[13]

In this context, the federal government decided to re-open its RCMP detachment at Craig Harbour in 1951. Concerned about continued hunting by Inughuit on Ellesmere Island, the Mounties now abandoned the practice of engaging employees from Greenland. In that year the Eastern Arctic patrol vessel, the *C.D. Howe*, stopped at Pond Inlet, where two Inuit men, Kayak and Ningiuk, were recruited to serve as special constables and taken north with their families. At Craig Harbour, the detachment was officially re-opened by Inspector H.A. Larsen in a solemn ceremony on 31 August 1951, and the police set up quarters in the old detachment house at the site (Figure 82). The supply of the post was carried out in difficult ice conditions, as a large sheet of pressure ice came across the ship's bows, dragged the anchor and began to force it toward the shore. With great difficulty, they prevented the ship from being grounded. The crew managed to manoeuvre the supply barge

Figure 82: "Re-opening RCMP post at Craig Harbour, Ellesmere Island, NWT, July 1951."
National Archives of Canada Photo no. PA-131770.

back to the *C.D. Howe* and to then push the larger vessel through a
large floe of newly formed ice, 9 to 13 cm thick and stretching 4 to 6
km, which threatened again to push them ashore and destroy the ship.[14]

Meanwhile, a committee of senior federal officials suggested that
Inuit employment on the arctic islands might strengthen Canadian
sovereignty in the region. In May 1952, at the Eskimo Affairs Conference, proposals for a "Policy on Employment of Eskimos" were tabled, including the topic "Exploration of the possibilities of finding
permanent employment in the Arctic for the average Eskimo who
could be trained in a particular field." Among the roles proposed for
Inuit were the following:

   i)   as Canadian citizens or as a branch of the Armed Services to
       occupy and patrol the Arctic for the purpose of sovereignty and
       security;

  ii)   as labourers and mechanics, radio meteorological stations, air fields,
       etc.;

 viii)   transfer of groups to underpopulated areas.[15]

Concerns about potential American challenges to sovereignty coincided with unease about ongoing occupation and hunting on Ellesmere Island by Inughuit from northwest Greenland. In the late 1940s, RCMP reports warned of continued hunting by Greenlanders on Ellesmere Island. In 1950, Danish scientist Christian Vibe published a monograph in which he reported that Inughuit hunters were making several excursions a year to the east coast of Ellesmere Island; 10 to 20 or more polar bears were taken on each trip. The hunters skinned the bears on the ice, cooking and consuming some of the meat, and feeding the raw remainder to their dogs.[16] In many cases, the visiting hunters were individuals and families who had served with Peary or later served with the RCMP on Ellesmere Island, as is apparent from the names of Inughuit persons visiting Bache Peninsula in 1927, recorded in the detachment diary.[17]

In this context, several federal officials perceived the potential to install Canadian Inuit on Ellesmere Island as a bulwark against potential rival claims to sovereignty that might flow from the Inughuit excursions. In 1950, Alex Stevenson, the officer in charge of the Eastern Arctic patrol asked RCMP Inspector H.A. Larsen "whether a number of native families might be moved from Baffin Island and re-established on Devon Island, Ellesmere Island and other islands of the Canadian archipelago." In the event the RCMP detachment at Dundas Harbour on Devon Island was closed, Stevenson proposed leaving some Inuit on Devon "and others established on Ellesmere Island, spreading out along the east coast as far as Bache Peninsula...It would even be possible to go up from Craig in the spring, spend the summer at Bache, then return in the fall or early winter." Apparently, Stevenson hoped that Canadian Inuit could be established along the route most frequently taken by Inughuit on their hunting trips to Ellesmere Island. He added:

> There is no doubt that country produce is plentiful in the aforementioned regions and Baffin Island Eskimos could easily live off the country. In this regard I understand that there is evidence that the Greenland Eskimos are hunting on Ellesmere Island and vicinity. Why not give the natives a chance to cover this country and also if it is considered necessary help improve the position regarding sovereignty rights.[18]

In October 1952, James Cantley, officer in charge of the northern segment of the Eastern Arctic Patrol, relayed in a report from personnel of the Eureka weather station that 12 Inughuit had visited the station on the west coast of Ellesmere Island. They had spent the winter at Bache Peninsula on Ellesmere's eastern coast. Cantley wrote:

There is no reason why more [Canadian] Eskimos should not be moved over to Ellesmere Island to live permanently. This was suggested to Inspector Larson and he expressed his willingness to have the Police detachment co-operate with the Department provided arrangements could be made to have the necessary supplies made available.[19]

In reply, Alex Stevenson described the report of unauthorized hunting as "disturbing"; he was also concerned by reports that six Inughuit had visited Craig Harbour the previous spring. Stevenson proposed that, if an RCMP detachment could be established in the Smith Sound area as well as at Craig Harbour, and Canadian Inuit could be relocated to inhabit these sites, such relocations could serve as a bulwark against these hunting excursions by the Greenlanders:

If Police detachments could be maintained at both Craig Harbour and Cape Sabine and arrangements could be made to have them supplied through the "loan fund," ten or twelve families could be transferred to Ellesmere Island and use made of the natural resources that are undoubtedly available there. The occupation of the island by Canadian Eskimos will remove any excuse Greenlanders may presently have for crossing over and hunting there.[20]

At this point, federal officials appear to have been less concerned about possible impacts of Inughuit hunting on wildlife populations as they were about the implied challenge by other countries to the territory. If citizens of a foreign country, in this case, Denmark, could transgress Canadian law, and Canada was seen as incapable of administering its laws in the region, then the possible claims of other nations, especially the United States, might be strengthened. On 10 June 1953, the Canadian government wrote to Denmark about the "illegal migration of certain Greenlanders to Ellesmere Island." Anxious to "prevent the intermingling of the Eskimos and Greenlanders," Canada proposed sending the Greenlanders—meaning, the Inughuit—back as soon as the ice formed in Upper Baffin Bay.[21]

A report to the Cabinet on activities in northern Canada was considered by the Advisory Committee on Northern Development on 16 March 1953. It included a report on plans for RCMP initiatives on the arctic islands:

The Force expects to continue the service we presently give in the north and to open new detachments when Canadian interests seem to call for such action. For instance—it is planned to open a detachment at Cape Herschel on the east coast of Ellesmere Island and another at Clyde River on the east coast of Baffin land this year. The Cape Herschel detachment will, it is hoped, encourage the move of some Canadian Eskimos into that part of Ellesmere Island and will also tend to prevent Greenland natives from making hunting excursions into Canadian territory.[22]

In 1989, the late Ross Gibson, the RCMP officer who selected Inuit at Inukjuak for relocation and accompanied them to Resolute Bay in 1953, expressed his own beliefs about the reasons behind the relocations in an interview:

> Because of the condition of the Natives, the Department of Northern Affairs and the Mounted Police decided that maybe we could move them [the Inuit] into the High Arctic, because the Arctic Archipelago was becoming the Queen Elizabeth Islands and we were sort of taking our sovereignty rights, stretching out and letting people know that we Canadians, that was part of our country, and this was part of the project of moving the Natives there and opening detachments.[23]

Whatever the original reasons for the relocations, several federal officials later expressed the view that the High Arctic settlements had helped Canada maintain an effective presence in the region. In 1960, C.M. Bolger, Administrator for the Arctic with the Department of Indian Affairs and Northern Development, signed a memorandum to the effect that Grise Fiord was then serving "a distinctly useful purpose in confirming, in a tangible manner, Canada's sovereignty over this vast region of the Arctic."[24] Earlier, Ben Sivertz, Director of the Northern Administration Branch, had argued that "Grise Fiord should be continued for sovereignty purposes."[25] Sivertz recognized the difficulties of supplying and providing medical services to this Ellesmere Island community and rejected the idea of further relocations to remote locations without pre-existing infrastructure of facilities and communications.[26] Instead, he hoped to establish "new colonies" in the High Arctic in the vicinity of the meteorological stations.[27]

Whether federal officials actually believed that sovereignty was a continuing issue in the High Arctic or simply viewed it as a useful justification for the continuation of federal programs in the region is difficult to determine definitively. The available documentary record appears to leave this issue unresolved.

In the 1950s, officials of the federal Department of Northern Development justified the relocations on the basis of providing new opportunities for Inuit to exploit the game resources of the High Arctic. Referring to game reports by the RCMP at the Ellesmere Island detachments, the planners of the relocation concluded that game animals in the vicinity of Jones Sound, the area of the RCMP detachment at Craig Harbour, could support several hunting families. They proposed an "experiment" which would help determine whether such relocations were viable and therefore might offer a solution to perceived Inuit overpopulation relative to game resources in more southerly regions. In the words of F.J.G. Cunningham, a director with the department:

> Our primary object is to find out how Eskimos from overpopulated areas can adapt themselves to conditions in the High Arctic where there is at present no Eskimo population and where natural food resources are reported to be much more readily available than they now are in southern areas.[28]

Federal officials argued that by moving several families north, they could relieve the pressure on an apparently depressed economic situation for Inuit on the eastern coast of Hudson Bay, at communities such as Inukjuak and Povungnituk. Other sources suggest that game animals had been depleted in these areas by that time. The artist James Houston, who moved into the Anglican mission at Port Harrison (Inukjuak), Québec in 1949, recalled the privations in that period: "Beyond any question many Eskimos knew real hardships at that time, especially since that area, after the disappearance of the caribou herds, was noticeably a poor hunting place."[29] Ross Gibson, who was stationed at Inukjuak before accompanying the Inuit north in 1953, recalled that at the time of the relocations, "foxes were scarce and prices were low...they [the Inuit] were really having a rough time."[30] Martha Flaherty, who was relocated with her family to Craig Harbour in 1955, remembered experiencing hunger before their departure.[31]

Federal officials asserted that the relocations would improve the hunting prospects for both the relocated Inuit and the families who remained in Quebec. However, few, if any, preparations were made for the subsistence or housing of the Inuit after their arrival on Ellesmere or Cornwallis islands. Before the relocation, R.C. Ripley, Air Officer Commanding of the RCAF Transport Command, expressed "considerable misgivings" regarding the plan. Noting that no arrangements had been made for housing or other assistance to the Inuit, he stated:

> They must have a properly balanced diet, clean healthy living accommodation and proper clothing, which will have to be supplied to them. Medical attention is not possible on Cornwallis other than the simplest first aid.[32]

Relocation of Canadian Inuit to the High Arctic

The relocation plan was finalized in the early summer of 1953. The organizers intended to collect three families from Inukjuak and one from Pond Inlet for relocation to Craig Harbour, Ellesmere Island, and one family from each of the source Inuit communities to the new RCMP detachment at Alexandra Fiord. At Inukjuak, 35 Inuit were picked up by the Eastern Arctic Patrol supply ship, the *C.D. Howe* on the 23 July 1953. At Pond Inlet, in northern Baffin Island, an additional 16 Inuit boarded. Reaching Craig Harbour, Ellesmere Island on the 29 August, the RCMP escorted six families, comprising 30 men, women, and children ashore.

These relocations coincided with federal plans to re-establish a second RCMP detachment on the central Ellesmere coast in the region of Smith Sound. The rationale for selecting this area was the need to address ongoing reports of hunting by Greenland Inughuit on Ellesmere Island. Since the principal route of entry was the crossing at Smith Sound, establishment of a police installation here would revive the RCMP presence originally asserted in this area with the Bache Peninsula detachment in 1927–32. In mid-August 1953, the Department of Transport icebreaker, the *D'Iberville*, entered Smith Sound and searched for a suitable site for the post on Cape Herschel. As no such site could be found, the expedition received orders from Ottawa to find a site farther north in the vicinity of Bache Peninsula. A site was finally identified on Alexandra Fiord on the south side of Buchanan Bay, where a Euro-Canadian constable and Ningiuk, an Inuit special constable and his family, were landed on 18 August to establish the new post.[33]

The architects of the relocation experiment had intended that several of the Inuit being relocated via the *C.D. Howe* would be moved to the new RCMP detachment at Alexandra Fiord immediately following its establishment. After leaving the first six Inuit families at Craig Harbour, the crew of the *C.D. Howe* transferred the four remaining families to the Department of Transport icebreaker *D'Iberville*, which had already left a constable and Ningiuk at the more northerly detachment. When the *D'Iberville* subsequently encountered heavy ice conditions on this second attempt to sail through Smith Sound, the RCMP was forced to abandon the plan to leave other Inuit families at this site. Improvising on the spot, they brought two families back to Craig Harbour to rejoin the group that had disembarked earlier, and the remaining Inuit were landed at Resolute Bay on the return voyage.[34] Inspector Larsen subsequently pursued the idea of transferring four or five Inuit families to Alexandra Fiord,[35] but a telegram from an officer at the detachment advised that the prevailing game conditions would not support more Inuit at that time. As well, "much rough ice in whole of

Buchanan Bay area and darkness has limited hunting activities to a certain extent."[36] Ultimately, federal officials decided to move only one additional Inuit family to join the small party already established at Bache Peninsula.[37]

Perspectives of the Relocated People

The synopsis of testimony by Inuit to the Royal Commission in 1993 represented the first occasion on which Inuit voices and perspectives on the 1953–55 relocations were given prominence in the debate surrounding this occurrence.[38] Oral histories carried out for Parks Canada within the communities of Grise Fiord, Pond Inlet, and Inukjuak also help to shape a picture of these events from the standpoint of the participants.

The oral testimony addresses a variety of issues, including perceptions of how participants were selected, conditions aboard ship en route to Ellesmere Island, living and hunting conditions after arrival, and whether, after relocation, Inuit people asked to be returned to their home communities. Among the more contentious issues raised were allegations of coercion, i.e., that Inuit were pressured to leave their home communities. Several people also believe that further coercion discouraged them from leaving their new domiciles in the High Arctic. They have indicated their view that the relocations were designed to use their presence in the new locations to reinforce Canada's sovereignty in the Arctic Archipelago. Other issues related to reports of privations and hardships at the remote destinations to which the people were moved.

Samuel Arnakallak, who moved with his family from Pond Inlet to Craig Harbour in 1953, spoke of the search for families from north Baffin Island in that year. He learned from Idlout, a fellow hunter from the Pond Inlet area, of the government's search for suitable men to go to the north. Arnakallak related he was told the government wanted three men with sufficient dogs, who had children "and were able to produce children but were not too old."[39] There was an apparent emphasis on finding families who would not only augment, but replenish the population of the fledgling settlement, contributing to a permanent settlement on Ellesmere Island.

Other people, particularly those from Quebec, recall the journey on the ship, which lasted two months, as a difficult one. Martha Flaherty, moved from Inukjuak as a young girl, five years of age, with her family in 1955, remembered it as a traumatic experience:

> When the weather was really bad it used to be scary. I remember one particular time [that] it was dark, rainy, stormy; everybody had to

wear life jackets and I was so scared, I thought we were going to die....And you know the pole of the ship, it almost touched the water...Sometimes, when it [was] really rough, all the dishes used to fly, and everyone was throwing up.[40]

A source of distress for the Inuit from Inukjuak, in particular, was the decision to separate families and friends, which Inuit informants maintain was only communicated to them after they had reached the High Arctic. Edith Patsauq Amaroalik related that after the relocated persons were picked up in Pond Inlet, they were assembled and told for the first time that they would be split into three groups with different destinations. Since they were interrelated, family members as well as friends would be separated from one another, a source of anguish:

When we were told that we [would] have to separate, Mary started crying right away. All those women, including women from Pond Inlet started crying when we were told that we will not be living in the same settlement. I did not cry unless I am made to cry. Once everyone was crying, all the dogs started howling on the ship. It was very frightening! We were at the bottom of the ship, in the forward lower deck, and a sad sight with the dogs howling and the women crying.[41]

The Inuit have testified that on their arrival, they discovered that there were no shelters in place, nor were materials made available for the manufacture of tools or housing. Anna Nungaq remembered that, after arriving at Craig Harbour, the RCMP moved the Inuit to the Lindstrom Peninsula site 60 km to the west.

[The] RCMP took us because we have no equipment to move ourselves. Then, they left us in front of huge mountains. I was very confused, lost, and did not know what to do. Huge mountains with a lot of huge rocks. Very different from here. No vegetation. We pitched our tents there. It was cold.[42]

Arnakallak stated that his family lived in sod-earth winter shelters on Baffin Island, but they needed wood to construct such dwellings. There was no wood available in the areas where they settled on Ellesmere Island, so they were unable to make warm dwellings. He also remembered that they were told that game animals would be abundant at the new location. After their arrival, Arnakallak found that it was true that marine mammals were more plentiful on Ellesmere Island than at Pond Inlet, but land mammals and other game were scarce.[43]

Ross Gibson, the former RCMP officer at Resolute Bay on Cornwallis Island, also asserted that no materials or facilities had been prepared for the relocated party, either for him or the Inuit in his charge. He had been told that the ship would be anchored for three weeks pending the setting up of the new settlement and police detachment. Instead, with the sea ice closing in, the ship departed three hours after the party had been left on the beach at Resolute Bay.

> Here I was with these people. Not a damned thing. The first night we put up these canvas tents, and I'll tell you, if I could have walked back to Ottawa the next day, I think I would have gone. But I was there and there wasn't anything I could do about it. There was no detachment building at that time. They [the RCMP administration] had made arrangements with DOT [the Department of Transport] that I could take residence there, but that was again another couple of miles away from where we had picked the camp. And my work certainly was not with the DOT. It was with the Eskimo. I had no transportation.[44]

Gibson expressed his frustration with the lack of planning or provision of facilities for the Inuit:

> There was no forethought put into it [the relocation] at all. You know, they just thought, well, all we have to do is get in touch with these people [the Inuit], and they're going to go. No, I never was happy with the way that the thing was done, ever. [There was] no planning at all. There was absolutely nothing. I don't know how they ever expected those people to live.[45]

Another source of unhappiness for the relocated Inuit was the lack of provisions or variety in the diet available to them on Ellesmere Island.

> It was very difficult, depressing, and confusing. All we ate was seal meat. When you are not used to eating seal meat alone, it's not very pleasant. Did we ever miss eating other food we used to have—birds, fish, caribou, berries from the land. We were hungry for our own food.[46]

Samwilly Elaijasialuk did not hold the RCMP responsible for the lack of provisions; he stated that the Mounties shared their own provisions with the Inuit. Rather, Mr. Elaijasialuk attributed more general neglect to the government:

> [The] RCMP is not to blame, it's the government that did wrong. RCMP tried their best to help us, they even gave us their own supply of flour. Once the flour arrived for Inuit, it would then be given to [the] RCMP to replace what we have used. RCMP did what they can do for us, especially when there was no transportation at all except by dog team.[47]

While federal officials had assumed that hunters from northern Baffin Island would be accustomed to 24-hour darkness, hunters from that region also found the winters on Ellesmere Island to be particularly dark, much more so than they had experienced. Gamaliel Aqiarak (Akeeagok), who moved to Grise Fiord from the Igloolik area in 1957, remembered his first winter at Grise Fiord as a difficult one:

> It was terrible, it was depressing. And it was very hard because it was dark. There was no day light and it was just terrible. In the wintertime it was very depressing and very discouraging especially when you wanted to go out hunting. And in the summer you couldn't even see when it got foggy. When we first got here it was very difficult.[48]

Hunting in the initial period, especially during the long, dark winters, imposed heavy demands on hunters and their families. The Inuit discovered that animals were often few and far between or accessible only for brief periods. Travelling was made difficult by variable sea-ice conditions. Due to ocean currents, leads opened in the ice of Jones Sound even during the winter and hunters were often thwarted from travelling, hampering food procurement. Anna Nungaq remembered:

> Getting food was sometimes a problem. The first year we were there we noticed this especially during the winter. Getting food depended on ice conditions. In Grise Fiord, when the ice freezes, it doesn't stay that way. But in Inukjuak, once the ice freezes, it stays frozen, so we had to adapt to unfamiliar ice conditions.[49]

Owing to the scarcity of food, the men were obliged to hunt in all seasons, including the winter.[50] The difficulties of hunting in the dark winters and the lack of hunting partners obliged men to take their spouses or children with them on hunting trips, a practice to which the Inuit from Quebec were unaccustomed.[51] Martha Flaherty recalled that due to shortages of food, she had to accompany her father on the hunt while she was still a child:

> I used to have to go [hunting] with my father when I was only seven, eight years old in the middle of winter, 50, 60 below. Sometimes he came home with nothing....We almost starved. The Police would think we were lying, but we didn't tell them. At that time, Inuit were such pushed-around people. Even if they're really starving or they're hungry, they're not going to say anything, so the Police would think we were fine....At that time, they [Inuit] were very shy.[52]

According to the relocated Inuit, many suffered from sadness or depression, persisting over many years. Anna Nungaq related her feelings about being moved to a strange environment:

> I hardly slept for years, cried, wanting to go home. I was extremely depressed. Practically for a year I slept very little, because I was so scared, threatened. I did not think there would ever be a day of light again. It is also very, very cold. Because I had never been in a place where there is no daylight at all, I was so scared and thought there would never be light again.[53]

Today, many Inuit who were relocated in the 1950s believe that the principal reason they were moved was the federal government's concern with maintaining Canadian sovereignty in the Arctic. A representative example of the expressed views was a statement by Anna Nungaq: "one of the reasons for moving us was to protect animals from Greenlanders. The Canadian Government did not want Greenlanders to hunt our animals."[54]

An issue arising from the controversies was whether Inuit had voluntarily agreed to move to the High Arctic or were manipulated into going. Testifying before the Royal Commission on Aboriginal Peoples, sociologist Hugh Brody interpreted the issue in light of the Inuit term *illira* or fear. Describing it as a mixture of awe and intimidation, Brody argued that this term characterized Inuit feelings toward Euro-Canadians during the era of paternalism in Inuit administration.[55]

Markusie Patsauq, who was relocated with his family from Inukjuak to Resolute Bay in 1953, stated in 1989: "In the past Inuit were afraid of white men, they did whatever they were asked to do, and the white men knew that."[56] Martha Flaherty described the relationship in similar terms, stating that, in the 1950s, Inuit people were not in a position to confront Euro-Canadians holding power over their lives.[57] In 1954, RCMP officers approached Abraham Pijamini, a hunter from Pinigat near Clyde River, Baffin Island, and asked him to serve as a special constable. Pijamini was extremely unhappy about this request because he felt he could not refuse Euro-Canadian authority figures. He later related his feelings at the time he was approached:

> At that time [prior to the RCMP's request] I was very happy, the way we survived. But I was disappointed and shocked the time I was asked to become a Special Constable or when the RCMP came to talk to me. At that time we were not hungry, we were physically fine and we did whatever we wanted to. We were not controlled by anyone outside our community. The first time the RCMP talked to me I was very hurt.[58]

Was pressure applied to Inuit people to move to the High Arctic? In reviewing the evidence, the Royal Commission concluded that the relocation plan was "inherently coercive," asserting:

> It was a plan designed to take people who were accustomed to an income economy, with the goods that income could purchase, and place them in a situation where they would be made to rely more heavily on game food, with all the hardship such a life naturally involved. The government did not need to use overt force. The imperative of survival achieved the desired objective.[59]

Other observers, such as Ross Gibson, have rejected the notion that the Inuit were deliberately coerced to relocate to the High Arctic.[60] Gibson was the RCMP officer who selected the families at Inukjuak for relocation to the High Arctic. Perhaps both perspectives have validity. In the 1950s, Inuit people, like other Aboriginal peoples, lacked the political power to assert their rights in exchanges with Euro-Canadians. Gibson may not have been aware of applying pressure, while the testimony of the Inuit suggests they felt they could not refuse officials who proposed to move them to "new hunting grounds," a reflection of their lack of power in the contact situation.

14
Change:
Adaptation to New Natural and
Cultural Environments, 1951–2000

Having arrived on Ellesmere Island in the 1950s, the Inuit at Craig Harbour, Alexandra Fiord, and then Grise Fiord confronted the enormous task of building a new life in a radically-different environment. The adjustment was particularly great for the Inuit from eastern Hudson Bay, whose homelands bore little resemblance to the climate, physiography, and ecology of the High Arctic, nearly 3,000 km north. The Inuit were expected to construct "traditional" Native dwellings, but they had no prior experience with the stone and sod winter dwellings typically built in the High Arctic. They were knowledgeable about snow-house construction, but the light precipitation in the region failed to produce enough snow for construction until winter was well advanced. Even when they were able to find suitable snow, the Inuit from Quebec were not aware of the method, common in the High Arctic, of lining snow houses with skins or canvas. Such an insulating layer was necessary in the harsh climate of the High Arctic region.[1] Families also lacked driftwood or suitable vegetation for fuel and initially had difficulty obtaining fresh water ice to melt for drinking.[2]

In addition to difficulties of adjustment for the persons being moved, the relocations reportedly caused additional problems for the communities they left behind. The departure of some of their leading hunters and leaders deprived the source communities of their procurement skills. In 1955, P.A.C. Nichols, an official with the Hudson's Bay Company, expressed his concern that the departure of Idlout and his party from Pond Inlet for Resolute Bay would remove "the mainstay of a large camp at Pond Inlet which always made a good living due largely to his leadership." Nichols also noted that Pond Inlet had suffered the loss of 39 people to the relocations of the previous two years and stated that, if this continued, he could foresee the area being reduced in population "to the point where it will be difficult from an economic standpoint to operate a trading post." On the positive side, he believed that the departure of Inuit from the game-depleted regions of eastern Hudson Bay would reduce the pressure on resources in these areas to the point that subsistence hunting would be viable for those who remained.[3]

In 1953 and succeeding years, Inuit who were being relocated arrived on Ellesmere in late August or early September, having spent the summer season aboard the *C.D. Howe* en route to Ellesmere Island. Their initial adjustment was therefore complicated by the fact that they were unable to exploit the summer season, the optimal time to hunt and stockpile resources for the winter. Akpaliapik, one of two Pond Inlet hunters who moved to Craig Harbour in the initial relocation of 1953, remembered that since they arrived too late to cache food during the summer, they had to hunt with particular urgency and intensity that fall and winter to provide food for their families.[4]

Aware of the difficulty of securing enough game in the fall, J. Cantley of the Arctic Services Division of the Department of Resources and Development, proposed in 1953 that the Inuit at Craig Harbour be allowed a "selective killing" of older bull muskoxen.[5] He suggested that RCMP officers at the detachment supervise the hunting to ensure that "the younger animals were left unmolested." Cantley's suggestion apparently reflected his belief that it would be less destructive to kill bull muskoxen than females or younger animals. These assumptions were later questioned by the Inuit from an ecological standpoint, as discussed later in this chapter. In any case, Larry Audlaluk, who moved to Craig Harbour from Quebec with his family in 1953 recalled that at that time, federal authorities would not allow any hunting of muskoxen "*unless* in extreme circumstances like starvation." Mr. Audlaluk recalled that the RCMP did permit hunting of caribou, but the hunt was limited to the late summer. He added: "bull caribou only were hunted and only one animal per hunter."[6] In the 1950s, federal officials did not consult with the Inuit regarding the development or implementation of such policies.

In a report prepared six months after the arrival of the first party, RCMP Corporal Sargent wrote that "the clothing of all natives, in the opinion of the writer, is not adequate at present in the form of skin clothing." Hunters had obtained adequate numbers of skins for their own apparel, but children had little or none at all. For this reason, he wired his superiors to request that 200 "clothing skins" be shipped to Craig Harbour. Sargent also stated that he hoped to avert an overkill of caribou in the area when other game was available for food. He indicated his desire to encourage the Inuit to wear more sealskin garments; "however, this may be easier said than done, as the Port Harrison natives appear very much in favour of 'white man's clothing.'"[7] Bedding was fashioned from caribou skins obtained by Inuit hunters during two fall hunting excursions, supplemented by skins supplied by the detachment.

Members of the community have cautioned that, to present the relocation experiment favourably, Sargent embroidered his reports with exaggerated remarks regarding the rapid adjustment of relocated Inuit to their new environment. An example was the constable's first report, subsequently published in the *RCMP Quarterly*, in which he asserted that within a year of their arrival the women from Port Harrison (Inukjuak) had learned the skills of making superior hunting boots from their counterparts from Baffin Island. However, Larry Audlaluk noted that the women from Inukjuak "already knew how to make good water proof kamiks (boots) and Cpt. [Constable] Sargent liked them so much he had pairs made almost every year."[8] In this case, the adaptations of Inuit had already occurred in their original homelands in northern Quebec and not as a result of the relocation.

Owing to the lack of suitable snow for snow-house construction, the Inuit arriving in 1953 were reportedly still occupying tents at the end of December during their first winter on Ellesmere Island.[9] An RCMP officer reported that the Inuit had insulated their tents with buffalo hides supplied by the detachment. Anna Nungaq remembered that her family lined their tent with muskox skins, but there were not enough of them, so the intended insulating layer was inadequate.[10] According to Martha Flaherty, willows were also gathered for insulation.[11]

Initially, two related Inukjuak families—headed by Paddy Aqiatasuk and Joalamie Aqiatasuq—shared one tent. Elijah Nutarak, step-son to Paddy, and his spouse Anna had their own tent, but they moved into the larger tent "because it was too cold."[12] This temporary dwelling sheltered 11 people and was warmed by three stone lamps (*qulliq*), tended by Anna Nungaq, Ikoomak, and their mother, Mary Aqiatasuk.[13]

In 1954, the RCMP reported that materials arrived with the *C.D. Howe* to enable additional improvements to the dwellings. According to this report, lumber was used to build flooring and to provide interior framing for the tents. In some cases, the roofs were covered with a double layer of canvas, over which buffalo hides supplied by the department were arranged. These structures were insulated on the outside by snow banking, and the inside walls lined with old magazines supplied by the detachment.[14] Larry Audlaluk, who had moved with his family the first year, has a different recollection, stating that no materials arrived with the ship. Rather, scrap wood was made available for framing material for the houses, while heather was gathered for use as insulation. As was their traditional practice, the families used caribou skins to cover the sleeping platforms and for bed covers, which they continued to use until the building of rental housing in the late 1960s.[15]

R.S. Pilot, a former RCMP constable who stayed for several months with Akpaliapik's family in 1955, described their dwelling as a small hut, about 4 m by 5 m, and 2 m high. He stated that it consisted of a canvas stretched over a wooden frame, with an outer structure of packing crates, which was covered over with sod. In this modest dwelling, three adults, one teenager, and three small children lived. Other than the sleeping platform, there was no furniture. Meals were cooked over a primus stove or a *qulliq*. The sleeping platform was covered with two or three layers of caribou skins. The entranceway measured about a metre high by two-thirds of a metre wide and led into a small porch where the family stored dog harnesses and seal meat. After a few weeks, Akpaliapik built a snow house adjacent to his own dwelling for Mr. Pilot to live in.[16]

Anna Nungaq described the simple materials used by her family to create the flooring and a cushioned surface for sleeping:

> We used rocks, or pebbles for the floor, and used just the skins for a mattress with rocks underneath. Because we pounded seal oil for the *qulliq* our floor would get all greasy sometimes, so they would open the edge of the tent to throw out the dirty rocks and put in the new ones. The rocks we were going to use for the floor would be steaming with the cold. There was no wood at that time for the floor.[17]

In December 1954, all but two of the Baffin Island families reportedly were still living in reinforced tents, although the tents had been improved by structural framing in the intervening period. Constructing the frames from scrap lumber, around which canvas was stretched to form an inside and outside lining, they filled the intervening space with moss. Magazines were used to line the interior of the structures, which was said to keep them "clean and fairly bright."[18] With the largest of these dwellings measuring 3 m x 3.6 m., and the smallest at 3 m x 2.5 m, these early dwellings were the approximate size of igloos.[19] Their size was partly the result of the lack of building materials, but also required by a continuing reliance on seal-oil lamps to heat the small spaces. These dwellings were also built to be low-lying, with only two metres from the peak of the ceiling to the floor. By keeping their houses low to the ground, the Inuit facilitated the snow banking of the structures in winter. This approach reduced the impact of the ferocious winds which periodically strike this exposed site on the coast. At the same time, the families from Inukjuak inhabited snow houses for the first three years. With the introduction of oil-burning stoves and the acquisition of sufficient materials, they moved into wooden dwellings by the fourth winter.[20]

At first, the Inuit women relied on traditional tools to maintain their households. The *qulliq* or seal-oil lamp was generally used as a source of light, for drying out clothes, in preparing skins, and for cooking, both in summer tents and winter dwellings.[21] Sixteen months after their arrival on Ellesmere the Inuit reportedly possessed an expanded range of household tools, including primus stoves, lanterns, gas and Coleman oil lamps. At this time, Corporal Sargent reported that sewing machines would be requisitioned for the following year.[22] The Inuit also fashioned stoves from oil drums, intending to burn moss during the winter, although this fuel was difficult and time-consuming to collect.

While the early shelters showed a resourceful application of traditional Inuit building principles and available materials, they were clearly not suitable for extended use. In early 1960, Constable Pilot described their limitations: "The problem these old houses present is the fact that during the early spring they become quite damp because of the accumulation of frost and ice through the lack of proper insulation and ventilation, they are very musty and are just a germ breeder during this period."[23] Mr. Pilot's remarks suggest that the periodic reports of respiratory illness in Grise Fiord in this period may have resulted in part from the crowded living conditions in these improvised shelters.[24] For these reasons, the federal government embarked on a program of building "rigid frame" dwellings in 1959.

Establishment of Grise Fiord

A resident of the community has related that, within a short period after arrival, the RCMP insisted that the Inuit residents move away from the detachment, reportedly to discourage "loitering" or requests for "handouts."[25] In any case, Craig Harbour was not a suitable location for their settlement. It was too distant from marine resources available at leads in Jones Sound, and too much time and resources were consumed travelling to suitable hunting grounds. In 1955, the police moved members of the community, with materials and belongings, in their utility boats,[26] and they re-established their community approximately 60 km along the coast to the west at the Lindstrom Peninsula, situated between Grise Fiord and Harbour Fiord, where they had already set up a hunting camp the previous year.[27] In this location, they had ready access to leads in the pack ice where pinnipeds and polar bears were present during the winter. It would become the site of the permanent community of Grise Fiord (Figure 83). The advantages of this location were demonstrated the first year when hunters secured 404 seals, 22 bearded seals (*oojook*), 27 harp seals, and 23 walruses. According to the RCMP, they took 11 beluga whales very near their settlement, and 28 caribou in the areas of Lee Point, Starnes Fiord, and Fram Fiord.[28] This represented a marked increase from the take of 102 seals in 1954, their first full year while based at Craig Harbour.[29] One resident of the

Figure 83: Grise Fiord in the late 1950s. National Archives of Canada, Photo No. PA-61670.

community has recalled that the majority of the killed animals were reserved for the food of the RCMP personnel or for use as dog food by their Husky teams.[30]

At the new Inuit communities, much of the productive labour of women was consumed in the search for basic necessities. Anna Nungaq related that her mother and mother-in-law worked very hard collecting moss for fuel. As it did not grow on the coast, they were obliged to climb the mountains to gather the moss. Owing to the rugged terrain, they were obliged to bag it and roll the bags down the slope.[31] Alternatively, according to Rynee Flaherty, low-lying willow branches growing in more protected areas were gathered for fuel. She stated: "All we had for lights were little lamps and it was so dark. It was a very sad time and I don't especially like to remember it."[32]

Drinking water was also difficult to secure. The search for fresh water ice became a daily preoccupation; the Inuit obtained it along the shore or from mountain glaciers.[33] According to Rynee Flaherty: "The big difference [between northern Quebec and Ellesmere Island] was that for drinking water there was only salt water, because it was so dark trying to get [to] icebergs from the mountains...and it was so dark when we tried to get ice for drinking water that we would hit rocks."[34]

Inuit special constables and their families encountered many similar difficulties at the new detachment established at Alexandra Fiord in

1953. Here they assisted the RCMP in its mission of monitoring Inughuit crossings from Greenland and their movements and hunting activities on Ellesmere Island. In practice, this proved to be more difficult than anticipated. In a 1958 report, the Alexandra Fiord detachment reported that Inughuit had been hunting in the area the previous winter, taking at least 10 polar bears in the Kane Basin along Ellesmere Island's eastern coast.[35] Two years later, an RCMP officer there reported that several Inughuit hunting parties had visited the detachment, including one that killed five bears in the vicinity of Makinson Inlet.[36] Noting an apparently sharp reduction in polar bear numbers, the officer observed:

> Little hope is held for an increase in the polar bear population in this area as long as the Greenlanders continue to slaughter them indiscriminately and after talking with these people for three consecutive springs the writer has no faith in them to observe any of the provisions of the NWT Game Ordinance that do not coincide with their wishes and requirements.[37]

The writer added that, while many patrols had been organized to intercept Inughuit hunters, locating their parties in the "rough ice and generally poor travelling conditions" had been difficult. Life at this remote post was lonely for all residents, but especially for the spouses of the special constables, who, like their predecessors at Bache Peninsula in the 1920s, were left alone when their husbands were on patrol. Annie Pijamini, the spouse of Special Constable Abraham Pijamini, stated:

> When we were just coming from Clyde River to Alexandra Fiord, my sewing machine and my radio that was operated by electricity were no longer useful. Even though I brought them over we couldn't use them because we didn't have any electricity in Alexandra Fiord. So I couldn't even use my radio. That was a terrible feeling. I couldn't use these machines anymore. The only machine I had, the sewing machine I had, was operated by electricity so it was useless. Plus, the only source of light we had was with the oil lamp. So they were just pieces of items that we had. We couldn't use them because there was no electricity anyway.[38]

As was the case at Craig Harbour, the Alexandra Fiord detachment was resupplied by the annual voyages of the Eastern Arctic Patrol ship. Assuming the ship was able to penetrate the perennial ice dam in Smith Sound and southern Kane Basin, it would approach as near to the detachment as ice and sea conditions permitted. The ship was met by the RCMP boat, into which supplies were offloaded for transport to the shore. Owing to the high winds that often occur in this area, the supply operation could be a very dangerous undertaking. With the limited navigation season and the ever-present risk of being trapped in ice, the ship needed to depart as soon as feasible. This sometimes meant taking the risk of meeting the vessel in stormy seas, a task which the Euro-Canadian officers sometimes delegated to their Inuit subordinates. Abraham Pijamini, a special constable with the RCMP at Alexandra Fiord between 1956 and 1962, recalled once such experience:

> It gets very difficult when it's windy up there because the wind is very strong. One time when it was very windy the RCMP head person asked us to go down to the ship [Police boat] to look after it. He wouldn't go himself. He asked me; the other RCMP [officer], and said that we could get help from the other Inuit. It was so rough that you could hardly see the bottom of the ship. Sometimes, you could hardly stand. But he asked us to go and we couldn't say no. He himself wouldn't go. It was particularly hard for me that time because nobody wanted to follow me. Nobody wanted to go with me; they wouldn't dare because they didn't think anybody would survive. I had to go by myself. I'll never forget that. It was very difficult to go to that ship one time. But other RCMP agreed to come with me so we put our life jackets on and we ended up going down there, but it was a difficult process because the wind was too strong. Sometimes, we would be blown away. We somehow got [to] the ship and took it toward the land. I particularly remember one time, when the wind came in it was like a tornado. It was coming from the mountain and it was so dark. When it hit the water it was white because it lifted all the water. From there, it started moving towards us and everything flew. Somehow, the RCMP and I got to the land.[39]

The relocated Inuit on Ellesmere Island experienced several early, demoralizing tragedies, which for a time appeared to place the community in jeopardy. In 1954, Corporal Sargent reported the death from a heart attack of an Inuit man, Paddy Aqiatusuk (Akteeeaktashuk), one of Canada's most famous Inuit sculptors,[40] who had travelled north with his wife and family the previous year. His death deprived the community of Inuit from Quebec of one of its leaders. In 1958, Grise Fiord was dealt a severe blow by the accidental drowning of two boys on 27 July. There are important differences in accounts by the RCMP and the Inuit as to the reasons for the accident. The RCMP claimed that the boys were playing on the shore-edge ice, but community members recall that they had been fishing for sculpin to supplement the "constant diet of mammals."[41] As a result of these deaths, R.S. Pilot reported that "morale was at a very low ebb at the native camp," and that several men expressed a desire to move away from the area. An additional drain on the community's morale at this time was the depletion of staple food items such as flour, rolled oats, sugar, milk, and tobacco, and the scarcity was another source of unhappiness. Reportedly, the arrival of the *C.D. Howe*, a new stock of trading store supplies, and two new Inuit families, helped lift the spirits of the people.[42] The community suffered another setback in 1960 when an epidemic of whooping cough caused one death and the "serious illness" of six other children.[43]

These tragedies apparently prompted several Inuit to request that they be returned to their home communities in Quebec or on Baffin Island. They asserted that at the time of the relocations they were promised return passage to their communities of origin, but were denied the opportunity to return to their homes. Federal officials denied that such promises were ever made or that any request to return was ever refused. In his annual report prepared in December 1954, Corporal Sargent stated that, up to that time, none of the Inuit had asked to be returned immediately to their communities of origin. However, he acknowledged that two families from Pond Inlet had expressed a wish to return at an unspecified future date. Fryer wrote: "Although they have no immediate desire to return they would like to go back possibly in a few years to help their aging parents and relatives." In the meantime, he stated, some families had asked that some of their relatives in Pond Inlet and Inukjuak be assisted in joining them on Ellesmere Island.[44]

Some Inuit, current or former residents of Grise Fiord, have questioned the reports of Constables Fryer and Sargent on these issues. They have suggested that Sargent wrote his reports to downplay the suggestion that Inuit people wished to return to their original homes. In their account, whenever Inuit expressed the desire to go back, Sargent attempted to dissuade them by proposing that, instead, it would be better to encourage their relatives to move to Grise Fiord.[45]

In 1955, an RCMP officer reported that Akpaliapik, the head of one of first families to move to Craig Harbour, had asked to return to Pond Inlet within two years. The previous year, he had requested that his brother Aqiarak (Akeeagok) be enabled to join them on Ellesmere. Since Aqiarak and his family had not yet arrived, Akpaliapik "may desire to return to them." If they did come, Akpaliapik "would have no present or near future desire to return."[46] At that point, even the leading hunters within the community wanted to leave Ellesmere Island if relatives or others did not arrive to make their tiny settlement a more viable community. Later that year, Aqiarak and his family moved to Ellesmere Island, and no further requests from Akpaliapik were recorded in the RCMP records in this period. However, the absence of written documentation did not necessarily indicate a change of heart. Members of the community subsequently related that, by this time, Akpaliapik and others, having met protracted resistance by the RCMP, had given up in their efforts to move back to their homelands.[47]

In 1959, the Inuk Elijah and his family expressed a desire to move to Resolute Bay to join his brother, Samwilly, who had left Grise Fiord the previous year. The RCMP discouraged him from moving, arguing that his brother had only gone to Resolute Bay to find a wife and, not having found one, would be returning in the spring. In the meantime, Samwilly asked his mother and brother at Grise Fiord to join him in Resolute. The RCMP officer in charge of the Grise Fiord detachment declared himself against such a move, stating that "it is known that others from this area would like to live at Resolute also, and if one moves it is felt that more will follow."[48] In 1960, Inuit people were again said to be considering departure from Ellesmere Island. Hunting was said to have been very poor the preceding season, with only 47 fox secured by the entire community.[49] J.F. Delaute, the Regional Administrator for the Department of Northern Affairs and National Resources, in a report on the Baffin Island Patrol that year, wrote of a conversation with RCMP Constable Donahue regarding the situation at Grise Fiord:

> There has been talk of their moving away if the hunting doesn't improve. He said they might stay if the hunting improved but if it didn't, he doubted that they would and that the only other inducement which would convince them, would be wage employment."[50]

Delaute suggested "that if the School were established at the Camp, it would be an inducement for the people to stay." In any case, concern over the possible move of the Inuit away from the region seems to have been a catalyst for the building of a school at Grise Fiord, as well as the conversion of the trading store to a co-operative.[51]

Beyond the documentary record prepared by RCMP officers, oral history has given voice to alternative perspectives by former and current residents of Grise Fiord. Various individuals testified to the Royal Commission on Aboriginal Peoples that they were thwarted in their efforts to return to their original homes in Quebec and Baffin Island. The Royal Commission asserted that in day-to-day life in the new communities of Grise Fiord and Resolute Bay, "small elements of coercion became additionally coercive when carried out by a police force."[52] Statements by numerous current and former residents of Grise Fiord that they experienced coercion are countered by assertions of former federal officials that no such pressure existed.

Writing before the public controversy over the relocations, Milton Freeman provided an account of pressure applied to at least one of the original families induced to move to Ellesmere Island in 1953.[53] Freeman wrote of a young hunter from Inukjuak, designated by the pseudonym Amarok, who was the youngest married hunter of the community. According to Freeman, he had not shown interest in emigrating, but "the police persisted in their attempts to get him to accompany the two families prepared to travel north, and so finally he gave in to the pressure of their demands." In 1959, the RCMP recruited Amarok to work as a special constable at Alexandra Fiord. He accepted on the understanding that, due to the isolated nature of the posting, he would be able to be "repatriated at a suitable time." Following the closure of the Alexandra Fiord detachment, Amarok returned to Grise Fiord in 1963. At this point, realizing he could not realize the same standard of living as a hunter that he could as a salaried employee, he requested relocation to Iqaluit or Churchill, where there were greater opportunities for waged employment.

His request apparently falling on deaf ears, Amarok asked to meet with the RCMP Inspector on his annual visit to Grise Fiord in 1966. Since an interpreter was not available, he could not express his concerns on that occasion. Writing again to the Inspector that winter, he indicated a series of issues he wished to discuss, including perceived interference by RCMP officers in the private affairs of Inuit. Yet, this request, too, was ignored. Not receiving a satisfactory reply in three years, Amarok wrote to the regional administrator in Iqaluit in 1967 to relay his request. At this time, non-RCMP Euro-Canadians at Grise Fiord assured him that the decision to move was his alone and he and his family departed soon after.[54] Freeman's article deals with many complexities of the contact situation not discussed here. For the present purpose, perhaps it is sufficient to note the resistance of federal officials to Inuit requests to return home, as late as 1967.

Development of Hunting, Fishing, and Trapping on Ellesmere Island

In addition to the people's needs for proper community facilities, family reunification, and other issues, the potential of the new community to persist on Ellesmere Island demanded rapid adaptation to hunting and natural resource use in rugged, unfamiliar terrain. The newcomers expected to find game in abundance on Ellesmere Island, but owing to the shortness of the autumn, they were unable to secure the desired numbers and variety of animals. In the first few years, little food was available other than seal meat. The lack of alternative foods was a hardship for the Inuit from Quebec, who were used to greater variety in their diet, including the flesh of birds, fish, caribou meat, and berries.[55]

451

Prior to their departure, they also consumed a few Western foods, including flour, tea, and rolled oats for breakfast.[56] R.S. Pilot, who arrived in 1955, recalled that the diet of the Inuit on Ellesmere Island at this time was largely confined to seal meat. Other game animals included caribou, narwhal, the fin of which was considered a delicacy, and occasional birds when they could be obtained, including ptarmigan, ducks, and geese.[57]

As with all other Aboriginal people who settled on Ellesmere Island from the time of the Thule culture, the Inuit in the 1950s relied heavily on husky dogs as the basis of their hunting culture. During the first year the number of dogs was inadequate; the RCMP reported that several of the Inuit from Quebec were "handicapped slightly in not having sufficient dogs for extended trapping purposes."[58] By the second year, the dog population increased so that each hunter had 8 or 10 animals. RCMP officers requested that hunters not expand their teams beyond this level. In late 1954, Corporal Sargent reported that three young men over the age of 17 were now to be given their own small teams. Each of the young hunters had purchased a 30-30 rifle and was now considered equipped to secure the required game for dog food.[59] Bob Pilot remembered that by the second year after their arrival, each of the Inuit men possessed harpoons, snow knives, and rifles,[60] although a resident of the community has stated that the hunters already possessed these tools before the relocations.[61]

Hunting trips with sled dogs were largely carried out by males, but women played an important role in preparing the food and extra clothing and harness required on the trail. Martha Kigugtak remembered:

> They always took food, because the dogs are not as fast as the vehicles right now. They made sure they took a lot. They had extra pairs of kamiks, extra clothes. They always carried more than one for one purpose. They made sure they carried two pair of kamiks [boots], two pair of mitts, everything. And then the strings for the dogs. They always carried skin ropes for the dogs.[62]

Hunting at Craig Harbour was initially hampered by the presence of open water in Jones Sound in the late summer when they arrived. Anna Nungaq remembered "The men could not hunt for a long time. There was a large open water not far so you could not go very far. Up there the water is salty, so it is easy to break."[63] Since dog teams could not be used until the ice had frozen sufficiently, the RCMP organized a hunting trip by boat to the vicinity of Jakeman Glacier. According to Constable A.C. Fryer, Inuit hunters found a herd of 50 walrus resting on large floating pans of ice in the Sound, and three of these animals were killed, enough to fill their boats.[64] Fryer reported that this trip was the first time that Inuit from Quebec experienced hunting and flensing walrus. He also reported that this hunting excursion initiated a cultural exchange between the two Inuit groups, as the Pond Inlet hunters reportedly taught their counterparts from Quebec the skills associated with these activities. He was apparently mistaken in this belief as the former residents of Inukjuak had long hunted walrus in Hudson Bay.[65]

Samuel Arnakallak, an Inuk who was relocated from Pond Inlet to Craig Harbour in 1953, also has a different recollection of this episode. He recalled that he and Akpaliapik, his compatriot from Baffin Island, killed the three walruses. According to Arnakallak, they gave the meat to the families from Inukjuak.[66] Subsequently, the RCMP officers accompanied the younger Inuit men on a caribou hunt to Fram Fiord. They secured 10 caribou, principally for skins, which were used in making winter clothing. During three additional hunting trips in the police power boat, the Inuit obtained six additional walrus, two bearded seal, and an unspecified number of "common" seals, presumably, harp seals.[67] Just before Christmas 1953, Corporal Sargent reported that the Inuit still had one and a half walrus and three narwhal in stores from the fall hunt. He wrote that they had secured 40 seals by hunting at seal holes (*utoq* hunting) and by setting nets at tight cracks in the ice.[68]

In this period, the main source of income for the Inuit was the trade in white fox furs. Between January 1954 and the arrival of the Eastern Arctic Patrol ship on 24 August, the Inuit traded the pelts of 365 white fox, four blue fox, and 19 ermine. Income from trapping was supplemented by the sale of 22 carvings. During the fall trapping season, they secured an additional 229 white fox, three blue fox, and four ermine and produced 44 carvings, a much larger number than the previous year. The take of fox furs represented an increase of 55 pelts over the same period in the preceding year, which was explained as the result of longer trap lines and an increase in the number of traps used by each hunter. The total trade value earned was $2,580 or $258 for each male over 16 years of age.[69]

By 1958, the Inuit had established trap lines across nearly the entire length of the southern coast of Ellesmere Island, from Hell Gate on the west to Craig Harbour on the east. According to Constable Bob Pilot, now the officer in charge of Grise Fiord RCMP detachment, maintenance of the trap lines demanded frequent travel, with the men leaving the settlement for 7 to 10 days at a time. The Inuit co-ordinated their travel so that at least two men remained at Grise Fiord to tend the dogs and to hunt seals in the vicinity.[70] The trap lines reportedly produced a good yield of skins in this period. In 1959, Constable Pilot wrote that the Inuit there had earned "good incomes" through the sale of white fox pelts over the previous year.[71]

The Influence of Modern Technology: The Snowmobile

While various Western technologies have changed the lives of Inuit people at Grise Fiord and other communities, few innovations have had a greater impact than the snowmobile, a vehicle whose introduction exerted a marked impact on circumpolar peoples in both Eurasia and North America.[72] For more than a thousand years after ca. AD 900, the Inuit and their ancestors, the Thule people, relied heavily on dog-sled transport for hunting and seasonal travel, a pattern reintroduced to Ellesmere Island by the relocations in the 1950s. Within an astonishingly short period in the 1960s, the use of sled dogs was eclipsed by the gas-powered snowmobile. Adoption of Euro-Canadian boats and motors occurred even before the spread of the snowmobile. By 1966, all but one of Grise Fiord hunters owned a canoe or boat, and only one hunter did not have an outboard motor.[73]

By the mid-1960s, the development of waged labour produced the preconditions for a further technological shift. Now engaged in a range of service vocations within the community, Grise Fiord men found much of their time to be taken up in these tasks and they therefore needed a faster means of reaching hunting grounds to secure country food for their families. At the same time, waged labour also generated sufficient cash earnings to pay for the new technology. In 1966, Samwilly Elijasialuk, who had worked for the Department of Public Works to maintain the first powerhouse and also worked in the local school, purchased the community's first Bombardier Ski-doo from Montreal.[74] In 1966, another Grise Fiord man who was a RCMP special constable and active hunter, purchased a Bombardier Ski-doo at Resolute Bay. His reasons were straightforward and pragmatic. Working eight hours a day for wages, he was also responsible for hunting for his own and his mother's households. Obtaining a Ski-doo enabled him to hunt after work hours, as well as make trips out to icebergs in the sound to chip and haul fresh-water ice back the community. This helped free up time for his brother and brother-in-law to go hunting, as he was able to supply their families with ice for drinking water while they were on the trail.[75]

Once these snowmobiles arrived, RCMP officers realized that further attempts to prevent their use would be futile. Having at first resisted its introduction, they now insisted that every hunter embrace the new technology and that the dogs of the community be shot, although no compensation was offered for the loss of the dogs or to help defray the costs of the new technology.[76] The police asserted that the destruction of the dogs was made necessary by several instances of dogs biting children, although residents of Grise Fiord have disputed these claims. Instead, they suggested that the reports of biting were concocted by Police officers to justify to their superiors the shift to snowmobiles, which in any case was by this time a *fait accompli*.[77] By December 1968, there were 16 snowmobiles in Grise Fiord, some of them individually owned, while in other cases hunters pooled their resources to purchase a machine.[78]

Reporting on the first year of general use, Constable Vitt of the Grise Fiord detachment noted that the snowmobiles enabled a caribou hunting trip to Baumann Fiord in October, when 10 animals were killed. The hunters brought back half the carcasses on the first trip, and later returned by Ski-doo to retrieve the remainder of the meat. According to Vitt, hunters also found the snowmobiles "ideal" for checking traplines during the dark winter months, as their headlamps made it much easier to follow the trail. Vitt noted: "What used to mean a week's trip by dogs to the end of the trapline and back now takes one day for the return trip."[79] Snowmobiles also enabled hunters to undertake some forms of hunting that previously were not feasible. Where, before 1967, Inuit hunters usually could not overtake caribou with dog teams, the snowmobile made it possible for them to take more of these animals. Snowmobiles also facilitated overland travel to caribou hunting grounds, enabling a higher harvest rate.[80] By 1968, increased use of snowmobiles enabled the hunters to increase the kill of caribou in the Baumann Fiord area to 37 animals.[81]

At the same time, the switch to snowmobiles also brought disadvantages unanticipated in the rush to modernization. Tookilkee Kigugtak, a senior hunter experienced in the use of both sled dogs and snowmobiles, preferred the use of dogs. Sled dogs could be taken over terrain inaccessible to the machines. Their keen sense of smell could help in tracking down game animals such as polar bears. Dogs also could find their way when hunters needed bearings on the trail, and could help them through dangerous areas. In Kigugtak's words: "The dogs were very good. They are much more knowledgeable than ski-doos. They know where to go even if it is very foggy....They knew where to go even if there were no tracks."[82] Twice, Kigugtak related, the dogs took him home when he was lost. "The dogs also were safer on thin ice. If they had previously fallen through the ice, they would learn quickly to avoid it the next time."

The relative merits and disadvantages of snowmobiles were summarized by Simon Akpaliapik, a former leader and hunter at Grise Fiord, in an interview published in the early 1980s:

> You could get trapped on the ice when it breaks up. Dogs know how to get around it, but with a skidoo it is dangerous....It would be better to

have dogs if you went hunting all the time. It is easy to feed them. But if you have a job and you go hunting only after work and on weekends, you are better off with a skidoo. We always keep some dogs around for fun, to make parkas, or for pets for the kids.[83]

From a strictly commercial standpoint, the adoption of the snowmobile did not represent a straightforward advantage. In a study published in 1972, biologist Roderick Riewe calculated the average costs of operating a dog team in the years 1965–67, as opposed to operating a snowmobile in 1969–72. He found that operators of dog teams spent on average $572.23 annually, while the cash income from the sale of furs totalled $550 per hunter. By contrast, operators of snowmobiles incurred annual costs of $1846.02, while cash earnings from furs increased only marginally to $890. These figures suggested that operators of snowmobiles were actually losing money on the trapline.[84] However, this was not the full story. All hunters at Grise Fiord in this period held wage-earning positions, and snowmobiles enabled them to hunt after work or on weekends and also greatly increased their range of hunting for subsistence.[85] As Freeman has pointed out, traditional food-gathering practices have assumed an importance beyond subsistence; they are also central to the culture and identity of Inuit.[86]

Another Western machine embraced by the Inuit was the motor boat, important for use in hunting walruses. In the early period, walrus hunting was carried out with a combination of modern technology, including guns and power boats and such traditional tools as the *avatuk*,[87] a large watertight bladder fashioned from sealskin, which, attached to the harpooned walrus, thwarted its efforts to escape by diving. In 1955, Akpaliapik purchased a trap boat from the RCMP for ten fox skins,[88] which was used by the community in hunting marine mammals. In that year Corporal Sargent wrote that three Inuit from Port Harrison were negotiating the purchase of a whale boat, to be paid for with their pooled resources from furs, to be deducted from their store accounts over the following three years.[89] In the event, the whaleboat was not sold at that time and remained the property of the RCMP until the mid-1970s, when it was tendered to Ookookoo Quaraq for purchase.[90] When an American visited Grise Fiord in 1962, he observed that, at that time, the Inuit were using two boats, a canoe, powered by a 10-horsepower motor, and a five-metre row boat, also fitted with a 10-horsepower engine. He erroneously described the canoe as a Peterhead, although no such boats were owned by either community members or the RCMP.[91] Both boats were transported to the walrus hunting waters off Craig Harbour on komatiks pulled by dog teams.[92]

Extension of Hunting Range

During the first 20 years after arrival, hunters at Grise Fiord steadily increased the range of their hunting activities as they gained knowledge of the region's coasts, ocean crossings, and interior passes of Ellesmere Island. The hunting range of the Grise Fiord Inuit was established in various ways: through excursions by hunters in the community, trips accompanying RCMP patrols, and sharing traditional knowledge with the Inughuit of Greenland. Gamaliel Aqiarak described the flexible, integrated approach to travel followed by Inuit hunters in his native Baffin Island, which they continued after moving to Ellesmere Island:

> We were always moving. We moved according to where the animals were. We would move to the best hunting areas. We would have sod houses in different towns, and that is how we moved. We moved according to the animals. That was how long we would live there. Inuit always moved around, following the animals. We would winter in a certain area if there were plenty of animals in that area. Or move to another one if there wasn't enough animals there. That is how they lived.[93]

After moving to Ellesmere Island, the Inuit no longer built sod dwellings and instead used snow houses or tents as temporary shelters on the trail, but the practice of moving from camp to camp continued.[94]

When zoologist Roderick Riewe conducted studies at Grise Fiord in the early 1970s, the routes of the Inuit hunters criss-crossed a territory with a surface area of 411,800 km². Measured in linear terms, there were then 1,190 km of winter routes in regular use; and a further 5,170 km of routes were used less frequently.[95] While overland passes were relatively fixed, routes traversing the ocean varied from year to year according to ice and snow conditions. Riewe's maps of hunting and travelling routes (Figures 84-86), document a remarkable range of land use within the first two decades. Even before the relocations of 1953, Inuit special constables with the RCMP at Craig Harbour initiated hunting and other patrols covering extensive portions of Jones Sound and other areas. These included a 1951 patrol from Craig Harbour to Resolute Bay via Dundas Harbour on Devon Island, shorter hunting trips in 1952 to Fram Fiord, Harbour Fiord, and Grise Fiord on Ellesmere Island's southern coast. In 1952, the Inuit with the RCMP also traversed southern Ellesmere Island between Grise and Baumann Fiords. After the arrival of the relocated families in 1953, Inuit special constables and other officers traversed the southern coast as far as Hell Gate between southeastern Ellesmere Island and North Kent Island. Together,

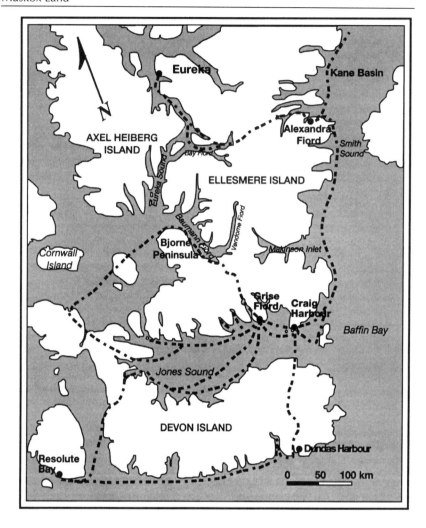

Figure 84: Map of major travelling and hunting routes of the Grise Fiord
Inuit, 1951–59. Map adapted and reproduced with the permission of
Dr. R.R. Riewe, Winnipeg.

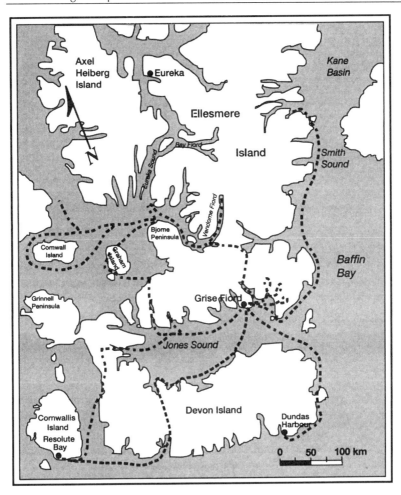

Figure 85: Map of major travelling and hunting routes of the Grise Fiord Inuit, 1960–69. Map adapted and reproduced with the permission of Dr. R.R. Riewe, Winnipeg.

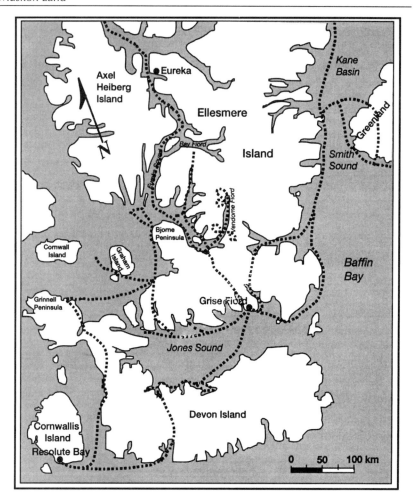

Figure 86: Map of major travelling and hunting routes of the Grise Fiord
Inuit, 1970–73. Map adapted and reproduced with the permission
of Dr. R.R. Riewe, Winnipeg.

they staged major patrols, including one which followed the southern Ellesmere coast to Devon Island, crossed the Grinnell Peninsula, before crossing the Belcher Channel, Graham Island, and the Hendriksen Strait to the Bjorne Peninsula, before returning to Craig Harbour.[96]

In his compilation, Riewe incorporated the itineraries of RCMP patrols of the 1950s and 1960s carried out by Inuit special constables and Euro-Canadians from Craig Harbour and Alexandra Fiord. Riewe's inclusion of these routes seems appropriate, given that Inuit usually took the lead navigational role during the patrols. Regarding the division of responsibilities, former Constable Bob Pilot has said of Special Constable Kayak: "when we were around the detachment, I was in charge, and when we were on the trail, he was in charge. We were the ones who did his bidding."[97] Many of these routes were established very early in their tenure on Ellesmere Island. In 1953, the hunters sledged along Ellesmere's eastern coast to Smith Sound and as far north as Dobbin Bay in 1957. Less frequently, Inuit hunters travelled across Devon Island and along its southern coast en route to Resolute Bay on adjacent Cornwallis Island.

According to Tookilkee Kigugtak, early hunters at Grise Fiord did not rely on maps but rather on an intuitive sense of where to find animals.[98] Riewe, recalling his sled excursions with Abraham Pijamini in southern Ellesmere Island, recalled his amazement that Pijamini was able to navigate easily through overland passes which they had not previously traversed. Pijamini utilized his environmental knowledge, but was also guided by the distant inukshuks he had discerned along the high mountain ridges left behind by earlier Aboriginal travellers.[99]

In the course of their travels, Inuit from Grise Fiord identified the location of various game and fish resources and, through observation over a period of years, learned their seasonal habits. Markosie Piunngittuk Inuualuk remembered that, in 1961 he, Ningiuk, and Aqiarak discovered charr in a lake near the east coast of Ellesmere Island. In the course of time, they learned that it was well stocked in the early fall, enabling them to harvest almost 100 fish. They also determined that this was a good place to find foxes.[100]

A 1976 survey of the land-use areal range for Inuit communities in the Eastern Arctic confirms the relative sparseness of game animals in the Jones Sound region and the vast territory Grise Fiord hunters needed to travel to secure game. Using data from 1953 to 1974, researchers found that Grise Fiord hunters covered an average of 6,864 square miles (17,780 km²) harvesting ringed seals, by far the largest hunting range of all Inuit communities in Nunavut.[101]

Adaptation to Political Action: The Muskox Controversy of 1967

Throughout their most recent occupation of Ellesmere Island, Inuit hunters at Grise Fiord had to deal with assorted hunting regulations drafted in the south, which they believed had negative impacts on both wildlife species and their ability to manage them. They were often short of food, yet these regulations prevented them from taking the very animals they had been promised they could hunt. In the hunters' view, bans or quotas on wildlife harvesting could threaten even the animals if applied paternalistically with inadequate ecological knowledge.

One example occurred shortly after their arrival on Ellesmere Island in the early 1950s. While accompanying Inuit hunting excursions in search of caribou, a RCMP officer insisted that Inuit shoot only male animals, not females and their young. Accordingly, the Inuit took only 20 per cent of the caribou, culling the adult males from each herd they encountered.[102] Based on their own experience, Inuit believed that such an approach was unwise, as all members of caribou herds were interdependent, and the death of the adult males would lead to the loss of the entire herd. They wished to shoot all members of a herd, rather than cull selectively. Ningiuk Killiktee, an Inuit special constable at Alexandra Fiord in this period, suggested that selective hunting of only one or two members of a herd would also make the others more wary, causing them to avoid feeding nearby. "The RCMP did not want us to finish off the caribou. They would tell us to leave some and I think they ran away and I think that's why there's not that much caribou."[103]

Anthropologist Milton Freeman advanced the interpretation that more serious ecological harm may have resulted from the downstream effects of the selective culling of caribou herds. Noting the important social dynamics of caribou herds as interdependent units, Freeman suggested that the remaining animals were made more vulnerable to wolf predation and other risks. In consequence, caribou herds were severely curtailed in areas of southern Ellesmere Island and the northern coast of Devon Island after a period of only a few years.[104]

Samwilly Elaijasialuk reported that his brother and another hunter, Joalamie, were hunting for wolves in a blizzard and nearly starved because they could not shoot muskoxen. Samwilly related that, while a member of the settlement council, he spoke to a visiting federal representative: "You send us all the way here from our own settlement, Inukjuak, in the first place. Who do you think should live, Inuit or the animals? I want you to think about this."[105]

A further source of unhappiness was a series of proposed experiments with the region's wildlife, such as the introduction of sport hunting into the region, without consultation with the Aboriginal users of the wildlife. In this regard, the regulations were not uniformly applied to all parties, as permits were occasionally issued to non-residents to take muskoxen or other protected species. An example was reported in May 1960, when a party from the Los Angeles Museum visited Eureka, on the west coast of Ellesmere Island and shot four muskoxen on a permit.[106] The issue came to the fore in 1967, when a series of federal actions relating to muskox and polar bear hunting triggered political action by Grise Fiord hunters to protect their interests. The proposed non-resident muskox kill had several components. Federal officials proposed that only male muskoxen would be harvested, as trophy animals were desired. Only old solitary males should be killed as they were assumed to be superfluous to reproduction. The muskoxen would need to be hunted in the vicinity of Grise Fiord, so that the community would benefit economically from the sport hunting. Meat generated by the kill would be given to the Inuit. A kill of 12 animals per year was indicated, based on the assumption that this level would not affect muskox population levels. It was further asserted that the selective culling of muskoxen would enable the Peary caribou population to increase, as it was assumed that both species fed on the same plant species.[107]

The Grise Fiord brief argued that the government was mistaken in these assumptions. The Inuit pointed out that food was never a problem in the summer months, when it was proposed that the sport hunting would take place. Rather, they asserted their need to hunt muskoxen in the winter, when food shortages were most acute. As well, the meat of muskoxen shot in June or July was inedible.[108] More significantly, the Inuit stated that the scientific rationale for regulations requiring them to hunt only older bulls was faulty. They had observed empirically that older bulls, through their ability to sense and avert danger, were essential to protecting the young of the herds. Therefore, it would be better to hunt all males in a given herd, but to do so on a selective basis. In support of this position, the community submitted impressive documentation of 51 separate sightings of muskoxen as recorded by Grise Fiord hunters at various locations in the year between March 1966 and March 1967.[109] Simonie, representing the community, closed with a clear, simple statement:

This is what I want to say concerning muskox. We want to be allowed to hunt them right now with our reasons being: we do not get enough to eat during cold winters because during these times seals are very hard to get; yet muskox are plentiful. It is unreasonable not being able to hunt muskox when there are pangs of hunger amongst our people and our dogs. It does not make sense fearing the Government and the Police when muskox are being killed by wolves. We now want to hunt them, during the present time. They would at least serve a use being eaten by people (rather than by wolves who are surely of less value?). The food that can be eaten by people is not always there; more often than not it is hard to get. Our land does not grow food like a garden. We are urging that we hunt muskox.[110]

In response to the protest, the Northwest Territories Council recommended to the federal government that the proposal for non-resident muskox hunting be withdrawn. Federal authorities acceded to this request, confirming the success of the community's challenge. Subsequent biological research has apparently corroborated the interpretations of the Grise Fiord Inuit of the implications of proposed sport hunting of muskox.[111]

Also in 1967, the Inuit at Grise Fiord protested the application of a new quota system for hunting polar bears. They expressed the view that their allotment of 17 bears was inordinately low in comparison to 50 bears allocated to Inuit at Resolute Bay.[112] It also imposed a significant reduction on their annual take of polar bears from the 45 bears reported killed by Grise Fiord hunters in 1966.[113] The Grise Fiord hunters noted that the number allocated to Resolute Bay was partly based on bears taken by Resolute Bay hunters in the area of Grise Fiord when travelling there to visit. As well, the hunters contended that Inuit at Resolute Bay had greater opportunities for waged employment at the air base there, and therefore did not need to take as many bears as Grise Fiord residents. Accordingly, they requested that five bears be transferred from the Resolute Bay quota and reallocated to their community. This was among the issues raised in letters of complaint to the Northwest Territories Council that year.[114]

The Inuit at Grise Fiord recalled the dispute over muskox regulations as an issue of basic survival. They had successfully protested perceived arbitrary measures affecting their opportunities to utilize the region's resources for necessary subsistence. Retrospectively, the event may have an even greater significance, as a watershed in the assertion of Inuit rights. The Inuit had demonstrated a need to be involved in decisions affecting their region and livelihood. Having achieved their objectives on the muskox issue, Inuit learned the potential of the political process to redress their concerns. Further grass-roots initiatives to protect their interests have continued in the organization of recent protests against oil exploration and dumping toxic wastes in the ocean in the vicinity of Grise Fiord, when the residents successfully prevented the contamination of nearby waters.[115] By these initiatives, Inuit demonstrated their capacity for direct political action, evidence of significant socio-cultural change since the 1950s.

15
Continuity Reasserted:
The Inuit, the Seasons, and the Land,
1951–2000

Inuit Adaptation to the High Arctic

In an article published on the community of Grise Fiord in 1969, arctic anthropologist Milton Freeman argued that its residents effectively adapted to life in a new environment.[1] Freeman's field work was first carried out in the 1960s, before the relocations were raised by Inuit as a major issue. At the same time, in other publications, Freeman identified a number of complicating factors in the relations between Inuit and Euro-Canadians at Grise Fiord, focussing on "patron" and "client" roles and dynamics of power relationships within this community. In view of the hardships and privations brought by the High Arctic relocations, it may be pertinent to ask whether the concept of adaptation is an entirely appropriate model for the study of Grise Fiord history. When humans are obliged by the decisions of others to try to survive in a new or difficult environment, can their process of adjustment to an artificially-induced situation be reasonably characterized as an "adaptation"? In answering this question, we may refer to the work of social scientists for guidance. Anthropologist Marshall Sahlins has observed that, in adapting to their environments, human societies inevitably confront constraints imposed by nature, culture, and a specific history. Assessments of the effectiveness or success of adaptations need to take into account the existing limitations within which a human society is obliged to operate in its particular contexts of time and place. Sahlins wrote:

> Adaptation implies maximizing the social life chances. But maximization is almost always a compromise, a vector in the internal structure of culture and the external pressure of environment. Every culture carries the penalties of a past within the frame of which, barring total disorganization, it must work out the future.[2]

In the case of Grise Fiord, the Inuit not only confronted the challenge of adapting to a new ecological region, they were obliged to adjust to entirely new cultural contexts. Specifically, residents were selected from both western Quebec and northern Baffin Island, groups with different dialects and customs. Their adaptation was complicated by the dynamics of inter-ethnic power relations in European–Inuit encounters. Another factor which apparently exerted pronounced effects on community life and social interaction was the role of Euro-Canadian RCMP officers in the community and their control over access to goods and services.

As well, Inuit from both northern Quebec and Baffin Island confronted the problems of adapting to rapidly changing cultural, technological, and political contexts at the same time that they were obliged to learn quickly how to exploit the natural resources of an alien environment. The benefits and disadvantages of modernization, and attendant pressures and stresses on Canadian Inuit, have been discussed in various works and will not be extensively covered here. Perhaps it is sufficient to note the complex character of the adjustments imposed by modernization,[3] the impact of which is still being addressed today. This discussion focusses on Inuit adaptations at Grise Fiord to a new natural environment and the role of traditional knowledge and approaches to problem solving that enabled a remarkable adjustment despite many difficulties.

At Grise Fiord, an early, effective method of maximizing resource harvesting was the co-ordination of hunting and trapping activities. Fur-bearing land mammals provided Grise Fiord residents with their principal source of cash from the 1950s to the 1980s. The white fox was dominant for the first decade, as trapping began soon after the arrival of the first group of Inuit in 1953. Polar bear skins became an increasingly important source of income after 1965, when the Inuit derived more than half their cash income from this source.[4] Traps were set on the outbound leg of bear, caribou, and muskoxen hunts and then checked on the return trip to the community. Hunters modulated their trapping activities according to the cycle of wildlife populations. Trap lines were extended during peaks in fox populations, but curtailed in areas of wolf predation, as in the vicinity of Baumann Fiord.[5]

While on the trail, the Inuit hunters also made effective use of the immemorial practice of caching to optimize their procurement activities. Practised by all Aboriginal occupants throughout the human history of Ellesmere Island, caching enabled hunters to store provisions for later consumption, allowing them to move quickly through hunting grounds and thus exploit a greater number and range of resources than was otherwise feasible. The senior hunter Pijamini has recently credited the practice of caching as the key factor that enabled Inuit to survive on Ellesmere Island over many years.[6]

Co-operation in hunting was essential to the successful exploitation of the region's resources. American Lewis Cotlow, who accompanied Akpaliapik and Markosie on a hunting excursion in 1962, marvelled at their teamwork in killing a polar bear. Coming upon the surface tracks of a bear while seal hunting on the pack ice, they followed the tracks for three hours until Akpaliapik spotted the bear. At this point, the two hunters turned their komatiks over so that the dogs would be restrained, and proceeded on foot. Encountering deeper snow, they ran in a crouched position, so that in striding forward their feet would thrust back rather than down, preventing them from sinking in the snow. After half an hour of following the bear's tracks over the hummocky pack ice, they eventually cornered it, then moved apart so they could spear it from either side. Approaching from two angles, the two hunters followed the bear to a crack in the ice, where they found it half-submerged itself in the water. Akpaliapik moved forward and lunged his harpoon, attached to a 15.5-metre line, into the bear's chest. He then withdrew the line while Markosie struck the bear in the head with his harpoon. Finally, Akpaliapik brought the hunt to a close with a forceful throw of the harpoon, killing the animal. Cotlow observed:

> It seemed to me that the bear epitomized everything the Eskimo had to struggle against in the open wilderness: hardship and uncertainly, an often pitiless nature which was for each member of the community a personal and implacable threat. It was that threat which made these people the most tightly-knit, yet most individualized human beings I had ever seen. It made them ready at any moment to give up possessions or comfort to a stranger. Not because of some abstract ideal: for them it was the only way of life that made sense. So each man threw into the communal lot his strength, wisdom and skill, as if nature had decreed, *Cooperate or die!*[7]

For a more detailed, vivid account of a hunting excursion undertaken by Grise Fiord men in the 1960s, readers may also wish to refer to Fred Bruemmer's *The Long Hunt*.[8]

Another important adjustment to the rigours of this environment was the refining of sledges in accordance with variable High Arctic travelling conditions. Responding to the variable surfaces encountered on the trail in this region, most Inuit hunters outfitted themselves with two sledges by the end of the 1950s. The runners of one of these sledges was fitted with steel shoes for travelling in the spring and fall, while the other sledge was equipped with hardwood or traditional whalebone shoes for winter sledging.[9] Hunters also applied traditional knowledge to repairing their equipment. In 1966, while accompanying a RCMP patrol to Resolute Bay, Inuit hunters damaged their komatik shoes made of whalebone. Improvising, they iced the runners with fresh caribou blood from an animal they had just killed. The following day, Abraham

Pijamini fashioned a more durable surface by inserting pieces of walrus liver between the cracks of the whalebone, allowing them to freeze, and rasping them with a file to the proper contour. RCMP Constable Hannan observed that "this proved to be a solid and permanent mend."[10] By the mid-1960s, the Grise Fiord hunters were replacing traditional whalebone runners with hardwood planks imported from the south,[11] but nevertheless retained ivory shoes to maintain a smooth surface for gliding over snow or ice. In other cases, Inuit adaptations involved innumerable on-the-spot improvisations to existing tools as the situation demanded. An example was recorded in a report on a 1966 RCMP patrol, during which four unruly sled dogs broke away. Special Constable Pijamini quickly improvised a sled by rolling his sleeping bag in a bearskin and, hitching up eight dogs, overtook the renegade pack.[12]

In the 1960s, Milton Freeman studied various material culture adaptations of the Grise Fiord Inuit that enabled a more effective occupation of the land, including the substitution of various technologies to save time and effort. Among their adaptations were changes in sledge design. Traditionally, the sledges of Inuit from northern Quebec were 4 to 5 m in length and 35 cm in width, while immigrants from Baffin Island employed longer sledges stretching to 5 to 6 m and 50 cm wide. Following a visit by several Inughuit from Greenland to Grise Fiord in 1958, several of the more innovative hunters from Inukjuak adopted Inughuit sledge design and constructed shorter and wider sledges measuring 3 m by 65 cm between the runners. These dimensions gave the sledges greater stability in the rough ice conditions of the High Arctic, where komatiks are more likely to overturn when negotiating the pressure ridges, particularly during the winter darkness between November and March. In addition, the Inuit from Inukjuak adopted the upright handlebars of Inughuit sledges, which were well suited to the driver's manoeuvring over rough ice conditions, particularly in the autumn or spring.[13] As in other aspects of daily life, the hunters at Grise Fiord adapted to High Arctic travel through careful observation, accumulation of ecological knowledge, and utilization of all sources of data at their disposal.

Traditions of Sharing and Flexible Social Organization

Sharing food resources was another effective method of mitigating the scarcity inherent in living off the land. In keeping with the uncertain character of hunting returns in the Arctic, the Inuit have institutionalized certain forms of sharing as pragmatic strategies to ensure the survival of the group. For example, sharing narwhal flesh by the entire community was customarily practised by the Igluligmiut,[14] one of the two founding groups at Grise Fiord. Other forms of sharing were organized along kinship lines and have been articulated by George Wenzel in his studies of the Inuit community at Clyde River, Baffin Island.[15] Another recent study of sharing among Baffin Islanders shows how extensive these practices have been, extending from sharing of food to reciprocity in hunting, financial relations, caregiving, and many other aspects of life.[16]

Sharing was also an important part of the culture of Quebec Inuit before the relocations. Rynee Flaherty, who was relocated to Grise Fiord with her spouse and family in 1955, remembered practices of sharing in Inukjuak before moving north. At Grise Fiord, survival during food shortages was facilitated by traditions of sharing the Inuit brought with them to the north:

> Whatever they had they would share it until it was gone. They made sure they weren't the only ones who had some. They made sure to share it with everyone....When there was starvation or when people were hungry that is what they used to do....They shared everything like seals, ptarmigan, caribou and so on. They made sure they shared it.[17]

In addition to the sharing of food, environmental knowledge was readily exchanged by the Aboriginal groups in the region. Gamaliel Aqiaraq (Akeeagok), who moved to Grise Fiord from Pond Inlet several years after the establishment of the community, recalled the help of his brother Akpaliapik in getting established:

> So I adapted to it. And I automatically fit in there because I was taught already. And I was told by my brother where to hunt. He gave me dog teams and everything. So that was fine. He would tell me which areas would be best for hunting. He also told me what to watch out for and what to look for so that was not as hard for me.[18]

Another example of co-operation was the exchange of knowledge between Inughuit visitors from northwest Greenland and Grise Fiord Inuit about Ellesmere Island's natural resources. In an interview in 1989, Anna Nungaq spoke of learning from the Inughuit the location of lakes with arctic charr:

> Because of them we learned about where the lakes with fish are. They know the land very good. Until they introduced us to the lakes we did not eat fish. They helped us a great deal. Because we did not know there were such fish we were craving for some fish all that time.[19]

Ms. Nungaq's memory is corroborated by the documentary record of RCMP files for Grise Fiord. In 1964, a RCMP report noted that Grise Fiord Inuit had fished at a lake near the southwest point of Makinson Inlet. They had first learned of this fishing place from an elderly Inughuit woman, Pudloo, from Northwest Greenland. She related that, as a child, her people had found this resource while migrating up the eastern coast of Ellesmere Island.[20]

The ability of Inuit to adjust to the rigours of life in this region owed much to the strengths of their distinctive culture. As the ethnographer W.E. Wilmott has noted, the flexible social organization of the Inuit was admirably suited to life in the High Arctic. Wilmott carried out his field work among the Inuit in the district of Inukjuak, Quebec, in the 1950s, only a few years after the first group of relocated persons departed for Ellesmere Island. Among other cultural practices, he observed flexible forms of family organization, including liberal approaches to adoption. In the context of higher mortality rates, Inuit adoption practices helped ensure a more balanced distribution of children than nature alone provided.[21]

Inuit flexibility extended to forms of community organization. Traditionally, Inuit groups were small, nomadic bands without clearly defined leadership. Membership in these groups varied somewhat from one year to the next, according to the decisions of individual families to live together. These patterns changed with the advent of the trapping economy and Inuit establishment in more permanent communities.[22] Nevertheless, traditions of community sharing and mutual assistance, common to smaller hunting groups, continued after the changes in settlement organization. These traditions were well suited to survival in a region where the sparseness of resources demanded strategies to maximize opportunities for the group as a whole.

Reliance on limited game resources on Ellesmere required sustainable approaches to their management. In addition to limiting the catch of particular species, the Inuit made maximum use of the harvested animals. Virtually all parts of game animals were utilized; nothing was wasted.[23] A case in point was the caribou. In addition to using the meat, according to Simon Akpaliapik:

> The sinew from the back and even from the leg tendons would be dried and saved for thread. There was no store-bought thread in those days, so any sinew and tendons that could be used when making clothes were saved for that purpose. Sinew and tendons were also used by my father to make harness and rope ties. The tendons were also useful as boot ties, because we had no yarn at that time. They would also be used as ties for pants. All parts of the caribou were very useful. Caribou

fat was used as fuel while we were inland. Caribou was our staple food. Even the bone marrow, if not consumed right away, was saved.[24]

Similarly, the entire carcass of captured seals was utilized. A 1961 report at Alexandra Fiord noted that 12 bearded seals taken during the previous year served many purposes: the meat was used for dog food and human consumption; skins were used to make soles of boots, dog harness, and traces.[25]

Inuit frugality extended to the conservation and re-use of materials for hunting and other purposes. For example, limited access to ammunition obliged saving and re-use of cartridges, for which Inuit have coined a term in Inuktitut: *aaqigait*.[26] Akpaliapik described this practice:

> After you have taken a shot, you save the cartridge. Then you need gun powder, a firing pin and point with you, to make new ones. After you have saved the cartridge, you need to dislodge the used firing pin. You put the new firing pin in, then a piece of paper is attached to the inside of the firing pin, then the point is attached. That is what *aaqigait* is. Making your own bullets. You must have everything that is needed. The gun powder has to be measured with a special measuring container."[27]

The need to conserve shells also influenced the nature of the hunt. In Akpaliapik's words, "it was necessary to get as close as possible to [caribou], in order to save ammunition."[28]

RCMP game reports from Craig Harbour between 1922 and 1940 and in the early 1950s reported both a diversity of species and numerical abundance of various species of game animals in the Jones Sound region. These reports figured prominently in the federal government's decision to relocate Inuit to Ellesmere Island in 1953. Yet, abundance is also a function of the accessibility of animals. Ellesmere Island is close to the northern extremity of many species, where animals tend to congregate in few and scattered pockets of biological productivity, such as polynyas. To exploit the scarce resources, Inuit needed to draw on an already extensive repertoire of environmental knowledge, while quickly developing specialized knowledge of the resources of this unfamiliar region. Successful adaptation to this harsh land depended on the capacity to hunt its wildlife in every season, utilizing a wide repertoire of skills and techniques.

The Seasonal Cycle at Grise Fiord in the 1970s

In the 1970s, zoologist Rick Riewe documented seasonal patterns of resource use at Grise Fiord. With some significant modifications, occasioned in part by the further advance of waged employment, these patterns have continued into the present day. From mid-April to mid-July, Inuit hunters hunted ringed seals by stalking. During this season, the seals spent much of the time fasting and basking on the surface of the ice; hunters stalked them in the traditional manner from behind hunting screens, the *utoq* method.[29] Another preferred method was *nunajak* hunting. Mother seals gave birth to their young in late April and nursed them in *nunajait* or hollows in the snow covering the sea ice. Formerly, hunters used dogs to locate these cavities; the hunters found the precise location by thrusting a probe into the snow, and then jumping on top to crush in the cavity. By June, bearded seals migrated to open leads in Jones Sound. The preferred hunting method was from boats. To prevent the seals from sinking, hunters aimed to shoot the animals in the nose. Thus injured, they could be readily approached to be harpooned and killed with a shot to the brain.[30] In other cases, the seals were hunted while they basked on the ice.[31]

In the spring, the Inuit also fished for charr in streams flowing into the fiords along the southern coast of Ellesmere Island. By the early 1960s, they had extended their fishing range to such sites as a small lake near Makinson Inlet on the eastern coast, discovered during hunting and trapping trips and through sharing knowledge with visiting Inughuit travellers from northwest Greenland. Other favoured places for fishing included a lake at Baad Fiord, discovered in 1970, and a third lake on the Truelove Lowland on Devon Island. They fished in the traditional way by jigging a lure made of a shiny object, such as used brass cartridges or a piece of walrus ivory on the end of a line, then spearing the fish with a leister as it approached. Another technique, practised by the Inuit from Quebec, was to set nets below the ice.[32]

Spring was also a time for collecting the eggs of glaucous and herring gulls at the nesting colonies known to the community, including, in the 1970s, the cliffs of Coburg and Smith islands, Makinson and Sverdrup inlets, Baumann Fiord, Grise and Starnes fiords, and Cape Combermere. According to zoologist Rick Riewe, hunters occasionally shot gulls while in pursuit of marine mammals, although these activities were limited to the Inuit hunters from Quebec, who had a taste for these birds.[33]

Hunting during the brief summers focussed on the ringed seal, the most abundant seal species in the region.[34] It was the preferred food source of Inuit at Grise Fiord and an important resource for hunters throughout the Canadian High Arctic.[35] With the opening of cracks in the sea ice around mid-June, ringed seals began to migrate farther from the floe edge of Baffin Bay. Hunters from Grise Fiord positioned themselves along the shore adjacent to the ice cracks and waited for the animals to surface at high tide. Firing from short distances, the hunters retrieved the seals with weighted triple hooks.[36] Another technique used in the early summer was netting seals in tidal cracks. In 1972, seven hunters maintained one to four nets each. Netted seals were used for dog food or skins.[37]

During the period of open water between mid-July and early October, the Inuit hunted ringed seals from the water in either of two ways. The more straightforward way was to navigate their boats at low speeds and shoot the seals on sight. Alternatively, they would remain stationary in their canoes on the water or pull the boats up on the ice pans to wait for the seals to approach. Various techniques were used to attract the animals. These included scratching the ice surface with a knife or banging on the canoe gunnels to imitate seal sounds.[38] By 1972, approximately 60% of all seals taken were obtained during the open-water season.

Grise Fiord hunters were also engaged extensively in hunting walruses during the period of open water. In the first three decades of the community's history, an average of 28 animals per year was taken, primarily for meat for dog food and ivory for carving. Through careful observation, hunters discovered that walruses moved from Baffin Bay into Jones Sound in June or July. Females and their young summered at the foot of the Jakeman Glacier, while adult males migrated to the vicinity of Hell Gate. Until 1967, when the need for dog food dropped after the introduction of the snowmobile, the walrus was hunted by various means, from boats or along the floe edge.[39] During the summers, the Inuit also hunted narwhals and belugas, primarily from boats. Migrating into Jones Sound from Baffin Bay after the ice breakup, the narwhals moved in pods of 30 to 150 animals. In the decade between 1962 and 1972, an annual average of nine narwhals was taken by Grise Fiord hunters, although these animals did not appear every year.[40] Arriving slightly later than the narwhals during the open-water season, the belugas moved to the vicinity of Grise Fiord from polynyas in Baffin Bay and Hell Gate–Cardigan Strait.

Autumn presented its own difficulties to hunters and demanded careful observation of weather patterns and sound judgment as to the potential risks involved. According to Tookilkee Kigugtak, if hunters considered the weather or ice conditions dangerous, they would not hunt.[41] With the formation of 10 cm of ice, the season of open-water sealing was over, and hunters turned to the *aglu* or breathing hole method of hunting, which continued until the following summer. After the sea froze, each ringed seal opened and maintained at least 10 breathing holes by chewing and clawing openings in the ice. As long as the ice was less than 10 to 15 cm thick, a seal could easily break through it to breathe. As the ice continued to thicken, the seal continued to eat and claw open its breathing holes or *aglus*. Hunting seals at breathing holes was typically carried out co-operatively. Having identified the breathing holes of a seal, two or more hunters typically worked together so that, if a seal sensed a hunter's presence at one hole and avoided capture, it could still be secured at the other. Walruses, too, were hunted during their fall migrations; they were pursued from canoes. Owing to considerable risk hunting walruses in herds, hunters stalked individual walruses or small groups of animals. Their technique was to wound the animal with a shot and then approach close enough to harpoon it. The harpoon was attached to a 10-gallon steel drum, a modern equivalent of bladder floats formerly fashioned from sealskins.[42]

Terrestrial mammals were also hunted in the fall. Due to seasonal travelling conditions, caribou were hunted in the area of Bjorne Peninsula and Makinson Inlet in October and November, an activity that ceased with the onset of winter, to be resumed in March.[43] The introduction of the snowmobile had a significant impact on caribou hunting. Following the reintroduction of muskox hunting, these animals, too, were hunted on extended trips in the fall, to northeastern Devon Island, Bjorne Peninsula, Sor Valley, Vendom Fiord, and Raanes Peninsula.[44] As was customary over many generations, arctic hares were generally hunted as an ancillary activity on excursions in search of larger game animals.[45] As well, in October, after the sea ice had again frozen sufficiently to permit snowmobile travel, Inuit returned to the lake near Makinson Fiord to catch charr.[46]

Despite the extended dark period, hunting in the winter was essential to sustaining the Canadian Inuit since their arrival on Ellesmere Island in 1951. In the 1970s, zoologist R.R. Riewe documented their major winter travelling and hunting routes in the first two decades of occupation. Riewe's data indicate an extensive and expanding use of the region's resources even during the dark period. Every year, Grise Fiord hunters have pursued the marine mammals that remain in the region throughout the winter. These include both animals that customarily overwintered in the area and others occasionally left stranded by a rapid build-up of sea ice in northern Baffin Bay before they were able to escape. In early December 1966, for example, Inuit and RCMP hunters took 40 beluga whales at breathing holes in Starnes Fiord. The hunters tried two methods. Initially, they harpooned the whales, but when fastening the line to the ice, the head of the weapon pulled out. The hunters tried an alternative method, using rope or dog lines to lassoo the animals. This method also proved superior from a conservation standpoint, as the whales that were lost were not wounded and would survive.[47]

The seasonal cycle of natural resource use at Grise Fiord in the 1970s is summarized in Figure 87, which illustrates both the wide range of resources utilized by the community and the hunting and procurement activities undertaken in every month of the year. Collectively, these activities demonstrated extensive adaptations by members of the community to optimize their utilization of a challenging environment within two decades of their arrival on Ellesmere Island. Their resource use was not limited to Ellesmere Island but also extended to neighbouring islands in the Queen Elizabeth Islands archipelago and the adjacent sea ice.

Inuit Knowledge and Survival in the High Arctic

The capacity of the relocated Inuit to persist in a new environment can also be credited to the pre-existing repertoire of hunting and survival skills they had developed in their regions of origin and carried with them to Ellesmere Island. Simon Akpaliapik, who moved to Ellesmere Island from Pond Inlet in 1953, related that, as a young child, he began to learn how to hunt from his father:

> I was five years old when I started hunting with my father. When I got tired he would carry me on his back. I was always asking to go hunting with him at that time. When he caught a caribou he would carry the meat and at the same time, he would have me on top of his load. That was how I began to learn, from experience. There were no schools at that time, so we learned by watching our parents.[48]

Hunting was an activity involving the whole family. Simon Akpaliapik, Tookilkee Kigugtak, and others recalled that Inuit men and women hunted together, on their native Baffin Island and also after they moved to Ellesmere Island. The women carried their needles and other tools of clothing preparation with them so that they could mend or prepare garments when the weather prevented hunting. During these excursions, Akpaliapik taught his children to hunt, passing on to them the techniques which he learned from his parents.

> I taught my two children how to hunt. I taught them by talking to them as we went hunting. That was how we learned then but today, it is different. There were not any white people around at that time, so we learned from watching what our parents did.
>
> The first thing I was taught was to hunt caribou during the summer. My father used to hunt caribou by foot, inland, because there weren't any caribou near the sea during summer. My whole family would go with the help of our dogs. The dogs would carry our things such as food, bedding, and our possessions.

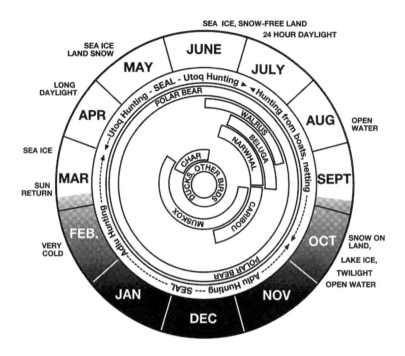

Figure 87: Grise Fiord: The Annual Harvesting Cycle in the 1970s (after Riewe (1976);
H. Myers (1981), and the Lancaster Sound Regional Land Use Plan (1989)).

> In the beginning of our journey, my father would carry our posses-
> sions inside a blanket, and my mother would carry the tent poles. She
> would wrap bedding (made from caribou skin) around the load to
> make it softer on her back.[49]

Akpaliapik described a remarkable range of seal-hunting techniques
that he learned while hunting with his father in northern Baffin Island,
revealing an extensive knowledge of the characteristics of game animals, as well as a sophisticated repertoire of methods for capturing
them. The most common approach was to capture seals at breathing
holes. Since seals maintained several breathing holes, hunting with
one or more partners reduced the required waiting time for the seals to
surface.[50] One role assumed by Akpaliapik was to make a feinting action to encourage the seal to emerge from the water while his father
waited at a breathing hole. His father instructed him that, when coming across a seal's breathing hole, he should walk away from it immediately at a fast pace. Then, a seal would often appear and his father

would spear it. When the sea ice was covered with snow, Akpaliapik's father would use a harpoon to find seal holes. On finding one, he would rig a string across the hole, attach it to a wire, and spread snow over the hole again so that it appeared undisturbed. When the seal came up, the wire would stand up, indicating its presence, and he would harpoon it.

In food shortage situations, Inuit hunters sometimes built a wind break around the breathing hole and stayed the night in the open in an attempt to secure a seal. Of his father, Akpaliapik remembered:

> When the seal finally came to where he was waiting, he would take care not to make any sound. If he had his arms tucked in his sleeves he would put his mitts on very carefully and take his harpoon from its resting place. Before he took his harpoon, he would carefully stand up, making sure he doesn't make a sound. He would then take his harpoon and harpoon the seal. That is how they used to do it when they waited all night.[51]

Akpaliapik also described the valuable role played by dogs in seal hunting, and how he taught his dogs to hunt for breathing holes:

> First of all, what you do to teach them would be to leave a piece of meat at a place where last summer's ice is, and cover it with snow. You do this without letting the dogs know. This way a dog would learn how to look for a scent on ice. You have to approach the area from its leeward side. This way you can teach a dog on a leash to look for and smell something. This is how I taught my dog to look for seal holes.[52]

Through trial and error, Akpaliapik found that, for this purpose, a piece of intestine was even better than a piece of meat; he would carry it with him whenever he wanted to train his dogs in this way. Another method of sealing was to punch through the compacted snow over a seal den, to expose the occupants, prior to lancing them. A simple tool fashioned for this purpose was a piece of ice shaped into a ball and attached to a rope. Swinging the rope, the hunter used the weight to crush the snow covering the seal den.

Inuit women also played important roles in teaching young men the skills of hunting. Akpaliapik's mother and his wife sewed *irqittaq* for him to use to break through the snow over seal dens during *utoq* hunting. *Irqittaq* is a piece of skin crimped and sewn on the soles of kamiks. It helped hunters avoid slipping on the ice when using their feet to punch through the compacted snow to expose a seal den. His mother also taught him how to help his father hunt at seal breathing holes during winter.[53]

Canadian Inuit on Ellesmere Island also learned from the exchange of ecological knowledge with Inughuit from northwestern Greenland, whom they encountered during excursions to Ellesmere Island. For example, Ningiuk Killiktee, a hunter from Pond Inlet, who served as a special constable with the RCMP at the Alexandra Fiord Detachment, related that he learned much about the region's ecology from Nukappiannguaq, the well-known Inughuit hunter who served with the RCMP for nearly 20 years at posts on Ellesmere Island, as well as with various High Arctic expeditions. In the 1950s, Nukappiannguaq, accompanied by other hunters from the Thule district, continued to cross Smith Sound to hunt along the eastern coast of Ellesmere Island. According to Ningiuk: "He used to talk about the land, where the walrus were and the danger areas. He used to tell us about them. I heard the land from him. I learned more from him and when we moved there I would go by what he said."[54] These exchanges provided a tangible link to the polar exploration era and helped revive a tradition of cultural exchange between Inuit and Inughuit, represented in the migration of Qitdlarssuaq a century before. Another fascinating outcome of the meetings of Inughuit and Inuit in this period was their discovery of common historical and ancestral links. In 1970, Ningiuk and Akpaliapik told some Inughuit people that their forefathers had included members of Qitlaq's party who had integrated into the Greenland population, particularly members of the family of Aqigssiarssuk, one of the original travellers in the nineteenth century.[55]

By any standards, Inuit at Grise Fiord—and formerly Craig Harbour and Alexandra Fiord—have made a remarkable adaptation to life on Ellesmere Island. Within only a short span, the transplanted Inuit established a viable economy rooted strongly in traditional patterns of natural resource harvesting. In the process, they acquired wide-ranging ecological knowledge of this remote region. Due to the relative sparseness of game animals at such a high latitude, the Inuit were obliged to strike out in all directions and in all seasons, extending their hunting activities over many hundreds of miles, the greatest areal range of natural resource use among Canada's Inuit communities. Their achievement seems particularly noteworthy given the difficulties of adjustment occasioned by the relocations in the 1950s. They had been placed in a situation in which rapid adaptation to an unfamiliar environment became a matter of sheer necessity for the group.

The Inuit were able to meet the challenge of an unfamiliar and difficult environment partly because they had already acquired many arctic survival skills that equipped them for future challenges. In Robin Ridington's terms, they "carried the world around in their heads." Hunters such as Akpaliapik, Aqiarak, Joalamee, Pijamini, Kigugtak, and others spent decades acquiring the knowledge of many techniques for securing game in their regions of origin. The relocated women, including Rynee Flaherty, Anna Nungaq, Martha Kigugtak, Annie Pijamini, and others also brought from their original homelands the skills of raising children, processing skins, and preparing food, all essential to the survival of the group. Clearly, the Inuit were obliged to make many specific adjustments to confront the particular challenges of the High Arctic, but, having already learned to be adaptable, they possessed the skills of experimentation and innovation essential to the adaptive process.

This story of adaptation occurred in the context of momentous technological and social change for Canadian Inuit. Alongside the need to adapt to the High Arctic environment, the Inuit at Grise Fiord managed such changes as the shift from traditional snow and sod shelters to frame houses, from skin clothing to Western dress, from dog teams to snowmobiles, and from government paternalism to management by Inuit people of their own political, educational, economic, and social institutions. A foreshadowing of these developments occurred during the muskox controversy of the 1960s, when the Inuit at Grise Fiord were finally able to exert a degree of control over political decisions affecting their lives and livelihood.

It is a story of group survival, rooted in shared traditions of hunting and co-operative patterns of natural resource use. Grise Fiord's history attests to the continuing value of Inuit survival skills, as developed over many generations. Contrasting with the larger society's preoccupation with continuous change and development, the history of this community demonstrates an accommodation to the seasons, to an endlessly repeatable cycle of natural resource harvesting as well as adaptation to local circumstances.

The history of Grise Fiord represents a synthesis of completely different histories and concepts of time. Born of Euro-Canadian geopolitics, notions of progress, and concepts of linear time, this community's survival owed more to the return to cyclical time, to connectedness to the seasons and an annual round of activities the relocated Inuit had developed long before setting foot on Ellesmere Island. With courage, resourcefulness, and mutual support, they renewed a process of adaption to the physical environment stretching back to the first arrival of Aboriginal people on Ellesmere Island, more than 4,000 years BP. In an interview in 1991, Martha Kigugtak, who moved to Grise Fiord with her family in the early 1960s, explained how, through many challenges, the Inuit at Grise Fiord have been able to maintain their community for nearly 50 years:

Since we have been here, although this is a very dark community it was alright. We got used to it. There are a lot of other people [Inughuit from Greenland] who hunt and catch polar bears and so on. That is part of our lives now. We did learn their way of life. But when I first got here I thought people were very brave. Also very hard workers and very brave. I guess that is how they survived. They're very brave. And we learned that technique too.[56]

Conclusion:

Ellesmere Island and the Times of History

In this book, I have tried to convey something of the complexity of reconstructing human history, particularly such a diverse history as that of the High Arctic in the contact era. It would be naïve to suppose that any written text could ever fully represent the past. Written history is like a palimpsest, a "piece of writing material or manuscript on which the original writing has been erased to make room for other writing." We can never have direct access to the original and are always dealing with fragments of evidence that may afford a glimpse into the past but cannot tell the full story. As well, the surviving evidence is coloured by the cultural or individual experience and presuppositions of the witnesses and then filtered again through the historian's perspectives and selected representational structures. Given the unavoidable impediments of fragmentary evidence and subjectivity of perception, the challenge for this study has been to find a way to represent the history of Ellesmere Island so that its many contours, cultures, and perspectives can be acknowledged and adequately expressed.

Previous writing on the post-contact era of the High Arctic has largely focussed on the factor of circumstance as it relates to narrative of the heroic age of exploration. Both the strengths and limitations of exploration narratives are reflected in their forms, which are shot through with the traditions of Western cultures, oriented to a linear story line and the charting of an adventure story or quest. Much of the literature of polar exploration bears the trappings of the traditional epic, a monumental prose poem narrating the progress of a hero[1] or the form of tragedy, a literary work with a fatal or disastrous conclusion. While the traditional forms have their merits, it must be acknowledged that, in themselves, they cannot provide a comprehensive portrait of human history. If it is true, as the literary critic Martin Green has argued, that the adventure stories of the last 200 years have provided much of the content of Anglo-American imperialism,[2] these works have also largely omitted alternative ways of conceptualizing or presenting the past.

To more fully represent the diversity of experience in arctic history, we require new models for approaching the past that are not subordinate to the prevailing master narratives. It is also the time to introduce different voices to further pluralize the story. Readers can readily discern a difference between the voice of Robert Peary, expressing the personal obsessions and national aspirations of the explorer and his country, and the voice of Hans Hendrik, discussing his role as a hunter, concerns about his family, and observations of daily life in the High Arctic. The voices of both individuals are legitimate expressions of their authors' thoughts and perspectives, as are the assorted quotations of other visitors to the region in the last 200 years. By giving due consideration to a range of voices, as well as the complexity of factors bearing on historical process, it may be possible to achieve a balanced and comprehensive account. The presentation of a wide-ranging selection of stories from Ellesmere Island's past may also assist readers in developing their own interpretations about the region's history to counterbalance the monolithic verities in exploration literature.

For this book, I have chosen to structure the events of High Arctic history as a complex interplay of environmental, cultural, and circumstantial factors. Circumstantial or short-term history still has its uses and, in Part II, the factors of personality and chance have been elaborated among the layers bearing on historical process, although the emphasis differs somewhat from other accounts. Alongside this more familiar narrative of events, the book identifies a series of continuities operating sometimes as imperceptible, yet irresistible forces in arctic history. The natural environment functioned as a player through the entire drama, as all groups inhabiting this region either came to terms with the relentless forces of climate and other physical forces, or perished in the attempt. Similarly, a treatment of the continuities of culture has been included to help explain the successes or failures of the approaches taken by different groups to life in the High Arctic. Alongside the continuities, the book attempts to isolate some of the key social, material, and ecological changes precipitated by the contact of Europeans and Aboriginal peoples in the region. It is at the intersection of these three great registers of human history, i.e. the short term of events, the long-term of natural environment and culture, and the medium term of social change, that individual and collective destinies have been shaped. While tracing the role of the different registers in a specific historical situation can be a daunting task, the formal reconstruction of the complexities of time holds the potential to more closely approximate the actual forces at play in the human past than any single approach to historical temporality.

There is no doubt that the contact of two groups of cultures, Inuit and European, brought about enormous changes in the social and material life of the region. In 1800, the High Arctic was entirely the domain of Aboriginal people. The Inughuit of northern Greenland and the Inuit of Canada, both successors to the Thule culture which expanded across the entire coastal arctic region of North America after ca. 1000 BP, developed ways of life that were admirably suited to this harsh region. Nevertheless, periodic cycles of climatic deterioration exerted dramatic effects on arctic ecology so that a succession of Aboriginal cultures were obliged in particular eras to retreat from the High Arctic. At the time of initial contact, the Inughuit were experiencing the stress of the Little Ice Age, a cooling episode of several hundred years' duration, which impeded their capacity to travel and exploit the region's resources. When Captain John Ross sailed to the Thule District in 1818, he encountered an isolated people of perhaps 200 individuals, entirely reliant on a limited repertoire of materials available within the region. Life was made difficult by increased levels of pack ice in Baffin Bay, which drove the Greenland whale beyond their range and also prevented driftwood from washing up on their shores. Under these trying circumstances, the Inughuit showed remarkable resourcefulness, as they carefully conserved and reused available old pieces of whalebone, ivory and driftwood in building sledges and fashioning tools.

Through interactions with Europeans the Inughuit gained access to a range of imported materials, enhancing their capacity to exploit their environment. Before 1900, they largely incorporated these materials within their pre-existing repertoire of tools. In the twentieth century, they adopted various Western technologies, including guns and, in the 1960s, motorboats and snowmobiles. Counterbalancing the material advantages, early contact also brought epidemics, which, for a time, inflicted considerable harm on Aboriginal peoples in the Arctic. Exchanges with Europeans also imposed considerable psychological stresses on individuals who served on various expeditions, as well as families left behind during their service in the far north. The phenomenon of "pibloktoq" and other examples of distress experienced by Aboriginal participants were indicative of various pressures placed on Inughuit people by American or European visitors to the region. At the same time, charting Inughuit demography over the past 150 years demonstrates the enduring resilience of this people, whose population rose progressively through the more favourable climatic period of the twentieth century. They persisted despite the epidemics and other stresses of contact and, in several respects, apparently succeeded in turning the contact situation to their own advantage.[3]

Today the Inuit and Inughuit are still the principal occupants of the High Arctic, but they now live in frame dwellings, travel in snowmobiles and aeroplanes, and utilize communications such as telephones, FAXes, and the Internet. Inuit people work in a wide range of occupations, although hunting still plays an important role in the subsistence and identity of Inuit in communities such as Grise Fiord. With the establishment of the Territory of Nunavut in 1999, the Inuit of Canada's Eastern Arctic achieved the status of Territorial self-government, a sign that at last they are securing the political authority to act on their own behalf. I have included a brief account of the muskox controversy at Grise Fiord in the 1960s to illustrate a breakthrough in terms of direct political action by Inuit people, a forerunner of subsequent efforts to gain a measure of power over decisions affecting their lives and livelihood.

Alongside enormous changes can be discerned equally strong strains of continuity in the history of the region. The most important changes to the lives of the Inughuit in the nineteenth century were the product of exchanges with Qitlaq's Inuit band from northern Baffin Island, who reintroduced traditional knowledge and skills lost in the Thule District. These changes did not represent a new departure so much as the renewal of long-standing patterns of adaptation to the Arctic developed over many generations. Even in the context of the many changes introduced during and after the Peary era, the more important impacts included the re-introduction of Inughuit people to hunting grounds on Ellesmere Island and other land masses of the Queen Elizabeth archipelago, a revival of earlier patterns of natural resource utilization by the Thule and Inuit peoples of the High Arctic. As late as the 1950s, the travels of Nukappiannguaq and other Inughuit to Ellesmere Island and their encounters with Canadian Inuit helped revive the traditions of cultural exchange between High Arctic peoples, thus contributing to a more effective utilization of their environment. It is a process that continues into the present.

If, as some historians have argued, the twentieth century was a period characterized by "the acceleration of historical time,"[4] a parallel trend toward *deceleration* can also be discerned in a succession of pragmatic accommodations to the High Arctic environment in the exploration era. We witness elements of this trend in Peary's wintering parties on Ellesmere in 1898–1902, in the RCMP operations at Craig Harbour and Bache Peninsula, and particularly in the re-occupation of Ellesmere Island by Canadian Inuit since the 1950s. To operate effectively in this environment, all groups were obliged, ultimately, to counterbalance the forward thrust of Western linear time with adaptations to the seasonal cycle and its rhythms (Figure 87). This trend finds parallels elsewhere in the world, as indigenous or vernacular traditions continue to persist even in the midst of the accelerating pace of Western technological change.

The more recent history of Grise Fiord suggests that, notwithstanding the onset of wage employment, most Inuit people on Ellesmere Island still rely to a great degree on "country food," the resources that have sustained them and their ancestors for countless generations. Their hunting range was extended by the use of Western innovations such as guns and snowmobiles, yet the pattern of resource procurement according to the seasons has remained notably consistent with practices of hunting and gathering developed throughout the region's history. The continuing importance of Aboriginal environmental knowledge is evident in the recurring patterns of resource use, concurrent with the adoption of useful Western innovations. In mediating between these categories and taking what is useful from both cultures, the Inuit today are synthesizing the different traditions that were brought together by contact, yet remained as solitudes for much of the past 200 years.

I have argued the need to acknowledge the role of all participants in the drama of High Arctic history. Over the past 20 years, a series of debates in the human sciences has challenged the prevailing Western models of writing as unrepresentative of the diversity of perspectives in human history. Various fields have begun to acknowledge alternative or parallel systems of knowledge, including Aboriginal cosmologies, which organize the world according to radically different ways of seeing, knowing, and believing. To encompass more than the story of celebrated explorers, the history of the High Arctic must be pluralized to represent the broad range of participants who played roles in its unfolding.

The words of Kuuttiikittoq (Kutsikitsoq) to Danish scientist Christian Vibe during the Van Hauen expedition of 1939–41 seem particularly relevant. Admittedly, we have Vibe's translated version, rather than Kuuttiikittoq's actual words, but it illustrates the point:

> Don't write too much about us. White men keep on running around with notebook and pencil, as though they were incapable of remembering anything, and they write down a whole mass of trivialities; and when they go home they feed the people with a lot of lies about us and have themselves been great heroes. You will perhaps do the same and give us all something to laugh about, till the stones come rolling down the mountains, when the priest tells us what you have written about us and about yourself. Lend me your pencil, and I will scratch it all out, for it is surely mostly lies.[5]

Kuuttiikittoq's admonitions are a corrective to the notion that a European-centred perspective can capture the whole truth of the history of contact with Indigenous cultures. The issue goes beyond voice; it relates to the ways knowledge is constructed and organized by a particular culture. At least two fundamentally different concepts of history are at play in the history of this region, each corresponding to distinctively different approaches to time. An understanding of the differences between these two concepts may hold the key to unlocking some of the answers to long-term trends in arctic history.

In the first instance, High Arctic history can be readily viewed as a European story of progress, breaking free from the past, competition, individualism, and upward mobility. It is the story of imperialism, played out by various actors on behalf of different countries, differing in degree but sharing a common approach to subordinating the Arctic to personal or larger national objectives. It is also a story of applying one culture's hierarchical structures to a region in which such notions were ill-suited, in which the destinies of whole groups were subjected to the rules and decisions of expedition leaders, whether imbued with wisdom or folly. The Western approach to history charts many attempts by explorers to impose European technology in the Arctic. They sought to overcome its physical environment through the techniques of modern industrial societies, often in defiance of climate and the seasons.

The other history is an Aboriginal history of group persistence, rooted in traditions of hunting and natural resource use, decisions by consensus, and accommodation to Indigenous ways of life. This history stresses survival skills built up over many generations, incorporating numerous responses to the opportunities and constraints presented by the natural environment and ecology. This version, too, acknowledges change, but incremental change through pragmatic adjustments to enable a more effective utilization of the environment. The two concepts of history find their counterparts in two different temporal registers: linear time and cyclical time, one oriented to continuous change and the other shaped in accordance with the seasons, an endlessly repeatable cycle of natural resource harvesting and land use. Diverging traditions of time are at play in the recent history of Ellesmere Island, co-existing but never completely reconciled. If we are to grasp the full dimensions of post-contact history, we need to untangle the intricate historical relationships arising from the interplay between these completely different temporal perspectives.

A theme explored in this book is human adaptation—adaptation to different cultural contexts, as well as to the natural environment. It is recognized that the concept of adaptation itself is problematic, a construct fraught with methodological and interpretive difficulties. Marshall Sahlins's interpretation of the concept of adaptation, discussed in Chapter 15, suggests how this theme may be addressed in a manner consistent with the complexity of human history. According to Sahlins, no individual or group operates in a vacuum but must act according to the pressures of the environment in relation to a pre-existing social or cultural context. Each culture carries a specific history, the "penalties of the past."

Notwithstanding the perennial Western dream of beginning anew with a "clean slate," individuals in every society must operate within limitations imposed by their own culture as well as the natural environment. In the contact era, Ellesmere Island witnessed a parade of individualists, who came north to "make a stake," each imagining himself to be the master of his own destiny. In travelling North, the newcomers nevertheless confronted the constraints imposed by the polar environment and either adapted to its exigencies or met defeat or disaster. Often blinded by their cultural presuppositions, explorers were unwilling or unable to make the necessary adjustments to arctic shelter, travelling techniques, and clothing that might have averted the tragic conclusions of some of these forays. In the failures of the Greely expedition, in particular, may be discerned the negative consequences of imposing European world views and models of social organization in an environment where such frameworks were ill-suited to survival.

More astute individuals, such as Robert Peary, recognized the value of Aboriginal techniques of adaptation and incorporated Inughuit models into all aspects of their material repertoire. Peary developed an attitude to arctic "living off the country" that paralleled the approach of his Inughuit companions.[6] His pragmatic adaptations involved both reshaping the existing universe of materials to meet new challenges and the development of conceptual solutions consistent with a profound knowledge of the polar environment. The complex of shelters built by his party at Fort Conger in 1900 survives today as an example of the "untamed thought" that seeks imaginative solutions in a situation of scarcity or necessity.

Yet Peary fell short of a viable long-term adaptation. He emulated Aboriginal settlement patterns in the design of his wintering complexes but failed to discern the importance of Inughuit community patterns to their long-term strategies of occupation in this region. While he was able, through various means, to harness much of the productive effort of this people to serve his own polar exploration objectives, the demands he imposed on them were not sustainable in the long run.[7] Peary's exploitative behaviour toward the Inughuit was matched by unparalleled destructiveness in his approaches to hunting arctic animals. By contrast, the Inughuit, like all arctic peoples, have always needed to be concerned with the long term. Their community patterns, such as sharing and reciprocity, developed over many generations, were essential to enhancing their life chances in this unforgiving environment. As the great historian Edward Gibbon observed more than 200 years ago, in the long run the persistence of human societies has probably owed less to "superior talents or national subordination" than to the capacity of "each village, each family, each individual" to develop the knowledge and abilities of self-sufficiency.[8]

Ultimately, the fundamental issue for all humans who inhabited the High Arctic over several thousand years has been the challenge of survival. All groups that persisted in this region necessarily developed strategies to enhance their life chances in this forbidding environment. Notwithstanding the periodic withdrawal of peoples from the High Arctic during periods of climatic stress, the archaeological record confirms that the Aboriginal peoples who inhabited the region demonstrated a capacity to survive, as witnessed in successive occupations lasting up to two centuries or more. The actions that enabled these people to persist were not the pre-programmed applications of Aboriginal culture, but rather a set of continually changing responses to pragmatic necessity. In an environment in which the variables of climate and resources are in continual flux, the optimal survival strategy appears to be not one of mastering specific technologies, but rather the development of an ethos of adaptability. In their documented applications of accumulated knowledge to everyday problem solving, the Aboriginal people of the High Arctic demonstrated the process by which humans have been able to survive in this region over thousands of years. Their stories have a universal resonance as examples of pragmatic strategies applied by humans to survive in challenging environments around the world.

In the last 200 years, the process of survival has been complicated by the clash of cultural traditions, the introduction of asymmetrical power relations, and the impact of Western technologies in the Arctic. These continuing factors pose completely new challenges to Indigenous cultures and their capacity to persist in this environment.[9] The problems are complex, and their resolution will depend on whether other cultures can respect the need of arctic peoples to have the power to manage the environment and ecosystems in which they operate.

The issue extends well beyond the survival of the human species and encompasses the larger ecosystem within which humans must function. Western ideologies have often placed humans in a relationship of opposition to nature. As Anthony Wilden noted in *System and Structure*, such a mindset is ultimately self-defeating, not only because of its exploitative features, but because "it substitutes short-range survival value (competition) for long-range survival value (co-operation)."[10] Few, if any, of the world's ecosystems have not been compromised by the scale of Western interventions over the last two centuries. The virtual extinction of the Greenland whale in Davis Strait and Baffin Bay and the extermination of caribou in northwestern Greenland by the early twentieth century are examples of the potentially catastrophic power of resource extraction driven by short-term imperatives. In addition, the explorers' slaughter of caribou and muskox on Ellesmere Island put severe stress on both of these species in that area. In the case of the Peary caribou, the effects are still evident, as this species was placed on the "Threatened" list in 1979.[11] Sometimes the penalties of the past are too great and their destructive impacts cannot readily be reversed, as in the failure of Greenland whale populations to regenerate even in 90 years since the end of commercial whaling in Baffin Bay. In the High Arctic, low species diversity and slow maturation rates for many of the region's organisms suggest a particular sensitivity to external stress. In this context, many species can replenish their numbers only after a protracted period of regeneration.

In retrospect, the vision of J.B. Harkin and Vilhjalmur Stefansson in promoting early wildlife conservation measures holds a continuing resonance. The federal government's steps to protect the muskox in 1917 and the establishment of a game preserve in the Arctic Islands in the 1920s represented a developing concern in the twentieth century with protecting the natural environment from thoughtless destruction by humans. At the same time, the interconnectedness of the human and natural history of the High Arctic demonstrates the need for sustainable approaches that respect both the natural environment and the Aboriginal cultures which have lived in this land for thousands of years. Anthropologist Milton Freeman has argued above all, Inuit should be regarded as ecologists:

> in respect to the Inuit in the Canadian Arctic, their native understanding is inherently ecological. They perceive the environment to be a complex system of interacting variables, and they appreciate that interference with one part of the system has implications for the other parts."[12]

As the testimony of the Grise Fiord Inuit during the muskox controversy of 1967 revealed, their empirical observations of the habits of muskox provided a sound basis for decision making regarding the management of this species, perhaps analogous to the many natural resource strategies developed by various peoples of the High Arctic over thousands of years. It may well be that only through careful stewardship of arctic animal populations, based on both Western science and traditional ecological knowledge,[13] keystone and other arctic species can be sustained in the long run.

In 1988, the Government of Canada established Ellesmere Island National Park Reserve, the forerunner of Quttinirpaaq National Park of

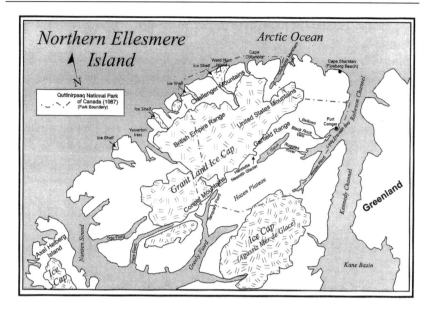

Figure 88: Map of northern Ellesmere Island, showing the boundaries of Quttinirpaaq National Park of Canada.

Canada (Figure 88). The second largest of Canada's national parks, it covers much of the northern part of the island, comprising 37,775 km^2, a vast area comparable in size to the entire country of Switzerland. Established to represent the eastern High Arctic natural region of Canada, Quttinirpaaq has a mandate to protect its constituent species, including muskox, Peary caribou, wolf, arctic fox, ermine, arctic hare and collared lemming, as well as a variety of migratory birds, including the horned lark, hoary redpoll, snow bunting, willow ptarmigan, and numerous others. In addition to its mandate to conserve the ecology of Quttinirpaaq National Park of Canada, Parks Canada has also undertaken to protect and present the important sites and cultural resources of human history within the park area, including pre-contact sites of the Independence and Thule cultures, and sites of the exploration era, including Fort Conger. In the agreement to establish the park reserve in 1986, the Government of Canada undertook to work closely with the communities of Grise Fiord and Resolute Bay in the development of park programs. At Quttinirpaaq National Park, there is an opportunity for Inuit and non-Inuit people to work together in partnership to foster the protection of this magnificent, yet fragile environment. The integration of Aboriginal traditional ecological knowledge and Western science offers the potential for a holistic approach to the management of the park's ecology and cultural resources.[14]

This history of Ellesmere Island ends where it began, with humans endeavouring to thrive and survive in the High Arctic environment. Throughout successive eras, this awesome landscape, the surrounding waters, and their component ecosystems established the basis for long-term human occupation, as they do today. Now, as before, the continuities of rugged terrain, ice, water, the rhythms of day and night, seasonal change, and the migration of arctic species continue to define the parameters of sustainable human life. Various cultures have come and gone, but in the last two centuries, Inuit and Inughuit people, like their Thule ancestors, have demonstrated their capacity for long-term occupation in this region. What has endured is a history of environmental and cultural adaptation, providing an important thread of continuity to a very diverse history.

The experience of Aboriginal peoples on Ellesmere Island over 4,000 years illustrates that High Arctic history is not a fixed phenomenon encased within the last 200 years of written records, but a dynamic entity, extending from remote antiquity to the present and into the future. To fully appreciate this history, we need to move beyond linear exploration narratives to acknowledge both the continuities of nature and culture, and the changes precipitated by cultural contact. In the process, it is hoped that the roles played by the Inuit, Inughuit, Europeans, and Euro-North Americans in the history of this region can become better known and understood by Canadians and all others with an interest in Canada's High Arctic. On a larger level, their individual and collective experience may serve as a tangible demonstration of the intricate workings of history, as the many layers of the past interact to shape the destinies of humans in their environment.

Colour Photographs

Figure 89: "MacMillan and Eskimo seated on boulder at Cape Sabine." Colourized
lantern slide from the Peary-MacMillan Arctic Museum, Bowdoin College
(Brunswick, Maine), Donald B. MacMillan Collection No. 3000.32.10.

Figure 90: "Eskimos hauling out a narwhal." Colourized lantern slide image courtesy of the Peary-MacMillan Arctic Museum, Bowdoin College, Donald B. MacMillan Collection No. 3000.32.1079.

Figure 91: "Mark-sing-wah (Mâsangguaq) at Cape York with bird net." Colourized lantern slide image courtesy of the Peary-MacMillan Arctic Museum, Bowdoin College, Donald B. MacMillan Collection No. 3000.32.1345.

Figure 92 : "Girl, black and white puppies (Shoo-ging-wah)." Colourized lantern slide image courtesy of the Peary-MacMillan Arctic Museum, Bowdoin College, Donald B. MacMillan Collection No. 3000.32.99.

Figure 93: "Following a lead" (North Pole expedition). Colourized lantern slide image courtesy of the Peary-MacMillan Arctic Museum, Bowdoin College, Donald B. MacMillan Collection No. 3000. 32.997.

Figure 94: "Eskimo boy fishing at Alida Lake." Colourized lantern slide image courtesy of the Peary-MacMillan Arctic Museum, Bowdoin College, Donald B. MacMillan Collection No.3000.32.495

Figure 95: "Eskimo with material from Fort Conger." Colourized lantern slide image courtesy of the Peary-MacMillan Arctic Museum, Bowdoin College, Donald B. MacMillan Collection No. 3000.32.5.

Figure 96: "Kahko in Spring at Cape Sheridan" ("Kahko after wading in stream"). Colourized lantern slide image courtesy of the Peary-MacMillan Arctic Museum, Bowdoin College, Donald B. MacMillan Collection No. 3000.32.1150.

Figure 97: Inughuit Sledgers on the Coastal Ice Foot of Eastern Ellesmere Island, Early Twentieth Century. Colourized lantern slide image courtesy of the Peary-MacMillan Arctic Museum, Bowdoin College, Donald B. MacMillan Collection No. 3000.32.13.

NOTES

Abbreviations

BCLSC   Bowdoin College Library, Special Collections (Brunswick, Maine)

LCMD   Library of Congress Manuscript Division (Washington, DC)

NAC   National Archives of Canada (Ottawa)

NGSL   National Geographic Society Library (Washington, DC)

PC, WCSC   Parks Canada, Western Canada Service Centre (Winnipeg)

USNA   United States National Archives (Washington, DC)

Introduction

1 Geoffrey Hattersley-Smith, *North Of Latitude Eighty: The Defence Research Board in Ellesmere Island* (Ottawa: The Defence Research Board, 1974).

2 Lyle Dick, "Defence Research Board Camps in Northern Ellesmere Island: Report on Historical Resources," Environment Canada Parks Service *Research Bulletin No. 292* (1991), pp. 1-36.

3 Trevor H. Levere, *Science and the Canadian Arctic: A Century of Exploration, 1818-1918* (Cambridge, England/New York: Cambridge University Press, 1993).

PART I
CONTINUITIES
The Natural Environment, Culture, and Human History

1 Fernand Braudel, *The Mediterranean and the Mediterranean World in the Age of Philip II*, Vols. I and II (Trans. Sîan Reynolds) (New York: Harper Torchbooks, 1975).

2 David Hackett Fischer, *The Great Wave: Price Revolutions and the Rhythm of History* (Oxford: Oxford University Press, 1996).

3 See, for example, Timo Myllyntaus and Mikko Saikko, Eds., *Encountering the Past in Nature: Essays in Environmental History* (Athens, Ohio: Ohio University Press, 2000); Char Miller and Hal Rothman, Eds., *Out of the Woods: Essays in Environmental History* (Pittsburgh: University of Pittsburgh Press, 1997); Richard H. Grove, *Ecology, Climate, and Empire: Colonialism and Global Environmental History, 1400-1940* (Cambridge, England: White Horse Press, 1997); Tom Griffiths and Libby Robin, Eds., *Ecology and Empire: Environmental History of Settler Societies* (Edinburgh: Keele University Press, 1997); Donald Worster, "Appendix: Doing Environmental History," in Donald Worster, Ed., *The Ends of the Earth: Perspectives on Modern Environmental History* (Cambridge, England: Cambridge University Press, 1988), pp. 289-307; and Richard White, "Historiographical Essay: American Environmental History: The Development of a New Historical Field," *Pacific Historical Review*, Vol. 54 (1985), pp. 297-335.

4 Raymond Williams, *Culture* (Glasgow: Fontana Paperbooks, 1981), pp. 10-14.

5 R.E. Allen, Ed., *The Concise Oxford Dictionary of Current English*, 8th ed. (Oxford, England: The Clarendon Press, 1990), p. 282.

6 Richard Slotkin, *The Fatal Environment: The Myth of the Frontier in the Age of Industrialization, 1800-1890* (New York: Atheneum Books, 1985), p. 21.

7 David Bidney, *Theoretical Anthropology* (New Brunswick, New Jersey: Transaction Publishers, 1967), p. 377.

Chapter 1: Geography and Climatic History of Ellesmere Island

1 Andrew Taylor, *Physical Geography of the Queen Elizabeth Islands, Canada*, Vol. I (New York: American Geographical Society, 1956), p. 11.

2 Robert P. Sharp, "Glaciers in the Arctic," *Arctic*, Vol. 9, Nos. 1 and 2 (1956), pp. 80, 107.

3 G.H. Miller, R.S. Bradley, and J.T. Andrews, "The Glaciation Level and Lowest Equilibrium Line Altitude in the High Canadian Arctic: Maps and Climatic Interpretation," *Arctic and Alpine Research*, Vol. 7, No. 2 (1975), map after p. 156.

4 Andrew Taylor, *Physical Geography of the Queen Elizabeth Islands*, Vol. V, pp. 14-15.

5 H.P. Trettin, *Precarboniferous Geology of the Northern Part of the Arctic Islands: Hazen Fold Belt and Adjacent Parts of Central Ellesmere Fold Belt, Ellesmere Island* (Ottawa: Geological Survey of Canada, 1994), Bulletin 430, p. 16, Figure 4.

6 R. Thorsteinsson and E.T. Tozer, "Geology of the Arctic Archipelago," in R.J.W. Douglas, Ed., *Geology and Economic Minerals of Canada*, Part B (Ottawa: Energy, Mines and Resources Canada, 1976), p. 588.

7 Jan Bednarski, "Geomorphology," in Parks Canada, Ellesmere Island National Park Reserve, "Resource Description and Analysis," Western Canada Service Centre, Parks Canada, Winnipeg, 1994, Vol. I, Chapter 3, pp. 3-5.

8 Andrew Taylor, *Physical Geography of the Queen Elizabeth Islands*, Vol. V, p. 26.

9 Ibid., Vol. III, pp. 38-41.

10 Ibid., Vol. III, pp. 42-43.

11 Ibid., Vol. III, pp. 33-35.

12 Adolphus Greely, *Three Years of Arctic Service*, Vol. I (New York: Charles Scribner's Sons, 1886), p. 276.

13 Andrew Taylor, *Physical Geography of the Queen Elizabeth Islands*, Vol. III, pp. 35-37.

14 Ibid., Vol. III, pp. 62-73.

15 Jan Bednarski, "Geomorphology," in Parks Canada, Ellesmere Island National Park Reserve, "Resource Description and Analysis," 1994, Vol. I, Chapter 3, pp. 3-9.

16 Andrew Taylor, *Physical Geography of the Queen Elizabeth Islands*, Vol. II, p. 44.

17 Jan Bednarski, "Geomorphology," in Ellesmere Island National Park Reserve, "Resource Description and Analysis," Parks Canada, Winnipeg, 1994, Vol. I, Chapter 3, pp. 3-12.

18 Moira Dunbar and Keith R. Greenaway, *Arctic Canada from the Air* (Ottawa: Defence Research Board, 1956), pp. 323-24.

19 Andrew Taylor, *Physical Geography of the Queen Elizabeth Islands*, Vol. II, pp. 55, 68.

20 Elisha Kent Kane, *Arctic Explorations: The Second Grinnell Expedition in Search of Sir John Franklin, 1853, '54, '55*, Vol. I (Philadelphia: Childs and Peterson, 1856), pp.175-76.

21 See Lauge Koch, "Contributions to the Glaciology of North Greenland," *Meddelelser om Grønland*, Vol. 65, No. 6 (1928), pp. 393-98.

22 *Sailing Directions for Northern Canada, including the Coast of Labrador North of St. Lewis Sound, the Northern Coast of the Canadian Mainland, and the Canadian Archipelago*, First Edition (Washington, DC: Government Printing Office, 1946), p. 56.

23 NAC, RG 18, Vol. 3014, Bache Peninsula Detachment Diary, 1927, Entry for Friday, 4 February 1927.

24 *Sailing Directions for Northern Canada* (1946), pp. 54-56.

25 Moira Dunbar, "Ice Regime and Ice Transport in Nares Strait," *Arctic*, Vol. 26, No. 4 (December 1973), pp. 288-89.

26 John W. Goodsell, *On Polar Trails: The Peary Expedition to the North Pole, 1908-09* (Ed. Donald W. Whisenhunt) (Austin, Texas: Eakin Press, 1983), p. 121.

27 Moira Dunbar and Keith R. Greenaway, *Arctic Canada From the Air*, pp. 448-60.

28 Moira Dunbar, "Ice Regime and Ice Transport in Nares Strait," pp. 288-89.

29 Louis Rey, "The Arctic Ocean: A 'Polar Mediterranean,'" in Louis Rey, Ed., *The Arctic Ocean: The Hydrographic Environment and The Fate of Pollutants* (London: Macmillan Press, 1982), pp. 3-36.

30 Gilbert M. Grosvenor, Ed., *National Geographic Atlas of the World* (Washington, DC: National Geographic Society, 1978), map: "Arctic Ocean Floor," pp. 170-71.

31 Moreau S. Maxwell, *Prehistory of the Eastern Arctic* (Orlando, Florida: Academic Press, Inc. 1985), p. 13.

32 Christian Vibe, "Arctic Animals in Relation to Climatic Fluctuations," *Meddelelser om Grønland*, Vol. 170, No. 5 (1967), pp. 15-17.

33 Moreau S. Maxwell, *Prehistory of the Eastern Arctic*, pp. 14-15.

34 Bill Thompson, "Climate," in Ellesmere Island National Park Reserve, "Resource Description and Analysis," Vol. I, Western Canada Service Centre, Parks Canada, Winnipeg, 1994, pp. 5-12.

35 J. Lotz and R.B. Sagar, "Meteorological Work in Northern Ellesmere Island," *Weather*, Vol. 15 (1960), p. 401.

36 Knud Rasmussen, *Greenland by the Polar Sea: The Story of the Thule Expedition from Melville Bay to Cape Morris Jesup* (Trans., Asta and Rowland Kenney) (London: William Henemann, 1921), p. 21.

37 Ibid., p. 21.

38 See Fernand Braudel, *The Mediterranean and the Mediterranean World in the Age of Philip II*, Vol. I, Preface to the First Edition, pp. 17-22; and pp. 231-75.

39 See H.H. Lamb, "Towards an Understanding of Climatic Change: Its Impact and History in the Modern World," in Knud Frydendahl, Ed., *Proceedings of the Nordic Symposium on Climatic Changes and Related Problems*, Danish Meteorological Institute Climatological Papers, No. 4 (1978), pp. 184-85.

40 The authors of a study tracing the Arctic's climatic history through the study of ice cores from the Greenland ice cap have identified a recurrent climatic oscillation of 63 years' duration, substantially corroborating Vibe's hypotheses based on faunal cycles of 66 years. See W. Dansgaard, J.J. Johnson, H.B. Clausen, and C.C. Langway, Jr., "Climatic Record Revealed By the Camp Century Ice Core," in Karl K. Turekian, Ed., *The Late Cenozoic Glacial Ages* (New Haven and London: Yale University Press, 1971), p. 42.

41 Louis Rey, "The Arctic Ocean: A 'Polar Mediterranean,'" p. 22.

42 John D. Jacobs, "Climate and the Thule Ecumene," in Allen P. McCartney, Ed., *Thule Eskimo Culture: An Anthropological Retrospective* (Ottawa: National Museum of Man, Mercury Series No. 88, 1979), pp. 528-35.

43 W. Dansgaard, S.J. Johnson, H.B. Clausen, and C.C. Langway, Jr., "Climatic Record Revealed By the Camp Century Ice Core," pp. 37-56.

44 Ibid.

45 Eigil Knuth, *Archaeology of the Musk-Ox Way* (Contributions du Centre d'Etudes Arctiques et Finno-Scandinaves, No. 5) (Paris: École Pratique des Hautes Études, Sorbonne, Sixième Section, Sciences Économiques et Sociales, 1967), pp. 17, .

46 Ian Stirling and T.G. Smith, "Interrelationships of Arctic Ocean Animals in the Sea Ice Habitat," in *Proceedings of the Circumpolar Conference on Northern Ecology*, Vol. II (Ottawa: National Research Council, 1975), pp. 37-47.

47 Thomas G. Stewart and John England, "Holocene Sea-Ice Variations and Paleo-environmental Change, Northernmost Ellesmere Island, NWT, Canada," *Arctic and Alpine Research*, Vol. 15, No. 1 (1983), p. 12; see also R.G. Barry, Wendy H Arundale, J.T. Andrews, Raymond S. Bradley, and Harvey Nichols, "Environmental Change and Cultural Change in the Eastern Canadian Arctic During the Last 5000 Years," *Arctic and Alpine Research*, Vol. 9, No.2 (1977), p. 205.

48 Moreau S. Maxwell, *Prehistory of the Eastern Arctic*, p. 305.

49 Moreau S. Maxwell, *An Archaeological Analysis of Eastern Grant Land, Ellesmere Island, Northwest Territories* (Canada, Department of Northern Affairs and Natural Resources, Bulletin No. 170 (1960), pp. 75-76.

50 Moreau S. Maxwell, *Prehistory of the Eastern Arctic*, p. 305.

51 Moreau S. Maxwell, "The House on the Ruggles," *The Beaver* Outfit 293 (Autumn, 1962), pp. 24-25.

52 Robert McGhee, "Thule Prehistory of Canada," in David Damas, Ed., *Handbook of North American Indians*, Vol. 5, "Arctic" (Washington, DC: The Smithsonian Institution, 1984), p. 375.

53 Lauge Koch, "The East Greenland Ice," *Meddelelser om Grønland*, Vol. 130, No. 3 (1945), p. 334.

54 Christian Vibe, "Arctic Animals in Relation to Climatic Fluctuations," *Meddelelser om Grønland*, Vol. 170, No. 5 (1967); see also Thomas McGovern, "The Economics of Extinction in Norse Greenland," in T.M.L. Wrigley, M.J. Ingram, and G. Farmer, *Climate and History: Studies in Past Climates and Their Impact on Man* (Cambridge, England: Cambridge University Press, 1981), p. 419.

55 Christian Vibe, "Arctic Animals in Relation to Climatic Fluctuations," pp. 163-66.

56 Ibid., pp. 91-92.

57 Ibid., p. 52.

Chapter 2: High Arctic Ecosystems and Human History

1 R.E. Allen, Ed., *The Concise Oxford Dictionary*, Eighth Edition (Oxford: Clarendon Press, 1990), p. 372.

2 John W. Bennett, *The Ecological Transition: Cultural Anthropology and Human Adaptation* (New York: Pergamon Press, 1975), pp. 35-36.

3 See E.F. Roots, "The Changing Arctic Marine Environment: Some Basic Considerations," in Louis Rey, Ed., *The Arctic Ocean*, pp. 226-29; and Milton M.R. Freeman, "Arctic Ecosystems," in David Damas, Ed., *Handbook of North American Indians*, Vol. 5, "Arctic" (Washington, DC: The Smithsonian Institution, 1984), p. 36.

4 M.J. Dunbar, "Arctic Marine Ecosystems," in Louis Rey, Ed., *The Arctic Ocean*, pp. 240-41.

5 For differing perspectives on the stability of arctic ecosystems, see Milton M.R. Freeman, "Arctic Ecosystems," in David Damas, Ed., *Handbook of North American Indians*, Vol. 5, "Arctic," p. 36, and M.J. Dunbar, "The Arctic Marine Ecosystem," in F.R. Engelhardt, Ed., *Petroleum Effects in the Arctic Environment* (London and New York: Elsevier Applied Science Publishers, 1985), pp. 26-27.

6 Robert Paine, "Animals as Capital: Comparisons Among Northern Nomadic Herders and Hunters," in Bruce Cox, Ed., *Cultural Ecology: Readings on the Canadian Indians and Eskimos* (Toronto: McClelland and Stewart, 1973), p. 305.

7 Ibid., p. 41.

8 J.R. Lotz, "Northern Ellesmere Island: An Arctic Desert," *Geografisker Annaler*, Vol. 44, Nos. 3-4 (1962), pp. 366-77.

9 L.C. Bliss, J. Svoboda, and D.I. Bliss, "Polar Deserts: Their Plant Cover and Plant Production in the Canadian High Arctic," *Holarctic Ecology*, Vol. 7 (1984), pp. 305-24.

10 R.L. Christie, *Geological Reconnaissance of Northeastern Ellesmere Island, District of Franklin*, Geological Survey of Canada, Memoir 331 (Ottawa: Department of Mines and Technical Surveys, 1964), p. 9.

11 Sylvia A. Edlund and Bea Taylor Alt, "Regional Congruence of Vegetation and Summer Climate Patterns in the Queen Elizabeth Islands, Northwest Territories, Canada," *Arctic*, Vol. 42, No. 1 (March, 1989), p. 11.

12 L.C. Bliss, J. Svoboda, and D.I. Bliss, "Polar Deserts. Their Plant Cover and Plant Production in the Canadian High Arctic," p. 321.

13 J.S. Tener, *Muskox in Canada: A Biological and Taxonomic Review* (Ottawa: Canadian Wildlife Service, 1965), p. 47.

14 N. Ronald Morrison, "Ecodistricts of Northen Ellesmere Island," Unpublished report, Parks Canada, National Parks Branch, Ottawa, 1984, p. 33.

15 Ibid., pp. 15-17.

16 Sylvia A. Edlund and Bea Taylor Alt, "Regional Congruence of Vegetation and Summer Climate Patterns in the Queen Elizabeth Islands, Northwest Territories, Canada," p. 17.

17 James H. Soper and John M. Powell, "Botanical Studies in the Lake Hazen Region, Northern Ellesmere Island, Northwest Territories, Canada," *Publications in Natural Sciences*, No. 5 (Ottawa: National Museum of Natural Sciences, 1985), p. 39.

18 D.B.O. Saville, "General Ecology and Vascular Plants of the Hazen Camp Area," *Arctic*, Vol. 17 (1964), p. 244.

19 G.R. Parker and R.K. Ross, "Summer Habitat Use by Muskoxen (*Ovibos moschatus*) and Peary Caribou (*Rangifer tarandus pearyi*) in the Canadian Arctic," *Polarforschung*, Vol. 46, No. 1 (1976), p. 24.

20 L.C. Bliss, "North American and Scandinavian Tundras and Polar Deserts," in L.C. Bliss, O.W. Heal, and J.J. Moore, Eds., *Tundra Ecosystems: A Comparative Analysis* (Cambridge, England: Cambridge University Press 1981), p. 18.

21 Ibid., p. 47.

22 A Gunn, F.L. Miller, and D.C. Thomas, "The Current and Future of Peary Caribou (*Rangifer tarandus pearyi*) on the Arctic Islands of Canada," *Biological Conservation*, Vol. 19 (1980-81), p. 290.

23 F.L. Miller and R.H. Parker, "Aerial surveys of Peary caribou and muskoxen on western Queen Elizabeth Islands, N.W.T.," *Canadian Wildlife Service Program Note No. 40* (1973); G.R. Parker, D.C. Thomas, E. Broughton, and D.R. Gray, "Crashes of Muskoxen and Peary Caribou Populations in 1973-74 on the Parry Islands, Arctic Canada," *Canadian Wildlife Service Program Note No. 56* (1975).

24 G.R. Parker and R.K. Ross, "Summer Habitat Use by Muskoxen (*Ovibos moschatus*) and Peary Caribou (*Rangifer tarandus pearyi*) in the Canadian Arctic," pp. 22-23.

25 Christian Vibe, "Arctic Animals in Relation to Climatic Fluctuations," p. 166.

26 I.A. McLaren, "Zooplankton of Lake Hazen, Ellesmere Island, and a Nearby Pond, with Special Reference to the Copepod Cyclops Scutifer Sars, *Canadian Journal of Zoology*, Vol. 42 (1964), pp. 613-29.

27 LGL Limited, *Biological Environment of Eastern Lancaster Sound and Western Baffin Bay: Components and Important Processes* (Ottawa: Department of Indian and Northern Affairs, Northern Affairs Program, 1983), p. 92.

28 H.D. Fisher, "Annual Report and Investigators' Summaries, No. 6, Hazen Lake," Unpublished Report, Fisheries Research Board of Canada, Arctic Unit, Montreal, Quebec, 1960, pp. 18-20.

29 J.A. Babaluk, N.M. Halden, J.D. Reist, A.H. Kristofferson, J.L.Campbell, and W.J. Teesdale, "Evidence for Non-Anadromous Behaviour of Arctic Charr (*Salvelinus alpinus*) from Lake Hazen, Ellesmere Island, Northwest Territories, Canada, Based on Scanning Proton Microprobe Analysis of Otolith Strontium Distribution," *Arctic*, Vol. 50, No. 3 (Sept. 1997), pp. 224-33.

30 LGL Limited, *Biological Environment of Eastern Lancaster Sound*, p. 92.

31 See, for example, Eigil Knuth, *Archaeology of the Musk-Ox Way*, pp. 31, 32a, 35; Moreau S. Maxwell, "The House on the Ruggles;" and Patricia D. Sutherland, "An Inventory and Assessment of the Prehistoric Archaeological Resources of Ellesmere Island National Park Reserve," Environment Canada, Parks Service, Microfiche Report Series No. 431 (1989).

32 See Moreau S. Maxwell, "The House on the Ruggles."

33 M.J. Dunbar, "The Arctic Marine Ecosystem," in F.R. Englehardt, Ed., *Petroleum Effects in the Arctic Environment* (London and New York: Elsevier Applied Science Publishers, 1985), p. 17.

34 See M.J. Dunbar, "The Biological Significance of Arctic Ice," in *Sikumiut: "The People Who Use the Sea Ice"* (Ottawa: Canadian Arctic Resources Committee,1982), pp. 8-10; and Moreau S. Maxwell, *Prehistory of the Eastern Arctic*, p. 68.

35 Elisha Kent Kane, *Arctic Explorations*, Vol. I, p. 454, note 6.

36 M.J. Dunbar, "The Biological Significance of Arctic Ice," in *Sikumiut*, p. 18; and Ian Stirling, "The Biological Importance of Polynyas in the Canadian Arctic," *Arctic*, Vol. 33, No. 2 (June 1980), p. 304.

37 Peter Schledermann, "Polynyas and Prehistoric Settlement Patterns," *Arctic*, Vol. 33, No. 2 (June 1980), Figure 2, p. 295.

38 Peter Schledermann, Personal communication with the author, 14 March 2001.

39 Christian Vibe, "The Marine Mammals and the Marine Fauna in the Thule District (Northwest Greenland) With Observations on Ice Conditions in 1939-41," *Meddelelser om Grønland*, Vol. 150, No. 6 (1950), pp. 16-17.

40 LGL Limited, *Biological Environment of Eastern Lancaster Sound and Western Baffin Bay: Components and Important Processes* (Ottawa: Department of Indian and Northern Affairs, Northern Affairs Program, 1983), p. 6.

41 Personal communication by Dr. Peter Schledermann to the author, 14 March 2001.

42 Ibid.

43 A.W. Mansfield, *Seals of Arctic and Eastern Canada* (Ottawa: Fisheries Research Board of Canada, Bulletin No. 137, 1967), p. 27.

44 Ibid., p. 19.

45 USNA, RG 401(1)(A), Robert E. Peary Papers, Papers Relating to Arctic Expeditions, 1886-1909, Greenland: 1893-95; Diaries, Reports and Notes: Astrup, Baldwin, Clark, Lee, Vincent, Greenland Expedition III, Folder 5, George H. Clark Notes, "Mammalogies, 1893-95," "Phoca Phoetida."

46 NAC, RG 18, Accn. 85-86/048, Vol. 56, File TA-500-20-10-1, RCMP Records, Reports on General Game Conditions, Alexandra Fiord Detachment Area, 30 June 1961, p. 1, and 30 June 1962, p. 2.

47 Ibid., Report on General Game Conditions, Alexandra Fiord Detachment Area, 30 June 1962, p. 1.

48 Christian Vibe, "The Marine Mammals and the Marine Fauna in the Thule District," p. 23.

49 NAC, RG 18, RCMP Records, Accn. 85-86/048, Vol. 56, File TA-500-20-10-1, General Game Conditions, Alexandra Fiord Detachment Area, 30 June 1962, p. 3.

50 Peter Freuchen and Finn Salomonsen, *The Arctic Year* (New York: G.P. Putnam's Sons, 1958), p. 276.

51 Kerwin J. Finley and Wayne E. Renaud, "Marine Mammals Inhabiting the Baffin Bay North Water in Winter," *Arctic*, Vol. 33, No. 4 (December 1980), p. 731.

52 Peter Schledermann, "Polynyas and Settlement Patterns," p. 295.

53 NAC, RG 18, RCMP Records, Accn. 85-86/048, Vol. 56, File TA-500-20-10-1, General Game Conditions, Alexandra Fiord Detachment Area, 30 June 1961, p. 2.

54 Christian Vibe, "Arctic Animals in Relation to Climatic Fluctuations," p. 57.

55 Ibid.

56 USNA, RG 401(1)(A), Robert E. Peary Papers, Papers Relating to Arctic Expeditions, 1886-1909: Greenland: 1893-95, Diary, Report, and Notes: Astrup, Baldwin, Clark, Lee, Vincent; 1893-95 Greenland Expedition III, Folder 5, George H. Clark Notes "Mammalogies, 1893-95."

57 USNA, RG 401(1)(A), Robert E. Peary Papers, Papers relating to Arctic Expeditions, 1886-1909, North Polar 1908-09, Expedition VIII, Box 1, Diaries and Journals, 1908-09, Diary of Dr. John Goodsell, 21 June – 12 October 1909, Entries for 23-25 July 1909.

58 On 7 October 1882, Dr. Octave Pavy reported that two narwhals had been spotted at Fort Conger. USNA, RG 27, Records of the Weather Bureau, Lady Franklin Bay Expedition Papers, Box 12, Pavy Notes and Letters, Pavy Diary Entry for 7 August 1882. In July 1909, on their return from Cape Sheridan, Peary's North Polar party spotted various narwhals, including two harpooned by native hunters on 24 July. USNA, RG 401(1)(A), Robert E. Peary Papers, Papers relating to Arctic Expeditions, 1886-1909, North Polar 1908-09, Expedition VIII, Box 1, Diaries and Journals, 1908-09, Diary of Dr. John Goodsell, 21 June – 12 October 1909, Entries for 23-25 July 1909.

59 Christian Vibe, "The Marine Mammals and the Marine Fauna in the Thule District," pp. 2-3.

60 P.R. Richard, M.P. Heide-Jørgensen, and S. St-Aubin, "Fall Movements of Belugas (*Delphinapterus leucas*) with Satellite-linked Transmitters in Lancaster Sound, Jones Sound, and Northern Baffin Bay," *Arctic*, Vol. 51, No. 1 (March 1998), pp. 5-16.

61 Gary F. Searing, Peter Schledermann, David Evans, and William Cross, "The Natural and Cultural Resources of Ellesmere Island National Park Reserve and Adjacent Areas: A Review of the Literature and Annotated Bibliography," Unpublished report, Parks Canada, Winnipeg, 1988.

62 Kerwin J. Finley and Wayne E. Renaud, "Marine Mammals Inhabiting the Baffin Bay," pp. 732-733.

63 Elisha Kent Kane, *Arctic Explorations*, Vol. I, p. 461, note 48.

64 M.J. Dunbar, *Ecological Development in Polar Regions: A Study in Evolution* (Englewood Cliffs, NJ: Prentice-Hall, 1968), p. 66.

65 Ibid., p. 68.

66 Marcel Mauss, *Seasonal Variations of the Eskimo: A Study in Social Morphology* (Trans. James J. Fox) (London, Boston and Henley: Routledge & Kegan Paul, 1979).

67 Ibid., pp. 36-52.

68 Ibid., pp. 55-56.

69 USNA, Robert E. Peary Papers, RG 401(1)(A), Papers Relating to Arctic Expeditions, 1886-1902, T.S. Dedrick Diaries, Notebooks and Other Papers, 1898-1901, VI, Box No. 4, Folder 6, Miscellaneous Papers of Dr. T.S. Dedrick: Field Notes, Letter of Dedrick, Mouth of Crozier River, to Robert Peary, Fort Conger, 21 February 1901, p. 1.

70 J. Lotz and R.B. Sagar, "Meteorological Work in Northern Ellesmere Island," p. 398.

71 Captain G.S. Nares, "Report of Proceedings," in *Journals and Proceedings of the Arctic Expedition, 1875-6, under the Command of Captain Sir George S. Nares*, Parliamentary Paper No. C-1636 (London: Queen's Printer, 1877), p. 18.

72 NAC, RG 18, Vol. 3012, File: Annual Reports, Bache Peninsula Detachment, 1927-28, Bache Peninsula Detachment Annual report, 1929-30, by Constable N. McLean, 29 July 1930.

73 Eigil Knuth, *Archaeology of the Musk-Ox Way*, p. 44.

74 Personal communication of Dr. Peter Schledermann to the author, 14 March 2001.

75 George Wenzel, "Archaeological Evidence for Prehistoric Inuit Use of the Sea-Ice Environment," in *Sikumiut*, pp. 49 ff.

76 For an account of a walrus hunt from the ice in this period, see Elisha Kent Kane, *Arctic Explorations*, Vol. I, pp. 409-17.

77 Dr. Edward Moss, *Shores of the Polar Sea: A Narrative of the Arctic Expedition of 1875-76* (London: Marcus Ward and Co., 1878), Chapter 8.

78 Peter Freuchen and Finn Salomonsen, *The Arctic Year*, pp. 215, 273-75.

79 Ibid., pp. 202-08.

80 Ibid., p. 202.

81 Ibid., pp. 277-81.

82 Eigil Knuth, *Archaeology of the Musk-Ox Way*, pp. 32a, 35; and Moreau Maxwell, *Prehistory of the Eastern Arctic*, p. 305.

83 Peter Freuchen and Finn Salomonsen, *The Arctic Year*, p. 292.

84 Ibid., p. 294.

85 Harry Whitney, *Hunting with the Eskimos* (New York: The Century Company, 1910), p. 79.

86 Wally Herbert, *Hunters of the Polar North: The Eskimo* (Amsterdam: Time-Life Books, 1981), p. 43.

87 Harry Whitney, *Hunting with the Eskimos*, pp. 82-83.

88 Peter Freuchen and Finn Salomonsen, *The Arctic Year*, pp. 330-31.

89 Donald L. Hardesty, *Ecological Anthropology* (New York: John Wiley and Sons, 1977), pp. 21-46; John W. Bennett, *The Ecological Transition: Cultural Anthropology and Human Adaptation* (New York: Pergamon Press, Inc., 1975).

90 Donald L. Hardesty, *Ecological Anthropology*, p. 21.

91 Ibid., p. 24.

92 Karl W. Butzer, *Archaeology as Human Ecology: Method and Theory for a Contextual Approach* (Cambridge, England: Cambridge University Press, 1982), Table 15-1, p. 290.

93 On this issue, see Donald L. Hardesty, *Ecological Anthropology*, pp. 43-44.

94 Robin Ridington, "Technology, World View, and Adaptive Strategy in a Northern Hunting Society," *Canadian Review of Sociology*, Vol. 19, No. 4 (1982), pp. 469-81.

95 Ibid., p. 471.

96 Robert Paine, "Animals as Capital: Comparisons Among Northern Nomadic Herders and Hunters," in Bruce Cox, Ed., *Cultural Ecology: Readings on the Canadian Indians and Eskimos* (Toronto: McClelland and Stewart, 1973), p. 303.

97 Eigil Knuth, *Archaeology of the Musk-Ox Way*; "The Ruins of the Musk-ox Way," *Folk*, Vol. 8-9 (1966-67), pp. 191-219; "An Outline of the Archaeology of Peary Land," *Arctic*, Vol. 5, No. 1 (1952), pp. 17-33; "Archaeology of the Farthest North," *Proceedings of the Thirty-Second International Congress of Americanists* (Copenhagen: Munksgaard, 1958), pp. 561-73.

98 See Moreau S. Maxwell, *Archaeological Analysis of Eastern Grant Land, Ellesmere Island, Northwest Territories* and *Prehistory of the Eastern Arctic*, op. cit.

99 Patricia D. Sutherland, "An Inventory and Assessment of the Prehistoric Archaeological Resources of Ellesmere Island National Park Reserve."

100 Peter Schledermann, *Crossroads to Greenland; 3000 Years of Prehistory in the Eastern High Arctic*, Komatik Series No. 2 (Calgary: The Arctic Institute of North America, 1990).

101 Karen M. McCullough, *The Ruin Islanders: Early Thule Culture in the Eastern High Arctic*, Archaeological Survey of Canada, Mercury Series Paper 141 (Ottawa: Canadian Museum of Civilization, 1989).

102 Patricia D. Sutherland, "An Inventory and Assessment of the Prehistoric Archaeological Resources of Ellesmere Island National Park Reserve," Vol. I, p. 15. Peter Schledermann does not use the term "Independence II" and has drawn attention to a more complex pattern of interrelationships of various cultures comprising the transition between Pre-Dorset and Dorset cultures in the High Arctic. Peter Schledermann, *Crossroads to Greenland*, pp. 23, 91-195.

103 Eigil Knuth, *Archaeology of the Muskox Way*, pp. 14-15.

104 Sutherland's findings are summarized in Robert McGhee, *Ancient People of the Arctic* (Vancouver: UBC Press and the Canadian Museum of Civilization, 1996), p. 70.

105 Peter Schledermann, *Voices in Stone: A Personal Journey into the Arctic Past* (Calgary: University of Calgary, Arctic Institute Komatik Series No. 5, 1996), "Palaeo-Eskimo Burin Types," p. 55.

106 Eigil Knuth, *Archaeology of the Musk-Ox Way*, p. 43.

107 Patricia D. Sutherland, "An Inventory and Assessment of the Prehistoric Archaeological Resources of Ellesmere Island National Park Reserve," p. 65.

108 Robert McGhee, *Ancient People of the Arctic*, p. 128.

109 For two contrary positions in this debate, see Milton M.R. Freeman, "A Critical View of Thule Culture and Ecologic Adaptation," in Allen P. McCartney, Ed., *Thule Eskimo Culture: An Anthropological Retrospective*, Archaeological Survey of Canada Mercury Paper No. 88 (Ottawa: National Museum, 1979), pp. 278-85; and Allen P. McCartney, "The Nature of Thule Eskimo Whale Use," *Arctic*, Vol. 33, No. 3 (September 1980), pp. 517-41.

110 Eigil Knuth, "Archaeology of the Farthest North," pp. 561-73.

111 George Wenzel, "Archaeological Evidence for Prehistoric Inuit Use of the Sea-Ice Environment," in *Sikumiut*, p. 46.

112 Peter Schledermann, *Voices in Stone*, pp. 122-30; see also Peter Schledermann, *The Viking Saga* (London: Weidenfeld and Nicolson, 1997), pp. 6-8.

113 Peter Schledermann, *Voices in Stone*, pp. 127-28. See also P. Schledermann and K.M. McCullough, "Culture Contact, Continuity, and Collapse: The Archaeology of North Atlantic Colonization, AD 800-1800: Native/Norse Contact in the Smith Sound Region," Unpublished paper, The Arctic Institute of North America, Calgary, 10 August 2000, pp. 1-23."

114 Vagn Fabtritius Buchwald and Gert Mosdal, "Meteorite Iron, Telluric Iron and Wrought Iron in Greenland," *Meddelelser om Grønland*, Man and Society, Vol. 9 (1985), pp. 3-49.

115 USNA, RG 401(1)(A), Robert E. Peary Papers, Papers Relating to Arctic Expeditions, 1886-1909, Diary Transcripts, 1871-1900, File "Diary (typed) 1899" [typescript transcription of Peary's diary entry for 25 June 1899].

116 Patricia Sutherland, "An Inventory and Assessment of the Prehistoric Archaeological Resources of the Ellesmere Island National Park Reserve," p. 33.

117 Peter Schledermann, personal communication with the author, 16 March 2001.

118 Peter Schledermann, personal communication with the author, 20 March 2001.

119 The comparative work of Joseph Bohlen, who studied explorers' responses to reduced light levels in the Arctic, suggests a strong relationship between the polar environment and human psychology, particularly in terms of the effects of the long winter darkness. Joseph Bohlen, "Biological Rhythms: Human Responses in the Polar Environment," *Yearbook of Physical Anthropology*, Vol. 22 (1979), 47-79. See also A.J.W. Taylor, "Polar Winters: Chronic Deprivation or Transient Hibernation?" *Polar Record*, Vol. 25, No. 154 (1989), pp. 239-46.

120 BCLSC, Donald B. MacMillan Collection, Diaries, Journals, Logs, Etc., Crocker Land Expedition, Journal No. 16, 2 July 1913 – 12 February 1914, Entry for 25 October 1913.

121 Elisha Kent Kane, *Arctic Explorations*, Vol. I, p. 152.

122 Ibid., p. 156.

123 William C. Godfrey, *Godfrey's Narrative of the Last Grinnell Arctic Exploring Expedition in Search of Sir John Franklin, 1853-4-5* (Philadelphia: J.T. Lloyd, 1860), p. 118.

124 Adolphus W. Greely, *Three Years of Arctic Service: An Account of the Lady Franklin Bay Expedition of 1881-84 and the Attainment of the Farthest North*, Vol. I (New York: Charles Scribner's Sons, 1886), p. 154.

125 Ibid., 155.

126 USNA, RG 27, Records of the Weather Bureau, Lady Franklin Bay Expedition Records, Volume 12, Transcriptions of Pavy Diaries, p. 398, Entry for 22 January 1882.

127 USNA, RG 401(1)(A), Robert E. Peary Papers, Papers Relating to Arctic Expeditions, 1886-1909; Greenland: 1898-1902, Box No. 3 of 6, Robert E. Peary Diaries 1901, Peary Diary, January–March 1901.

128 USNA, RG 401(1)(A), Robert E. Peary Papers, Papers Relating to Arctic Expeditions, Greenland, 1898-1902, T.S. Dedrick Diaries, Notebooks, and Other Papers, VI, Folder 6, Field notes, Miscellaneous Papers, Letter of T.S. Dedrick, Mouth of Crozier River, to Robert Peary, Fort Conger, 27 February 1901.

129 USNA, RG 401(1)(A), Robert E. Peary Papers, Papers Relating to Arctic Expeditions, 1886-1909; Greenland: 1898-1902, Box No. 3 of 6, Robert E. Peary Diaries 1901, Peary Diary, January–March 1901, Entry for 10 March 1901, at Fort Conger.

130 Harry Whitney, *Hunting with the Eskimos* (New York: The Century Company, 1910), p. 79.

131 Ibid., pp. 82-83.

132 Ibid., pp. 83-84.

133 Dr. Frederick A. Cook, *My Attainment of the Pole* (New York and London: Mitchell and Kennerley, 1913), p. 92.

134 Ibid., pp. 93-94.

135 Lyle Dick, "'Pibloktoq' (Arctic Hysteria): A Construction of European-Inuit Relations?" *Arctic Anthropology*, Vol. 32 No. 2 (1995), p. 13.

136 See Charles Bernheimer and Claire Kehane, Eds., *In Dora's Case: Freud—Hysteria—Feminism* (New York: Columbia University, 1985); and Carroll Smith-Rosenberg, *Disorderly Conduct: Visions of Gender in Victorian America* (New York and Oxford: Oxford University Press, 1985).

Chapter 3: Inughuit Culture in the High Arctic, 1800 to 1900

1 Elisha Kent Kane, *Arctic Explorations*, Vol II, p. 211. Kane acknowledged that his informal census might have slightly understated the numbers, but as three Inughuit individuals corroborated the tally, he concluded that his population estimates were reasonably accurate. See also Rolf Gilberg, "The Polar Eskimo Population, Thule District, North Greenland," *Meddelelser om Grønland*, Vol. 203, No. 3 (1976), Table 3, p. 15.

2 Captain John Ross, *A Voyage of Discovery Made Under the Orders of the Admiralty in His Majesty's Ships* Isabella *and* Alexander *for the Purpose of Exploring Baffin's Bay and Inquiring into the Probability of a North-West Passage*, Vol. I (London: John Murray, 1819), p. 80. See also C.R. Markham, "The Arctic Highlanders," *Transactions of the Ethnological Society of London*, Vol. 4 (1866), pp. 125-37.

3 Emil Bessels, "The Northernmost Inhabitants of the Earth," *The American Naturalist*, Vol. 18 (1884), pp. 861-82.

4 A.L. Kroeber, "The Eskimo of Smith Sound," *American Museum of Natural History Bulletin*, Vol. 12, No. 21 (1900), p. 265 ff.

5 Knud Rasmussen, *The People of the Polar North* (Trans. and ed., G. Herring) (London: Kegan Paul, Trench, Trübner and Co., 1908).

6 Robert E. Peary, *The North Pole* (New York: Greenwood Press, 1910), pp. 63-71.

7 Rolf Gilberg, "Polar Eskimo," in David Damas, Ed., *Handbook of North American Indians*, Vol. 5, "Arctic," p. 593.

8 Wendell H. Oswalt, "Technological Complexity: The Polar Eskimos and the *Tareumiut*," *Arctic Anthropology*, Vol. 24, No. 2 (1987), p. 91.

9 Peter C. Sutherland, *Journal of a Voyage in Baffin's Bay and Barrow Straits in the Years 1850-51, Performed by HM Ships* Lady Franklin *and* Sophia *Under the Command of Mr. William Penny, in Search of the Missing Crews of HM Ships* Erebus *and* Terror, Vol. I (London: Longman, Brown, Green, and Longmans, 1852), p. 257.

10 Ibid., pp. 257-58.

11 Christian Vibe, "Arctic Animals in Relation to Climatic Fluctuations," *Meddelelser om Grønland*, Vol. 170, No. 5 (1967), p. 52, cited in Rolf Gilberg, "Changes in the Life of the Polar Eskimos Resulting From a Canadian Immigration into the Thule District, North Greenland, in the 1860s," *Folk*, Vols.16-17 (1974-75), p. 159.

12 Karl W. Butzer, *Archaeology as Human Ecology*, p. 292.

13 Elisha Kent Kane, *Arctic Explorations*, Vol. II, pp. 109-10.

14 A tabulation of the basis for Inughuit subsistence from the ethnographic record indicated a wide variety of foods obtained by this group, through i) collecting, including plants (berries, lichen, seaweed, sorrel, willow, flowers, scurvy grass, and possibly other plants), birds (auks, eiders, gulls, terns, and many others), and mammals (dog); ii) hunting, including caribou rumen contents, muskox stomach contents, and ptarmigan intestinal contents; birds (dovekies, eiders, murrs, gulls, geese (brant and snow), ravens, and rock ptarmigan), and mammals (polar bear, fox, hare, and, in the post-contact era, muskox and caribou); and iii) fishing or marine extraction, including shellfish (mussels, walrus shellfish stomach contents); fish (salmon, lake trout, shark, halibut, cod, sea scorpion), and mammals (seals [ringed, bearded, etc.], walrus, beluga, and narwhal). See Gregory Allen Reinhardt, "The Dwelling as Artifact: Analysis of Ethnographic Eskimo Dwellings, with Archaeological Implications," (PhD dissertation, University of California, Los Angeles, 1986), Table 4.5, p. 79.

15 Christian Vibe, "The Marine Mammals and the Marine Fauna in the Thule District," p. 83.

16 Emil Bessels, "The Northernmost Inhabitants of the Earth," *The American Naturalist*, Vol. 18 (1884), p. 873.

17 Knud Rasmussen, *Greenland by the Polar Sea*, p. 16.

18 Captain John Ross, *A Voyage of Discovery*, pp. 130-31.

19 Knud Rasmussen, *Greenland by the Polar Sea*, pp. 22-25.

20 Isaac Israel Hayes, *An Arctic Boat Journey in the Autumn of 1854* (Ed., Dr. Norton Shaw) (London: Richard Bentley, 1860), p. 262.

21 Robert E. Peary, *Northward over the "Great Ice": A Narrative of Life and Work Along the Shores and upon the Interior Ice-Cap of Northern Greenland in the Years 1886 and 1891-1897* (New York: Frederick A. Stokes Company, 1898), Vol. II, pp. 428-30.

22 For a discussion of the relationships of breathing hole sealing and aggregation of Inuit settlements in the Central Arctic region, see David Damas, "Environment, History, and Central Eskimo Society," in David Damas, Ed., *Contributions to Anthropology: Ecological Essays*, National Museum of Canada, Bulletin No. 320, Ottawa, 1969, pp. 40-64.

23 Benjamin Hoppin, *A Diary Kept While With the Peary Arctic Expedition of 1896* (New Haven: n.p., 1897), pp. 20-23.

24 Marcel Mauss, *Seasonal Variations of the Eskimo*, p. 66.

25 Kwang-Chih Chang, "A Typology of Settlement and Community Patterns in Some Circumpolar Societies," *Arctic Anthropology*, Vol. 1, No. 1 (1962), pp. 28-41. See also the essay and panel discussion in June Helm, "Relationship between Settlement Pattern and Community Pattern," in David Damas, Ed., *Contributions to Anthropology: Ecological Essays*, pp. 151-62.

26 USNA, RG 401(1)(A), Robert E. Peary Papers, Papers Relating to Arctic Expeditions, 1886-1909, Greenland: 1898-1902, T.S. Dedrick Diaries, Notebooks, and Other Papers VI, Folder 2, Dedrick Diaries, 1899, Entry for 13 December 1899 [at Etah].

27 Marcel Mauss, *Seasonal Variations of the Eskimo*, pp. 53-75.

28 Knud Rasmussen, *The People of the Polar North*, p. 174.

29 Eivind Astrup, *With Peary Near the Pole* (London: C. Arthur Pearson, Ltd., 1898), p. 278.

30 USNA, RG 401(1)(A), Robert E. Peary Papers, Papers Relating to Arctic Expeditions, 1886-1909, Greenland: 1898-1902, T.S. Dedrick Diaries, Notebooks, and Other Papers VI, Folder 2, Dedrick Diaries, 1899, Diary Entry for 13 December 1899.

31 Jean Malaurie, *The Last Kings of Thule* (Trans. Adrienne Foulke) (Chicago: University of Chicago Press, 1982), pp. 114-18.

32 Marcel Mauss, *Seasonal Variations of the Eskimo*, p. 59.

33 Knud Rasmussen, *The People of the Polar North*, p. 146.

34 Ibid., pp. 107-08.

35 Jean Malaurie, *The Last Kings of Thule*, pp. 131-33.

36 Emil Bessels, "The Northernmost Inhabitants of the Earth," *The American Naturalist*, Vol. 18 (1884), p. 877.

37 USNA, RG 401(1)(A), Robert E. Peary Papers, Papers Relating to Arctic Expeditions, 1886-1909, Greenland: 1898-1902, T.S. Dedrick Diaries, Notebooks, and Other Papers VI, Folder 2, Dedrick Diaries, 1899, Diary Entry for 3 October 1899.

38 Robert E. Peary, *Northward Over the "Great Ice,"* Vol. II, p. 268.

39 Elisha Kent Kane, *Arctic Explorations*, Vol. II, pp. 201-03.

40 Peter Freuchen and Finn Salomonsen, *The Arctic Year*, p. 200.

41 Ibid., p. 201.

42 W. Elmer Ekblaw, "The Material Response of the Polar_Eskimo to Their Far Arctic Environment," *Annals of the Association of American Geographers*, Vol.17, No. 4, December, 1927, p. 163.

43 August Sonntag, *Professor Sonntag's Thrilling Narrative of the Grinnell Exploring Expedition to the Arctic Ocean in the Years 1853, 1854, and 1855, In Search of Sir John Franklin, Under the Command of Dr. E.K. Kane, USN* (Philadelphia: J.H.C. Whiting, n.d.) p. 111.

44 Harrison Hunt and Ruth Hunt Thompson, *North to the Horizon: Searching for Peary's Crocker Land* (Camden, Maine: Down East Book, 1980), p. 23.

45 Nicholas Senn, *In the Heart of the Arctic* (Chicago: W.B. Conkey Company, 1907), pp. 212-13.

46 Ibid., pp. 211-12.

47 Ibid., p. 211.

48 Ibid., p. 173.

49 Ibid., p. 84.

50 Marcel Mauss, *Seasonal Variations of the Eskimo*, Chapter 2, pp. 36-52.

51 Captain John Ross, *A Voyage of Discovery*, p. 103.

52 Elisha Kent Kane, *Arctic Explorations*, Vol. I, pp. 409-10.

53 Ibid., Vol. I, p. 244.

54 Clements Markham, "On the Arctic Highlanders," in *A Selection of Papers on Arctic Geography and Ethnology* (London: John Murray, 1875), p. 182.

55 Robert E. Peary, *Northward over the "Great Ice,"* Vol. II, pp. 420-22.

56 Captain John Ross, *A Voyage of Discovery*, pp. 131-32.

57 Edward Shackleton, *Arctic Journeys: The Story of the Oxford University Ellesmere Land Expedition, 1934-5* (London: Hodder and Stoughton, Ltd., 1936), p. 194.

58 Christian Vibe, "The Marine Mammals and the Marine Fauna of the Thule District," pp. 72-73. The methods described by Vibe were witnessed in the Second World War era, when guns were used in *utoq* hunting. Apart from the use of firearms, post-contact Inughuit techniques for stalking seals were largely unchanged from the pre-contact period.

59 Elisha Kent Kane, *Arctic Explorations*, Vol. II, p. 64.

60 Ibid., Vol. I, pp. 417-18.

61 Peter Freuchen, *Book of the Eskimos* (Ed. Dagmar Freuchen) (New York: Fawcett Premier, 1973), p. 33.

62 Jean Malaurie, *The Last Kings of Thule*, Part 2, pp. 439-40, n. 23.

63 Map by Kallihirua (Erasmus York), "Drawn on board HMS *Assistance* during the winter of 1850-51," reproduced in Clements Markham, "On the Arctic Highlanders," in *A Selection of Papers on Arctic Geography and Ethnology* (1875), insert between pages 184 and 185.

64 Richard Vaughan, *Northwest Greenland: A History* (Orono, Maine: University of Maine Press, 1991), p. 18.

65 Captain John Ross, *A Voyage of Discovery*, p. 102.

66 USNA, RG 401(1)(A), Robert E. Peary Papers, Papers Relating to Arctic Expeditions, 1886-1909; Greenland, 1898-1902, T.S. Dedrick Diaries, Notebooks, and Other Papers, 1898-1901, Box. No. 4 of 6, Dr. T.S. Dedrick Diary, 28 June to 23 August 1900, at Fort Conger, Entry for 22 July 1900.

67 Captain John Ross, *A Voyage of Discovery*, p. 101.

68 C.R. Markham, "The Arctic Highlanders," (1866), pp. 130-31.

69 See also Kane's discussion of an Inughuaq's use of the *toq* during a walrus hunt in the 1850s. Elisha Kent Kane, *Arctic Explorations*, Vol. II, pp. 413-14.

70 Hans Hendrik, *Memoirs of Hans Hendrik, the Arctic Traveller, serving under Kane, Hayes, Hall and Nares, 1853-1876* (Ed. Henry Rink) (London: Trübner and Co., Ludgate Hill, 1878), p. 34.

71 BCLSC, Donald B. MacMillan Collection, Diaries, Journals, Logs, Etc., Diary No. 56 "Ethnological Notes," p. 324.

72 Ibid., p. 333.

73 Elisha Kent Kane, *Arctic Explorations*, Vol. II, p. 204.

74 Ibid. Vol. I, pp. 205-06.

75 Nicholas Senn, *In the Heart of the Arctic*, p. 116.

76 BCLSC, Donald B. MacMillan Collection, Diaries, Journals, Logs, Etc., Diary No. 56, "Ethnological Notes."

77 See Robert E. Peary, *Northward Over the "Great Ice,"* Vol. II, pp. 267-71.

78 Elisha Kent Kane, *Arctic Explorations*, Vol. I, p. 380.

79 See the illustration of an Inughuit dwelling, entrance tunnel, and snow-domed porch at Navdlortoq in Erik Holtvedt, "Contributions to Polar Eskimo Ethnography," *Meddelelser om Grønland*, Vol. 182. No. 2 (1967), Figure 9, p. 17.

80 Sherard Osborn, *Stray Leaves from an Arctic Journal; or, Eighteen Months in the Polar Regions, in Search of Sir John Franklin's Expedition, In the Years 1850-51* (London: Longman, Brown, Green, and Longmans, 1852), pp. 250-51; For further descriptions of the interiors of Inughuit wintering dwellings in the mid-nineteenth century, see: Elisha Kent Kane, *Arctic Explorations*, Vol. II, pp. 113-15; Isaac Israel Hayes, *An Arctic Boat Journey in the Autumn of 1854* (Ed. Dr. Norton Shaw) (London: Richard Bentley, 1860), pp. 126-28; and C.R. Markham, "The Arctic Highlanders," (1866), p. 130.

81 Isaac Israel Hayes, *An Arctic Boat-Journey in the Autumn of 1854*, pp. 27-28.

82 Ibid.

83 Elisha Kent Kane, *Arctic Explorations*, Vol. I, p. 122.

84 H.P. Steensby, "Contributions to the Ethnology and Anthropogeography of the Polar Eskimos," *Meddelelser om Grønland*, Vol. 34, No. 7 (1910), p. 287.

85 BCLSC, Donald B. MacMillan Collection, Diaries, Journals, Logs, Etc., MacMillan North Polar Diaries, No. 7, Field Diary, 19 April to 31 May 1909, Entry for 18 May 1909, at Cape Morris Jesup, northern Greenland.

86 USNA, RG 401(56), Papers of Hugh J. Lee, Reports on Greenland Eskimos, 1893-95, "Arctic Highlanders — Houses and Tents, Igloos and Tupiks," Unpublished manuscript, 28 October 1894.

87 W. Elmer Ekblaw, "The Material Response of the Polar Eskimo to Their Far Arctic Environment," pp. 161-62.

88 Daniel W. Streeter, *An Arctic Rodeo* (New York: G.P. Putnam's Sons, 1929), pp. 155-56.

89 Isaac Israel Hayes, *An Arctic Boat-Journey in the Autumn of 1854*, p. 215.

90 Ibid., p. 216.

91 Benjamin Hoppin, *A Diary Kept While With the Peary Arctic Expedition of 1896* (New Haven: n.p., 1897), p. 20.

92 Isaac Israel Hayes, *An Arctic Boat-Journey in the Autumn of 1854*, p. 217.

93 Elisha Kent Kane, *Arctic Explorations*, Vol. II, p. 142.

94 Peter Freuchen, *Book of the Eskimos*, p. 33.

95 W. Elmer Ekblaw, "Eskimo Dogs — Forgotten Heroes," *Natural History* (Journal of the American Museum of Natural History), Vol. 37 (January, 1936), p. 173.

96 Wally Herbert, *Hunters of the Polar North* (Amsterdam: Time-Life Books, 1981), pp. 62-63.

97 H.P. Steensby, "Contributions to the Ethnology and Anthropogeography of the Polar Eskimos," p. 354.

98 Rolf Gilberg, "Polar Eskimo," in David Damas, Ed., *Handbook of North American Indians*, Vol. 5, "Arctic," p. 580.

99 Ibid.

100 Frank Wilbert Stokes, "An Arctic Studio (77° 44' N. Lat.)," *The Century Magazine*, Vol. 52, New Series, Vol. 30 (1896), p. 414.

101 See the illustration "Wild Dog Team" in Elisha Kent Kane, *Arctic Explorations*, Vol. I, p. 210.

102 W. Elmer Ekblaw, "Eskimo Dogs — Forgotten Heroes," p. 175.

103 Peter Freuchen, *Arctic Adventure: My Life in the Frozen North* (New York: Farrar and Rinehart, 1935), p. 44.

104 W. Elmer Ekblaw, "The Material Response of the Polar Eskimo to their Far Arctic Environment," p. 20.

105 Elisha Kent Kane, *Arctic Explorations*, Vol. I, pp. 123-24.

106 H.P. Steensby, "Contributions to the Ethnology and Anthropogeography of the Polar Eskimos," p. 300.

107 Knud Rasmussen, *The People of the Polar North*, p. 146.

108 Ibid., p. 150.

109 Ibid., pp. 146-57. See also Daniel Merkur, *Becoming Half-Hidden: Shamanism and Initiation Among the Inuit* (Stockholm: Almqvist and Wiksell International, 1985), pp. 70-117; and Peter Freuchen, *Book of the Eskimos* (Ed. Dagmar Freuchen) (New York: Ballantine Books, 1983), pp. 167-71.

110 In an account of the belief system of Netsilik Inuit society, Asen Balikci argued that their taboos served a number of cultural functions, including reduction of anxiety attending childbirth or hunting, a symbolic explanation for misfortune, and the strengthening of spiritual beliefs. Asen Balikci, "Netsilik," in David Damas, Ed., *Handbook of North American Indians*, Vol. 5, "Arctic," p. 426. With regard to the Inughuit, on the other hand, the French scientist Jean Malaurie argued that when the climate became warmer and game animals became more abundant, the Inughuit responded by lifting a series of food, hunting and sex taboos, enabling the population to rise. See Jean Malaurie, *The Last Kings of Thule*, p. 123.

111 Knud Rasmussen, *The People of the Polar North*, pp. 121-22.

112 USNA, RG 401(56), Papers of Hugh J. Lee, "Arctic Highlanders, Customs — Igluetah." [location: 8E1, Row 4/11/E, Box labelled "Reports on Greenland — Eskimos 1893-95."]

113 Knud Rasmussen, *The People of the Polar North*, p. 153.

114 Ibid., p. 101.

115 Ibid., p. 123.

116 John MacDonald, *The Arctic Sky: Inuit Astronomy, Star Lore, and Legend* (Toronto/Iqaluit: Royal Ontario Museum/Nunavut Research Institute, 1998), p. 193.

117 Elisha Kent Kane, *Arctic Explorations*, Vol. I, p. 426.

118 H.P.Steensby, "Contributions to the Ethnology and Anthropogeography of the Polar Eskimos," p. 376.

119 Ibid., p. 376.

120 Edmund Carpenter, *Eskimo* (*Explorations 9*) (Toronto: University of Toronto Press, 1960), pp. 66-67.

121 Edmund Carpenter, "Space Concepts of the Aivilik Eskimos," *Explorations*, Vol. 5 (1955), p. 132.

122 Ibid., p. 138-39.

123 Elisha Kent Kane, *Arctic Explorations*, Vol. II, p. 211.

124 Ibid., Vol. II, p. 260.

125 In the Keewatin region, for example, the Inuit developed songs, incorporating the place names along travel routes, such as the Kazan River. Among other purposes, the songs served as an aide-memoire to maintain their knowledge of the routes. Darren Keith, "The Fall Caribou Crossing Hunt, Kazan River, Northwest Territories," Unpublished Paper, Historic Sites and Monuments Board of Canada Agenda Papers, Fredericton, New Brunswick, 6 and 7 July 1995, Vol. 3, pp. 843-83, especially 857-59.

126 Renée Fossett, "Mapping Inuktut: Inuit Voices of the Real World," in Jennifer S.H. Brown and Elizabeth Vibert, Eds., *Reading Beyond Words: Contexts for Native History* (Peterborough, Ontario: Broadview Press, 1996), pp. 74-94.

127 Edmund Carpenter, "Space Concepts of the Aivilik Eskimos," p. 140.

128 Milton M.R. Freeman, "Arctic Ecosystems," in David Damas, Ed., *Handbook of North American Indians*, Vol. 5, "Arctic," pp. 36-48.

129 Elisha Kent Kane, *Arctic Explorations*, Vol. I, pp. 426-27.

130 Christian Vibe, "Arctic Animals in Relation to Climatic Fluctuations," p. 13 ff.

131 See the discussion in Milton M.R. Freeman, Eleanor E. Wein, and Darren E. Keith, *Recovering Rights: Bowhead Whales and Inuvialuit Subsistence in the Western Canadian Arctic* (Edmonton: Canadian Circumpolar Institute and Fisheries Joint Management Committee, 1992), p. 47.

132 Elisha Kent Kane, *Arctic Explorations*, Vol. II, p. 427.

133 Ibid., Vol. II, pp. 212-14.

134 Kenneth Longley Rawson, *A Boy's-Eye View of the Arctic* (New York: Macmillan, 1926), p. 104.

Chapter 4: Inuit on Ellesmere Island and Exchanges with Inughuit in the Nineteenth Century

1 Knud Rasmussen, *The People of the Polar North*, p 27.

2 BCLSC, Donald B. MacMillan Collection, Diaries, Journals, Logs, Etc., Diary No. 56, "Ethnological Notes," pp. 100-1.

3 Inuuterssuaq Uvdloriaq, *The Narrative of Qitdlarssuaq* (Translated by Kenn and Navarana Harper, n.d.).

4 Guy Mary-Rousselière, *Qitdlarssuaq: l'histoire d'une migration polaire* (Montréal: Les Presses de l'Université de Montréal, 1980).

5 Robert Peterson, "The Last Eskimo Immigration into Greenland," *Folk*, Vol. 4 (1962), pp. 95-110.

6 Guy Mary-Rousselière, *Qitdlarssuaq: l'histoire d'une migration polaire*, p. 29.

7 Robert Peterson, "The Last Eskimo Immigration into Greenland," pp. 105-6.

8 Knud Rasmussen, *The People of the Polar North*, p. 27.

9 Jean Malaurie, *The Last Kings of Thule*, p. 202.

10 Guy Mary-Rousselière, *Qitdlarssuaq*, pp. 36-37.

11 Inuuterssuaq Uvdloriaq, *The Narrative of Qitdlarssuaq*, p. 2 [Note: since this translated version of the narrative was not paginated, I have assigned page numbers from the beginning of the section "The Narrative of Qitdlarssuaq and his Party."]

12 Ibid., pp. 6-13.

13 Ibid., *p. 12.*

14 Guy Mary-Rousselière, *Qitdlarssuaq*, p. 47.

15 Knud Rasmussen, *The People of the Polar North*, p. 29.

16 Capt. Sir Leopold M'Clintock, *The Voyage of the* Fox *in the Arctic Seas in Search of Franklin and His Companions* (London: John Murray, 1869), pp. 121-22.

17 Inuuterssuaq Uvdloriaq, *The Narrative of Qitdlarssuaq, p. 18.*

18 Knud Rasmussen, *The People of the Polar North*, p. 29. For a detailed discussion of the hardships and suffering experienced by the party that returned to Ellesmere Island, see Inuuterssuaq Uvdloriaq, The Narrative of Qitdlarssuaq, p. 50 ff.

19 Knud Rasmussen, *The People of the Polar* North, p. 30.

20 BCLSC, Donald B. MacMillan Collection, Diaries, Journals, Logs, Etc., Diary No. 56, "Ethnological Notes," p. 101.

21 Rolf Gilberg, "Changes in the Life of the Polar Eskimos Resulting From a Canadian Immigration into the Thule District, North Greenland, in the 1860s," *Folk*, Vols.16-17 (1974-75), *p. 163.*

22 Vagn Fabritius Buchwald and Gert Mosdal, "Meteorite Iron, Telluric Iron and Wrought Iron in Greenland," pp. 3-49.

23 Rolf Gilberg, "Polar Eskimo," in David Damas, Ed., *Handbook of North American Indians* Vol. 5, "Arctic," p. 578; see also Knud Rasmussen, *The People of the Polar North*, pp. 31-33.

24 Rolf Gilberg, "Changes in the Life of the Polar Eskimos Resulting from a Canadian Immigration into the Thule District, North Greenland, in the 1860s," p. 164.

25 Eivind Astrup, *With Peary Near the Pole*, pp. 131.

26 Rolf Gilberg, "Changes in the Life of the Polar Eskimos Resulting From a Canadian Immigration into the Thule District, North Greenland, in the 1860s," p. 164.

27 Eivind Astrup, *With Peary Near the Pole*, p. 133-34.

28 Ibid., p. 165.

29 Ibid., p. 166.

30 Elisha Kent Kane, Arctic Explorations, Vol. II, p. 208.

31 H.P. Steensby, "Contributions to the Ethnology and Anthropogeography of the Polar Eskimos," p. 292.

32 Robert E. Peary, "The Discovery of the North Pole: The Fall Hunting; Preparing for the Long Night," Hampton's Magazine, Vol. 24, No. 4 (April 1910), p. 502; see also Robert Bartlett's description of Inughuit spear fishing in Bowdoin College Library, Special Collections, Robert Abrams Bartlett Papers, Books, Articles, Etc. by Robert A. Bartlett, "From the Crow's Nest": "The First Roosevelt Expedition" (1905-06), p. 16.

33 Emil Bessels, "The Northernmost Inhabitants of the Earth," p. 869.

34 James W. VanStone, "The First Peary Collection of Polar Eskimo Material Culture," Fieldiana: Anthropology, Vol. 63, No. 2 (December 1972), pp. 48, 52.

35 Rolf Gilberg, "Polar Eskimo," in David Damas, Ed., Handbook of North American Indians, Vol. 5, "Arctic," p. 578.

36 James W. VanStone, "New Evidence Concerning Polar Eskimo Isolation," American Anthropologist, Vol. 74 (1972), p. 1064.

37 Robert N. Keely Jr., In Arctic Seas: The Voyage of the Kite with the Peary Expedition Together with a Transcript of the Log of the Kite (London: Gay and Bird, 1893), pp. 167 ff.

38 Herbert Patrick Lee, Policing the Top of the World (Toronto: McClelland and Stewart, 1928), pp. 170-71.

39 Knud Rasmussen, The People of the Polar North, pp. 206-7.

40 Henry W. Feilden, "Ethnology," in Captain Sir G.S. Nares, Narrative of a Voyage to the Polar Sea During 1875-6 in HM Ships Alert and Discovery, Vol. II (London: Sampson Low, Marston, Searle, and Rivington, 1878), Appendix 1, p. 188.

41 C.H. Davis, Ed., Narrative of the North Polar Expedition, US Ship Polaris, Captain Charles Francis Hall, Commanding (London: Trübner and Co., 1881), p. 477 [Narrative for April, 1873].

42 Franz Boas, "The Configuration of Grinnell Land and Ellesmere Land," Science, Vol. 5, No. 108 (27 February 1885), pp. 170-71.

43 Franz Boas, The Central Eskimo (Lincoln, Nebraska: University of Nebraska Press, 1964), p. 52.

44 Ibid., p. 53.

45 NAC, RG 18, RCMP Records, Accn. No. 83-84/68, Box 22, File G 567-44, Patrol Report, Grise Fiord, NWT, to Makinson Inlet, NWT, 30 September to 12 October 1964, pp. 3-4.

46 Emil Bessels, "Smith Sound and its Exploration," Proceedings of the United States Naval Institute, Vol. 10, No. 3, Whole No. 30 (1884), p. 412.

47 Emil Bessels, "The Northernmost Inhabitants of the Earth," p. 863.

48 Emil Bessels, Die Amerikanische Nordpol-Expedition (Leipzig, 1879); cited in Guy Marie-Rousselière, Qitdlarssuaq: l'histoire d'une migration polaire, p. 147.

49 Captain Sir G.S. Nares, Narrative of a Voyage to the Polar Sea During 1875-6 in HM Ships Alert and Discovery, Vol. I (London: Sampson Low, Marston, Searle, and Rivington, 1878), p. 56.

50 Emil Bessels, "Smith Sound and its Exploration," pp. 414, 415-46.

51 USNA, RG 401(1)(A), Robert E. Peary Papers, Papers Relating to Arctic Expeditions, 1886-1909 Peary Diary Transcripts, 1871-1900, "Diary (typed) 1899," Entry for 25 June 1899.

52 Rolf Gilberg, "Polar Eskimo," in David Damas, Ed., Handbook of North American Indians, Vol. 5, "Arctic," p. 580.

53 Dr. I. I. Hayes, The Open Polar Sea: A Narrative of a Voyage of Discovery Towards the North Pole (New York: Hurd and Houghton, 1867), p. 385.

54 Johan Carl Christian Petersen, Dr. Kane's Voyage to the Polar Lands (Ed., Oscar M. Villarejo) (Philadelphia: University of Pennsylvania Press, 1965), p. 82.

55 USNA, RG 401(1)(A), Robert E. Peary Papers, Papers Relating to Arctic Expeditions, 1886-1909, Greenland: 1893-95, Diary — Report and Notes: Astrup, Baldwin, Clark, Lee, Vincent, 1893-95, Greenland Expedition III, Folder 5, George H. Clark Notes, "Mammalogies."

56 Fitzhugh Green, *Peary: The Man Who Refused to Fail* (New York and London: G. Putnam's Sons, 1926), pp. 178-79.

57 Moreau S. Maxwell, *An Archaeological Analysis of Eastern Grant Land, Ellesmere Island, Northwest Territories*, p. 73.

58 Ibid., pp. 75-76.

59 Patricia Sutherland, "An Inventory and Assessment of the Prehistoric Archaeological Resources of Ellesmere Island National Park Reserve," Vol. I, p. 33.

Chapter 5: European Cultures in the High Arctic, 1818–1940

1 Fernand Braudel, *Capitalism and Material Life 1400–1800* (Trans., George Weidenfeld and Nicolson Ltd.) (New York: Harper Colophon Books, 1967), p. 63.

2 See Robin Ridington, "Technology, World View, and Adaptive Strategy in a Northern Hunting Society," pp. 469-81.

3 British historian E.J. Hobsbawm has argued that nineteenth-century capitalism was not simply a newly ascendant form of economics, world commerce, and monetary exchange, but a cultural complex permeating all aspects of social, political, and ideological organization in the societies that embraced it. E.J. Hobsbawm, *The Age of Capital, 1843-1875* (New York: Mentor Books, 1979), p. 279.

4 Immanuel Wallerstein, *The Modern World System*, Volume III, *The Second Era of Great Expansion of the Capitalist World Economy* (New York: Academic Press, 1988).

5 Here, we might refer to the literature on the historical study of world systems. Various historians, including Fernand Braudel, Immanuel Wallerstein, and Eric Hobsbawm, have written on Europe's expansion into the New World after 1500. For Wallerstein, European expansionism constituted a modern world system, characterized by a "*ceaseless* accumulation of capital." Immanuel Wallerstein, "World System versus World Systems: A Critique," in Andre Gunder Frank and Barry K. Gills, Eds., *The World System: Five Hundred Years or Five Thousand?* (London and New York: Routledge, 1993), pp. 292-96. On the other hand, economic historians Andre Gunder Frank and Barry Gills have argued that a world economic system devoted to surplus accumulation has been in place for 5,000 years. Andre Gunder Frank and Barry K. Gills, "The 5,000-Year World System," in ibid., pp. 3-55. These observers agree that there is a world economic system, focussed on accumulation, for which communication and trade networks were world-wide by the sixteenth century.

6 L.P. Kirwan, *A History of Polar Exploration* (Harmondsworth, Middlesex, England, 1962), pp. 92-93.

7 Ibid., p. 96ff. See also Christopher Lloyd, *Mr. Barrow of the Admiralty: A Life of Sir John Barrow 1764-1848* (London: Collins, 1970), p. 124 ff; and Fergus Fleming, *Barrow's Boys* (London: Granta Books, 1998), pp. 1-61.

8 Angelo Heilprin, *The Arctic Problem and Narrative of the Peary Relief Expedition of the Academy of Natural Sciences of Philadelphia* (Philadelphia: Contemporary Publishing Co., 1893), p. 11.

9 See Richard Slotkin, *The Fatal Environment: The Myth of the Frontier in the Age of Industrialization, 1800-1890* (New York: Atheneum Books, 1985).

10 Ibid.

11 Eugene S. Ferguson, "Expositions of Technology, 1851-1900," in Melvin Kranzberg and Carroll W. Pursell, Jr., Eds., *Technology in Western Civilization*, Vol. I, "*The Emergence of Modern Industrial Society*" (New York, London, and Toronto: Oxford University Press, 1967), pp. 708-16.

12 E.J. Hobsbawm, *The Age of Empire, 1875-1914* (London: Cardinal Books, 1989), pp. 142-64.

13 US House of Representatives, 45th Congress, *Report No. 96*, 2nd Session, "Expedition to the Arctic Seas," 22 January 1878 — Recommended to the Committee on Naval Affairs, p. 6.

14 *Proceedings of the* Proteus *Court of Inquiry on the Greely Relief Expedition of 1883* (Washington, DC: Government Printing Office, 1884), Appendix, p. 145.

15 Ibid., p. 147.

16 Henry W. Howgate, "Plan for the Exploration of the Arctic Regions," *Journal of the American Geographical Society of New York*, Vol. 10 (1878), p. 279.

17 Charles C. Bates and John F. Fuller, *America's Weather Warriors, 1814-1985* (College Station, Texas: Texas A&M University Press, 1986), p. 9.

18 L.P. Kirwan, *A History of Polar Exploration*, p. 201.

19 "Peary's Own Story of the Discovery of the North Pole," *Hampton's Magazine*, Vol. 23, No. 6 (December 1909), p. 814.

20 See L.P. Kirwan, *A History of Polar Exploration*, pp. 198-99.

21 Theon Wright, *The Big Nail: The Story of the Cook-Peary Feud* (New York: The John Day Company, 1970), p. 114.

22 Between 1870 and 1900, the number of metropolitan daily newspapers in the United States increased from 971 to 2,226. Monthly popular magazines also proliferated in this era. Thomas J. Schlereth, *Victorian America: Transformations in Everyday Life* (New York: HarperCollins, 1991), p. 182.

23 See A.A. Hoehling, *The* Jeannette *Expedition: An Ill-Fated Journey to the Arctic* (London/ New York/ Toronto: Abelard-Schuman, 1967); and Leonard F. Guttridge, *Icebound: The* Jeannette *Expedition's Quest for the North Pole* (Annapolis, Maryland: Naval Institute Press, 1986).

24 See the discussion in Beau Riffenburgh, *The Myth of the Explorer: The Press, Sensationalism, and Geographical Discovery* (London and New York/Cambridge: Belhaven Press/Cambridge University, Scott Polar Research Institute, 1993), pp. 69-76.

25 Dr. Frederick A. Cook, *My Attainment of the Pole* (New York and London: Mitchell and Kennerley, 1908), p. 74.

26 Letter quoted in Herbert L. Bridgeman, "Ten Years of the Peary Arctic Club," *National Geographic Magazine*, Vol. 19, No. 9 (September 1908), p. 665.

27 Robert E. Peary, *Secrets of Polar Travel* (New York: The Century Company, 1917), p. 87.

28 Stephen Kern, *The Culture of Time and Space (London, 1983)*.

29 The role of clocks in the development of modern European societies has been explored by writers such as David S. Landes, *Clocks and the Making of the Modern World* (Cambridge, Massachusetts: Harvard University Press, 1983), and Stephen Kern, *The Culture of Time and Space*.

30 Lawrence Wright, *Clockwork Man* (London: Elek Books, 1968), *p. 150*.

31 Samuel L. Macey, *Clocks and the Cosmos: Time in Western Life and Thought* (Hamden, Connecticut Archon Books, 1980).

32 United States, House of Representatives, *Congressional Record*, Proceedings and Debates of the First Session of the Sixty-Fourth Congress, Vol. 53, Part 14 (Washington, DC: Government Printing Office, 1916), p. 271.

33 David Hackett Fischer, "Massachusetts Time Ways: The Puritan Idea of 'Improving the Time,'" in *Albion's Seed: Four British Folkways in America* (New York and Oxford: Oxford University Press, 1989), pp. 158-66.

34 D.W. Meinig, *The Shaping of America: A Geographical Perspective on 500 Years of History*, Vol. I, "Atlantic America, 1492-1800" (New Haven: Yale University Press, 1986), p. 232.

35 J.B. Harley, "Maps, Knowledge, and Power," in Denis Cosgrove and Stephen Daniels, Eds., *The Iconography of Landscape: Essays on the Symbolic Representation, Design and Use of Past Environments* (Cambridge, England: Cambridge University Press, 1988), pp. 277-312.

36 NAC, RG 85, Vol. 584, File 571, "Canadian Sovereignty over Arctic Islands, 1921-23," Letter of Hanlsey R. Holmden to J.D. Craig· International Boundaries Commission, 17 January 1923.

37 Otto Sverdrup, *New Land: Four Years in the Arctic Regions* (New York: Longmans, Green, and Co., 1904), Vol. I, p. 358.

38 Michael Lewis, *The Navy in Transition, 1814-1864: A Social History* (London: Hodder and Stoughton, 1965), pp. 131-206.

39 "Plan of House at Fort Conger," in Adolphus W. Greely, *Three Years of Arctic Service: An Account of the Lady Franklin Bay Expedition of 1881-84 and the Attainment of the Farthest North*, Vol. I (New York: Charles Scribner's Sons, 1886), p. 90.

40 Eugene L. Rasor, *Reform in the Royal Navy: A Social History of the Lower Deck, 1850 to 1880* (Hamden, Connecticut: The Shoe String Press, 1976), pp. 112-23.

41 Captain Albert Hastings Markham, *The Great Frozen Sea* (London: Isbister and Company, 1878), p. 303.

42 United States, *Proceedings of the* Proteus *Court of Inquiry on the Greely Relief Expedition of 1883* (Washington, DC: Government Printing Office, 1884), Appendix, p. 148.

43 Adolphus W. Greely, *Three Years of Arctic Service: An Account of the Lady Franklin Bay Expedition of 1881-84 and the Attainment of the Farthest North*, Vol. I (New York: Charles Scribner's Sons), p. 85.

44 USNA, RG 27, Records of the Weather Bureau, Lady Franklin Bay Expedition, Box. No. 12, Diaries of Dr. Octave Pavy, Entry for 20 February 1883.

45 See Robert E. Peary, *Secrets of Polar Travel* (New York: The Century Company, 1917), pp. 44-50.

46 Jean Malaurie, *The Last Kings of Thule*, p. 202. See also Chapter 7.

47 USNA, RG 401(1)(A), Robert E. Peary Papers, Papers Relating to Arctic Expeditions, 1886-1909, Greenland: 1898-1902, R.E. Peary Diaries, 1900-1902, Peary Diary, 1-16 November 1900, n.d. [at Fort Conger].

48 Everett S. Allen, *Arctic Odyssey: The Life of Rear Admiral Donald B. MacMillan* (New York: Dodd, Mead and Company, 1962), p. 167.

49 Edmund Otis Hovey, "The Personnel of the Crocker Land Expedition," *The American Museum Journal*, Vol. 13 (1913), p. 179.

50 Everett S. Allen, *Arctic Odyssey*, p. 167.

51 Lisa Bloom, *Gender on Ice: American Ideologies of Polar Expeditions* (Minneapolis: University of Minnesota Press, 1993), p. 32.

52 USNA, RG 27, Records of the Weather Bureau, Lady Franklin Bay Expedition Papers, Vol. No. 2, Manuscript of Expedition Report, Narrative, and Appendices, Transcription of Memorandum of A.W. Greely, 1st Lieutenant ASO Commanding, to Acting Assistant Surgeon O. Pavy, 9 March 1883.

53 Robert E. Peary, *Secrets of Polar Travel*, p. 57.

54 Peary, Robert E., "Moving on the North Pole—Outlines of My Arctic Campaign," *McClure's Magazine*, (March 1899), p. 418.

55 Theodore Roosevelt, "Introduction," in Robert E. Peary, *The North Pole* (New York: Greenwood Press, 1910), p. vii.

56 Quoted in Nancy J. Fogelson, "Robert E. Peary and American Exploration in the Arctic, 1886-1910," *Fram: the Journal of Polar Studies*, Vol. 2, Part 1 (1985), p. 134.

57 J.H. MacBrien, "The Mounties in the Arctic," *Canadian Geographical Journal*, Vol. 10. No. 3 (March 1935), p. 159.

58 Steve Hewitt, "The Masculine Mountie: The Royal Canadian Mounted Police as a Male Institution, 1914-1939," *Journal of the Canadian Historical Association*, New Series, Vol. 7 (1997), pp. 153-74.

59 See Lisa Bloom, *Gender on Ice*, pp. 34-35.

60 Fernand Braudel, *Capitalism and Material Life 1400-1800* (Trans. Miriam Kochan) (New York: Harper Colophon Books, 1967), p. 300.

61 Clive Holland, *Arctic Exploration and Development, c. 500 BC to 1915* (New York and London: Garland Publishing, Inc., 1994), p. 41; Miller Graf, *Arctic Journeys: A History of Exploration for the Northwest Passage* (New York: Peter Lang, 1992), pp. 46-47.

62 Kenneth R. Andrews, *Trade, Plunder, and Settlement: Maritime Enterprise and the Genesis of the British Empire, 1480-1630* (Cambridge, England: Cambridge University Press, 1986), p. 30.

63 W.E. May and Leonard Holder, *A History of Marine Navigation* (New York: W.W. Norton and Company, 1973), p. 32.

64 William Edwin Parry, *Journal of a Voyage of Discovery to the Arctic Regions Performed between the 4th of April and the 18th of November 1818 in His Majesty's Ship* Alexander, *William Edwin Parry, Esq, Lieutenant and Commander*, p. 73.

65 Ibid., p. 8.

66 W.E. May and Leonard Holder, *A History of Marine Navigation*, pp. 38-39.

67 Elisha Kent Kane, *Arctic Explorations*, Vol. II, Appendix 10, "Methods of Survey," p. 400.

68 Isaac I. Hayes, *Physical Observations in the Arctic Seas* (Washington, DC: Smithsonian Institution, Smithsonian Contributions to Knowledge, Vol. 196, 1865), p. 10.

69 Ibid., p. 68.

70 Ibid., p. 5.

71 Isaac I. Hayes, *Physical Observations in the Arctic Seas*, pp. 168-69; Elisha Kent Kane, *Arctic Explorations*, Vol. II, Appendix 10, "Methods of Survey," pp. 406-7.

72 Archaeologist Peter Schledermann has argued that Norse archaeological artifacts at sites investigated in the Bache Peninsula region indicate that Norse Greenlanders may have reached this area by boat by the thirteenth century. If the Vikings did sail to Smith Sound in this period, there is no evidence that their knowledge was transferred to subsequent European explorers in the region, who appear to have begun with a clean slate. See Peter Schledermann, *Voices in Stone: A Personal Journey into the Arctic Past* (Calgary: University of Calgary, Arctic Institute Komatik Series No. 5, 1996), pp. 126-30.

73 W.E. May and Leonard Holder, *A History of Marine Navigation*, p 37.

74 Moira Dunbar and M.J. Dunbar, "The History of the North Water," *Proceedings of the Royal Society of Edinburgh*, Series B, Vol. 72 (1972), p. 232.

75 *Arctic Voyages, Being An Account of Discoveries in the North Polar Seas in the Years 1818, 1819, and 1820, with An Account of the Esquimaux People* (Dublin: Richard B. Webb, 1831), p. 21.

76 Anonymous, *Journal of a Voyage of Discovery to the Arctic Regions, Performed Between the 4th of April and the 18th of November 1818* (London: Richard Phillips, 1819?) Facsimile Reproduction, the Shorey Book Store, Seattle, 1964), p. 49ff.

77 Clements Markham, *The Lands of Silence: A History of Arctic and Antarctic Exploration* (Cambridge, England: Cambridge University Press, 1921), p.189.

78 Clements R. Markham, *The Threshold of the Unknown Region* (London: Sampson Low, Marston, Low, and Searle, 1875), pp. 142-43.

79 Sir John Leslie, *Narrative of Discovery and Adventure in the Polar Seas and Regions, with Illustrations of their Climate, Geology, and Natural History, and an Account of the Whale Fishery* (Edinburgh: Oliver and Boyd, 1835), p. 423.

80 Liz Cruwys, "Henry Grinnell and the American Franklin Searches," *The Polar Record*, Vol. 26, No. 158, (1974), pp. 211-16.

81 Isaac Israel Hayes, *The Open Polar Sea*, pp. 7-8.

82 Chauncy C. Loomis, *Weird and Tragic Shores: The Story of Charles Francis Hall, Explorer* (New York: Alfred A. Knopf, 1971), p. 235.

83 E. Vale Blake, *Arctic Experiences: Containing Captain George E. Tyson's Wonderful Drift on the Ice Floe, A History of the* Polaris *Expedition, the Cruise of the* Tigress, *and Rescue of the* Polaris *Survivors* (New York: Harper and Brothers, 1874).

84 John Edwards Caswell, "The RGS and the British Arctic Expedition, 1875-76," *Geographical Journal*, Vol. 143, Part 2 (July 1977)· p. 205.

85 Captain Albert Hastings Markham, *The Great Frozen Sea*, pp. 2-3.

86 Adolphus W. Greely, *Three Years of Arctic Service*, Vol. I (New York: Charles Scribner's Sons, 1886), p. 37; Emil Bessels, "Smith Sound and its Exploration," *Proceedings of the United States Naval Institute*, Vol. 10, No. 3, Whole No. 30 (1884), p. 420.

87 See *Proceedings of the* Proteus *Court of Inquiry on the Greely Relief Expedition of 1883*.

88 John Maxtone-Graham, *Safe Return Doubtful: The Heroic Age of Polar Exploration* (New York: Charles Scribner's Sons, 1988), p. 128-29.

89 Ibid., p. 134.

90 Ibid., p. 131, and Plate 2, insert between pages 210 and 211.

91 Ibid., p. 130.

92 Robert E. Peary, *Secrets of Polar Travel*, pp. 87-88; Robert E. Peary, *Nearest the Pole* (London: Hutchinson, 1907), p. 365 ff.

93 Robert E. Peary, *Nearest the Pole*, p. 360.

94 Ibid., p. 125.

95 Letter of Robert E. Peary, 11 January 1903, quoted in Fitzhugh Green, *Peary: The Man Who Refused to Fail* (New York and London: G. Putnam's Sons, 1926), p. 194.

96 John Edward Weems, *Race for the Pole* (New York: Henry Holt and Company, 1960), p. 26.

97 W. Gillies Ross, "Whalemen, Whale Ships, and the Search for Franklin," in Patricia D. Sutherland, Ed., *The Franklin Era in Canadian Arctic History, 1845-1859* (Ottawa: National Museum of Man, Mercury Series No. 131, 1985), p. 60.

98 Ibid.

99 Johan Carl Christian Petersen, in Oscar Villarejo, Ed., *Dr. Kane's Voyage to the Polar Lands*, p. 59.

100 Elisha Kent Kane, *Arctic Explorations*, Vol. I, pp. 112-13.

101 Ibid., p. 114.

102 Ibid., p. 98.

103 Isaac Israel Hayes, *The Open Polar Sea*, pp. 102-5; 277-352.

104 Michael Pearson, Sledges and Sledging in Polar Regions," *Polar Record*, Vol. 31, No. 176 (1995), p. 8.

105 C.S. Mackinnon, "The British Man-Hauled Sledging Tradition," in Patricia D. Sutherland, Ed., *The Franklin Era in Canadian Arctic History 1845-1859* (Ottawa: National Museum of Man, Mercury Series No. 131, 1985), pp. 135-36.

106 Geoffrey Hattersley-Smith, "The British Arctic Expedition, 1875-76," *Polar Record*, Vol. 18, No. 113 (1976), p. 123.

107 Captain Albert Hastings Markham, *The Great Frozen Sea: A Personal Narrative of the Voyage of the Alert During the Arctic Expedition of 1875-6* (London: Daldy, Isbister and Co., 1878), pp. 343-4.

108 Ibid., p. 344.

109 Captain A.H. Markham, "On Sledge Travelling," *Proceedings of the Royal Geographical Society* (Great Britain), 12 December 1876, pp. 118-19.

110 Adolphus W. Greely, *Three Years of Arctic Service*, Vol. I, p. 309.

111 Capt. Albert Hastings Markham, *The Great Frozen Sea*, p. 180.

112 Dr. Edward L. Moss, *Shores of the Polar Sea: A Narrative of the Arctic Expedition of 1875-6* (London: Marcus Ward and Co., 1878) [Mimeographed transcription in the library of Canadian Forces Base, Alert, NWT, p. 31].

113 Ibid., pp. 37-38.

114 Capt. Albert Hastings Markham, *The Great Frozen Sea*, pp. 180-81.

115 Letter of Dr. Belgrave Ninnis, Staff Surgeon, HMS *Discovery*, to the Director General of the Medical Department, 26 September 1876, in *Journals and Proceedings of the Arctic Expedition, 1875-6, Parliamentary Paper C-1636* (London: Harrison and Sons, Queen's Printer, 1877), pp. 464-65.

116 United Kingdom, Parliament, *Report of the Committee Appointed by the Lords Commissioners of the Admiralty to Enquire into the Causes of the Outbreak of Scurvy in the Recent Arctic Expedition, Parliamentary Paper C-1722* (London: Her Majesty's Stationery Office, 1877).

117 USNA, RG 27, Weather Bureau, Correspondence, 1870-1912, Miscellaneous Series, Lady Franklin Bay 700 (1883), Box No. 818, 3278-4212, Folder 3278 +, Garlington-Greely Expedition, Memoranda (taken from pigeon hole of desk of Asst. Chief Clerk, 26 May 1886), Office of the Chief Signal Officer, Washington, DC, 27 May 1880.

118 Adolphus W. Greely, *Three Years of Arctic Service*, Vol. I, pp. 82-91.

119 USNA, RG 27, Records of the Weather Bureau, Lady Franklin Bay Expedition, Box No. 12, Diaries of Dr. Octave Pavy, Entry for 19 May 1883.

120 Adolphus W. Greely, *Three Years of Arctic Service*, Vol. I, pp. 156-57.

121 USNA, RG 27, Records of the Weather Bureau, Lady Franklin Bay Expedition, Box No. 12, Diaries of Dr. Octave Pavy.

122 Adolphus W. Greely, *Three Years of Arctic Service*, Vol. I, pp. 181-82.

123 Ibid., Vol. II, pp. 149 ff.

124 Ibid., pp. 171-74.

125 Ibid., p. 195.

126 Ibid., pp. 206-7.

127 "The Work of the Arctic Expedition," *The Geographical Magazine*, Vol. 2 (March 1875), p. 70.

128 Ibid.

129 NAC, Papers of Captain George Strong Nares, RN, Relating to the Arctic Expedition of 1875-76, Nares' Expedition Journal, n.d., n.p.

130 A.H. Markham related that, in December 1875, four individuals who had experienced exposure during the fall sledging forays were still on the sick list and three of these had lost a big toe to amputation. Captain A. H. Markham, *The Great Frozen Sea*, p. 226.

131 Great Britain, Admiralty, *Journals and Proceedings of the Arctic Expedition, 1875-6*, "Report of General Proceedings from 26 August 1875 to 30 March 1875," p. 49.

132 Ibid., Letter of P. Aldrich to G.S. Nares, 15 July 1876, pp. 173-74.

133 Ibid., Letter of A.H. Markham to G.S. Nares, 1 July 1876, p. 125.

134 Capt. Sir George S. Nares, *Narrative of a Voyage to the Polar Sea*, Vol. I, pp. 280-81.

135 Dr. Edward L. Moss, *Shores of the Polar Sea* (mimeographed transcription in the library of Canadian Forces Base Alert, NWT), p. 31.

136 Great Britain, Admiralty, *Journals and Proceedings of the Arctic Expedition, 1875-6*, Memorandum of Commander A.H. Markham to Captain G.S. Nares, HMS *Alert* (in Winter Quarters), 18 October 1875, p. 87.

137 David L. Brainard, "Farthest North With Greely," in Rudolf Kersting, Comp., *The White World: Life and Adventures Within the Arctic Circle Portrayed by Famous Living Explorers* (New York: Lewis, Scribner, and Company, 1902), p. 63.

138 Great Britain, Admiralty, *Journals and Proceedings of the Arctic Expedition, 1875-6*, Letter of Dr. Thomas Colan to Director-General of the Medical Department, 27 October 1876, p. 461.

139 Ibid., p. 462.

140 Capt. Sir George S. Nares, *Narrative of A Voyage to the Polar Sea*, Vol. II, Appendix 17, p. 353.

141 Elisha Kent Kane, *Arctic Explorations*, Vol. II, p. 210.

PART II
CIRCUMSTANCE
History of Events on Ellesmere Island, 1818-1940

1 Fernand Braudel, *The Mediterranean and the Mediterranean World in the Age of Philip II*, Vol. II, p. 901.
2 Benjamin Disraeli, *Vivien Grey*, Book 6, Ch. 7, p. 17, quoted in Burton Stevenson, Ed., *The Home Book of Quotations, Classical and Modern* (New York: Dodd, Mead and Co., 1964, p. 273.
3 Herodotus, *The Histories* (Trans., Aubrey de Sélincourt) (Harmondsworth, Middlesex, England: Penguin Books, Ltd., 1954), Book 7, Section 49, p. 434.

Chapter 6: Early Exploration of the High Arctic by Europeans, 1818-90

1 Immanuel Wallerstein, *The Modern World System*, Volume III, T*he Second Era of Great Expansion of the Capitalist World Economy* (New York: Academic Press, 1988).
2 M.J. Ross, *Polar Pioneers: John Ross and James Clark Ross* (Montreal and Kingston: McGill-Queen's University Press, 1994), p. 28.
3 William Edwin Parry, *Journal of a Voyage of Discovery to the Arctic Regions*, p. 49.
4 Captain John Ross, *A Voyage of Discovery*, Vol. I, p. 80.
5 Ibid., p. 85.
6 Ibid., p. 86.
7 Sir John Leslie, *Narrative of Discovery and Adventure in the Polar Seas and Regions, with Illustrations of their Climate, Geology, and Natural History, and an Account of the Whale Fishery* (Edinburgh: Oliver and Boyd, 1835), pp. 450-51.
8 Charles Edward Smith, Ed., *From the Deep of the Sea, Being the Diary of the Late Charles Edward Smith, MRCS, Surgeon of the Whale-Ship Diana of Hull* (London: H. & C. Black, Ltd., 1922), p. 83, note.
9 W. Gillies Ross, "The Annual Catch of Greenland (Bowhead Whales) in Waters North of Canada 1719-1915: A Preliminary Compilation," *Arctic*, Vol. 32, No. 2 (June 1979), Table 3, p. 105.
10 NAC, RG 85, Vol. 584, File 573-1, Letter of Knud Rasmussen, c/o Royal Danish Consulate General, Montreal, to O.S. Finnie, Ottawa, 5 May 1925.
11 George W. Corner, *Doctor Kane of the Arctic Seas* (Philadelphia: Temple University Press, 1972), p. 76.
12 Ibid., pp. 76-77.
13 Ibid., pp. 79-80.
14 Richard Vaughan, *Northwest Greenland: A History*, p. 33.
15 George W. Corner, *Doctor Kane of the Arctic Seas*, pp. 88-101.
16 Commander E.A. Inglefield, *A Summer Search for Sir John Franklin; With a Peep into the Polar Basin* (London: Thomas Harrison, 1853), p. 42.
17 Ibid., p. 65.
18 Andrew Taylor, *Geographical Discovery and Exploration in the Queen Elizabeth Islands* (Canada: Department of Mines and Technical Surveys, Geographical Branch Memoir No. 3, 1955), p. 45.
19 Commander E.A. Inglefield, *A Summer Search for Sir John Franklin*, pp. 216-23.
20 L.H. Neatby, *The Conquest of the Last Frontier* (Toronto: Longmans Canada, Ltd. 1966), p. 14.
21 Liz Cruwys, "Profile: Henry Grinnell," *The Polar Record*, Vol. 27, No. 161 (1991), p. 116.
22 Ibid., p. 108.
23 L.H. Neatby, *Conquest of the Last Frontier*, p. 56.
24 John Edwards Caswell, *Arctic Frontiers: United States Exploration in the Far North* (Norman, Oklahoma: University of Oklahoma Press, 1956), p. 21.

25 Elisha Kent Kane, *Arctic Explorations*, Vol. I, p. 18.

26 Ibid., Vol. II, Appendix 2, "Preliminary Report of Past Assistant Surgeon Kane to the Secretary of the Navy," p. 301.

27 Johan Carl Christian Petersen, *Dr. Kane's Voyage to the Polar Lands*, p. 78.

28 "Report of a Sledge Journey to the Northwest Coasts of Smith's Strait by Dr. I.I. Hayes and William Godfrey," in Elisha Kent Kane, *Arctic Explorations*, Vol. II, p. 365.

29 Isaac Israel Hayes, *An Arctic Boat Journey*, p. 22.

30 Elisha Kent Kane, *Arctic Explorations*, Vol. 2, pp. 365-73.

31 "Mr. Morton's Report of Journey to North and East During the Months of June and July, 1854," in Ibid., pp. 376-77.

32 Isaac Israel Hayes, *An Arctic Boat Journey*, p. 24.

33 Elisha Kent Kane, *Arctic Explorations*, Vol. I, p. 298.

34 Sir Clements Markham, *The Lands of Silence: A History of Arctic and Antarctic Exploration* (Cambridge, England: Cambridge University Press, 1921), p. 299.

35 Elisha Kent Kane, *Arctic Explorations*, Vol. II, Appendix No. 2, pp. 311, 315.

36 George W. Corner, *Doctor Kane of the Arctic Seas* (Philadelphia: Temple University Press, 1971), p. 262.

37 William C. Godfrey, *Godfrey's Narrative of the Last Grinnell Arctic Exploring Expedition in Search of Sir John Franklin, 1853-4-5* (Philadelphia: J.T. Lloyd, 1860), pp. 64-66.

38 John Edwards Caswell, *United States Explorations in the Far North*, p.29.

39 See, for example, Elisha Kent Kane, *Arctic Explorations*, Vol. II, pp. 21-25.

40 Elisha Kent Kane, *The United States Grinnell Expedition in Search of Sir John Franklin* (1857), and *Arctic Explorations*, Vols. I and II (1856).

41 John Edwards Caswell, *United States Explorations in the Far North*, p. 32.

42 Isaac Israel Hayes, *The Open Polar Sea*, p. 1.

43 John Edwards Caswell, *United States Explorations in the Far North*, p. 33.

44 Isaac Israel Hayes, *The Open Polar Sea*, p. 2.

45 John Edwards Caswell, *United States Explorations in the Far North*, p. 35.

46 Ibid., pp. 34-36.

47 Andrew Taylor, *Geographical Discovery and Exploration in the Queen Elizabeth Islands*, p. 61.

48 Isaac Israel Hayes, *The Open Polar Sea*, p. 308.

49 Ibid., p. 316.

50 Ibid., p. 345.

51 Ibid., p. 351.

52 Ibid., p. 62, n. 1.

53 Walter Lafeber, *The New Empire: An Interpretation of American Expansion, 1860-1898* (Ithaca and New York: Cornell University Press, 1963), pp. 32-33.

54 Miller Graf, *Arctic Journeys: A History of Exploration for the Northwest Passage* (New York: Peter Lang, 1992), p. 190.

55 George M. Robeson, *Instructions for the Expedition Toward the North Pole* (Washington, DC: Government Printing Office, 1871), p. 4.

56 Chauncy C. Loomis, *Weird and Tragic Shores: The Story of Charles Francis Hall, Explorer* (New York: Alfred A. Knopf, 1971), pp. 257-58.

57 Ibid., p. 235.

58 Ibid., p. 275.

59 E. Vale Blake, *Arctic Experiences: Containing Capt. George E. Tyson's Wonderful Drift on the Ice Floe, A History of the* Polaris *Expedition, The Cruise of the* Tigress, *and Rescue of the* Polaris *Survivors* (New York: Harper and Brothers, 1874), p. 161.

60 Chauncy C. Loomis, *Weird and Tragic Shores*, p. 283.

61 John Maxtone-Graham, *Safe Return Doubtful*, pp. 46-49.

62 "Examination of Captain Tyson," *Report to the President of the United States of the Action of the Navy Department in the Matter of the Disaster to the United States Exploring Expedition Toward the North Pole, Accompanied By a Report of the Examination of the Rescued Party, Etc.* (Washington, DC: Navy Department, 1873).

63 E. Vale Blake, *Arctic Experiences*, p. 209.

64 Ibid., "Daily Journal of Sergeant Meyer, Kept While Drifting on the Ice," pp. 122-23.

65 E. Vale Blake, *Arctic Experiences*, p. 302.

66 Sir Clements Markham, *The Lands of Silence*, p. 303.

67 John Edwards Caswell, "The RGS and the British Arctic Expedition, 1875-76," *Geographical Journal*, Vol. 143, Part 2 (July 1977), pp. 200-4.

68 Quoted in Ibid., p. 204.

69 "Sailing Orders," in Capt. Sir G.S. Nares, *Narrative of a Voyage to the Polar Sea*, Vol. I (London: Sampson Low, Marston, Searle, & Rivington, 1878), p. xi.

70 NAC, Papers of Captain George Strong Nares, RN (later Vice-Admiral Sir George Nares, KCB) Relating to the Arctic Expedition of 1875-76 (Microfilm Reel No. A-394), Vol. I, News clipping, Letter of John Rae to the *Times*, 27 May 1875.

71 Beau Riffenburgh, *The Myth of the Explorer: The Press, Sensationalism, and Geographical Discovery*, p. 82.

72 Capt. Sir G.S. Nares, *Narrative of a Voyage to the Polar Sea*, Vol. I, pp. 19-23.

73 Great Britain, Admiralty, *Journals and Proceedings of the Arctic Expedition, 1875-76, under the Command of Captain Sir George S. Nares*, "Report of Proceedings between 22 July 1875 and 27 October 1876," by Captain G.S. Nares, p. 13.

74 Ibid., "Lieutenant Reginald B. Fulford, Report of Proceedings, 7th October [1875]," pp. 100-102.

75 NAC, Reginald Baldwin Fulford Journal, 29 May 1875 to 30 September 1876 (Microfilm Reel No. A-1176).

76 Capt. Albert Hastings Markham, *The Great Frozen Sea*, pp. 175-78.

77 Dr. Edward L. Moss, *Shores of the Polar Sea* (mimeographed copy), p. 31.

78 Ibid., pp. 35-36.

79 Capt. Sir G.S. Nares, *Narrative of a Voyage to the Polar Sea*, Vol. I, pp. 212-13.

80 Dr. Edward L. Moss, *Shores of the Polar Sea* (mimeographed copy), pp. 35-37.

81 Ibid., p.34.

82 Capt. Albert Hastings Markham, *The Great Frozen Sea*, Appendix "A," pp. 416-23.

83 Ibid., pp. 196-97.

84 NAC, Papers of Captain George Strong Nares (Microfilm No. A-394, Memorandum of G.S. Nares to the Commander in Chief re: Amusements, 27 April 1875.)

85 NAC, Reginald Baldwin Fulford Journal, 29 May 1875 to 30 September 1876.

86 Dr. Edward L. Moss, *Shores of the Polar Sea* (mimeographed copy), p. 47.

87 NAC, Papers of Captain George Strong Nares, RN, Memo to Thos. Rawlings and the Crew of HM Sledge Marco Polo, and to Edw. Lawrence and the Crew of HM Sledge Victoria, from Nares, HMS *Alert* Winter Quarters, Lat. 82° 27' N., long. 61° 22' W., n.d.

88 NAC, Papers of Captain George Strong Nares, RN, Relating to the Arctic Expedition of 1875-76, Memorandum of Captain N.F. Stephenson, HMS *Discovery*, to Captain G.S. Nares, HMS *Alert*, 21 March 1876.

89 Great Britain, Admiralty, *Journals and Proceedings of the Arctic Expedition, 1875-6*, "Northern Sledge Party—Orders to Commander Markham," by Captain G.S. Nares, 3 April 1876, p. 118.

90 Ibid., "Journal," accompanying memorandum of Commander A.H. Markham to Captain G.S. Nares, 1 July 1876, p. 126.

91 Dr. Edward L. Moss, *Shores of the Polar Sea* (mimeographed copy), p. 53.

92 Capt. Albert Hastings Markham, *The Great Frozen Sea*, pp. 324-25.

93 Ibid., p. 342.

94 Clements Markham, "The Arctic Expedition, IX: The Work," *The Geographical Magazine*, Vol. 3 (December 1876), p. 319.

95 Capt. Albert Hastings Markham, *The Great Frozen Sea*, p. 309.

96 NAC, Papers of Captain George Strong Nares, Memorandum from Captain George Nares to Lieut. Pelham Aldrich, 3 April 1876.

97 Great Britain, Admiralty, *Journals and Proceedings of the Arctic Expedition, 1875-6*, Report of Lieutenant Pelham Aldrich to Captain G.S. Nares, 17 July 1876, pp. 171-72.

98 Ibid., Eastern Sledge Party—Lieut. L.A. Beaumont, Orders to, 20th April..., Memorandum to Lieutenant Lewis A. Beaumont from Captain G.S. Nares, 20 April 1876, pp. 338-39.

99 Ibid., Memorandum of Lieutenant L.A. Beaumont to Captain H.F. Stephenson, 17 August 1876, p. 354.

100 Ibid., Memorandum of Lieutenant L.A. Beaumont to Lieutenant R.B. Fulford, Hall's Rest, Polaris Bay, 12 July 1876, p. 434.

101 Ibid., Memorandum of R.W. Coppinger, M.D. to Captain H.F. Stephenson, HMS *Discovery*, 12 September 1876, p. 424.

102 Ibid., Memorandum of Lieutenant Reginald B. Fulford to Captain H.F. Stephenson, HMS *Discovery*, n.d., p. 434.

103 NAC, Papers of Captain George Strong Nares, Memorandum to the Officers and Ships Company, HMS *Alert* at Floeberg Beach, from Captain George Nares, 16 June 1876.

104 United Kingdom, Parliament, *Report of the Committee Appointed by the Lords Commissioners of the Admiralty to Enquire into the Causes of the Outbreak of Scurvy in the Recent Arctic Expedition*, Parliamentary Paper C-1722 (London: Her Majesty's Stationery Office, 1877).

105 E.J.C. Kendall, "Scurvy During Some British Polar Expeditions, 1875-1917," The Polar Record, Vol. 7, No. 51 (September 1951), p. 474.

106 D. Murray Smith, *Arctic Explorations from British and Foreign Shores from the Earliest Times to the Expedition of 1875-76* (Edinburgh: Thomas C. Jack, Grange Publishing Works, 1877), pp. 823-24.

107 A.H. Markham, *Life of Sir Clements R. Markham* (1917), cited in Margaret Deacon and Ann Savours, "Sir George Strong Nares (1831-1915)," *Polar Record*, Vol. 18, No. 113 (1976), p. 136. See also Geoffrey Hattersley-Smith, "The British Arctic Expedition, 1875-76," *Polar Record*, Vol. 18, No. 113 (1976), pp. 124-125, and Trevor H. Levere, *Science and the Canadian Arctic: a Century of Exploration, 1818–1918*.

108 NAC, Papers of Captain George Strong Nares, Copy of the journal article "The Polar Indictment," *The Navy Royal and Mercantile*, Vol. 33, No. 5, 9 December 1876.

109 Richard Slotkin, *The Fatal Environment: The Myth of the Frontier in the Age of Industrialization, 1800–1890* (New York: Atheneum Books, 1985), pp. 3-5.

110 In her book on the Philadelphia exposition, Dee Brown discerned two overriding myths in American popular literature of the 1870s: the myths of the Western hero and the Alger hero, both masters of their own destiny. Dee Brown, *The Year of the Century: 1876* (New York: Charles Scribner's Sons, 1976), pp. 66-72.

111 Richard Slotkin, *The Fatal Environment*, p. 433 ff.

112 I.I. Hayes, "Address on Arctic Exploration," *Journal of the American Geographical and Statistical Society of New York*, Vol 2, Part 2 (1870), p. 23.

113 Ibid., p. 23.

114 Robert M. Utley, *Frontier Regulars: The United States Army and the Indian* (Lincoln and London: University of Nebraska Press, 1973), pp. 22-23.

115 Ibid., 23.

116 Letter of Elias Loomis to H.W. Howgate, 14 January 1877, in H.W. Howgate, Comp., *Proposed Legislation, Correspondence, and Action of Scientific and Commercial Associations in Reference to Polar Colonization* (Washington, DC: Beresford, Printer, 1877), p. 5.

117 Ari Hoogenboom, *The Presidency of Rutherford B. Hayes* (Lawrence, Kansas: University of Kansas, 1988), p. 183.

118 United States, House of Representatives, 44th Congress, 2nd session, *Report No. 181*, "Expedition to the Arctic Seas," Report to accompany Bill HR 4339 "to authorize and equip an expedition to the Arctic Seas," 22 February 1877.

119 Ibid., Exhibit E, Letter of Dr. Isaac Israel Hayes, Arctic Explorer, Albany, New York, to Capt. H.W. Howgate, Washington, DC, 12 February 1877.

120 Ibid., p. 11.

121 Ibid., p. 12.

122 Captain Henry W. Howgate, *Polar Colonization* (Washington, DC: Beresford, Printer, 1877), pp. 15-16.

123 United States, House of Representatives, 45th Congress, 2nd Session, *Report No. 96*, "Expedition to the Arctic Seas." Report to Accompany Bill HR 447, by Benjamin A. Willis, 22 January 1878, p. 5.

124 Emil Bessels, "Smith Sound and its Exploration," *Proceedings of the United States Naval Institute*, Vol. 10, No. 3, Whole No. 30 (1884), p. 414.

125 Ibid., 415-16.

126 Captain H.W. Howgate, Ed., The Cruise of the Florence, or Extracts from the Journal of the Preliminary Arctic Expedition of 1877–78 (Washington, DC: James J. Chapman, 1879), p. 5.

127 Ibid., p. 8.

128 William Barr, *The Expeditions of the First International Polar Year, 1882–83* (Calgary: The Arctic Institute of North America, Technical Paper No. 29, 1985), pp. 2-3.

129 United States, House of Representatives, 46th Congress, 2nd session, *Report No. 453* "Expedition to the Arctic Seas," Report to accompany Bill HR 3534 "to authorize and equip an expedition to the Arctic Seas," 9 March 1880, p. 3.

130 Ibid., p. 7.

131 Ibid., p. 8.

132 USNA, RG 27, Weather Bureau Correspondence, 1870-1912, Miscellaneous Series, Lady Franklin Bay 700 (1883), Box No. 818, 3278-4212, Folder 32781/2 Mis. 1883 Garlington–Greely Expedition, memoranda taken from pigeon hole of desk of Asst. Chief Clerk 5/26/86, File with 700 Misc. 1881, "Proceedings of a Board which convened at Washington, DC. May 27, 1880, by authority of Instructions No. 33, Current Series, from this office," [Signed] J.P. Story, A.W. Greely, R.W.D. Bryan, H.C. Chester, and Octave Pavy.

133 B.F. (Benjamin Franklin) Da Costa, "'Inventio Fortunata': Arctic Exploration, With an Account of Nicholas of Lynn," Paper read before the American Geographical Society, Chickering Hall, 15 May 1880. Reprinted from the *Bulletin of the American Geographical Society*, New York, 1881, pp. 35-36.

134 "An Act to Authorize and Equip an Expedition to the Arctic Seas," 46th Congress, 2nd Session, H.R. 3534, in LCMD, Papers of Albert J. Myers, A.J. Myers Correspondence, 1879-1880, Microfilm Reel No. 3.

135 USNA, RG 27, Weather Bureau Correspondence, 1870-1912, Miscellaneous Series, Lady Franklin Bay 700 (1883), Box No. 818, 3278-4212, Folder 32781/2 Mis. 1883 Garlington–Greely Expedition, "Proceedings of a Board which convened at Washington, DC. May 27, 1880."

136 Adolphus W. Greely, *Three Years of Arctic Service*, Vol. I, p. 37.

137 USNA, RG 27, Records of the Weather Bureau, Lady Franklin Bay Expedition, Box no. 12, Pavy Notes and Letters, Notes dated 21 January 1883.

138 USNA, RG 27, Weather Bureau Correspondence, 1870-1912, Miscellaneous Series, Lady Franklin Bay 700 (1883), Box No. 818, 3278-4212, Folder 32781/2 Mis. 1883 Garlington–Greely Expedition, "Proceedings of a Board which convened at Washington, DC, May 27, 1880."

139 Adolphus Greely, *Three Years of Arctic Service*, Vol. I, pp. 82-91.

140 Adolphus W. Greely, *Report on the Proceedings of the United States Expedition to Lady Franklin Bay, Grinnell Land*, Vol. I, p. 7.

141 USNA, RG 27, Weather Bureau Correspondence, 1870-1912, Miscellaneous Series, Lady Franklin Bay 700 (1883), Box No. 818, 3278-4212, Folder 32781/2 Mis. 1883 Garlington–Greely Expedition, memoranda taken from pigeon hole of desk of Asst. Chief Clerk 5/26/86, File with 700 Misc. 1881, Memorandum of Adolphus Greely, Fort Conger, Grinnell Land, to the Chief Signal Officer of the Army, Washington, DC, 17 August 1881.

142 William Barr, *The Expeditions of the First International Polar Year, 1882-83*, p. 13.

143 Lieutenant James Lockwood Expedition Journal, quoted in Charles Lanman, *Farthest North, or The Life and Explorations of Lieutenant James Booth Lockwood of the Greely Arctic Expedition* (New York: D. Appleton and Company, 1885), p. 215.

144 USNA, RG 27, Records of the Weather Bureau, Lady Franklin Bay Expedition Records, Box No. 12, Pavy Notes and Letters, Diary Transcription, Entry for 22 January 1882, p. 221.

145 "Lieutenant Lockwood's abstract of sledge journey on the north coast of Greenland, with general remarks on the same," in Adolphus W. Greely, *Report on the Proceedings of the United States Expedition to Lady Franklin Bay, Grinnell Land*, Vol II, p. 186.

146 Ibid.

147 Adolphus Greely, *Three Years in Arctic Service*, Vol. I, p. 335.

148 Ibid., cited in Donald B. MacMillan, *How Peary Reached the Pole: The Personal Story of His Assistant* (Boston and New York: Houghton Mifflin, 1934), p. 210.

149 Adolphus Greely, *Three Years in Arctic Service*, Vol. I, pp. 275-76.

150 Ibid., p. 289.

151 Ibid., p. 367.

152 Ibid., p. 379.

153 Ibid., p. 383.

154 Ibid., p. 401.

155 Ibid., pp. 410-13.

156 Lieutenant James Lockwood Expedition Journal, quoted in Charles Lanman, *Farthest North*, pp. 276-77.

157 USNA, RG 27, Records of the Weather Bureau, Lady Franklin Bay Expedition Papers, Box No. 12, Pavy Notes and Letters, Diary Transcription, Entry for 1 April [1883], p. 188.

158 Adolphus W. Greely, *Report on the Proceedings of the United States Expedition to Lady Franklin Bay, Grinnell Land*, Vol. I, "Appendix No. 62—Dr. Pavy's Letter of March 8, 1883," Fort Conger, Grinnell Land, p. 242.

159 USNA, RG 27, Records of the Weather Bureau, Box No. 2, Manuscript of Expedition Report, Narrative, and Appendices, Transcription of memorandum of A.W. Greely, 1st Lieutenant ASO Commanding, to Acting Assistant Surgeon O. Pavy, 9 March 1883; copied in Adolphus W. Greely, *Report on the Proceedings of the United States Expedition*, Vol. I, p. 243.

160 Leonard Guttridge, *Ghosts of Cape Sabine: The Harrowing True Story of the Greely Expedition* (New York: G.P. Putnam's Sons, 2000), p. 157.

161 Ibid., p. 158.

162 USNA, RG 27, Records of the Weather Bureau, Lady Franklin Bay Expedition, Box No. 13, Journals and Diaries, Private Henry Biederbick Diary, Entry for 15 April 1883, p. 18.

163 L.H. Neatby, *Conquest of the Last Frontier*, pp. 242-45.

164 USNA, RG 27, Papers of General David Brainard, Journal, 1881-84. Handwritten statement by Brainard, dated 19 January 1883, Fort Bidwell, California [inserted into Vol. II].

165 Ibid.

166 Adolphus W. Greely, *Report on the Proceedings of the United States Expedition to Lady Franklin Bay, Grinnell Land*, Vol. I, pp. 63-64.

167 USNA, RG 27, Records of the Weather Bureau, Lady Franklin Bay Expedition, Box No. 13, Journals and Diaries, Lieutenant Frederick Kislingbury Diary Transcription, Entry for 3-4 October 1883, p. 144.

168 David Brainard Diary, Entry for 27 October 1883. Published in Bessie Rowland James, Ed., *Six Came Back: The Arctic Adventure of David L. Brainard* (Indianapolis/ New York: Bobbs-Merrill, 1940), p. 193.

169 See Adolphus Greely, *Three Years of Arctic Service*, Vol. II, p. 211 ff.; Bessie Rowland James, *Six Came Back: The Arctic Adventure of David L. Brainard*, pp. 190-297; and L.H. Neatby, "The Greely Ordeal," *The Beaver*, Outfit 292 (Autumn 1961), pp. 4-11.

170 Leonard Guttridge, *Ghosts of Cape Sabine*, pp. 217-89.

171 On 21 September, Jens shot three seals, two of which were approximately 70 kg and the other 35 kg. Soon after, he brought home another 75-kg seal. At a critical time in April 1884, Jens and Private Long shot a polar bear, which may have nourished the group sufficiently to enable the ultimate survival of a minority of the men. USNA, RG 27, Records of the Weather Bureau, Lady Franklin Bay Expedition Papers, Box 12, Extracts from Greely's Journal, Entry for 21 September 1883; Box No. 19, OCSO Correspondence With or About Members of the Expedition, "The Physician's Handbook" [Translation of Dr. Pavy's notes] No. 1/6226 O.C.S.O. Mis. 1884, Original sent Mrs. Pavy, 6 March 1886, Octave Pavy's Entry for 21 September 1883; Leonard Guttridge, *Ghosts of Cape Sabine*, p. 216; and David Brainard Diary, Entry for 11 April 1884, published in Bessie Rowland James, Ed., *Six Came Back: The Arctic Adventure of David L. Brainard*, p. 250.

172 Greely wrote that, in April 1884, Sergeant Brainard caught 210 kg of shrimp and one kg of seaweed for the group. Adolphus W. Greely, *Report on the Proceedings of the United States Expedition to Lady Franklin Bay, Grinnell Land*, Vol. I, p. 86.

173 USNA, RG 27, Records of the Weather Bureau, Lady Franklin Bay Expedition, Box No. 13, Journals and Diaries, Private Henry Biederbick Diary, Entries for 11-12 April 1884.

174 Adolphus W. Greely, *Report on the Proceedings of the United States Expedition to Lady Franklin Bay, Grinnell Land*, Vol. I, p. 90.

175 USNA, RG 27, Records of the Weather Bureau, Lady Franklin Bay Expedition Papers, Box No. 12, Extracts from Lieutenant Greely's Journal, Entry for 24 September 1883, p. 10.

176 Ibid., Entry for 2 October 1883, p. 20.

177 Ibid., Entry for 3 October 1883, pp. 21-22.

178 USNA, RG 27, Records of the Weather Bureau, Box 19, OCSO Correspondence With or About Members of the Expedition, Private Bender Diary (translation), signed George Leyerzapf, or Jacob Bender, Entries for 11 and 12 May 1884.

179 USNA, RG 27, Records of the Weather Bureau, Lady Franklin Bay Expedition, Vol. 13, Diary of Private Charles Henry, p. 64.

180 USNA, RG 27, Records of the Weather Bureau, Lady Franklin Bay Expedition, Box No. 13, Journals and Diaries, Lieutenant Frederick Kislingbury Diary Transcription, Entry for 12 May 1884, p. 144.

181 USNA, RG 27, Records of the Weather Bureau, Lady Franklin Bay Expedition, Box 19, OCSO Correspondence With or About Members of the Expedition, Private Bender Diary (translation), signed George Leyerzapf, or Jacob Bender, Entry for 12 May 1884.

182 182 Adolphus W. Greely, *Report on the Proceedings of the United States Expedition to Lady Franklin Bay, Grinnell Land*, Vol. I, Appendix No. 118, p. 90.

183 Ibid. p. 363.

184 Ibid.

185 Sergeant David Brainard Diary, Entry for 6 June 1884, reproduced in *Six Came Back: The Arctic Adventures of David L. Brainard*, p. 289.

186 USNA, RG 27, Records of the Weather Bureau, Lady Franklin Bay Expedition, Box No. 13, Journals and Diaries, Private Henry Biederbick Diary, Entry for 6 June 1884.

187 USNA, RG 27, Records of the Weather Bureau, Lady Franklin Bay Expedition, Box No. 12, Extracts from Greely's Journal, Entries for 9 and 10 April 1884.

188 Sergeant David Brainard Diary, Entry for 7 June 1884, reproduced in *Six Came Back: The Arctic Adventures of David L. Brainard*, p. 291.

189 USNA, RG 27, Records of the Weather Bureau, Lady Franklin Bay Expedition, Box No. 13, Journals and Diaries, Private Henry Biederbick Diary, Entry for 15 April 1884.

190 Ibid., Lieutenant Frederick Kislingbury Diary Transcription, Entry for 30 April 1884, p. 137.

191 Transcription of Letter of Private Maurice Connell to Captain Johnson, in William Cary Brown Papers, Western Historical Collections, University of Colorado. Quoted in Richard N. Ellis, "The Greely Expedition: The Last Days," *The Beaver*, Outfit 304, No. 4 (Spring 1974), p. 33.

192 Leonard F. Guttridge, *Ghosts of Cape Sabine*, p. 218.

193 Commander W.S. Schley and Professor J.R. Soley, *The Rescue of Greely* (New York: Charles Scribner's Sons, 1886), p. 223.

194 Ibid., p. 235.

195 Winfield S. Schley, *Report of Winfield S. Schley, Commander, US Navy, Commanding Greely Relief Expedition of 1884* (Washington, DC: Government Printing Office, 1887), p. 50.

196 USNA, RG 27, Papers of General David L. Brainard, Journal, 1881-84, Vol. III, Entry for Friday, 6 June 1884, p. 99.

197 *The New York Times*, 12 August 1884, p. 1.

198 Ibid., p. 294, Quoted in William R. Hunt, *To Stand at the Pole: The Dr. Cook-Admiral Peary North Pole Controversy* (New York: Stein and Day, 1981), p. 98.

199 USNA, RG 27, Lady Franklin Bay Expedition Papers, Box No. 19, OCSO Correspondence With or About Members of the Expedition, Letter of M. Stone, Leland University, New Orleans, to General A.J. Warner, Washington, DC, 9 February 1885.

200 Ibid., Letter of Lilla May Pavy, Lexington, Missouri, to the Secretary of War, Washington, 9 October 1885.

201 Ibid., Letters on Dr. Pavy, his death, etc., n.d.

202 Adolphus Greely, *Three Years of Arctic Service*, Vol. II, p. 335.

203 Leonard Guttridge, *Ghosts of Cape Sabine*, p. 297.

204 Ibid., pp. 300-301.

205 USNA, RG 27, Records of the Weather Bureau, Lady Franklin Bay Expedition Papers, Box 12, Octave Pavy Notes and Letters, Pavy Diary Transcription.

206 Adolphus Greely, *Three Years of Arctic Service*, Vols. I and II.

207 USNA, RG 27, Papers of General David Brainard, Journal, 1881-84. Handwritten statement by Brainard, dated 19 January 1883, Fort Bidwell, California [inserted in Vol. 2].

208 Rev. William A. McGinley, Comp., *Reception of Lieut. A.W. Greely, USA, and His Comrades, and of the Arctic Relief Expedition, at Portsmouth, NH, on August 1 and 4, 1884* (Washington, DC: Government Printing Office, 1884), pp. 3-13.

209 Ibid., p. 55.

210 Ibid., p. 54. For an illuminating discussion of the political machinations behind this event, see Leonard Guttridge, *Ghosts of Cape Sabine*, pp. 290-95.

211 A.W. Greely, "Arctic Exploration, with Reference to Grinnell Land," *Proceedings of the Royal Geographical Society*, Vol. 8, No. 3 (March 1886), pp. 156-76.

212 Ibid.

213 Ibid., p. 173.

214 Adolphus Greely, *Three Years of Arctic Service*, Vol. I, p. 335.

215 William Barr, *The Expeditions of the First International Polar Year, 1882-83*, pp. 28-29.

216 In January 1927, the Inughuit men Nukappiannguaq and Aqioq, then working for the RCMP detachment at Bache Peninsula, tried to cross from Cape Camperdown, Ellesmere Island to Greenland. They were prevented from doing so by very rough moving pack ice and open water extending far to the north of Smith Sound into Kane Basin. NAC, RG 18, Vol. 3014, Bache Peninsula Detachment Diary, Entry for 17 January 1927.

217 William R. Hunt, *To Stand at the Pole*, pp. 15-16.

218 Andrew Taylor, *Geographical Discovery and Exploration in the Queen Elizabeth*, p. 86.

219 Henry G. Bryant, "The Peary Auxiliary Expedition of 1894," *Bulletin of the Geographical Club of Philadelphia*, Vol. 1, No. 5 (June, 1895), pp. 153-54.

220 William Barr, "Robert Stein's Expedition to Ellesmere Island, 1899-1901," *The Polar Record*, Vol. 21, No. 132 (1982), pp. 253-54.

221 Ibid., p. 259.

222 Ibid., p. 271. See also W. Barr and W. Blake, Jr., "The Site of Fort Magnesia, Payer Harbour, Pim Island, NWT," *The Polar Record*, Vol. 26, No. 156 (1990), pp. 39-42.

223 Otto Sverdrup, *New Land: Four Years in the Arctic Regions* (Trans., Ethel Harriet Hearn) (London: Longmans, Green and Co., 1904), Vol. I, pp. 122-43.

224 Andrew Taylor, *Geographical Discovery and Exploration in the Queen Elizabeth Islands*, p. 93.

225 J. Gordon Hayes, *The Conquest of the North Pole: Recent Arctic Exploration* (London: Thornton Butterworth, Ltd., 1934), p. 43.

226 Ibid., p. 98.

227 Sir Clements Markham, "The Promotion of Further Discovery in the Arctic and the Antarctic Regions" (Address to the Royal Geographic Society), *The Geographical Journal*, Vol. 4, No. 1 (July 1894), p. 7.

228 Ibid., p. 13.

Chapter 7: *"Mine* at Last": Robert E. Peary's Polar Expeditions, 1890–1909

1 See Robert E. Peary, *Northward Over the Great Ice*, Vols. I and II; *Nearest the Pole: A Narrative of the Polar Expedition of the Peary Arctic Club in the SS Roosevelt, 1905-06* (New York: Doubleday, Page & Co., 1907); *The North Pole: Its Discovery in 1909 Under the Auspices of the Peary Arctic Club* (New York: Greenwood Publishers, 1910); "The Discovery of the North Pole," *Hampton's Magazine*, Vol. 24, January to September 1910 [serialized in nine consecutive issues]; and *Secrets of Polar Travel* (1917).

2 See, for example, Josephine Diebitsch Peary, *My Arctic Journal: A Year Among Ice-Fields and Eskimos* (New York: Contemporary Publishing Co., 1893); Eivind Astrup, *With Peary Near the Pole*; George Borup, *A Tenderfoot With Peary* (New York: Frederick A. Stokes, 1911); Robert A. Bartlett, *The Log of "Bob" Bartlett* (New York: Blue Ribbon Books, 1928); Fitzhugh Green, *Peary: The Man Who Refused to Fail* (G.P. Putnam's Sons, 1926); Donald B. MacMillan, *How Peary Reached the Pole* (Boston and New York: Houghton Mifflin Company, 1934); Mattthew A. Henson, *A Negro Explorer at the Pole* (Arno Press and the New York Times, 1969); William Henry Hobbs, *Peary* (New York: The Macmillan Company, 1936); J. Gordon Hayes, *The Conquest of the North Pole: Recent Arctic Exploration* (London: Thornton Butterworth, Ltd., 1934); and John Edwards Caswell, *Arctic Frontiers*.

3 H.P. Steensby, "The Polar Eskimos and the Polar Expeditions," p. 900.

4 Kenn Harper, *Give Me My Father's Body: The Life of Minik, The New York Eskimo* (Iqaluit, NWT: Blacklead Books, 1986).

5 Robert E. Peary, "Moving on the North Pole—Outlines of My Arctic Campaign," *McClure's Magazine* (March 1899), p. 418.

6 USNA, RG 401(1)(A), Robert E. Peary Papers, Papers Relating to Arctic Expeditions, 1886–1909, Greenland Expedition 1898-1902, Robert E. Peary Diaries, August 1900–1902, Loose Notes: "Correspondence, Memoranda, etc, in re: Dr. at B[lack] R[ock] V[ale] and L[ake] Hazen, Jan. and Feb. 1901."

7 USNA, RG 401(1)(A) Robert E. Peary Papers, Papers Relating to Arctic Expeditions, 1886-1909, Expeditions: Greenland 1886, Notebook 1886, Equipment Lists, Notebook, Planning Notes, 1885-86, Notes dated 21 November 1885.

8 Ibid., Notes dated 21 November 1885.

9 Ibid., Notes dated 13 October 1885.

10 John Edward Weems, *Race for the Pole* (New York: Henry Holt and Co., 1960), p. 27.

11 Robert E. Peary, "The Party and the Outfit for the Greenland Journey," *Journal of the American Geographical Society of New York*, Vol. 23 (1898), p. 260.

12 John Edward Weems, *Race for the Pole*, p. 27.

13 Ibid.

14 USNA, RG 401(1)(A), Robert E. Peary Papers, Papers Relating to Arctic Expeditions, 1886-1909, Diary Transcripts, 1871-1900, "Diary (typed) 1900," Letter of Instruction to Matt, 15 February 1900 [typed after the 28 February 1900 diary entry].

15 Donald B. MacMillan, *How Peary Reached the Pole* (Boston and New York: Houghton Mifflin Co., 1934), p. 61.

16 Robert E. Peary, "The Discovery of the North Pole," *Hampton's Magazine*, Vol. 24, No. 1 (January 1910), p. 9.

17 John Edwards Caswell, *Arctic Frontiers: United States Exploration in the Far North* (Norman: University of Oklahoma Press, 1956), p. 213.

18 Henry G. Bryant, "The Peary Auxiliary Expedition of 1894," *Bulletin of the Geographical Club of Philadelphia*, Vol. 1, No. 5 (June 1895), pp. 156-57; Elisha Kent Kane, Arctic Explorations, Vol. I, "Chart exhibiting the discoveries of the Second American Grinnell Expedition in Search of Sir John Franklin," insert between pp. 4-5.

19 See Robert E. Peary, *Northward Over the "Great Ice,"* Vols. I and II (New York: Frederick A. Stokes Company, 1898).

20 USNA, RG 401(1)(A), Robert E. Peary Papers, Papers Relating to Arctic Expeditions, 1886-1909, Diary Transcripts, 1871-1900, "Diary (typed) 1898," File: Letter to the President and Members of the Peary Arctic Club, New York City, Etah, Foulke Fjord, August 1898.

21 Robert E. Peary, "Moving on the North Pole—Outlines of My Arctic Campaign," *McClure's Magazine*, (March 1899), pp. 417-26.

22 Ibid.

23 Sturgis B. Rand, "Robert E. Peary and his Campaign for the Pole," *McClure's Magazine*, February 1902, p. 361.

24 Fitzhugh Green, *Peary: The Man Who Refused to Fail*, p. 173.

25 Robert E. Peary, "Report of R.E. Peary, CE, USN, on Work Done in the Arctic in 1898-1902," *Bulletin of the American Geographical Society of New York*, Vol. 35 (1903), p. 496.

26 Ibid., pp. 498-503.

27 Robert E. Peary, "Sledging Over the Polar Pack," *Outing*, Vol. 41, No. 4 (January 1903), p. 396.

28 Ibid., p. 404.

29 USNA, RG 401(1)(A), Robert E. Peary Papers, Papers Relating to Arctic Expeditions, 1886-1909, Diary Transcripts, 1871-1900, File "Diary (typed) 1899" [typescript transcription of Peary's diary entry for 6 January 1899].

30 J. Gordon Hayes, Robert Edwin *Peary: A Record of His Explorations, 1886-1909* (London: Grant Richards and Humphrey Toulmin, 1929), p. 269.

31 Pierre Berton, *The Arctic Grail: The Quest for the North West Passage and the North Pole, 1818–1909* (Toronto: McClelland and Stewart, 1988), p. 525.

32 William Herbert Hobbs, *Peary*, p. 213.

33 Pierre Berton, *The Arctic Grail*, p. 525.

34 Bradley Robinson, *Dark Companion* (London: Hodder and Stoughton, Ltd., 1948), p. 138.

35 [Dedrick's version, January 1899] "The moon was gone when we got to Conger, and Lieut. having a painful neuritis which rendered his arm useless the last two days, allowed his feet to escape his attention, and after building fire in house at Fort Conger and eating, he pulled off his foot gear and nearly all his toes were frozen and part of foot too. I worked with them and got the frost out of them, but the toes were frozen badly. I took the dead tissues from three and a half [toes] on right foot and parts [of] three on left foot and left the bones protruding."

    [later, back at Cape D'Urville] "Three weeks ago I etherized Peary and disarticulated three toes back into foot & cut off diseased bone back into tissue nearly to foot joint (inch back toward ankles from web of toe) of four other toes. This leaves stumps of toes for all but three [toes]."

    USNA RG 401(1)(A) Robert E. Peary Papers, Papers Relating to Arctic Expeditions, 1886-1909, Greenland: 1898-1902, T.S. Dedrick Diaries, Notebooks, and Other Papers, 1898-1901, Miscellaneous Papers of T.S. Dedrick: Field Notes, Vol. VI, Folder 6. [Peary's version, Friday, 6 January 1899] "I had become suspicious that one of my feet was touched by frost, and having Angoodloo remove my kamiks, was deeply annoyed to find that the toes on both feet were apparently seriously frost-bitten. As a consequence my coffee was taken while I sat on the water tank with the doctor carefully removing the frost from my frozen feet in bowls of ice water.... Have been able to take a partial bath, discard the perspiration-saturated clothing & put on dry and warm woolen clothing which we find here. The change is very refreshing & enables me [to] forget temporarily that I am doomed to some amps [amputations]." USNA, Robert E. Peary Papers, RG 401(1)(A) Papers Relating to Arctic Expeditions, 1886–1909, Greenland: 1898-1902, T.S. Dedrick Diaries, Notebooks, and Other Papers, 1898–1901, Robert E. Peary Diary, January 1899, at Fort Conger. "Copied July 1934, M.A.P." [Marie Agnihito Peary?]

36 See John Edward Weems, *Peary: The Explorer and the Man* (Boston: Houghton Mifflin Company, 1967), p. 337, note 5.

37 See William Herbert Hobbs, *Peary*, pp. 217-20.

38 USNA, RG 401(1)(A), Robert E. Peary Papers, Diary Transcripts, 1871–1900, "Diary (typed), 1900," Entry for 4 March 1900.

39 USNA, RG 401(1)(A), Robert E. Peary Papers, Diary Transcripts, 1871–1900, File "Diary (typed) 1900," Letter to Warmbath, Cape Lawrence, 18 March 1900 [typescript following the transcription of Peary's diary entry for 18 March 1900].

40 USNA, RG 401(1)(A), Robert E. Peary Papers, Diary Transcripts, 1871–1900, File "Diary (typed) 1900," Typescript transcription of Peary's diary entry for 25 March 1900.

41 Ibid., Typescript transcription of Peary's diary entry for 23 March 1900.

42 William Herbert Hobbs, Peary, p. 224.

43 Fitzhugh Green, *Peary: The Man Who Refused to Fail*, p. 217.

44 Ibid., pp. 217-18.

45 NAC, RG 85, Vol. 584, File No. 571, Copy of letter of Knud Rasmussen, Copenhagen, to The Administrator of the Colonies in Greenland, 8 March 1920.

46 Fitzhugh Green, *Peary: The Man Who Refused to Fail*, p. 216.

47 USNA, RG 401(1)(A), Robert E. Peary Papers, Papers Relating to Arctic Expeditions, 1886-1909, Greenland, 1898-1902, T.S. Dedrick Diaries, Notebooks and Other Papers, 1898-1901, Box 4 of 6, Dedrick Diary, 28 June - 23 August 1900, Entry for 28 June 1900.

48 USNA, RG 401(1)(A), Robert E. Peary Papers, Papers Relating to Arctic Expeditions, 1886-1909, Greenland: 1898-1902, Peary Diary Entry for 14 September 1900.

49 Peary's fall hunting trip in 1900 to the interior of northern Ellesmere Island is described in USNA, RG 401(1)(A), Robert E. Peary Papers, Papers Relating to Arctic Expeditions, 1886-1909, Greenland, 1898-1902, Peary Diary, 16 September to 22 October 1900. See also Robert E. Peary, Living Off the Country," *Century Magazine* (October 1917), p. 913.

50 USNA, RG 401(1)(A), Robert E. Peary Papers, Papers Relating to Arctic Expeditions, 1886-1909 Greenland, 1898-1902, T.S. Dedrick Diaries, Notebooks and Other Papers, 1898-1901, Vol. VI, Folder 6, Miscellaneous Papers of T.S. Dedrick and Field Notes, Diary Entry for 5 October 1900 [at Fort Conger].

51 Ibid.

52 USNA, RG 401(1)(A), Robert E. Peary Papers, Papers Relating to Arctic Expeditions, 6-1902, T.S. Dedrick Diaries, Notebooks and Other Papers, 1898-1901, VI, Box No. 4, Folder 6, Miscellaneous Papers of Dr. T.S. Dedrick: Field Notes, Letter of Dedrick, Mouth of the Crozier River, to Robert Peary, Fort Conger, 21 February 1901, p. 1.

53 Ibid., p. 5.

54 Fitzhugh Green, *Peary: The Man Who Refused to Fail*, p. 224.

55 USNA, RG 401(1)(A), Robert E. Peary Papers, Papers Relating to Arctic Expeditions, 1886-1909, Greenland: 1898-1902, Peary Diary Entry for Tuesday, 9 April 1901.

56 William Herbert Hobbs, *Peary*, p. 239.

57 Ibid., p. 242.

58 USNA, RG 401(1)(A), Robert E. Peary Papers, Papers Relating to Arctic Expeditions, 1886–1909, Greenland: 1898–1902, Peary Diary Entry for 17 November 1901.

59 USNA, RG 401(1)(A), Robert E. Peary Papers, Papers Relating to Arctic Expeditions, 1886–1909, Greenland, 1898-1902, R.E. Peary Diaries, Field Notes, 1899–1902, Peary Diary for 20 January to 5 March 1902, Entry for 29 January 1902.

60 Ibid., Entry for 21 April 1901.

61 William Herbert Hobbs, *Peary*, p. 246.

62 Harold Horwood, *Bartlett: The Great Canadian Explorer* (Garden City, NY and Toronto: Doubleday, 1977), p. 65.

63 Robert E. Peary, *Nearest the Pole*, pp. 4-6.

64 William Henry Hobbs, *Peary* (New York: Macmillan, 1936), p. 260.

65 Nicholas Senn, *In the Heart of the Arctic* (Chicago: W.B. Conkey Company, 1907), p. 261.

66 Ibid.

67 Ibid., pp. 173-74.

68 BCLSC, Robert Abrams Bartlett Papers, Books, Articles, Etc. by Robert A. Bartlett, "From the Crow's Nest": "The First Roosevelt Expedition" (1905-06), p. 5.

69 Ibid., pp. 6-8.

70 Robert E. Peary, *Nearest the Pole*, p. 49.

71 USNA, RG 401(1)(A), Robert E. Peary Papers, Papers Relating to Arctic Expeditions, 1886-1909, North Polar, 1905-06, Diaries, Journals and Logs; Correspondence and Instructions, 1905-06, Dr. Louis Wolf, Journal, 1905-06, 14 July to 23 December 1905, Entry for 14 September 1905.

72 Ibid., Entry for 17 September 1905.

73 Robert E. Peary, *Nearest the Pole*, pp. 56-57.

74 Robert E. Peary, *Nearest the Pole*, p. 64; See also BCLSC, Special Collections, Robert Abrams Bartlett Papers, Books, Articles, Etc. by Robert A. Bartlett, "From the Crow's Nest": "The First Roosevelt Expedition" (1905-06), p. 15.

75 Caroline J. Phillips, "Eastern Canadian High Arctic Exploration as an Example of Frontier Change, With Particular Emphasis on the Robert Peary North Pole Expeditions," M.A. Thesis, University of Manitoba, 1987, pp. 64; John Edward Weems, *Peary: The Explorer and the Man* (Boston: Houghton Mifflin Company, 1967), pp. 212-13.

76 BCLSC, Special Collections, Robert Abrams Bartlett Papers, Books, Articles, Etc. by Robert A. Bartlett, "From the Crow's Nest": "The First Roosevelt Expedition" (1905-06), p. 16.

77 Ibid., p. 15.

78 See Patricia D. Sutherland, "An Inventory and Assessment of the Prehistoric Archaeological Resources of the Ellesmere Island National Park Reserve," Vol. I, p. 17 and Figure 4-13.

79 Caroline J. Phillips, "Eastern Canadian High Arctic Exploration as an Example of Frontier Change, With Particular Emphasis on the Robert Peary North Pole Expeditions," MA Thesis, University of Manitoba, 1987, p. 66.

80 USNA, RG 401(1)(A), Robert E. Peary Papers, Papers Relating to Arctic Expeditions, 1886-1909, North Polar: 1905–06, Box 1, File: "Letters Rec[eived]. Henson, 1905–06," Letter of Matthew Henson to Robert Peary, 16 December 1905.

81 BCLSC, Robert Abrams Bartlett Papers, Books, Articles, Etc. by Robert A. Bartlett, "From the Crow's Nest": "The First Roosevelt Expedition" (1905-06), p. 16.

82 Robert E. Peary, *Nearest the Pole*, pp. 59-60.

83 Ibid., p. 61.

84 Ibid., p. 173.

85 William Henry Hobbs, *Peary*, p. 273.

86 Bradley Robinson, *Dark Companion* (London: Hodder and Stoughton, Ltd., 1948), p. 188.

87 Ibid., p. 189.

88 USNA, RG 401(1)(A), Robert E. Peary Papers, Papers Relating to Arctic Expeditions, 1886-1909, North Polar: 1905-06, Box 1, Peary Journal Notes, April 1906, Entry for Wednesday, 4 April 1906.

89 Ibid., Entry for Wednesday, 11 April 1906.

90 William Henry Hobbs, *Peary*, p. 282.

91 Jean Malaurie, *The Last Kings of Thule*, p. 202.

92 BCLSC, Robert Abrams Bartlett Papers, Books, Articles, Etc. by Robert A. Bartlett, "From the Crow's Nest": "The First Roosevelt Expedition" (1905-06), p. 36.

93 Fitzhugh Green, *Peary: The Man Who Refused to Fail* (New York: G.P. Putnam's Sons, 1924), p. 224.

94 Jean Malaurie, *The Last Kings of Thule*, p. 202.

95 William Herbert Hobbs, *Peary*, pp. 301-2.

96 Robert E. Peary, *Nearest the Pole*, p. 190.

97 Theon Wright, *The Big Nail: The Story of the Cook-Peary Feud* (New York: The John Day Company, 1870), p. 113.

98 Ibid., pp. 115-17.

99 Dr. Frederick Cook, *My Attainment of the Pole* (New York and London: Mitchell Kennerley, 1908), p. 159.

100 Jean Malaurie, *The Last Kings of Thule*, p. 52.

101 Dr. Frederick Cook, *My Attainment of the Pole*, p. 263.

102 Ibid., p. 271.

103 Ibid., p. 287.

104 Theon Wright, *The Big Nail*, p. 155.

105 Dr. Frederick A. Cook, *My Attainment of the Pole*, and *Return from the Pole* (New York: Pellagrini and Cudahy, 1951).

106 Theon Wright, *The Big Nail*, p. 159.

107 Dr. Frederick Cook, *My Attainment of the Pole*, p. 336.

108 H.P. Steensby, "Contributions to the Ethnology and Anthropogeography of the Polar Eskimos," p. 302.

109 "The Testimony of Inuutersuaq Ulloriaq," in Wally Herbert, *The Noose of Laurels: The Discovery of the North Pole* (London, Sydney, Aukland and Toronto: Hodder and Stoughton, 1989), pp. 333-38.

110 See Frederick Cook, *My Attainment of the Pole*, pp. 314-437.

111 Howard S. Abramson, *Hero in Disgrace: The Life of Arctic Explorer Frederick A. Cook* (New York: Paragon House, 1991); Sheldon Cook-Dorough, "Frederick Albert Cook: Discoverer of the North Pole," *Fram: The Journal of Polar Studies*, Vol. 2, Part 1 (1985), pp. 141-58; Andrew A. Freeman, *The Case for Doctor Cook* (New York: Coward-McCann, Inc., 1961).

112 William Henry Hobbs, *Peary*, pp. 371-83; Harold Horwood, *Bartlett: The Great Canadian Explorer* (Garden City, New York and Toronto: Doubleday, 1977), pp. 95-102.

113 John Edward Weems, *Race for the Pole* (New York: Henry Holt and Company, 1960); Theon Wright, *The Big Nail*; Wally Herbert, *The Noose of Laurels*.

114 See, for example, William R,. Hunt, *To Stand at the Pole: The Dr. Cook—Admiral Peary North Pole Controversy* (New York: Stein and Day, 1981).

115 Harold Horwood, *Bartlett: The Great Canadian Explorer*, pp. 78-79.

116 William Herbert Hobbs, *Peary*, pp. 313-14.

117 Harold Horwood, *Bartlett: The Great Canadian Explorer*, p. 80.

118 Robert E. Peary, *The North Pole*, p. 88.

119 Caroline J. Phillips, "Eastern Canadian High Arctic Exploration as an Example of Frontier Change," Table 3, p. 70.

120 Kenn Harper, *Give Me My Father's Body*, pp. 167-68.

121 John W. Goodsell, *On Polar Trails: The Peary Expedition to the North Pole, 1908–09* (Ed., Donald W. Whisenhunt) (Austin, Texas: Eakin Press, 1983), p. 112.

122 Robert E. Peary, *The North Pole*, p. 127.

123 Donald B. MacMillan, *How Peary Reached the Pole*, p. 101.

124 BCLSC, Robert Abrams Bartlett Papers, "From the Crow's Nest": "The First Roosevelt Expedition" (1905-06), p. 15.

125 BCLSC, Donald B. MacMillan Collection, Diaries, Journals, Logs, Etc., MacMillan Diary No. 7, Field Diary, 19 April - 31 May 1909 (note at front of diary); and ibid., copy of record placed by MacMillan and George Borup at Cape Morris Jesup, 23 May 1909.

126 Hans P. Steensby, "The Polar Eskimos and the Polar Expeditions," p. 900.

127 John W. Goodsell, *On Polar Trails*, pp. 112-13.

128 John W. Goodsell, *On Polar Trails*, p. 110.

129 Caroline J. Phillips, "Eastern Canadian High Arctic Exploration as an Example of Frontier Change," p. 101.

130 John W. Goodsell, *On Polar Trails*, p. 112.

131 William Herbert Hobbs, *Peary*, p. 317.

132 John W. Goodsell, *On Polar Trails*, pp. 116-17.

133 Matthew Henson, *A Negro Explorer at the North Pole*, p. 79.

134 Quoted in Wally Herbert, *The Noose of Laurels*, p. 228.

135 John W. Goodsell, *On Polar Trails*, p. 122.

136 BCLSC, Robert Abrams Bartlett Papers, "From the Crow's Nest": "The Conquest of the Pole" (1908–09), p. 15.

137 John W. Goodsell, *On Polar Trails*, p. 125.

138 Matthew Henson, *A Negro Explorer at the North Pole*, p. 133.

139 USNA, RG 401(1)(A), Robert E. Peary Papers, Diary Transcripts, 1971-1900, "Diary (typed) 1898" [Note: this portion of Peary's diary transcriptions is mislabelled as it clearly relates to his trek over the ice pack in 1909, rather than 1898].

140 Ibid.

141 BCLSC, Donald B. MacMillan Collection, Diaries, Journals, Logs, Etc., No. 3, Diary, North Pole Expedition, 17 July 1908 to 2 October 1909, Entry for 2 October 1909, p. 278.

142 Ibid., Diary Entry for 20 August 1909, Etah.

143 W. Henry Lewin, *The Great North Pole Fraud* (London: C.W. Daniel Co. Ltd., 1935); Thomas Hall, *Has the North Pole Been Discovered?* (Boston: Badger, 1917).

144 For a treatment of the coverage of the Cook-Peary controversy in the popular media, see Beau Riffenburgh, *The Myth of the Explorer: The Press, Sensationalism, and Geographical Discovery*, pp. 165-90.

145 See, for example, Randall J. Osczevski, "Frederick Cook's Polar Journey: A Reconstruction," *Polar Record*, Vol. 26, No. 158 (1990), pp. 225-32; J. Gordon Hayes, *Robert Edwin Peary: A Record of His Explorations, 1886–1909* (London: Grant Richards and Humphrey Toulmin, 1929). J. Gordon Hayes, *The Conquest of the North Pole: Recent Arctic Exploration* (London: Thornton Butterworth, Ltd., 1934).

146 Fitzhugh Green, *Peary: The Man Who Refused to Fail*; William Henry Hobbs, *Peary*; and Donald B. MacMillan, *How Peary Reached the Pole*.

147 John Edward Weems, *Race for the Pole*; John Edward Weems, *Peary: The Explorer and the Man*; Theon Wright, *The Big Nail: The Story of the Cook-Peary Feud* (New York: The John Day Company, 1970); Dennis Rawlins, *Peary at the North Pole: Fact or Fiction?* (Washington/New York: Robert B. Luce, Inc., 1973); William R.Hunt, *To Stand at the Pole: The Dr. Cook-Admiral Peary North Pole Controversy* (New York: Stein and Day, 1981); Wally Herbert, *The Noose of Laurels*; Robert M. Bryce, *Cook and Peary: The Polar Controversy Resolved* (Mechanicsburg, Pennsylvania: Stackpole Books, 1997).

148 See, for example, "Year-Long Study Backs Explorer's North Pole Claim," *The Winnipeg Free Press*, 12 December 1989, p. 15, and the discussion of recent claims and controversies in Robert M. Bryce, Cook and *Peary: The Polar Controversy Resolved*, pp. 757-61.

149 Dennis Rawlins, *Peary at the North Pole: Fact or Fiction?*

150 Jean Malaurie, *The Last Kings of Thule*, p. 52.

151 United States, *Congressional Record*, Proceedings and Debates of the Sixty-First Congress, Vol. 46, Part 3, Third Session (Washington, DC: Government Printing Office, 1911), pp. 2,700-2,725; United States, House of Representatives, Sixty-First Congress, Third Session, Report No. 1961 (Washington, DC: Government Printing Office, 1911), pp. 410-31; United States, *Congressional Record*, Proceedings and Debates of the Sixty-Fourth Congress, Vol. 53, Part 14 (Washington, DC: Government Printing Office, 1916), Appendix, pp. 268-327.

152 Edmund Morris, *The Rise of Theodore Roosevelt* (New York: Coward, McCann, and Geoghegan, 1979), pp. 662-87; Lewis L. Gould, *The Presidency of Theodore Roosevelt* (Lawrence, Kansas: University Press of Kansas, 1991), pp. 6-7.

153 See, for example, *Hampton's Magazine*, January 1910, inside back cover.

154 Robert E. Peary, *Secrets of Polar Travel*, pp. 76-77.

Chapter 8: Assertion of Canadian Sovereignty Over the High Arctic, 1895–1940

1 V. Kenneth Johnson, "Canada's Title to the Arctic Islands," *Canadian Historical Review*, Vol. 14 (1933), p. 30.

2 Quoted in Nancy Fogelson, "Robert E. Peary and American Exploration in the Arctic 1886-1910," *Fram: The Journal of Polar Studies*, Vol. 2, No. 1 (1985), p. 137.

3 See Gordon Smith, "The Historical and Legal Background of Canada's Arctic Claims," PhD Dissertation, Columbia University, New York, 1952.

4 NAC, RG 85, Vol. 584, File 571, Memorandum of Hensley R. Holmden, Maps Division, to A.G. Doughty, Deputy Minister and Dominion Archivist, re: the Arctic Islands, 26 April 1921, pp. 33-34.

5 William R. Morrison, *Showing the Flag: The Mounted Police and Canadian Sovereignty in the North, 1894–1925* (Vancouver: University of British Columbia Press, 1985), p. 91.

6 A.P. Low, *Report on the Dominion Government Expedition to Hudson Bay and the Arctic Islands on Board the D.G.S.* Neptune, *1903–04* (Ottawa: Government Printing Bureau, 1906), pp. 47-48.

7 NAC, RG 85, Vol. 584, File 573-1, Letter of J.E. Bernier, Quebec, to O.S. Finnie, Ottawa, 26 March 1925.

8 See the discussion in C.J. Taylor, "Canadian Sovereignty Over its Arctic Islands," Unpublished agenda paper, Historic Sites and Monuments Board of Canada Agenda Papers, June 1981 Meeting, Parks Canada, Hull, 1981, pp. 328-43.

9 Captain J.E. Bernier, *Report on the Dominion of Canada Government Expedition to the Arctic Islands and Hudson Strait on Board the GS Arctic*, (Ottawa: King's Printer, 1910), p. 273.

10 Ibid., pp. 16-17.

11 Robert E. Peary, *Nearest the Pole*, p. 202. Of his view from the summit, Peary wrote: "North stretched the well-known ragged surface of the polar pack, and northwest it was with a thrill that my glasses revealed the faint white summits of a distant land which my Eskimos claimed to have seen as we came along from the last camp."

12 Fitzhugh Green, "The Crocker Land Expedition," *Natural History* (Journal of the American Museum of Natural History), Vol. 28 (1928), p. 463.

13 Harrison Hunt and Ruth Hunt Thompson, *North to the Horizon: Searching for Peary's Crocker Land* (Camden, Maine: Down East Book, 1980), pp. 14-15.

14 Donald B. MacMillan, *Four Years in the White North* (New York and London: Harper Brothers, 1918), p. 47.

15 Harrison Hunt and Ruth Hunt Thompson, *North to the Horizon*, p. 31.

16 Donald B. MacMillan, *Four Years in the White North*, p. 48.

17 Elmer Ekblaw, "Of Unbroken Shores: The Traverse of Grant Land and Ellesmere Lands," in Donald B. MacMillan, *Four Years in the White North* (New York and London: Harper Brothers, 1918), pp. 333-70.

18 Ibid., pp. 342-52; 364.

19 Ibid., p. 370.

20 J. Gordon Hayes, *The Conquest of the North Pole: Recent Arctic Exploration* (London: Thornton Butterworth, Ltd., 1934), p. 144.

21 William Barr, *Back from the Brink: The Road to Muskox Conservation in the Northwest Territories* (Calgary: The Arctic Institute of North America, 1991), p. 43.

22 Quoted in ibid., p. 89.

23 NAC, RCMP Records, RG 18, Accn. 84-85/084, Vol. 32, File G-516-37, Letter of George Comer, East Haddam, Conn., to Vilhjalmur Stefansson, 29 May 1919.

24 Ibid., Letter of W.W. Cory to A.A. McLean, Comptroller of the RCMP, 18 July 1919.

25 Ibid., Discussion Paper, Arctic Technical Board, received 25 November 1920, fol. 35.

26 Ibid., Minutes of a Special Meeting of the Technical Advisory Board, 1 October 1920, p.1.

27 Ibid., Letter to Sir Basil Thomson, Scotland House, London, 18 January 1921.

28 NAC, RG 85, Vol. 1203, fols. 401-3, Letter of J.B. Harkin to W.W. Cory, 16 June 1920, Quoted in William Barr, *Back from the Brink*, p. 90.

29 NAC, RG 18, Accn. No. 84-85/084, Vol. 32, File G-516-37, Minutes of a Special Meeting of the Technical Advisory Board, 1 October 1920, p.16.

30 NAC, RG 85, Vol. 584, File 571, Memorandum of J.B. Harkin to W.W. Cory, Deputy Minister, Department of the Interior, 7 April 1921.

31 Ibid.

32 Ibid., Minutes of a Special Meeting of the Technical Advisory Board, 1 October 1920, p. 8.

33 NAC, RG 18, Accn. No. 84-85, Vol. 32, File G-516-37, Minutes of a Special Meeting of the Technical Advisory Board, 1 October 1920, p. 7.

34 Ibid., pp. 34-5.

35 NAC, RG 15, Vol. 1, File "Arctic Islands," Report of J.B. Harkin to the Minister of the Interior, "Recommendations." Photocopy provided by Shelagh Grant in "Inuit Relocations to the High Arctic 1953-1960: Errors Exposed," Vol. I (bound collection of documents submitted to the Royal Commission on Aboriginal Peoples, June 1993, Revised August 1993). I would like to thank Professor Grant for this reference.

36 Ibid.

37 NAC, RG 18, Accn. 84-85/084, Vol. 32, File G-516-37, "Memorandum on the Sovereignty of the Polar Islands," n.d.

38 NAC, RG 18, Accn. 84-85/084, Vol. 33, File G 516-37, Part 4, Memorandum of Commissioner, RCMP, to Staff Sergeant Joy, 6 July 1921.

39 Ibid., "Canadian Sovereignty in the Arctic," RCMP report re: "Establishing of, closing of, and re-opening of the most northerly detachments in Canadian Arctic."

40 NAC, RG 18, Accn 84-85/084, Vol. 33, File G-516-37, Part 2, Memorandum for the Minister in Control of the RCM Police from Cortlandt Starnes, Assistant Commissioner, 13 June 1922.

41 NAC, RG 18, Accn. 84-85/084, Vol. 32, File G-516-37, Memorandum of A. Bowen Perry, Commissioner, to President of the Privy Council, 9 February 1921.

42 NAC, RG 18, Accn 84-85/084, Vol. 33, File G-516-37, Part 2, Memorandum for the Minister in Control of the RCM Police from Cortlandt Starnes, Assistant Commissioner, 13 June 1922.

43 Ibid., Memorandum of J.D. Craig, Officer in Charge of Expedition, on board CGS Arctic, to the Officer Commanding, Headquarters Division, RCMP, Ottawa, 27 September 1927.

44 James de Jonge, "Building on the Frontier: The Mounted Police in the Canadian North," *SSAC Bulletin*, Vol. 17, No. 2 (June 1992), p. 51.

45 Herbert Patrick Lee, *Policing the Top of the World*, pp. 190-93.

46 F.D. Henderson, "Canada's Arctic Islands," *The Canadian Magazine*, Vol. 65, No. 4 (April 1928), p. 11.

47 Ibid., pp. 207-8.

48 NAC, RG 85, Vol. 348, File 201-1-8, "The 1923 Expedition to the Arctic," by J.D. Craig [unpublished typescript], pp. 17-18.

49 Ibid., p. 23.

50 NAC, RG 18, Accn. 84-85/084, Vol. 33, File G-516-37, Part 3, "Statement of Position, Canada's Arctic Islands, April 1925," p. 1.

51 Ibid., Letter of W.D. Cory, Deputy Minister of the Interior to Col. Cortlandt Starnes, Commissioner, RCMP, 29 June 1925.

52 Ibid., Memorandum of O.S. Finnie to J.D. Craig, 27 November 1924.

53 BCLSC, Donald B. MacMillan Collection, Diaries, Journals, and Logs, Etc., Field Notebook No. 32, March – July 1924.

54 Ibid., Entry for 4 June 1924.

55 NAC, RG 85, Vol. 85, File No. 202-2 [1], Memorandum of O.S. Finnie to J.D. Craig, 13 March 1924.

56 Ibid., Memorandum of N.R. Daly, Departmental Solicitor to O.S. Finnie, 10 March 1925.

57 Ibid., "Suggestions re: Procedure to be Followed in Cases of Explorers and Scientists Desiring to Enter the North West Territories of Canada" [1925].

58 Christian Vibe, *Arctic Animals in Relation to Climatic Fluctuations*, p. 54.

59 Donald B. MacMillan, "The MacMillan Expedition Returns," *The National Geographic Magazine*, Vol. 48, No. 5 (November 1925), pp. 477-78.

60 Everett S. Allen, *Arctic Odyssey: The Life of Rear Admiral Donald B. MacMillan* (New York: Dodd, Mead, 1962), p. 258.

61 D.H. Dinwoodie, "Arctic Controversy: The 1925 Byrd-MacMillan Expedition Example," *Canadian Historical Review*, Vol. 52, No. 1 (March 1972), p. 55.

62 Raimund E. Goerler, Ed., *To the Pole: The Diary and Notebook of Richard E. Byrd, 1925–1927* (Columbus: Ohio University Press, 1998), "The Greenland Expedition of 1925," p. 20.

63 Ibid., p. 54.

64 Ibid., p. 55.

65 "MacMillan Hopes to Win Arctic Race," *New York Times*, 22 April 1925. News clipping inserted into NAC, RG 85, Vol. 584, File No. 573-1.

66 Edwin P. Hoyt, *The Last Explorer: The Adventures of Admiral Byrd* (New York: The John Day Company, 1968), p. 74.

67 Ibid., p. 22.

68 NAC, RG 18, Accn. 84-85/084, Vol. 33, File G-516-37, Part 3, "Statement of Position, Canada's Arctic Islands, April 1925," p. 1.

69 Richard E. Byrd's Diary of 1925, Entries for 10, 13, and 17 August 1925, reproduced in Raimund E. Goerler, Ed., *To the Pole: The Diary and Notebook of Richard E. Byrd, 1925–1927*, "The Greenland Expedition of 1925," pp. 36-37.

70 Edwin P. Hoyt, *The Last Explorer: The Adventures of Admiral Byrd*, pp. 86-91.

71 Ibid., p. 91.

72 Richard E. Byrd, "Flying over the Arctic," *National Geographic Magazine*, Vol. 48, No. 5 (November 1925), p. 519.

73 Nancy Fogelson, *Arctic Exploration and International Relations, 1900–1932* (Fairbanks: University of Alaska Press, 1992), p. 95.

74 NAC, RG 18, Accn 84-85/084, Vol. 33, File G-516-37, Part 1, Memorandum: "Arctic Possession—U.S. Attitude (Secret)," 27 August 1947.

75 D.H. Dinwoodie, "Arctic Controversy: The 1925 Byrd-MacMillan Expedition Example," p. 60. For a recent treatment of this expedition from an American perspective, see John H. Bryant and Harold N. Cones, *Dangerous Crossings: The First Modern Polar Expedition, 1925* (Annapolis, Maryland: Naval Institute Press, 2000).

76 NAC, RG 85, Vol. 584, File 571, Part 7, Letter of O.S. Finnie to Cortlandt Starnes, 20 April 1925.

77 NAC, RG 85, Vol. 584, File 573-1, Letter of Knud Rasmussen, c/o Royal Danish Consulate General, Montreal, to O.S. Finnie, Ottawa, 5 May 1925.

78 NAC, RG 18, Accn. 84-85/084, Vol. 33, File G-516-37, Part 3, Letter of C.E. Wilcox, Inspector Commanding Ellesmere Sub-District, on board the CGS Arctic, to the Officer Commanding, Headquarters Division, RCMP, Ottawa, 25 August 1925.

79 R.C. Fetherstonhaugh, *The Royal Canadian Mounted Police* (New York: Carrick and Evans, 1938), pp. 211-12; William R. Morrison, *Showing the Flag: the Mounted Police and Canadian Sovereignty in the North, 1894–1925* (Vancouver: University of British Columbia Press, 1985), pp. 169-70.

80 NAC, RG 85, Vol. 347, File 200-2, Report by External Affairs, "The Question of Ownership of the Sverdrup Islands," 28 October 1929, p. 10; cited in Shelagh Grant, "Inuit Relocations to the High Arctic, 1953-1960: 'Errors Exposed,'" Unpublished manuscript, Vol. I, Report and Chronology, revised 30 August 1993, p. 23, n. 61.

81 William R. Morrison, "Eagle Over the Arctic: Americans in the Canadian North," *Canadian Review of American Studies* (March 1987), p. 67.

82 NAC, RG 85, Vol. 348, File 201-1-8, "The 1923 Expedition to the Arctic," typed manuscript by J.D. Craig, 22 February 1926, p. 18.

83 See J. Jones, "Arctic Adventure: Inspector A.H. Joy," *The Scarlet and Gold*, 57th Edition (1975), pp. 26-37; 46-56.

84 NAC, RG 18, Accn. 84-85/084, Vol. 33, File G-516-37, Part 3, Memorandum of Cortlandt Starnes, Commissioner, respecting Police posts in the Eastern Arctic Sub-district of the R.C.M. Police, 25 June 1925.

85 See, for example, the Bache Peninsula Detachment Diary for 1928 in NAC, RG 18, Vol. 3015, Entries for June and July 1928.

86 NAC, RG 18, Accn. No. 84-85/084, Vol. 33, File No. G-516-37, Part 2, Memorandum from Inspector C.E. Wilcox, Ellesmere Island [Craig Harbour] Detachment, NWT, to the Officer Commanding, Headquarters Division, Ottawa, 28 August 1922.

87 Ibid., Memorandum of C.E. Wilcox, Inspector Commanding Ellesmere Island and Baffin Land, to the Officer Commanding, Headquarters Division, 1 August 1923.

88 Ibid., p. 16.

89 NAC, RG 18, Accn. 84-85/084, Vol. 33, File G-516-37, Part 2, Memorandum of C.E. Wilcox, Inspector Commanding Ellesmere Island and Baffin Land, to the Officer Commanding, Headquarters Division, 1 August 1923.

90 NAC, RG 85, Vol. 348, "The 1923 Expedition to the Arctic Islands," by J.D. Craig,

91 Ibid., p. 19.

92 NAC, RG18 (Accn. 84-85/084), Vol. 33, File G-516-37, Part 3, Report of Inspector C.E. Wilcox, Pond Inlet, to the Officer Commanding, Headquarters Division, 4 September 1925.

93 NAC, RG85, Vol. 348, "The 1923 Expedition to the Arctic Islands," Unpublished report by J.D. Craig, 22 February 1926, p. 15.

94 NAC, RG18, Vol. 3015, Bache Peninsula Detachment Diary for 1928, "Natives' Credit Account 1926-27" [inserted at end of diary].

95 NAC, RG 18, Vol. 3014, Bache Peninsula Detachment Diary for 1927, Entry for 3 January 1927.

96 Ibid., Entries for 8 and 9 January 1927.

97 Ibid., Entry for 12 January 1927.

98 NAC, RG 18, Accn. 84-85/084, Vol. 33, File G-516-37, Part 3, Letter of C.E. Wilcox, on board CGS Arctic, to the Officer Commanding, RCMP, Ottawa, 25 August 1925.

99 See Donald B. MacMillan, *Four Years in the White North*, passim.

100 Lauge Koch, "Report on the Danish Jubilee Expedition North of Greenland, 1920-23," *Meddelelser om Grønland*, Vol. 70 (1927).

101 See, for example, assorted accounts in Harwood Steele, *Policing the Arctic: The Story of the Conquest of the Arctic by the Royal Canadian (formerly North-West) Mounted Police* (Toronto: The Ryerson Press, n.d.), pp. 257, 333, and 337.

102 NAC, RG 18, Vol. 3012, File "Annual Reports, Bache Peninsula Detachment, 1927–28," Annual Report, 1931-32, by H.W. Stallworthy, Bache Peninsula, to the Officer Commanding, Headquarters Division, RCMP, Ottawa, 3 August 1932, p. 4.

103 Ibid., p. 5.

104 NAC, RG 18, Accn. 84-85/084, Vol. 33, File G-516-37, Part 3, Memorandum of Inspector C.E. Wilcox to the Officer Commanding, Headquarters Division, RCMP, 25 August 1925.

105 Ibid., Part 2, Memorandum of Inspector C.E. Wilcox, Fram Fiord, Ellesmere Island, to the Officer Commanding, Headquarters Division, RCMP, Ottawa, 20 August 1922.

106 NAC RG 18, Vol. 3014, Bache Peninsula Detachment Diary for 1927, Entry for 18 May 1927.

107 NAC, RG 18, Vol. 3012, File Annual Reports, Bache Peninsula Detachment, 1927-28, Bache Peninsula Detachment Annual Report, 1929-30, by Constable N. McLean, 29 July 1930.

108 NAC, RG 18, Vol. 3014, Bache Peninsula Detachment Diary for 1927, Entries for 1-17 September 1927.

109 Ibid., Entry for 19 September 1927.

110 Ibid., Entry for 17 October 1927.

111 NAC, RG 18, Vol. 3012, File Annual Reports, Bache Peninsula Detachment, 1927-28, Bache Peninsula Detachment Annual Report, 1929-30, by Constable N. McLean, 29 July 1930.

112 NAC, RG 18, Vol. 3014, Bache Peninsula Detachment Diary for 1927, Entries for 12 January, 19 May, and 2 June 1927.

113 Ibid., Entries for 3 January to 17 February 1927.

114 Ibid., see, for example, the entries for 20, 21, and 24 May and 11, 22, and 23 June 1927.

115 Ibid., Entry for 3 July 1927.

116 Ibid., Entries for 24 and 25 February 1927.

117 NAC, RG 18, Vol. 3012, Bache Peninsula Annual Reports, Annual Report for 1930–1931, by Corporal H.W. Stallworthy, p. 4.

118 Herbert Patrick Lee, *Policing the Top of the World*, pp. 148, 165, 183-85, and 207.

119 NAC, RG 18, Vol. 3663, File G-567-25, Memorandum of Constable P. Dersch, Craig Harbour, to the Officer Commanding, Headquarters Division, RCMP, Ottawa, 10 December 1925.

120 NAC, RG 18, Vol. 3013, Bache Peninsula Patrol Repots, 1926-32, "Patrol on West Coast of Ellesmere Island," by Constable E. Anstead 22 May 1929, pp. 2-4.

121 NAC, RG 18, Vol. 3014, Bache Peninsula Detachment Diary, 1927, Entry for 23 July 1927.

122 NAC, RG 18, Vol. 3012, Bache Peninsula Patrol Reports, "Report re: Patrol to Craig Harbour via West Coast of Ellesmere Island," 4 May 1930, by Constable N. McLean, 4 May 1930, p. 2.

123 NAC, RG 18, Vol. 3013, Bache Peninsula Patrol Reports, 1926-32, "Patrol in Search of German Arctic Expedition from Bache Peninsula to Cornwall Island, Makinson Inlet and Return," by Constable R.W. Hamilton, 12 July 1932, p. 5.

124 See, for example, ibid., "Patrol on West Coast of Ellesmere Island," by E. Anstead, 22 May 1929, p. 3. Three bears were shot at Ulvingen on the west side of Stor Island, off Axel Heiberg Island's eastern coast.

125 NAC, RG 18, Vol. 3012, Bache Peninsula Annual Reports, Annual Report for 1930-1931, by Corporal H.W. Stallworthy, p. 3.

126 NAC, RG 85, Vol. 584, File 573-1, Letter of Knud Rasmussen, c/o Royal Danish Consulate General, Montreal, to O.S. Finnie, Ottawa, 5 May 1925.

127 NAC, RG 18, Accn. 84-85/084, Vol. 33, File G-516-37, Part 3, Letter of Inspector Commanding Ellesmere Island Sub-District, on board CGS *Arctic*, to L. Rosendahl, Governor, North Greenland, 10 August 1925.

128 NAC, RG 85, Vol. 835, File 7423, Memorandum: "Eastern Arctic Expedition, 1932," 31 August 1932.

129 NAC, RG 85, Vol. 835, File 7424, "Eastern Arctic Expedition, 1932," Report on Craig Harbour, 1 September 1932.

130 NAC, RG 18, Accn. 84-85/084, Vol. 33, File G-516-37, Part 4, Memorandum of Inspector A.H. Joy, Bache Peninsula, to the Commissioner, RCMP, Ottawa, 6 August 1928.

131 NAC, RG 18, Vol. 3012, File: Annual Reports, Bache Peninsula Detachment, 1927–28, Bache Peninsula Detachment Annual Report, 1927-28, by Constable E. Anstead, 17 July 1928, pp. 1-2.

132 NAC, RG 18, Accn. 84-85/084, Vol. 33, File G-516-37, Part 4, "Report re: Annual Arctic Expedition" by Constable A.M. McKellar, 17 August 1929.

133 NAC, RG 18, Vol. 3012, Bache Peninsula Annual Reports, Annual Report for 1930-1931, by Corporal H.W. Stallworthy, n.d., p. 3.

134 NAC, RG 18, Vol. 3013, Bache Peninsula Patrol Repots, 1926-32, "Report re: Patrol on West Coast of Ellesmere Island, 1928," by Constable E. Anstead, 18 May 1928.

135 NAC, RG 18, Vol. 3012, Bache Peninsula Annual Reports, Annual Report for 1927–28, by Corporal E. Anstead, 17 July 1928, p. 4.

136 NAC, RG 18, Vol. 3012, Bache Peninsula Patrol Reports, "Report re: Patrol to Craig Harbour and Southern Ellesmere District," by Constable G.T. Makinson, 25 July 1928, p. 2.

137 NAC, RG 18, Vol. 3012, Bache Peninsula Annual Reports, Annual Report for 1929–30, by Constable N. McLean, n.d., p. 2.

138 Ibid., Annual Report for 1930–1931, by Corporal H.W. Stallworthy, p. 4.

139 NAC, RG 18, Vol. 3014, Bache Peninsula Detachment Diary for 1927, Entries for 2, 4, 5, and 6 February 1927.

140 Ibid., Entry for 15 January 1927.

141 NAC, RG 18, Vol. 3663, File No. G-567-25, "Craig Harbour Patrol Reports, 1925–1956," "Patrols—Craig Harbour Detachment," by Corporal H. Kearney, 30 June 1934, p. 2.

142 NAC, RG 18, Vol. 3012, File: "Annual Reports, Bache Peninsula Detachment, 1927-28," Bache Peninsula Detachment Annual Report, 1929-30, by Constable N. McLean, 29 July 1930.

143 Ibid.

144 Ibid., Annual Report for 1930-1931, by Corporal H.W. Stallworthy, p. 5.

145 W.R. Morrison, *Showing the Flag*, pp. 169-70.

146 NAC, RG 18, Vol. 3663, File No. G-567-25, "Craig Harbour Patrol Reports, 1925–1956," "Patrol to Grethasoer, Bay Fiord, and Axel Heiberg Island," by Staff Sergeant A.H. Joy, 10 June 1926.

147 Ibid., p. 6.

148 NAC, RG 18, Vol. 3013, Bache Peninsula Patrol Reports, 1926-32, Report re: "Patrol to King Christian Island," by Staff Sergeant A.H. Joy, 1 June 1927; See also NAC, RG 18, Accn. 84-85/084, File G-516-37, Part 4, "Canadian Sovereignty in the Arctic," n.d., p. 2.

149 J.H. MacBrien, "The Mounties in the Arctic," *Canadian Geographical Journal*, Vol. 10. No. 3 (March 1935), p. 165.

150 William R. Morrison, *Showing the Flag*, p. 170.

151 NAC, RG 18, Vol. 3012, File: Annual Reports, Bache Peninsula Detachment, Bache Peninsula Detachment Annual Report for 1929-30, by Constable N. McLean, 29 July 1930.

152 Ibid., Annual Report for 1930-1931, by Corporal H.W. Stallworthy, p. 3.

153 Harwood Steele, *Policing the Arctic*, pp. 315-16.

154 NAC, RG 18, Vol. 3013, Bache Peninsula Patrol Reports, 1926-32, "Patrol in Search of German Arctic Expedition from Bache Peninsula to Cornwall Island, Makinson Inlet and Return," by Constable R.W. Hamilton, 12 July 1932, p. 5.

155 J. Gordon Hayes, *The Conquest of the North Pole*, p. 147.

156 NAC, RG 18, Vol. 3013, Bache Peninsula Patrol Reports, 1926-32, "Patrol in Search of German Arctic Expedition from Bache Peninsula to Cornwall Island, Makinson Inlet and Return," by Constable R.W. Hamilton, 12 July 1932, p. 4.

157 Ibid., "Patrol report: Bache Peninsula to Head of Flagger River, Craig Harbour, and Makinson Inlet, Ellesmere Island," by Corporal H.W. Stallworthy, 31 May 1931, p. 5.

158 NAC, RG 18, Vol. 3663, File No. G-567-25, "Craig Harbour Patrol Reports, 1925-1956," "Report re: Patrol to Kane Basin Detachment," by Corporal T.R. Michelson, 1 August 1925.

159 NAC, RG 18, Vol. 3012, Bache Peninsula Annual Reports, Annual Report for 1927-28, by Corporal E. Anstead, 17 July 1928, p. 1.

160 NAC, RG 18, Vol. 3013, Bache Peninsula Patrol Reports, 1926-32, "Patrol Report: Bache Peninsula to Head of Flagger [Flagler?] River, Craig Harbour, and Makinson Inlet, Ellesmere Island," by Corporal H.W. Stallworthy, 31 May 1931.

161 Ibid., "Report re: Patrol on West Coast of Ellesmere Island, 1928," by Constable E. Anstead, 18 May 1928, p. 3.

162 Ibid., p. 7.

163 Ibid., "Patrol on West Coast of Ellesmere Island," by E. Anstead, 22 May 1929, p. 2.

164 Ibid., p. 3.

165 NAC, RG 18, Vol. 3013, Bache Peninsula Patrol Reports, 1926-32, "Patrol Report: Bache Peninsula to Head of Flagger [Flagler?] River, Craig Harbour, and Makinson Inlet, Ellesmere Island," by Corporal H.W. Stallworthy, 31 May 1931, p. 6.

166 Harwood Steele, *Policing the Arctic*, p. 9.

Chapter 9: Adventurers, Big-Game Hunters, and Scientists on Ellesmere Island, 1934–40

1 John Wright, "British Polar Expeditions, 1919-39," *Polar Record*, Vol. 26, No. 157 (1990), pp. 77-84.

2 Alfred Stephenson, "British Polar Exploration 10 Years Before and After World War II: A Comparison," *The Polar Record*, Vol. 20, No. 127 (1981), p. 318.

3 Noel Humphreys, "Ellesmere Land and Grinnell Land," *The Geographical Journal*, Vol. 87, No. 5 (January–June 1936), p. 386.

4 Edward Shackleton, *Arctic Journeys: The Story of the Oxford University Ellesmere Land Expedition, 1934-5* (London: Hoddard and Stoughton, 1936), p. 33.

5 NAC, RG 18, Accn. 85-86/048, Vol. 43, File G-804-44, Report of H.W. Stallworthy re: Oxford University Ellesmere Land Expedition, 1934, 15 November 1935, p. 6.

6 "The Oxford University Ellesmere Land Expedition," *The Geographical Journal*, Vol. 87, No. 5 (May, 1936), p. 389.

7 NAC, RG 18, Accn. 85-86/084, Box 33, File G-804-13, "Oxford [University] Ellesmere Land Expedition, General Plan."

8 Ibid., Memorandum of G.T. Henn, Departmental Secretary, RCMP, 22 September 1933.

9 NAC, RG 18, Accn. 85-86/048, Vol. 43, File G-804-44, Report of Sergeant H.W. Stallworthy re: Oxford University Ellesmere Land Expedition, 15 November 1935, p. 5.

10 Ibid., p. 13.

11 "The Oxford University Ellesmere Land Expedition," *The Geographical Journal*, Vol. 87, No. 5 (May, 1936), p. 392.

12 Ibid., p. 391.

13 NAC, RG 18, Accn. 85-6/048, Vol. 43, File G-04-4, Report of Sergeant H.W. Stallworthy re: Oxford University Ellesmere Land Expedition, 15 November 1935, p. 14.

14 Ibid., p. 18.

15 Edward Shackleton, *Arctic Journeys*, p. 241.

16 "The Oxford University Ellesmere Land Expedition," Appendix V: "Dogs and Sledges," by Edward Shackleton, The Geographical Journal, Vol. 87, No. 5 (May, 1936), p. 439.

17 Edward Shackleton, *Arctic Journeys*, p. 247.

18 A.W. Moore, "The Sledge Journey to Grant Land," *The Geographical Journal*, Vol. 87, No. 5 (May, 1936), p. 423.

19 Ibid., pp. 253-4.

20 Edward Shackleton, *Arctic Journeys*, pp. 252-6; A.W. Moore, "The Sledge Journey to Grant Land," pp. 425-7.

21 NAC, RG 85, Vol. 818, File 7022, Part 3, [News clipping] *The Telegraph Journal*, 5 November 1937.

22 Ibid., [News clipping] "Riches of Arctic Declared Great," *Montreal Daily Star*, 2 November 1937.

23 Ibid., [News clipping] *The Halifax Chronicle*, 4 November 1937.

24 Edward Shackleton, "Personal View," *The Manchester Evening News*, 22 April 1937.

25 NAC, RG 85, Vol. 818, File No. 7022, Part 2, "Plans for Expedition to Canadian Arctic," Proposal accompanying letter of Edward Shackleton, Hampton Court Palace, Middlesex, to Sir James MacBrien, Commissioner, RCMP, Ottawa, 31 January 1936.

26 Ibid., p. 2.

27 Ibid.

28 Ibid., Letter of Edward Shackleton, Chicago, to Dr. Camsell, Deputy Minister, Mines and Resources, Ottawa, 24 November 1937, pp. 3-4.

29 Ibid., Memorandum for File re: November 18, 1937 Meeting of the Northwest Territories Council, 19 November 1937, p. 2.

30 See Geoffrey Hattersley-Smith, *North Of Latitude Eighty: The Defence Research Board in Northern Ellesmere Island* (Ottawa: The Defence Research Board, 1974); and Lyle Dick, "Defence Research Board Camps in Northern Ellesmere Island: Report on Historical Resources," Environment Canada Parks Service *Research Bulletin No. 292* (1991), pp. 1-6.

31 31 NAC, RG 85, Vol. 872, File 8729, Part 2, Letter of Arthur R. Hinks, Secretary, Royal Geographical Society, to Col. Vanier, 27 May 1936.

32 Ibid., Memorandum of Sergeant Stallworthy to the Officer Commanding, RCMP, Moncton Division, 24 March 1937.

33 Ibid., p. 2

34 NAC, RG 85, Vol. 872, File 8729, Part 1, Letter of A.R. Hinks, Secretary, Royal Geographical Society, to Col. Georges Vanier, 6 December 1937.

35 Ibid., Handwritten statement by David Haig-Thomas, Kudligssat, North Greenland, 21 July 1937.

36 "The Oxford University Ellesmere Land Expedition: Discussion," *The Geographical Journal*, Vol. 87, No. 5 (May, 1936), p. 442.

37 David Haig-Thomas, Tracks in the Snow (London: Hodder and Stoughton, 1939), p. 19.

38 Ibid., p. 26.

39 Ibid., pp. 78-81.

40 Ibid., p. 15.

41 Ibid., p. 155.

42 David Haig-Thomas, "Expedition to Ellesmere Island, 1937-38," *Geographical Journal*, Vol. 95 (1940), pp. 269-70.

43 NAC, RG 85, Vol. 872, File 8729, Part 1, Memorandum of Major D.L. McKeand to R.A. Gibson, 20 January 1939.

44 NAC, RG 85, Vol. 872, File 8729, Part 2, Sworn statement of Nukappiannguaq, 23 August 1939.

45 Ibid., Extracts from the Minutes of the Northwest Territories Council, 17 October 1939.

46 Ibid., Sworn statement of Nukappiannguaq, 23 August 1939.

47 Ibid., Letter of Arthur R. Hinks, Secretary, Royal Geographical Society, to the Secretary, Office of the High Commissioner for Canada, 14 February 1949, pp. 2-3.

48 Ibid., Memorandum of Commissioner S.T. Wood re: *Tracks in the Snow*, 11 December 1939.

49 Ibid., Letter of Lance Corporal R.W. Hamilton, Craig Harbour, NWT, to David Haig-Thomas, London, England, 20 November 1939.

50 David Haig-Thomas, *Tracks in the Snow*, p. 175.

51 NAC, RG 18, Vol. 3663. File G-567-25, Memorandum of Inspector Martin, to the Commissioner, RCMP, 18 October 1939.

52 David Haig-Thomas, *Tracks in the Snow*, p. 175.

53 NAC, RG 85, Vol. 877, File 8904, "MacGregor Expedition 1937-38" [News clipping], *The Detroit Free Press*, 21 February 1939, "Weather Detective Forecasts End of Clouded Predictions."

54 Ibid., Letter of C.J. MacGregor to the [Right] Hon. W.L. Mackenzie King, Prime Minister of Canada, 8 May 1937 (copy).

55 Ibid., Letter of C.J. MacGregor to Charles Camsell, Commissioner, Northwest Territories, 15 May 1937.

56 Ibid., Letter of C.J. MacGregor to R.A. Gibson, Deputy Commissioner, Northwest Territories, 29 October 1938.

57 Ibid.

58 Ibid., News clipping: "Weather Detective Forecasts End of Clouded Predictions," *The Detroit Free Press*, 21 February 1939.

59 Ibid., Memorandum of R.N. Yates, A/L/Cpl., on board RMS Nascopie, to the Officer Commanding, RCM Police "G" Division, Ottawa, 15 September 1938.

60 "Danish Thule and Ellesmere Land Expedition, 1939-40," *The Polar Record*, No. 18 (July 1939), pp. 111-12.

61 NAC, RG 85, Vol. 916, File 11036, Letter of G. Holler, Consul General of Denmark to O.D. Skelton, Undersecretary of State for External Affairs, 22 March 1939.

62 Ibid., Letter of G.B. Holler, Consul General of Denmark to O.D. Skelton, Undersecretary of State for External Affairs, 25 March 1939.

63 Ibid., Letter of A.E. Porsild, Chief Botanist, National Museum of Canada, to R.A. Gibson, Deputy Commissioner [Northwest Territories], 26 November 1948.

64 "Record of Danish Thule and Ellesmere Land Expedition, 1939," Retrieved and reproduced in G. Hattersley-Smith, Ed., Operation Tanquary Preliminary Report, 1964 (Ottawa: Defence Research Board 1967), Figure 5.

65 NAC, RG 85, Vol. 916, File 11036, Christian Vibe and Gud. Thorlaksson, "The Danish Thule and Ellesmere Island Expedition 1939-41" (translated from *Grønlandsposten*, No. 5, pp. 56-57.

66 Ibid., Memorandum of Trevor Lloyd, Acting Consul for Canada in Greenland, Godthaab, to the Secretary of State for External Affairs, Ottawa, 23 April 1945, p. 1.

67 Ibid., "Notes on Van Hauen Expedition," from Niels Rasmussen, 27 May 1946.

68 See Vibe's "The Marine Mammals and the Marine Fauna in the Thule District (Northwest Greenland) With Observations on Ice Conditions in 1939-41 (1950), and "Arctic Animals in Relation to Climatic Fluctuations" (1967).

69 "Contributions to the Geology of Northwest Greenland, Ellesmere Island and Axel Heiberg Island," *Meddelelser om Grønland*, Vol. 149, No. 7 (1950), pp. 1-85; and "Geological Investigations in Ellesmere Island, 1952," *Arctic*, Vol. 5 (1952), pp. 199-210.

70 Christy Collis, "The Voyage of the Episteme: Narrating the North," in *Essays on Canadian Writing*, No. 59 (Fall 1996), Theme Issue: "Representing North," p. 31.

71 Ibid., p. 32.

72 John England, "The First Expeditions to Lady Franklin Bay, Northeast Ellesmere Island, NWT, Canada," *Arctic and Alpine Research*, Vol. 5, No. 2 (1973), p. 144.

73 B.T. Alt, R.M. Koerner, D.A. Fisher, and J.C. Bourgeois, "Arctic Climate During the Franklin Era, As Deduced from Ice Cores," in Patricia D. Sutherland, Ed., The Franklin Era in Canadian Arctic History (Ottawa: National Museum of Man, Mercury Series, No. 131 (1985), pp. 69-92.

74 United States, Sailing Directions for Baffin Bay and Davis Strait, Comprising the West Coast of Greenland From the Eastern Entrance of Prince Christian Sound to Cape Morris Jesup and the East Coasts of Baffin, Bylot, Devon, and Ellesmere Islands from Resolution Island to Cape Joseph Henry, First Edition (Washington, DC: Government Printing Office, 1947), p. 513.

75 Robert E. Peary, The North Pole, p. 333.

PART III

CHANGE

The Interplay of Cultures and the Environment, 1818–1940

1 Fernand Braudel, "History and the Social Sciences: The Long Durée," in On History (Trans. Sarah Matthews) (Chicago: University of Chicago Press, 1980), p. 27 ff.

2 Fernand Braudel, The Mediterranean and the Mediterranean World in the Age of Philip II, Vol. II, p. 704.

Chapter 10: Material and Technological Adaptations of the Contact Era

1 D.W. Meinig, "A Geographical Transect of the Atlantic World, ca 1750," in Eugene D. Genovese and Leonard Hochberg, Eds., Geographic Perspectives in History (Oxford: Basil Blackwell, Ltd., 1989), p. 200.

2 Anthony Wilden, System and Structure: Essays in Communication and Exchange, 2nd Edition (London: Tavistock Publications, 1980) pp. 367, 507.

3 Captain John Ross, A Voyage of Discovery, p. 147.

4 Ibid.

5 Inuuterssuaq Uvdloriaq, The Narrative of Qitdlarssuaq, pp. 88-89.

6 Richard Vaughan, Northwest Greenland: A History, pp. 68-69.

7 BCLSC, Donald B. MacMillan Collection, Diary No. 56, "Ethnological Notes," p. 324, Section entitled "Harpoon"; citing J.E. Nourse, Narrative of the Second Arctic Expedition Made by Charles Francis Hall: His Voyage to Repulse Bay, Sledge Journeys in the Straits of Fury and Hecla and to King William's Land and Residence Among the Eskimos During the Years 1864–69 (Washington, DC: Government Printing Office, 1879), p. 62.

8 Clements Markham, "On the Arctic Highlanders," in A Selection of Papers on Arctic Geography and Ethnology (London: John Murray, 1875), pp. 176-77.

9 Sherard Osborn, Stray Leaves from an Arctic Journal, p. 204.

10 LCMD, William S. Lovell, Journal of a Cruise in the Arctic Regions in Search of Sir John Franklin, 1850–1855 [unpublished manuscript], Entry for 17 July 1855.

11 Commander E.A. Inglefield, A Summer Search for Sir John Franklin, p. 61.

12 Ibid., p. 62.

13 Ibid., p. 61.

14 Lieut. Parker Snow, Voyage of the Prince Albert in Search of Sir John Franklin: A Narrative of Every-Day Life in the Arctic Seas (Paris: A. and W. Galignant and Co. and Baudry's European Library, 1851), p. 25.

15 Sir Allen Young, The Two Voyages of the Pandora in 1875 and 1876, p. 157.

16 Elisha Kent Kane, Arctic Explorations, Vol. I, p. 442.

17 Richard Vaughan, Northwest Greenland: A History, p. 65.

18 Captain Sir G.S. Nares, Narrative of a Voyage to the Polar Sea During 1875-6 in HM Ships Alert and Discovery, Vol. I, pp. 41-42.

19 Sir Allen Young, *The Two Voyages of the Pandora in 1875 and 1876*, p. 158.

20 A. Barclay Walker, *The Cruise of the Esquimaux, Steam Whaler to Davis Straits and Baffin Bay, April-October 1899* (Liverpool: The Liverpool Printing and Stationary Company Ltd., 1900), p. 29.

21 Angelo Heilprin, *The Arctic Problem and Narrative of the Peary Relief Expedition of the Academy of Natural Sciences of Philadelphia* (Philadelphia: Contemporary Publishing Co., 1893), p. 102.

22 USNA, RG 401(1)((A), Robert E. Peary Papers, Peary Diary Transcripts, 1871-1900, "Diary (typed) 1900," Letter of Instruction to Matt [Henson], 15 February 1900.

23 USNA, RG 401(1)(A), Robert E. Peary Papers, Papers Relating to Arctic Expeditions, Diary Transcripts 1871-1900, File: "Diary (typed) 1899," "Memoranda for Henson during journey from *Windward* to Fort Conger with five Eskimos and five sledges," 3 April 1899.

24 H.P. Steensby, "Contributions to the Ethnology and Anthropogeography of the Polar Eskimos," *Meddelelser om Grønland*, Vol. 34, No. 7 (1910), pp. 348-49.

25 Quoted in Daniel W. Streeter, *An Arctic Rodeo* (New York: G.P. Putnam's Sons, 1929), p. 151.

26 USNA, RG 401(1)(A), Robert E. Peary Papers, Papers Relating to Arctic Expeditions, 1886-1909, T.S. Dedrick, Diaries, Notebooks, and Other Papers, 1898-1901, Miscellaneous Papers of T.S. Dedrick, Field Notes, VI, Folder 6, "Trade with Natives, Anortok, Fall 1901."

27 BCLSC, Donald B. MacMillan Collection, Diaries, Journals, Logs, Etc., Crocker Land Expedition, MacMillan "Journal No. 3," 12 April 1916 to 2 April 1917, Entry for 22 October 1916, p. 202.

28 LCMD, William S. Lovell, "Journal of a Cruise in the Arctic Regions in Search of Sir John Franklin, 1850-1855," Entry for 17 August 1851 [about 12 miles south of Etah].

29 Sir Allen Young, *The Two Voyages of the Pandora in 1875 and 1876*, p. 194.

30 Eivind Astrup, *With Peary Near the Pole*, p. 103.

31 Ibid., p. 135.

32 H.P. Steensby, "Contributions to the Ethnology and Anthropogeography of the Polar Eskimos," p. 356.

33 W. Elmer Ekblaw, "The Material Response of the Polar Eskimo to their Far Arctic Environment," pp. 8-9.

34 Ibid., pp. 72-73.

35 Christian Vibe, "The Marine Mammals and the Marine Fauna in the Thule District," p. 72.

36 NAC, RG 18, Accn. 84-85/084, Vol. 33, File G-516-37, Part 3, Letter of Knud Rasmussen to O.D. Skelton, Undersecretary of State for External Affairs, 5 May 1925, pp. 1-2; see also Peter Freuchen, *Arctic Adventure: My Life in the Frozen North* (New York: Farrar and Rinehart, 1935), p. 32.

37 Peter Freuchen, I Sailed with Rasmussen (New York: Julian Messner, 1958), pp. 57-72.

38 Rolf Gilberg, "The Polar Eskimo Population, Thule District, North Greenland," *Meddelelser om Grønland*, Vol. 203, No. 3 (1976), p. 47.

39 Malaurie, *The Last Kings of Thule*, pp. 120-21.

40 Ibid., p. 120.

41 See Knud Rasmussen's letter of 8 March 1920, quoted in William Barr, *Back from the Brink*, p. 88.

42 David Haig-Thomas, *Tracks in the Snow*, p. 15; see also Dr. Frederick A. Cook, *My Attainment of the Pole*, p. 196.

43 Knud Rasmussen, *Greenland by the Polar Sea*, p. 17.

44 NAC, RG 85, Vol. 759, File 4829, pp. 459-60 [Transcript of Donald B. MacMillan's testimony before the Musk-ox Commission]. I would like to thank Kenn Harper of Iqaluit and Rene Wissink, formerly with Ellesmere Island National Park Reserve, for this reference.

45 See, for example, Harry Whitney, *Hunting with the Eskimos*, pp. 272-329; and Harrison J. Hunt, North to the Horizon, pp. 65-70.

46 Knud Rasmussen, *Greenland by the Polar Sea*, p. 17.

47 Peter Freuchen, *Book of the Eskimos*, p. 91.

48 NAC, RCMP Records, RG18, Accn. 84-85/084, Vol. 32, File G-516-37, Letter of George Comer, East Haddam, Connecticut, to Vilhjalmur Stefansson, 29 May 1919.

49 Donald MacMillan, *Four Years in the White North* (New York and London: Harper Brothers, 1918), p. 307. The quoted passage is from MacMillan's expedition journal.

50 NAC, RG 85, Vol. 584, File No. 571, Copy of letter of Knud Rasmussen, Copenhagen, to the Administrator of the Colonies in Greenland, 8 March 1920.

51 Peter Freuchen, *Book of the Eskimos*, p. 303.

52 NAC, RG 85, Vol. 584, File No. 571, Copy of Letter of Knud Rasmussen, Copenhagen, to the Administrator of the Colonies in Greenland, 8 March 1920.

53 Donald B. MacMillan, "Geographical Report of the Crocker Land Expedition, 1913-1917," *Bulletin of the American Museum of Natural History*, Vol. 56, "1926-1929" (1930), pp. 426-27.

54 Christian Vibe, "The Marine Mammals and the Marine Fauna in the Thule District," pp. 76-77.

55 Ibid., p. 18.

56 Ibid., p. 8.

57 Christian Vibe, "Arctic Animals in Relation to Climatic Fluctuations," p. 54.

58 NAC, Department of Indian and Northern Affairs Records, File 401-23-1, Vol. 10, Passage of Greenland Eskimos Through Canadian Territory, Memorandum by Constable J.L. Gubbels, RCMP Detachment, Grise Fiord, 22 May 1968.

59 Personal communication with Renee Wissink, former Chief Park Warden, Ellesmere Island National Park Reserve, July 1990. See also Memorandum of R. Popko, Northwest Territories, Department of Renewable Resources, Pond Inlet, NWT, re: "Polar Bear Hunting by Greenlanders in Canada," 11 May 1987 [Copy on file at the Western Canada Service Centre, Parks Canada, Winnipeg].

60 NAC, Defence Research Board Records, RG 24, Vol. 4235, File DRBS-3-780-43 (Vol. 1), Memorandum of G.S. Hume to O.M. Solandt, 22 January 1953, p. 2.

61 Captain Sir G.S. Nares, *Narrative of a Voyage to the Polar Sea During 1875-6 in HM Ships* Alert *and* Discovery, Vol. I, pp. 53-54.

62 BCLSC, Donald B. MacMillan Collection, Diaries, Journals, Logs, Etc., "Crocker Land" Expedition Diary No. 19/5, 12 February 1914 – 26 March 1915, Entry for 14 February 1914.

63 Peter Freuchen, *Arctic Adventure: My Life in the Frozen North* (Farrar and Rinehart, 1935), p. 292.

64 BCLSC, Donald B. MacMillan Collection, Diaries, Journals, Logs, Etc., "Crocker Land" Expedition, Journal No. 3, 12 April 1916 - 2 April 1917, Entry for 22 January 1917, p. 278.

65 Harry Whitney, *Hunting With the Eskimos*, p. 244.

66 BCLSC, Robert Abrams Bartlett Papers, Books, Articles, Etc. by Robert A. Bartlett, "From the Crow's Nest": "The First Roosevelt Expedition" (1905-06), p. 33.

67 Peter Freuchen, *Arctic Adventure*, p. 170.

68 Hans Hendrik, *Memoirs of Hans Hendrik*, p. 37.

69 John Edwards Caswell, *Arctic Frontiers*, pp. 109-10.

70 USNA, RG 27, Records of the Weather Bureau, Lady Franklin Bay Expedition Papers, Vol. 2, "Manuscripts of Reports, Narratives, and Appendices," Report on a Sledge Journey from the 19 March to the 2 May, 1882, by Dr. Octave Pavy to the Commanding Officer, LFB Expedition, Received at Fort Conger, 23 July 1882.

71 Great Britain, Admiralty, *Journals and Proceedings of the Arctic Expedition, 1875-6*, Letter of R.W. Coppinger to Captain H.F. Stephenson, HMS *Discovery* at Barden Bay, 12 September 1876, p. 423.

72 Ibid., p. 424.

73 Captain Leopold M'Clintock, *The Voyage of the* Fox *in the Arctic Seas: A Narrative of the Fate of Sir John Franklin and His Companions* (London: John Murray, 1859).

74 Elisha Kent Kane, *Arctic Explorations*, Vol. II, p. 98.

75 See Robert E. Peary, *Secrets of Polar Travel*, p. 197.

76 Ibid., p. 198.

77 Otto Sverdrup, *New Land*, Vol. I, p. 110.

78 Robert A. Bartlett, *The Log of Bob Bartlett: The True Story of Forty Years of Seafaring and Exploration* (New York: G.P. Putnam's Sons, 1928), p. 188.

79 Robert E. Peary, *Secrets of Polar Travel*, p. 73.

80 Ibid., p. 179.

81 Robert E. Peary, "Living Off the Country," *Century Magazine* (October, 1917), pp. 907-19; and *Secrets of Polar Travel*, Chapter 8, pp. 206-39.

82 Robert E. Peary, *Secrets of Polar Travel*, p. 229.

83 Ibid., p. 78.

84 See Lauge Koch, *Report on the Danish Bicentenary Jubilee Expedition North of Greenland 1920–23* (Copenhagen: C.A. Reitzels, Forlag, 1927), pp. 12-13.

85 Nicholas Senn, *In the Heart of the Arctic*, pp. 212-13.

86 Barbara F. Schweger, "Clothing the Early Expeditions: An Essential Contribution by the Native Seamstresses," *Yukon Historical Museums Association Proceedings*, No. 2 (1984), pp. 52-53.

87 Ibid., p. 51.

88 USNA, RG 401(1)(A), Robert E. Peary Papers, Papers Relating to Arctic Expeditions, 1886-1909 North Polar: 1905-06, Box 1, File "Letters Rec[eived]. Henson, 1905-06." List appended to letter of Matthew Henson, SS *Roosevelt*, Cape Sheridan, to Robert Peary, 16 December 1905.

89 Robert E. Peary, *Secrets of Polar Travel*, pp. 167-73.

90 August Sonntag, *Professor Sonntag's Thrilling Narrative of the Grinnell Exploring Expedition to the Arctic Ocean in the Years 1853, 1854, and 1855, In Search of Sir John Franklin, Under the Command of Dr. E.K. Kane, USN* (Philadelphia: J.H.C. Whiting, n.d.), p. 125.

91 USNA, RG401(1)(A), Robert E. Peary Papers, Papers Relating to Arctic Expeditions, 1886-1909, Greenland: 1898-1902, Peary Diaries, 1900-02, Peary Diary, 16 September to 22 October 1900, Entries for 3 and 9 October 1900.

92 Informal comments by Abraham Pijamini on presentation by Lyle Dick on the "Muskox Land" book manuscript, Grise Fiord, Nunavut, 25 May 2001.

93 Robert E. Peary, *Secrets of Polar Travel*, pp. 228-29.

94 Ibid., p. 207.

95 Ibid.

96 Robert E. Peary, *Nearest the Pole*, p. 80.

97 Robert E. Peary, *Northward Over the "Great Ice"*, Vol I, p. lxxvii.

98 Robert E. Peary, "Moving on the North Pole: Outlines of My Arctic Campaign," *McClure's Magazine*, (March 1899), p. 424.

99 See Guy Mary-Rousselière, "Iglulik," in David Damas, Ed., *Handbook of North American Indians*, Vol. 5 "Arctic," p. 433; J.E. Nourse, Ed., *Narrative of the Second Arctic Expedition Made by Charles Francis Hall*, pp. 128, 371; Franz Boas, *The Central Eskimo* (Lincoln, Nebraska: University of Nebraska Press, 1964), pp. 138-39; and Captain Leopold M'Clintock, *The Voyage of the* Fox *in the Arctic Seas*, pp. 258-59. See also "Communal Igloos" in Peter Nabokov and Robert Easton, *Native American Architecture* (New York/ Oxford: Oxford University Press, 1989), p. 197.

100 Robert E. Peary, "Report of R.E. Peary, USN, on Work Done in the Arctic in 1898-1902," *Bulletin of the American Geographical Society*, Vol. 35 (December 1903), p. 508.

101 Robert E. Peary, *Nearest the Pole*, p. 61.

102 Robert E. Peary, "In Greely's Old Camp at Fort Conger," *McClure's Magazine*, Vol. 14 (January 1900), p. 239.

103 Ibid., pp. 239-40.

104 USNA, RG 401(1)(A) Robert E. Peary Papers, Papers Relating to Arctic Expeditions,1886-1909, Greenland 1898-1902, Dr. T.S. Dedrick Diaries, Notebooks, and Other Papers, Diary of 17 January to 21 May 1899, Entry for 11 May 1899.

105 Robert E. Peary, *Secrets of Polar Travel*, p. 153.

106 USNA, RG 410(1)(A), Robert E. Peary Papers, Papers Relating to Arctic Expeditions, 1886-1909, Greenland, 1898-1902, Peary Diary, July-August 1900.

107 Virgil Broodhagen, Caroline Parmenter, and Larry Konotopetz, "Fort Conger, Ellesmere Island, NWT, As Found Recording," Unpublished Report, Drawings, and Photographs, Canadian Parks Service, Prairie and Northern Region, July, 1979, Photograph negative no. R3-11-18; and C. Phillips Parmenter, M. Burnip, and R. Ferguson, "Preliminary Report of the Second Season (1977) of Historical Archaeological Investigations in the High Arctic," Canadian Parks Service, National Historic Parks and Sites Branch Manuscript Report, Ottawa, 1978), pp. 235-36, 241.

108 C. Phillips Parmenter, M. Burnip, and R. Ferguson, "Preliminary Report of the Second Season (1977) of Historical Archaeological Investigations in the High Arctic," pp. 235-36.

109 USNA, RG 401(1)(A), Robert E. Peary Papers, Papers Relating to Arctic Expeditions, Greenland 1898-1902, Peary Diary Entry for 26 August 1900.

110 USNA, RG 401(1)(A), Robert E. Peary Papers, Papers Relating to Arctic Expeditions, Greenland 1898-1902, T.S. Dedrick Diaries and Other Papers, 1898-1901, Miscellaneous Papers and Field Notes, Entry for 25 October 1900.

111 Amos Rapoport, *House Form and Culture* (Englewood Cliffs, NJ: Prentice Hall, 1969), p. 98.

112 Robert E. Peary, *Secrets of Polar Travel*, pp. 155-56.

113 USNA, RG 401(1)(A), Robert E. Peary Papers, Papers Relating to Arctic Expeditions, 1886-1909, Greenland, 1898-1902, Peary Diary Entry for 20 December 1900.

114 Robert E. Peary, *Secrets of Polar Travel*, p. 154.

115 For a detailed discussion of Peary's development of the complex at Fort Conger, see Lyle Dick, "The Fort Conger Shelters and Vernacular Adaptation to the High Arctic," *Society for the Study of Architecture in Canada Bulletin*, Vol. 16, No. 1 (March 1991), pp. 13-23.

116 USNA, RG 401(1)(A), Robert E. Peary Papers, Papers Relating to Arctic Expeditions, 1886-1909, Greenland, 1898-1902, Peary Diary, January-April 1901, "My Domicile at Conger," pp. 1-5.

117 Robert E. Peary, *Secrets of Polar Travel*, pp. 154-55.

118 Ibid., p. 155; and USNA, RG 401(1)(A) Robert E. Peary Papers, Papers Relating to Arctic Expeditions, 1886-1909, Greenland, 1898-1902, Peary Diary, January-April 1901, "My Domicile at Conger."

119 Ibid., Greenland: 1898-1902, Box No. 3 of 6, Robert E. Peary Diaries 1900-01, Peary Diary Entry for 25 December 1900; see also Peary's own plan of the complex in USNA, RG 401(1)(A), Robert E. Peary Papers, Papers Relating to Arctic Expeditions, 1886-1909, Greenland, 1898-1902, Papers Relating to Expedition Plans, Supplies, Field Operations, LFB [Lady Franklin Bay], and Fort Conger, Cartographic Activities, Etc., 1898-1902, Box 6 of 6, File labelled "Drawing, Ft. Conger, Layout, Sled."

120 Walter Ekblaw, "Of Unknown Shores: The Traverse of Grant and Ellesmere Lands," in Donald B. MacMillan, Four Years in the White North, Appendix B; Large Koch, "Report on the Danish Jubilee Expedition North of Greenland, 1920-23," *Meddelelser om Grønland*, Vol. 70 (1927), pp. 60-63; and Edward Shackleton, *Arctic Journeys*, p. 241.

121 USNA, RG 401(1)(A), Robert E. Peary Papers, Papers Relating to Arctic Expeditions, 1886–1909, Greenland, 1898-1902, T.S. Dedrick Diaries, Notebooks, and Other Papers, VI, Folder 6, Field Notes, Miscellaneous Papers, Letter of T.S. Dedrick, Mouth of Crozier River, to Robert Peary, Fort Conger, 27 February 1901, pp. 4-5.

122 Ibid.

123 Robert E. Peary, *Secrets of Polar Travel*, pp. 157-58.

124 Quoted in Kwang-Chih Chang, "A Typology of Settlement and Community Patterns in Some Circumpolar Societies," p. 37.

125 H.P. Steensby, "The Polar Eskimos and the Polar Expeditions," *Fortnightly Review*, Vol. 92 (November 1909), pp. 891-902.

126 Ibid., p. 892.

Chapter 11: Intercultural Relations in the Contact Era

1 For an excellent account of the stresses of contact for an Inughuit person transplanted into American society, see Kenn Harper, *Give Me My Father's Body*.

2 Johan Carl Christian Petersen, *Dr. Kane's Voyage to the Polar Lands*, p. 150.

3 Hans Hendrik, *Memoirs of Hans Hendrik*, p. 32.

4 Johan Carl Christian Petersen, *Dr. Kane's Voyage to the Polar Lands*, p. 150.

5 L.H. Neatby, *Conquest of the Last Frontier*, p. 75.

6 USNA, RG 27, Records of the Weather Bureau, Lady Franklin Bay Expedition Papers, Box 12, Octave Pavy Notes and Letters, Pavy Diary Entry for 17 December 1881.

7 Hans Hendrik, *Memoirs of Hans Hendrik*, p. 24.

8 Elisha Kent Kane, *Arctic Explorations*, Vol. I, pp. 144-45.

9 Ibid.

10 Hans Hendrik, *Memoirs of Hans Hendrik*, pp. 37-38.

11 Ibid., p. 90.

12 NAC, Reginald Baldwin Fulford Journal, 29 May 1875 to 30 September 1876, Entry for 20 January 1876.

13 NAC, Sir Albert Hastings Markham Fonds, Notebooks, n.d., Microfilm reel A-822.

14 NAC, Pelham Aldrich Journals, 29 May 1875 to 14 August 1876, Entries for July 1875, Microfilm reel A-822 [by permission of the Scott Polar Research Institute, Cambridge, Ms. 278/1].

15 USNA, RG 27, Records of the Weather Bureau, Lady Franklin Bay Expedition Papers, Box 12, Octave Pavy Notes and Letters, Pavy Diary Entry for 6 December 1881.

16 Ibid., Entry for 7 December 1881.

17 Adolphus W. Greely, *Report on the Proceedings of the United States Expedition to Lady Franklin Bay, Grinnell Land*, Vol. I, "Report of the Commanding Officer," p. 14

18 LCMD, Papers of Adolphus Washington Greely, Military Papers, Container No. 71, Summary of the Journal of Lieutenant A.W. Greely, Commanding Lady Franklin Bay Expedition, August 1881 to July 1882, Entry dated 13 December 1881.

19 USNA, RG 27, Records of the Weather Bureau, Lady Franklin Bay Expedition Papers, Box 12, Octave Pavy Notes and Letters, Pavy Diary Entry for 6 December 1881.

20 USNA, RG 27, Records of the Weather Bureau, Lady Franklin Bay Expedition Papers, Box 2, "Manuscripts of Reports, Narratives, and Appendices," Lieutenant Adolphus Greely Journal, Volume 1, Entry for 8 December 1881.

21 USNA, RG 27, Records of the Weather Bureau, Lady Franklin Bay Expedition Papers, Box 12, Pavy Notes and Letters, Pavy Diary Entry for 8 December 1881.

22 USNA, RG 27, Records of the Weather Bureau, Lady Franklin Bay Expedition Papers, Box 2, "Manuscripts of Reports, Narratives, and Appendices," Lieutenant Adolphus Greely Journal, Volume 1, Entry for 13 December 1881.

23 USNA, RG 27, Papers of General David L. Brainard, Journal, 1881-84, Vol. I, Entry for 18 December 1881.

24 USNA, RG 27, Records of the Weather Bureau, Lady Franklin Bay Expedition Papers, Box 2, "Manuscripts of Reports, Narratives, and Appendices," Lieutenant Adolphus Greely Journal, Volume 1, Entry for 15 December 1881.

25 Ibid.

26 USNA, RG 27, Papers of General David L. Brainard, Journal, 1881-84, Vol. I, Entry for 15 December 1881.

27 24 USNA, RG 27, Records of the Weather Bureau, Lady Franklin Bay Expedition Records, Box 12, Extracts from Adolphus Greely's Journal, Entry for 4 January 1883.

28 USNA, RG 27, Papers of General David L. Brainard, Journal, 1881-84, Vol. I, Entry for 18 December 1881.

29 Lyle Dick, "'Pibloktoq' (Arctic Hysteria): A Construction of European-Inuit Relations?" *Arctic Anthropology* (1995), Vol. 32 No. 2, 1995, pp. 1-42.

30 USNA, RG 401(1)(A), Robert E. Peary Papers. Papers Relating to Arctic Expeditions, 1886-1909, Greenland, 1898-1902, Robert E. Peary Diaries, 1900-1901, Diary Entries for 11-21 April 1900.

31 Ibid.

32 Ibid., Entries for 22 April to 4 May 1900.

33 USNA, RG 401(1)(A) Robert E. Peary Papers, Papers Relating to Arctic Expeditions, 1886-1909, Greenland, 1898-1902. T.S. Dedrick Diaries, Notebooks and Other Papers, 1898-1901, VI, Box 4 of 6, Dedrick Diary, 28 June to 23 August 1900, Entry for 7 July 1900.

34 Jean Blodgett, *The Coming and Going of the Shaman: Eskimo Shamanism and Art* (Winnipeg, Manitoba: Winnipeg Art Gallery, 1978), p. 203.

35 Jane M. Murphy, *An Epidemiological Study of Psychopathology in an Eskimo Village.* PhD dissertation, Cornell University, Ithaca, NY, 1960, p. 90.

36 USNA, RG 401(1)(A) Robert E. Peary Papers, Papers Relating to Arctic Expeditions, 1886-1909. Greenland, 1898-1902. T.S. Dedrick Diaries and Field Notebooks, 1900, Diary Entry for 23 September 1900.

37 Ibid., Entry for 26 September 1900.

38 Ibid., Entry for 25 October 1900.

39 A.A. Brill, "Piblockto or Hysteria Among Peary's Eskimos," *Journal of Nervous and Mental Disease*, Vol. 40 (1913), p. 517.

40 Jean Malaurie, *The Last Kings of Thule*, p. 202.

41 BCLSC, Robert Abrams Bartlett Papers, Books, Articles, Etc. by Robert A. Bartlett, "From the Crow's Nest": "The First Roosevelt Expedition" (1905-06), p. 36.

42 Fitzhugh Green, *Peary: The Man Who Refused to Fail*, p. 224.

43 Jean Malaurie, *The Last Kings of Thule*, p. 202.

44 Robert E. Peary, *The North Pole*, p. 127.

45 George Borup, *A Tenderfoot With Peary* (New York: Frederick A. Stokes, 1911), p. 87.

46 Donald B. MacMillan, *How Peary Reached the Pole* (Boston and New York: Houghton Mifflin, 1934), p. 101.

47 Frederick A. Cook, *My Attainment of the Pole*; Knud Rasmussen, *Foran Dagens Oje: Liv I Grønland* (Copenhagen: Nordisk Forlag, 1915); H.P. Steensby, "Contributions to the Ethnology and Anthropogeography of the Polar Eskimos"; Harry Whitney, *Hunting With the Eskimos*; Jean Malaurie, *The Last Kings of Thule*; and Wally Herbert, *Hunters of the Polar North: The Eskimo* (Amsterdam: Time-Life Books, 1981).

48 Peter Freuchen, *Book of the Eskimo*, p. 56.

49 Only a few years after the 1909 expedition, Peary's rival Dr. Frederick Cook wrote that Ahngmaloktok and other former employees accused Peary of leaving a party "to die of cold and hunger" at Fort Conger. Cook was hardly a disinterested observer, but Inughuit reports of perceived abandonment by Peary may partially explain the anxiety represented in the epidemic. Dr. Frederick A. Cook, *My Attainment of the Pole*, p. 454.

50 Barbara Winstead, "Hysteria," in C.S. Widom, Ed., *Sex Roles and Psychopathology* (New York: Plenum Press, 1984), p. 81.

51 BCLSC, Robert Abrams Bartlett Papers, Books, Articles, Etc. by Robert A. Bartlett, "From the Crow's Nest": "The First Roosevelt Expedition" (1905-06), p. 14.

52 A.A. Brill, "Piblockto or Hysteria Among Peary's Eskimos," p. 516.

53 USNA, RG 401(1)(A), Robert E. Peary Papers Relating to Arctic Expeditions, 1886-1909, Greenland, 1898-1902, Peary Diary, March-April 1901, Entry for 11 March 1901.

54 BCLSC, Robert Abrams Bartlett Papers, "From the Crow's Nest": "The First Roosevelt Expedition," p. 22.

55 USNA, RG 401(1)(A), Robert E. Peary Papers, Papers Relating to Arctic Expeditions, 1886-1909 North Polar: 1905-06, Diaries, Journals and Logs; Correspondence and Instructions, 1905-06 [Box 1 of 2], Dr. Louis Wolf Journal, 1905-06, Entry for 16 February 1906 [at Cape Sheridan].

56 55 Hans P. Steensby, "The Polar Eskimos and the Polar Expeditions," *Fortnightly Review*, Vol. 92 (1909), p. 892.

57 Rolf Gilberg, "Polar Eskimo," in David Damas, Ed., *Handbook of North American Indians*, Vol. 5, "Arctic," p. 590; See also H.P. Steensby, "The Polar Eskimos and the Polar Expeditions," pp. 891-902.

58 NAC, RG 18, Vol. 3015, Bache Peninsula Detachment Daily Journal, Entry for 6 April 1928.

59 Ibid., Entry for 19 April 1928.

60 Lyle Dick, "'Pibloktoq' (Arctic Hysteria): A Construction of European-Inuit Relations?" *Arctic Anthropology*, Vol. 32, No. 2 (1995), Appendix B, pp. 41-42.

61 Ibid., pp. 18-23.

62 Laurence J. Kirmayer and Harry Minas, "The Future of Cultural Psychiatry: An International Perspective," *Canadian Journal of Psychiatry*, Vol. 45, No. 5 (June 2000), p. 239; and L.J. Kirmayer, "Cultural Psychiatry: From Museums of Exotica to the Global Agora," *Current Opinion in Psychiatry*, Vol. 11, No. 2 (1998), pp. 183-89.

63 Alan M. Klein, "Adaptive Strategies and Process on the Plains: The 19th Century Cultural Sink," PhD. Dissertation, University of New York at Buffalo, Buffalo, NY, 1977.

64 USNA, RG 401(1)(A) Robert E. Peary Papers. Papers Relating to Arctic Expeditions, 1886-1909, Expeditions: Greenland 1886, Notebook 1886, Equipment Lists, Notebook, Planning Notes, 1885-86, Notes dated 13 October 1885.

65 Ibid.

66 USNA, RG 401(1)(A), Robert E. Peary Papers, Papers Relating to Arctic Expeditions, 1886–1909, Greenland, 1898-1902, Box No. 2 of 6, Peary Diary Transcriptions, 1898–1902, Diary entry for Tuesday, 31 July 1900.

67 Peter Freuchen, *Vagrant Viking: My Life and Adventures* (New York: Julian Messner, 1953), p. 89.

68 Ibid., p. 90.

69 Robert E. Peary, *Northward Over the "Great Ice"*, Vol. I, p. 500, and Vol. II, p. 394. See also the photographs entitled "Flashlight Study" in Vol. II, pp. 366-67.

70 Ibid., p. 406.

71 LCMD, Papers of Evelyn Briggs Baldwin, Container No. 7, Polar Expedition Records, 1893-1915, Baldwin Diary, 20 August 1893 to 15 December 1893, Entry for 21 November 1893.

72 Ibid., Entries for 22 and 23 November 1893.

73 Ibid., Entries for 28 November and 10 December 1893.

74 BCLSC, Photographs NP-24 and NP-25 by Donald B. MacMillan, both labelled "Alnayah with 'Piblock-to' (Arctic Hysteria)," Cape Sheridan, 1908-09.

75 USNA, RG 401(1)(A), Robert E. Peary Papers, Papers Relating to Arctic Expeditions, 1886–1909, Greenland, 1898-1902, T.S. Dedrick Diaries, Notebooks and Other Papers, Letter of Dedrick to Peary, 27 February 1901; Lyle Dick, "The Fort Conger Shelters and Vernacular Adaptation to the High Arctic," *SSAC Bulletin* (Society for the Study of Architecture in Canada), Vol. 16, No. 1 (March 1991), p. 22.

76 USNA, RG 401(1)(A), Robert E. Peary Papers, Robert E. Peary Papers, Papers Relating to Arctic Expeditions, 1886-1909, Greenland, 1898-1902, Peary Diary Entry for 5 April 1901.

77 NAC, RG 18, Vol. 3015, Bache Peninsula Detachment Diary for 1928, Entries for 24 March, 6 April, and 19 April 1928.

78 Peter Freuchen, *Book of the Eskimos*, p. 117.

79 Robert E. Peary, The North Pole, p. 74.

80 NAC, RG 18, Accn. 84-85/084, Vol. 33, File G-516-37, Part 3, Letter of C.E. Wilcox, Inspector Commanding Ellesmere Sub-District, on board the CGS Arctic, to the Officer Commanding, Headquarters Division, RCMP, Ottawa, 25 August 1925.

81 NAC, RG 85, File 6887, Letter of Cortlandt Starnes, Commissioner, RCMP, to O.S. Finnie, Director, North-West Territories and Yukon, 31 July 1931.

82 NAC, RG 85, File 6887, Letter of Knud Rasmussen, Copenhagen, to O.S. Finnie, Ottawa, 16 July 1930.

83 Robert E. Peary, The North Pole, pp. 252-53.

84 See Peter Freuchen, Adventures in the Arctic, pp. 200-01; and Vagrant Viking (Trans. Johan Hambro) (New York: Julian Messner, 1953), p. 138.

85 NGSL, Adolphus Greely Collection, Notebook, Accn. no. 13439, News clipping: "Reports on Killing of Peary's Aide: Rasmussen Sends Results of Inquiry Into Marvin Murder to Danish Legation" [1926].

86 Ibid., News clipping: George Palmer Putnam, "Eskimo Killed Prof. Marvin, Peary Aide; Confesses Arctic Crime of 17 Years Ago; Victim, Reported Drowned, Was Shot," The New York Times, 25 September 1926, pp. 1-2.

87 Ibid., pp. 1-2.

88 Ibid., p. 2.

89 Ibid., p. 2.

90 Ibid., News clipping: "Reports on Killing of Peary's Aide: Rasmussen Sends Results of Inquiry Into Marvin Murder to Danish Legation" [1926].

91 BCLSC, Robert Abrams Bartlett Papers, Books, Articles, Etc. by Robert A. Bartlett, "From the Crow's Nest": "The Conquest of the Pole" (1908-09), p. 14.

92 Ibid., p. 6.

93 Captain Thomas F. Hall, "The Murder of Professor Ross G. Marvin," in W. Henry Lewin, The Great North Pole Fraud (London: The C.W. Daniel Company, 1935), p. 169.

94 Robert Peary, Note to Ross Marvin, 11 March 1909, quoted in Donald B. MacMillan, How Peary Reached the Pole, p. 182.

95 Harrison J. Hunt and Ruth Hunt Thompson, North to the Horizon: Searching for Peary's Crocker Land, p. 57.

96 BCLSC, Donald B. MacMillan Collection, Diaries, No. 19/5, Crocker Land Expedition, MacMillan Diary, 12 February 1914 to 26 March 1915, Entry for 4 May 1914.

97 BCLSC, Donald B. MacMillan Collection, Correspondence 1914, MacMillan, Etah, Greenland, to D.L. Brainard, 25 August 1914.

98 Harrison J. Hunt and Ruth Hunt Thompson, North to the Horizon, p. 57.

99 BCLSC, Donald B. MacMillan Collection, Diary No. 25, Fitzhugh Green's Field Notebook, 7 February 1914 to 20 May 1914.

100 Ibid.

101 Ibid., Entry for Friday, 1 May 1914.

102 BCLSC, Donald B. MacMillan Collection, Diaries, No. 19/5, Crocker Land Expedition, MacMillan Diary, 12 February 1914 to 26 March 1915.

103 Ibid., Diary No. 25, Fitzhugh Green's Field Notebook, Entry for 4 May 1914.

104 Kenn Harper, Give Me My Father's Body, pp. 201-2.

105 Donald B. MacMillan, Four Years in the White North, p. 92.

106 BCLSC, Donald B. MacMillan Collection, Diaries, Journals, Logs, Etc., Crocker Land Expedition, Journal No. 17, 12 February 1914 to 26 March 1915, p. 83.

107 Kenn Harper, Give Me My Father's Body, p. 202.

108 Fitzhugh Green, "The Crocker Land Expedition: The Story of the Last Extensive Dog-Sledge Expedition in the Arctic," Natural History (American Museum of Natural History) Vol. 28 (1928), p. 475.

109 NGSL, Adolphus Greely Collection, Notebook, Accn. no. 13439, News clipping: "Doubts Marvin 'Cracked' in Arctic: Fitzhugh Green Thinks Eskimoes Become Panicky Over the Shortage of Food: Tells How He Shot One: Explorer Declares Native

Tried to Run Away With Provisions After a Storm," *The New York Times*, 25 September 1926, p. 2.

110 Everett S. Allen, *Arctic Odyssey: The Life of Rear Admiral Donald B. MacMillan*, p. 182.

111 Donald B. MacMillan, "Geographical Report of the Crocker Land Expedition, 1913–1917," *Bulletin of the American Museum of Natural History*, Vol. 56, "1926–29," (1930), p. 400.

112 These episodes are suggestive of the Greenlandic Native tradition, reported by ethnographers in the nineteenth century, of the *kivitoq*. According to this tradition, persons estranged from other members of their communities often went into self-imposed exile to live like hermits. See Henrik Rink, *Tales and Traditions of the Eskimo* (Ed. Robert Brown) (Edinburgh and London: William Blackwood and Sons, 1875), pp. 260-62.

113 See Lyle Dick, "The Fort Conger Shelters and Vernacular Adaptation to the High Arctic," p. 22.

114 Robert E. Peary, *The North Pole*, p. 333.

Chapter 12: Cultural Contact and High Arctic Ecology, 1818-1940

1 Robert Anstruther Goodsir, *An Arctic Voyage to Baffin's Bay and Lancaster Sound in Search of Friends with Sir John Franklin* (London: John Van Voorst, 1850), pp. 58-59.

2 Elisha Kent Kane, *The United States Grinnell Expedition*, p. 132.

3 Lieut. W. Parker Snow, *Voyage of the* Prince Albert, p. 55.

4 Sherard Osborn, *Stray Leaves from an Arctic Journal*, pp. 265-66.

5 Hans Hendrik, *Memoirs of Hans Hendrik*, p. 44.

6 Rolf Gilberg, "The Polar Eskimo Population, Thule District, North Greenland," *Meddelelser om Grønland*, Vol. 203, No. 3 (1976), 27-28.

7 Robert E. Peary, *Northward Over the "Great Ice,"* Vol. II, p. 514.

8 Rolf Gilberg, "The Polar Eskimo Population, Thule District, North Greenland," p. 29.

9 USNA, Robert E. Peary Papers, RG 401(1)(A), Papers Relating to Arctic Expeditions, 1886-1909, Greenland, 1898-1902, Peary Diary Entry for 6 January 1902.

10 Ibid.

11 NAC, RG 18, Accn. 85-86/084, Vol. 33, File G-516-37, Part 2, Memorandum of C.E. Wilcox, Craig Harbour Detachment, to the Officer Commanding, Headquarters Division, RCMP, Ottawa, 13 August 1923; NAC, RG 85, Vol. 348, File 201-1-8, J.D. Craig, "The 1923 Expedition to the Arctic Islands," unpublished manuscript, 22 February 1926, p. 21.

12 NAC, RG 18, Accn. No. 84-85/084, Vol. 33, File G-516-37, Part 3, Fol. 422. Messages filed by Harwood Steele, Godhavn, Greenland, to the Northwest Territories and Yukon Branch, 10 August 1925.

13 NAC, RG 18, Vol. 3014, Bache Peninsula Detachment Diary for 1927, Entry for 18 June.

14 Rolf Gilberg, "The Polar Eskimo Population, Thule District," p. 29.

15 Ibid.

16 Ibid.

17 Ibid.

18 BCLSC, Donald B. MacMillan Collection, Diaries, No. 19, Crocker Land Expedition, Diaries, Diary 12 February 1914 to 26 March 1915, Entry for 14 February 1914.

19 Interview with Dr. Milton Freeman by Lyle Dick, Edmonton, March 1989.

20 Rolf Gilberg, "The Polar Eskimo Population, Thule District," p. 52.

21 Sir John Leslie, *Narrative of Discovery and Adventure in the Polar Seas and Regions, with Illustrations of their Climate, Geology, and Natural History, and an Account of the Whale Fishery* (Edinburgh: Oliver and Boyd, 1835), p. 445.

22 Richard Vaughan, "Bowhead Whaling in Davis Strait and Baffin Bay During the 18th and 19th Centuries," *Polar Record*, Vol. 23, No. 144 (1986), p. 294.

23 Basil Lubbock, *The Arctic Whalers* (Glasgow: Brown, Son, and Ferguson, Ltd., 1937), pp. 255-56.

24 For an account of the disaster of 1830, when 22 whaling ships were lost in the pack ice of northern Baffin Bay, see Sir John Leslie, *Narrative of Discovery and Adventure in the Polar Seas and Regions*, pp. 450-57.

25 See W. Gillies Ross, "The Annual Catch of Greenland (Bowhead) Whales in Waters North of Canada 1719-1915," Arctic, Vol. 32, No. 2 (June 1979), Table 3, pp. 102-6.

26 Ibid., p. 112.

27 Ibid.

28 Edward Mitchell and Randall R. Reeves, "Catch History and Cumulative Catch Estimates of Initial Population Size of Cetaceans in the Eastern Canadian Arctic," *Report of the International Whaling Commission*, Vol. 31 (1981), p. 648.

29 Richard Vaughan, *The Arctic: A History* (Dover, New Hampshire: Alan Sutton Publishing, 1994), p. 95.

30 NAC, Canada, Department of Marine and Fisheries, 1894-1908, File 1536, Part 1, Fol. 392, J.E. Bernier, Pond Inlet, to Hon. L.P. Brodeur, Minister of Marine and Fisheries, 2 October 1906.

31 Basil Lubbock, The Arctic Whalers, p. 450.

32 Edward Mitchell and Randall R. Reeves, "Catch History and Cumulative Catch Estimates," p. 651.

33 Robert E. Peary, "Living Off the Country," pp. 915-16.

34 Ibid., pp. 907-19.

35 Christian Vibe, "The Marine Mammals and the Marine Fauna in the Thule District," p. 22.

36 Robert E. Peary, "Living Off the Country," p. 909.

37 Christian Vibe, "The Marine Mammals and the Marine Fauna in the Thule District," p. 22.

38 Robert E. Peary, "Living Off the Country," pp. 908-10.

39 William Henry Hobbs, *Peary*, p. 241.

40 Christian Vibe, "The Marine Mammals and the Marine Fauna in the Thule District," pp. 22-23.

41 Capt. Sir G.S. Nares, *Narrative of a Voyage to the Polar Sea*, Vol. I, p. 113.

42 Ibid., Vol. II, Appendix 17, pp. 352-53.

43 A.W. Greely, "Arctic Exploration, with Reference to Grinnell Land," p. 160.

44 The account of Peary's fall hunting trip to the interior of northern Ellesmere Island is derived from USNA, Robert E. Peary Papers, RG 401(1)(A), Papers Relating to Arctic Expeditions, 1886-1909, Greenland, 1898-1902, Peary Diary, 16 September to 22 October 1900. See also Robert E. Peary, "Living Off the Country," p. 913.

45 R.E. Peary, *North Polar Exploration: Field Work of the Peary Arctic Club, 1898–1902* (Washington: The Smithsonian Institution, 1903). The assorted kills included: one muskox killed at Buchanan Bay in September 1898 (p. 430); 15 killed at Buchanan Bay in early October 1989 (431); one bull killed at Bache Peninsula in March 1899 (p. 435); 16 muskoxen killed at Muskox Bay, May 1899 (p. 436); 12 killed at the Bellows and Black Rock Vale in May 1899 (p. 436); eight muskoxen killed at Buchanan Bay June 1899 (p. 437); seven muskoxen killed at Princess Marie and Buchanan Bay in July 1899 (p. 438); 27 muskoxen killed near Fort Conger in March 1900 (p. 441), six muskoxen killed near Fort Conger on18 May 1900 (p. 445); 33 muskoxen killed near Conger in May and June 1900 (p. 449); 20 muskoxen killed near Black Rock Vale and Lake Hazen in August and early September 1900 (p. 449); 92 muskoxen killed around Lake Hazen in October 1900 (p. 449); and 12 muskoxen killed at Buchanan Bay and November 1901 (p. 450).

46 USNA, Robert E. Peary Papers, RG 401(1)(A), Papers Relating to Arctic Expeditions, 1886–1909, Greenland: 1898–1902, T.S. Dedrick Diaries, Notebooks and Other Papers, 1898–1901, VI, Box No. 4, Folder 6, Miscellaneous Papers of Dr. T.S. Dedrick: Field Notes, Letter of Dedrick, Mouth of Crozier River, to Robert Peary, Fort Conger, 21 February 1901, p. 1.

47 USNA, Robert E. Peary Papers, RG 401(1)(A), Papers Relating to Arctic Expeditions, 1886-1909, Greenland, 1898-1902, Peary Diary Entry for 15 April 1901.

48 Ibid., Peary Diary Entries for 16 and 17 May 1902.

49 William Barr, *Back from the Brink*, p. 80. The expedition's muskoxen hunting activities are detailed in Otto Sverdrup, New Land, Vol. I, pp. 47, 50-51, 55, 161-63, 262, 483, and Vol. II, pp. 6, 10-11, 22-25, 62, 74, 77, 138, 140, 209, 271, 282, 293, and 381.

50 Otto Sverdrup, *New Land*, Vol. I, pp. 262-64.

51 Robert E. Peary, *Nearest the Pole*, pp. 46-47.

52 BCLSC, Papers of Robert Abrams Bartlett, "From the Crow's Nest": "The First Roosevelt Expedition" (1905-06), p. 15.

53 Ibid., p. 16.

54 USNA, RG 401(1)(A), Robert E. Peary Papers, Papers Relating to Arctic Expeditions, 1886–1909, North Polar, 1905–06, Box No. 1, Letters Received, Henson, 1905–06, Letter of Matthew Henson to Robert Peary, 16 December 1905.

55 William Barr, *Back from the Brink*, p. 80.

56 Robert E. Peary, "Living Off the Country," p. 913.

57 Matthew Henson, *A Negro Explorer at the North Pole*, p. 156.

58 BCLSC, Donald B. MacMillan Collection, Diaries, North Pole, 19 April to 31 May 1909, Entry for 19 May 1909.

59 Robert E. Peary, *Secrets of Polar Travel*, pp. 228-29.

60 William Barr, *Back from the Brink*, p. 81.

61 Dr. Frederick Cook, *My Attainment of the Pole*, pp. 165, 172-73, 185.

62 William Barr, *Back from the Brink*, p. 81.

63 Walter Ekblaw, "Of Unknown Shores: The Traverse of Grant and Ellesmere Lands," in Donald B. MacMillan, *Four Years in the White North*, Appendix B, p. 351. See also J. Gordon Hayes, *The Conquest of the North Pole: Recent Arctic Exploration*, pp. 139-41.

64 BCLSC, Donald MacMillan Collection, Diaries, Crocker Land Expedition, No. 19/5. 12 February 1914 to 26 March 1915, Entry for 22 March 1914.

65 Ibid., Entries for 22 March and 1 April 1914.

66 Ibid., Entry for 1 April 1914.

67 Harrison J. Hunt and Ruth Hunt Thompson, *North to the Horizon*, pp. 68-69.

68 NAC, RG 18, Accn. 84-85/084, Vol. 33, File G-516-37, Part 3, Letter of W.D. Cory, Deputy Minister of the Interior to Col. Cortlandt Starnes, Commissioner, RCMP, 29 June 1925.

69 BCLSC, Donald B. MacMillan Collection, Diaries, Journals, and Logs, Etc., Field Notebook No. 32, March to July 1924, Entry for 4 June 1924.

70 William Barr, *Back from the Brink*, p. 82.

71 Clarence F. Wyckoff, "A Caribou Hunt on Peary's 1898-1902 Expedition," *Arctic*, Vol. 5, No. 3 (October 1952), p. 180.

72 BCLSC, Donald B. MacMillan Collection, Diaries, Journals, Logs, Etc., Crocker Land Expedition, Journal No. 16, 2 July 1913 to 12 February 1914, Entry for 25 October 1913.

73 Knud Rasmussen, *Greenland by the Polar Sea*, p. 16.

74 Robert E. Peary, "Living Off the Country," p. 916.

75 Eivind Astrup, who served on this expedition, related that these caribou were taken "that autumn, before the darkness hindered us." Eivind Astrup, *With Peary Near the Pole*, p. 21.

76 Robert E. Peary, "Living Off the Country," p. 917.

77 Clarence F. Wyckoff, "A Caribou Hunt on Peary's 1898-1902 Expedition," pp. 178-82.

78 USNA, Robert E. Peary Papers, RG 401(1)(A), Papers Relating to Arctic Expeditions, 1896-1902, Greenland, 1898-1902, Peary Diary Entries for 16 and 17 May 1902.

79 Ibid.

80 John W. Goodsell, *On Polar Trails*, p. 135.

81 Robert E. Peary, "Living Off the Country," p. 917.

82 Matthew Henson, *A Negro Explorer at the North Pole*, p. 156.

83 Robert E. Peary, "Living Off the Country," p. 917.

84 BCLSC, Donald B. MacMillan Collection, Diaries, Journals, Logs, Etc., Crocker Land Expedition, Journal No. 16, 2 July 1913 to 12 February 1914, Entry for 15 October 1913.

85 Ibid., Diary No. 19, Crocker Land Expedition, Journal No. 3, 12 April 1916 to 2 April 1917, Entry for 22 October 1916, p. 226.

86 John S. Tener, "Queen Elizabeth Islands Game Survey, 1961," Canadian Wildlife Service, *Occasional Papers, No. 4* (Ottawa, Department of Northern Affairs and Natural Resources, National Parks Branch, 1963), p. 36.

87 BCLSC, Donald B. MacMillan Collection, Diaries, Journals, Logs, Etc., Diary No. 19, Crocker Land Expedition, Journal No. 3, 12 April 1916 to 2 April 1917, p. 59.

88 NAC, RG 85, Vol. 759, File 4829, Donald B. MacMillan's testimony before the Muskox Commission, p. 265. I would like to thank Kenn Harper and Renee Wissink for this reference.

89 NAC, RG 85, Vol. 584, File No. 571, Copy of Letter of Knud Rasmussen, Copenhagen, to the Administrator of the Colonies in Greenland, 8 March 1920.

90 Knud Rasmussen, Greenland by the Polar Sea, p. 17.

91 NAC, RG 85, Vol. 584, File No. 571, Copy of Letter of Knud Rasmussen, Copenhagen, to the Administrator of the Colonies in Greenland, 8 March 1920.

92 Christian Vibe, "The Marine Mammals and the Marine Fauna in the Thule District," pp. 22-23.

93 Jean Malaurie, *The Last Kings of Thule*, p. 220.

94 Godfred Hansen, "Den Tredje Thuleekspedition: Norges Depotekspedition Til Roald Amundsen," in Roald Amundsen, *Nordostpassagen* (Copenhagen: Kristiana Gyldendalske Boghandel, 1921), pp. 439-62.

95 See, for example, Harwood Steele, *Policing the Arctic*; and R.C. Fetherstonhaugh, *The Royal Canadian Mounted Police* (New York: Carrick & Evans, 1938).

96 NAC, RG 85, Vol. 764, File 5086, News clipping from *The Christian Science Monitor*, 8 March 1928.

97 Fernand Braudel, *The Mediterranean and the Mediterranean World in the Age of Philip II*, Vol. II, p. 763.

98 Fernand Braudel, *Capitalism and Material Life*, p. 63. For a comparable distinction from a systems ecological perspective, see Anthony Wilden's discussion of "hot" and "cool" societies in *System and Structure*, pp. 406-12.

PART IV

CIRCUMSTANCE, CHANGE, AND CONTINUITY

The Inuit on Ellesmere Island, 1951-2000

1 See, for example, André Picard, "The Internal Exiles of Canada," *The Globe and Mail* (Toronto), 7 September 1991, p. D3.

2 Marc Hammond, "Report of Findings on an Alleged Promise of the Government to Finance the return of Inuit from Resolute Bay and Grise Fiord to their Original Homes in Port Harrison and Pond Inlet," Ottawa, 1984; Hickling Corporation, "Assessment of the Factual Basis of Certain Allegations Made before the Standing Committee on Aboriginal Affairs Concerning the Relocation of Inukjuak Inuit in the 1950s," prepared for the Department of Indian and Northern Affairs, 1990; M. Gunther, "The 1953

Relocations of the Inukjuak Inuit to the High Arctic—A Documentary Analysis and Evaluation," prepared for the Department of Indian and Northern Affairs and Northern Development, Ottawa, 1992.

3 Shelagh D. Grant, "A Case of Compounded Error: The Inuit Resettlement Project, 1953, and the Government Response, 1990," *Northern Perspectives* (Canadian Arctic Resources Committee), Vol. 19, No. 1 (Spring 1991), pp. 3-29.

4 Keith Lowther, "An Exercise in Sovereignty: The Canadian Government and the Relocation of Inuit to the High Arctic in 1953," in W. Peter Adams and Peter G. Johnson, Eds., *Student Research in Canada's North*, Proceedings of the National Student Conference on Northern Studies, November 18–19, 1986 (Ottawa: Association of Canadian Universities for Northern Studies, 1986), pp. 517-22; and Alan R. Marcus, "Out in the Cold: The Legacy of Canada's Relocation Experiment in the High Arctic, 1953–90," M. Phil. thesis, Scott Polar Research Institute, University of Cambridge, 1990.

5 Daniel Soberman, *Report to the Canadian Human Rights Commission on the Complaints of the Inuit People Relocated from Inukjuak and Pond Inlet, to Grise Fiord and Resolute Bay in 1953 and 1955* (Ottawa: Canadian Human Rights Commission, 1991).

6 Royal Commission on Aboriginal Peoples, *The High Arctic Relocation: A Report on the 1953–55 Relocation* (Ottawa: Royal Commission on Aboriginal Peoples, 1994).

Chapter 13: Circumstance: Inuit Relocation to the High Arctic, 1951-2000

1 Diamond Jenness, *Eskimo Administration: II. Canada* (Ottawa: Arctic Institute of North America, Technical Paper No. 14, 1964), pp. 59-60.

2 NAC, RG 85, Vol. 72, File 201-1 [11], Memorandum of D.L. McKeand, Department of the Interior, Lands, Northwest Territories and Yukon Branch to Mr. Turner, 5 February 1936.

3 Ibid., p. 61.

4 Farley Mowat, "Dark Odyssey of Soosie," in *The Snow Walker* (Toronto: McClelland and Stewart, 1975).

5 Ernie Lyall, *An Arctic Man: Sixty-Five Year in Canada's North* (Halifax: Goodread Biographies, 1979), pp. 97-102.

6 See Shelagh D. Grant, *Sovereignty or Security? Government Policy in the Canadian North, 1936–1950* (Vancouver: University of British Columbia Press, 1988), pp. 103-28; 211-37.

7 Ibid, p. 144.

8 Ibid., pp. 185-86, 230.

9 During a visit to Alert in the 1950s, Ross Gibson observed that Canadian officials were very concerned that the displayed Canadian flag not be exceeded in dimensions by the American flag flown at this station. PC, WCSC, Grise Fiord Oral History Project, Interview with Ross Gibson by Lyle Dick, Victoria, British Columbia, 20 March 1989, Side 4.

10 NAC, RG 25, Accn. no. 90-91/109, Vol. 58, File 50197-40/1, Document reproduced in Shelagh Grant, "Inuit Relocations to the High Arctic 1953-1960: 'Errors Exposed,'" Vol. I (Bound collection of documents submitted to the Royal Commission on Aboriginal Peoples, June 1993, revised August 1993).

11 D. Barry, Ed., *Documents on Canada's External Relations, 1952* (Ottawa: Department of External Affairs and International Trade, 1990), Vol. 18, p. 1194, quoted in Frank James Tester and Peter Kulchyski, Tammarniit *(Mistakes): Inuit Relocation in the Eastern Arctic, 1939–63* (Vancouver: University of British Columbia Press, 1994), pp. 128-29.

12 NAC, RG 2, Vol. 2652, File: "Jan-Feb 1953," reproduced in Shelagh Grant, "Inuit Relocations to the High Arctic 1953-1960: 'Errors Exposed,'" Vol. I, Cabinet Conclusions of Meeting, 22 January 1953, p. 14.

13 Ibid.

14 "Canadian Eastern Arctic Patrol, 1951," *The Polar Record*, Vol. 7, No. 47 (January 1954), pp. 43-44.

15 NAC, RG 85, Vol. 294, File 1005-7 (5), "Agenda," Eskimo Affairs Conference, 19-20 May 1952, cited in Shelagh D. Grant, "Inuit Relocations to the High Arctic, 1953–1960: 'Errors Exposed,'" Vol. 1, Report and Chronology, submitted to the Royal Commission on Aboriginal Peoples (Revised 30 August 1993), p. 42.

16 Christian Vibe, "The Marine Mammals and the Marine Fauna in the Thule District," p. 95.

17 NAC, RG 18, File 3014, Bache Peninsula Detachment Diary for 1927, Entries for 17 May and 2 June.

18 NAC, RG 85, Vol. 79, File No. 201[25-A], "Extracts from Report of A. Stevenson, Officer-in-Charge, Eastern Arctic Patrol, 1950: Outline of Purpose and Particulars of Patrol—Past and Present," pp. 6-7.

19 NAC, RG 85, Vol. 1207, File 201-1-8/3, 1952 Eastern Arctic Patrol Report (Northern Section) by James Cantley, Officer in Charge, cited in Shelagh D. Grant, "Inuit Relocations to the High Arctic, 1953–1960: 'Errors Exposed,'" Vol. 1, Report and Chronology, submitted to the Royal Commission on Aboriginal Peoples (Revised 30 August 1993), pp. 43-44.

20 NAC, RG 85, Vol. 176, File 40-2-20, "Eastern Arctic Patrol," 1952 Report, p. 8.

21 NAC, Indian and Northern Affairs Records, File 401-23-1, Part 6, Letter of Canadian Legation to Royal Danish Ministry for Foreign Affairs, 10 June 1953.

22 NAC, MG 30, E133, Vol. 294, File: "First Report 1953" (Advisory Committee on Northern Development), cited in Royal Commission on Aboriginal Peoples, *The High Arctic Relocation: Summary of Supporting Information*, Vol. II, p. 587.

23 PC, WCSC, Grise Fiord Oral History Project, Interview with Ross Gibson by Lyle Dick, Victoria, British Columbia, 20 March 1989, Side 1.

24 NAC, RG 85, Vol. 1962, File no. A-1012-13, Part 1, Memorandum of C.M. Bolger to B.G. Sivertz, 15 November 1960.

25 Ibid., Memorandum of C.M. Bolger, Administrator of the Arctic, to the Director, Northern Administration Branch, Department of Northern Affairs and Natural Development, 4 October 1960.

26 Ibid.

27 Ibid., Memorandum of B.G. Sivertz to C.M. Bolger re: "Relocation of Eskimo Groups in the High Arctic."

28 NAC, RG 85, Vol. 1070, File 251-4. Part 1, Memorandum of F.J.G. Cunningham for C.W. Jackson, 4 August 1953.

29 James Houston, "Port Harrison, 1948," in *Port Harrison / Inukjuak* (Exhibition Catalogue) (Winnipeg: The Winnipeg Art Gallery, 1976), p. vii.

30 PC, WCSC, Grise Fiord Oral History Project, Interview with Ross Gibson by Lyle Dick, Victoria, British Columbia, 20 March 1989, Side 1.

31 PC, WCSC, Grise Fiord Oral History Project, Interview with Martha Flaherty by Lyle Dick, Ottawa, 27 February 1989, Side 1.

32 NAC, RG 85, Vol. 1070, File 251-4, Part 1, Memorandum from Robert C. Ripley, Air Officer Commanding of the RCAF Transport Command, Lachine, Quebec, to the Chief of the Air Staff, Ottawa, 6 July 1953.

33 "Supply of Settlements in the Canadian Arctic, 1953," *The Polar Record*, Vol. 7, No. 50 (May 1955), p. 392.

34 Ibid., pp. 391-92.

35 NAC, RG 18, Accn. 85-86/048, Vol. 55, File No. TA-500-8-1-1, "Game Conditions— Alexandra Fiord," Teletype Message of Inspector H.A. Larsen, "G" Division to NCO, RCMP, Alexandra Fiord, 28 January 1954.

36 Ibid., Teletype Message from A/Corporal Jones, Alexandra Fiord to OC, "G" Division, 31 January 1954.

37 Ibid., Teletype Message of H.A. Larsen, "G" Division, to NCO, RCMP, Alexandra Fiord, 16 March 1954.

38 Royal Commission on Aboriginal Peoples, *The High Arctic Relocation: Summary of Supporting Information*, Vol. II, pp. 17-116.

39 Ibid., p. 78.

40 PC, WCSC, Grise Fiord Oral History Project, Interview with Martha Flaherty by Lyle Dick, Ottawa, 27 February 1989, Side 1.

41 PC, WCSC, Grise Fiord Oral History Project, Interview with Edith Patsauq Amaroalik by Martha Flaherty, Inukjuak, PQ, 6 November 1989, English translation by Martha Flaherty, p. 4.

42 PC, WCSC, Grise Fiord Oral History Project, Interview with Anna Nungaq by Martha Flaherty, Inukjuak, PQ, 14 November 1989, English translation by Martha Flaherty, p. 5.

43 Ibid.

44 PC, WCSC, Grise Fiord Oral History Project, Interview with Ross Gibson by Lyle Dick, Victoria, British Columbia, 20 March 1989, Side 2.

45 Ibid., Side 1.

46 PC, WCSC, Grise Fiord Oral History Project, Interview with Anna Nungaq by Martha Flaherty, Inukjuak, PQ, 14 November 1989, English translation by Martha Flaherty, p. 8.

47 PC, WCSC, Grise Fiord Oral History Project, Interview with Samwilly Elaijasialuk by Martha Flaherty, Inukjuak, PQ, 15 November 1989, English translation by Martha Flaherty, p. 3.

48 PC, WCSC, Grise Fiord Oral History Project, Interview with Gamaliel Aqiarak by Liza Ningiuk, Grise Fiord, Nunavut, 29 January 1990, English translation by Martha Flaherty, p. 6.

49 "Anna Nungaq About Moving to Grise Fiord," *Inuktitut*, No. 49 (December 1981), p. 10.

50 PC, WCSC, Grise Fiord Oral History Project, Interview with Tookilkee Kigugtak by Liza Ningiuk, Grise Fiord, Nunavut, 3 March 1991, English Translation by Martha Flaherty, p. 3.

51 PC, WCSC, Grise Fiord Oral History Project, Grise Fiord Oral History Project, Interview with Martha Flaherty by Lyle Dick, Ottawa, 27 February 1989, Side 1.

52 Ibid.

53 PC, WCSC, Grise Fiord Oral History Project, Interview with Anna Nungaq by Martha Flaherty, Inukjuak, PQ, 14 November 1989, English translation by Martha Flaherty, pp. 8-9.

54 Ibid., p. 14.

55 Royal Commission on Aboriginal Peoples, *The High Arctic Relocation: A Report on the 1953–55 Relocation*, Vol. I, pp. 13-14.

56 PC, WCSC, Grise Fiord Oral History Project, Interview with Markusie Patsauq by Martha Flaherty, Inukjuak, PQ, 17 November 1989, English translation by Martha Flaherty, p. 5.

57 PC, WCSC, Grise Fiord Oral History Project, Interview with Martha Flaherty by Lyle Dick, Ottawa, 27 February 1989, Side 1. 0

58 PC, WCSC, Grise Fiord Oral History Project, Interview with Abraham Pijamini, by Liza Ningiuk, Grise Fiord, Nunavut, 28 February 1991, English translation by Martha Flaherty.

59 Royal Commission on Aboriginal Peoples, *The High Arctic Relocation: A Report on the 1953–55 Relocations*, Vol. I, p. 138.

60 PC, WCSC, Grise Fiord Oral History Project, Interview with Ross Gibson by Lyle Dick, Victoria, British Columbia, 20 March 1989.

Chapter 14: Change: Adaptation to New Natural and
Cultural Environments, 1951–2000

1 Milton M.R. Freeman, "Patrons, Leaders and Values in an Eskimo Settlement," in Symposium on the Contemporary Cultural Situation of the Northern Forest Indians of North America and the Eskimo of North America and Greenland, in *Proceedings of the 38th International Congress of Americanists* (Stuttgart-München, 1968), Vol. 3, p. 114.

2 Milton M.R. Freeman, "Tolerance and Rejection of Patron Roles in an Eskimo Settlement," in Robert Paine, Ed., *Patrons and Brokers in the East Arctic*, Newfoundland Social and Economic Papers No. 2 (St. John's: Memorial University, 1971), p. 40.

3 NAC, RG 85, Vol. 1070, File 251-4, Part. 2, Letter of P.A.C. Nichols to B.G. Sivertz, 24 May 1955.

4 "Notes from Simeonie Akpaliapik's Conversation," in Royal Commission on Aboriginal Peoples, *The High Arctic Relocation: Summary of Supporting Information*, Vol. I, p. 218.

5 NAC, RG 85, Vol. 1070, File 251-4, Part 1, Memorandum from J. Cantley for Mr. Burton, 10 July 1953.

6 Larry Audlaluk, Unpublished notes on the text of the "Muskox Land" book manuscript, February/March 2001, p. 1.

7 NAC, RG 18, Vol. 1446, File 1000/133, Part 1, Report Re: Eskimo Conditions, Craig Harbour Area, 31 December 1953, p. 3.

8 Larry Audlaluk, Unpublished notes on the text of the "Muskox Land" book manuscript, February/March 2001, p. 2.

9 NAC, RG 18, Accn. 85-86/048, Vol. 55, File TA 500-8-1-5, "Conditions Amongst the Eskimos Generally," Report of Craig Harbour detachment re: Eskimo Conditions, Craig Harbour Area, period ending 31 December 1953.

10 PC, WCSC, Grise Fiord Oral History Project, Interview with Anna Nungaq by Martha Flaherty, Inukjuak, PQ, 14 November 1989, English translation by Martha Flaherty, p. 6.

11 PC, WCSC, Grise Fiord Oral History Project, Interview with Martha Flaherty by Lyle Dick, Ottawa, 27 February 1989, Side 1.

12 PC, WCSC, Grise Fiord Oral History Project, Interview with Anna Nungaq by Martha Flaherty, Inukjuak, PQ, 14 November 1989, English translation by Martha Flaherty, p. 6.

13 Ibid.

14 NAC, RG 18, Accn. 85-86/048, Vol. 55, File TA-500-8-1-5, Report of Corporal G.K. Sargent re: Eskimo Conditions, Craig Harbour Area, 31 December 1954, p. 2.

15 Larry Audlaluk, Unpublished notes on the text of the "Muskox Land" book manuscript, February/March 2001, p.2.

16 PC, WCSC, Grise Fiord Oral History Project, Interview with Robert Pilot by Lyle Dick, Pembroke, Ontario, 14 February 1989, Side 1.

17 PC, WCSC, Grise Fiord Oral History Project, Interview with Anna Nungaq by Martha Flaherty, Inukjuak, PQ, 14 November 1989, English translation by Martha Flaherty, pp. 10-11.

18 NAC, RG18, Accn. 85-86/048, Vol. 55, File TA 500-8-1-5, Report of Cpl. G.K. Sargent Re: Eskimo Conditions, Craig Harbour Area, Period ending 31 December 1954, p. 2.

19 NAC, RG 18, Accn. 85-86/048, Vol. 56, File TA-500-20-10-1, Memorandum of Cst. R.S. Pilot, Grise Fiord, to the Officer Commanding, "G" Division, 10 January 1960, p. 1.

20 Milton M.R. Freeman, "The Grise Fiord Project," p. 677.

21 PC, WCSC, Grise Fiord Oral History Project, Interview with Anna Nungaq by Martha Flaherty, Inukjuak, PQ, 14 November 1989, English translation By Martha Flaherty, p. 9.

22 NAC, RG18, Accn. 85-86/048, Vol. 55, File TA 500-8-1-5, Report of Cpl. G.K. Sargent Re: Eskimo Conditions, Craig Harbour Area, Period ending 31 December 1954, pp. 2-3.

23 Ibid., Annual Report, Grise Fiord Area, by R.S. Pilot, 19 January 1960, p. 3.

24 See, for example, NAC, RG 18, Accn. 85-86/048, Vol. 55, File TA 500-8-1-5, "Conditions Amongst the Eskimos Generally," Annual Report for 1958, p. 3; Annual Report for 1959, p. 4; and RG 85, Vol. 1446, File 1000/133, Part 1, "Craig Harbour Area General File (and Grise Fiord, NWT)," Urgent report of P.E. Moore, MD, 16 November 1960, and Memorandum, B.G. Sivertz to Deputy Minister, 18 November 1960.

25 Larry Audlaluk, Unpublished notes on the text of the "Muskox Land" book manuscript, February/March 2001, p. 2.

26 Ibid., p. 2.

27 NAC, RG 18, Accn. 85-86/048, Vol. 55, File TA 500-8-1-5, Report re: Eskimo Conditions, Craig Harbour Area, from 31 December 1953 to 31 December 1954, by Corporal G.K. Sargent, Craig Harbour, 31 December 1954.

28 Ibid., Report re: Eskimo Conditions, Craig Harbour Area, Period ending 31 December 1955, by Corporal G.K. Sargent, Craig Harbour, 2 January 1956.

29 Ibid., Report re: Eskimo Conditions, Craig Harbour Area, from 31 December 1953 to 31 December 1954, by Corporal G.K. Sargent, Craig Harbour, 31 December 1954.

30 Larry Audlaluk, Unpublished notes on the text of the "Muskox Land" book manuscript, February/March 2001, p. 2.

31 PC, WCSC, Grise Fiord Oral History Project, Interview with Anna Nungaq by Martha Flaherty, Inukjuak, PQ, 14 November 1991, English translation by Martha Flaherty, p. 6.

32 PC, WCSC, Grise Fiord Oral History Project, Interview with Rynee Flaherty by Larry Audlaluk, Grise Fiord, 1 December 1991, English translation by Martha Flaherty, pp. 9-10.

33 Ibid.

34 Ibid.

35 NAC, RG 18, RCMP Records, Accn. 85-86/048, Vol. 56, File No. TA-500-20-10-1, Alexandra Fiord Detachment, Report re: General Game Conditions, 10 July 1958, p. 2.

36 Ibid., Alexandra Fiord Detachment, Report on Game Conditions, July 1959 to June 1960, p. 3.

37 Ibid., p. 4.

38 PC, WCSC, Grise Fiord Oral History Project, Interview with Annie Pijamini by Iga Kigugtak, Grise Fiord, Nunavut, 7 January 1991, English translation by Martha Flaherty, p. 13.

39 PC, WCSC, Grise Fiord Oral History Project, Interview with Abraham Pijamini by Liza Ningiuk, Grise Fiord, Nunavut, 28 February 1991, English translation by Martha Flaherty, pp. 21-22.

40 James Houston, "Akeeaktashuk," in James H. Marsh, Ed., *The Canadian Encyclopedia* (Revised edition) (Edmonton: Hurtig Publishers, 1988), p. 47.

41 Larry Audlaluk, Unpublished notes on the text of the "Muskox Land" book manuscript, February/March 2001, p. 3.

42 NAC, RG 18 Accn. 85-86/048, Vol. 55, File TA 500-8-1-5, Annual Report for 1958 of Cst. R.S. Pilot re: Conditions Amongst Eskimos Generally, Grise Fiord Area, 19 January 1959.

43 NAC, RG 18, Vol. 1446, File. 1000/133, Part 1, Memorandum of B.G. Sivertz to the Deputy Minister (copy), 18 November 1960; Report re: Conditions Amongst Eskimos Generally, Annual report by J.T. Parsons, Inspector, 7 January 1961.

44 NAC, RG 18 Accn. 85-86/048, Vol. 55, File TA-500-8-1-5, Report of Corporal G.K. Sargent re: Eskimo Conditions, Craig Harbour Area, 31 December 1954, p. 5.

45 Larry Audlaluk, Unpublished notes on the text of the "Muskox Land" book manuscript, February/March 2001, p. 3.

46 NAC, RG 18, Accn. 85-86/048, Vol. 55, File TA 500-8-1-5, Report by Corporal G.K. Sargent re: Eskimo Conditions, Craig Harbour Area, 31 December 1955, p. 3.

47 Larry Audlaluk, Unpublished notes on the text of the "Muskox Land" book manuscript, February/March 2001, p. 3

48 Ibid.

49 NAC, RG 85, Vol. 1912, File A-1011-1, Part 1, Memorandum of J.H. Leedham for the Administrator of the Arctic, 7 June 1960, p. 5.

50 Ibid., Memorandum of J.F. Delaute for the Administrator of the Arctic, 6 June 1960, pp. 6-7.

51 Ibid.

52 Royal Commission on Aboriginal Peoples, *The High Arctic Relocation: A Report on the 1953–55 Relocation*, Vol. I, pp. 138-39.

53 M.M.R. Freeman, "Adaptive Innovation Among Recent Eskimo Immigrants in the Eastern Canadian Arctic," *Polar Record*, Vol. 14, No. 93 (1969), pp. 769-81; and "Tolerance and Rejection of Patron Roles in an Eskimo Settlement," in Robert Paine, Ed., *Patrons and Brokers in the Eastern Arctic* (St. John's, Newfoundland: Memorial University, 1971).

54 Milton M.R. Freeman, "Patrons, Leaders and Values in an Eskimo Settlement," in Symposium on the Contemporary Cultural Situation of the Northern Forest Indians of North America and the Eskimo of North America and Greenland, in *Proceedings of the 38th International Congress of Americanists* (Stuttgart-München, 1968), Vol. 3, pp. 113-124.

55 Ibid., p. 8.

56 PC, WCSC, Grise Fiord Oral History Project, Interview with R.S. Pilot by Lyle Dick, Pembroke, Ontario, 14 February 1989.

57 Larry Audlaluk, Unpublished notes on the text of the "Muskox Land" book manuscript, February/March 2001, p. 3.

58 NAC, RG18, Vol. 1446, File 1000/133, Part 1, Report Re: Eskimo Conditions, Craig Harbour Area, 31 December 1953, p. 4.

59 NAC, RG18, Accn. 85-86/048, Vol. 55, File TA 500-8-1-5, Report of Cpl. G.K. Sargent Re: Eskimo Conditions, Craig Harbour Area, Period ending 31 December 1954, p. 2.

60 Ibid., pp. 2-3.

61 Larry Audlaluk, Unpublished notes on the text of the "Muskox Land" book manuscript, February/March 2001, p. 3.

62 PC, WCSC, Grise Fiord Oral History Project, Interview with Martha Kigugtak by Larry Audlaluk, Grise Fiord, Nunavut, 1 December 1991, English translation by Martha Flaherty, p. 4.

63 PC, WCSC, Grise Fiord Oral History Project, Interview with Anna Nungaq by Martha Flaherty, Inukjuak, PQ, 14 November 1989, English translation by Martha Flaherty, p. 6.

64 Cst. A.C. Fryer, "Eskimo Rehabilitation Program at Craig Harbour," *The RCMP Quarterly*, Vol. 20, No. 2 (October 1954), p. 139. See also the original manuscript of Fryer's article in: NAC, RG18 Accn. 85-86/048, Vol. 55, File TA500-8-1-5.

65 Larry Audlaluk, Unpublished notes on the text of the "Muskox Land" book manuscript, February/March 2001, p. 4.

66 PC, WCSC, Grise Fiord Oral History Project, Pond Inlet Oral History Project, Interview with Samuel Arnakallak by Elisapee Ootoova, Pond Inlet, English translation by Philip Paneak, pp. 8-9.

67 A.C. Fryer, "Eskimo Rehabilitation Program at Craig Harbour," p. 140.

68 NAC, RG 18, Accn. 85-86/048, Vol. 55, File TA 500-8-1-5, Cablegram of A/Cpl. Sargent to Officer Commanding, "G" Division, 24 December 1953.

69 Ibid., Report of G.K. Sargent re: Eskimo Conditions, Craig Harbour Area, 31 December 1953.

70 Ibid., Annual Report, Grise Fiord Area, Year Ending 31 December 1958, by Constable R.S. Pilot, 19 January 1959.

71 NAC, RG 18, Accn. No. 85-86/048, Vol. 54, File TA-500-20-10-1. Memorandum of Cst. R.S. Pilot, Grise Fiord Detachment, to the Officer Commanding, "G" Division, 18 February 1959.

72 For an in-depth analysis of the social, economic, and political impact of the introduction of the snowmobile on the Skolt Lapps in northern Finland, see Pertti J. Pelto, *The Snowmobile Revolution: Technology and Change in the Arctic* (Menlo Park, California: Cummings Publishing Co., 1973).

73 NAC, RG 18, Accn. 85-86/048, Vol. 55, File TA 500-8-1-5, Report re: Conditions Amongst Eskimos Generally, Year Ending 31 Dec. 1966, by Corporal L.B. Schollar, 8 February 1967, p. 4.

74 Larry Audlaluk, Unpublished notes on the text of the "Muskox Land" book manuscript, February/March 2001, p. 4.

75 Pertti J. Pelto, "Snowmobiles: Technological Revolution in the Arctic," in H. Russell Bernard and Pertti J. Pelto, *Technology and Social Change* (New York: Macmillan, 1972), p. 185. This author's discussion of snowmobiles at Grise Fiord was based on a report by Milton M.R. Freeman.

76 PC, WCSC, Grise Fiord Oral History Project, Interview with Tookilkee Kigugtak by Liza Ningiuk, Grise Fiord, Nunavut, 3 March 1991, English translation by Martha Flaherty, p. 16.

77 Larry Audlaluk, Unpublished notes on the text of the "Muskox Land" book manuscript, February/March 2001, p. 4.

78 NAC, RG 18, Accn. 85-86/048, Vol. 55, File TA 500-8-1-5, Annual Report, Year Ending 31 December 1968, by Corporal V.R. Vitt, 6 January 1969, p. 4.

79 Ibid., Report re: Conditions Amongst the Eskimos Generally, Year Ending 31 December 1967, Grise Fiord Detachment, by V.R. Vitt, 15 January 1968, p. 5.

80 NAC, RG 85 M, Accn. 77803/16, File no. S17LR, "Grise Fiord," Unpublished report entitled "Inuit Land Use and Occupancy in the Eastern High Arctic: Grise Fiord," by Roderick R. Riewe, October 1974, p. 22.

81 NAC, RG 18, Accn. 85-86/048, Vol. 55, File TA 500-8-1-5, Annual Report, Year Ending 31 December 1968, by Corporal V.R. Vitt, 6 January 1969, p. 4.

82 PC, WCSC, Grise Fiord Oral History Project, Interview with Tookilkee Kigugtak by Liza Ningiuk, Grise Fiord, Nunavut, 3 March 1991, English translation by Martha Flaherty, p. 14.

83 Quoted in Ulli Steltzer, *Inuit: The North in Transition* (Vancouver/Toronto: Douglas and McIntyre, 1982), p. 36.

84 R.R. Riewe, "The Utilization of Wildlife in the Jones Sound Region by the Grise Fiord Inuit," in L.C. Bliss, Ed., *Truelove Lowland, Devon Island, Canada: A High Arctic Ecosystem* (Edmonton: University of Alberta Press, 1977), p. 640.

85 Kenn Harper, "A History of Human Occupation," in *Socio-Economic Characteristics and Conservation Interests of the Lancaster Sound Region* (Ottawa: Department of Indian and Northern Affairs, Lancaster Sound Regional Study, Background Report No. 3, 1980), p. 34.

86 M.M.R. Freeman, "Effects of Petroleum Activities on the Ecology of Arctic Man," in F.R. Engelhardt, Ed., *Petroleum Effects in the Arctic Environment* (London and New York: Elsevier Applied Science Publishers, 1985), pp. 245-73.

87 Lewis Cotlow, *In Search of the Primitive* (Boston and Toronto: Little, Brown, and Company, 1966), p. 434.

88 Larry Audlaluk, Unpublished notes on the text of the "Muskox Land" book manuscript, February/March 2001, p. 4.

89 NAC, RG 18, Accn. 85-86/048, Vol. 55, File TA 500-8-1-5, Copy of Teletype message from Corporal Sargent, Craig Harbour, 21 February 1955.

90 Larry Audlaluk, Unpublished notes on the text of the "Muskox Land" book manuscript, February/March 2001, p. 4.

91 Ibid., p. 4.

92 NAC, RG 18, Accn. 85-86/048, Vol. 55, File TA 500-8-1-5, Copy of Teletype message from Corporal Sargent, Craig Harbour, 21 February 1955.

93 PC, WCSC, Grise Fiord Oral History Project, Interview with Gamaliel Aqiarak, by Lisa Ningiuk, Grise Fiord, 1991, English translation by Martha Flaherty, p. 15.

94 Larry Audlaluk, Unpublished notes on the text of the "Muskox Land" book manuscript, February/March 2001, p. 4.

95 R.R. Riewe, "The Utilization of Wildlife in the Jones Sound Region by the Grise Fiord Inuit," in L.C. Bliss, Ed., *Truelove Lowland, Devon Island, Canada: A High Arctic Ecosystem* (Edmonton: University of Alberta Press, 1977), p. 629.

96 R.R. Riewe, "The Utilization of Wildlife in the Jones Sound Region by the Grise Fiord Inuit," Fig. 1, p. 626.

97 PC, WCSC, Grise Fiord Oral History Project, Grise Fiord Oral History Project, Interview with Robert Pilot by Lyle Dick, Pembroke, Ontario, 14 February 1989, Side 3.

98 PC, WCSC, Grise Fiord Oral History Project, Interview with Tookilkee Kigugtak by Liza Ningiuk, Grise Fiord, Nunavut, 3 March 1991, English translation by Martha Flaherty, p. 4.

99 Telephone interview with Dr. Roderick R. Riewe by Lyle Dick, Winnipeg, 31 August 1995.

100 NAC, RG 85M, 77803/16, S17LIT, Transcript of Interview with Markosie Piunngittuk Inaaluk by Roderick Riewe, English translation by Minnie Freeman, 1971?, p. 2.

101 See Milton M.R. Freeman, "Effects of Petroleum Activities on the Ecology of Arctic Man," in F.R. Englehardt, Ed., *Petroleum Effects in the Arctic Environment* (London and New York: Elsevier Applied Science Publishers, 1985), Table 1, p. 252.

102 PC, WCSC, Pond Inlet Oral History Project, Pond Inlet Oral History Project, Interview with Ningiuk Killiktee by Lucy Quasa, Pond Inlet, NWT, 18 May 1994, English translation, p. 12.

103 Ibid.

104 M.M.R. Freeman, "Traditional Land Users as a Legitimate Source of Environmental Expertise," in J.G. Nelson, R.D. Needham, S.H. Nelson, and R.C. Scace, Eds., *The Canadian National Parks: Today and Tomorrow; Conference II: Ten Years Later,* Vol. I (Waterloo, Ontario: University of Waterloo, 1979), Discussion, pp. 364-65.

105 PC, WCSC, Grise Fiord Oral History Project, Interview with Samwilly Elaijasialuk by Martha Flaherty, Inukjuak, PQ, Quebec, 15 November 1989, English translation by Martha Flaherty, p. 2.

106 NAC, RG 18, RCMP Records, Accn. 85-86/048, Vol. 56, File TA-500-20-10-1, Alexandra Fiord Detachment, Report by Constable P. Sims re: Game Conditions, July 1959 to June 1960, 30 June 1960, p. 4.

107 M.M.R. Freeman, "Traditional Land Users as a Legitimate Source of Environmental Expertise," pp. 356-57.

108 Northwest Territories Council, Debates, 34th Session, "Brief, Grise Fiord Hunters—Muskox Hunting," Tabled Document No. 13, 1967, p. 452.

109 Ibid., "Survey of Muskox Numbers in Jones Sound region, March 1966 to March 1967" [appended to Brief—Grise Fiord Hunters], pp. 461-62.

110 Ibid., p. 460.

111 M.M.R. Freeman, "Traditional Land Users as a Legitimate Source of Environmental Expertise," p. 357.

112 NAC, RG 85, Accn. 85-86/220, Box 7, File A-401-3, Part 2, Memorandum of L. Elkin, A/Regional Administrator, to the Administrator of the Arctic, 12 September 1967.

113 NAC, RG 85, Accn. 85-86/220, Box 7, File A-400-1/133, Copy of Memorandum re: Annual Report on Game Conditions to the Officer Commanding, Frobisher Bay, by Constable V.R. Vitt, Grise Fiord, 3 August 1967, p. 2.

114 NAC, RG 18, RCMP Records, Accn. 85-86/048, File TA 500-8-1-5, "Conditions Amongst Eskimos Generally—Annual Report, Year Ending 31 December 1967—Grise Fiord Detachment," by Constable V.R. Vitt, Grise Fiord, 15 January 1968, p. 7.

115 In the spring of 1993, Grise Fiord residents again demonstrated their preparedness to take collective action, this time in the interest of protecting their environment. Federal officials had approved a permit to allow Panarctic Oil and Gas to dump 400 tonnes of scrap metal waste on the sea ice near Lougheed Island, some 400 km west of Grise Fiord. Community members expressed strong opposition to the permit, as they argued that their community was in the path of ocean currents. As a hunting community that depended heavily on harvesting marine mammals, the Inuit felt they had good reason to be concerned with the possible consequences of industrial contamination of game animals on which they relied. Eventually, on 15 April 1993, the federal Minister of the Environment, who said he was impressed with the protest which had been mounted, revoked Panarctic's permit. See *The Globe and Mail* (Toronto), 16 April 1993, and *Nunatsiaq News* (Iqaluit), 23 April 1993, p. 3.

Chapter 15: Continuity Reasserted: The Inuit, the Seasons, and the Land, 1951–2000

1 M.M.R. Freeman, "Adaptive Innovation Among Recent Eskimo Immigrants in the Eastern Canadian Arctic," *Polar Record*, Vol. 14, No. 93 (1969), pp. 769-81.

2 Quoted in John W. Bennett, *The Ecological Transition: Cultural Anthropology and Human Adaptation* (New York: Pergamon Press, 1976), p. 246.

3 See, for example, M.M.R. Freeman, "Effects of Petroleum Activities on the Ecology of Arctic Man," pp. 265-67; and Lance W. Roberts, "Becoming Modern: Some Reflections on Inuit Social Change," in Ian A.L. Getty and Antoine S. Lussier, Eds., *As Long as the Sun Shines and Water Flows: A Reader in Canadian Native Studies* (Vancouver: University of British Columbia Press, 1983), pp. 299-314.

4 NAC, RG 85M, Accn. 77803/16, File S17LR: "Grise Fiord." Roderick R. Riewe, "Inuit Land Use and Occupancy in the Eastern High Arctic: Grise Fiord" (1974), p. 30.

5 Heather Myers, "The Use of Biological Resources by Certain Arctic and Subarctic Peoples," M. Phil. thesis, Scott Polar Research Institute, Cambridge, England, 1981, pp. 23-24.

6 Informal comments by Abraham Pijamini on presentation by Lyle Dick on the "Muskox Land" book manuscript, Grise Fiord, Nunavut, 25 May 2001.

7 Lewis Cotlow, *In Search of the Primitive*, pp. 439-42.

8 Fred Bruemmer, The Long Hunt (Toronto: The Ryerson Press, 1969).

9 NAC, RG 18, Accn. 85-86/048, Vol. 55, File TA-500-1-5, "Conditions Among Eskimos Generally," Annual Report, Grise Fiord Area, NWT, Year Ending 31 December 1958, by Constable R.S. Pilot, p. 3.

10 NAC, RG 18, RCMP Records, Accn. 83-84/68, Vol. 22, File G 567-44, Patrol Report, Grise Fiord to Resolute Bay, NWT, 4 February to 15 March 1966, Entries for 15 and 16 February 1966, p. 4.

11 Lewis Cotlow, *In Search of the Primitive*, p. 415.

12 NAC, RG 18, RCMP Records, Accn. No. 83-84/68, Vol. 22, File G 567-44, Patrol Report, Grise Fiord to Resolute Bay, NWT, 4 February to 15 March 1966, Entries for 15 and 16 February 1966, pp. 1-2.

13 Milton M.R. Freeman, "Adaptive Innovation Among Recent Eskimo Immigrants in the Eastern Canadian Arctic," pp. 769-81.

14 David Damas, *Igluligmiut Kinship and Local Groupings: A Structural Approach* (Ottawa: National Museum of Canada, Bulletin No. 196, 1963).

15 George W. Wenzel, "*Ningiqtuq*: Resource Sharing and Generalized Reciprocity in Clyde River, Nunavut," *Arctic Anthropology*, Vol. 32, No. 2 (1995), pp. 43-60.

16 Jill Oakes and Rick Riewe, "The Informal Economy of Baffin Island: Sharing Practices of Yesterday and Today," in *Culture, Economy and Society: Case Studies in the Circumpolar Region* (Millbrook, Ontario: The Cider Press, 1997), pp. 79-126.

17 PC, WCSC, Grise Fiord Oral History Project, Grise Fiord Oral History Project, Interview with Rynee Flaherty by Larry Audlaluk, Grise Fiord, Nunavut, December 1991, English translation by Martha Flaherty, p. 6.

18 PC,WCSC, Grise Fiord Oral History Project, Interview with Gamaliel Aqiarak (Akeeagok) by Liza Ningiuk, Grise Fiord, Nunavut, 29 January 1990. English language translation by Martha Flaherty, p. 5.

19 PC, WCSC, Grise Fiord Oral History Project, Interview with Anna Nungaq by Martha Flaherty, Inukjuak, PQ, 14 November 1989, English translation by Martha Flaherty, p. 15.

20 NAC, RG 18, RCMP Records, Accn. No. 83-84/68, Box 22, File G 567-44, Patrol Report, Grise Fiord, NWT to Makinson Inlet, NWT, 30 September to 12 October 1964, pp. 3-4.

21 See W.E. Wilmott, "The Flexibility of Inuit Social Organization," *Anthropologica*, Vol. 2, No. 1 (1960), pp. 48-59.

22 Ibid., pp. 52-53.

23 PC, WCSC, Grise Fiord Oral History Project, Interview with Anna Nungaq by Martha Flaherty, Inukjuak, PQ, 14 November 1989, English translation by Martha Flaherty, p. 11.

24 PC, WCSC, Pond Inlet Oral History Project, Interview with Simon Akpaliapik by Hannah Quaraq, Pond Inlet, Nunavut, April 19, 1994, Transcribed by Pierre Quasa, English translation by Elisapee Ootoova, p. 2.

25 NAC, RG 18, RCMP Records, Accn. No. 85-86/048, Vol. 56, File No. TA-500-20-10-1, Alexandra Fiord Detachment, Report re: General Game Conditions, 30 June 1961, p. 2.

26 PC, WCSC, Pond Inlet Oral History Project, Interview with Simon Akpaliapik by Hannah Quaraq, Pond Inlet, Nunavut, April 19, 1994, Transcribed by Pierre Quasa, English translation by Elisapee Ootoova, p. 3.

27 Ibid., p. 3.

28 Ibid.

29 Roderick R. Riewe and Charles W. Amsden, "Harvesting and Utilization of Pinnipeds by Inuit Hunters in Canada's Eastern High Arctic," in Allen P. McCartney, Ed., *Thule Eskimo Culture: An Anthropological Retrospective* (Ottawa: National Museum of Man, Archaeological Survey of Canada Paper No. 88, 1979), p. 335.

30 Ibid., p. 338.

31 Roderick R. Riewe, "Grise Fiord," in Milton Freeman, Ed., *Inuit Land Use and Occupancy Project,* Vol. I, "Land Use and Occupancy" (Ottawa: Department of Indian and Northern Affairs, 1976), p. 178.

32 NAC, RG 85 M, Accn. 77803/16, File no. S17LR, "Grise Fiord," Unpublished report entitled "Inuit Land Use and Occupancy in the Eastern High Arctic: Grise Fiord," by Roderick R. Riewe, October 1974, pp. 13-15.

33 Ibid., pp. 17-18.

34 Roderick R. Riewe and Charles W. Amsden, "Harvesting and Utilization of Pinnipeds by Inuit Hunters in Canada's Eastern High Arctic," p. 327.

35 Heather Myers, "The Use of Biological Resources by Certain Arctic and Subarctic Peoples," M. Phil. Thesis, The Scott Polar Research Institute, Cambridge, England, 1981, p. 11.

36 Roderick R. Riewe and Charles W. Amsden, "Harvesting and Utilization of Pinnipeds by Inuit Hunters in Canada's Eastern High Arctic," p. 336.

37 Ibid.

38 NAC, RG 85 M, Accn. 77803/16, File no. S17LR, "Grise Fiord," Unpublished report entitled "Inuit Land Use and Occupancy in the Eastern High Arctic: Grise Fiord," October 1974, by Roderick R. Riewe, p. 35.

39 Roderick W. Riewe, "The Utilization of Wildlife in the Jones Sound Region by the Grise Fiord Inuit," p. 635.

40 Ibid., p. 32.

41 PC, WCSC, Grise Fiord Oral History Project, Interview with Tookilkee Kigugtak by Liza Ningiuk, Grise Fiord, 3 March 1991, English Translation by Martha Flaherty, p. 3.

42 Roderick Riewe, "Grise Fiord," in Milton Freeman, Ed., *Inuit Land Use and Occupancy Project*, Vol. I, "Land Use and Occupancy" (Ottawa: Department of Indian and Northern Affairs, 1976), p. 184.

43 NAC, RG 85 M, Accn. 77803/16, File no. S17LR, "Grise Fiord," Unpublished report entitled "Inuit Land Use and Occupancy in the Eastern High Arctic: Grise Fiord," by Roderick R. Riewe, October 1974, p. 22.

44 Ibid., p. 24.

45 Roderick Riewe, "Grise Fiord," in Milton Freeman, Ed., *Inuit Land Use and Occupancy Project*, Vol. 1, "Land Use and Occupancy," p. 179.

46 NAC, RG 85 M, Accn. 77803/16, File no. S17LR, "Grise Fiord," Unpublished report entitled "Inuit Land Use and Occupancy in the Eastern High Arctic: Grise Fiord," by Roderick R. Riewe, October 1974, p. 14.

47 NAC, RG 18, Accn. 83-84/68, Box 22, File G 567-44, Patrol Report, Grise Fiord to Starnes Fiord, NWT and Return, 28 November to 2 December 1966, "Remarks," p. 2.

48 Ibid; and PC, WCSC, Pond Inlet Oral History Project, Interview with Simon Akpaliapik by Hannah Quaraq, Pond Inlet, Nunavut, April 19, 1994, Transcribed by Pierre Quasa, English translation by Elisapee Ootoova, pp. 1-2.

49 PC, WCSC, Pond Inlet Oral History Project, Interview with Simon Akpaliapik by Hannah Quaraq, Pond Inlet, NWT, April 19, 1994, Transcribed by Pierre Quasa, English translation by Elisapee Ootoova, pp. 1-2.

50 Milton M.R. Freeman, "Contemporary Inuit Exploitation of the Sea-Ice Environment," in *Sikumiut*, p. 80.

51 PC, WCSC, Pond Inlet Oral History Project, Interview with Simon Akpaliapik by Hannah Quaraq, Pond Inlet, Nunavut, April 19, 1994, Transcribed by Pierre Quasa, English translation by Elisapee Ootoova, pp. 5-6.

52 Ibid., p. 7.

53 Ibid., p. 5.

54 PC, WCSC, Pond Inlet Oral History Project, Interview with Ningiuk Killiktee by Lucy Quasa, co-ordinated by Lynn Cousins, Pond Inlet, Nunavut, 18 May 1994, English translation, p. 10.

55 Inuuterssuaq Uvdloriaq, *The Narrative of Qitdlarssuaq*, p. 88.

56 PC, WCSC, Grise Fiord Oral History Project, Interview with Martha Kigugtak by Larry Audlaluk, Grise Fiord, Nunavut, 11 December 1991, English translation by Martha Flaherty, p. 15.

Conclusion: Ellesmere Island and the Times of History

1 J.A. Cuddon, *A Dictionary of Literary Terms* (Harmondsworth, England: Penguin Books, 1979), p. 225. As Russian critic Mikhail Bakhtin has pointed out, the epic does not represent the past so much as it involves the transferral of a represented world onto the past. M.M. Bakhtin, "The Epic and the Novel," in *The Dialogic Imagination: Four Essays* (Ed., Michael Holquist) (Austin, Texas: University of Texas Press, 1981), pp. 3-38.

2 Martin Green, *Dreams of Adventure, Deeds of Empire* (New York: Basic Books, 1979), p. 3.

3 For an account of the more recent history of the Inughuit, see Richard Vaughan, *Northwest Greenland: A History*, pp. 151-68.

4 Charles S. Maier, "Consigning the Twentieth Century to History: Alternative Narratives for the Modern Era," *American Historical Review*, Vol. 105, No. 3 (June 2000), p. 11.

5 M.J. Dunbar, Review of *Langthen og Nordpaa*, by Christian Vibe, *Arctic*, Vol. 2, No.1 (May 1949), p. 61.

6 Elsewhere, I have discussed Peary's approach as an example of anthropologist Claude Lévi-Strauss's concept of bricolage, an imaginative, pragmatic application of the materials at hand to arrive at conceptual solutions attuned to specific environmental and cultural contexts. In contrast to the Western engineer, the bricoleur or handyman pragmatically reworks materials within pre-existing mental structure to arrive at a suitable solution. Lévi-Strauss criticized both the ethnocentric classification of such approaches as "primitive" and its binary opposite, that is, i.e. the rejection of European culture in favour of "going native." Both Western and Aboriginal approaches have their merits, and one should not be privileged over the other. Lyle Dick, "The Fort Conger Shelters and Vernacular Adaptation to the High Arctic," p. 23. See also Claude Lévi-Strauss, The Savage Mind (Chicago: University of Chicago Press, 1966), pp. 16-36; and David Pace, Claude Lévi-Strauss: The Bearer of Ashes (London: ARK Paperbacks, 1986), pp. 139-43.

7 British anthropologist Roy Ellen has provided a useful distinction between the *cumulative* adaptation of individuals and the *manipulative* adaptation of powerful individuals or collectivities within a group. At the primary level, adaptations occur through the cumulative practice of individuals, such as preparing and wearing suitable garments in a cold environment. In the event others then adopt these practices, one can speak of an adapting population. On the other hand, manipulative adaptation involves the exploitation of others to achieve individual goals. If taken to an extreme, the exploited group may withdraw from the relationship, terminating the basis for continued adaptation. Such manipulation is less evident in smaller, tribal societies than more complex, socially differentiated societies, as all members of smaller societies have an obvious interest in the continued success and survival of the group. Roy Ellen, *Environment, Subsistence, and System: The Ecology of Small Formations* (Cambridge, England: Cambridge University Press, 1982), pp. 246-47. As anthropologist John W. Bennett noted, a key variable is *power* and how it is applied to exert control over human societies and nature. John W. Bennett, *The Ecological Transition: Cultural Anthropology and Human Adaptation*, p. 27.

8 Edward Gibbon, *The Decline and Fall of the Roman Empire*, Vol. II, *Barbarism and the Fall of Rome* (Abridged version edited by Jacob Sloan) (New York: Collier Books, 1962), p. 382.

9 See, for example, the essays in Milton M.R. Freeman, Ed., *Endangered Peoples of the Arctic: Struggles to Survive and Thrive* (Westport, Connecticut and London: Greenwood Press, 2000); and Minority Rights Group, Ed., *Polar Peoples: Self-Determination and Development* (London: Minority Rights Publications, 1994).

10 Anthony Wilden, *System and Structure*, 2nd Edition, p. 116.

11 A. Gunn, A., F.L. Miller and D.C. Thomas, "The Current and Future of Peary Caribou (*Rangifer tarandus pearyi*) on the Arctic Islands of Canada," *Biological Conservation*, Vol. 19 (1980-81), p. 293.

12 M.M.R., Freeman, "Traditional Land Users as a Legitimate Source of Environmental Expertise," in J.G. Nelson, R.D. Needham, S.H. Nelson, and R.C. Scace, Eds., *The Canadian National Parks: Today and Tomorrow; Conference II: Ten Years Later*, Vol. I (Waterloo, Ontario: University of Waterloo, 1979), p. 348.

13 For a useful discussion of the differing perspectives of Western science and Aboriginal traditional knowledge, see Milton M.R. Freeman, "Appeal to Tradition: Different Perspectives on Arctic Wildlife Management," in Jens Brøsted et al., Eds., *Native Power: The Quest for Autonomy and Nationhood of Indigenous Peoples* (Bergen: Universitetsforlaget, 1985), pp. 265-81.

14 As the anthropologist Milton Freeman has pointed out, when co-management paradigms are introduced, it is important to ensure that they do not undermine preexisting Indigenous management practices considered essential to continued sustainability. Milton M.R. Freeman, "Issues Affecting Subsistence Security in Arctic Societies," *Arctic Anthropology*, Vol. 34, No. 1 (1997), p. 13.

BIBLIOGRAPHY

Unpublished Textual and Iconographic Sources

Bowdoin College Library, Special Collections (Brunswick, Maine)

Robert Abrams Bartlett Papers: Books, Articles, Etc. by Robert A. Bartlett
"From the Crow's Nest: The First Roosevelt Expedition" (1905–06)
"From the Crow's Nest: The Conquest of the Pole" (1908–09).

Donald B. MacMillan Collection
Correspondence, 1914.
Diaries, Journals, Logs, Etc.,
MacMillan Diary No. 3, Diary, North Pole Expedition, 17 July 1908 - 2 October 1909
MacMillan Diary No. 7, North Pole, 19 April - 31 May 1909, Entry for 19 May 1909 [at Fort Conger].
"Crocker Land" Expedition, Journal No. 16, 2 July 1913 - 12 February 1914.
"Crocker Land" Expedition, Diary No. 19/5, 12 February 1914 - 26 March 1915.
"Crocker Land" Expedition, MacMillan Journal No. 3, 12 April 1916 - 2 April 1917.
Diary No. 56, MacMillan "Ethnological Notes."
Diary No. 25, Fitzhugh Green's Field Notebook, 7 February 1914 - 20 May 1914.
MacMillan Field Notebook No. 32, March - July 1924.

National Archives of Canada (Ottawa), Textual Archives

Pelham Aldrich Journals, 29 May 1875 to 14 August 1876 (Microfilm reel A-822).
[by permission of the Scott Polar Research Institute, Cambridge, Ms. 278/1].

Reginald Baldwin Fulford Journal, 29 May 1875 to 30 September 1876 (Microfilm reel A-1176).

Sir Albert Hastings Markham Fonds, Notebooks and Journal for the period 3 April - 8 May 1876 (Microfilm reel A-822).

Papers of Captain George Strong Nares, RN (later Vice-Admiral Sir George Nares, KCB) Relating to the Arctic Expedition of 1875-76 (Microfilm Reel No. A-394).

RG 85M, 77803/16, S17L1T, Accn. 1977-0110, Inuit Land Use and Occupancy Project
Transcript of Interview with Markosie Piunngittuk Inaaluk by Roderick Riewe, English-language translation by Minnie Freeman, 1971?
Transcript of Interview with Tukiqiq (Tookilkee Kigugtak) by Roderick Riewe, English translation by Minnie Freeman, 1971?
Transcript of Interview with Tukiqiq (Tookilkee Kigugtak) by Roderick Riewe, English translation by Minnie Freeman, 1971?
Transcript of Interview with Akeeagok (Gamaliel Aqiarak) by Milton Freeman, English translation by Minnie Freeman, 1971?
Transcript of Interview with Piyamini (Abraham Pijamini) by Minnie and Milton Freeman, English-language translation by Minnie Freeman, 1971?

RG 85 M, Accn. 77803/16, File no. S17LR, "Grise Fiord"
Unpublished report entitled "Inuit Land Use and Occupancy in the Eastern High Arctic: Grise Fiord," by Roderick R. Riewe, October 1974.

National Archives of Canada (Ottawa), Government Records

Department of Marine and Fisheries, 1894-1908
File 1536, fol. 392, Part 1.

RG 18, Royal Canadian Mounted Police Records
Accn. No. 83-84/68, Vol. 22, File G 567-44; Accn. No. 83-84/68, Box 22, File G 567-44; Accn. 85-86/048, Vol. 56; Accn. 84-85/084, Vol. 32, File G-516-37; Accn. No. 84-85/084, Vol. 32; File G-516-37, Parts 1-2; Accn. 85-86/084, Vol. 33, File G-516-37, Parts 3-4; Accn. No. 85-86/084, Vol. 33, File G-804-13; File G-516-37, Part 2; Accn. No. 85-86/048, Vol. 43, File G 804-44; Vol. 54, File TA-500-20-10-1; Accn. No. 85-86/048, Vol. 55, File TA 500-8-1-1, File TA 500-8-1-5; File TA 500-20-10-1; Accn. 85-86/084, Vol. 43, File G 804-44; Vol. 1446, File 1000/133, Part 1; Vol. 3014; Vol. 3015; Vol. 3012; Vol. 3663, File G 567-25.

RG 24, Defence Research Board Records
Vol. 4235, File DRBS-3-780-43 (Vol.1) RG 85, Vol. 72, File 201-1 [11].

RG 85 Indian and Northern Affairs Records (incorporates the records of the former Department of Northern Affairs and Natural Development)
Vol. 10; File 401-23-1; Vol. 72, File 201-1 [11]; Vol. 79, File 201 [25-A]; Vol. 85, File 202-2-1; Vol. 176, File 40-2-20; Vol. 294, File 1005-7 (5); Vol. 348, File 201-1-8; Vol. 584, File 571; Vol. 584, File 571, Part 7; Vol. 584, File 573-1; Vol. 759, File 4829;Vol. 764, File 5086; Vol. 818, File 7022, Parts 2 and 3; Vol. 835, Files 7423, 7424; Vol. 872, File 8729, Parts 1 and 2; Vol. 877, File 8904, Vol. 916, File 11036; Vol. 1070, File 251-4, Parts 1 and 2; Vol. 1203; Vol. 1446, File 1000/133, Pt. 1; Vol. 1912, File A-1011-1, Part 1; Vol. 1962, File A-1012-13, Part 1; and Accn. 85-86/220, Box 7, File A-401-3, Part 2.

McGill University Archives (Montreal)

MG 4112, Accn. 88-041 and Accn 87-089, Maxwell Dunbar Papers
Unpublished Work, 1970-1981, "The State of the Environment in Northern Canadian Seas: Beaufort Sea to the Strait of Belle Isle," by M.J. Dunbar, 1982.

The Library of Congress Manuscript Division (Washington, DC)

Papers of Evelyn Briggs Baldwin
Container No. 7, Polar Expedition Records, 1893-1915, Baldwin Diary [handwritten], 20 August 1893 - 15 December 1893.

Papers of Adolphus Washington Greely
Military Papers, Container No. 71, Summary of the Journal of Lieutenant A.W. Greely, Commanding Lady Franklin Bay Expedition, August 1881 to July 1882.
Military Papers, Container No. 95, Arctic Files, 1877-1915.

Papers of Albert J. Myers
Reel No. 3, A.J. Myers Correspondence, 1879-1880.

William S. Lovell
"Journal of a Cruise in the Arctic Regions in Search of Sir John Franklin, 1850-1855."

National Geographic Society Library (Washington, DC)

Adolphus Greely Collection,
Notebook, Accn. No. 13439, News clipping: "Reports on Killing of Peary's Aide: Rasmussen Sends Results of Inquiry into Marvin Murder to Danish Legation" [1926].

Robert E. Peary Photographic Collection
US National Archives (Washington, DC)

RG 27, Papers of General David L. Brainard
Journal, 1881-84.

RG 27, Records of the Weather Bureau
Weather Bureau Correspondence, 1870-1912, Miscellaneous Series, Lady Franklin Bay, Vol. 2, Manuscript of Expedition Report, Narrative, and Appendices.
Weather Bureau Correspondence, 1870-1912, Miscellaneous Series, Lady Franklin Bay 700 (1883), Box No. 818, 3278-4212, Folder 32781/2, Mis. 1883 Garlington-Greely Expedition, memoranda taken from pigeon hole of desk of Asst. Chief Clerk 5/26/86, File with 700 Misc. 1881, "Proceedings of a Board which convened at Washington, DC, 27 May 1880, by authority of Instructions No. 33, Current Series, from this office."

RG 27, Records of the Weather Bureau, Lady Franklin Bay Expedition Papers
Box 2, "Manuscripts of Reports, Narratives, and Appendices," Lieutenant Adolphus Greely Journal, Vol.1.
Box 12, Translation of Dr. Octave Pavy's Loose Notes.
Box 12, Extracts from Lieutenant Adolphus Greely's Journal.
Box 13, Private Henry Biederbick Diary.
Box 13, Private Charles B. Henry Diary.
Box 13, Lieutenant Frederick F. Kislingbury Diary.
Box 17, Illustrations Relating to the Expedition.
Box 19, OCSO Correspondence with or About Members of the Expedition.
Box 19, Translation of Diary of Private Jacob Bender.
Box 19 "The Physician's Handbook, 1880 " (Translation of Octave Pavy's Notes)
Box 22, Journals and Diaries, Lieutenant Adolphus Greely Journal, Vol. 1.

RG 401(1)(A), Robert E. Peary Papers
Papers Relating to Arctic Expeditions, 1886-1909.
Greenland 1886, Notebook 1886, Equipment Lists, Notebook, Planning Notes, 1885-86.
Greenland: 1891-92; Diaries and Reports: Astrup, Cook, Gibson, and Verhoef, Greenland Expedition (II), Folder 8, Dr. Frederick A. Cook, Surgeon and Ethnologist. Notes, dated 22 September 1892, p. 4 [on board the *Kite*]
Greenland: 1893-95, Diaries and Field Notebooks, Box 1, "Logbook for 5 March - 26 April 1894" [Note: the logbook incorporates a wider range of dates than is indicated in its title.]
Greenland: 1893-95; Diaries, Reports and Notes: Astrup, Baldwin, Clark, Lee, Vincent, Greenland Expedition III, Folder 5, George H. Clark Notes, "Mammalogies, 1893-95."
Greenland: 1898-1902, Box No. 3 of 6, Robert E. Peary Diaries 1900-01.
Greenland, 1898-1902, Peary Diary, July-August 1900.
Greenland: 1898-1902, Peary Diary, 1-16 November 1900.
Greenland: 1898-1902, Peary Diary, January-April 1901.
Greenland: 1898-1902, Peary Diary, 20 January-5 March 1902.
Greenland: 1898-1902, Peary Diaries, 1898-1902, "Journal Entries by Peary, Portion of 1900" [typescript].
Greenland: 1898-1902, T.S. Dedrick Diaries, Notebooks, and Other Papers VI, Folder 2, Dedrick Diaries, 1899.
Greenland, 1898-1902, T.S. Dedrick Diaries, Notebooks and Other Papers, 1898-1901, VI, Box 4 of 6, Dr. T.S. Dedrick Diary, 28 June-23 August 1900 [at Fort Conger].
Greenland, 1898-1902, T.S. Dedrick Diaries, Notebooks and Other Papers, 1898-1901, VI, Box No. 4, Folder 6, Miscellaneous Papers of Dr. T.S. Dedrick: Field Notes.
Greenland, 1898-1902, Peary Diary, January-April 1901, "My Domicile at Conger," pp. 1-5.
Greenland, 1898-1902, Papers Relating to Expedition Plans, Supplies, Field Operations, LFB [Lady Franklin Bay], and Fort Conger, Cartographic Activities, Etc., 1898-1902.
Greenland: 1898-1902, Box No. 2 of 6, Peary Diary Transcriptions, 1898-1902.
Greenland - Ellesmere Island, 1898-1902, Photographs.

North Polar: 1905-06, Box 1, Peary Journal Notes, April 1906.

North Polar: 1905-06, Box 1, File "Letters Rec[eived], Henson, 1905-06."

North Polar: 1905-06, Diaries, Journals and Logs; Correspondence and Instructions, 1905-06 [Box 1 of 2], Dr. Louis Wolf Journal, 1905-06 [Cape Sheridan].

North Polar 1908-09, Expedition VIII, Box 1, Diaries and Journals, 1908-09, Diary of Dr. John Goodsell, 21 June - 12 October 1909.

North Polar 1908-09, Diaries, Logs, and Journals, 1908-09, Box 1, Peary Diary Transcript, 2 March-23 April 1909.

Peary Diary Transcripts, 1871-1900, "Diary (typed) 1899"

Peary Diary Transcripts, 1871-1900, "Diary (typed) 1900."

Peary Diary Transcripts, 1871-1900, "Diary (typed) 1901."

Peary Diary Transcripts, 1871-1900, "Diary (typed) 1902."

Peary Diary Transcripts, 1871-1900, "Diary (typed) 1898." [Note: this transcript is mislabelled and actually is Peary's diary for his foray over the pack ice in 1909.]

RG 401(56), Papers of Hugh J. Lee

Reports on Greenland Eskimos, 1893-95, "Arctic Highlanders — Houses and Tents, Igloos and Tupiks," Unpublished manuscript, 28 October 1894.

Reports on Greenland Eskimos, 1893-95, "Arctic Highlanders, Customs — Igluetah." [location: 8E1, Row 4/11/E, Box labelled "Reports on Greenland — Eskimos 1893-95."].

American Museum of Natural History (New York City)

Donald B. MacMillan "Crocker Land" Expedition Photographic Collection.

Unpublished Oral History Sources

Parks Canada, Western Canada Service Centre (Winnipeg), Grise Fiord Oral History Project, Interviews with current or former residents of Grise Fiord, Ellesmere Island

Interview with Edith Patsauq Amaroalik by Martha Flaherty, Inukjuak, PQ, 16 November 1989 (English translation by Martha Flaherty).

Interview with Anna Nungaq by Martha Flaherty, Inukjuak, PQ, 14 November 1989 (English translation by Martha Flaherty).

Interview with Samwilly Elaijasialuk by Martha Flaherty, Inukjuak, PQ, 15 November 1989, (English translation by Martha Flaherty).

Interview with Markusie Patsauq by Martha Flaherty, Inukjuak, PQ, 17 November 1989 (English translation by Martha Flaherty).

Interview with Gamaliel Aqiarak (Akeeagok) by Liza Ningiuk, Grise Fiord, Nunavut, 29 January 1990 (English translation by Martha Flaherty).

Interview with Rynee Flaherty by Larry Audlaluk, Grise Fiord, Nunavut, 1 December 1991 (English translation by Martha Flaherty).

Interview with Tookilkee Kigugtak by Liza Ningiuk, Grise Fiord, Nunavut, 3 March 1991 (English translation by Martha Flaherty).

Interview with Martha Kigugtak by Larry Audlaluk, Grise Fiord, Nunavut, 1 December 1991 (English translation by Martha Flaherty).

Interview with Annie Pijamini by Iga Kigugtak, Grise Fiord, Nunavut, 7 January 1991 (English translation by Martha Flaherty).

Interview with Abraham Pijamini, by Liza Ningiuk, Grise Fiord, Nunavut, 28 February 1991 (English translation by Martha Flaherty).

Interview with Martha Flaherty by Lyle Dick, Ottawa, Ontario, 27 February 1989.

Interview with Ross Gibson by Lyle Dick, Victoria, British Columbia, 20 March 1989.

Interview with Robert Pilot by Lyle Dick, Pembroke, Ontario, 14 February 1989

Parks Canada, Western Canada Service Centre (Winnipeg), Pond Inlet Oral History Project, coordinated by Lynn Cousins, Interviews of former residents of Grise Fiord, Ellesmere Island

Interview with Samuel Arnakallak by Elisapee Ootoova, Pond Inlet, Nunavut (English translation by Philip Paneak).

Interview with Ningiuk Killiktee by Lucy Quasa, Pond Inlet, Nunavut, 18 May 1994.

Interview with Simon Akpaliapik by Hannah Quaraq, Pond Inlet, Nunavut, 19 April 1994 (Transcribed by Pierre Quasa, English translation by Elisapee Ootoova).

Parks Canada, Nunavut Field Unit (Iqaluit)

Larry Audlaluk, Unpublished notes on the text of the "Muskox Land" book manuscript, February/March 2001.

Published Primary Sources

Anonymous, *Journal of a Voyage of Discovery to the Arctic Regions, Performed Between the 4th of April and the 18th of November 1818* (London: Richard Phillips, 1819?) (Facsimile Reproduction, The Shorey Book Store, Seattle, 1964).

Astrup, Eivind, *With Peary Near the Pole* (London: C. Arthur Pearson, Ltd., 1898).

Bartlett, Robert A., *The Log of Bob Bartlett: The True Story of Forty Years of Seafaring and Exploration* (New York: G.P. Putnam's Sons, 1928).

Bernier, Captain J.E., *Report on the Dominion of Canada Government Expedition to the Arctic Islands and Hudson Strait on Board the GS Arctic* (Ottawa: King's Printer, 1910).

Bessels, Emil, "The Northernmost Inhabitants of the Earth: An Ethnographic Sketch," *The American Naturalist*, Vol. 18 (1884), pp. 861-82.

Bessels, Emil, "Smith Sound and its Exploration," *Proceedings of the United States Naval Institute*, Vol. 10, No. 3, Whole No. 30 (1884).

Blake, E. Vale, *Arctic Experiences: Containing Capt. George E. Tyson's Wonderful Drift on the Ice Floe, A History of the Polaris Expedition, The Cruise of the Tigress, and Rescue of the Polaris Survivors* (New York: Harper and Brothers, 1874).

Boas, Franz, *The Central Eskimo* (Lincoln, Nebraska: University of Nebraska Press, 1964).

Boas, Franz, "The Configuration of Grinnell Land and Ellesmere Land," *Science*, Vol. 5, No. 108 (27 February 1885), pp. 170-71.

Borup, George, *A Tenderfoot With Peary* (New York: Frederick A. Stokes, 1911).

Brainard, David L., "Farthest North With Greely," in Rudolf Kersting, Comp., *The White World: Life and Adventures Within the Arctic Circle Portrayed by Famous Living Explorers* (New York: Lewis, Scribner, and Company, 1902).

Bridgeman, Herbert L., "Ten Years of the Peary Arctic Club," *National Geographic Magazine*, Vol. 19, No. 9 (September 1908).

Brill, A.A., "Piblockto or Hysteria Among Peary's Eskimos," *Journal of Nervous and Mental Disease*, Vol. 40 (1913), pp. 514-20.

Bryant, Henry G., "The Peary Auxiliary Expedition of 1894," *Bulletin of the Geographical Club of Philadelphia* Vol. 1, No. 5 (June, 1895), pp. 141-64.

Byrd, Richard E., "Flying over the Arctic," *National Geographic Magazine*, Vol. 48, No. 5 (November 1925), pp. 519-32.

Cook, Dr. Frederick A., *My Attainment of the Pole* (New York and London: Mitchell and Kennerley, 1913).

Cook, Dr. Frederick A., *Return from the Pole* (New York: Pellagrini and Cudahy, 1951).

Da Costa, B.F. (Benjamin Franklin), "'Inventio Fortunata': Arctic Exploration, With an Account of Nicholas of Lynn," Paper read before the American Geographical Society, Chickering Hall, 15 May 1880. Reprinted from the *Bulletin of the American Geographical Society*, New York, 1881, pp. 1-36.

"Danish Thule and Ellesmere Land Expedition, 1939-40," *The Polar Record*, No. 18 (July 1939), pp. 111-12.

Davis, C.H., Ed., *Narrative of the North Polar Expedition, US Ship* Polaris, *Captain Charles Francis Hall, Commanding* (London: Trübner and Co., 1881).

Ekblaw, W. Elmer, "The Material Response of the Polar Eskimo to Their Far Arctic Environment," *Annals of the Association of American Geographers*, Vol. 17, No. 4 (December 1927).

Ekblaw, Walter, "Of Unknown Shores: The Traverse of Grant and Ellesmere Lands," in Donald B. MacMillan, *Four Years in the White North* (New York and London: Harper Bros., 1918), Appendix B.

Ellis, Richard N., "The Greely Expedition: The Last Days," *The Beaver*, Outfit 304, No. 4 (Spring 1974), p. 33.

Freuchen, Peter, *Arctic Adventure: My Life in the Frozen North* (New York: Farrar and Rinehart, 1935).

Godfrey, William C., *Godfrey's Narrative of the Last Grinnell Arctic Exploring Expedition in Search of Sir John Franklin, 1853-4-5* (Philadelphia: J.T. Lloyd, 1860).

Goodsell, John W., *On Polar Trails: The Peary Expedition to the North Pole, 1908-09* (Ed., Donald W. Whisenhunt) (Austin, Texas: Eakin Press, 1983).

Goodsir, Robert Anstruther, *An Arctic Voyage to Baffin's Bay and Lancaster Sound in Search of Friends with Sir John Franklin* (London: John Van Voorst, 1850).

Great Britain, Admiralty, *Journals and Proceedings of the Arctic Expedition, 1875-6, Under the Command of Captain Sir George S. Nares*, Parliamentary Paper C-1636 (London: Harrison & Sons, Queen's Printer, 1877).

Greely, A.W., "Arctic Exploration, with Reference to Grinnell Land," *Proceedings of the Royal Geographical Society*, Vol. 8, No. 3 (March 1886), pp. 156-76.

Greely, Adolphus W., *Report on the Proceedings of the United States Expedition to Lady Franklin Bay, Grinnell Land*, Vols. I and II (Washington, DC: Government Printing Office, 1888).

Greely, Adolphus, *Three Years of Arctic Service*, Vols. I and II (New York: Charles Scribner's Sons, 1886).

Green, Fitzhugh, "The Crocker Land Expedition: The Story of the Last Extensive Dog-Sledge Expedition in the Arctic," *Natural History* (American Museum of Natural History) Vol. 28 (1928), pp. 463-75.

Haig-Thomas, David, "Expedition to Ellesmere Island, 1937-38," *Geographical Journal*, Vol. 95 (1940), pp. 265-77.

Haig-Thomas, David, *Tracks in the Snow* (London: Hodder and Stoughton, 1939).

Hall, Thomas, *Has the North Pole Been Discovered?* (Boston: Badger, 1917).

Hall, Captain Thomas F., "The Murder of Professor Ross G. Marvin," in W. Henry Lewin, *The Great North Pole Fraud* (London: C.W. Daniel Company, 1935).

Hansen, Godfred, "Den Tredje Thuleekspedition: Norges Depotekspedition Til Roald Amundsen," in Roald Amundsen, *Nordostpassagen* (Copenhagen: Kristiana Gyldendalske Boghandel, 1921), pp. 439-62.

Hayes, I.I., "Address on Arctic Exploration," *Journal of the American Geographical and Statistical Society of New York*, Vol 2, Part 2 (1870).

Hayes, Isaac Israel, *An Arctic Boat Journey in the Autumn of 1854* (Ed., Dr. Norton Shaw) (London: Richard Bentley, 1860).

Hayes, Dr. I. I., *The Open Polar Sea: A Narrative of a Voyage of Discovery Towards the North Pole in the Schooner* United States (New York: Hurd and Houghton, 1867).

Hayes, Isaac I., *Physical Observations in the Arctic Seas* (Washington, DC: Smithsonian Institution, Smithsonian Contributions to Knowledge, Vol. 196, 1865).

Heilprin, Angelo, *The Arctic Problem and Narrative of the Peary Relief Expedition of the Academy of Natural Sciences of Philadelphia* (Philadelphia: Contemporary Publishing Co., 1893).

Hendrik, Hans, *Memoirs of Hans Hendrik, the Arctic Traveller, Serving under Kane, Hayes, Hall and Nares, 1853-1876* (Trans. and ed., Dr. Henry Rink) (London: Trübner and Co., Ludgate Hill, 1878).

Henderson, F.D., "Canada's Arctic Islands," *The Canadian Magazine*, Vol. 65, No. 4 (April 1928), pp. 10-11, 42.

Henson, Matthew, *A Negro Explorer at the North Pole* (New York: Arno Press and the New York Times, 1969).

Hoppin, Benjamin, *A Diary Kept While With the Peary Arctic Expedition of 1896* (New Haven: n.p., 1897).

Hovey, Edmund Otis, "The Personnel of the Crocker Land Expedition," *The American Museum Journal*, Vol. 13 (1913).

Howgate, Captain H.W., Ed., *The Cruise of the* Florence, *or Extracts from the Journal of the Preliminary Arctic Expedition of 1877-'78* (Washington, DC: James J. Chapman, 1879).

Howgate, Henry W., "Plan for the Exploration of the Arctic Regions," *Journal of the American Geographical Society of New York* , Vol.10 (1878).

Howgate, Captain Henry W., *Polar Colonization* (Washington, DC: Beresford, Printer, 1877?).

Howgate, H.W., Comp., *Proposed Legislation, Correspondence, and Action of Scientific and Commercial Associations in Reference to Polar Colonization* (Washington, DC: Beresford, Printer, 1877?).

Humphreys, Noel, "Ellesmere Land and Grinnell Land," *The Geographical Journal*, Vol. 87, No. 5 (January to June 1936).

Hunt, Harrison and Ruth Hunt Thompson, *North to the Horizon: Searching for Peary's Crocker Land* (Camden, Maine: Down East Book, 1980).

Inglefield, Commander E.A., *A Summer Search for Sir John Franklin: With a Peep into the Polar Basin* (London: Thomas Harrison, 1853).

James, Bessie Rowland, Ed., *Six Came Back: The Arctic Adventure of David L. Brainard* (Indianapolis / New York: Bobbs-Merrill, 1940).

Kane, Elisha Kent, *The United States Grinnell Expedition in Search of Sir John Franklin: A Personal Narrative* (New York: Sheldon, Blakeman and Co., 1857).

Kane, Elisha Kent, *Arctic Explorations: The Second Grinnell Expedition in Search of Sir John Franklin, 1853, '54, '55*, Vols. I and II (Philadelphia: Childs and Peterson, 1856).

Keely Jr., Robert N., *In Arctic Seas: The Voyage of the* Kite *with the Peary Expedition Together with a Transcript of the Log of the* Kite (London: Gay and Bird, 1893).

Koch, Lauge, *Report on the Danish Bicentenary Jubilee Expedition North of Greenland 1920-23* (Copenhagen: C.A. Reitzels, Forlag, 1927).

Kroeber, A.L., "The Eskimo of Smith Sound," *American Museum of Natural History Bulletin*, Vol. 12, No. 21 (1899), pp. 265-27.

Lanman, Charles, *Farthest North, or The Life and Explorations of Lieutenant James Booth Lockwood, of the Greely Arctic Expedition* (New York: D. Appleton and Company, 1885).

Lee, Herbert Patrick, *Policing the Top of the World* (Toronto: McClelland and Stewart, 1928).

Leslie, Sir John, *Narrative of Discovery and Adventure in the Polar Seas and Regions, with Illustrations of their Climate, Geology, and Natural History, and an Account of the Whale Fishery* (Edinburgh: Oliver and Boyd, 1835).

Lewin, W. Henry, *The Great North Pole Fraud* (London: C.W. Daniel Company, 1935).

Low, A.P., *Report on the Dominion Government Expedition to Hudson Bay and the Arctic Islands on Board the DGS* Neptune, *1903-04* (Ottawa: Government Printing Bureau, 1906)

MacBrien, J.H., "The Mounties in the Arctic," *Canadian Geographical Journal*, Vol. 10. No. 3 (March 1935), pp. 157-66.

MacMillan, Donald B., *Four Years in the White North* (New York and London: Harper Brothers, 1918).

MacMillan, Donald B., "Geographical Report of the Crocker Land Expedition, 1913-1917," *Bulletin of the American Museum of Natural History*, Vol. 56, "1926-1929" (1930), pp. 379-35.

MacMillan, Donald B.,"The MacMillan Expedition Returns," *The National Geographic Magazine*, Vol. 48, No. 5 (November 1925), pp. 477-518.

Markham, Captain Albert Hastings, *The Great Frozen Sea: A Personal Narrative of the Voyage of the* Alert *During the Arctic Expedition of 1875-6* (London: Daldy, Isbister and Co., 1878).

Markham, Captain A.H., "On Sledge Travelling," *Proceedings of the Royal Geographical Society* (Great Britain), 12 December 1876, pp. 118-19.

Markham, Clements, "The Arctic Expedition, IX: The Work," *The Geographical Magazine*, (December 1876), pp. 313-24.

Markham, Clements, Compiler, *Arctic Voyages, Being An Account of Discoveries in the North Polar Seas in the Years 1818, 1819, and 1820, with An Account of the Esquimaux People* (Dublin: Richard B. Webb, 1831).

Markham, C.R. "The Arctic Highlanders," *Transactions of the Ethnological Society of London*, Vol. 4 (1866), pp. 125-37.

Markham, Clements, *The Lands of Silence: A History of Arctic and Antarctic Exploration* (Cambridge, England: Cambridge University Press, 1921).

Markham, Clements, "On the Arctic Highlanders," in *A Selection of Papers on Arctic Geography and Ethnology* (London: John Murray, 1875), pp. 175-87.

Markham, Sir Clements,"The Promotion of Further Discovery in the Arctic and the Antarctic Regions" (Address to the Royal Geographic Society), *The Geographical Journal*, Vol. 4, No. 1 (July 1894), pp. 1-25.

Markham, Clements R., *The Threshold of the Unknown Region* (London: Sampson Low, Marston, Low, and Searle, 1875).

M'Clintock, Capt. Sir Leopold, *The Voyage of the* Fox *in the Arctic Seas in Search of Franklin and His Companions* (London: John Murray, 1859).

McGinley, Rev. William A., Comp., *Reception of Lieut. A.W. Greely, USA, and His Comrades, and of the Arctic Relief Expedition, at Portsmouth, NH, on August 1 and 4, 1884* (Washington: Government Printing Office, 1884), pp. 3-58.

Moss, Dr. Edward, *Shores of the Polar Sea: A Narrative of the Arctic Expedition of 1875–76* (London: Marcus Ward and Co., 1878).

Nares, Captain Sir G.S., *Narrative of a Voyage to the Polar Sea During 1875-6 in HM Ships* Alert *and* Discovery, Vols. I and II (London: Sampson Low, Marston, Searle, and Rivington, 1878).

Nares, Captain G.S., "Report of Proceedings," in Great Britain, Admiralty, *Journals and Proceedings of the Arctic Expedition, 1875-6, under the Command of Captain Sir George S. Nares*, Parliamentary Paper No. C-1636 (London: Queen's Printer, 1877).

New York Times (New York), 12 August 1884, p. 1.

Northwest Territories Council, Debates, 34th Session, "Brief, Grise Fiord Hunters — Muskox Hunting," Tabled Document No. 13, 1967.

Nourse, J.E., *Narrative of the Second Arctic Expedition Made by Charles Francis Hall: His Voyage to Repulse Bay, Sledge Journeys in the Straits of Fury and Hecla and to King William's Land and Residence Among the Eskimos During the Years 1864-69* (Washington, DC: Government Printing Office, 1879).

Osborn, Sherard, *Stray Leaves from an Arctic Journal; or, Eighteen Months in the Polar Regions, in Search of Sir John Franklin's Expedition, In the Years 1850-51* (London: Longman, Brown, Green, and Longmans, 1852).

Parry, William Edwin, *Journal of a Voyage of Discovery to the Arctic Regions Performed between the 4th of April and the 18th of November 1818 in His Majesty's Ship* Alexander, *William Edwin Parry, Esq, Lieutenant and Commander* (Seattle: Shorey Book Store Facsimile Reproduction, 1964).

Peary, Josephine Diebitsch, *My Arctic Journal: A Year Among Ice-Fields and Eskimos* (New York: Contemporary Publishing Co., 1893).

Peary, Robert E., "The Discovery of the North Pole," *Hampton's Magazine*, Vol. 24 (January to September 1910).

Peary, Robert E., "In Greely's Old Camp at Fort Conger," *McClure's Magazine*, Vol. 14 (January 1900), pp. 238-40.

Peary, Robert E., "Living Off the Country," *Century Magazine* (October, 1917), pp. 907-19.

Peary, Robert E., "Moving on the North Pole — Outlines of My Arctic Campaign," *McClure's Magazine*, (March 1899), pp. 417-26.

Peary, Robert E., *Nearest the Pole: A Narrative of the Polar Expedition of the Peary Arctic Club in the SS* Roosevelt, *1905-06* (London: Hutchinson & Co., 1907).

Peary, R.E., *North Polar Exploration: Field Work of the Peary Arctic Club, 1898-1902* (Washington, DC: The Smithsonian Institution, 1903).

Peary, Robert E., *The North Pole: Its Discovery in 1909 Under the Auspices of the Peary Arctic Club* (New York: Frederick A. Stokes Co., 1910).

Peary, Robert E., *Northward over the "Great Ice": A Narrative of Life and Work Along the Shores and upon the Interior Ice-Cap of Northern Greenland in the Years 1886 and 1891-1897*, Vols. I and. II (New York: Frederick A. Stokes Company, 1898).

Peary, Robert E.,"The Party and the Outfit for the Greenland Journey," *Journal of the American Geographical Society of New York*, Vol. 23 (1898), pp. 256-65.

"Peary's Own Story of the Discovery of the North Pole," *Hampton's Magazine*, Vol. 23, No. 6 (December 1909).

Peary, Robert E., "Report of R.E. Peary, USN, on Work Done in the Arctic in 1898-1902," *Bulletin of the American Geographical Society*, Vol. 35 (December 1903), pp. 496-534.

Peary, Robert E., *Secrets of Polar Travel* (New York: The Century Company, 1917).

Peary, Robert E., "Sledging Over the Polar Pack," *Outing*, Vol. 41, No. 4 (January 1903), pp. 395-405.

Petersen, Johan Carl Christian, *Dr. Kane's Voyage to the Polar Lands* (Ed. Oscar M. Villarejo) (Philadelphia: University of Pennsylvania Press, 1965).

Rand, Sturgis B., "Robert E. Peary and his Campaign for the Pole," *McClure's Magazine*, February 1902, pp. 354-63.

Rasmussen, Knud, *Foran Dagens Oje: Liv I Grønland* (Copenhagen: Nordisk Forlag, 1915).

Rasmussen, Knud, *Greenland by the Polar Sea: The Story of the Thule Expedition from Melville Bay to Cape Morris Jesup* (Trans., Asta and Rowland Kenney) (London: William Henemann, 1921).

Rasmussen, Knud, *The People of the Polar North* (Trans. and ed., G. Herring) (London: Kegan Paul, Trench, Trübner and Co., 1908).

Rawson, Kenneth Longley, *A Boy's-Eye View of the Arctic* (New York: Macmillan, 1926).

Rink, Henrik, *Tales and Traditions of the Eskimo* (Ed., Robert Brown) (Edinburgh and London: William Blackwood and Sons, 1875).

Robeson, George M., *Instructions for the Expedition Toward the North Pole* (Washington: Government Printing Office, 1871).

Ross, Captain John, *A Voyage of Discovery Made Under the Orders of the Admiralty in His Majesty's Ships* Isabella *and* Alexander *for the Purpose of Exploring Baffin's Bay and Inquiring into the Probability of a North-West Passage*, Vol. I (London: John Murray, 1819).

Shackleton, Edward, *Arctic Journeys: The Story of the Oxford University Ellesmere Land Expedition, 1934-5* (London: Hodder and Stoughton, Ltd., 1936).

Shackleton, Edward, "The Oxford University Ellesmere Land Expedition," Appendix V: "Dogs and Sledges," *The Geographical Journal*, Vol. 87, No. 5 (May 1936), pp. 437-40.

Schley, Winfield S., *Report of Winfield S. Schley, Commander, US Navy, Commanding Greely Relief Expedition of 1884* (Washington, DC: Government Printing Office, 1887).

Schley, Commander W.S. and Professor J.R. Soley, *The Rescue of Greely* (New York: Charles Scribner's Sons, 1886).

Senn, Nicholas, *In the Heart of the Arctic* (Chicago: W.B. Conkey Company, 1907).

Smith, Charles Edward, Ed., *From the Deep of the Sea, Being the Diary of the Late Charles Edward Smith, M.R.C.S., Surgeon of the Whale-Ship* Diana *of Hull* (London: H. & C. Black, Ltd., 1922).

Smith, D. Murray, *Arctic Explorations from British and Foreign Shores from the Earliest Times to the Expedition of 1875-76* (Edinburgh: Thomas C. Jack, Grange Publishing Works, 1877).

Snow, Lieut. W. Parker, *Voyage of the* Prince Albert *in Search of Sir John Franklin: A Narrative of Every-Day Life in the Arctic Seas* (Paris: A. and W. Galignant and Co.; and Baudry's European Library, 1851).

Sonntag, August, *Professor Sonntag's Thrilling Narrative of the Grinnell Exploring Expedition to the Arctic Ocean in the Years 1853, 1854, and 1855, In Search of Sir John Franklin, Under the Command of Dr. E.K. Kane, USN* (Philadelphia: J.H.C. Whiting, n.d.).

Steele, Harwood, *Policing the Arctic: The Story of the Conquest of the Arctic by the Royal Canadian (formerly North-West Mounted Police)* (Toronto: The Ryerson Press, 1935).

Steensby, H.P., "The Polar Eskimos and the Polar Expeditions," *Fortnightly Review*, Vol. 92 (November 1909), pp. 891-902.

Steensby, H.P., "Contributions to the Ethnology and Anthropogeography of the Polar Eskimos," *Meddelelser om Grønland*, Vol. 34, No. 7 (1910), pp. 255-405.

Stokes, Frank Wilbert, "An Arctic Studio (77o 44' N. Lat.)," *The Century Magazine*, Vol. 52, New Series, Vol. 30 (1896), pp. 408-14.

Streeter, Daniel W., *An Arctic Rodeo* (New York: G.P. Putnam's Sons, 1929).

Sutherland, Peter C., *Journal of a Voyage in Baffin's Bay and Barrow Straits in the Years 1850-51, Performed by HM Ships* Lady Franklin *and* Sophia *Under the Command of Mr. William Penny, in Search of the Missing Crews of HM Ships* Erebus *and* Terror, Vol. I (London: Longman, Brown, Green, and Longmans, 1852).

Sverdrup, Otto, *New Land: Four Years in the Arctic Regions*, Vols. I and II (Longmans, Green, and Co.: 1904).

United Kingdom, Parliament, *Journals and Proceedings of the Arctic Expedition, 1875-6*, Parliamentary Paper C-1636 (London: Harrison and Sons, Queen's Printer, 1877).

United Kingdom, Parliament, *Report of the Committee Appointed by the Lords Commissioners of the Admiralty to Enquire into the Causes of the Outbreak of Scurvy in the Recent Arctic Expedition*, Parliamentary Paper C-1722 (London: Her Majesty's Stationery Office, 1877).

United States, House of Representatives, 45th Congress, 2nd Session, *Report No. 96*, "Expedition to the Arctic Seas," 22 January 1878 — Recommended to the Committee on Naval Affairs.

United States, House of Representatives, 45th Congress, 2nd Session, *Report No. 96*, "Expedition to the Arctic Seas," Report to Accompany Bill HR 447, by Benjamin A. Willis, 22 January 1878.

United States, House of Representatives, 44th Congress, 2nd Session, *Report No. 181*, "Expedition to the Arctic Seas," Report to accompany Bill H.R. 4339 "to authorize and equip an expedition to the Arctic Seas," 22 February 1877.

United States, House of Representatives, 46th Congress, 2nd Session, *Report No. 453*, "Expedition to the Arctic Seas," Report to accompany Bill HR 3534 "to authorize and equip an expedition to the Arctic Seas," 9 March 1880.

United States, *Congressional Record*, Proceedings and Debates of the Sixty-First Congress, Vol. 46, Part 3, Third Session (Washington, DC: Government Printing Office, 1911), pp. 2700-25.

United States, House of Representatives, Sixty-First Congress, Third Session, *Report No. 1961* (Washington, DC: Government Printing Office, 1911), pp. 410-31.

United States, House of Representatives, *Congressional Record*, "Proceedings and Debates of the First Session of the Sixty-Fourth Congress," Vol. 53, Part 14 (Washington, DC: Government Printing Office, 1916), Appendix, pp. 268-327.

United States, *Proceedings of the* Proteus *Court of Inquiry on the Greely Relief Expedition of 1883* (Washington, DC: Government Printing Office, 1884).

United States Navy, *Report to the President of the United States of the Action of the Navy Department in the Matter of the Disaster to the United States Exploring Expedition Toward the North Pole, Accompanied By a Report of the Examination of the Rescued Party, Etc.* (Washington, DC: Navy Department, 1873).

Walker, A. Barclay, *The Cruise of the* Esquimaux, *Steam Whaler to Davis Straits and Baffin Bay, April - October 1899* (Liverpool: The Liverpool Printing and Stationery Company Ltd., 1900).

Whitney, Harry, *Hunting with the Eskimos: The Unique Record of a Sportsman's Year Among the Northernmost Tribe — the Big Game Hunting, the Native Life, and the Battle for Existence Through the Long Arctic Night* (New York: The Century Company, 1910).

Wyckoff, Clarence F., "A Caribou Hunt on Peary's 1898-1902 Expedition," *Arctic*, Vol. 5, No. 3 (October 1952), pp. 178-82.

Young, Sir Allen, *The Two Voyages of the* Pandora *in 1875 and 1876* (London: Edward Stafford, 1879).

Secondary Sources

Abramson, Howard S., *Hero in Disgrace: The Life of Arctic Explorer Frederick A. Cook* (New York: Paragon House, 1991).

Allen, Everett S., *Arctic Odyssey: The Life of Rear Admiral Donald B. MacMillan* (New York: Dodd, Mead and Company, 1962).

Alt, B.T., R.M. Koerner, D.A. Fisher, and J.C. Bourgeois, "Arctic Climate During the Franklin Era, As Deduced from Ice Cores," in Patricia D. Sutherland, Ed., *The Franklin Era in Canadian Arctic History* (Ottawa: National Museum of Man, Mercury Series, No. 131, 1985), pp. 69-92.

Andrews, Kenneth R., *Trade, Plunder, and Settlement: Maritime Enterprise and the Genesis of the British Empire, 1480-1630* (Cambridge, England: Cambridge University Press, 1986).

"Anna Nungaq About Moving to Grise Fiord," *Inuktitut*, No. 49 (December 1981), pp. 5-12.

Babaluk, J.A., N.M. Halden, J.D. Reist, A.H. Kristofferson, J.L. Campbell, and W.J. Teesdale, "Evidence for Non-Anadromous Behaviour of Arctic Charr (*Salvelinus alpinus*) from Lake Hazen, Ellesmere Island, Northwest Territories, Canada, Based on Scanning Proton Microprobe Analysis of Otolith Strontium Distribution," *Arctic*, Vol. 50, No. 3 (Sept. 1997), pp. 224-33.

Bakhtin, M.M., "The Epic and the Novel," in *The Dialogic Imagination: Four Essays* (Ed., Michael Holquist) (Austin, Texas: University of Texas Press 1981), pp. 3-38.

Balikci, Asen, "Netsilik," David Damas, Ed. *Handbook of North American Indians*, Vol. 5, "Arctic" (Washington, DC: The Smithsonian Institution, 1984), pp. 415-30

Barr, William, *Back from the Brink; The Road to Muskox Conservation in the Northwest Territories*, Komatik Series, No. 3 (Calgary: the Arctic Institute of North America, 1991).

Barr, William, *The Expeditions of the First International Polar Year, 1882-83* (Calgary: The Arctic Institute of North America, Technical Paper No. 29, 1985).

Barr, W., and W. Blake, Jr., "The Site of Fort Magnesia, Payer Harbour, Pim Island, NWT," *Polar Record*, Vol. 26, No. 156 (1990), pp. 39-42.

Barr, William, "Robert Stein's Expedition to Ellesmere Island, 1899-1901," *Polar Record*, Vol. 21, No. 132 (1982), pp. 253-74.

Barry, R.G., Wendy H Arundale, J.T. Andrews, Raymond S. Bradley, and Harvey Nichols, "Environmental Change and Cultural Change in the Eastern Canadian Arctic During the Last 5000 Years," *Arctic and Alpine Research*, Vol. 9, No. 2 (1977).

Bates, Charles C., and John F. Fuller, *America's Weather Warriors, 1814-1985* (College Station, Texas: Texas A&M University Press, 1986).

Bednarski, Jan "Geomorphology," in Parks Canada, Ellesmere Island National Park Reserve, "Resource Description and Analysis," Western Canada Service Centre, Parks Canada, Winnipeg, 1994, Vol. I, Chapter 3, pp. 3-5. 1994, Vol. I, Chapter 3.

Bennett, John W., *The Ecological Transition: Cultural Anthropology and Human Adaptation* (New York: Pergamon Press, 1976).

Bernheimer, Charles, and Claire Kehane, Eds., *In Dora's Case: Freud – Hysteria – Feminism* (New York: Columbia University, 1985).

Berton, Pierre, *The Arctic Grail: The Quest for the North West Passage and the North Pole, 1818-1909* (Toronto: McClelland and Stewart, 1988).

Bidney, David, *Theoretical Anthropology* (New Brunswick, New Jersey: Transaction Publishers, 1967).

Bliss, L.C., J. Svoboda, and D.I. Bliss, "Polar Deserts, Their Plant Cover and Plant Production in the Canadian High Arctic," *Holarctic Ecology*, Vol. 7 (1984), pp. 305-24.

Bliss, L.C., "North American and Scandinavian Tundras and Polar Deserts," in L.C. Bliss, O.W. Heal, and J.J. Moore, Eds., *Tundra Ecosystems: A Comparative Analysis* (Cambridge, England: Cambridge University Press 1981), pp. 8-24.

Blodgett, Jean, *The Coming and Going of the Shaman: Eskimo Shamanism and Art* (Winnipeg, Manitoba: Winnipeg Art Gallery, 1978).

Bloom, Lisa, *Gender on Ice: American Ideologies of Polar Expeditions* (Minneapolis: University of Minnesota Press, 1993).

Bohlen, Joseph, "Biological Rhythms: Human Responses in the Polar Environment," *Yearbook of Physical Anthropology*, Vol. 22 (1979), pp. 47-79.

Braudel, Fernand, *Capitalism and Material Life 1400-1800* (Trans., George Weidenfeld and Nicolson Ltd.) (New York: Harper Colophon Books, 1967).

Braudel, Fernand, *The Mediterranean and the Mediterranean World in the Age of Philip II* (Trans. Sîan Reynolds) (New York: Harper Torchbooks, 1975).

Braudel, Fernand, *On History* (Trans., Sarah Matthews) (Chicago: University of Chicago Press, 1980).

Broodhagen, Virgil, Caroline Parmenter, and Larry Konotopetz, "Fort Conger, Ellesmere Island, NWT, As Found Recording," Unpublished Report, Drawings, and Photographs, Canadian Parks Service, Prairie and Northern Region, July, 1979.

Brown, Dee, *The Year of the Century: 1876* (New York: Charles Scribner's Sons, 1976).

Brown, Robert Craig, and Ramsay Cook, *Canada, 1896-1921: A Nation Transformed* (Toronto: McClelland and Stewart, 1974).

Bruemmer, Fred, *The Long Hunt* (Toronto: The Ryerson Press, 1969).

Bryant, John H. and Harold N. Cones, *Dangerous Crossings: The First Modern Polar Expedition, 1925* (Annapolis, Maryland: Naval Institute Press, 2000).

Bryce, Robert M., *Cook and Peary: The Polar Controversy Resolved* (Mechanicsburg, Pennsylvania: Stackpole Books, 1997).

Buchwald, Vagn Fabtritius, and Gert Mosdal, "Meteorite Iron, Telluric Iron and Wrought Iron in Greenland," *Meddelelser om Grønland*, Man and Society Vol. 9 (1985), pp. 3-49.

Butzer, Karl W., *Archaeology as Human Ecology: Method and Theory for a Contextual Approach* (Cambridge, England: Cambridge University Press, 1982).

"Canadian Eastern Arctic Patrol, 1951," *The Polar Record*, Vol. 7, No. 47 (January 1954), pp. 43-44.

Carpenter, Edmund, *Eskimo* (*Explorations 9*) (Toronto: University of Toronto Press, 1960).

Carpenter, Edmund, "Space Concepts of the Aivilik Eskimos," *Explorations*, Vol. 5 (1955), pp. 131-45.

Caswell, John Edwards, *Arctic Frontiers: United States Exploration in the Far North* (Norman, Oklahoma: University of Oklahoma Press, 1956).

Caswell, John Edwards, "The RGS and the British Arctic Expedition, 1875-76," *Geographical Journal*, Vol. 143, Part 2 (July 1977), pp. 200-10.

Chang, Kwang-Chih, "A Typology of Settlement and Community Patterns in Some Circumpolar Societies," *Arctic Anthropology*, Vol. 1, No.1 (1962), pp. 28-41.

Christie, R.L., *Geological Reconnaissance of Northeastern Ellesmere Island, District of Franklin*, Geological Survey of Canada, Memoir 331 (Ottawa: Department of Mines and Technical Surveys, 1964).

Collis, Christy, "The Voyage of the Episteme: Narrating the North," in *Essays on Canadian Writing*, No. 59 (Fall 1996), Theme Issue: "Representing North," pp. 26-45.

Cook-Dorough, Sheldon, "Frederick Albert Cook: Discoverer of the North Pole," *Fram: The Journal of Polar Studies*, Vol. 2, Part 1 (1985), pp. 141-58.

Corner, George W., *Doctor Kane of the Arctic Seas* (Philadelphia: Temple University Press, 1972).

Cotlow, Lewis, *In Search of the Primitive* (Boston and Toronto: Little, Brown, and Company, 1966).

Cruwys, Liz, "Henry Grinnell and the American Franklin Searches," *The Polar Record*, Vol. 26, No. 158 (1974), pp. 211-16.

Cruwys, Liz, "Profile: Henry Grinnell," *Polar Record*, Vol. 27, No. 161 (1991).

Cuddon, J.A., *A Dictionary of Literary Terms* (Harmondsworth, England: Penguin Books 1979).

Damas, David, "Environment, History, and Central Eskimo Society," in David Damas, Ed., *Contributions to Anthropology: Ecological Essays*, National Museum of Canada, Bulletin No. 320, Ottawa, 1969, pp. 40-64.

Damas, David, *Igluligmiut Kinship and Local Groupings: A Structural Approach* (Ottawa: National Museum of Canada, Bulletin No. 196, 1963).

Dansgaard, W., J.J. Johnson, H.B. Clausen, and C.C. Langway, Jr., "Climatic Record Revealed By the Camp Century Ice Core," in Karl K. Turekian, Ed., *The Late Cenozoic Glacial Ages* (New Haven and London: Yale University Press, 1971), pp. 37-56.

Deacon, Margaret, and Ann Savours, "Sir George Strong Nares (1831-1915)," *Polar Record*, Vol. 18, No. 113 (1976), pp. 127-41.

De Jonge, James, "Building on the Frontier: The Mounted Police in the Canadian North," *SSAC Bulletin* (Society for the Study of Architecture in Canada), Vol. 17, No. 2 (June 1992), pp. 42-54.

Dick, Lyle, "Defence Research Board Camps in Northern Ellesmere Island: Report on Historical Resources," Environment Canada Parks Service, *Research Bulletin No. 292* (1991), pp. 1-36.

Dick, Lyle, "The Fort Conger Shelters and Vernacular Adaptation to the High Arctic," *SSAC Bulletin* (Society for the Study of Architecture in Canada), Vol. 16, No. 1 (March 1991), pp. 13-23.

Dick, Lyle, "'Pibloktoq' (Arctic Hysteria): A Construction of European-Inuit Relations?" *Arctic Anthropology*, Vol. 32 No. 2 (1995), pp. 1-42.

Dick, Lyle, "A Severe Look at the History of a Severe Land," *The Globe and Mail* (Toronto Edition), 3 December 1988, p. C-4.

Dinwoodie, D.H., "Arctic Controversy: The 1925 Byrd-MacMillan Expedition Example," *Canadian Historical Review*, Vol. 52, No. 1 (March 1972).

Dolan Jr., Edward, *White Battleground: The Conquest of the Arctic* (Toronto: Dodd, Mead, and Co., 1961).

Dunbar, M.J., "The Arctic Marine Ecosystem," in F.R. Engelhardt, Ed., *Petroleum Effects in the Arctic Environment* (London and New York: Elsevier Applied Science Publishers, 1985), pp. 1-35.

Dunbar, M.J., "Arctic Marine Ecosystems," in Louis Rey, Ed., *The Arctic Ocean: The Hydrographic Environment and the Fate of Pollutants* (London and Basingstoke: Macmillan Press Ltd., 1982), pp. 232-62.

Dunbar, M.J., "The Biological Significance of Arctic Ice," in Sikumiut: *"The People Who Use the Sea Ice"* (Ottawa: Canadian Arctic Resources Committee, 1982), pp. 7-30.

Dunbar, M.J., *Ecological Development in Polar Regions: A Study in Evolution* (Englewood Cliffs, N.J.: Prentice-Hall, 1968).

Dunbar, M.J., Review of *Langthen og Nordpaa*, by Christian Vibe, *Arctic*, Vol. 2 , No. 1 (May 1949), pp. 60-63.

Dunbar, Moira, and M.J. Dunbar, "The History of the North Water," *Proceedings of the Royal Society of Edinburgh*, Series B, Vol. 72 (1972), pp. 231-41.

Dunbar, Moira, and Keith R. Greenaway, *Arctic Canada from the Air* (Ottawa: Defence Research Board, 1956).

Dunbar, Moira, "Ice Regime and Ice Transport in Nares Strait," *Arctic*, Vol. 26, No. 4 (December 1973).

Edlund, Sylvia A., and Bea Taylor Alt, "Regional Congruence of Vegetation and Summer Climate Patterns in the Queen Elizabeth Islands, Northwest Territories, Canada," *Arctic*, Vol. 42, No. 1 (March, 1989), pp. 3-23.

Ekblaw, W. Elmer, "Eskimo Dogs — Forgotten Heroes," *Natural History* (Journal of the American Museum of Natural History), Vol. 37 (January 1936), pp. 173-84.

Ekblaw, W. Elmer, "The Material Response of the Polar Eskimo to their Far Arctic Environment, *Annals of the Association of American Geographers*, Vol. 18, No. 1 (March 1928).

Ellen, Roy, *Environment, Subsistence, and System: The Ecology of Small Formations* (Cambridge, England: Cambridge University Press, 1982).

England, John, "The First Expeditions to Lady Franklin Bay, Northeast Ellesmere Island, NWT, Canada," *Arctic and Alpine Research*, Vol. 5, No. 2 (1973), pp. 133-44.

Ferguson, Eugene S., "Expositions of Technology, 1851-1900," in Melvin Kranzberg and Carroll W. Pursell, Jr., Eds., *Technology in Western Civilization*, Vol. I, "The Emergence of Modern Industrial Society" (New York, London, and Toronto: Oxford University Press, 1967), pp. 708-16.

Fetherstonhaugh, R.C., *The Royal Canadian Mounted Police* (New York: Carrick & Evans, 1938).

Finley, Kerwin J., and Wayne E. Renaud, "Marine Mammals Inhabiting the Baffin Bay North Water in Winter," *Arctic*, Vol. 33, No. 4 (December 1980), pp. 724-38.

Fischer, David Hackett, *Albion's Seed: Four British Folkways in America* (New York and Oxford: Oxford University Press, 1989).

Fischer, David Hackett, *The Great Wave: Price Revolutions and the Rhythm of History* (Oxford and New York: Oxford University Press, 1996).

Fisher, H.D., "Annual Report and Investigators' Summaries, No. 6, Hazen Lake," Unpublished Report, Fisheries Research Board of Canada, Arctic Unit, Montreal, Quebec, 1960, pp. 18-20.

Fleming, Fergus, *Barrow's Boys* (London: Granta Books, 1998).

Fogelson, Nancy, *Arctic Exploration and International Relations, 1900-1932* (Fairbanks: University of Alaska Press, 1992), pp. 131-40.

Fogelson, Nancy J., "Robert E. Peary and American Exploration in the Arctic, 1886-1910," *Fram: the Journal of Polar Studies*, Vol. 2, Part 1 (1985).

Fossett, Renée, "Mapping Inuktut: Inuit Voices of the Real World," in Jennifer S.H. Brown and Elizabeth Vibert, Eds., *Reading Beyond Words: Contexts for Native History* (Peterborough, Ontario: Broadview Press, 1996), pp. 74-94.

Frank, Andre Gunder, and Barry K. Gills, Eds., *The World System: Five Hundred Years or Five Thousand?* (London and New York: Routledge, 1993).

Freeman, Andrew A., *The Case for Doctor Cook* (New York: Coward-McCann, Inc., 1961).

Freeman, M.M.R., "Adaptive Innovation Among Recent Eskimo Immigrants in the Eastern Canadian Arctic," *Polar Record*, Vol. 14, No. 93 (1969), pp. 769-81.

Freeman, Milton M.R., "Appeal to Tradition: Different Perspectives on Arctic Wildlife Management," in Jens Brøsted et al., Eds., *Native Power: The Quest for Autonomy and Nationhood of Indigenous Peoples* (Bergen: Universitetsforlaget, 1985), pp. 265-81.

Freeman, Milton M.R., "Arctic Ecosystems," in David Damas, Ed., *Handbook of North American Indians*, Vol. 5, "Arctic" (Washington, DC: The Smithsonian Institution, 1984), pp. 36-48.

Freeman, Milton M.R., "Contemporary Inuit Exploitation of the Sea-Ice Environment," in *Sikumiut: "The People Who Use the Sea Ice"* (Ottawa: Canadian Arctic Resources Committee, 1984), pp. 73-96.

Freeman, Milton M.R., "A Critical View of Thule Culture and Ecologic Adaptation," in Allen P. McCartney, Ed., *Thule Eskimo Culture: An Anthropolical Retrospective*, Archaeological Survey of Canada Mercury Paper No. 88 (Ottawa: National Museum, 1979), pp. 278-85.

Freeman, Milton M.R., "Effects of Petroleum Activities on the Ecology of Arctic Man," in F.R. Englehardt, Ed., *Petroleum Effects in the Arctic Environment* (London and New York: Elsevier Applied Science Publishers, 1985), pp. 245-73.

Freeman, Milton M.R., "Issues Affecting Subsistence Security in Arctic Societies," *Arctic Anthropology*, Vol. 34, No. 1 (1997), pp. 7-17.

Freeman, Milton, Ed., *Endangered Peoples of the Arctic: Struggles to Survive and Thrive* (Westport, Connecticut and London: Greenwood Press, 2000).

Freeman, Milton M.R., "Patrons, Leaders and Values in an Eskimo Settlement," in Symposium on the Contemporary Cultural Situation of the Northern Forest Indians of North America and the Eskimo of North America and Greenland, in *Proceedings of the 38th International Congress of Americanists*, Vol. 3 (Stuttgart-München, 1968).

Freeman, Milton M.R., "Tolerance and Rejection of Patron Roles in an Eskimo Settlement," in Robert Paine, Ed., *Patrons and Brokers in the East Arctic*, Newfoundland Social and Economic Papers No. 2 (St. John's: Memorial University, 1971), pp. 34-54.

Freeman, Milton M.R., Eleanor E. Wein, and Darren E. Keith, *Recovering Rights: Bowhead Whales and Inuvialuit Subsistence in the Western Canadian Arctic* (Edmonton: Canadian Circumpolar Institute and Fisheries Joint Management Committee, 1992).

Freeman, M.M.R., "Traditional Land Users as a Legitimate Source of Environmental Expertise," in J.G. Nelson, R.D. Needham, S.H. Nelson, and R.C. Scace, Eds., *The*

Canadian National Parks: Today and Tomorrow; Conference II: Ten Years Later, Vol. I, (Waterloo, Ontario: University of Waterloo, 1979), pp. 345-61.

Freuchen, Peter, *Adventures in the Arctic* (Ed., Dagmar Freuchen) (New York: Julian Messner, Inc., 1960).

Freuchen, Peter, and Finn Salomonsen, *The Arctic Year* (New York: G.P. Putnam's Sons, 1958).

Freuchen, Peter, *Book of the Eskimos* (Ed., Dagmar Freuchen) (New York: Fawcett Premier, 1973).

Freuchen, Peter, *I Sailed with Rasmussen* (New York: Julian Messner, 1958).

Freuchen, Peter, *Vagrant Viking: My Life and Adventures* (New York: Julian Messner, 1953).

Fryer, Constable A.C., "Eskimo Rehabilitation Program at Craig Harbour," *The RCMP Quarterly*, Vol. 20, No. 2 (October 1954), p. 139.

Gibbon, Edward, *The Decline and Fall of the Roman Empire*, Vol. II, *Barbarism and the Fall of Rome* (Abridged version edited by Jacob Sloan) (New York: Collier Books, 1962).

Gilberg, Rolf, "Changes in the Life of the Polar Eskimos Resulting From a Canadian Immigration into the Thule District, North Greenland, in the 1860s," *Folk*, Vols.16-17 (1974-75), pp. 159-70.

Gilberg, Rolf, "Polar Eskimo," in David Damas, Ed., *Handbook of North American Indians*, Vol. 5 (Washington, DC: The Smithsonian Institution, 1984), pp. 577-94.

Gilberg, Rolf, "The Polar Eskimo Population, Thule District, North Greenland," *Meddelelser om Grønland*, Vol. 203, No. 3 (1976).

The Globe and Mail (Toronto), 16 April 1993.

Goerler, Raimund E., Ed., *To the Pole: The Diary and Notebook of Richard E. Byrd, 1925-1927* (Columbus: Ohio University Press, 1998).

Gould, Lewis L., *The Presidency of Theodore Roosevelt* (Lawrence, Kansas: University Press of Kansas, 1991).

Graf, Miller, *Arctic Journeys: A History of Exploration for the Northwest Passage* (New York: Peter Lang, 1992).

Grainger, E.H., "On the Age, Growth, Migration, Reproductive Potential, and Feeding Habits of the Arctic Char (*Salvelinus alpinus*) in Frobisher Bay, Baffin Island, "*Journal of the Fisheries Resources Board of Canada*, Vol. 1 (1953), pp. 326-70.

Grant, Shelagh D., "A Case of Compounded Error: The Inuit Resettlement Project, 1953, and the Government Response, 1990," *Northern Perspectives* (Canadian Arctic Resources Committee), Vol. 19, No. 1 (Spring 1991), pp. 3-29.

Grant, Shelagh, "Inuit Relocations to the High Arctic, 1953-1960: 'Errors Exposed,'" Unpublished manuscript, Vol. I, Report and Chronology, Author's submission to the Royal Commission on Aboriginal Peoples, June 1993, Revised August 1993.

Grant, Shelagh D., *Sovereignty or Security? Government Policy in the Canadian North, 1936-1950* (Vancouver: University of British Columbia Press, 1988).

Gray, D.R., "Crashes of Muskoxen and Peary Caribou Populations in 1973-74 on the Parry Islands, Arctic Canada," *Canadian Wildlife Service Program Note No. 56* (1975).

Green, Fitzhugh, *Peary: The Man Who Refused to Fail* (New York and London: G. Putnam's Sons, 1926).

Green, Martin, *Dreams of Adventure, Deeds of Empire* (New York: Basic Books, 1979).

Griffiths, Tom, and Libby Robin, Eds., *Ecology and Empire: Environmental History of Settler Societies* (Edinburgh: Keele University Press, 1997).

Grosvenor, Gilbert M., Ed., *National Geographic Atlas of the World* (Washington, DC: National Geographic Society, 1978).

Grove, Richard H., *Ecology, Climate, and Empire: Colonialism and Global Environmental History, 1400-1940* (Cambridge, England: White Horse Press, 1997).

Gunn, A., F.L. Miller and D.C. Thomas, "The Current and Future of Peary Caribou (*Rangifer tarandus pearyi*) On the Arctic Islands of Canada," *Biological Conservation*, Vol. 19 (1980-81), pp. 283-96.

Gunther, M., "The 1953 Relocations of the Inukjuak Inuit to the High Arctic—A Documentary Analysis and Evaluation," prepared for the Department of Indian and Northern Affairs and Northern Development, Ottawa, 1992.

Guttridge, Leonard, *Ghosts of Cape Sabine: The Harrowing True Story of the Greely Expedition* (New York: G.P. Putnam's Sons, 2000).

Guttridge, Leonard F., *Icebound: The* Jeannette *Expedition's Quest for the North Pole* (Annapolis, Maryland: Naval Institute Press, 1986).

Haig-Thomas, David, *Tracks in the Snow* (London: Hodder and Stoughton, 1939).

Hammond, Marc, "Report of Findings on an Alleged Promise of the Government to Finance the return of Inuit from Resolute Bay and Grise Fiord to their Original Homes in Port Harrison and Pond Inlet," Ottawa, 1984.

Hardesty, Donald L., *Ecological Anthropology* (New York: John Wiley and Sons, 1977).

Harley, J.B., "Maps, Knowledge, and Power," in Denis Cosgrove and Stephen Daniels, Eds., *The Iconography of Landscape: Essays on the Symbolic Representation, Design and Use of Past Environments* (Cambridge, England: Cambridge University Press, 1988), pp. 277-312.

Harper, Kenn, *Give Me My Father's Body: The Life of Minik, The New York Eskimo* (Iqaluit, NWT: Blacklead Books, 1986).

Harper, Kenn, "A History of Human Occupation," in *Socio-Economic Characteristics and Conservation Interests of the Lancaster Sound Region* (Ottawa: Department of Indian and Northern Affairs, Lancaster Sound Regional Study, Background Report No. 3, 1980).

Hattersley-Smith, Geoffrey, "The British Arctic Expedition, 1875-76," *Polar Record*, Vol. 18, No. 113 (1976), pp. 117-26.

Hattersley-Smith, Geoffrey, *North Of Latitude Eighty: The Defence Research Board in Ellesmere Island* (Ottawa: The Defence Research Board, 1974).

Hattersley-Smith, G., Ed., *Operation Tanquary Preliminary Report, 1964* (Ottawa: Defence Research Board 1967).

Hayes, J. Gordon, *The Conquest of the North Pole: Recent Arctic Exploration* (London: Thornton Butterworth, Ltd., 1934).

Hayes, J. Gordon, *Robert Edwin Peary: A Record of His Explorations, 1886-1909* (London: Grant Richards and Humphrey Toulmin, 1929).

Helm, June, "Relationship between Settlement Pattern and Community Pattern," In David Damas, Ed., *Contributions to Anthropology: Ecological Essays* (Ottawa: National Museums of Canada Bulletin No. 230, Anthropological series No. 86, 1969), pp. 151-62.

Herbert, Wally, *Hunters of the Polar North: The Eskimo* (Amsterdam: Time-Life Books, 1981).

Herbert, Wally, *The Noose of Laurels: The Discovery of the North Pole* (London, Sydney, Aukland, and Toronto: Hodder and Stoughton, 1989).

Herodotus, *The Histories* (Trans., Aubrey de Sélincourt) (Harmondsworth, Middlesex, England: Penguin Books, Ltd., 1954).

Hewitt, Steve, "The Masculine Mountie: The Royal Canadian Mounted Police as a Male Institution, 1914-1939," *Journal of the Canadian Historical Association*, New Series, Vol. 7 (1997), pp. 153-74.

Hickling Corporation, "Assessment of the Factual Basis of Certain Allegations Made before the Standing Committee on Aboriginal Affairs Concerning the Relocation of Inukjuak Inuit in the 1950s," Prepared for the Department of Indian and Northern Affairs, 1990.

Hobbs, William Henry, *Peary* (New York: Macmillan, 1936).

Hobsbawm, E.J., *The Age of Capital, 1843-1875* (New York: Mentor Books, 1979).

Hobsbawm, E.J., *The Age of Empire, 1875-1914* (London: Cardinal Books, 1989).

Hoehling, A.A. *The* Jeannette *Expedition: An Ill-Fated Journey to the Arctic* (London/New York/Toronto: Abelard-Schuman, 1967).

Holland, Clive, *Arctic Exploration and Development, c. 500 BC to 1915* (New York and London: Garland Publishing, Inc., 1994)

Holtved, Erik, "Contributions to Polar Eskimo Ethnography," *Meddelelser om Grønland*, Vol. 182. No. 2 (1967).

Hoogenboom, Ari, *The Presidency of Rutherford B. Hayes* (Lawrence, Kansas: University of Kansas, 1988).

Horwood, Harold, *Bartlett: The Great Canadian Explorer* (Garden City, New York and Toronto: Doubleday, 1977).

Houston, James, "Akeeaktashuk," In James H. Marsh, Ed., *The Canadian Encyclopedia*, Revised Edition (Edmonton: Hurtig Publishers, 1988), p. 47.

Hunt, William R., *To Stand at the Pole: The Dr. Cook-Admiral Peary North Pole Controversy* (New York: Stein and Day, 1981).

Jacobs, John D., "Climate and the Thule Ecumene," in Allen P. McCartney, Ed., *Thule Eskimo Culture: An Anthropological Retrospective* (Ottawa: National Museum of Man, Mercury Series No. 88, 1979), pp. 528-35.

Jenness, Diamond, *Eskimo Administration: II. Canada* (Ottawa: Arctic Institute of North America, Technical Paper No. 14, 1964).

Johnson, V. Kenneth, "Canada's Title to the Arctic Islands," *Canadian Historical Review*, Vol. 14 (1933), pp. 24-41.

Jones, J., "Arctic Adventure: Inspector A.H. Joy," *The Scarlet and Gold*, 57th Edition (1975), pp. 26-37; 46-56.

Keith, Darren,"The Fall Caribou Crossing Hunt, Kazan River, Northwest Territories," Unpublished Paper, Historic Sites and Monuments Board of Canada Agenda Papers, Fredericton, New Brunswick, 6 and 7 July 1995, Vol. 3, pp. 843-83.

Kendall, E.J.C., "Scurvy During Some British Polar Expeditions, 1875-1917," *The Polar Record*, Vol. 7, No. 51 (September 1951), pp. 467-85.

Kern, Stephen, *The Culture of Time and Space* (London, 1983).

Kirmayer Laurence J., and Harry Minas, "The Future of Cultural Psychiatry: An International Perspective," *Canadian Journal of Psychiatry*, Vol. 45, No. 5 (June 2000), pp. 438-46.

Kirmayer, L.J., "Cultural Psychiatry: From Museums of Exotica to the Global Agora," *Current Opinion in Psychiatry*, Vol. 11, No. 2 (1998), pp. 183-89.

Kirwan, L.P., *A History of Polar Exploration* (Harmondsworth, Middlesex, England, 1962).

Klein, Alan M., "Adaptive Strategies and Process on the Plains: The 19th Century Cultural Sink," Ph.D. Dissertation, University of New York at Buffalo, Buffalo, NY, 1977.

Knuth, Eigil, "Archaeology of the Muskox Way," *Contributions du Centre d'Études Arctiques et Finno-Scandinaves*, No. 5 (Paris, 1969).

Knuth, Eigil, *Archaeology of the Musk-Ox Way* (Contributions du Centre d'Etudes Arctiques et Finno-Scandinaves, No. 5) (Paris: École Pratique des Hautes Études, Sorbonne, Sixième Section, Sciences Économiques et Sociales, 1967).

Knuth, Eigil, "The Ruins of the Musk-ox Way," *Folk*, Vol. 8-9 (1966-67), pp. 191-219.

Knuth, Eigil, "An Outline of the Archaeology of Peary Land," *Arctic*, Vol. 5, No. 1 (1952), pp. 17-33.

Knuth, Eigil, "Archaeology of the Farthest North," *Proceedings of the Thirty-Second International Congress of Americanists* (Copenhagen: Munksgaard, 1958), pp. 561-73.

Koch, Lauge, "Contributions to the Glaciology of North Greenland," *Meddelelser om Grønland*, Vol. 65, No. 6 (1928).

Koch, Lauge, "The East Greenland Ice," *Meddelelser om Grønland*, Vol. 130, No. 3 (1945).

Lafeber, Walter, *The New Empire: An Interpretation of American Expansion, 1860-1898* (Ithaca and New York: Cornell University Press, 1963).

Lamb, H.H., "Towards an Understanding of Climatic Change: Its Impact and History in the Modern World," in Knud Frydendahl, Ed., *Proceedings of the Nordic Symposium on Climatic Changes and Related Problems*, Danish Meteorological Institute Climatological Papers, No. 4 (1978).

Lancaster Sound Regional Land Use Planning Commission, *The Lancaster Sound Proposed Regional Land Use Plan* (Pond Inlet, Nunavut: Lancaster Sound Regional Land Use Planning Commission, 1989).

Landes, David S., *Clocks and the Making of the Modern World* (Cambridge, Massachusetts: Harvard University Press, 1983).

Levere, Trevor H., *Science and the Canadian Arctic: A Century of Exploration, 1818-1918* (Cambridge, England / New York: Cambridge University Press, 1993).

Lévi-Strauss, Claude, *The Savage Mind* (Chicago: University of Chicago Press, 1966).

Levin, David, *History as Romantic Art* (Stanford, California: Stanford University Press, 1959).

Lewis, Michael, *The Navy in Transition, 1814-1864: A Social History* (London: Hodder and Stoughton, 1965).

LGL Limited, *Biological Environment of Eastern Lancaster Sound and Western Baffin Bay: Components and Important Processes* (Ottawa: Department of Indian and Northern Affairs, Northern Affairs Program, 1983).

Lloyd, Christopher, *Mr. Barrow of the Admiralty: A Life of Sir John Barrow 1764-1848* (London: Collins, 1970).

Loomis, Chauncy C., *Weird and Tragic Shores: The Story of Charles Francis Hall, Explorer* (New York: Alfred A. Knopf, 1971).

Lotz, J., and R.B. Sagar, "Meteorological Work in Northern Ellesmere Island," *Weather*, Vol. 15 (1960).

Lotz, J.R., "Northern Ellesmere Island: An Arctic Desert," *Geografisker Annaler*, Vol. 44, Nos. 3-4 (1962), pp. 366-77.

Lowther, Keith, "An Exercise in Sovereignty: The Canadian Government and the Relocation of Inuit to the High Arctic in 1953," in W. Peter Adams and Peter G. Johnson, Eds., *Student Research in Canada's North*, Proceedings of the National Student Conference on Northern Studies, November 18-19, 1986 (Ottawa: Association of Canadian Universities for Northern Studies, 1986), pp. 517-22.

Lubbock, Basil, *The Arctic Whalers* (Glasgow: Brown, Son, and Ferguson, Ltd., 1937).

Lyall, Ernie, *An Arctic Man: Sixty-Five Year in Canada's North* (Halifax: Goodread Biographies, 1979).

MacDonald, John, *The Arctic Sky: Inuit Astronomy, Star Lore, and Legend* (Toronto/Iqaluit: Royal Ontario Museum/Nunavut Research Institute, 1998).

Macey, Samuel L., *Clocks and the Cosmos: Time in Western Life and Thought* (Hamden, Connecticut, 1980).

Mackinnon, C.S., "The British Man-Hauled Sledging Tradition," in Patricia D. Sutherland, Ed., *The Franklin Era in Canadian Arctic History 1845-1859* (Ottawa: National Museum of Man, Mercury Series No. 131, 1985), pp. 129-40.

MacMillan, Donald B., *How Peary Reached the Pole: The Personal Story of His Assistant* (Boston and New York: Houghton Mifflin, 1934).

Maier, Charles S., "Consigning the Twentieth Century to History: Alternative Narratives for the Modern Era," *American Historical Review*, Vol. 105, No. 3 (June 2000), pp. 807-31.

Malaurie, Jean, *The Last Kings of Thule* (Trans., Adrienne Foulke) (Chicago: University of Chicago Press, 1982).

Mansfield, A.W., *Seals of Arctic and Eastern Canada* (Ottawa: Fisheries Research Board of Canada, Bulletin No. 137, 1967).

Marcus, Alan R., "Out in the Cold: The Legacy of Canada's Relocation Experiment in the High Arctic, 1953–90," M.Phil. Thesis, Scott Polar Research Institute, University of Cambridge, 1990.

Mary-Rousselière, Guy, *Qitdlarssuaq: l'histoire d'une migration polaire* (Montréal: Les Presses de l'Université de Montréal, 1980).

Mary-Rousselière, Guy, "Iglulik," in David Damas, Ed., *Handbook of North American Indians*, Vol. 5, "Arctic" (Washington, DC: Smithsonian Institution, 1984), p. 431-46.

Mauss, Marcel, *Seasonal Variations of the Eskimo: A Study in Social Morphology* (Trans., James J. Fox) (London, Boston and Henley: Routledge & Kegan Paul, 1979).

Maxtone-Graham, John, *Safe Return Doubtful: The Heroic Age of Polar Exploration* (New York: Charles Scribner's Sons, 1988).

Maxwell, Moreau S., *An Archaeological Analysis of Eastern Grant Land, Ellesmere Island, Northwest Territories* (Canada, Department of Northern Affairs and Natural Resources, Bulletin No. 170, 1960).

Maxwell, Moreau S., "The House on the Ruggles," *The Beaver* Outfit 293 (Autumn, 1962), pp. 20-27.

Maxwell, Moreau S., *Prehistory of the Eastern Arctic* (Orlando, Florida: Academic Press, Inc. 1985).

May, W.E., and Leonard Holder, *A History of Marine Navigation* (New York: W.W. Norton and Company, 1973).

McCartney, Allen P., "The Nature of Thule Eskimo Whale Use," *Arctic*, Vol. 33, No. 3 (September 1980), pp. 517-41.

McCullough, Karen M., *The Ruin Islanders: Early Thule Culture in the Eastern High Arctic*, Archaeological Survey of Canada, Mercury Series Paper 141 (Ottawa: Canadian Museum of Civilization, 1989).

McGhee, Robert, *Ancient People of the Arctic* (Vancouver: UBC Press and the Canadian Museum of Civilization, 1996).

McGhee, Robert, "Thule Prehistory of Canada," in David Damas, Ed., *Handbook of North American Indians*, Vol. 5, "Arctic" (Washington, DC: The Smithsonian Institution, 1984), pp. 369-76.

McGovern, Thomas, "The Economics of Extinction in Norse Greenland," in T.M.L. Wrigley, M.J. Ingram and G. Farmer, *Climate and History: Studies in Past Climates and Their Impact on Man* (Cambridge, England: Cambridge University Press, 1981).

McLaren, I.A., "Zooplankton of Lake Hazen, Ellesmere Island, and a Nearby Pond, with Special Reference to the Copepod Cyclops Scutifer Sars, *Canadian Journal of Zoology*, Vol. 42 (1964), pp. 613-29.

Meinig, D.W., "A Geographical Transect of the Atlantic World, ca. 1750," in Eugene D. Genovese and Leonard Hochberg, Eds., *Geographic Perspectives in History* (Oxford: Basil Blackwell, Ltd., 1989).

Meinig, D.W., *The Shaping of America: A Geographical Perspective on 500 Years of History*, Vol. I: Atlantic America, 1492-1800 (New Haven, Connecticut: Yale University Press, 1986).

Merkur, Daniel, *Becoming Half-Hidden: Shamanism and Initiation Among the Inuit* (Stockholm: Almqvist and Wiksell International, 1985).

Miller, Char, and Hal Rothman, Eds., *Out of the Woods: Essays in Environmental History* (Pittsburgh: University of Pittsburgh Press, 1997).

Miller, F.L., and R.H. Parker, "Aerial Surveys of Peary Caribou and Muskoxen on Western Queen Elizabeth Islands, NWT," *Canadian Wildlife Service Program Note No. 40* (1973).

Miller, G.H, R.S. Bradley, and J.T. Andrews, "The Glaciation Level and Lowest Equilibrium Line Altitude in the High Canadian Arctic: Maps and Climatic Interpretation," *Arctic and Alpine Research*, Vol. 7, No. 2 (1975).

Mitchell, Edward, and Randall R. Reeves, "Catch History and Cumulative Catch Estimates of Initial Population Size of Cetaceans in the Eastern Canadian Arctic," *Report of the International Whaling Commission*, Vol. 31 (1981).

Minority Rights Group, Ed., *Polar Peoples: Self-Determination and Development* (London: Minority Rights Publications, 1994).

Moore, A.W.,"The Sledge Journey to Grant Land," *The Geographical Journal*, Vol. 87, No. 5 (May 1936).

Morris, Edmund, *The Rise of Theodore Roosevelt* (New York: Coward, McCann, and Geoghegan, 1979).

Morrison, N. Ronald, "Ecodistricts of Northen Ellesmere Island," Unpublished report, Parks Canada, National Parks Branch, Ottawa, 1984.

Morrison, William R., "Eagle Over the Arctic: Americans in the Canadian North," *Canadian Review of American Studies* (March 1987), pp. 61-75.

Morrison, William R., *Showing the Flag: the Mounted Police and Canadian Sovereignty in the North, 1894-1925* (Vancouver: University of British Columbia Press, 1985).

Mowat, Farley, "Dark Odyssey of Soosie," *The Snow Walker* (Toronto: McClelland and Stewart, 1975).

Mowat, Farley, *Ordeal by Ice: The Search for the Northwest Passage* (Toronto: McClelland and Stewart, 1976).

Murphy, Jane M., An Epidemiological Study of Psychopathology in an Eskimo Village, PhD dissertation, Cornell University, Ithaca, N.Y., 1960.

Myers, Heather, "The Use of Biological resources by Certain Arctic and Subarctic Peoples," M. Phil. Thesis, Scott Polar Research Institute, Cambridge, England, 1981.

Myllyntaus, Timo, and Mikko Saikko, Eds., *Encountering the Past in Nature: Essays in Environmental History* (Athens, Ohio: Ohio University Press, 2000).

Nabokov, Peter and Robert Easton, *Native American Architecture* (New York/Oxford: Oxford University Press, 1989).

Neatby, L.H., *Conquest of the Last Frontier* (Toronto: Longmans Canada, 1966).

Neatby, L.H., "The Greely Ordeal," *The Beaver*, Outfit 292 (Autumn 1961), pp. 4-11.

Nunatsiaq News (Iqaluit), 23 April 1993

Oakes, Jill, and Rick Riewe, *Culture, Economy and Society: Case Studies in the Circumpolar Region* (Millbrook, Ontario: The Cider Press, 1997).

Osczevski, Randall J., "Frederick Cook's Polar Journey: A Reconstruction," *Polar Record*, Vol. 26, No. 158 (1990), pp. 225-32.

Oswalt, Wendell H., "Technological Complexity: the Polar Eskimos and the *Tareumiut*," *Arctic Anthropology*, Vol. 24, No. 2 (1987), pp. 82-98.

"The Oxford University Ellesmere Land Expedition," *The Geographical Journal*, Vol. 87, No. 5 (May, 1936), p. 389.

"Oxford University Ellesmere Land Expedition," *The Polar Record*, No. 11 (January 1936), pp. 56-60.

Pace, David, *Claude Lévi-Strauss: The Bearer of Ashes* (London: ARK Paperbacks, 1986).

Paine, Robert, "Animals as Capital: Comparisons Among Northern Nomadic Herders and Hunters," in Bruce Cox, Ed., *Cultural Ecology: Readings on the Canadian Indians and Eskimos* (Toronto: McClelland and Stewart, 1973).

Parker, G.R., D.C. Thomas, E. Broughton, and D.R. Gray, "Crashes of Muskoxen and Peary Caribou Populations in 1973-74 on the Parry Islands, Arctic Canada," *Canadian Wildlife Service Program Note No. 56* (1975).

Parker, G.R. and R.K. Ross, "Summer Habitat Use by Muskoxen (*Ovibos moschatus*) and Peary Caribou (*Rangifer tarandus pearyi*) in the Canadian Arctic, *Polarforschung*, Vol. 46, No. 1 (1976), pp. 12-25.

Parmenter, C. Phillips, M. Burnip, and R. Ferguson, "Preliminary Report of the Second Season (1977) of Historical Archaeological Investigations in the High Arctic," Canadian Parks Service, National Historic Parks and Sites Branch Manuscript Report, Ottawa, 1978.

Pearson, Michael, Sledges and Sledging in Polar Regions," *The Polar Record*, Vo. 31, No. 176 (1995), pp. 3-24.

Pelto, Pertti J., and Ludger Müller-Wille, "Snowmobiles: Technological Revolution in the Arctic," in H. Russell Bernard and Pertti J. Pelto, *Technology and Social Change* (New York: Macmillan, 1972).

Pelto, Pertti J., *The Snowmobile Revolution: Technology and Change in the Arctic* (Menlo Park, California: Cummings Publishing Co., 1973).

Peterson, Robert, "The Last Eskimo Immigration into Greenland, *Folk*, Vol. 4 (1962), pp. 95-110.

Phillips, Caroline J., "Eastern Canadian High Arctic Exploration as an Example of Frontier Change, With Particular Emphasis on the Robert Peary North Pole Expeditions," MA thesis, University of Manitoba, 1987.

Picard, André, "The Internal Exiles of Canada," *The Globe and Mail* (Toronto), 7 September 1991, p. D3.

Rapoport, Amos, *House Form and Culture* (Englewood Cliffs, N.J.: Prentice Hall, 1969).

Rasor, Eugene L., *Reform in the Royal Navy: A Social History of the Lower Deck, 1850 to 1880* (Hamden, Connecticut: The Shoe String Press, 1976).

Rawlins, Dennis, *Peary at the North Pole: Fact or Fiction?* (Washington/New York: Robert B. Luce, Inc., 1973).

Reinhardt, Gregory Allen, "The Dwelling as Artifact: Analysis of Ethnographic Eskimo Dwellings, with Archaeological Implications," PhD dissertation, University of California, Los Angeles, 1986.

Rey, Louis, Ed., *The Arctic Ocean: The Hydrographic Environment and The Fate of Pollutants* (London: Macmillan Press, 1982).

Richard, P.R., M.P. Heide-Jørgensen, and S. St-Aubin, "Fall Movements of Belugas (*Delphinapterus leucas*) with Satellite-linked Transmitters in Lancaster Sound, Jones Sound, and Northern Baffin Bay," *Arctic*, Vol. 51, No. 1 (March 1998), pp. 5-16.

Ridington, Robin, "Technology, World View, and Adaptive Strategy in a Northern Hunting Society," *Canadian Review of Sociology*, Vol. 19, No 4 (1982), pp. 469-81.

Riewe, Roderick R., "Grise Fiord," in Milton Freeman, Ed., *Inuit land Use and Occupancy Project*, Vol. I, "Land Use and Occupancy" (Ottawa: Department of Indian and Northern Affairs, 1976), pp. 178-84.

Riewe, Roderick R. and Charles W. Amsden, "Harvesting and Utilization of Pinnipeds by Inuit Hunters in Canada's Eastern High Arctic," in Allen P. McCartney, Ed., *Thule Eskimo Culture: An Anthropological Retrospective* (Ottawa: National Museum of Man, Archaeological Survey of Canada Paper No. 88, 1979), pp. 324-36.

Riewe, R.R., "The Utilization of Wildlife in the Jones Sound Region by the Grise Fiord Inuit," in L.C. Bliss, Ed., *Truelove Lowland, Devon Island, Canada: A High Arctic Ecosystem* (Edmonton: University of Alberta Press, 1977), pp. 623-44.

Riffenburgh, Beau, *The Myth of the Explorer: The Press, Sensationalism, and Geographical Discovery* (London and New York/Cambridge: Belhaven Press/Cambridge University, Scott Polar Research Institute, 1993).

Roberts, Lance W., "Becoming Modern: Some Reflections on Inuit Social Change," in Ian A.L. Getty and Antoine S. Lussier, Eds., *As Long as the Sun Shines and Water Flows: A Reader in Canadian Native Studies* (Vancouver: University of British Columbia Press, 1983), pp. 299-314.

Robinson, Bradley, *Dark Companion* (London: Hodder and Stoughton, Ltd., 1948).

Roots, E.F. ,"The Changing Arctic Marine Environment: Some Basic Considerations," in Louis Rey, Ed., *The Arctic Ocean: The Hydrographic Environment and the Fate of Pollutants* (London and Basingstoke, Macmillan Press Ltd., 1982), pp. 226-29.

Ross, W. Gillies,"The Annual Catch of Greenland (Bowhead) Whales in Waters North of Canada 1719-1915," *Arctic*, Vol. 32, No. 2 (June 1979).

Ross, W. Gillies, "Whalemen, Whaleships, and the Search for Franklin," in Patricia D. Sutherland, Ed., *The Franklin Era in Canadian Arctic History, 1845-1859* (Ottawa: National Museum of Man, Mercury Series No. 131, 1985), pp. 54-68.

Royal Commission on Aboriginal Peoples, *The High Arctic Relocation: A Report on the 1953-55 Relocation*, Vols. I and II (Ottawa: Royal Commission on Aboriginal Peoples, 1994).

Saville, D.B.O., "General Ecology and Vascular Plants of the Hazen Camp Area," *Arctic*, Vol. 17 (1964), pp. 237-58.

Schledermann P., and K.M. McCullough, "Culture Contact, Continuity, and Collapse: The Archaeology of North Atlantic Colonization, A.D. 800-1800: Native/Norse Contact in the Smith Sound Region," Unpublished paper, The Arctic Institute of North America, Calgary, 10 August 2000, pp. 1-23.

Schledermann, Peter, *Crossroads to Greenland; 3000 Years of Prehistory in the Eastern High Arctic*, Komatik Series No. 2 (Calgary: The Arctic Institute of North America, 1990).

Schledermann, Peter, "Polynyas and Prehistoric Settlement Patterns," *Arctic*, Vol. 33, No. 2 (June, 1980), pp. 292-302.

Schledermann, Peter, *The Viking Saga* (London: Weidenfeld and Nicolson, 1997).

Schledermann, Peter, *Voices in Stone: A Personal Journey into the Arctic Past* (Calgary: University of Calgary, Arctic Institute Komatik Series, No. 5, 1996).

Schlereth, Thomas J., *Victorian America: Transformations in Everyday Life* (New York: HarperCollins, 1991).

Schweger, Barbara F., "Clothing the Early Expeditions: An Essential Contribution by the Native Seamstresses," *Yukon Historical Museums Association Proceedings*, No. 2 (1984).

Searing, Gary F., Peter Schledermann, David Evans, and William Cross, "The Natural and Cultural Resources of Ellesmere Island National Park Reserve and Adjacent Areas: A Review of the Literature and Annotated Bibliography," Unpublished report, Parks Canada, Winnipeg, 1988.

Sharp, Robert P., "Glaciers in the Arctic," *Arctic*, Vol. 9, Nos. 1 and 2 (1956), pp. 78-117.

Slotkin, Richard, *The Fatal Environment: The Myth of the Frontier in the Age of Industrialization, 1800-1890* (New York: Atheneum Books, 1985).

Smith, Gordon, "The Historical and Legal Background of Canada's Arctic Claims," PhD dissertation, Columbia University, New York, 1952."

Smith-Rosenberg, Carroll, *Disorderly Conduct: Visions of Gender in Victorian America* (New York and Oxford: Oxford University Press, 1985).

Soberman, Daniel, *Report to the Canadian Human Rights Commission on the Complaints of the Inuit People Relocated from Inukjuak and Pond Inlet, to Grise Fiord and Resolute Bay in 1953 and 1955* (Ottawa: Canadian Human Rights Commission, 1991).

Soper, James H., and John M. Powell, "Botanical Studies in the Lake Hazen Region, Northern Ellesmere Island, Northwest Territories, Canada," *Publications in Natural Sciences*, No. 5 (Ottawa: National Museum of Natural Sciences, 1985), pp. 1-65.

Steltzer, Ulli, *Inuit: The North in Transition* (Vancouver/Toronto: Douglas and McIntyre, 1982).

Stephenson, Alfred, "British Polar Exploration 10 Years Before and After World War II: A Comparison," *Polar Record*, Vol. 20, No. 127 (1981), pp. 317-28.

Stewart, Thomas G., and John England, "Holocene Sea-Ice Variations and Paleo-environmental Change, Northernmost Ellesmere Island, NWT," *Arctic and Alpine Research*, Vol. 15, No. 1 (1983), pp. 1-17.

Stirling, Ian, "The Biological Importance of Polynyas in the Canadian Arctic," *Arctic*, Vol. 33, No. 2 (June, 1980).

Stirling, Ian, and T.S. Smith, "Interrelationships of Arctic Ocean Animals in the Sea Ice Habitat," in *Proceedings of the Circumpolar Conference on Northern Ecology*, Vol. II (Ottawa: National Research Council, 1975).

"Supply of Settlements in the Canadian Arctic, 1953," *The Polar Record*, Vol. 7, No. 50 (May 1955), p. 392.

Sutherland, Patricia D., "An Inventory and Assessment of the Prehistoric Archaeological Resources of Ellesmere Island National Park Reserve," Environment Canada, Parks Service, Microfiche Report Series No. 431, 1989.

Taylor, A.J.W., "Polar Winters: Chronic Deprivation or Transient Hibernation?" *Polar Record*, Vol. 25, No. 154 (1989), pp. 239-46.

Taylor, Andrew, *Geographical Discovery and Exploration in the Queen Elizabeth Islands* (Canada: Department of Mines and Technical Surveys, Geographical Branch Memoir No. 3, 1955).

Taylor, Andrew, *Physical Geography of the Queen Elizabeth Islands, Canada*, Vols. I-V (New York: American Geographical Society, 1956).

Taylor, C.J., "Canadian Sovereignty Over its Arctic Islands," Unpublished agenda paper, Historic Sites and Monuments Board of Canada Agenda Papers, June 1981 Meeting, Parks Canada, Hull, 1981, pp. 328-43.

Tener, J.S., *Muskox in Canada: A Biological and Taxonomic Review* (Ottawa: Canadian Wildlife Service, 1965).

Tener, John S., "Queen Elizabeth Islands Game Survey, 1961," Canadian Wildlife Service, *Occasional Papers, No. 4* (Ottawa, Department of Northern Affairs and Natural Resources, National Parks Branch, 1963), pp. 1-50.

Tester, Frank James, and Peter Kulchyski, Tammarniit *(Mistakes): Inuit Relocation in the Eastern Arctic, 1939-63* (Vancouver: University of British Columbia Press, 1994).

Thompson, Bill, "Climate," in Ellesmere Island National Park Reserve, "Resource Description and Analysis," Western Canada Service Centre, Parks Canada, Winnipeg, 1994, Vol. I, pp. 5-12.

Thorsteinsson, R. and E.T. Tozer, "Geology of the Arctic Archipelago," in R.J.W. Douglas, Ed., *Geology and Economic Minerals of Canada*, Part B (Ottawa: Energy, Mines and Resources Canada, 1976), pp. 547-590.

Todd, A.L., *Abandoned: The Story of the Greely Arctic Expedition, 1881-84* (New York: McGraw-Hill, 1961).

Trettin, H.P., *Precarboniferous Geology of the Northern Part of the Arctic Islands: Hazen Fold Belt and Adjacent Parts of Central Ellesmere Fold Belt, Ellesmere Island* (Ottawa: Geological Survey of Canada, 1994).

Troelsen, J.C., "Contributions to the Geology of Northwest Greenland, Ellesmere Island and Axel Heiberg Island," *Meddelelser om Grønland*, Vol. 149, No. 7 (1950), pp. 1-85.

Troelsen, J.C., "Geological Investigations in Ellesmere Island, 1952," *Arctic*, Vol. 5 (1952), pp. 199-210.

United States, *Sailing Directions for Baffin Bay and Davis Strait, Comprising the West Coast of Greenland From the Eastern Entrance of Prince Christian Sound to Cape Morris Jesup and the East Coasts of Baffin, Bylot, Devon, and Ellesmere Islands from Resolution Island to Cape Joseph Henry*, First Edition (Washington, DC: Government Printing Office, 1947).

United States, *Sailing Directions for Northern Canada, including the Coast of Labrador North of St. Lewis Sound, the Northern Coast of the Canadian Mainland, and the Canadian Archipelago*, First Edition (Washington, DC: Government Printing Office, 1946).

Utley, Robert M., *Frontier Regulars: The United States Army and the Indian* (Lincoln and London: University of Nebraska Press, 1973).

Uvdloriaq, Inuuterssuaq, *The Narrative of Qitdlarssuaq* (Trans, Kenn and Navarana Harper, n.d.).

VanStone, James W., "The First Peary Collection of Polar Eskimo Material Culture," *Fieldiana: Anthropology*, Vol. 63, No. 2 (December 1972).

VanStone, James W., "New Evidence Concerning Polar Eskimo Isolation," *American Anthropologist*, Vol. 74 (1972).

Vaughan, Richard, *The Arctic: A History* (Dover, New Hampshire: Alan Sutton Publishing, 1994).

Vaughan, Richard, "Bowhead Whaling in Davis Strait and Baffin Bay During the 18th and 19th Centuries," *Polar Record*, Vol. 23, No. 144 (1986), pp. 289-99.

Vaughan, Richard, "How Isolated Were the Polar Eskimos in the Nineteenth Century?" in Louwrens Hacquebord and Richard Vaughan, Eds., *Between Greenland and America: Cross-Cultural Contacts and the Environment in the Baffin Bay Area* (Groningen, the Netherlands: University of Groningen, 1987), pp. 95-107.

Vaughan, Richard, *Northwest Greenland: A History* (Orono, Maine: University of Maine Press, 1991).

Vibe, Christian, "Arctic Animals in Relation to Climatic Fluctuations," *Meddelelser om Grønland*, Vol. 170, No. 5 (1967).

Vibe, Christian, "The Marine Mammals and the Marine Fauna in the Thule District (Northwest Greenland) With Observations on Ice Conditions in 1939-41," *Meddelelser om Grønland*, Vol. 150, No. 6 (1950).

Wallerstein, Immanuel, *The Modern World System*, Vol. III, *The Second Era of Great Expansion of the Capitalist World Economy* (New York: Academic Press, 1988).

Weems, John Edward, *Peary: The Explorer and the Man* (Boston: Houghton Mifflin Company, 1967).

Weems, John Edward, *Race for the Pole* (New York: Henry Holt and Company, 1960).

Wenzel, George, "Archaeological Evidence for Prehistoric Inuit Use of the Sea-Ice Environment," in Sikumiut: *"The People Who Use the Sea Ice"* (Ottawa: Canadian Arctic Resources Committee, 1982).

Wenzel, George W., *"Ningiqtuq*: Resource Sharing and Generalized Reciprocity in Clyde River, Nunavut," *Arctic Anthropology*, Vol. 32, No. 2 (1995), pp. 43-60.

White, Richard, "Historiographical Essay: American Environmental History: The Development of a New Historical Field," *Pacific Historical Review*, Vol. 54 (1985), pp. 297-335.

Wilden, Anthony, *System and Structure: Essays in Communication and Exchange*, 2nd Edition (London: Tavistock Publications, 1980).

Williams, Raymond, *Culture* (Glasgow, Fontana Paperbooks, 1981).

Wilmott, W.E., "The Flexibility of Eskimo Social Organization," *Anthropologica*, Vol. 11, No. 2 (1960), pp. 48-59.

The Winnipeg Art Gallery, *Port Harrison / Inukjuak* (Exhibition Catalogue) (Winnipeg: The Winnipeg Art Gallery, 1976).

Winstead, Barbara, "Hysteria," in C.S. Widom, Ed., *Sex Roles and Psychopathology* (New York: Plenum Press, 1984), pp. 73-100.

Worster, Donald, "Appendix: Doing Environmental History," in Donald Worster, Ed., *The Ends of the Earth: Perspectives on Modern Environmental History* (Cambridge, England: Cambridge University Press, 1988), pp. 289-307.

Wright, John, "British Polar Expeditions, 1919-39," *The Polar Record*, Vol. 26, No. 157 (1990), pp. 77-84.

Wright, Lawrence, *Clockwork Man* (London: Elek Books, 1968).

Wright, Theon, *The Big Nail: The Story of the Cook-Peary Feud* (New York: The John Day Company, 1970).

"Year-Long Study Backs Explorer's North Pole Claim," *The Winnipeg Free Press*, 12 December 1989, p. 15.

INDEX

Lyle Dick has been a historian with Parks Canada for many years. He lives in Vancouver, BC, where he is currently the West Coast Historian for Parks Canada's Western Canada Service Centre. He has researched, written, and published extensively in the fields of Arctic history, Western Canadian history, and historiography. Lyle Dick has also received numerous awards for endeavours and accomplishments in his chosen fields.